THE NEW SPIRIT OF

THE NEW SPIRIT OF CAPITALISM

LUC BOLTANSKI and ÈVE CHIAPELLO

Translated by GREGORY ELLIOTT

VERSO

London • New York

Ouvrage publié avec le concours du Ministère français
chargé de la culture – Centre national du livre.

This work was published with the help of the French
Ministry of Culture – Centre national du livre.

This work, published as part of the program of aid for publication,
received support from the French Ministry of Foreign Affairs and
the Cultural Service of the French Embassy in the United States.

Further support was gratefully received through a research
fund allocated by the HEC Foundation, Paris.

First English edition published by Verso 2005 © Verso 2005
Translation © Gregory Elliott 2004, 2007
This paperback edition published by Verso 2007 © Verso 2007
First published as *Le nouvel esprit du capitalisme* © Editions Gallimard 1999

1 3 5 7 9 10 8 6 4 2

Verso
UK: 6 Meard Street, London W1F 0EG
USA: 180 Varick Street, New York, NY 10014-4606
www.versobooks.com

Verso is the imprint of New Left Books

ISBN-13: 978-1-84467-165-6

British Library Cataloguing in Publication Data
A catalogue record for this book is available from the British Library

Library of Congress Cataloging-in-Publication Data
A catalog record for this book is available from the Library of Congress

Printed and bound in the USA by Courier Stoughton, Inc.

For Ariane
For Guy

CONTENTS

PREFACE TO THE ENGLISH EDITION   ix

ACKNOWLEDGEMENTS   xxix

PROLOGUE   xxxv

GENERAL INTRODUCTION: ON THE SPIRIT OF CAPITALISM   1
AND THE ROLE OF CRITIQUE

PART I: THE EMERGENCE OF A NEW IDEOLOGICAL CONFIGURATION   55

1 MANAGEMENT DISCOURSE IN THE 1990s   57

2 THE FORMATION OF THE PROJECTIVE CITY   103

PART II: THE TRANSFORMATION OF CAPITALISM AND THE   165
           NEUTRALIZATION OF CRITIQUE

3 1968: CRISIS AND REVIVAL OF CAPITALISM   167

4 DISMANTLING THE WORLD OF WORK   217

5 UNDERMINING THE DEFENCES OF THE WORLD OF WORK   273

PART III: THE NEW SPIRIT OF CAPITALISM AND THE NEW FORMS   343
            OF CRITIQUE

6 THE REVIVAL OF THE SOCIAL CRITIQUE   345

7 THE TEST OF THE ARTISTIC CRITIQUE   419

CONCLUSION: THE FORCE OF CRITIQUE   483

POSTSCRIPT: SOCIOLOGY *CONTRA* FATALISM   529

APPENDICES   537

BIBLIOGRAPHY   559

NAME INDEX   589

SUBJECT INDEX   597

PREFACE TO
THE ENGLISH EDITION

1. 1994–2003

Nearly ten years have passed since we organized the work programme that led to the publication of *Le nouvel esprit du capitalisme* five years later. So it is perhaps worth offering a brief sketch of some of the features of the period in which this book took shape. The various decisions about theoretical positioning we took in order to tackle recent economic and social changes can in fact be clarified by recalling certain elements of the French intellectual and political context at the end of the 1980s and beginning of the 1990s.

The reference to capitalism

A first feature – which, given our subject matter, is not unimportant – was quite simply that virtually no one, with the exception of a few allegedly archaic Marxists (an 'endangered species'), referred to capitalism any longer. The term was simply struck from the vocabulary of politicians, trade unionists, writers and journalists – not to mention social scientists, who had consigned it to historical oblivion. In this regard, especially striking was the fact that – to take but one example – the discourse of political ecology, originally associated with violent attacks on the 'power of capital', seemed to have forgotten the link, still obvious ten years earlier, between the destruction of natural resources and the 'pursuit of profit at any price'. If anglophone authors, particularly Americans, continued to use the term,[1] no doubt because it was less associated with communism in their intellectual and political culture than it is in ours, sociologists and economists in the old world preferred to forget it. Obviously, this was in startling contrast to the ubiquitous reference to capitalism in the 1960s and 1970s. In order to get a clearer idea of what we were aiming to do, we must go back over the fate of the reference to capitalism in French sociology in the last thirty years.

In the 1960s and 1970s, reference to capitalism was inspired, in various degrees of orthodoxy, by Marxism, which became – especially with the revival occasioned by Althusserianism – a dominant paradigm. This paradigm sometimes presented itself as a 'return to the original sources', aimed at restoring the thought of Marx in all its purity; and sometimes grafted itself on to other traditions and authors – in particular, Durkheim and Weber on the one hand, Freud and Nietzsche on the other. These different 'schools' shared a dual ambition whose contradictory character is invariably neither theorized, nor even acknowledged. On the one hand, their aim was to reactivate a positivist conception of the social world and a scientistic vision of history (the social world is constituted by 'structures', inhabited by 'laws', and propelled by 'forces' that escape the consciousness of social actors; and history itself follows a course that does not directly depend upon the volition of the human beings subject to it). On the other hand, they sought to remain in the closest possible contact with the social movements that developed in these years and to be their critical vanguard. According to this conception, sociology there-fore had to be both scientific and critical.

Now, in our view, this dual orientation comes up against the problem of values and, in particular, moral values and ideals. Because it aims to dig beneath the consciousness of actors and unveil structures, laws and forces that are beyond their control, the scientific approach can deal with moral values and ideals only as 'ideologies' – that is to say, in this conception, as a more or less hypocritical cover for relations of force (invariably without explaining why such masks are necessary). Contrariwise, the critical impulse presupposes ref-erence to ideals with which the reality to be criticized can be compared.

The same antinomy recurs at the level of action. Stressing historical struc-tures, laws and forces tends to minimize the role of intentional action. Things are what they are. Yet the critical approach becomes meaningless if one does not believe that it can serve to inflect human beings' action, and that this action can itself help to change the course of things in the direction of further 'liberation'. This tension is especially evident in the sociology of domination elaborated by Pierre Bourdieu, which aims to unveil the 'mechanisms' through which a universal 'domination', presented as an iron law, is exercised, while at the same time seeking to advance the work of individual liberation, con-ceived as an emancipation from external powers and intervention. But if, in the final analysis, all relations are reducible to conflicts of interest and relations of force, and this is a 'law' immanent in the order of the 'social', what is the point of unmasking them in the indignant tones of critique, as opposed to registering them with the dispassion of the entomologist studying ant societies?

Confronted with these aporias, and in a context of the waning of protest movements and the decline of Marxism, some 1980s sociology and political science, which we participated in within the framework of the Political and Moral Sociology Group, sought to restart work on the question of action and moral values.[2] In the realm of action, the issue was to find a language that made it possible to describe people's actions not as the realization of potentialities inscribed in structures, or as the execution of a ready-made programme (which boils down to denying that such things as actions actually exist), but inasmuch as they presuppose that decisions and risks are taken in the light of the uncertain situations in which people find themselves. In the realm of moral values, it was a question of taking the normative principles and ideals that people claim to adhere to seriously, without reducing them to mere ideological masks or expressions of false consciousness. Finally, the same currents aimed to broach the issue of social order and the way it is 'achieved' (an issue that no sociology can avoid), without reducing it a priori to an interplay of forces over which actors have no control.

The prospect of restoring critique was not alien to this enterprise. If one accepts that, if it is to be credible, critique presupposes normative fulcra, then it is necessary, if the critiques developed by actors are to be taken seriously, to model the normative exigencies their critiques point towards. A *critical sociology* indifferent to the values that actors claim to adhere to must therefore be replaced by a *sociology of critique*. It must also be made clear that this move had no intention of putting critique in the dock, but, on the contrary, sought to render its foundations more solid. The detour via a sociology of critique had heuristic intentions, not a political design.

The 1980s sociologies that stressed action and moral values were often directed towards a pragmatic analysis of the actions, justifications and critiques developed by people in concrete situations – bringing out the operations implemented by actors to 'perform' or 'construct' the 'social', reduce the uncertainty of situations, make and consolidate agreements, criticize existing arrangements, and so on. Such analyses have been accused (often by sociologists who remain attached, albeit usually implicitly, to philosophies of history proximate to Marxism) on the one hand of neglecting relations of force, thereby offering an irenic vision of the social world; and on the other of locking themselves into a description of micro-situations amenable to observation, thereby neglecting processes that are realized on a broader canvas, involving a multiplicity of actors, and over the long term.

This applies to references to 'capitalism', which disappeared from the sociological currents we have just briefly described. Dethroned from its status of key concept of the 1970s, 'capitalism' has been reduced to an inferior status – a somewhat indecent swearword – because it implied a Marxist terminology that many sociologists wished to forget, but also because it referred to something too 'large', too 'bulky' to be immediately observable and describable via the observation of specific situations.

Fifteen years on, we may nevertheless ask whether sociology can really dispense with referring to substantial entities, grasped over the long term, without sacrificing much of the light it is supposed to cast on the present. A sociology that makes do with describing the configuration of various concrete situations, and the way in which people construct these arrangements, can clearly serve to inspire various sorts of 'repairs' to the social fabric, made on a day-by-day basis by working 'participants' or social 'engineers'. But it does not make it possible to aid the construction of wider collective projects – something that formed part of sociology's mission from the outset.

Abandonment of any reference to capitalism in the 1980s was also accompanied by a kind of astonishment at the changes under way in the economic and social sphere – changes that could nevertheless not be ignored. Lacking a macro-sociological perspective, sociology struggled to construct mediations between a comprehensive 'mutation' (often referred to in an idiom of economic or technological necessity, or even in terms of biological evolutionism) and local transformations affecting the main components of everyday life (working conditions, unemployment, life cycle, income, inequalities, education, emotional and family life, etc.). These links were simply not established or, at any rate, were not organized in such a way as to form a system.

Similar remarks could be made about the term 'social class'. At the heart of European sociology from 1950 to 1980, it had suddenly disappeared, even though new forms of inequality were proliferating during the 1980s. What was particular about these was, if we might put it thus, that they were visible to the naked eye: Europeans discovered with amazement and anxiety that their towns in turn were filling up with the homeless people whose presence in the great American metropolises had shocked them, but without them ever seriously envisaging the possibility that such figures might one day come to populate their own familiar public spaces. This was the context in which a different theme was popularized – 'exclusion' – that was intended, at a theoretical level at least, to reconcile belief in the virtual disappearance of social classes (especially the proletariat), supposedly replaced by a 'large middle class', and the reality of tangible poverty associated with inner-city ghettoization.

These various remarks clarify our endeavour in *Le nouvel esprit du capitalisme*. We sought to construct a framework that makes it possible to combine approaches in terms of *critical sociology*, referring to supra-individual entities (especially capitalism) with the capacity to affect a large number of people over a long period, and approaches derived from pragmatic sociology, stressing action, the normative exigencies that intentional actions claim to be inspired by, and critical operations in particular, by pursuing the programme of a *sociology of critique*. Feeling the need to return to the issue of capitalism, we did not drop the contributions of pragmatic sociology: this book is presented as an attempt to integrate the two approaches. In particular, we employed the analytical framework presented in *De la justification*,[3] which highlights the critical and justificatory operations performed by people in everyday situations, and offers a model of general conventions and forms of equivalence that make it possible to confer legitimacy on justification and critique. But rather than describing critical operations in limited situations on a case-by-case basis, our objective was to highlight the role played by critique in the dynamic of capitalism, and to construct a model of normative change.

The book focuses on the years 1965 to 1995. This period is especially auspicious for such a project. It was initially marked (1965–75) by an intensive critical movement, coinciding with a crisis of capitalism. Then, in a subsequent phase (1975–90), critique was brought to heel concurrently with a transformation and revival of capitalism. This revival finally led, in the 1990s, to the gradual construction of a new normative fulcrum – a new 'city' in the sense given the term by *De la justification*.

On a more practical level, our intention was on the one hand to paint a picture rendering the changes under way more intelligible, and on the other hand to explain with the same schemas the interpretative deficit, and especially the silence of critique, which seemed to us to be key characteristics of the period we were living through.

Studying critique and being critical

To reconstruct a critical sociology on the basis of the sociology of critique by hybridizing it with the old thematic of capitalism: such was our ambition. So what analytical objects did we select to pursue this project? Starting out from the question posed by the lack of social critique that seemed to us to be characteristic of the 1980s and the beginning of the 1990s, we developed a dual analysis. In the first instance, we analysed the role of critique in the changes in historical capitalism, basing this work on a more general model of normative change whose construction was one of the main theoretical objectives of our work. Second, we sought to deepen (by displacing it to a macro-social level, by comparison with the theoretical framework of *De la justification*) the role played by the coexistence of comparatively incompatible forms of critique in the dynamic relationship between capitalism and critique. Here we encounter the distinction, which constitutes a leitmotiv of this book, between social critique (associated with the history of the working-class movement, and stressing exploitation) and what we have called the artistic critique (derived from intellectual and artistic circles, especially nineteenth-century Parisian Bohemia, this takes the dehumanization of the capitalist sphere as its particular target). In so doing, we were not so naive as to be unaware that, in its descriptive aspects, our work was, by force of circumstance, going to acquire a political dimension. Besides, regardless of whether they wish it to be so, is this not true of all enterprises – for example, in the case of nineteenth-century fiction – whose object is to compose a picture of 'society', given that a representation, however 'naturalistic' in intent, is also always an interpretation which, by this very token, opens up the possibility of a judgement?

It is still incumbent on us to clarify the kind of critique we wanted to revitalize, and our position as 'critics' (and not simply 'analysts of critique'). First of all, what is the relationship between sociological analysis and social action? We deliberately limited ourselves when it came to setting out the practical implications of our analyses (what we were bound to say is contained in a twelve-page Postscript). This was in order to avoid both the arrogance of the expert adviser to the Prince and pontificator, and the irresponsibility of armchair revolutionaries (Max Weber denounced 'professorial socialists' in his time) basing their power on a dual, 'scientific' and 'political', legitimacy – something which, as is well known, has led to unprecedented forms of intellectual terrorism in the recent past. But we nevertheless hope that our work will be able to contribute to a renewal of critique – not only its content, but also its forms and aims. Here we took as our model Karl Polanyi and Albert Hirschman, whose works were a constant source of support.

In order to pursue the line we had marked out, the main sacrifice we had to make doubtless involved the radicalism and totalizing designs which, especially for researchers trained in the continental tradition, possess a seductive power that is difficult to resist. In contrast, we strove to dissect the details – for example, those of the new mechanisms of exploitation (thereby following the Lévi-Straussian precept that 'the truth is in the detail'). One consequence of this determination to stick to details, combined with a lack of financial resources to assemble a huge work team (but such gigantic projects often have the deleterious effect of industrializing research), was that we were obliged to restrict ourselves for the most part to the French case. An ideal programme would have allowed for comparison between several countries over the same period and with the same methods. It remains to be pursued.

This is also to say that the forms of critique indicated by our analyses (if they must be characterized, they might be dubbed 'reformist') are not 'revolutionary' – if, as has frequently been the case since the early nineteenth century, by 'revolutionary' is meant a position offering a portrayal of the human condition in the capitalist sphere and, more generally, in contemporary industrial society which is so alien to human destiny or, if you prefer, so 'alienated', that critique's sole possible objective is the creation of a 'new man'.[5] In particular, we reject one of the implications of this conception, which is that it releases critique from the requirement of developing the normative standpoint that grounds it, inasmuch as it is bound up with the belief that no normative position is attainable in the world as currently constituted, or even really imaginable as long as the revolution remains to be made. Critique alone is then accessible; this has the inestimable advantage that one can subject everything to critique without ever having to disclose one's own normative presuppositions. When it is not simply nihilistic or mundane, such a position ultimately invariably comes down to making 'Science' – whether it be the

Science of history in the sense of dialectical materialism or, today, an abso-lutist social Science – and, indirectly, those in whom the Revolutionary and the Scientist are conjoined, who are supposed to have the requisite materials in their possession, the final arbiters of human action. And this occurs at the expense of a common sense of justice, which is certainly the most widely shared thing in the world. Here we follow Michael Walzer's analysis in his fine book on social critique in the twentieth century, *The Company of Critics*.

We are confirmed in this position by what our analyses have taught us of capitalism's ability to assimilate critique. There is no ideology, however radical its principles and formulations, that has not eventually proved open to assim-ilation – and all the more readily the more comprehensive it was, abandoning the prosaic, tedious terrain ('petty-bourgeois' would once have been the term) of everyday conflicts (over working conditions, the defence of jobs, the dis-tribution of value added, schooling, living conditions that make it possible to bear and raise children, etc.), in favour of vast prophetic demands.

In particular, this explains why we have examined so closely the mecha-nisms that aim to introduce new forms of security and justice into a universe where flexibility, mobility and network forms of organization had become basic reference points – mechanisms proposed by jurists or economists, among others, which were being discussed in the second half of the 1990s. At a the-oretical level, analysis of these mechanisms allowed us to give substance to the projective city – a new normative fulcrum that we think is in the process of being formed – while from a more practical standpoint, it enabled us to identify some of the points which critique seemed best placed to latch on to.

We must, however, clear up a misunderstanding whose implications are as much political as theoretical. Our aim in writing this book was never to help establish the 'projective city' or even, as we have been criticized for doing, to seek to offer 'capitalism' a new, immediately available 'city'. Our work was pri-marily intended to be descriptive, and for the most part we made do with assembling mechanisms proposed by a fairly wide range of authors from dif-ferent disciplines (management, law, sociology, etc.), which aim to establish tests making it possible to realize the projective city. What might be called our 'personal' position on this point is expressed not in the body of the text, which is given over to description, but in the Postscript. We believe that anything that makes it possible to diminish the insecurity of wage-earners even mar-ginally is better than nothing – first because suffering will thereby be reduced, and we have no time for *la politique du pire*; but also because, as the whole history of the working-class movement has shown, it is when insecurity dimin-ishes that conditions conducive to a revival of critique develop. We are not experts in political strategy. But that is why the option of instituting mecha-nisms which lead to greater security for wage-earners, even if these mechanisms come to a compromise with demands for flexibility, currently seems to us a pretty reasonable option, on condition that it is accompanied by theoretical and practical work, based on these mechanisms, preparing for a more vigorous revival of critique.

So we have no qualms about acknowledging that we assign critique a 'reformist' role in the first instance. For, once the metaphysical constructions that sustained the messianic expectation of 'revolution' have been renounced, and, in particular, once anticipations of a 'new man' have been abandoned, how are demands for 'reform' radically different from 'revolutionary' commitment? Reforms can also be radical, and change the existing order of things fairly profoundly. In fact, underlying this whole debate between 'reform' and 'revolution' is a problem that remains largely implicit today: the legitimacy of using violence. It remains implicit because those who, after two world wars and episodes of mass extermination in the fascist and communist countries, still advocate large-scale use of violence are fewer and farther between than in Sorel's time. But if support for violence on grounds of revolutionary necessity is rejected, how are reformist movements to be distinguished from revolutionary ones?

How do things stand with critique? Expansion and confusion

At the start of this Preface, we underlined the changed context between the first half of the 1990s and the period we are now living through. It is especially intriguing where critique is concerned.

First of all, since our book was first published in France at the end of 1999, we have witnessed a very rapid revival of critique – certainly more rapid and intense than we could have anticipated when we wrote Chapter 6, devoted to the resurgence of critique after 1995. Especially noteworthy has been the speed with which critiques developed in different countries have converged on a comprehensive critique of globalization, with its high points of Seattle, Genoa or Porto Alegre.

On the other hand, however, we have witnessed virtual stagnation when it comes to establishing mechanisms capable of controlling the new forms of capitalism and reducing their devastating effects. In France, the belated arrival of the euphoria created by the 'new economy', which can be fairly precisely dated to the end of 1999 – or a little more than two years before the collapse of the NASDAQ in April 2002 – certainly played a significant role in the Socialist government's shelving of most of the measures envisaged.[6] In all likelihood, this played a role in the spectacular failure of the established left at the Presidential elections in April 2002 and the 'protest' vote by a significant section of the electorate for the extreme right or the extra-parliamentary extreme left.

The same could be said of mechanisms intended to have a global impact, whose implementation seems an even more utopian prospect for the moment. In this respect, things have not changed very much compared with the years when we wrote our book; and the least one can say is that the new spirit of capitalism is taking its time about rectifying itself as regards its ability to offer not only what we call 'stimulation' (which it affords less and less as the new mechanisms become commonplace), but also security and justice.

In retrospect, it might be thought that our work is thus simultaneously rather timid when it comes to a resumption of critique, which has been more rapid than we foresaw; and decidedly over-optimistic about the effects of critique, which for the time being are not immediately obvious, to say the least.

Moreover, the relative absence of a coherent theoretical analysis and precise empirical analyses of the way that capitalism has been reinvigorated over the last thirty years might possibly explain – at least in part – the present paradoxical situation, which is characterized by an undeniable redeployment of critique and a no less patent disarray of that critique. We can detect an initial sign of this disarray in the nostalgia, prevalent among old activists, for the good old days of communism, when the threat posed to the Western democracies by the armies of the countries of actually existing communism was thought to 'give the bosses pause', while some young activists are attracted by archaic forms of revolutionary discourse.

In our opinion, another such sign consists in the temptation to transform a critique of capitalism itself (centred on economic mechanisms, forms of work organization, and profit extraction) into a critique of 'imperialism'. In France, this move has translated into a resurgence of vulgar anti-Americanism. It is always disturbing to see indignation detached from the concrete, often conflictual sites it applies to, making way for a consensus in the face of an external enemy, even when it concerns 'globalization' and its 'agents'.

For the time being, it is also difficult to make out what direction the renewal of what we have called the 'artistic critique' might take. If the exhaustion of the forms assumed by this critique in France over the last fifty years (with its marked stress on the revolutionary dimension of individual liberation, especially in sexual matters) is fairly generally acknowledged – certainly more clearly so than five or ten years ago – the issue of which symptoms should be considered in order to identify the currently dominant modes of 'alienation' remains very blurred. This contributes in significant measure to maintaining the confusion between the markers via which, until recently, left- or right-wing political identifications were readily discerned. For example, in the case of recent mobilizations around the Confédération paysanne, we have seen a movement defending agriculture against the depredations of globalization and GMOs, which it has been possible to identify as both 'leftist' and 'reactionary', depending on whether stress is laid on its rather contradictory positions in favour of fair trade at a world level or the protection of traditional French agriculture.

2. REPLIES TO SOME CRITIQUES

Since its publication three and a half years ago, this book has been subject to a certain number of critiques by colleagues at home and abroad. Despite their diversity, certain themes recur in these critiques, perhaps because they highlight the most obvious defects of our work. But in some cases at least, the critiques latch on to points that typify the approach we sought to develop, so that they indicate the connection between our enterprise and other recent theoretical endeavours in the social sciences. This is why it is worth taking them up and briefly noting the responses we think we are in a position to make.

Conventions economics and regulation theory

An initial critique, which is fairly typical of the very lively debates among unorthodox economists in the French intellectual arena, maintains that our position is awkwardly poised between two recent currents in economic analysis: conventions economics, whose development has been very closely related to the efforts we ourselves have made to develop a pragmatic sociology of critique;[7] and the works of the Regulation School.[8] An important aspect of our work was indeed the quite deliberate pursuit of a synthesis (reckoned impossible by some) between these two approaches.

From conventions theory we derived the need to clarify the conventions, in the sense of principles of equivalence, that allow for the comparison of persons (and of goods), in so far as they constitute the often largely invisible bedrock of economic relations, but also of the judgements that different actors make about them. For example, transactions rest on different quality conventions. As for production, it is based on different co-ordination conventions.

From the spirit (if not the letter) of Regulation theory we took the macroeconomic and macro-social orientation, and also the structuralist orientation that underlines the existence of regimes of accumulation – that is to say, translating back into our language, the fact that certain conventions and tests have a strategic position at a given moment in time, and in a particular social formation. These conventions and tests are established, in the sense that they are organized into a system, orchestrated by legal mechanisms, and anchored in organizations. But rather than conferring a quasi-mechanical *modus operandi* on these systems, which tends to hypostatize them, we integrate into our descriptions the interpretations and critiques to which these conventions and tests are subjected by the actors whom they engage.

The underestimation of technological innovations

We have likewise been criticized for not giving technological changes – particularly the new information technologies – and their impact on the production of wealth the space they warrant. We do not ignore the increased effectiveness and efficiency brought about by the new ways of organizing firms, which have been made possible, especially but not exclusively, by the new information technologies. We even begin our book by registering a regeneration of capitalism. Moreover, the management literature we studied is full of praise for these 'economic' benefits.

But we have tried to pose the problem differently, so as not to isolate an independent variable in the shape of technology. As has been cogently demonstrated in the new sociology of science, technological changes are far from being independent of other dimensions of social existence. If, for example, we follow Bruno Latour's analyses, we see that numerous aspects which might readily be characterized as 'moral' are embedded in technological options. The same could be said of 'consumer demand' and its more or less 'unstable' character. For the process of rapid change in consumer tastes and, consequently, demand, is not unconnected (at least this is the thesis defended in *Le nouvel esprit du capitalisme*) with demands pertaining to the artistic critique – especially those related to the requirement of 'authenticity' – which translated into a quest for consumption that individualizes its consumer, in contrast to all forms of 'mass' production. To put it in a nutshell, our intention in this work was not to deny the role of technological change in the development of capitalism, which would have been quite absurd, but – in accordance with a Polanyesque way of thinking – to break with a fatalistic vision of technological determinism.

The relationship to Marxism: Beyond the base/superstructure dichotomy

Other queries revolve around whether our book can be regarded as forming part of the vague return of Marxism in the social sciences (in the guise of a 'ghost', to adopt Derrida's term, or the 'spectre' Žižek refers to). Some critics – aligned, one suspects, with the anti-Marxists – have condemned the resurgence in our work of a crypto-Marxism that dare not speak its name. We shall leave them to their fantasies. Others, this time pro-Marxists, have accused us of a 'spiritualist deviation': we allegedly make 'ideas' and 'spiritual tendencies' the motor of history.

More seriously, authors motivated by the best of intentions have sought to make sense of our work by interpreting it with the categories of 'base' and 'superstructure'. Yet the theoretical architecture we sought to put in place – as early as the preliminary work elaborated in *De la justification* – aimed precisely to render such a dichotomy redundant. Our starting point, inspired by Max Weber, Karl Polanyi and Louis Dumont, sought precisely to revive the problematic of the dynamic of capitalism without using these Marxist categories, whose limits had become apparent in the 1970s and which, in particular, do not seem to us to tackle the problem of ideology correctly.[9] Effecting a marked separation between ideas and the real world, and ignoring their interconnection, their interwoven, conjoint production, their reciprocal influence, such a conception always prompts a lapse into narrow definitions of ideology as a mask or mirror, constantly posing the question of the chicken and the egg. It prevents researchers from engaging with the complexity and indeterminacy of the production of historical realities in order patiently to untangle its threads.

The sense we give to the term 'ideology'

On the subject of the same critical register, it is worth dwelling, however briefly, on the use we make of the term 'ideology', which has given rise to numerous misunderstandings. As Raymond Boudon explains in his study of the subject,[10] discussions of ideology always revolve around the question of whether it should be defined by reference to the criterion of truth or error. Those who criticize us for rescuing the notion of ideology from the obscurity to which it had been consigned at the end of the 1970s are no exception, since for them ideology is manifestly a set of false ideas – that is to say, ideas which a scientific approach has the capacity to invalidate. Now, we explicitly rejected such a conception. As we state on several occasions, the spirit of capitalism not only legitimates the accumulation process; it also constrains it. We might also say that it can legitimate it only because it constrains it. And this is because we credit people with genuine critical capacities, and critique has an impact on the world. We start out from the principle that people are able by themselves to measure the discrepancy between discourses and what they experience, to the point where capitalism must, in a way, offer – in practice – reasons for accepting its discourse.

To make things clearer still, let us recall that we distinguish between three components in what we term the 'spirit of capitalism', one of which refers to justice and specifies how capitalist mechanisms are geared towards the common good.[11] This 'justice' element refers directly to the concept of 'city' and the notion of test, initially developed in *De la justification* and reworked in this book. This model was never intended exclusively for the analysis of discourses, in complete abstraction from any actual implementation of the principles of justice referred to. Thus, operating in tandem with a notion of ideology as deception we find a portrayal of justifications in terms of cities as idle, empty words. So we would have a world of discourses and justifications as so many veils and shams, designed to deceive as many people as possible and conceal the relations of force or underlying structures that determine us; and the real world, which only scientists, whether economists or sociologists, have access to, since they are the only ones who have the privilege of being able to extricate themselves from the social world. This is definitely not our view.

Yet those who have criticized us for accepting the validity of a management literature whose role is 'purely ideological', and which consequently bears little relation to the changes that have occurred in the organization of work and production, largely rely on a conception of ideology as a mask serving to veil reality. On this point, our position is as follows: we think that a sufficient number of reliable and convergent statistical indicators now exist (supplied in particular by Labour Ministry surveys, which we cite abundantly in Chapter 4) to maintain that the trends recommended in 1990s management literature are widely diffused. It is therefore wrong to consider only the 'ideological' dimension of this literature, without perceiving its practical impact. This does not mean that the changes advocated have all been effected at the same pace, or (especially) that they have been implemented with the same intensity, in the various sectors. Starting out from the management literature allowed us to delineate the ideal type of the new organization of production. (Is not 'mass production' likewise an 'ideal type', whose concrete forms are rarely a certified copy?) How far this model is realized in practice (according to sectors, regions, etc.) would itself make an extremely interesting object of study.

A specifically French book?

The same applies to the limited scope of our analyses, restricted to France, which has been regretted by numerous anglophone commentators. Is *Le nouvel esprit du capitalisme* yet another of those very French products which (like José Bové's Roquefort) do not travel well, and are a speciality of French intellectuals? Confining ourselves to France, far from being fortuitous, was the result of a deliberate and, to be frank, polemical choice. In reaction against the numerous publications which, in the course of the 1990s, claimed to offer a general survey of globalization, we decided to impose restrictions on ourselves. Because they did not study the tensions at work, and the decisions and policies aimed at overcoming them, at a manageable level, some of these texts virtually presented 'globalization' as the 'inevitable' outcome of 'forces' external to human agency.

We, in contrast, were convinced that understanding the process leading to 'globalization' required a detailed analysis of multiple changes and conflicts which had occurred in seemingly very disparate domains; and that description of these changes could be seriously undertaken only in a fairly limited time-span (five years) and on a small scale (the two of us worked alone, without a large team behind us), at the level of one country – especially because, at country level, the constraints bound up with national histories play a not insignificant role. That said, we are also persuaded that basically rather similar processes have affected the principal industrialized countries in the Western world. Once again, we hope that future work, with a similar methodological approach, will make it possible to enrich a fine-grained vision of the way in which, under the impact of local variables, new constraints have been established that local economic and political actors can, in all good faith, have a sense of being subjected to from without, as if they were forces that it was difficult – even impossible – for them to oppose.

The place of networks and its interpretation

Other critiques have focused on the role we attributed to networks, and – this is not the same thing – to the references to networks in the managerial literature published at the end of the 1980s. So we have been criticized either – in a realistic spirit analogous to a critique already mentioned – for not taking the role played by the new network-based technologies sufficiently seriously; or, on the contrary, for accepting the validity of a reticular ideology which presents processes of mediation and mediating roles that have always existed as if they were novelties. Our concern was precisely to avoid these equally reductionist interpretations.

With respect to works, often adopting a broadly determinist position, that endeavour to define the social effects of new technologies based on a network architecture, we adopted a position that might be called Durkheimian (though it is also James Beniger's, for example, in his important book *The Control Revolution*). It consists in emphasizing the social conditions and, more particularly, the social conflicts that provoked or encouraged the adoption or development of a particular technology. In this respect, it is striking to see how the critique of close modalities of hierarchical surveillance at the end of the 1960s and beginning of the 1970s preceded the full development of technologies allowing for effective remote control in real time by ten or twenty years.

Conversely, to those critics who reprove us for accepting the validity of managerial discourse on networks, we can answer that this critique is anticipated in the book. As we took the trouble to make clear on several occasions, we certainly do not think – and here we follow the work of Fernand Braudel – that networks and the role played by mediators are novel phenomena. What is new, on the other hand, is precisely the societal project, to which much of the book is given over, aiming to make the network a normative model. If you like, it can be said that this involves an 'ideology', but on condition that this term is construed in the sense – indicated above – which emphasizes the fact that 'ideologies', if they are to be successful, must be rooted in organizational, institutional or legal mechanisms which give them a 'real' existence.

Other interpretations of our work reckon to have detected in it a sort of hostility to networks articulated from an implicitly centralist and statist position (a critique often addressed by American political scientists which, particularly since Stanley Hoffman's works thirty years ago, has become a kind of commonplace). We are supposedly unaware of the beneficial effects of 'spatially bounded micro-networks'. But we are not certain that we have understood the argument, since in our view it is very difficult to understand what is meant by it from a strictly formal standpoint. As works by French philosophers of networks like Michel Serres or, in other respects, Gilles Deleuze have shown, one of the basic properties of networks is that they are open. Moreover, an American theoretician of the sociology of networks like Harrison White adopts the same basic premiss. The space of the network, constituted by those who compose it, is not the same as a geographical space: it is open, indeterminate and shifting. The difficulty in establishing a scale of justice in networks stems precisely from the fact that it is not always known who is on the inside and who is on the outside; that these contours change constantly; and that the parties to the network only very rarely have an overall view of it, each of them knowing only that section of the network which they frequent. Consequently, attempts to structure networks always involve a minimal formalization of a list of parties to it and the creation, if not of a state, then at least of a regulatory instance accepted by the 'members' – that is to say, of a second, overarching level that lays down 'the law'. In the process of so doing, it is clear that the network loses its fluidity, its openness, and thus its reticular character. To note this is not be a centralizer at heart.

Nevertheless, the issue of the relations beween networks and territories deserves a much closer examination than we conducted in the book. For it is clear that networks have real territorial bases, and that territories are not equal when it comes to their capacity to accommodate nodes where wealth, produced by networks extending beyond them, is accumulated. Moreover, regulation, which is organized and conceived in primarily territorial fashion today, is all the more ineffective to the extent that the branches of the network precisely extend beyond these territorial borders.

The same could be said of self-organization within networks, which is frequently presented today as a quasi-'revolutionary' emancipatory force (for example, in the case of the Internet or, to take a more specific example, debates about free software). The self-organization that develops in networks can certainly prove auspicious for innovation and innovators (as Michel Callon's works, which we cite, have indicated). But there is very little chance of it providing acceptable solutions in terms of social justice on its own, precisely because the network does not offer an overarching position allowing for consideration of those who find themselves on its margins, or even disconnected.

The dual ontology of the social world

The questions raised by the way we use the notion of network refer, in the end, to a central aspect of our approach on the theoretical level, which has gone comparatively unremarked – so that it has escaped comment or criticism – but that is nevertheless at the heart of critiques of our work and the responses we are in a position to make. For us, this dimension of our research is pretty fundamental, because it concerns what might be called the ontology of the social. To put it rapidly and crudely, social theory, especially French social theory (but in this respect French thought has had considerable influence on social science at a global level over the last thirty years), has periodically oscillated between two paradigms that appear to be incompatible. Without being confined to them, these paradigms refer to the two epochs in French sociology we mentioned at the beginning of this Preface, when we recalled the fate of the reference to capitalism over the last thirty years.

The first emphasizes force and the relations of force that are regarded as underlying the institutions, and legal and normative fulcra, on which actors claim to base their actions. In this type of paradigm, moral exigencies, modes of justification, and institutional forms are treated as veils concealing reality – that is to say, as an interplay of interests and relations of force – or are simply forgotten and passed over in silence. In both cases, the question as to why human beings in society seem to attach so much importance to normativity if, in fact, it plays no role in determining their actions, has remained unresolved, no satisfactory response having been offered. Models that stress force and relations of force have taken several forms. In the 1960s and 1970s, they were associated with the revival of Marxism through an injection of structuralism. More recently, they have instead been based upon a reticular or rhizomorphous ontology, especially in the form given it by Deleuze on the basis of an original reinterpretation of Spinoza and Nietzsche, whose works only belatedly had specific effects on social theory, so that they were only really important from, let us say, the mid-1980s. This second version has the advantage over the first that it eliminates some of the most unacceptable aspects of 'classical' Marxism – in particular, the base/superstructure dichotomy.

By contrast, the second paradigm, which was redeployed at the end of the 1970s and in the 1980s, when the decline of Marxism reopened the field of theoretical reflection, intends to underscore the real social role played by political institutions and political philosophy, by law, morality and, in general, normativity. In particular, it has relied on the *oeuvre* of Habermas Mark 2, but also in France on those of the historian François Furet, who played an important role in the return to political theory, and the philosopher Paul Ricoeur.

What is distinctive about these two paradigms is that they are based on two quite different conceptions (which often remain implicit) of what one might call the metaphysics of the social world. The first, especially in its rhizomorphous forms, is based on an ontology containing only one tier or plane (the 'plane of immanence'). It knows only singularities or flows, the relationship between which assumes a reticular form and whose movements and relations are governed by a logic of forces. The second, in contrast, is intelligible only on condition that it posits a two-tier space, the first of which is occupied by singular entities – in particular, people – while the second is composed of principles of parity that make it possible to compare singular entities, to constitute them as categories or classes, and to make normative judgements about the relations between them. It is precisely this two-tier structure that is condemned by the first paradigm as succumbing to the illusion of transcendence.

Neither of these paradigms seems to us to be wholly satisfactory or adequate for explaining the social dynamic. Moreover, that is why, in our opinion, we witness a periodic alternation between them. This is attested today, for example, by a reversion to an ontology of force which, keen to demarcate itself from Marxism, often takes its inspiration from Carl Schmidt – an author whose stand in favour of Nazism long excluded him from the intellectual scene, but who has recently made a comeback in left-wing or ultra-left thought that is as sensational as it is astonishing.

The originality of the model of change we propose is that it seeks to integrate the two paradigms we have just schematically invoked into a single theoretical framework. We have in fact tried to articulate two regimes of action in the social world. We called the first the *regime of categorization.* Set in motion by the impact of critique on the most important tests at a given moment in time, it relies on a two-tier metaphysic and leads to activating principles of equivalence (often by calling them into question), strengthening institutions, producing law, and prompting the deployment of moral justifications, which are expressed in particular in terms of justice. This is the framework in which – in the French case, for example – we interpret the large number of joint agreements, decrees and laws augmenting the mechanisms of security and justice for workers that were signed, issued or voted following the events of May 1968.

But this regime of categorization does not exhaust action on the social. We have also sought to highlight the role performed by a different regime, which we have called the *regime of displacement.* Dispensing with generalization and moral judgement, this regime is deployed on a single plane and generates forms the most satisfactory image of which is afforded by rhizomorphous algorithms. We sought to show how, in the case to hand – the revival of capitalism from the second half of the 1970s – the increasing strictness of tests induced by intensive recourse to instruments from the regime of categorization led a number of actors to turn away from established tests, and to seek new routes to profit by acting in accordance with modalities characteristic of a regime of displacement – that is, in particular, by multiplying networks.

Our theoretical position exposes us to being criticized, or at least ill understood or misunderstood: (1) first of all by those, often inspired by Habermas, who stress the search for forms (if only procedural forms) conducive to co-ordination on a normative basis, so as to make a convergence of judgements possible; (2) but also by those who stress interests and relations of force from a structuralist standpoint; and finally (3) by those who, likewise abandoning the issue of normativity as if it were groundless, put all the emphasis on the creativity of networks. It is a matter for some concern, although readily intelligible on a fundamental level, that today we are witnessing a convergence on the last position both by authors who are fascinated by the proliferation and inventiveness of the technological and economic mechanisms currently being deployed before our very eyes (i.e. authors fascinated by the renewal of capitalism) and by authors who want to revive revolutionary activity against capitalism by anchoring it in new theoretical bases and who, rather as the Althusserians used structuralism to revamp the image of Marxism in the 1960s, rely on the ontology of networks to revive it by plugging it into *Lebensphilosophie*.

Some revisions on the issue of 'the lateness of critique'

To conclude, we would like to turn from responding to critiques to formulating an autocritique. It is as follows. Where tests are concerned, we equipped our actors with capacities for both displacement and categorization. Categorization consists in comparing singular events in a particular respect in order to connect them in a series. It is one of the basic operations people perform when they seek to give meaning to the world they live in, by deriving from it major invariants and a certain simplified image of the way it operates. Capacities for categorization are essential for 'tightening up tests'. Contrariwise, displacements refer to people's actions inasmuch as they are not categorized and, more especially, in so far as they do not form part of established, identified and highly categorized tests – a feature which gives them a local, largely invisible character. Circumvention of established tests presupposes the existence of displacements. It would have been logical to distribute these capacities evenly to all our actors. Yet this is not the case because, in the story we tell, for the most part it is capitalism that displaces and critique that categorizes. Accordingly, critique is inevitably always late, for in order to be effective it must analyse the displacements operated by capitalism and order them in a sequence, categorize them in order to reveal them and condemn them as unjust. With this unequal distribution of relative capacities for displacement and categorization, we can see how it is possible to topple over into a clash of the kind 'displacement–capitalism–material world' versus 'categorization–critique–ideal world'.

What is involved is a flaw in our exposition: capacities for categorization and displacement, as anthropological capacities, are obviously uniformly distributed. As for capitalism's capacity for categorization, is not this what was at work in the construction of the first, and then the second, response by employers to the 'crisis of governability' following May 1968 (see Chapter 3)? And is it not precisely what management authors are doing when they seek to outline some of the new world's basic rules? Hence capitalism and its critiques simultaneously, and interactively, take charge of the definition/ categorization of the world.

Symmetrically, critique has significant capacities for displacement and inventiveness. The outflanking of the trade unions by their rank and file, and the great difficulties explaining what was occurring experienced by analysts in the 1970s, should be taken up again. If, thirty years later, it seems to us that these events can be understood as the artistic critique descending into the street, it appeared to observers at the time as basically pertaining to the order of displacement – that is to say, one of those moments when no one knows what is happening, or how to characterize it.

Besides being necessary theoretically, this kind of rebalancing of our model would result in giving critique its full due, and would help to check the all too common drift towards reducing critique to the world of ideas and capitalism to the world of things.

On this point, as on many others, *Le nouvel esprit du capitalisme* may be read as a research programme rather than a fully finished work; as a summons to future work for the purposes of extending, clarifying or invalidating our suggestions, rather than as a dogmatic, self-sufficient *summa*.

Paris, 27 May 2003

Notes

1. As indicated, for example, by the title of Oliver Williamson's work, *The Economic Institutions of Capitalism*, published in 1985.

2. A research centre at the École des hautes études en sciences sociales and the Centre national de la recherche scientifique, founded by Luc Boltanski in 1985. See François Dosse, *L'empire du sens. L'humanisation des sciences humaines* (La Découverte, Paris 1995), for a history of French social science in these years.

3. See Luc Boltanski and Laurent Thévenot, *De la justification. Les économies de la grandeur*, Gallimard, Paris 1991.

5. See Luc Boltanski, 'The Left after May 1968 and the Longing for Total Revolution', *Thesis Eleven*, no. 69, May 2002, pp. 1–20.

6. Among the measures that were implemented, mention should be made of the mechanisms of VAE (*Validation des acquis de l'expérience*), which allow people who have accumulated skills in their working lives to obtain equivalent qualifications without having to return to school. These mechanisms can be interpreted as attempts to give practical effect to the promise of employability, which is central in the projective city. Firms, for their part, have continued to work on the new management of human resources around the notion of skills.

7. See Olivier Favereau and Emmanual Lazega, eds, *Conventions and Structures in Economic Organization: Markets, Networks and Hierarchies*, Edward Elgar, Cheltenham and Northampton (MA) 2002.

8. See Robert Boyer and Yves Saillard, *Théorie de la régulation. L'état des savoirs*, La Découverte, Paris 1995.

9. See Ève Chiapello, 'Reconciling Two Principal Meanings of the Notion of Ideology: The Example of the "Spirit of Capitalism"', *European Journal of Sociology*, vol. 6, no. 2, 2003, pp. 155–71.

10. *L'idéologie ou l'origine des idées reçues*, Fayard, Paris 1986.

11. The other components involve propositions in terms of security and stimulation.

ACKNOWLEDGEMENTS

This work has been brought to a conclusion thanks to the contributions and help of numerous people who, in their various ways, have given us the benefit of their time, their knowledge and their solicitude – when it was not also their friendship, their affection or, especially in the case of those closest to us, their unflagging endurance (and these forms of assistance are no less vital for completing a long-term project). We take the opportunity to thank them all.

In preparing this work, we enjoyed the financial support of the HEC group and the HEC foundation, the backing of Gilles Laurent, then head of research, and of Bernard Ramanantsoa, director-general of the HEC group, as well as the support of the political and moral sociology group (EHESS–CNRS), where the group secretary Danielle Burre, in particular, was endlessly helpful.

Without the aid of Sophie Montant, we would not have been able – or not in a reasonable time-scale, at least – to complete the demanding and often thankless task of constructing the corpus of management texts and preparing the computer files for processing by the Prospero@ program. Its inventors – Francis Chateauraynaud and Jean-Pierre Charriaud – taught us how to use it proficiently.

Yves-Marie Abraham, sociologist and doctoral student at HEC, and Marie-Noëlle Godet, engineer at the CNRS (GSPM), helped us complete our documentation – the former by assembling a statistical dossier; the latter by perusing the political and trade-union press of the 1970s and 1980s.

The final version of this book is the fruit of a protracted, thankless labour of clarification, refinement and also distillation, in order to make the transition from a manuscript almost too bulky to transport to an object which, while not exactly aerodynamic, is nevertheless manageable. That labour owes a lot to discussion with close friends, especially Laurent Thévenot, and our various readers. Francis Chateauraynaud, Bruno Latour, Cyril Lemieux and Peter Wagner read extracts or earlier versions and criticized them vigorously: thank you. Isabelle Baszanger, Thomas Bénatouïl, Alain Desrosières and François Eymard-Duvernay took on the unrewarding task of reading everything and suggesting clarifications, amendments and additions. Throughout the writing of this book, we have had the benefit of Élisabeth Claverie's pertinent remarks and emotional support. But without a doubt the most constant support was that provided by Lydie Chiapello and Guy Talbourdet, who read the manuscript several times with unfailing vigilance. The final version bears the stamp of their wisdom.

We have jointly presented and tested out a number of the themes developed in this book in various seminars, particularly the seminar on 'Ordres et classes' conducted by Robert Descimon at the EHESS (where we found the stringent but insightful criticisms of P.-A. Rosental stimulating); and at the seminar on 'Possible worlds' organized at the École normale supérieure by Thomas Bénatouïl and Élie During. Above all, we have drawn upon the weekly seminar at the EHESS conducted by Luc Boltanski. The opportunity thus afforded us to submit this work for discussion at various stages of its development represented an incalculable advantage. We have also benefited from work presented in this seminar by doctoral students or researchers belonging to other institutions. Particularly useful were the comments and presentations of Yves-Marie Abraham (on financial markets); Thomas Bénatouïl (on the relationship between pragmatic and critical sociology); Damien de Blic (on financial scandals); Damien Cartron (on techniques for the close supervision of work); Sabine Chalvon-Demersay (on contemporary representations of the family); Julien Coupat (on Situationism); Emmanuel Didier (on the formation of the notion of exclusion); Claude Didry (on redundancy plans); Pascal Duret (on sporting contests); Arnaud Esquerre (on the notion of manipulation); François Eymard-Duvernay and Emmanuelle Marchal (on recruitment methods); Francis Ginsbourger and Francis Bruggeman (on second assessments undertaken at the request of works councils); Christophe Hélou (on resistance to supervision); Jacques Hoarau (on Marx and morality); Dominique Linhardt and Didier Torny (on traceability in a network world); Thomas Périlleux (on the reorganization of an arms factory); Claudie Sanquer (on skills appraisals); Isabelle Saporta and Éric Doidy (on the new social movements); and David Stark (on the recombination of the Hungarian economic fabric in network form). We hope they will accept our thanks for their contributions here, along with the other participants in these seminars, whose comments and criticisms were likewise very useful.

We also benefited from interviews at the INSEE with Alain Desrosières, Jean-David Fermanian, Baudouin Seys and Maryvonne Lemaire.

Finally, we must thank our editor, Éric Vigne, who had confidence in us and proved unyielding when it came to pruning passages of superfluous scholarship, pointless notes or unnecessary digressions. As presented to readers today, this book owes a lot to him.

To conclude, we must confess that as we wrote virtually every page of this book we could not help asking ourselves what Albert Hirschman, whose work, more than any other, sustained us throughout this long journey, would think of it. Hence it is only fitting that it should be dedicated to him. May he find in these hundreds of pages practical homage to the irreplaceable role he has played in the formation of the inclinations, which are not merely intellectual, that have guided us throughout: as a researcher, thanks to the concepts he has introduced into socioeconomic analysis – especially the importance he has long assigned critique – and also, by his example, as a human being.

We have known, we have had contact with a world (as children we partook of it), where a man condemned to poverty was at least secure in poverty. It was a kind of unspoken contract between man and fate, and before the onset of modern times fate had never reneged on this contract. It was understood that those who indulged in extravagance, in caprice, those who gambled, those who wished to escape poverty, risked everything. Since they gambled, they could lose. But those who did not gamble could not lose. They could not have suspected that a time would come, that it was already here – and this, precisely, is modern times – when those who do not gamble lose all the time, even more assuredly than those who do.

(Charles Péguy, *L'Argent*)

PROLOGUE

This book, the idea for which was conceived at the beginning of 1995, was born out of the perplexity, shared by numerous observers, created by the coexistence of a deterioration in the economic and social position of a growing number of people and a booming, profoundly restructured capitalism. This perplexity was increased by the state of social critique, to which sociology, as a kindred discourse, is rarely indifferent. For social critique has not seemed so helpless for a century as it has been during the last fifteen years, whether in evincing indignation but without backing it up with alternative proposals; or (most frequently) in simply giving up on denouncing a situation whose problematic character (to say the very least) could not escape it, as if it were tacitly admitting its inevitability.

In many respects, we are living today in a situation that is the reverse of the late 1960s and early 1970s. Then capitalism was experiencing a fall in growth and profitability bound up, at least according to Regulationist analyses, with a slowdown in productivity gains that was associated with a continuous increase in real wages proceeding at the same pace as before.[1] Critique, for its part, was at its zenith, as demonstrated by the events of May 1968, which combined a social critique of a fairly classical Marxist stamp with demands of a very different kind, appealing to creativity, pleasure, the power of the imagination, to a liberation affecting every dimension of existence, to the destruction of the 'consumer society', and so on. As for the macroeconomic environment, it was that of a full-employment society whose leaders endlessly repeated that it was 'progress-orientated', a society in which people had hopes of a better life for their children, and where demands developed – backed up by denunciation of unequal opportunities for access to the education system – for social advancement open to all via a democratized republican school system.

The questions behind this book derive from the well-nigh total reversal of this situation and the weak critical resistance that was ultimately mounted against it. Ranging beyond the disarming impact of a left-wing government on critique,[2] we wanted to understand in more detail why critique had not 'latched on' to the situation; why it was incapable of understanding the developments that occurred; why it suddenly fizzled out towards the end of the 1970s, leaving the field free for the reorganization of capitalism for close on two decades, while restricting itself to the less than glorious (albeit necessary) role of echoing mounting social problems; and, finally, why many of the 'class of '68' felt so at ease in the emerging new society that they made themselves its spokesmen and egged on the transformation.

But before embarking upon the kind of answers we have given to these questions, it seems to us worthwhile in this preamble to sketch – on the basis of macroeconomic indicators or statistics – a rapid picture of the context (full of contrasts, to say the least) underlying not only our analyses, but also the questions (not to mention consternation) that have spurred on our work over the last four years.

A revived capitalism and a worsening social situation

Contrary to the frequent recourse to the stock theme of 'crisis', which has regularly been invoked since 1973, albeit in different contexts, we believe that the last twenty years have instead been marked by a flourishing capitalism. In this period, capital has had multiple investment opportunities offering profit rates often in excess of earlier eras. These years have been auspicious for all those with savings (a capital): profits, which disappeared during the great depression of the 1930s and which, in subsequent decades, did not recover on account of inflation, are back.

Certainly, growth has slowed on a long-term basis,[3] but the returns to capital are increasing. The profit rate[4] of non-individual firms, which had declined sharply in the 1960s and 1970s (- 2.9 points from 1959 to 1973; - 7.8 points between 1973 and 1981), was restored in the 1980s (+ 10 points from 1981 to 1989), and has been maintained since (- 0.1 points from 1989 to 1995). Between 1984 and 1994, GDP in 1994 constant francs grew by 23.3 per cent. Social contributions increased in the same proportion (+ 24.3 per cent), but not net wages (+ 9.5 per cent). In the same ten years, property income (rent, dividends, capital gains) rose by 61.1 per cent, and unredistributed profits[5] by 178.9 per cent. Taddei and Coriat – taking up the progress in the profit rate of firms, and recalling the downward trend in corporation tax (from 50 per cent to 42 per cent in 1988, and then 34 per cent in 1992, with a rise, however, to 41.1 per cent in 1997), as well as the stagnation in the rates of employers' social security contributions since 1987 – show that at the beginning of the 1990s France offered rates of return on capital markedly higher than at the beginning of the 1980s.[6] According to these authors, the finances of French firms have very largely recovered under the dual impact of reduced taxation and a division between profits and wages that is much more advantageous to firms.

In the same years, financial dealers rediscovered 'a freedom of action they had not known since 1929 and sometimes even since the nineteenth century'.[7]

The deregulation of financial markets, their decompartmentalization, and the creation of 'new financial products' have multiplied the possibilities of purely speculative profits, whereby capital expands without taking the form of invest- ment in productive activity. The so-called 'crisis years' were thus marked by the fact that capital profitability was now better guaranteed by financial invest- ments than industrial investment (which suffered, moreover, on account of interest rates). We have witnessed an increase in power on the part of certain operators like pension funds, which for a long time were fairly stable owners of a mass of shares, but which have been made very prominent by market transformations (their means are considerable) and impelled to alter their *modus operandi* to conform to 'the model of undiluted financial profit-taking'.[8] The liquid assets concentrated in the hands of mutual investment funds (SICAV), insurance companies and pension funds are such that their capacity to influ- ence the markets in accordance with their interests is a recognized fact.[9] These developments in the financial sphere are inseparable from the evolution of quoted firms, which are subjected to the same profit imperatives by the markets, and themselves take an ever larger slice of their profits through purely financial transactions. Between 1983 and 1993, the stock-market valu- ation of Paris (the number of share certificates multiplied by their price) rose from 225 to 2,700 billion francs for shares and from 1,000 to 3,900 billion francs for bonds.[10]

Multinational firms, too, emerged as winners from these years of redeploy- ment of world capitalism. The slowdown in the world economy over almost thirty years has not really affected them, and their share of world GDP, itself rising, has continued to grow: from 17 per cent in the mid-1960s to more than 30 per cent in 1995.[11] It is reckoned that they control two-thirds of interna- tional trade, approximately half of which comprises intragroup exports[12] between parent companies and subsidiaries, or between two subsidiaries of the same group. Their share of 'research and development' expenditure is unquestionably even greater. Their development has been secured over the last ten years mainly by mergers and acquisitions on a world scale, accelerat- ing the process of concentration and the constitution of global oligopolies. One of the most striking phenomena since the 1980s, especially post-1985, is the growth in direct foreign investment, which is distinguished from the inter- national exchange of goods and services by the fact that there is a transfer of property rights and an assumption of power locally. But while the impact of multinationals is a major economic phenomenon, there is virtually no study devoted to them. The United Nations Centre on Transnational Corporations (UNCTNC) was wound up at the beginning of 1993 at the request of the US government. Some of the incumbents were transferred to UNCTAD in Geneva, where a much-reduced work programme has been pursued.[13] While between two and five hundred firms, closely corresponding to the list supplied by Fortune magazine each year, dominate the world economy, the definition of a multinational company imposed on researchers has been consistently relaxed, submerging the handful of ultra-powerful companies that has remained immune from the crisis in an ocean of firms.[14]

Finally, capitalist restructuring over the last two decades – which, as we have seen, occurred around financial markets and merger-acquisition activities in a context of favourable government policies as regards taxation, social security and wages – was also accompanied by significant incentives to greater labour flexibility. Opportunities for hiring on a temporary basis, using a temporary workforce, flexible hours, and a reduction in the costs of layoffs, have developed considerably in all the OECD countries, gradually whittling down the social security systems established during a century of social struggles. At the same time, the new communication technologies, data communications in the forefront, have made it possible to handle orders in real time at a planetary level, providing for a hitherto unknown global capacity to adapt. A whole model of managing large firms has been transformed under this pressure, generating a new way of making profits.

World capitalism, understood as the possibility of making capital yield a profit through economic investment, is thus in good health. As for societies, to adopt the separation of the social and the economic that we have lived with for more than a century,[15] they are in rather poor shape. The data here are much more familiar, beginning with the French unemployment rate: 3 per cent of the working population in 1973, 6.5 per cent in 1979, around 12 per cent today. In February 1998, there were slightly more than three million unemployed in the sense of ANPE's category 1,[16] which is far from counting all job-seekers registered with ANPE, and does not include those unemployed persons exempted from seeking work on account of their age, those who have taken early retirement, those on a training course or a government-sponsored contract (or something comparable). The number of people 'without work' must thus in fact be estimated at five million in 1995,[17] as against 2.45 million in 1981.[18] The average situation in Europe is scarcely better.[19] The United States has a lower rate of unemployment, but whereas wage-earners in France have pretty much maintained their purchasing power, it has undergone a marked decline there. While American GDP *per capita* grew by 36 per cent between 1973 and mid-1995, the hourly wage for non-managerial work, representing the majority of jobs, fell by 14 per cent. At the century's close, the real wage of non-*cadres* in the USA will have returned to what it was fifty years earlier, whereas GDP will have more than doubled in the same period.[20] Throughout the OECD zone, we are witnessing a downward alignment of pay. In countries like France, where policies have sought to maintain the purchasing power of the minimum wage, the unemployment figures have regularly increased, with the deterioration in living conditions first and foremost affecting the unemployed and the ever-increasing number of part-time workers. (They accounted for 15.6 per cent of the employed working population in

1995, as against 12.7 per cent in 1992 and 9.2 per cent in 1982.) Of the latter, 40 per cent would like to work more. The employment of those with jobs is also much more insecure. The number of 'atypical jobs' (fixed-term contracts, apprentices, temps, paid trainees, beneficiaries of state-aided contracts and government-sponsored contracts in the civil service) has doubled between 1985 and 1995.[21]

If the number of households living below the poverty threshold[22] has gone down (from 10.4 per cent of households in 1984 to 9.9 per cent in 1994), the structure of the population affected has developed in significant ways. Poverty affects old people less and less, and people of working age more and more. The changes in the population covered by social minima constitute a good reflection of alterations in the pattern of poverty: it went up from three million people (2.3 million households) at the end of 1970 to nearly six million by the end of 1995 (or 3.3 million households).[23] The average number of people per household on benefit has gradually increased from 1.3 to 1.8, while the proportion of couples and families has risen. The minima for the unemployed (*Allocation de solidarité spécifique*) and the RMI (*Revenu minimum d'insertion*)[24] account for the greater part of this increase, while the number of those on old-age benefits was halved between 1984 and 1994 with the arrival in retirement of age groups who had paid contributions all their working lives. Even so, it should be stressed that the outlay has not matched the increase in the number of beneficiaries: as in 1982, 1 per cent of GDP was devoted to them in 1995 (whereas between 1970 and 1982 it had progressed from 0.3 to 1 per cent). As a percentage of expenditure on social welfare, the share devoted to the minima in 1995 was even inferior to what it was in 1982.[25]

The effect of all these developments (impoverishment of the population of working age, regular increase in unemployment and job insecurity, stagnation in income from work), at a time when incomes from profits were rising, was that inequalities in the distribution of income once again began to grow in France from the second half of the 1980s – a trend that had begun prior to this date in other countries.[26]

These dramatic changes in the economic situation of households were accompanied by a series of problems that were particularly concentrated in certain suburbs (ghettoization, the *de facto* creation of extra-legal zones conducive to mafia activity, the development of violence among increasingly young children, the problem integrating populations of immigrant origin); and by striking (because highly conspicuous) phenomena in the daily life of those living in large towns and cities (for example, the increase in begging and homelessness,[27] often among the young and, in the case of a sizeable number of them, people with qualifications that should give them access to a job). This irruption of poverty in public areas plays an important role in the new standard representation of French society. These extreme situations, although as yet directly affecting only a relatively small number of people, aggravate the sense of insecurity of all those who feel themselves threatened with the loss of employment, either on their own account or that of someone close to them – spouse or children in particular. In other words, in the final analysis it affects a large proportion of the working population.

During these years of social regression, the family developed in ways whose effects are still far from having been calculated.[28] It became a much more fluid and fragile institution, compounding job insecurity and the general sense of insecurity.[29] This development is doubtless partially independent of the evolution of capitalism, although the search for maximum flexibility in firms chimed with a depreciation of the family as a factor of temporal and geographical inflexibility, so that, as we shall see later, similar ideological schemas are mobilized to justify adaptability in work relations and mobility in emotional life. It remains the case that the changes which have occurred in the economic sphere and in the domain of private life are sufficiently aligned for the family environment to seem ever less capable of functioning as a safety net, particularly when it comes to guaranteeing children positions equivalent to those of their parents. And the school system, to which the task of reproduction has been overwhelmingly transferred since the 1960s, is not in a position to satisfy the hopes once invested in it.

The imperilment of the postwar model of society, and ideological disarray

These changes endanger the compromise established in the postwar years around the theme of the rise of the 'middle classes' and '*cadres*', which represented a satisfactory solution to the anxieties of the petty bourgeoisie. Small employers and self-employed people impoverished, even ruined, by the crisis of 1929, or occupants of intermediate posts in firms threatened with unemployment – many of these members of the middling social categories, also scared by the rise of communism, whose menace the 1936 strikes had rendered tangible – regarded fascism as the sole bastion against the excesses of liberalism in the second half of the 1930s. The development of the state's role as the Second World War drew to a close, and the advent of the large firm, offered them a new opportunity to live a 'bourgeois' lifestyle compatible with the growth of a wage-labour economy.

In fact, we know that up to approximately the middle of the interwar period a salary was rarely the sole or even main means of support for members of the bourgeoisie, who also had significant inheritance income; and that the money they received by virtue of belonging to an organization was not regarded as a 'wage', the terms 'wage' and 'wage-earners' being in practice reserved for blue-collar workers. These inheritances, composed especially of property but also, to a growing extent during the interwar years, of transferable stocks and shares (bonds, debentures), were gradually wiped out, first of all by currency devaluation in the 1920s, and then by the crisis of the 1930s. Engineers and, with them, ever larger fractions of the bourgeoisie then entered the sphere of the wage-earning class, which in the first instance represented a significant drop in their standard of living. This situation persisted until the establishment in the postwar years of a new organization of economic resources brought with it a new lifestyle for the higher professions, based upon new security systems that were no longer personal but social: the retirement of *cadres*; the growing importance of academic qualifications in the determination of wages and careers; regular career enhancement in the course of working life (facilitating access to credit); social insurance systems reinforced by mutual insurance companies; stability of wage income through the institutionalization of procedures for revising wages in line with the latest consumer price trends; quasi-guarantee of employment in large organizations guaranteeing their *cadres* 'career plans' and offering social services (canteens, shopping co-operatives, holiday camps, sports clubs).[30] There thus emerged a new chance to live the 'bourgeois' life, this time within the wage-earning class.

The popular classes did not benefit to the same extent from mechanisms inspired by a concern to further their access to consumption and integrate them more fully into the economic cycle, as well as to divert them from communism. But they did experience a steady increase in their purchasing power in the same period and also, especially from the 1960s, in opportunities for secondary education for their children.

Some key components of this compromise – qualifications, careers and retirement – have been shattered over the last twenty years. The effects of these changes were naturally deplored, but they did not really alter the certain conviction on the part of the ruling elites that they derived from an imperative necessity, as long as they affected only the most vulnerable members of the popular classes – women, immigrants, disabled people, young people without academic qualifications (the 'casualties of progress' in the 1970s; individuals incapable of 'adapting' to intensifying international competition in the 1980s).[31] Contrariwise, when, in the 1990s, the bourgeoisie found itself affected, they were regarded as alarming.

Increased unemployment among university graduates and *cadres* has become patent, although it is infinitely lower than that of the less privileged. Furthermore, if firms still offer career prospects to those individuals they deem the most talented, they now refrain from guaranteeing them in the long term. Unemployment and early retirement among those over the age of fifty-five, which is one of the most striking aspects of French unemployment, attests to that. The guarantees offered by academic qualifications, which nevertheless still afford good insurance against unemployment, were likewise called into question when it was observed that, with equivalent qualifications, the young invariably accede to positions inferior to those of their elders at the same age – and this often at the end of a succession of casual jobs, which now marks the entry of new generations into working life. To fears about work have now been added anxieties about the level of retirement pensions.

Given that access to the living conditions exemplified by the bourgeoisie has, since the nineteenth century, been one of the most important spurs that made the effort demanded of other classes bearable, the demoralizing effect of this new order of things – echoed by the media in the form of news reports, novels, films, TV dramas – is fairly widespread. Increasing scepticism about the ability of capitalist institutions – international organizations like the OECD, the IMF or the World Bank, multinationals or the financial markets – to maintain, in the case of currently educated generations, their parents' economic living standards and, more generally, their lifestyle, is one of its most obvious expressions. It has been accompanied, particularly over the last three years, by a growing social demand for critical thinking that can give shape to this diffuse anxiety and furnish, at the very least, tools for understanding the situation and, ideally, an orientation to action – that is to say, in this case, some hope.

Yet it must be observed that belief in progress (associated with capitalism since the beginning of the nineteenth century in various forms), which from the 1950s constituted the credo of the middle classes, whether they were professedly left- or right-wing, has found no substitute, apart from a scarcely inspiring invocation of the 'harsh laws of economics', rapidly stigmatized as *la pensée unique*. In the same period, the old anti-systemic critical ideologies – to adopt Immanuel Wallerstein's terminology – failed in their role of destabilizing the capitalist order, and no longer seemed to be the vector of credible alternatives.

Ideological disarray has thus been one of the most evident features of recent decades, marked by the decline of the representations associated with the socioeconomic compromise established after the war, without any critical thought seemingly being in a position to track the changes under way. In part, as we shall see more clearly later, this is because the only critical resources available were built up to denounce the kind of society that reached its zenith at the turn of the 1960s and 1970s – that is to say, just before the great transformation, whose effects are today making themselves felt with all their force, set in. For now, the critical apparatuses to hand offer no wide-ranging alternative. All that remains is raw indignation, humanitarian work, suffering turned into a spectacle, and – above all since the strikes of December 1995 – action focused on specific issues (housing, the *sans-papiers*, etc.). These still lack the refurbished analytical models and social utopia to assume the scope of appropriate representations.

If, in the short term, capitalism is doing all the better, its forces having found a way in the space of a few years largely to liberate themselves from some of the obstacles accumulated over the past century, it could also very well be led into one of those potentially terminal crises that it has already experienced. And this time it is not certain that what would come out of it – and at what cost? – would be a 'better world', as was the case with the developed countries in the postwar decades. Leaving aside the systemic effects of an unbridled freeing-up of the financial sphere, which is beginning to cause concern even among those in charge of capitalist institutions, it seems to us scarcely open to doubt that at an ideological level – to which this book is primarily devoted – capitalism will face increasing difficulties, if it does not restore some grounds for hope to those whose engagement is required for the functioning of the system as a whole. In the postwar years, capitalism was compelled to transform itself to respond to the anxiety and insistent demands of generations of the bourgeoisie and petty bourgeoisie, whose expectations of upward social mobility (whether underpinned by savings or reduced fertility),[32] or of preserving the advantages they had acquired, had been disappointed. Obviously, a social system that can no longer satisfy the classes it is supposed to serve in the first instance (i.e., in the case of capitalism, the bourgeoisie) is menaced, whatever the reasons for this failure, not all of which are under the control of the actors who possess (or believe they possess) power.

In writing this book, we have not set ourselves the objective of proposing solutions to correct the most shocking features of the condition of labour today, or even of adding our voices to the clamour of denunciation, even though these are worthy tasks. Our aim is to understand the waning of critique over the last fifteen years, and its corollary: the currently dominant fatalism, whether the recent changes are presented as inevitable but ultimately beneficial mutations, or as the product of systemic constraints whose results are ever more disastrous, but without it being possible to predict a change in trends.

Political organizations of both left and right, as well as trade unions and intellectuals, one of whose vocations is to influence economic processes in such a way as to create the conditions of a good life for human beings, have not done the analytical work involved in understanding why they were unable to prevent a redeployment of capitalism that proved so costly in human terms; whether deliberately or inadvertently, they have even encouraged this shift. Consequently, they have had no alternative but to choose between two positions that are, in our view, unsatisfactory: on the one hand, the utopia of reverting to an idealized past (with its nationalizations, its relatively non-internationalized economy, its project of social solidarity, its state planning, and its vocal trade unions); on the other, often enthusiastic backing for technological, economic and social changes (which open France up to the world, create a more liberal and tolerant society, multiply opportunities for individuals to flourish, and constantly force back the limits of the human condition). Neither of these two positions enables genuine resistance to the damage inflicted by the new forms assumed by economic activity – the former, because it is blind to what makes neo-capitalism seductive for a large number of people, and underestimates the break that has occurred; the latter, because it minimizes their destructive effects. Although the two are engaged in controversy with each other, they have the common effect of diffusing a sense of impotence and, by imposing a dominant problematic (critique of neo-liberalism versus generally positive balance-sheet of globalization), closing down the field of possibilities.

Our ambition has been to strengthen the resistance to fatalism, without thereby encouraging any retreat into nostalgia for the past, and to provoke in readers a change of *mindset* by helping them to consider the problems of the period differently, from an alternative perspective – that is to say, as so many processes on which it is possible to have some purchase. To this end, it seemed useful to us to open the black box of the last thirty years, in order to observe the way that human beings make their own history. In returning to the moment when things were decided, and making it clear that they could have taken a different turn, history represents the quintessential tool for *denaturalizing* the social; as a result, it goes hand in hand with critique.

We have sought, on the one hand, to describe a unique conjuncture when capitalism was able to extricate itself from a number of fetters linked to its previous mode of accumulation and the demands for justice it prompted; and on the other, basing ourselves on this historical period, to establish a model of change in the values on which both the success and the tolerability of capitalism depend – a model with claims to more general validity.

We have thus revisited the allegedly inevitable developments of the last twenty years, highlighting the problems businessmen had to face, particularly as a result of an unprecedented rise in the level of critique since the war; their attempts to confront or evade these problems; the role of proposals and analyses derived from that critique in the solutions they opted for or were able to implement. In the course of this work, opportunities to resist micro-changes with ominous consequences also emerged that were missed by those who should have been especially vigilant about the risks entailed by these transformations – in particular, because they did not realize that the 'recuperation-implementation' by capitalism of some of their proposals required them in turn to reinvest in analysis and shift ground.

In this sense, our intention was not merely sociological, directed towards knowledge, but geared to a revival of political action, understood as the formation and implementation of a collective will regarding our way of life. While it is certainly the case that not every action is possible at any given moment, nothing is possible when people lose sight of the specificity and legitimacy of the distinctive domain of action[33] – understood as choices guided by values in unique (hence uncertain) conjunctures, whose consequences are in part unforeseeable – and replace it by retreat, whether contented or terrified, optimistic or pessimistic, into the receptive matrix of determinism, social, economic or biological. This also explains why we have not sought to conceal what we opt for and what we reject behind a sham scientism, or to create an insurmountable boundary (formerly labelled 'epistemological') between 'factual judgements' and 'value judgements'. For, as Max Weber taught us, without the aid of a 'viewpoint' involving values, how would it even be possible to select what warrants being noted, analysed or described amid the confused flow of events?

Notes

1. See Michel Juillard, 'Régimes d'accumulation', in Robert Boyer and Yves Saillard, eds, *Théorie de la régulation. L'état des savoirs*, La Découverte, Paris 1995, pp. 225–33; Juillard and Boyer, 'Les États-Unis: adieu au fordisme!', in ibid., pp. 378–88; and Benjamin Coriat, 'France: un fordisme brisé mais sans successeur', in ibid., pp. 389–97.

2. Moreover, the draining effect attributed to the left's accession to power at the beginning of the 1980s is not as obvious as is often claimed. In other historical conjunctures, the left's arrival in office occurred at the same time as an intense revival of critique: simply think of France in 1936, or, closer to us in time if not space, Chile at the start of the 1970s.

3. From the 1970s to the 1980s, the average annual rate of growth in GDP declined by a third in Japan, the USA and the countries of the European Union alike. It has declined by approximately another third since.

4. Source: Gilbert Cette and Selma Mahfouz, 'Le partage primaire du revenu: un constat descriptif sur longue période', *Économie et statistique*, nos 296–297, June–July 1996, pp. 165–84. This rate of margin is defined by the share of the gross surplus of exploitation in value added, which serves to remunerate providers of capital (capital and debts) and to pay taxes on profits. The rest of value added serves in the main for the remuneration of wage-labour, and for financing the social security system, which, as is well known, impacts more heavily on wages than other incomes; as well as – in very small measure – for the payment of various taxes. In their study, the authors subsequently exclude the impact of the development of financial burdens on profit – an evolution that has been unfavourable as a result of the real interest rates obtaining in recent years, as well as the structural effect bound up with the expansion of wage-labour in the economy (all sorts of forms of work having historically been gradually reduced to the generic form of the wage-earning class, this translates on an accounting level into a different way of recording expenses that can bias perception of the evolution of value added). The development of returns to capital (in the form of the development of a corrected rate of margin) referred to above is what is recorded once all the effects that might lead to querying whether what is involved is the evolution of the profits on capital have been excluded.

5. So-called 'unredistributed' profits remain at the disposal of the firms that have made them, whether they make investments with them or place them in financial markets. In all cases, the value of stocks increases and offers potential surplus-values to capital holders. The figures mentioned are taken from *Alternatives économiques*, 'Les chiffres de l'économie et de la société 1995–1996', winter 1995.

6. See Dominique Taddei and Benjamin Coriat, *Made in France. L'industrie française dans la compétition mondiale*, Librairie générale française, Paris 1993.

7. François Chesnais, *La Mondialisation du capital*, Syros, Paris 1994, p. 15.

8. Ibid., p. 222.

9. Chesnais thus analyses the rise in American interest rates in 1994 as 'a sign of the ability of parasitic rentier interests ... to defend their positions whatever the cost for the world economy, and to prevent the amount of their drain on value (expressed by interest rates that are positive in real terms) being dented ... even by a rise in prices of 1 or 2%': ibid., p. 21.

10.   See Philippe Fremeaux, 'Le bilan économique des années Mitterrand', *Alternatives économiques*, February 1995, pp. 14–22.

11.   See Frédéric Clairmont, 'Vers un gouvernement planétaire des multinationals. Ces deux cents sociétés qui contrôlent le monde', *Le Monde diplomatique*, April 1997.

12.   Source: UNCTAD, cited by Philippe Fremeaux, 'Mondialisation: les inégalités contre la démocratie', *Alternatives économiques*, no. 138, June 1996, pp. 30–33.

13.   Chesnais, *La Mondialisation du capital*, p. 53.

14.   We have thus passed from a definition of the multinational as a large firm possessing industrial subsidiaries in at least six countries to that of a firm possessing only one. In its last study, UNCTC counted 37,000 multinationals, only to restrict the inquiry a few pages later to a mere 100 firms that on their own were responsible for a third of direct foreign investment in 1990; ibid., p. 53.

15.   On this question, see, for example, Louis Dumont, *Homo aequalis*, Gallimard, Paris 1977, and Karl Polanyi, *Origins of Our Time: The Great Transformation*, Victor Gollancz, London 1945.

16.   Category 1 of the Agence nationale pour l'emploi (ANPE) contains unemployed job-seekers, who are available immediately, seeking full-time work on a permanent basis, and who have worked fewer than 78 hours in the previous month.

17.   In the same period, category 1 of ANPE recorded 'only' 2.9 million unemployed.

18.   See CERC-Association, 'Chiffres le chômage', *Dossiers du Cerc-Association*, no. 1, 1997.

19.   The average rate of unemployment (in the ILO definition) in the Europe of the fifteen EU members was 10.8 per cent in January 1997, but with significant disparities from country to country (for example, 21.7 per cent in Spain; 15 per cent in Finland; 12.5 per cent in France; 12.2 per cent in Italy; 11.6 per cent in Ireland; 9.6 per cent in Germany; 7.3 per cent in Portugal; 7.1 per cent in the United Kingdom; 4.4 per cent in Austria). See Louis Maurin, 'La grosse déprime de l'emploi', *Alternatives économiques*, no. 149, June 1997, pp. 27–29.

20.   See Lester Thurow, *Head to Head: The Coming Economic Battle among Japan, Europe and America*, Nicholas Brealey, London 1993.

21.   On part-time jobs, see Laurent Bisault *et al.*, 'Le développement du travail à temps partiel', *Données sociales 1996*, INSEE, Paris 1996, pp. 225–33; and on atypical jobs, see Brigitte Belloc and Christine Lagarenne, 'Emplois temporarires et emplois aidés', in ibid., pp. 124–30.

22.   The poverty threshold is defined as a pre-tax income by unit of consumption inferior to half of the average income. Consumption units are counted here according to the so-called Oxford scale: the first adult is worth 1, the second 0.7, and each child under fifteen 0.5.

23.   See CERC-Association, 'Les minima sociaux. 25 ans de transformation', *Dossiers du Cerc-Association*, no. 2, 1997.

24.   In its first year, the *Revenu minimum d'insertion* was granted to 400,000 people (1989). The number benefiting from it in 1995 was 946,000, covering 1.8 million people, and 48 per cent of beneficiaries were under the age of 35.

25.   This situation is explained by the fact that the purchasing power of the old minima has barely been maintained, and has even diminished in the case of those allocated to the unemployed (the purchasing power for the *allocation de solidarité spécifique* fell by 15 per cent between 1982 and 1995, and the allowance for integration into work by 20 per cent); and that the new minima directed at new poor populations (RMI) have been fixed at a level inferior to the old.

26.   The altered trend in inequalities (from a reduction to a sometimes very rapid increase) set in from the end of the 1960s in the United States, from the mid-1970s in Japan, from the late 1970s in the United Kingdom, and at the beginning of the 1980s in Germany, Italy and Sweden: CERC-Association, 'Tendances de la distribution des revenus dans une perspective internationale', *La Note de Cerc-Association*, no. 1, October 1994.

27.   INED estimated in 1996 that approximately 8,000 persons 'of no fixed abode' were living in Paris (*Alternatives économiques*, special issue no. 3, 'Les chiffres de l'économie et de la société 1996–1997', winter 1996).

28. See Évelyne Sullerot, *Le grand remue-ménage: la crise de la famille*, Fayard, Paris 1997.

29. Between 1981 and 1994, the number of marriages declined from 315,000 to 254,000 a year, while the number of divorces rose from 87,600 to 115,000. Moreover, the statistics indicate that unmarried cohabiting couples separate more frequently than married couples. Births outside marriage rose from 12.7 per cent in 1981 to 34.9 per cent in 1993 (Maurin, 'Le bilan social des années Mitterrand'). The 'enquête sur les situations familiales' (ESF) conducted in 1985, but only published in 1994, revealed that two million children were living apart from their fathers, while barely 2 per cent had ever lived with him. Thus, this high figure is bound up not with fathers abandoning pregnant mothers, but with parents separating, which, as the inquiry also shows, occurs at an increasingly early age for the children, multiplying the years of childhood lived after family break-up. The ESF inquiry reckoned that the probability of living in a new family doubled in a few years. Moreover, 3 per cent of those born between 1967 and 1971, and 8 per cent of those born between 1971 and 1975, and then 11 per cent of those born between 1976 and 1980, had experienced two break-ups in five years. See Sullerot, *Le grand remue-ménage*.

30. See Luc Boltanski, *The Making of a Class: Cadres in French Society*, trans. Arthur Goldhammer, Cambridge University Press/Éditions de la Maison des Sciences de l'Homme, Cambridge 1987.

31. The proof of this is that aid mechanisms (unemployment insurance, social benefits, etc.) were primarily relied on to take care of populations, without questioning the legitimacy of the changes that had led to their worsened social situation. The effects were acted on without examining the causes, in the manner of nineteenth-century charity, which was accompanied by a refusal to perceive the level of wages as the cause of industrial poverty. It was already the case then that wages derived from the operation of the market were necessarily just; their verdict was final; and they had to be adapted to.

32. Saving, creating a business, and reducing fertility were the ways of becoming bourgeois suggested to the popular classes by the nineteenth century. Taking up the same combination, the postwar period replaced creating a business by schooling, and directed saving towards financing children in education. Consequently, children were no longer able to bring a wage into the family household.

33. See Hannah Arendt, *The Human Condition*, University of Chicago Press, Chicago 1958.

the more safety-nets, the more raw capitalism can get away with murder...

GENERAL INTRODUCTION

ON THE SPIRIT OF CAPITALISM AND
THE ROLE OF CRITIQUE

The subject of this book is the *ideological changes that have accompanied recent trans-formations in capitalism*. It suggests an interpretation of the dynamic that runs from the years following the events of May 1968, when the critique of capitalism was expressed loud and clear, to the 1980s when, with critique silenced, the organizational forms on which the functioning of capitalism rests were profoundly altered, right up to the faltering search for new critical foundations in the second half of the 1990s. It is not merely descriptive, but proposes, by way of this historical example, a more general theoretical framework for understanding the way in which the ideologies associated with economic activity are altered. We stipulate that the term 'ideology' is to be construed here not in the reductionist sense to which it has often been reduced in the Marxist vulgate – that is to say, a moralizing discourse, intended to conceal material interests, which is constantly contradicted by practice – but as developed, for example, in the work of Louis Dumont: a set of shared beliefs, inscribed in institutions, bound up with actions, and hence anchored in reality.

We shall perhaps be criticized for tackling a transformation of global scope on the basis of a local example: France in the last thirty years. We certainly do not believe that the French case single-handedly encapsulates all the transformations of capitalism. However, far from being convinced by the approximations and broad brushstrokes that make up the ordinary run of discourses on globalization, we have sought to establish the model of change presented here on the basis of analyses which are pragmatic in character – that is to say, capable of taking account of the ways in which people engage in action, their justifications, and the meaning they give to their actions. Yet the influence of national political conjunctures and traditions on the orientation of economic practices, and the ideological forms of expression accompanying them, remains so strong that such an undertaking remains practically unrealizable at a global or even continental level, essentially for lack of time and resources. No doubt this is why general approaches are often led to assign preponderant importance to explanatory factors – typically of a technological, macroeconomic or demographic kind – which are treated as forces external to the human beings and nations that experience them, in the way one endures a storm. For this historical neo-Darwinism, 'mutations' are imposed on us in much the same way as they are imposed on species: we must adapt or die. But human beings do not only endure history; they make it. And we wanted to see them at work.

We are not claiming that what has occurred in France is a paradigm for the rest of the world, or that the models we have established on the basis of the French situation possess a universal validity as such. Nevertheless, we have good reason to believe that rather similar processes have marked the evolution of the ideologies accompanying the redeployment of capitalism in the other developed countries, in accordance with modalities that stem in each instance from the specificities of political and social history, which only detailed regional analyses can bring out with the requisite precision.

We have sought to clarify *the relations that were established between capitalism and its critiques* in order to interpret certain phenomena in the ideological sphere over recent decades: the waning of critique at a time when capitalism was undergoing significant restructuring whose social impact could not go unnoticed; the new enthusiasm for enterprise, orchestrated by Socialist governments, during the 1980s and the depressive repercussions of the 1990s; the difficulties faced by attempts to reconstruct critique today on new bases and – for now – its fairly limited mobilizing power, at a time when sources of indignation are not wanting; the profound transformation in managerial discourse and justifications of the development of capitalism since the mid-1970s; and the emergence of new representations of society, of novel ways of putting people and things to the test and, therewith, of new ways of succeeding or failing.

sic !

To carry out this work, the notion of *spirit of capitalism* rapidly became essential for us, since (as we shall see) it makes it possible to articulate the two central concepts on which our analyses are based – *capitalism and critique* – in a dynamic relation. Below we present the different concepts on which our construction is founded, as well as the springs of the model we have developed to account for ideological transformations as regards capitalism over the last thirty years, but which seem to us to possess a wider significance than the French situation studied in isolation.

THE SPIRIT OF CAPITALISM

A minimal definition of capitalism

Of the different characterizations of capitalism (or, today frequently, capitalisms) over the last century and a half, we shall employ the minimal formula stressing an *imperative to unlimited accumulation of capital by formally peaceful means*. The constant reintroduction of capital into the economic circuit with a view to deriving a profit – that is to say, increasing the capital, which will in turn be reinvested – is the basic mark of capitalism, endowing it with the dynamic and transformative power that have fascinated even the most hostile of observers. *Mahil 2008 ...*

Capital accumulation does not consist in amassing riches – that is to say, objects desired for their use-value, their ostentatious function, or as signs of power. The concrete forms of wealth (property, plant, commodities, money, etc.) have no interest in and of themselves and can even, by dint of their lack of liquidity, represent an obstacle to the only objective that really matters: the constant transformation of capital, plant and various purchases (raw materials, components, services, etc.) into output, of output into money, and of money into new investments.[1]

This detachment of capital from material forms of wealth gives it a genuinely abstract character, which helps make accumulation an interminable process. In so far as enrichment is assessed in accounting terms, the profit accumulated in a span of time being calculated as the difference between the balance-sheets of two different periods,[2] there exists no limit, no possible satiation,[3] contrary to when wealth is directed towards consumer needs, including luxuries.

No doubt there is another reason for the insatiable character of the capitalist process, underlined by Heilbroner.[4] Because capital is constantly reinvested and can expand only in circulation, the capitalist's ability to recover his outlay with a profit is under constant threat, particularly as a result of the actions of other capitalists with whom he competes for consumers' spending power. This dynamic creates constant anxiety, and offers the capitalist a very powerful self-preservation motive for continuing the accumulation process interminably.

The rivalry between traders seeking to make a profit, however, does not necessarily yield a market in the classical sense, where the conflict between a multiplicity of agents taking decentralized decisions is resolved by transactions disclosing equilibrium prices. In the minimal definition employed here, capitalism is to be distinguished from market self-regulation based upon conventions and institutions, particularly of a legal and political character, aimed at ensuring equal terms between traders (pure, perfect competition), transparency, symmetry of information, a central bank guaranteeing a stable exchange rate for credit money, and so on. Capitalism is indeed based on transactions and contracts, but these contracts can only sustain discreet arrangements to the advantage of the parties, or contain *ad hoc* clauses, without publicity or competition. Following Fernand Braudel, we shall therefore distinguish between capitalism and the market economy. On the one hand, the market economy was constructed 'step by step', and predates the appearance of capitalism's norm of unlimited accumulation.[5] On the other hand, capitalist accumulation cedes to market regulation only when more direct routes to profit are closed to it. Accordingly, recognition of the beneficent powers of the market, and acceptance of the rules and constraints on which its 'harmonious' operation depends (free trade, prohibition of cartels and monopolies, etc.), may be regarded as pertaining to a form of self-limitation by capitalism.[6]

In the framework of the minimal definition of capitalism employed here, the capitalist is, in theory, anyone who possesses a surplus and invests it to make a profit that will increase the initial surplus. The archetypal example is the shareholder who puts money into a firm and expects a return. But investment does not necessarily take this legal form: think, for example, of investment in rental property, or the purchase of Treasury bonds. Small shareholders, savers who do not want their 'money to lie idle' but 'to make a little bit on it' – as popular parlance has it – thus belong to the group of capitalists by the same token as the big property-owners who come more readily to mind under this description. In its broadest sense, the capitalist group thus encompasses all those who possess a property income[7] – a group, however, that constitutes a minority only beyond a certain level of savings. Although it is difficult to estimate, given existing statistics, it can be reckoned that it represents only around 20 per cent of French households, in what is one of the wealthiest countries in the world.[8] As one can easily imagine, on a world scale the percentage is much lower.

In this essay, we shall nevertheless reserve the term 'capitalists' first and foremost for the main actors responsible for the accumulation and expansion of capital, who directly pressurize firms to make maximum profit. Obviously, their numbers are much smaller. They comprise not only big shareholders, private individuals who are able to affect the running of business single-handedly by virtue of their influence, but also legal entities (represented by a few influential individuals, primarily the directors of firms), which, via their shareholdings, own or control the most substantial portions of global capital (holding companies and multinationals – including banks – through the mechanism of subsidiaries and interests, investment funds, or pension funds). Major employers, the salaried directors of large firms, fund managers, or large shareholders – the influence of such people on the capitalist process, the practices of firms, and the profit rates extracted is beyond doubt, unlike that of the small shareholders mentioned above. Although they constitute a population that is itself characterized by significant asset inequalities, albeit on the basis of a very advantageous situation on average, they deserve to be called capitalists inasmuch as they make the requirement of profit maximization their own, and relay its constraints to the people and legal entities over whom they exercise controlling power. Leaving to one side for the moment the issue of the systemic constraints upon capitalists and, in particular, the question of whether the directors of firms can do anything other than conform to the rules of capitalism, we shall merely note that they do so conform, and that their action is guided largely by the pursuit of substantial profits for their own capital and that entrusted to them.[9]

We shall also characterize capitalism by the wage-earning class. Marx and Weber alike place this form of organizing labour at the centre of their definition of capitalism. We shall consider the wage-earning class independently of the contractual legal forms it can assume. What matters is that part of the population – possessing little or no capital, and to whose benefit the system is not naturally geared – derives income from the sale of its labour (not the sale of the products of its labour); that it does not possess means of production, and hence depends upon the decisions of those who do in order to work (for, by virtue of property rights, the latter can refuse use of these means to them); and, finally, that in the framework of the wage relation, and in exchange for its remuneration, it surrenders all property rights over the fruits of its efforts, which are said to accrue in their entirety to the owners of capital.[10] A second important feature of the wage-earning class is that the wage-earner is theoretically free to refuse to work on the terms offered by the capitalist, just as the latter is free not to offer work on the terms demanded by the worker. The upshot is that, while the relation is unequal in the sense that the worker cannot survive for long without working, it is nevertheless markedly different from forced labour or slavery, and thus always involves a certain amount of voluntary subjection.

In France, as on a world scale, the wage-earning class has gone on expanding throughout the history of capitalism, to the point where today it involves an unprecedented percentage of the working population.[11] On the one hand, it gradually replaces self-employed labour, in the front rank of which, historically, was agriculture.[12] On the other hand, the working population has itself greatly expanded as a result of the entry into the wage-earning class of women, who perform work outside the home in growing numbers.[13]

The Necessity of a Spirit for Capitalism

In many respects, capitalism is an absurd system: in it, wage-earners have lost ownership of the fruits of their labour and the possibility of pursuing a working life free of subordination. As for capitalists, they find themselves yoked to an interminable, insatiable process, which is utterly abstract and dissociated from the satisfaction of consumption needs, even of a luxury kind. For two such protagonists, integration into the capitalist process is singularly lacking in justifications.

Now, albeit to an unequal extent depending upon the direction in which profit is sought (greater, for example, in the case of industrial than commercial or financial profits), capitalist accumulation demands the mobilization of a very large number of people whose prospects of profit are low (especially when their initial capital is small or nonexistent), and each of whom is assigned only minute responsibility – or, at any rate, responsibility that is difficult to assess – in the overall accumulation process. Consequently, when they are not downright hostile to capitalist practices, they are not particularly motivated to engage in them.

Some people can invoke a material motive for participating – more obviously in the case of wage-earners who need their wages in order to live than in that of large property owners whose activity, above a certain threshold, is no longer bound up with satisfying personal needs. On its own, however, this does not prove much of a spur. Work psychologists have regularly emphasized that pay is insufficient to induce commitment and stimulate enthusiasm for the task, the wage constituting at most a motive for staying in a job, not for getting involved in it.

Similarly, duress is insufficient to overcome actors' hostility or indifference, especially when the commitment demanded of them assumes active engagement, initiative and voluntary sacrifices, as is ever more frequently the case not simply with *cadres* but with all wage-earners. Thus, the hypothesis of 'enforced commitment' under the threat of hunger and unemployment does not seem to us to be very plausible. For if the 'slave' factories that still exist the world over are unlikely to disappear in the short term, reliance on this form of setting people to work seems problematic, if for no other reason than that most of the new ways of profit-making and new occupations invented in the last thirty years, which today generate a substantial portion of global profits, stress what human resources management calls 'workforce participation'.

In fact, the quality of the commitment one can expect depends upon the arguments that can be cited to bring out not only the advantages which participation in capitalist processes might afford on an individual basis, but also the collective benefits, defined in terms of the common good, which it contributes to producing for everyone. We call *the ideology that justifies engagement in capitalism* 'spirit of capitalism'.

This spirit is currently undergoing a significant crisis, demonstrated by growing social confusion and scepticism, to the extent that safeguarding the accumulation process, which is ultimately threatened by any narrowing of its justification to a minimal argument in terms of compulsory submission to economic laws, presupposes the formation of a new, more inspiring ideological corpus. At all events, this is valid for the developed countries, which remain at the core of the accumulation process and reckon on remaining the main suppliers of skilled personnel, whose positive involvement is imperative. Capitalism must be in a position to guarantee these people a minimum of security in sheltered zones – places to live in, have a family, bring up children, and so on – like the residential quarters of the commercial cities of the northern hemisphere, shop windows of capitalist success for new arrivals from the periphery, and hence a crucial element in the global ideological mobilization of the sum total of productive forces.

For Max Weber, the 'spirit of capitalism' refers to the set of ethical motivations which, although their purpose is foreign to capitalist logic, inspire entrepreneurs in activity conducive to capital accumulation.[14] Given the singular, even transgressive character of the kinds of behaviour demanded by capitalism when compared with the forms of life exhibited in most human societies,[15] Weber was led to defend the idea that the emergence of capitalism presupposed the establishment of a new moral relationship between human beings and their work. This was defined in the manner of a vocation, such that, regardless of its intrinsic interest and qualities, people could devote themselves to it firmly and steadily. According to Weber, it was with the Reformation that the belief became established that people performed their religious duty in the first instance by practising an occupation in the world, in temporal activities, in contrast to the extra-mundane religious life favoured by the Catholic ethos. This new conception made it possible to circumvent the question of the purpose of effort in work (boundless enrichment) at the dawn of capitalism, and thereby overcome the problem of commitment posed by the new economic practices. The conception of work as *Beruf* – a religious vocation demanding fulfilment – furnished a normative support for the merchants and entrepreneurs of nascent capitalism, and gave them good reasons – a 'psychological motivation', as Weber puts it[16] – for devoting themselves tirelessly and conscientiously to their task; for undertaking the pitiless rationalization of their affairs, inextricably bound up with the pursuit of maximum profit; and for pursuing material gain, a sign of success in fulfilling their vocation.[17] It also served them in so far as workers imbued with the same ideal proved obedient, tireless in their work, and – convinced as they were that man must perform his duty where Providence has placed him – did not seek to question the situation in which they found themselves.

We shall leave to one side the important post-Weberian debate, essentially revolving around the actual influence of Protestantism on the development of capitalism and, more generally, of religious beliefs on economic practices, and draw above all from Weber's approach the idea that people need powerful moral reasons for rallying to capitalism.[18]

Albert Hirschman reformulates the Weberian question ('[h]ow then does it come about that activity which, in the most favourable case, is barely morally tolerable, becomes a "calling" in the manner practiced by Benjamin Franklin?') as follows: '[h]ow did commercial, banking, and similar money-making pursuits become honorable at some point in the modern age after having stood condemned or despised as greed, love of lucre, and avarice for centuries past?'[19] Rather than appealing to *psychological motives* and the search by new elites for a means of guaranteeing their *personal salvation*, however, Hirschman evokes grounds that touched on the political sphere before impinging upon the economy. Profitable activities had been highly esteemed by elites in the eighteenth century on account of the *sociopolitical benefits* they anticipated from them. In Hirschman's interpretation, the secular thinking of the Enlightenment justifies profit-making activities in terms of society's common good. Hirschman thus shows how the emergence of practices in tune with the development of capitalism was interpreted as conducive to a mellowing of manners and a perfecting of modes of government. Given the inability of religious morality to quell human passions, the powerlessness of reason to govern human beings, and the difficulty of subjugating the passions by means of sheer repression, there remained the solution of using one passion to counter the others. In this way, lucre, hitherto first-placed in the order of disorders, was awarded the privilege of being selected as the innocuous passion which the task of subjugating aggressive passions henceforth rested upon.[20]

Weber's works stressed capitalism's need to furnish individual reasons, whereas Hirschman's emphasize justifications in terms of the common good. For our part, we shall employ both dimensions, construing the term 'justification' in a sense that makes it possible to encompass both individual justifications (wherein a person finds grounds for engaging in capitalist enterprise) and general justifications (whereby engagement in capitalist enterprise serves the common good).

The question of the moral justifications of capitalism is not only relevant historically, for shedding light on its origins or, in our day, for arriving at a better understanding of the ways in which the peoples of the periphery (developing countries and former socialist countries) are converted to capitalism. It is also of the utmost importance in Western countries like France, whose population is nevertheless integrated into the capitalist cosmos to an unprecedented extent. In fact, systemic constraints on actors are insufficient on their own to elicit their engagement.[21] Duress must be internalized and justified; and this is the role sociology has traditionally assigned to socialization and ideologies. Contributing to the reproduction of the social order, they have in particular the effect of enabling people not to find their everyday universe uninhabitable – one of the conditions of a durable world. If, contrary to prognoses regularly heralding its collapse, capitalism has not only survived, but ceaselessly extended its empire, it is because it could rely on a number of shared representations – capable of guiding action – and justifications, which present it as an acceptable and even desirable order of things: the only possible order, or the best of all possible orders. These justifications must be based on arguments that are sufficiently strong to be accepted as self-evident by enough people to check, or overcome, the despair or nihilism which the capitalist order likewise constantly induces – not only in those whom it oppresses but also, on occasion, in those who have responsibility for maintaining it and, via education, transmitting its values.

The spirit of capitalism is precisely the set of beliefs associated with the capitalist order that helps to justify this order and, by legitimating them, to sustain the forms of action and predispositions compatible with it. These justifications, whether general or practical, local or global, expressed in terms of virtue or justice, support the performance of more or less unpleasant tasks and, more generally, adhesion to a lifestyle conducive to the capitalist order. In this instance, we may indeed speak of a *dominant ideology*, so long as we stop regarding it as a mere subterfuge by the dominant to ensure the consent of the dominated, and acknowledge that a majority of those involved – the strong as well as the weak – rely on these schemas in order to represent to themselves the operation, benefits and constraints of the order in which they find themselves immersed.[22]

While, following the Weberian tradition, we put the ideologies on which capitalism rests at the centre of our analyses, we shall employ the notion of the spirit of capitalism in a way that departs from canonical usages. In fact, in Weber the notion of spirit takes its place in an analysis of the 'types of practical rational behaviour', the 'practical incentives to action',[23] which, constitutive of a new *ethos*, made possible a break with traditional practices, generalization of the tendency to calculation, the lifting of moral condemnations of profit, and the switch to the process of unlimited accumulation. Our perspective – intent not upon explaining the genesis of capitalism but on understanding the conditions in which it can once again secure for itself the actors required for profit creation – will be different. We shall set aside the predispositions towards the world required to participate in capitalism as a cosmos – means–end compatibility, practical rationality, aptitude for calculation, autonomization of economic activities, an instrumental relation to nature, and so on – as well as the more general justifications of capitalism produced in the main by economic science, which we shall touch on later. Today, at least among economic actors in the Western world, they pertain to the common skills which, in accordance with institutional constraints imposed as it were from without, are constantly reproduced through processes of familial and educational socialization. They constitute the ideological platform from which historical variations can be observed, even if we cannot exclude the possibility that changes in the spirit of capitalism sometimes involve the metamorphosis of certain of its most enduring aspects. *Our intention is to study observed variations, not to offer an exhaustive description of all the constituents of the spirit of capitalism.* This will lead us to detach the category of spirit of capitalism from the substantial content, in terms of *ethos*, which it is bound up with in Weber, in order to treat it as a form that can contain different things at different points in the development of the modes of organizing firms and processes of extracting capitalist profit. We shall thus seek to integrate some very diverse historical expressions of the spirit of capitalism into a single framework, and pose the question of their transformation. We shall highlight the way in which an existence attuned to the requirements of accumulation must be marked out for a large number of actors to deem it worth the effort of being lived.

We shall, however, remain faithful throughout this historical journey to the methodology of Weberian ideal types in systematizing and underlining what seems to us to be specific about one epoch by comparison with those that preceded it, and in attaching more importance to variations than constants, but without ignoring the more stable features of capitalism.

Thus, the persistence of capitalism, as a mode of co-ordinating action and a lived world, cannot be understood without considering the ideologies which, in justifying and conferring a meaning on it, help to elicit the good will of those on whom it is based, and ensure their engagement – including in situations where, as is the case with the developed countries, the order they are integrated into appears to rest virtually in its entirety on mechanisms congruent with capitalism.

What the spirit of capitalism is composed of

When it comes to lining up reasons for being in favour of capitalism, one candidate immediately presents itself: none other than economic science. From the first half of the nineteenth century down to the present, have not those in charge of capitalist institutions initially looked to economic science, and particularly its dominant currents – classical and neo-classical – for justifications? The strength of the arguments they found there stemmed precisely from the fact that they were presented as non-ideological, not directly dictated by moral motives, even if they involved reference to end results generally conformable to an ideal of justice for the best and of well-being for the greatest number. As Louis Dumont has shown, the development of economic science, whether classical economics or Marxism, contributed to constructing a representation of the world that is radically novel compared with traditional thinking, marking 'the radical separation of the economic aspects of the social fabric and their constitution as an autonomous domain'.[24] This made it possible to impart substance to the belief that the economy is an autonomous sphere, independent of ideology and morality, which obeys positive laws, ignoring the fact that such a conviction was itself the product of an ideological endeavour, and that it could have been formed only by incorporating – and then partially masking by scientific discourse – justifications whereby the positive laws of economics are in the service of the common good.[25]

In particular, the view that the pursuit of individual interests serves the general interest has been the object of an enormous, incessant labour, which has been taken up and extended throughout the history of classical economics. This separation between morality and economics, and the incorporation into economics in the same gesture of a consequentialist ethics,[26] based upon the calculation of utilities, made it possible to supply a moral sanction for economic activities solely by dint of the fact that they are profitable.[27] If we may be allowed a rapid summary, for the purposes of explaining the development of the history of economic theory which interests us here more clearly, it can be said that the incorporation of utilitarianism into economics made it possible to regard it as self-evident that 'whatever served the individual served society. By logical analogy, whatever created a profit (and thereby served the individual capitalist) also served society.'[28] In this perspective, regardless of the beneficiary, increased wealth is the sole criterion of the common good.[29] In its everyday usage, and the public pronouncements of the agents mainly responsible for explaining economic activities – heads of firms, politicians, journalists, and so on – this vulgate makes it possible to combine individual (or local) profit and overall benefit, in a way that is at once sufficiently tight and sufficiently vague to circumvent demands for justification of the activities that contribute to accumulation. It regards it as self-evident that the specific – but not readily calculable – moral cost (devotion to the passion for material gain) of establishing an acquisitive society (a cost that still preoccupied Adam Smith) is amply offset by the quantifiable benefits of accumulation (material goods, health, etc.). It also allows it to be argued that the overall increase in wealth, regardless of the beneficiary, is a criterion of the common good, as is attested on a daily basis by the presentation of the health of a country's firms, measured by their profit rate, their level of activity and growth, as a criterion for measuring social well-being.[30] This enormous social labour, performed in order to establish individual material advancement as a – if not the – criterion of social well-being, has allowed capitalism to wrest unprecedented legitimacy, for its designs and mainspring were thus legitimated simultaneously.

Works of economic science likewise make it possible to argue that, as between two different economic organizations geared to material well-being, capitalist organization is the most efficient. Free enterprise and private property in the means of production in fact introduce competition, or a risk of competition, into the system from the outset. And from the moment it exists, competition, without even having to be pure and perfect, is the surest means for customers to benefit from the best service at the lowest cost. Likewise, although they are orientated towards capital accumulation, capitalists find themselves obliged to satisfy consumers in order to achieve their own ends. Thus it is that, by extension, competitive private enterprise is always deemed more effective and efficient than non-profit-making organizations (but this at the undisclosed price of transforming the art lover, the citizen, the student, children with respect to their teachers, from recipients of social services into ... consumers); and that the privatization and maximum commodification of all services appear to be the socially optimal solution, since they reduce the waste of resources and require anticipation of customers' expectations.[31]

To the themes of utility, general well-being and progress, which have been available for mobilization in virtually unchanged fashion for two centuries, and to the justification in terms of incomparable efficiency when it comes to supplying goods and services, we must obviously add the reference to the emancipatory power of capitalism and political freedom as the collateral of economic freedom. The kinds of arguments advanced here refer to the liberation represented by wage-earning by comparison with serfdom, the room for freedom permitted by private property, or the fact that in the modern age political liberties have only ever existed sporadically in any country which was openly and fundamentally anti-capitalist, even if they are not possessed by every capitalist country.[32]

Obviously, it would be unrealistic not to include these three central supporting pillars of capitalism – material progress, effectiveness and efficiency in the satisfaction of needs, and a mode of social organization conducive to the exercise of economic freedom compatible with liberal political regimes – in the spirit of capitalism.

But, precisely by virtue of their very general and stable character over time, these reasons[33] do not seem to us to be sufficient to engage ordinary people in the concrete circumstances of life, especially working life, or to equip them with the resources in terms of arguments that allow them to face the condemnation or criticism which might be personally addressed to them on the spot. It is not obviously the case that individual wage-earners genuinely rejoice because their labour serves to increase the nation's GDP, makes it possible to improve the well-being of consumers, or because they are part of a system that creates room for free enterprise, for buying and selling. And this, to put it no higher, is because they find it difficult to make the connection between these general benefits and the living and working conditions they, and those close to them, experience. Unless people become directly wealthy by making the most of the possibilities of free enterprise – something that is reserved for a small minority – or, thanks to a job they willingly chose, achieve sufficient financial comfort to take full advantage of the consumer opportunities offered by capitalism, too many mediations are wanting for the suggestion of engagement to fire their imagination,[34] and become embodied in the deeds and gestures of everyday life.

By comparison with what (paraphrasing Weber) might be called professorial capitalism, which trots out neo-liberal dogma from on high, the expressions of the spirit of capitalism of interest to us here must be integrated into descriptions that are sufficiently substantial and detailed, and contain adequate *purchase*, to '*sensitize*' those to whom they are addressed. In other words, they must both coincide with people's moral experience of daily life and suggest models of action they can grasp. We shall see how management discourse, which aims to be formal and historical, general and local, which mixes general precepts with paradigmatic examples, today constitutes the form *par excellence* in which the spirit of capitalism is incorporated and received.

This discourse is first and foremost addressed to *cadres*, whose support for capitalism is particularly indispensable for running firms and creating profits. The high level of commitment demanded of them cannot be obtained purely through duress; moreover, less subject to immediate necessity than blue-collar workers, they can mount passive resistance, engage only reluctantly, even undermine the capitalist order by criticizing it from within. There is also the risk that the offspring of the bourgeoisie, who constitute the quasi-natural breeding ground for the recruitment of *cadres*, will *defect*, to use Hirschman's term,[35] heading for occupations that are less integrated into the capitalist mechanism (the liberal professions, arts and sciences, public service), or even partially withdraw from the labour market – especially since they possess various resources (educational, patrimonial and social).

In the first instance, capitalism must therefore perfect its legitimating apparatus with respect to *cadres* or future *cadres*. If, in the ordinary course of working life, a majority of them are persuaded to subscribe to the capitalist system because of financial constraints (notably fear of unemployment, especially if they are in debt and responsible for a family), or the classical mechanisms of sanctions and rewards (money, various benefits, career ambitions, etc.), it is plausible to reckon that the exigencies of justification are particularly developed in periods like the present. Such periods are characterized by strong numerical growth in the category, with the arrival in firms of numerous young *cadres* from the education system, whose motivation is weak and who are in search of normative incentives;[36] and, on the other hand, by profound developments compelling experienced *cadres* to retrain – something that is easier if they can give meaning to the changes of direction imposed upon them, and experience them as freely undertaken.

Being simultaneously wage-earners and spokesmen for capitalism, particularly with respect to the other members of firms, *cadres* are, on account of their position, privileged targets of criticism – especially from their subordinates – and are themselves often inclined to lend it an attentive ear. They cannot make do with the material benefits granted them, and must also have arguments to justify their position and, more generally, the selection procedures from which they emerged, or which they themselves employ. One of the constraints on their justification is the preservation of a culturally tolerable distance between their own condition and that of the workers whom they have to manage. (This was demonstrated, for example, at the turn of the 1970s by the reluctance of a number of young engineers from the *grandes écoles*, trained in a more permissive fashion than earlier generations, to supervise unskilled and semi-skilled workers who were assigned highly repetitive tasks and subject to harsh factory discipline.)

The justifications of capitalism that interest us here are thus not so much those referred to above, which capitalists or academic economists might elaborate for external consumption, particularly in the political world, but first and foremost those addressed to *cadres* and engineers. Now, if they are to be effective, the justifications in terms of the common good that they require must be based on localized criteria. Their judgements refer to the firm they work for and the extent to which the decisions taken in its name are defensible as regards their consequences – in the first instance, for the common good of

the wage-earners it employs, and then for the common good of the geographical and political community it forms part of. Unlike liberal dogmas, these
localized justifications are subject to alteration, because they must conjugate
concerns formulated in terms of justice with practices bound up with historical states of capitalism, and the specific ways of making profit in any particular
period. They must at one and the same time stimulate an inclination to act
and provide assurance that the actions thus performed are morally acceptable.
At any moment in time, the spirit of capitalism is thus expressed in a certainty
imparted to *cadres* about the 'right' actions to be performed to make a profit,
and the legitimacy of these actions.

Over and above the justifications in terms of the common good they need
in order to respond to criticism and explain themselves to others, as Weberian
entrepreneurs *cadres*, and especially young *cadres*, require personal reasons for
commitment. To make commitment to it worthwhile, to be attractive, capitalism must be capable of being presented to them in the form of activities which,
by comparison with alternative opportunities, can be characterized as 'stimulating' – that is to say, very generally, and albeit in different ways in different periods,
as containing possibilities for self-realization and room for freedom of action.

However, as we shall see more clearly later, this expectation of *autonomy*
comes up against another demand, with which it is often in tension, corresponding this time to an expectation of *security*. In fact, capitalism must also be able
to inspire *cadres* with confidence about the prospects of enjoying the well-being
it promises them over the long term (as long, if not longer, than the alternative social situations they have abandoned), and of guaranteeing their children
access to positions that allow them to preserve the same privileges.

In terms that vary greatly historically, the spirit of capitalism peculiar to
each age must thus supply resources to assuage the anxiety provoked by the
following three questions:

- How is committed engagement in the processes of accumulation a source
  of enthusiasm, even for those who will not necessarily be the main beneficiaries of the profits that are made?
- To what extent can those involved in the capitalist universe be assured of
  a minimum of security for themselves and their children?
- How can participation in capitalist firms be justified in terms of the
  common good, and how, confronted with accusations of injustice, can the
  way that it is conducted and managed be defended?

The different historical states of the spirit of capitalism

The changes in the spirit of capitalism that are currently emerging, to which
this book is devoted, are certainly not the first. Over and above the kind of
archaeological reconstruction to be found in Weber's work of the *ethos* that

inspired the original capitalism, we possess at least two stylized or typological descriptions of the spirit of capitalism. Each of them defines the different components identified above and indicates, for its time, what an inspiring adventure capitalism could represent: how it seemed to be the bearer of solid foundations for building the future, and of responses to expectations of a just society. It is these different combinations of autonomy, security and the common good that we shall now evoke very schematically.

The first description, undertaken at the end of the nineteenth century – in novels as much as the social sciences proper – is focused on the person of the bourgeois entrepreneur and a description of bourgeois values. The image of the entrepreneur, the captain of industry, the conquistador,[37] encapsulates the heroic elements of the portrait,[38] stressing gambles, speculation, risk, innovation. On a broader scale, for more numerous social categories the capitalist adventure is embodied in the primarily spatial or geographical liberation made possible by the development of the means of communication and wage-labour, which allow the young to emancipate themselves from local communities, from being enslaved to the land and rooted in the family; to escape the village, the ghetto, and traditional forms of personal dependence. In return, the figure of the bourgeois and bourgeois morality afford elements of security in an original combination, combining novel economic propensities (avarice or parsimony, the spirit of saving, a tendency to rationalize daily life in all its aspects, development of capacities for book-keeping, calculation, prediction) with traditional domestic predispositions: the importance attached to the family, lineage, inheritance, the chastity of daughters in order to avoid misalliances and the squandering of capital; the familial or patriarchal nature of relations with employees[39] – what will subsequently be denounced as paternalism – whose forms of subordination remained largely personal in firms that were generally small in size; the role accorded charity in relieving the sufferings of the poor.[40] As for justifications aspiring to greater generality and referring to constructions of the common good, they owed less to economic liberalism, the market,[41] or scientific economics, whose diffusion remained fairly limited, than to a belief in progress, the future, science, technology, and the benefits of industry. A vulgar utilitarianism was employed to justify the sacrifices required by the market in pursuit of progress. Precisely this amalgam of very different, even incompatible propensities and values – thirst for profit and moralism, avarice and charity, scientism and familial traditionalism – which is at the root of the bourgeois self-division François Furet refers to,[42] underlay what was to be most unanimously and enduringly denounced in the bourgeois spirit: its hypocrisy.

A second characterization of the spirit of capitalism was most fully developed between the 1930s and the 1960s. Here, the emphasis is less on the individual entrepreneur than on the organization. Centred on the development at the beginning of the twentieth century of the large, centralized and bureaucratized industrial firm, mesmerized by its gigantic size, its heroic figure is the manager.[43] Unlike the shareholder seeking to increase his personal wealth, he is preoccupied by the desire endlessly to expand the size of the firm he is responsible for, in order to develop mass production, based on economies of scale, product standardization, the rational organization of work, and new techniques for expanding markets (marketing). Particularly 'exciting' for young graduates were the opportunities offered by organizations for attaining positions of power from which one could change the world and, for a large majority, liberation from need, the fulfilment of desires thanks to mass production and its corollary: mass consumption.

In this version, the security dimension was supplied by a faith in rationality and long-term planning – the priority task for managers – and, above all, by the very gigantism of the organizations, which constituted protective environments not only offering career prospects, but also taking care of everyday life (subsidized accommodation, holiday camps, training bodies), modelled on the army (a type of organization of which IBM represented the paradigm in the 1950s and 1960s).

As for the reference to a common good, it was provided in coming to terms not only with an ideal of industrial order embodied by engineers – belief in progress, hope invested in science and technology, productivity and efficiency – that was even more resonant than in the earlier version; but also with an ideal which might be described as civic in the sense that the stress fell on institutional solidarity, the socialization of production, distribution and consumption, and collaboration between large firms and the state in pursuit of social justice. The existence of salaried managers and the development of categories of technicians, 'organizers'; the construction in France of the category of *cadres*;[44] the increase in the number of owners constituted by legal entities rather than actual persons; or the limits introduced into ownership of firms with, in particular, the development of rights for wage-earners and the existence of bureaucratic rules restricting employers' prerogatives as regards workforce management – these developments were interpreted as so many indices of a profound change in capitalism, marked by an attenuation of class struggle, a separation between the ownership of capital and control of the firm, which was transferred to the 'technostructure',[45] and as signs of the appearance of a new capitalism, propelled by a spirit of social justice. We shall have frequent occasion to return to the specificities of this 'second' spirit of capitalism.

Changes in the spirit of capitalism thus proceed in tandem with profound alterations in the living and working conditions, and the expectations – whether for themselves or for their children – of workers, who play a role in the process of capitalist accumulation in firms, without being its privileged beneficiaries. Today, the security supplied by academic qualifications has diminished, retirement pensions are under threat, and careers are no longer guaranteed. The mobilizing power of the 'second spirit' is in question, while the forms of accumulation have once again been profoundly transformed.

If our analysis is accepted, one probable ideological trend in the current situation can be identified, since it is based upon the system's capacity for survival and restricted to adjustments within the framework of the capitalist regime – from which, following the end of the communist illusion, no feasible exits exist for now – not even in theory. It is the formation in the developed countries of a spirit of capitalism that is more capable of attracting support (and hence also more directed towards justice and social well-being), with a view to seeking to regalvanize workers and, at a minimum, the middle class.

The 'first' spirit of capitalism – associated, as we have seen, with the figure of the bourgeois – was in tune with the essentially familial forms of capitalism of an age when gigantic size was very rarely sought after. Owners and employers were personally known to their employees; the fate and life of the firm were closely associated with those of a family. As for the 'second' spirit, which was organized around the central figure of the director (or salaried manager) and *cadres*, it was bound up with a capitalism of large firms, already sufficiently imposing for bureaucratization and the use of an abundant, increasingly academically qualified managerial staff to be a central element. But only some of them (a minority) may be characterized as multinationals. Shareholding became more impersonal, with numerous firms finding themselves detached from the name and destiny of a particular family. The 'third' spirit, in its turn, will have to be isomorphic with a 'globalized' capitalism employing new technologies, to cite only the two aspects most frequently mentioned as characteristic of capitalism today.

The way out of the ideological crisis that set in during the second half of the 1930s, with the loss of momentum of the first spirit, could not have been predicted. The same is true of the crisis we are currently experiencing. The need to restore meaning to the accumulation process, and combine it with the requirements of social justice, comes up in particular against the tension between the collective interest of capitalists as a class and their particular interests as atomized operators competing in a market.[46] No market operator wants to be the first to offer a 'good life' to those he hires, since his production costs would thereby be increased, and he would be at a disadvantage in the competition pitting him against his peers. On the other hand, the capitalist class as a whole has an interest – especially where *cadres* are concerned – in overall measures that make it possible to retain the commitment of those on whom profit creation depends. We may thus reckon that the formation of a third spirit of capitalism, and its embodiment in various mechanisms, will depend largely upon the interest multinationals, which are currently dominant, have in the preservation of a peaceful zone at the centre of the world system, maintained as a breeding ground for *cadres*, where the latter can develop, raise children, and live in security.

The origin of the justifications incorporated into the spirit of capitalism

We have mentioned how important it is for capitalism to be able to rely on a justificatory apparatus attuned to the concrete forms taken by capital accumulation in a given period, which indicates that the spirit of capitalism incorporates schemas other than those inherited from economic theory. These schemas, while they permit defence of the principle of accumulation in abstraction from all historical specificity,[47] lack sufficient mobilizing power.

But capitalism cannot find any resources within itself with which to justify grounds for commitment and, in particular, to formulate arguments directed towards a demand for justice. In fact, capitalism is doubtless the sole – or at least the main – historical form organizing collective practices to be completely detached from the moral sphere, in the sense that it identifies its purpose in itself (capital accumulation as an end in itself) and not by reference, not simply to a common good, but even to the interests of a collective entity such as a people, a state, or a social class. Justification of capitalism thus assumes reference to constructions of a different order, whence derive requirements that are quite distinct from those imposed by the pursuit of profit.

To maintain its powers of attraction, capitalism therefore has to draw upon resources external to it, beliefs which, at a given moment in time, possess considerable powers of persuasion, striking ideologies, even when they are hostile to it, inscribed in the cultural context in which it is developing. The spirit sustaining the accumulation process at a given point in history is thus imbued with cultural products that are contemporaneous with it and which, for the most part, have been generated to quite different ends than justifying capitalism.[48]

Faced with a demand for justification, capitalism mobilizes 'already-existing' things whose legitimacy is guaranteed, to which it is going to give a new twist by combining them with the exigency of capital accumulation. Accordingly, it is pointless to search for a clear separation between impure ideological constructs, intended to serve capitalist accumulation, and pure, utterly uncompromised ideas, which would make it possible to criticize it. Frequently, the same paradigms find themselves engaged in condemnation and justification of what is condemned.

We can compare the process whereby ideas that were initially alien – even hostile – to capitalism were incorporated into it with the process of acculturation described by Dumont, when he shows how the dominant modern ideology of individualism was diffused by forging compromises with pre-existing cultures. From the encounter and clash between two sets of ideas-values, new representations are born that are a 'a sort of synthesis, which may be more radical or less so, a sort of alloy of the two kinds of ideas and values, the ones being of holistic inspiration, and autochthonous, the others being borrowed from the predominant individualistic configuration'. One remarkable effect of this acculturation is that 'the individualistic representations do not by any means get diluted or become less pungent as they enter into those combinations. Quite to the contrary, they become more adaptable and even stronger through these associations with their contraries.'[49] If we transpose this analysis to the study of capitalism (whose principle of accumulation goes hand in glove with individualistic modernity), we shall see how the spirit that drives it possesses two aspects, one 'turned inside', as Dumont puts it – that is to say, in this context, turned towards the accumulation process, which is legitimated – and the other turned towards the ideologies with which it is imbued, which furnish it with precisely what capitalism lacks: reasons for participating in the accumulation process that are rooted in quotidian reality, and attuned to the values and concerns of those who need to be actively involved.[50]

In Dumont's analysis, the members of a holistic culture confronted with an individualistic culture find themselves under challenge, and feel the need to defend themselves, justify themselves, in the face of what seems to them like a critique and a challenge to their identity. In other respects, however, they can be attracted by the new values, and the prospects of individual liberation and equality afforded by these values. Out of this process of attraction–resistance–search for self-justification, new compromise representations are generated.

The same observations may be made about the spirit of capitalism. It is transformed to respond to the need for justification by people who are engaged in the capitalist accumulation process at a given moment, but whose values and representations, inherited as a cultural legacy, are still associated with earlier forms of accumulation – with traditional society in the case of the birth of the 'first spirit', or with a previous spirit in the case of the transition to subsequent spirits of capitalism. What is at stake is making the new forms of accumulation attractive to them (the *exciting* dimension of any spirit), while taking account of their need to justify themselves (by relying on reference to a common good), and erecting defences against those features of the new capitalist mechanisms that they perceive as threatening the survival of their social identity (the security dimension).

In many respects, the 'second spirit' of capitalism, constructed at the same time as the supremacy of the large industrial firm became established, has characteristics that would have been disowned by neither communism nor fascism, which were nevertheless the most powerful movements critical of capitalism at the time when this 'second spirit' began to be instituted.[51] Economic *dirigisme*, a common aspiration, was to be implemented by the welfare state and its planning bodies. Mechanisms for consistent control of the allocation of value added between capital and labour were put in place with national accounting,[52] which is consistent with Marxist analyses. As for the hierarchical *modus operandi* in force in large, planned firms, it would long retain the stamp of a compromise with traditional domestic values – something that could only serve to reassure traditionalist reaction. Respect and deference in return for welfare and assistance formed part of the hierarchical contract in its traditional forms – much more so than wages in exchange for work, which encapsulates the liberal, Anglo-American manner of conceiving the employment relation. In this way, the principle of boundless accumulation found some points of convergence with its enemies, and the resulting compromise guaranteed capitalism its survival by offering hesitant populations the opportunity to participate in it more enthusiastically.

Cities as normative supports for constructing justifications

Inasmuch as they are subject to an imperative of justification, social arrangements tend to incorporate reference to a kind of very general convention directed towards a common good, and claiming universal validity, which has been modelled on the concept of the *city*.[53] Capitalism is no exception to this rule. What we have called the spirit of capitalism necessarily contains reference to such conventions, at least in those of its dimensions that are directed towards justice. In other words, considered from a pragmatic point of view, the spirit of capitalism assumes reference to two different logical levels. The first contains an agent capable of actions conducive to profit creation, whereas the second contains an agent equipped with a greater degree of reflexivity, who judges the actions of the first in the name of universal principles. These two agents obviously denote the same actor, described as capable of engaging in operations of increasing generality. Without this competence, it would in fact be impossible for actors to understand the critiques directed at capitalism in so far as it is profit-orientated, or to construct justifications to foil such critiques.

In view of the central character of the concept of the city here, we are now going to go back over the work where the model of cities was presented. The concept of the city is orientated towards the question of justice. It is intended to be modelled on the kind of operations that actors engage in during disputes with one another, when they are faced with a demand for justification. This demand for justification is inextricably linked to the possibility of critique. The justification is necessary to back up the critique, or to answer it when it condemns the unjust character of some specific situation.

To characterize what is meant by justice here, and in order to give ourselves the opportunity to compare seemingly very different disputes with one and the same notion, we shall say that disputes over justice always have as their object the ranking of *status* in a situation.

To explain what we understand by status, let us take a trivial example – for instance, the problem of distributing the food between those who are present at a meal. The issue of the order in which the dish is offered to guests is unavoidable, and has to be settled publicly. Unless the significance of this sequence is neutralized by the introduction of a rule adjusting the temporal order to a spatial order (everyone serves themselves in turn, 'without any fuss'), the temporal sequence lends itself to being interpreted as an order of precedence according to the comparative status of the persons, as in serving the elderly first and children last. But observance of this order can present tricky problems, and give rise to disputes when several different principles of ranking order are in opposition. If the sequence is to run smoothly, the guests must therefore be in agreement about the comparative status of people as disclosed by the order they are served in.[54] Yet this agreement on status presupposes a more fundamental agreement on a *principle of equivalence*, by recourse to which the status of those present can be established. Even if the principle of equivalence is not explicitly mentioned, it must be sufficiently clear and present in everyone's mind for the episode to unfold naturally. These principles of equivalence are designated by the term *principes supérieurs communs*, borrowed from Rousseau.

These principles of status cannot emerge from a local, contingent arrangement. Their legitimacy depends upon their robustness – that is to say, their capacity for validity in an a priori unlimited number of particular situations, bringing together beings with the most varied qualities. That is why the principles of equivalence that have a claim to validity in a society at a given point in time are orientated, in some sense by their very structure, towards universal validity.

If, at a given point in time, a multiplicity of legitimate forms of status exists, their number is nevertheless not unlimited. Six logics of justification, six 'cities', have been identified in contemporary society. To define them, the work we are basing ourselves on here shuttled between two types of sources. On the one hand, there were empirical data collected by fieldwork on conflicts and disputes; supplying a corpus of arguments and situational mechanisms, this guided intuition towards the kind of justifications often used in everyday life. On the other hand, there were constructions, systematically developed in political philosophy, which possess a high level of logical coherence; this allows them to be put to profitable use in the task of modelling shared competence.[55]

In the *inspirational city*, high status pertains to the saint who achieves a state of grace, or the artist who receives inspiration. It reveals itself in the clean body prepared by ascesis, whose inspired manifestations (holiness, creativity, artistic sense, authenticity, etc.) constitute the privileged form of expression. In the *domestic city*, high status depends upon people's seniority in a chain of personal dependencies. In a system of subordination established on a domestic model, the political bond between beings is conceived as a generalization of the generational link, combining tradition and proximity. The 'great man' is the elder, the ancestor, the father, to whom respect and fidelity are due, and who vouchsafes protection and support. In the *reputational city*, high status depends exclusively on the opinion of others – that is to say, on the number of people who confer their trust and esteem. The 'great man' in the *civic city* is the representative of a collective whose general will he expresses. In the *commercial city*, the 'great man' is he who enriches himself by supplying highly desirable commodities in a competitive market, by successfully passing the market test. In the *industrial city*, high status is based upon efficiency, and defines a scale of professional abilities.

When it refers to the common good, the second spirit of capitalism invokes justifications that rest upon a compromise between the industrial city and the civic city (and, secondarily, the domestic city), whereas the first spirit was rooted in a compromise between domestic and commercial justifications.

Along similar lines, we shall have to identify the conventions with a universal vocation and the modes of reference to the common good assumed by the third spirit of capitalism, which is in the process of being formed. As we shall see, however, capitalism's new justificatory discourses are only imperfectly conveyed by the six cities that have been identified. In order to describe the 'residue', which cannot be interpreted in the language of the six existing cities, we have been led to model a seventh city, making it possible to create equivalences and justify positions of comparative status in a network world. In contrast to the work mentioned above, however, to systematize the arguments used we have relied not on a major text of political philosophy,[56] but on a corpus of management texts from the 1990s – the fact that they are intended for *cadres* makes them an especially obvious receptacle for the new spirit of capitalism – and on an analysis of various concrete proposals being advanced today to improve social justice in France. We are in fact contemporaneous with an intense effort, in which the social sciences are actively participating, to reconstruct a model of society. While it wants to be realistic – that is to say, attuned to people's experience of the social world they are thrust into, and compatible with a certain number of commonplaces rightly or wrongly regarded as self-evident (firms require flexibility, the system of contributory pension schemes cannot survive for much longer, the unemployment of the unskilled is here to stay, etc.) – this model possesses a normative character in the sense that it is directed towards greater justice.

We shall therefore have to demonstrate how the new spirit of capitalism arises on hitherto unused principles of equivalence. We shall also have to indicate the process of cultural assimilation of themes and constructs already present in the ideological environment, deriving in particular from the critical discourses addressed to capitalism, through which this spirit was structured and progressively became more firmly entrenched, to the point of forming a novel ideological configuration.

The spirit of capitalism legitimates and constrains the accumulation process

We have seen how capitalism is obliged, if it is to succeed in engaging the people who are indispensable to the pursuit of accumulation, to incorporate a spirit that can provide attractive, exciting life prospects, while supplying guarantees of security and moral reasons for people to do what they do. And this composite amalgam of grounds and reasons turns out to be variable over time, depending upon the expectations of those who must be mobilized and the hopes they have grown up with, as well as the forms taken by accumulation in different periods. The spirit of capitalism must meet a demand for self-justification, particularly in order to resist anti-capitalist critique; and this involves reference to conventions of general validity as to what is just or unjust.

This is an appropriate moment in our analysis to make it clear that the spirit of capitalism, far from simply occupying the position of a 'dash of spirit', a spiritualist 'point of honour', or a 'superstructure' – as is assumed by a Marxist approach to ideology – plays a key role in the capitalist process, which it serves by restraining that process. In fact, the justifications that make it possible to mobilize the relevant parties fetter accumulation. If the justifications proffered are taken seriously, not all profit is legitimate, not all enrichment is just, not all accumulation, even substantial and rapid accumulation, is licit. Max Weber already endeavoured to show how capitalism, thus fettered, was clearly distinguished from a passion for gold indulged in unrestrainedly, and that one of its specific characteristics was precisely the rational moderation of this impulse.[57]

The internalization of a certain spirit of capitalism by actors thus places constraints on accumulation processes that are not purely formal, conferring a specific framework on them. In this way, the spirit of capitalism simultaneously furnishes a justification of capitalism (in opposition to challenges that are intended to be radical) and a critical fulcrum making it possible to condemn the discrepancy between the concrete forms of accumulation and normative conceptions of the social order.

If it is to be taken seriously in the light of the numerous critiques directed at capitalism, justification of the forms in which capitalism has operated historically must equally be subject to reality tests. To withstand such tests, the justification of capitalism must be able to lean upon various mechanisms – collections of objects, rules and conventions – of which law might be an expression at the national level, and which, not being limited to framing the pursuit of profit, are orientated towards justice. Thus, the second spirit of capitalism was inseparably bound up with mechanisms of career management in large firms, the establishment of contributory pension schemes, and the extension to an ever greater number of situations of the legal form of the wage-labour contract, so that workers enjoyed the benefits accruing to this condition.[58] In the absence of these mechanisms, no one could genuinely have believed in the promises of the second spirit.

The constraints placed on capitalism by the spirit of capitalism thus operate in two ways. On the one hand, the internalization of justifications by capitalist actors introduces the possibility of self-criticism, and favours the self-censure and self-elimination of incompatible practices within the accumulation process itself. On the other hand, the establishment of mechanisms that are *constraining*, but are the only things that can impart credibility to the spirit of capitalism, makes it possible to establish various reality tests, and thereby to provide tangible evidence in response to condemnations.

We shall give two examples, especially apt for our purposes, of the way that reference to demands expressed in terms of the common good (to a city, according to the model we employ) is able to constrain the accumulation process. In a *commercial city*, first of all, profit is valid, and the order derived from the confrontation between different persons pursuing profit is just, only if the market test meets strict conditions of equality of opportunity, such that success can be attributed to merit — that is to say, in this instance, the ability to seize the opportunities offered by the market and the attractions of the goods and services offered — and not to a sheer balance of power. Foremost among these constraints we may cite everything that ensures competition — for example, the absence of a dominant position, of prior arrangements and cartels, or transparency of information, and the availability of capital prior to the test that is not grossly unequal (which would, for example, justify inheritance tax). It is therefore only under very strict conditions that the market test may be deemed legitimate. Yet not only does observance of these conditions not make any specific contribution to profit creation; it can put a brake on it. We could say the same about the way reference to an *industrial city* makes it possible to justify capitalist forms of production by placing on them constraints which do not derive from the immediate requirements of accumulation; constraints, for example, like planning of a more or less long-term character, putting resources by for the future, and measures aimed at reducing risks or avoiding waste.

In taking the effects of the justification of capitalism by reference to a common good seriously, we distance ourselves both from critical approaches for which only capitalism's tendency to unlimited accumulation at any price is real, and the sole function of ideologies is to conceal the reality of all-powerful economic relations of force; and from apologetic approaches which, confusing normative supports and reality, ignore the imperatives of profit and accumulation, and place the demands for justice faced by capitalism at its heart.

These two positions are not unrelated to the ambiguity of the term 'legitimate', with its two derivatives: legitimation and legitimacy. In the first case, legitimation is turned into a mere operation of retrospective concealment, which must be unmasked in order to arrive at the reality. In the second, the communicative relevance of arguments and the legal rigour of procedures are latched on to, but without questioning the conditions of performance of the reality tests to which great men — that is, in a capitalist world, primarily the rich — owe their status, when such status is deemed legitimate. As we define it, the notion of the spirit of capitalism makes it possible to surmount an opposition that has dominated a considerable amount of the sociology and philosophy of the last thirty years, at least when it comes to works at the inter-section of the social and the political: the opposition between theories, often Nietzscheo–Marxist in inspiration, which see in society only violence, relations of force, exploitation, domination and conflicts of interest;[59] and theories, inspired instead by contractualist political philosophies, which have empha-sized forms of democratic debate and the conditions of social justice.[60] In works deriving from the first current, the description of the world seems too grim to be true: such a world would not be habitable for very long. But in works related to the second, the social world is, it must be confessed, a little too rosy to be credible. The first theoretical orientation frequently deals with capitalism, but without acknowledging any normative dimension to it. The second takes account of the moral requirements that stem from a legitimate order, yet, underestimating the importance of interests and relations of force, tends to ignore the specificity of capitalism, whose contours are blurred by virtue of the fact that they are grounded in the intricate conventions on which social order always rests.

CAPITALISM AND ITS CRITIQUES

The notion of the spirit of capitalism equally allows us to combine in one and the same dynamic the development of capitalism and the critiques that have been made of it. In fact, in our construction we are going to assign critique the role of a motor in changes in the spirit of capitalism.

If capitalism cannot do without an orientation towards the common good, whence it derives reasons for commited engagement, its lack of concern for norms means that the spirit of capitalism cannot be generated exclusively out of its own resources. As a result, it needs its enemies, people whom it outrages and who are opposed to it, to find the moral supports it lacks and to incor-porate mechanisms of justice whose relevance it would otherwise have no reason to acknowledge. The capitalist system has proved infinitely more robust than its detractors – Marx at their head – thought. But this is also because it has discovered routes to its survival in critiques of it. For example, did not the new capitalist order derived from the Second World War share with fascism and communism the features of assigning great importance to the state, and a certain economic *dirigisme*? It is probably this surprising capacity for survival by absorbing part of the critique that has helped to disarm anti-capitalist forces. The paradoxical consequence is that in periods when capitalism seems triumphant – as is the case today – it displays a fragility that emerges precisely when real competitors have disappeared.

Moreover, the very concept of critique escapes theoretical polarization between interpretations in terms of relations of force and of legitimate rela-tions. In effect, the idea of critique is meaningful only when there is a difference between a desirable and an actual state of affairs. To give critique the place that falls to it in the social world, we must stop reducing justice to force, or allowing ourselves to be blinded by the existence of justice to the point where we ignore relations of force. To be valid, critique must be capable of justifying itself – that is to say, clarifying the normative supports that ground it – especially when it is confronted with the justifications that those who are subject to critique supply for their action. Hence it continues to refer to justice, for if justice is a delusion, what is the point of criticizing?[61] On the other hand, however, critique presents a world in which the requirement of justice is incessantly contravened. It unmasks the hypocrisy of moral pretensions that conceal the reality of relations of force, exploitation and domination.

The effects of critique on the spirit of capitalism

The potential impact of critique on the spirit of capitalism seems to be of at least three sorts.

First of all, it can *delegitimate previous spirits and strip them of their effectiveness*. Thus, Daniel Bell argues that American capitalism encountered major difficulties at the end of the 1960s, as a result of a growing tension between ways of relating to work derived from the Protestant asceticism it continued to rely on, and the blossoming of a mode of existence, based on immediate consumer pleasure stimulated by credit and mass production, which wage-earners in capitalist firms were encouraged to adopt in their private lives.[62] According to this analysis, the materialistic hedonism of the consumer society clashed head-on with – that is, criticized – the values of toil and saving that were supposed, at least implicitly, to support life at work, and thus undermined modes of engagement associated with the then dominant spirit of capitalism, which consequently found itself partially delegitimated. There ensued a significant demobilization of wage-earners as a result of altered expectations and aspirations.

A second effect of critique is that, in opposing the capitalist process, it compels its spokesmen to justify that process in terms of the common good. And the more violent and convincing the critique for a large number of people, the more the justifications advanced in response will have to be combined with reliable mechanisms that guarantee *a positive improvement in terms of justice*. If those who speak for the social movements make do, in response to their demands, with superficial declarations that are not followed by concrete actions (empty words, as they say); if the expression of finer feelings suffices to calm indignation, then there is no reason for improving the mechanisms that are supposed to render capitalist accumulation more in keeping with the common good. And when capitalism is obliged to respond positively to the points raised by critique, to try to placate it and maintain the support of its troops, who are in danger of listening to the denunciations, *by the same gesture it incorporates some of the values in whose name it was criticized*. The dynamic impact of critique on the spirit of capitalism here takes the form of a strengthening of the justifications and associated mechanisms which, while it does not challenge the principle of accumulation itself, or the need for profits, partially satisfies the critique and integrates into capitalism constraints that correspond to the points of most concern to its detractors. The price paid by critique for being listened to, at least in part, is to see some of the values it had mobilized to oppose the form taken by the accumulation process being placed at the service of accumulation, in accordance with the process of cultural assimilation referred to above.

A final potential impact of critique rests upon a much less optimistic analysis of the reactions of capitalism. We may suppose that, in certain conditions, it can *elude the requirement of strengthening the mechanisms of justice* by making itself more difficult to decipher, by 'clouding the issue'. According to this scenario, the response to critique leads not to the establishment of more just mechanisms but to a change in the modes of profit creation, such that the world is momentarily disrupted with respect to previous referents, and in a state that is extremely difficult to decipher. Faced with new arrangements whose emergence was not anticipated, and of which it is difficult to say whether they are more or less favourable to wage-earners than the earlier social mechanisms, critique finds itself disarmed for a time. The old world it condemned has disappeared, but people do not know what to make of the new one. Here critique acts as a spur hastening the transformation of modes of production, which then enter into tension with the expectations of wage-earners shaped on the basis of previous processes. This calls for an ideological reconstruction to demonstrate that the world of work does indeed still possess a 'meaning'.

We shall have occasion to invoke these three types of effects to account for the transformations in the spirit of capitalism over the last thirty years.

The model of change we shall employ rests upon the interplay between three terms. The first represents critique, and can be parametrized according to what it denounces (the objects of denunciation being, as we shall see, pretty various in the case of capitalism) and its vigour. The second corresponds to capitalism inasmuch as it is characterized by the mechanisms for organizing work, and ways of making a profit associated with it, at a given period. The third likewise denotes capitalism, but this time in so far as it integrates mechanisms intended to maintain a tolerable space between the means employed to generate profits (second term) and demands for justice relying on conventions whose legitimacy is acknowledged. Each of the poles of this three-term opposition can develop: critique can change its object, decrease or increase in virulence; capitalism can maintain or change its mechanisms of accumulation; it can also improve them in the direction of greater justice, or dismantle the guarantees that have hitherto been offered.

A critique that is exhausted or defeated, or loses its vigour, allows capitalism to relax its mechanisms of justice and alter its production processes with total impunity. A critique that increases in vigour and credibility compels capitalism to strengthen its mechanisms of justice, unless – assuming the political and technological environment permits it – this instead constitutes an incentive to blur the rules of the game by capitalism transforming itself.

Change in the mechanisms of capitalist accumulation has the effect of temporarily disarming critique. But there is also a good chance that it will lead, in the medium term, to the reformulation of a new spirit of capitalism to restore the involvement of wage-earners, who, with these developments, have lost the reference-points they clung on to in order to have a hold over their work. Equally, it is not impossible for a transformation in the rules of the capitalist game to alter the expectations of wage-earners, and thereby undermine the mechanisms of accumulation – as in the case analysed by Bell.[63]

On the other hand, the establishment of mechanisms ensuring greater justice placates critique when it comes to the contents of the demands advanced hitherto. By the same token, however, this can also prompt it to switch to other problems – a move that is invariably accompanied by reduced vigilance about old points of protest, thereby opening up new opportunities for capitalism to change the rules of the game, and entailing an erosion of the benefits that have been obtained, leading, in the medium term, to a revival of critique.

At the heart of this three-sided game, functioning as a recording chamber, resonance-box, and crucible where new compromises are formed, we find the spirit of capitalism. It is renegotiated, challenged, or even destroyed prior to emerging anew, through transformation of the mechanisms geared towards profit and justice alike, and continuous metamorphosis in the need for justification under fire from critique. Study of the spirit of capitalism and its evolution is thus an especially appropriate entry point into analysis of the conjoint dynamic of capitalism and its critiques, which we have placed at the heart of this work.

There is one notion that will help us to articulate the three terms of capitalism, spirit of capitalism and critique: that of the *test*, which, in addition, represents an excellent vehicle for integrating exigencies of justice and relations of force into the same framework without reductionism.

Tests of strength and legitimate tests

The notion of the test breaks with a narrowly determinist conception of the social, whether based on the omnipotence of structures or, in a culturalist perspective, the domination of internalized norms. From the viewpoint of action, it puts the emphasis on the various degrees of uncertainty haunting situations in social life.[64]

For our project, the notion of the test has the advantage of allowing us to circulate between relations of force and legitimate orders with the same theoretical instruments. The test is always a test of strength. That is to say, it is an event during which beings, in pitting themselves against one another (think of an arm-wrestling match between two people, or the confrontation between a fisherman and the trout that seeks to elude him), reveal what they are capable of and, more profoundly, what they are made of. But when the situation is subject to justificatory constraints, and when the protagonists judge that these constraints are being genuinely respected, the test of strength will be regarded as legitimate.

We shall say in the first instance (the test of strength) that at its conclusion the disclosure of power is conveyed by the determination of a certain degree of *strength*; and in the second (the legitimate test), by a judgement as to the respective *status* of people. Whereas the attribution of strength defines a state of affairs without any moral implications, the attribution of a status assumes a judgement that bears not only on the respective strength of the opposing parties, but also on the just character of the order disclosed by the test.

The transition from tests of strength to tests of legitimate status presupposes a social labour identifying and characterizing different kinds of strength, which must be amenable to being distinguished and separated from one another. In fact, to be open to assessment from the standpoint of justice, a test must first of all be specified, be a test of *something* – of this or that, a competition on the running track or in Latin – and not indeterminate, open to a confrontation between beings in any respect whatsoever, and using any kind of force they choose (which is arguably one possible characterization of violence). If what is put to the test is not specified in advance, the test is adjudged unsound, unreliable, and its outcome is open to challenge. Thus, whereas in the logic of tests of strength the opposing forces meet, are deployed and displaced, constrained only by the resistance of other forces, tests of status are valid (just) only if they involve forces of the same kind. We may no longer examine the strength of money by means of art, or the strength of reputation or intelligence by money, and so on. To be not only strong but also enjoy high status, it is necessary to commit the kind of strength that is appropriate in the test one is submitting to. To ensure the justice of a test is thus to arrange it and control its performance in such a way as to prevent interference by external forces.

In a society where a large number of tests are subject to conditions defining what is a legitimate test, the strength of the strong is diminished. For the strictness of the tests tends to hamper the possibilities of those who, possessing various unspecified strengths, can transfer them, confuse them, exchange them and extend them, depending simply on the strategic necessities of the situation. For example, one cannot pay literary critics and be recognized as an inspired, great writer, or become principal private secretary just because one is the minister's cousin. The idea of winning by any and all means has to be abandoned.

It is nevertheless the case that tests of strength and legitimate tests are not to be conceived as discrete oppositions. There is a *continuum* between them, such that tests may be deemed more or less just, and it is always possible to unmask the action of underlying forces that contaminate a test claiming legitimacy. (We see this, for example, with the disclosure of the social handicaps or advantages that influence the results of educational tests, without examiners explicitly taking account of them.)

The notion of test places us at the heart of the sociological perspective, one of whose most persistent questions – which no theory has dodged – concerns the selection process governing the differential distribution of persons between positions of unequal value, and the more or less just character of this distribution. (This is where sociology rejoins questions of political philosophy.) It also has the advantage of allowing for changes of scale, depending on whether the object of analysis is test situations in their singularity, interactions treated as unique events (some particular exchange between a candidate and a recruiting agent) – handling which calls upon the procedures of micro-sociology; or attempts to describe relatively stable classes of test in a manner which, from the viewpoint of a sociology of action, takes up the traditional questions of macro-sociology. The notion of test thus makes it possible to shift between the micro and the macro, in the sense that it is inflected towards both sectoral mechanisms or unique situations and societal arrangements. For the major trends in social selection rest, in the last analysis, on the character of the tests that a society recognizes at a given moment in time. It is thus no exaggeration to think that a society (or the state of a society) may be defined by the character of the tests it sets itself, through which the social selection of people is conducted, and by conflicts over the more or less just nature of those tests.

Critique and tests are intimately related. Critique leads to tests in so far as it challenges the existing order and casts suspicion upon the status of the opposing beings. But tests – especially when they claim legitimacy – are vulnerable to critique, which reveals the injustices created by the action of hidden forces.

The impact of critique on capitalism operates by means of the effects it has on the central tests of capitalism. This is the case with the tests on which the division between wages and profits depends, in a certain state of the labour and company law that they are supposed to respect; or, to take another example, with recruitment tests, which provide access to positions regarded as more or less advantageous.

The role of critique in the dynamic of tests

We may say that there are two ways of criticizing tests.

The first is *corrective* in intent: critique reveals those features of the tests under challenge that infringe justice and, in particular, the forces mobilized by certain of the protagonists without the others being aware of it, thereby securing an undeserved advantage. In this instance, the objective of the critique is to improve the justice of the test – *to make it stricter* – to increase the degree to which it is conventionalized, to develop its regulatory or legal supervision. Established tests – for example, political elections, educational exams, sporting contests and joint negotiations between social partners – are the fruit of such effort, refining their justice in order to admit only those forces deemed compatible with the definition of the test. But by the same token, these tests always remain open to improvement, and hence to critique. The work of refinement is in effect interminable, because the number of respects in which people can be apprehended is ontologically limitless.[65]

A second manner of criticizing tests may be dubbed *radical*. In this instance, what is at stake is no longer correcting the conditions of the test with a view to making it more just, but suppressing it and ultimately replacing it with a different test. In the first case, critique takes the criteria the test is supposed to satisfy seriously, in order to demonstrate that its conduct deviates in various respects from its definition – or, if you like, its concept – and to help bring it more into line with the claims it is supposed to meet. In the second case, it is the validity of the test itself – strictly speaking, what conditions its existence – that is subject to challenge. From this second critical position, the critique that aims to rectify the test will itself often be criticized as *reformist*, in contrast to a radical critique that has historically proclaimed itself *revolutionary*.

With respect to the model of economies of status on which we base our discussion here,[66] corrective critique is one that takes the city with reference to which the test is constructed seriously. What is involved is, as it were, a critique internal to the city. Contrariwise, radical critique is critique performed in the name of different principles, pertaining to another city, from those on which the test in its currently accepted definition claims to base its judgements.

First of all we shall discuss the possible fate of a corrective critique that is reformist in intent. In so far as the tests under criticism claim legitimacy (so that they are justified by the same normative positions as those invoked by the critique), it is not possible for those responsible for controlling their practical conduct endlessly to ignore the observations made about them. If they are to remain legitimate, these tests must incorporate a response to the critique. This reply can consist either in demonstrating that the critique is mistaken (it is then necessary to adduce convincing evidence of this); or in making the test stricter and refining it to make it more consonant with the model of justice that supports judgements claiming legitimacy. This is the case, for example, when an exam that was not anonymous is made so, or when disclosures of information prior to stock-market transactions (insider trading) are prohibited.

But there exists another potential reaction when one is faced with corrective critique of a test, and this consists not in satisfying it, but in seeking to circumvent it. This is a possible move by certain beneficiaries of the test whose critique has revealed that they succeeded illegitimately, and who see their prospects diminish accordingly. It may also be made by the organizers of the test, or those on whom the cost of its organization mainly falls,[67] who believe that the anticipated increase in justice (and hence legitimacy) will not compensate for the higher cost of the test (reinforcement of controls and precautions, refinement of the evaluative criteria); or that, independently of the expected benefit in terms of justice, the cost has become prohibitive.

A number of actors can thus have an interest in reducing the importance assigned to the test, in marginalizing it, above all if it proves difficult to put an end to the critical enterprise, whose revival compels continual tightening of the test and an increase in its cost. Rather than challenge the established tests head-on, which would be too costly – especially in terms of legitimacy – they are prompted to seek new paths to profit by effecting *displacements* that are local, small-scale, virtually invisible, multiple. These displacements may be geographical (relocation to regions where the workforce is cheap and labour law is undeveloped or accorded little respect) if, for example, the firms do not wish to improve the division between wages and profits in the way demanded by the critique. (The same could be said of new environmental requirements.) It may also be a question of altering the criteria of success in the firm, so as to evade the procedures associated with career management, or of abolishing formal recruitment tests (making decisions on the basis of a written examination, or psycho-technical tests), which are reckoned to be too costly. These displacements, which alter a course of tests,[68] have the effect of reducing the costs associated with the maintenance of strict tests and increasing the advantages of those who are in a position to commit miscellaneous resources, and find themselves liberated from the fetters that had hitherto hampered the use they could make of their strengths. In a capitalist society, the strong are first and foremost the owners of capital, and history has repeatedly shown that in the absence of legislative and regulatory obstacles they tend to use their economic power to wrest a dominant position in all spheres, leaving wage-earners with only the meanest share of the value added that has been created. Hence under capitalism it is obviously the party of profit that invariably emerges victorious from these micro-displacements.

This manner of reacting to critique, by creating displacements, also has the effect of temporarily disarming it by presenting it with a world it no longer knows how to interpret. The critique and critical apparatuses associated with an earlier state of the spirit of capitalism in fact have little purchase on the new tests, which have not been subject to a labour of recognition, institutionalization and codification. For one of the first tasks of critique is precisely to identify the most important tests in a given society, to clarify – or press the protagonists to clarify – the principles underlying these tests, and then proceed to a critique that is corrective or radical, reformist or revolutionary, depending on the options and strategies of those conducting it.

After a multiplicity of micro-displacements, locally circumventing the most costly tests or those most subject to critique, capitalist accumulation finds itself partially released from the fetters placed on it by the constraint of the common good. But by the same token it finds itself stripped of the justifications that made it desirable for a large number of actors – unless this redeployment of tests chimes with themes deriving from a radical critique intent upon abolishing the old tests, likewise in the name of the common good, but invoking different values. A displacement of this sort loses legitimacy in terms of the old principles, but can rely on principles of legitimacy employed by another side of the critique. Short of steering clear of the capitalist regime entirely, the only possible fate of radical critique (preserving a stubborn and interminable oppositional stance, easily characterized as 'unrealistic' by its detractors) is to be used as a source of ideas and legitimacy for escaping the unduly normative and, for some actors, costly framework inherited from a prior state of capitalism.

We can thus envisage *situations where critique in its entirety finds itself disarmed* in a single move: one form, characterized as corrective here (which does not mean it necessarily conceives itself as reformist), because the tests to which it was adapted disappear or fall into disuse; the other, called radical here (which does not mean it is exclusive to those who call themselves 'revolutionaries'), because the development of the dominant ideas takes a direction that it demanded, and it finds itself partially satisfied. As we shall see later, in our view this is what occurred in France in the 1980s.

Even so, such a situation does not seem set to last, for the redeployment of capitalism creates new problems, new inequalities, new injustices: not because it is inherently unjust, but because the question of justice is not pertinent in the framework within which it develops – the norm of capital accumulation is amoral – unless critique compels it to justify and control itself.

Interpretative schemas are gradually reconstructed, making it possible to give meaning to these transformations and favouring a revival of critique by facilitating identification of the problematic new modalities of accumulation. The resumption of critique leads to the construction of new normative fulcra that capitalism must come to terms with. This compromise is asserted in the expression of a new form of the spirit of capitalism, which, like its predecessors, contains exigencies of justice.

The birth of a new spirit of capitalism thus comes about in two stages, although this is a merely analytical distinction, since they broadly overlap. In the first, we witness the sketching of a general interpretative schema of the new mechanisms and the establishment of a new cosmology, allowing people to get their bearings and deduce some elementary rules of behaviour. In the second, this schema is going to be *refined in the direction of greater justice*; with its organizing principles established, the reformist critique will strive to make the new tests that have been identified stricter.

The historical forms of the critique of capitalism

If we are to understand the historical conjuncture our work focuses on, we must now define more precisely the content of the critiques addressed to capitalism. For the orientation of a particular dynamic of capitalism, and the meaning of the transformations that affect its spirit, can be thoroughly understood only if we consider the kind of critiques it is vulnerable to. The necessity of furnishing capitalism with justifications, and casting it in an attractive light, would not in fact impose themselves with such urgency if capitalism had not from the outset been confronted with large-scale critical forces. Anti-capitalism is in fact as old as capitalism: 'Throughout the course of its development, it accompanies it like its shadow. Without courting the slightest paradox, it may be argued that anti-capitalism is the most significant expression of capitalism in the eyes of history'.[69]

Without resuming in detail the history of the critiques to which capitalism has been subject – a task that would far exceed the framework of this book – we must, in order to understand the formation of the new spirit of capitalism, recall the main themes around which the principal forms of anti-capitalism are constructed (these themes have been fairly constant since the first half of the nineteenth century).

The formulation of a critique presupposes a bad experience prompting protest, whether it is personally endured by critics or they are roused by the fate of others.[70] This is what we call the source of *indignation*. Without this prior emotional – almost sentimental – reaction, no critique can take off. On the other hand, it is a long way from the spectacle of suffering to articulated critique; critique requires a theoretical fulcrum and an argumentative rhetoric to give voice to individual suffering and translate it into terms that refer to the common good.[71] This is why there are actually two levels in the expression of any critique: a primary level – the domain of the emotions – which can never be silenced, which is always ready to become inflamed whenever new situations provoking indignation emerge; and a secondary level – reflexive, theoretical and argumentative – that makes it possible to sustain ideological struggle, but assumes a supply of concepts and schemas making it possible to connect the historical situations people intend to criticize with values that can be universalized. When we allude to critique being disarmed, it is to this second level that we are referring. Given that the work of critique consists in translating indignation into the framework of critical theories, and then voicing it (something that assumes other conditions which we shall not examine here), we can understand why, even when the critical forces seem to be in a state of complete collapse, the capacity for indignation can remain intact. It is particularly prevalent among young people, who have not yet experienced the closure of the horizon of possibilities that goes with growing older, and who may constitute the ground on which a revival of criticism becomes possible once again. This is where the guarantee of a constant renewal of critical work is to be found.

While capitalism has changed since its formation, its 'nature'[72] has not been radically transformed. As a result, the sources of indignation that have continually fuelled criticism of it have remained pretty much the same over the last two centuries. They are essentially of four sorts:

(a) capitalism as a source of *disenchantment* and *inauthenticity* of objects, persons, emotions and, more generally, the kind of existence associated with it;

(b) capitalism as a source of *oppression*, inasmuch as it is opposed to the freedom, autonomy and creativity of the human beings who are subject, under its sway, on the one hand to the domination of the market as an impersonal force fixing prices and designating desirable human beings and products/services, while rejecting others; and on the other hand to the forms of subordination involved in the condition of wage-labour (enterprise discipline, close monitoring by bosses, and supervision by means of regulations and procedures);

(c) capitalism as a source of *poverty* among workers and of *inequalities* on an unprecedented scale;

(d) capitalism as a source of *opportunism* and *egoism* which, by exclusively encouraging private interests, proves destructive of social bonds and collective solidarity, especially of minimal solidarity between rich and poor.

One of the difficulties faced by critical work is that it is virtually impossible to combine these different grounds for indignation and integrate them into a coherent framework. Consequently, most critical theories privilege one line over the others and deploy their arguments accordingly. Thus, the emphasis is sometimes placed on the industrial dimensions of capitalism (critique of product standardization, technology, the destruction of nature and authentic ways of living, factory discipline, bureaucracy, etc.), such that the same criticisms can be extended to a denunciation of 'real socialism'; and sometimes on its commercial dimensions (critique of impersonal domination by the market, of the omnipotence of money, which renders everything equivalent and turns the most sacred entities – artworks, and especially human beings – into commodities; which subjects politics to the process of commodification, making it an object of marketing and advertising like any other product). Similarly, the normative references mobilized to account for indignation are different, even difficult to reconcile. Whereas the critique of egoism and disenchantment is often accompanied by a nostalgia for traditional or orderly societies, particularly their communitarian aspects, indignation at oppression and poverty in a wealthy society is based on the values of freedom and equality which, while they are foreign to the principle of unbounded accumulation characteristic of capitalism, have historically been associated with the rise of the bourgeoisie and the development of capitalism.[73]

Consequently, the bearers of these various grounds for indignation and normative fulcra have been different groups of actors, although they can often be found associated in a particular historical conjuncture. Thus, we may distinguish between an *artistic critique* and a *social critique*.[74]

The former, which is rooted in the invention of a bohemian lifestyle,[75] draws above all upon the first two sources of indignation that we mentioned briefly above: on the one hand the disenchantment and inauthenticity, and on the other the oppression, which characterize the bourgeois world associated with the rise of capitalism. This critique foregrounds the loss of meaning and, in particular, the loss of the sense of what is beautiful and valuable, which derives from standardization and generalized commodification, affecting not only everyday objects but also artworks (the cultural mercantilism of the bourgeoisie) and human beings. It stresses the objective impulse of capitalism and bourgeois society to regiment and dominate human beings, and subject them to work that it prescribes for the purpose of profit, while hypocritically invoking morality. To this it counterposes the freedom of artists, their rejection of any contamination of aesthetics by ethics, their refusal of any form of subjection in time and space and, in its extreme forms, of any kind of work.

The artistic critique is based upon a contrast between attachment and detachment, stability and mobility, whose paradigmatic formulation is found in Baudelaire. On the one hand, we have the bourgeoisie, owning land, factories and women, rooted in possessions, obsessed with preserving their goods, endlessly concerned about reproducing, exploiting and increasing them, and thereby condemned to meticulous forethought, rational management of space and time, and a quasi-obsessive pursuit of production for production's sake. On the other hand, we have intellectuals and artists free of all attachments, whose model – the *dandy*, a product of the mid-nineteenth century – made the absence of production (unless it was self-production) and a culture of uncertainty into untranscendable ideals.[76]

The second critique, inspired by socialists and, later, by Marxists, draws instead on the second two sources of indignation that we have identified: the egoism of private interests in bourgeois society and the growing poverty of the popular classes in a society of unprecedented wealth – a mystery that will find its explanation in theories of exploitation.[77] Basing itself on morality and, often, on themes inspired by Christianity, the social critique rejects – sometimes violently – the immorality or moral neutrality, the individualism, and even the egoism or egotism of artists.[78]

Drawing as they do upon different ideological and emotional sources, the four thematics whose major features we have just mentioned are not directly compatible. Depending on the historical conjuncture, they may find themselves associated, but often at the cost of a misunderstanding that can easily be denounced as incoherence; alternatively, they may enter into tension with one another.

One example of amalgamation is intellectual critique in postwar France as articulated in a journal like *Les Temps modernes*, which was eager to remain at the forefront of all struggles, and reconcile Communist Party workerism and moralism with the aristocratic libertinism of the artistic avant-garde. In this instance, an essentially economic critique condemning bourgeois exploitation of the working class went hand in hand with a critique of mores, denouncing the oppressive and hypocritical nature of bourgeois morality (especially in matters of sexuality), and an aesthetic critique discrediting the sybaritism of a bourgeoisie with academic tastes. An insistence on *transgression* (for which the figure of Sade was the mandatory symbol for a large number of writers on the non-Communist left, from the beginning of the 1940s down to the mid-60s)[79] served as intermediary between these different themes, which nevertheless gave rise to misunderstandings or conflicts when the sexual or aesthetic transgression to which intellectuals and artists were particularly attached collided with the moralism and aesthetic traditionalism of working-class elites. Workers sequestering their employer, homosexuals kissing in public, or artists displaying trivial objects transferred from their usual context into a gallery or museum – when it came down to it, were not all these forms of one and the same *transgression* of the bourgeois order?

In other political conjunctures, however, the different traditions critical of capitalism can easily diverge and come into tension, even violent conflict. Thus, while the critique of individualism and its communitarian corollary can easily drift towards fascism (many examples of this can be found among intellectuals in the 1930s), the critique of oppression can gently lead those for whom it represents the preponderant point of attack towards acceptance – at least tacitly – of liberalism, as was the case with a number of intellectuals from the ultra-left in the 1980s. Having correctly recognized in Soviet communism another form of alienation, and having made the struggle against totalitarianism their principal battle, they did not anticipate, or were not able to recognize, the reassertion of liberal control over the Western world.

Each of these critiques may be regarded as more *radical* in its attitude towards the Enlightenment modernity in which capitalism – by the same token as democracy, but in different respects – claims to be rooted.

While it shares its individualism with modernity, the artistic critique presents itself as a radical challenge to the basic values and options of capitalism.[80] As a rejection of the disenchantment generated by the processes of rationalization and commodification of the world inherent in capitalism, it presupposes their interruption or abolition, and hence involves a total abandonment of the capitalist regime. The social critique, for its part, seeks above all to solve the problem of inequalities and poverty by breaking up the operation of individual interests. If various solutions to this problem might seem radical, they do not presuppose halting industrial production, the invention of new artefacts, or the enrichment of the nation and material progress, and thus represent a less comprehensive rejection of the frameworks and options of capitalism.

However, notwithstanding the dominant tendency of each of these critiques – towards reform of, or abandonment of, the capitalist regime – it will be observed that each of them possesses a modernist and an anti-modernist aspect. For this reason, the tension between a radical critique of modernity, which leads to 'protesting against the age without participating in it', and a modernist critique that risks leading to 'participating in the age without challenging it', is a constant feature of critical movements.[81] The artistic critique is anti-modernist when it stresses disenchantment, and modernist when it is concerned with liberation. Rooting itself in the liberal values derived from the spirit of Enlightenment, it denounces the falsity of an order that pretends to accomplish the modern project of liberation only the better to betray it. Far from liberating the human potentialities of autonomy, self-organization and creativity, capitalism excludes people from running their own affairs, subjects human beings to the domination of instrumental rationality, and keeps them imprisoned in an 'iron cage';[82] demanding the active participation of the producers, it consistently denies and destroys it.[83] The social critique is rather modernist when it underscores inequalities and anti-modernist when, fixing on the lack of solidarity, it is constructed as a critique of individualism.

The incompleteness of critique

These features of the traditions that are critical of capitalism, and the impossibility of constructing a perfectly articulated, overarching critique impartially based on the four sources of indignation we have identified, explain the inherent ambiguity of critique: even in the case of the most radical movements, it shares 'something' with what it seeks to criticize. This stems from the simple fact that the normative references on which it is based are themselves in part inscribed in the world.[84] But the same reasons account for the fallibility of critique. It can, for example, watch the world move towards a situation that will prove disastrous without intervening. Or it may regard the changes under way at a given moment favourably, because they bring about improvement in some significant respect that had been a source of indignation, without noticing that the situation is simultaneously deteriorating in another respect. In particular, in the context of the period that concerns us here, they may not notice that capitalism has indeed developed in the direction of reducing the oldest forms of oppression, but at the price – belatedly detected – of intensifying inequalities.

Accordingly, the dialectic of capitalism and its critiques necessarily proves interminable as long as we remain in the capitalist regime, which seems the most probable eventuality in the medium term. Partially attended to and integrated on certain points, circumvented or countered on others, critique must constantly shift and forge new weapons. It must continually resume its analysis in order to stay as close as possible to the properties that characterize the capitalism of its time. In many respects, this is a sophisticated form of the labour of Sisyphus, assigned to all those who are not content with a given social condition, and think that human beings must seek to improve the society they live in – something that is in itself a recent idea.[85] But the effects of critique are real. The boulder does indeed go up the full length of the slope, even if it always risks rolling back down by another path whose direction most often depends on the way it has been rolled up.[86] Moreover, even if we went so far as to accept a pessimistic interpretation of the dynamic of capitalism and its critiques, whereby, in the final analysis, 'in so far as capitalism is a source of indignation, it always pulls through it', we would find some consolation in this observation taken from the work of Karl Polanyi:

> Why should the ultimate victory of a trend be taken as proof of the ineffectiveness of the efforts to slow down its progress? And why should the purpose of these measures not be seen precisely in that which they achieved, i.e. in the slowing down of the rate of change? That which is ineffectual in stopping a line of development altogether is not, on that account, altogether ineffectual. The rate of change is often of no less importance than the direction of the change itself; but while the latter frequently does not depend upon our volition, it is the rate at which we allow change to take place which may well depend upon us.[87]

While we acknowledge that critique possesses a certain effectiveness, in this book we shall not directly tackle a question dealt with by political science and social history: the conditions on which the degree of effectiveness of critique in determinate historical situations depends.[88] Although we shall not ignore the set of factors that condition the vigour and effectiveness of critique, we have focused predominantly on its specifically ideological dimension – that is to say, on the way in which the formulation of indignation and the condemnation of contraventions of the common good operates. This choice brings with it the risk of finding ourselves accused of being interested exclusively in 'discourse', to the exclusion of what is supposedly 'real'. But it nevertheless highlights an essential part of the work of critique: the codification of 'what is not going well' and the search for the causes of this situation, with the aim of proceeding to solutions. Besides, this is the relevant level of analysis in a study devoted to the spirit of capitalism. Thus, when we refer to critique being disarmed, what is involved is ideological neutralization (critique no longer knows what to say), not physical neutralization (it knows what to say, but cannot say it or does not succeed in making itself heard).

Alterations in the spirit of capitalism independent of critique

It remains for us to dispel a final ambiguity as to the dynamic of the spirit of capitalism. We have made critique one of its most powerful motors. In obliging capitalism to justify itself, critique compels it to strengthen the mechanisms of justice it contains, and to refer to certain kinds of common good in whose service it claims to be placed. But we have equally seen that the impact of critique could be indirect, spurring capitalism to 'displace itself' more rapidly – that is to say, alter the nature of the key tests in order to evade the critique to which it is subject. Here the spirit of capitalism is affected only by the repercussion of changes that initially focused on capitalism.

But if changes in capitalism are likewise a significant source of alteration in its spirit, we have to acknowledge that not all its displacements can be related to critique. The dynamic of capitalism itself is only partially bound up with critique – or, at least, critique in the sense in which we have construed it up to now, which supposes that one gives voice ('voice' in Hirschman's conceptualization).[89] To account for the dynamic of capitalism, it is important to add the impact of critique of the 'exit' variety in Hirschman – that is, competition. The 'exit' critique, which is a refusal to buy on the part of the consumer or customer in the broad sense, a refusal of employment by the potential wage-labourer, or a refusal to serve by the independent service provider, is one to which capitalism more readily submits. In this instance too, however, it seeks to evade the obstacles critique creates – for example, by constituting monopolies or cartels so as to ignore the desire to defect, which can then no longer find an outlet. The rivalry that competition keeps up between capitalists compels them endlessly to seek advantage over their competitors – by technological innovations, the search for new products or services, improvements in existing ones, and an alteration in ways of organizing work. Thus we find here a cause of constant change in capitalism that conforms to the process of 'creative destruction' described by Schumpeter.

The effectiveness of the 'voice' critique – which, all things being equal, is expressed in harder and more costly tests, and by a fall in profits – is thus not the only reason for capitalism's displacements, even if it may play a crucial role in certain epochs. The impact of the 'voice' critique on profits is real. But capitalism's displacements are bound up with all the opportunities that emerge for increasing gains, and the most advantageous solution at a given point in time is not necessarily to renege on previously conceded benefits. On the other hand, the constant pressure of competition, and anguished observation of the strategic moves made in their markets, are a powerful spur to those in charge of firms in their endless search for new ways of doing things. Consequently, competition will be advanced as minimal justification for the transformation of capitalism, for reasons that are valid and yet scarcely acceptable to those engaged in the capitalist process, since it makes them mere playthings.

Having defined the main tools of our research, we may now embark upon a description of the changes in the spirit of capitalism over the last thirty years, in its relations with the critiques directed at the accumulation process in this period.

Notes

1 See Robert Heilbroner, *The Nature and Logic of Capitalism*, Norton, New York and London 1985.

2 The balance-sheet is the accounting instrument which, at a given point in time, inventories all the wealth invested in a concern. The importance of the accountancy tool for the functioning of capitalism – to the point that some have made its sophistication one of the origins of capitalism – is a feature very generally emphasized by analysts. See, for example, Max Weber, *The Protestant Ethic and the Spirit of Capitalism*, trans. Stephen Kalberg, Fitzroy Dearborn, Chicago and London 2001, pp. 25–6; or *General Economic History*, trans. Frank H. Knight, George Allen & Unwin, London 1927, p. 276.

3 As Georg Simmel observes, in effect money alone never holds any disappointment in store, on condition that it is intended not for expenditure but for accumulation as an end in itself: 'as a thing absolutely devoid of quality, [money] cannot hide either surprise or disappointment as does any object, however miserable' (quoted in A.O. Hirschman, *The Passions and the Interests*, Princeton University Press, Princeton 1977, p. 56). If satiation accompanies the realization of desire in an intimate knowledge of the thing desired, this psychological effect cannot be created by a calculable figure that remains abstract.

4 See Heilbroner, *The Nature and Logic of Capitalism*, pp. 53 ff.

5 Fernand Braudel, *The Wheels of Commerce*, trans. Sian Reynolds, Harper and Row, New York 1982, p. 228.

6 Examples of the way in which capitalist agents infringe market rules in order to make profits, which is beyond any possible comparison with ordinary commercial activities, abound in Braudel, for whom '[t]he capitalist game only concerned the unusual, the very special, or the very long distance connection – sometimes lasting months or even years': the use of protection 'to break into a resistant circuit' and 'ward off rivals'; privileged information and circuits of confidential information, as well as 'the acquiescence of the state', making it possible 'regularly, quite naturally and without any qualms, to bend the rules of the market economy'; and so on (*The Wheels of Commerce*, pp. 456, 384, 400).

Similarly, the *grande bourgeoisie* of the nineteenth century, despite its apparent adherence to the 'liberal credo', as Karl Polanyi puts it (*Origins of Our Time: The Great Transformation*, Victor Gollancz, London 1945), is only really in favour of *laissez-faire* in the labour market. As for the rest, in their struggle with one another capitalists use all the means at their disposal and, in particular, political control of the state, in order to restrict competition, to curb free trade when it is unfavourable to them, to occupy monopoly positions and retain them, and to benefit from geographical and political imbalances in such a way as to drain maximum profit towards the centre. See Pierre Rosanvallon, *Le Libéralisme économique. Histoire de l'idée de marché*, Seuil, Paris 1979, pp. 208–12; Immanuel Wallerstein, *Historical Capitalism*, Verso, London 1983.

7 According to the INSEE's definition, this notion covers 'the totality of physical and financial investments made by private individuals when they put buildings, money, land at someone else's disposition in exchange for a monetary payment', and excludes property for use (main residence, liquid cash and cheques) and the professional property of self-employed persons (farmers, liberal professionals, artisans, shopkeepers).

8 In January 1996, 80 per cent of households possessed a savings account, but the amounts in them rapidly reached a ceiling and were intended for popular savings first and foremost;

38 per cent had a housing plan or savings account (most with a view to purchasing their main residence). On the other hand, typical capitalist investments involved around only 20 per cent of households: 22 per cent possessed stocks and shares (bonds, government loans, SICAV (Société d'Investissement à Capital Variable) or FCP (Fonds Communs de Placement), shares outside SICAV), and 19 per cent property other than their main residence. See *INSEE Première*, no. 454, May 1996. That said, the households able to draw from their rental property an income equal to the average French income, assimilating them to fairly comfortable rentiers (or better), represent less than 5 per cent of the totality of households, and are doubtless closer to 1 than to 5 per cent (see Alain Bihr and Roland Pfefferkorn, 'Peut-on définir un seuil de richesse?', *Alternatives économiques*, special issue no. 25, 'Les riches', autumn 1995).

9   Since the work of Berle and Means, it has been recognized that if the behaviour of managers is not necessarily to maximize shareholder interests, at the very least they behave in such a way as to provide them with a satisfactory return, if not the maximum.

10   Moreover, according to Heilbroner (*The Nature and Logic of Capitalism*, pp. 65–77), this last aspect is the best concealed form of capitalist exploitation, since the whole remaining margin made on the product, whatever the amount, reverts to the capitalist by virtue of the property rules pertaining to the labour contract.

11   According to the figures cited by Gérard Vindt ('Le salariat avant guerre: instabilité et précarité', *Alternatives économiques*, no. 141, October 1996, pp. 58–61), the wage-earning class represented 30 per cent of the active population in 1881, 40 per cent in 1906, 50 per cent in 1931, and stands at more than 80 per cent today. The INSEE (*Annuaire statistique de la France*, Paris 1998 [CD-ROM version]) gives a figure of 76.9 per cent of wage-earners in the population for 1993, to which must be added the 11.6 unemployed (table C.01-1).

12   Thévenot has offered a very fine-grained analysis by socio-professional category of the development of the wage-earning class in the 1970s. In 1975, wage-earners represented 82.7 per cent of total employment, as against 76.5 per cent in 1968. The only category of non-wage-earners to expand was that of liberal professions – even though it grew slowly on account of the barriers to entry into these professions – while all the other categories (employers in industry and commerce, artisans and small shopkeepers – i.e. employing fewer than three wage-earners – farmers, home helps) contracted. And the wage-earning class likewise grew in traditional liberal professions such as doctors, almost as many of whom in 1975 were wage-earners (in hospitals especially) as private practitioners, whereas wage-earners represented little more than a half of medical personnel seven years earlier. The expansion of the wage-earning class is linked in part to the appearance of large firms in traditional sectors like commerce that destroy the small independents. The significant reduction in the number of wage-earners in agriculture and household employees likewise confirms that the majority of the growth in the wage-earning class is related to growth in activity of an employer class that is ever more 'anonymous' and less 'personal' – i.e. in industrial and service companies – but also to the development of public services (particularly teaching). See Laurent Thévenot, 'Les categories sociales en 1975: l'extension du salariat', *Économie et statistique*, no. 91, July/August 1977, pp. 3–31.

13   Women today represent 45 per cent of the working population, as against 35 per cent in 1968. Their rate of activity (percentage of those over fifteen years of age belonging to the active population) has continually increased over the last thirty years (François Jeger-Madiot, 'L'emploi et le chômage des familles professionnelles', *Données statisiques 1996*, INSEE, Paris 1996, pp. 117–23).

14   It appears that the expression 'spirit of capitalism' was used for the first time by Werner Sombart, in the first edition of his *The Quintessence of Capitalism*. But in Sombart, for whom it is generated 'from the conjunction of the "Faustian spirit" and the "bourgeois spirit"', it assumes a very different sense from that given it by Weber. The spirit of capitalism is more focused on the demiurgic character of the big businessman in Sombart, whereas Weber lays greater stress on the work ethic. See Hinnerk Bruhns, 'Économie et religion chez Werner Sombart et Max

Weber', in Gérard Raulet, ed., *L'éthique protestante de Max Weber et l'esprit de la modernité*, Éditions de la MSH, Paris 1997, pp. 95–120.

15 '[O]nly a human lifetime in the past it was futile to double the wages of an agricultural laborer in Silesia who mowed a certain tract of land on a contract in the hope of inducing him to increase his exertions. He would simply have reduced by half the work expected because with this half he would have been able to earn twice as much as before': Weber, *General Economic History*, p. 355. See also Polanyi, *Origins of Our Time*, on the transformation of land and labour into commodities.

16 Weber, *The Protestant Ethic and the Spirit of Capitalism.*

17 '[A]sceticism … defined the pursuit of riches, if viewed as an *end* in itself, as the peak of reprehensibility. At the same time, it also viewed the acquisition of wealth, when it was the *fruit* of work in a vocational calling, as God's blessing. Even more important for this investigation, the religious value set on restless, continuous, and systematic work in a vocational calling was defined as absolutely the highest of all ascetic means for believers to testify to their elect status, as well as simultaneously the most certain and most visible means of doing so. Indeed, the Puritan's sincerity of belief must have been the most powerful lever conceivable working to expand the life outlook that we are here designating as the spirit of capitalism': ibid., p. 116.

18 The main sources and presentation of these polemics are to be found in Philippe Besnard, *Protestantisme et capitalisme. La controverse post-weberienne*, Armand Colin, Paris 1970; Malcom H. MacKinnon, 'The Longevity of the Thesis: A Critique of the Critics', in H. Lehmann and G. Roth, eds, *Weber's Protestant Ethic: Origins, Evidence, Contexts*, Cambridge University Press, Cambridge, 1993, pp. 211–44; Annette Disselkamp, *L'Éthique protestante de Max Weber*, Presses Universitaires de France, Paris 1994; in the introduction by Jean-Claude Passeron and the presentation by J.-P. Grossein of a volume of works by Weber devoted to the sociology of religions (Sociologies des religions, Gallimard, Paris 1996); and in the collective work of the Research Group on Weimar Culture published under the direction of Gérard Raulet, *L'Éthique protestante de Max Weber et l'esprit de la modernité*, which also supplies an abundance of information on the intellectual climate in which *The Protestant Ethic* was composed. Moreover, this controversy, doubtless one of the most prolific in the entire history of the social sciences, is not over: it has focused above all on the validity of the link between motives of religious inspiration and economic practices. To critical arguments that challenge the correlation between Protestantism and capitalism, maintaining (in K. Samuelson and Joseph Schumpeter, for example) that capitalism developed before the emergence of Protestantism or in regions of Europe where the influence of the Reformation was weak, and, consequently, under the impact of a constellation of phenomena unrelated to religion (not to mention the Marxist critique, which makes capitalism the cause of the emergence of Protestantism), defence of Weber has replied with arguments that stress the distinction between *causes* and *affinities* (Weber is argued not to have sought to provide a causal explanation, but simply to have demonstrated the affinities between the Reformation and capitalism – for example, in Reinhard Bendix and Raymond Aron), as well as the difference between *capitalism* and *the spirit of capitalism* (Weber's subject was not the causes of capitalism, but the moral and cognitive changes that favoured the emergence of a mentality exploited by capitalism – for example, in Gordon Marshall).

19 Weber, *The Protestant Ethic and the Spirit of Capitalism*, p. 34; Hirschman, *The Passions and the Interests*, p. 9.

20 This reversal was possible thanks to the transformation of this passion into an 'interest', an amalgam of egoism and rationality, with the virtues of constancy and predictability. Trade was deemed liable to induce a certain moderation of behaviour, the merchant desiring peace for the prosperity of his business and maintaining benevolent relations during his transactions with the customers whom it is in his interest to satisfy. The passion for money thus emerges as a good deal less destructive than the search for glory or great deeds. It is also the case that traditionally only the nobility was deemed capable of the latter: 'anyone who did not belong to the

nobility could not, *by definition*, share in heroic virtues or violent passions. After all, such a person had only interests and not glory to pursue, and everybody *knew* that this pursuit was bound to be *doux* in comparison with the passionate pastimes and savage exploits of the aristocracy' (Hirschman, *The Passions and the Interests*, p. 63). The idea of a modern erosion of the violent, noble passions in favour of an exclusive interest in money was rather widespread, and also sufficiently valid, it seems, to provoke at the end of the eighteenth century and the beginning of the nineteenth the Romantic critique of the bourgeois order as empty, cold, mean, 'materialist', and precisely stripped of all passionate character, of all features hitherto judged positively on account of their political advantages. As for theses about *le doux commerce*, developed in the eighteenth century, if they seem old-fashioned to us today, it is because it became obvious in the course of the nineteenth century, particularly given the poverty of the working-class housing estates and colonization, that bourgeois passion had nothing gentle about it, but on the contrary produced unprecedented devastation.

21 Here we distance ourselves from the Weberian position according to which when capitalism is firmly in the saddle, it has less need of moral justification (*The Protestant Ethic and the Spirit of Capitalism*, pp. 18–19), which his contemporary Werner Sombart also subscribed to (*The Quintessence of Capitalism*, trans. M. Epstein and T. Fisher Unwin, London 1915), while remaining faithful to an interpretative sociology that stresses the meaning which social organization possesses for actors and, consequently, the importance of justifications and ideological constructs.

22 The issue of whether the beliefs associated with the spirit of capitalism are true or false, which is key in many theories of ideology, especially when dealing with an object as conflictual as capitalism, is not central to our reflection, which seeks to describe the formation and transformation of the justifications of capitalism, not to assess their intrinsic truth. To temper this relativism, let us add that a dominant ideology in a capitalist society remains rooted in the reality of things, inasmuch as it helps to inflect people's action, and thus fashion the world they act in, but where it is transformed depending on their experience, positive or negative, of their action. As Louis Dumont observes, a dominant ideology can therefore just as easily be declared 'false' in view of its incomplete character, because it is better suited to the interests of some social groups than others, or its tendency to amalgamate constructs of diverse origins and antiquity without articulating them in a coherent fashion, as it can be declared 'true' in the sense that each of the elements composing it has been (and still can be) pertinent in a given time or place, under certain conditions. Here we adopt Hirschman's solution: confronted with seemingly irreconcilable theories about the impact of capitalism on society, he shows that they can be made to coexist in the same representation of the world once it is acknowledged that capitalism is a contradictory phenomenon, with the ability simultaneously to limit and strengthen itself. He suggests that, however incompatible, each of the theories can possess its 'moment of truth' or its 'country of truth' and be pertinent in a country, or group of countries, for a certain period (see A. O. Hirschman, *L'économie comme science morale et politique*, Hautes Études-Gallimard-Seuil, Paris 1984, p. 37).

23 Weber, quoted in Pierre Bouretz, *Les Promesses du monde. Philosophie de Max Weber*, Gallimard, Paris 1996, pp. 205–6.

24 Louis Dumont, *Homo aequalis*, Gallimard, Paris 1977, p. 15.

25 In fact, paradoxically, it was in being constituted as a 'science' on the model of the natural sciences in the nineteenth century that classical economics was orchestrated to validate actions, at the cost of forgetting the political philosophy which had served as its matrix and transforming the conventions underlying market forms of agreement into positive laws separated from people's volition. See Luc Boltanski and Laurent Thévenot, *De la justification. Les économies de la grandeur*, Gallimard, Paris 1991, pp. 43–6.

26 According to consequentialist moral theories, acts must be judged morally according to their consequences (an act is good if it produces more good than evil, and if the balance is superior to an alternative act that has not been able to be realized as a result of the first act). These are generally contrasted with theories that can be called deontological, and which make

it possible to judge acts according to their conformity to a list of rules, commandments, or rights and duties. Consequentialist theories make it possible to resolve the thorny problem of the conflict of rules in deontological theories, and to pass over the question of the foundation and origin of these rules. On the other hand, they are vulnerable to other problems like the inventory of the set of consequences, or the measurement and aggregation of the accruing quantities of good and evil. The utilitarianism of Jeremy Bentham (1748–1832) is the classic example of consequentialist theory, as well as the best known; it grounds the evaluation of an action on calculation of the utility produced by the action.

27 This extremely solid assemblage was the outcome of the alliance, which was initially marginal and unnecessary but then very widely accepted, of classical economics and utilitarianism, supported by an 'evolutionist materialism', referring sometimes to Darwin and sometimes to Condorcet or Comte (Joseph Schumpeter, *A History of Economic Analysis*, Allen & Unwin, London 1986, pp. 436–8). According to Schumpeter, this mixture of liberal credence in the virtues of *laissez-faire*, Social Darwinism and vulgar utilitarianism constituted the mould that the world vision of the entrepreneurial bourgeoisie rested in. Thus, utilitarianism, combined with economic liberalism and Social Darwinism, could in vulgarized form become the main resource for simultaneously liberating oneself from common morality and imparting a moral design to actions in pursuit of profit.

28 Heilbroner, *The Nature and Logic of Capitalism*, p. 115.

29 One of the reasons why any increase in the wealth of any member of society is supposed to bring about an improvement in the overall well-being of society itself is that this wealth has not been removed from another by a form of theft, for example, as the idea of a sum total of stable wealth would have it. It has been created from start to finish, to the point where the sum total of society's wealth is increased. Pareto's work in the domain of economics, which extends and renews the Walrasian approach, resulting in a redefinition of economic optimality, illustrates how the question of who is enriched by this increase in wealth was rendered increasingly pointless in classical economics. One consequence of the abandonment in Pareto of a measurable utility at the turn of the nineteenth and twentieth centuries is that it is now impossible to compare the utilities of two different individuals, and hence to reply to the question of whether increase at a given point is more beneficial for society than it would be at another. Similarly, Pareto's theory of equilibrium allows it to be argued that it is impossible to assess in terms of overall well-being the effect of a transfer in wealth from one point to another, for the loss of utility of some members cannot be compensated by a gain in utility by other members. It is clear that there are two possible uses of Paretian equilibrium theory: either one sticks to what it asserts, acknowledging that no distribution of wealth which is good in itself exists that could be scientifically determined by economics, and accepts existing distributions; or one registers the inability of economic science to decide such a question, and transfers it to the political level without qualms. It is thus that Pareto, genuinely without intending to, supplied arguments for supporters of the welfare state.

30 This comes down to regarding the country in general as an 'enterprise', a highly reductionist but frequent metaphor. Orio Giarini demonstrates how far removed the notion of GNP is from that of social well-being, even accepting reduction of the latter exclusively to an increase in living standards: see *Dialogue sur la richesse et le bien-être*, report to the Club of Rome, Economica, Paris 1981; 'La notion de valeur économique dans la société post-industrielle: éléments pour la recherche de nouveaux paradigmes', *Économies et sociétés*, February 1983, pp. 299–334. Incorporating the accounting value added of all firms, it does not indicate, for example, that some value added is linked to markets making reparation for the damage done by other sectors of the economy; the sum total of the value added of those that have destroyed the environment and those that clean it up cannot, in any case, claim to convey a real improvement for citizens, although it increments the GNP indicator twice over. 'There is instead a transfer of expenses, which have had the effect of a real net increase in wealth and well-being … to other

expenses, which are essential for keeping the system running' ('La notion de valeur économique dans la société post-industrielle', p. 308). Other value added that is now counted in is simply bound up with the commodification of activities that had formerly been kept outside the monetary sphere (like the development of ready-made meals that in part replace family cooking, a market that certainly creates monetary profits but does not necessarily improve living standards). Giarini goes so far as to affirm: 'There is very often a zero growth or negative growth in real wealth and well-being even when the economic indicators of gross national product are positive' (ibid., p. 310).

31   This position, according to which market organization is always the most efficient, has been developed recently by the theoreticians of the economics of bureaucracy (see Xavier Greffe, 'La gestion du non-marchand', *Revue française de gestion*, September/October 1979, pp. 53–63; Guy Terny, 'Éléments d'une théorie de la bureaucratie', *Vie et sciences économiques*, no. 87, 1980, pp. 147–97, for an introduction).

32   Milton Friedman, in his celebrated essay *Capitalism and Freedom* (University of Chicago Press, Chicago 1962), is one of the fervent defenders of the thesis that political freedoms are possible only in the framework of capitalist relations: 'Economic arrangements play a dual role in the promotion of a free society. On the one hand, freedom in economic arrangements is itself a component of freedom broadly understood, so economic freedom is an end in itself. In the second place, economic freedom is also an indispensable means towards the achievement of political freedom' (p. 8). But he also acknowledges that capitalism in itself does not definitely guarantee freedom: 'History suggests only that capitalism is a necessary condition for political freedom. Clearly it is not a sufficient condition. Fascist Italy and Fascist Spain, Germany at various times in the last seventy years, Japan before World Wars I and II, tsarist Russia in the decades before World War I – are all societies that cannot conceivably be described as politically free. Yet, in each, private enterprise was the dominant form of economic organization. It is therefore clearly possible to have economic arrangements that are fundamentally capitalist and political arrangements that are not free' (p. 10).

33   It is likely that this justificatory apparatus is enough to engage capitalists and is also deployed whenever conflict has reached a very high level of generality (involving the rationale of the system, and not of some particular action or decision), as well as whenever no more immediate justification of dispute can be found – which is the case, in our view, when the spirit of capitalism is weak.

34   On the necessity, if ideologies are to be able to serve action, of integrating them into discursive forms containing mediations that are many and varied enough to nurture the imagination in the face of the concrete situations of existence, see Luc Boltanski, *Distant Suffering: Morality, Media and Politics*, trans. Graham Burchell, Cambridge University Press, Cambridge 1999, pp. 73–6.

35   See A.O. Hirschman, *Exit, Voice and Loyalty*, Harvard University Press, Cambridge (MA) 1970.

36   The number of *cadres* increased significantly between the 1982 and 1990 censuses. The category of 'administrative and commercial *cadres*' gained 189,000 people, that of 'engineers and technical enterprise *cadres*' more than 220,000, and that of 'intermediate administrative and commercial enterprise professions' more than 423,000. A percentage of the numbers accounting for the growth in these subcategories derives from social strata that are traditionally more distant from – even hostile to – capitalism, as in the case of teachers' children. As is well known, the latter are especially well prepared for the educational tests that open the doors to higher education and the *grandes écoles*, but less well prepared normatively than the children of the business bourgeoisie for the exercise of hierarchical and/or economic power. As numerous studies have shown, the increase in the number of those with university degrees does not have purely numerical consequences. It also alters the character of those who hold them as a result, in particular, of a change in their social origin under the impact of the democratization of access to higher education. Consequently, the

'signalling' effect of degrees (Michel Spence, 'Job Market Signalling', *The Quarterly Journal of Economics*, vol. 87, no. 3, pp. 355–74) is disrupted. In fact, a degree provides not only information about the kind of knowledge that has supposedly been acquired, but also about a type of culture in the anthropological sense of the term, and finally a type of human being. Mere knowledge of the possession of a degree no longer provides the tacit and lateral information about its holder that previously made it possible to 'get an idea' intuitively – i.e. based on ordinary social experience – of the kind of person 'one is dealing with', because those with the same degree can differ very markedly from one another, and above all from elders with the same qualification, in most other respects.

37 See Sombart, *The Quintessence of Capitalism*, pp. 51–6.

38 See, for example, Charles Morazé's book *Les Bourgeois conquérants* (Armand Colin, Paris 1957), especially the foreword and the section devoted to the railways (pp. 205–16).

39 Braudel, *The Wheels of Commerce*, p. 438.

40 See Giovanna Procacci, *Gouverner la misère. La question sociale en France, 1789–1848*, Seuil, Paris 1993.

41 With reference to economic liberalism as expounded in the English political economy of the nineteenth century, especially in Adam Smith, Rosanvallon writes: 'Nineteenth-century industrial society fashioned a world wholly opposed to this representation' (*Le Libéralisme économique*, p. 222).

42 See François Furet, *The Passing of an Illusion*, trans. Deborah Furet, University of Chicago Press, Chicago 1999.

43 See Adolf Berle and Gardiner Means, *The Modern Corporation and Private Property* (Macmillan, London 1932); James Burnham, *The Managerial Revolution* (John Day, New York 1941) for an initial description; and Alfred D. Chandler, *The Visible Hand: The Managerial Revolution in American Business* (Harvard University Press, Cambridge [MA] 1977) for a more recent historical work on the advent of salaried management.

44 See Luc Boltanski, *The Making of a Class: Cadres in French Society*, trans. Arthur Goldhammer, Cambridge University Press/Éditions de la Maison des Sciences de l'Homme, Cambridge 1987.

45 See J.K. Galbraith, *American Capitalism: The Concept of Countervailing Power*, Houghton Mifflin, Boston 1952; *The New Industrial estate*, Hamish Hamilton, London 1967.

46 Wallerstein, *Historical Capitalism*, pp. 17–18.

47 Microeconomics is in fact remarkable in that its dominant current does not concern itself with history and social transformations at all. It was, moreover, precisely in opposition to Carl Menger and the Austrian School that, at the instigation of Gustav Schmoller, the German Historical School was constituted, to which Sombart and Weber were attached. These economist-sociologists were concerned to found an interpretative position between sheer historical empiricism and marginalist abstraction, and 'to be able to deal with economic facts from the perspective of a theory – that is to say, to seek, with the help of concepts and ideal types constructed on the basis of historical material, to discover the very principles of economic systems and processes' (see Bruhns, 'Économie et réligion chez Werner Sombart et Max Weber', pp. 195–210). Traces of this intellectual project, seeking to reconcile theoretical and historical approaches, can be found in Regulation economics and conventions economics, which explains, moreover, why these currents find themselves marginalized by the dominant forms of microeconomics.

48 Here we follow the approach adopted by Weber: 'we must … be prepared to note that the cultural influences of the Reformation were to a great extent (and perhaps even predominantly from our particular vantage point) the unforeseen and even unwanted results of the [theological] labor of the Reformation figures. Indeed, the cultural influences stood often quite distant from, or precisely in opposition to, all that the religious reformers had in mind' (*The Protestant Ethic and the Spirit of Capitalism*, p. 48).

49 Louis Dumont, *German Ideology: From France to Germany and Back*, University of Chicago Press, Chicago and London 1994, pp. 14–15.

50 'These new representations have two aspects: one particularly directed within, and self-justificatory; the other turned towards the dominant culture, and universalist': ibid., p. 29.

51 See Polanyi, *Origins of Our Time*.

52 See Alain Desrosières, *La Politique des grands nombres*, La Découverte, Paris 1993.

53 See Boltanski and Thévenot, *De la justification*.

54 The requirement for justice can be reduced to a requirement for equality. Since Aristotle, we have known that equality in the polity does not necessarily signify an absolutely identical distribution between all the members of the city of that which possesses value, whether material or immaterial goods. What it involves, as Michel Villey puts it so well, is a 'just proportion between the quantity of the things distributed and the various qualities of the persons' (*Le Droit et les droits de l'homme*, Presses Universitaires de France, Paris 1983, p. 51; see also Michael Walzer, *Spheres of Justice*, Martin Robertson, Oxford 1983). Defining a relationship as unjust or just – which is what critique and justification do – thus presupposes a definition of what the value of things and persons consists in, a scale of values that requires clarification in the event of a dispute.

55 Bringing together data collected on the ground from ordinary people and scholarly texts belonging to the tradition of intellectual culture (a labour that does not frighten anthropologists of exotic societies) was supported by some reflection on the place of tradition in our society and, more specifically, in our political universe. It can in fact be shown that the constructions of political philosophy are today inscribed in institutions and mechanisms (for example, polling stations, workshops, the media or concerts, family gatherings, etc.) , which are constantly informing actors as to what they must do in order to behave normally. The inspirational city has been constructed on the basis of Saint Augustine's *City of God* and the treatises he devoted to the problem of grace. The domestic city was established through a commentary on Bossuet's *La Politique tirée des propres paroles de l'écriture sainte*. The reputational city was constructed starting from Hobbes's *Leviathan*, particularly the chapter devoted to honour. The civic or collective city is analysed in Rousseau's *Social Contract*. The commercial city is extracted from Adam Smith's *The Wealth of Nations*. The industrial city was established on the basis of Saint-Simon's *oeuvre*.

56 There are possibly one or more texts that would have done the job. But it must be admitted that the highly contemporary character of the construct that we have sought to outline, and also the role played by the social sciences themselves in elaborating this new sphere of legitimacy, would have made the choice of a paradigmatic author and text particularly sensitive. Furthermore, in this instance, in contrast to the classical texts, we could not rely on a tradition of exegesis, and justify the choice by an established reputation and the consequences it has for the inscription of themes from political philosophy in the reality of the social world.

57 See Weber, *The Protestant Ethic and the Spirit of Capitalism*; *General Economic History*; *Sociologie des religions*.

58 See François Gaudu, 'Travail et activité', *Droit social*, no. 2, February 1997, pp. 119–26.

59 This first current, constituted in its present form in the 1950s, which inherits the legacy of Marxism in the interpretation of the Frankfurt School and the apocalyptic post-Nietzscheanism of the first third of this century, tends to reduce all normative exigencies to the level of conflicts of interest (between groups, classes, peoples, individuals, etc.). It is in this sense that the current interprets itself as being a radical critique. In this perspective, which in large measure is that adopted by Pierre Bourdieu today, normative exigencies, devoid of autonomy, are simply the disguised expression of relations of forces: they add 'their force to power relations', which assumes actions in a permanent state of illusion, split personality, or bad faith (the first axiom of 'Foundations of a Theory of Symbolic Violence' reads: 'Every power to exert symbolic violence, i.e. every power which manages to impose meanings and to impose them as legitimate by concealing the power relations which are the basis of its force, adds its own specifically symbolic force to those power relations': Pierre Bourdieu and Jean-Claude Passeron, *Reproduction in Education, Society and Culture*, trans. Richard Nice, Sage, London 1977, p. 4).

60   This second current, which has developed over the last fifteen years, in large measure in reaction to the first and starting out from the aporias produced by the hermeneutics of suspicion (see Paul Ricœur, *The Conflict of Interpretations*, Northwestern University Press, Evanston [IL] 1974), has significantly extended the analysis of the principles of justice and the normative bases of judgement. But it must be said that it has often done so at the expense of a deficit in the examination of real social relations and the conditions of realization of the exigencies of justice (for which these theories were scarcely equipped) and an underestimation of relations of force.

61   On this point, we can adopt Jacques Bouveresse's position: 'In the sense in which there is a dialectic of "Enlightenment", one might equally speak of a dialectic of democratic discourse, by virtue of which it ends up itself denouncing its own ideals as illusory and false. When intellectuals who are regarded as convinced democrats openly proclaim that the only observable reality, with which one must come to terms, consists in power and domination, what objection can be made to those who decide definitively to cast aside the mask? ... When the principles of liberty, equality and justice only end up obtaining purely formal approval and commitment, hedged around with all sorts of sceptical reservations, ironic insinuations, self-criticisms, self-suspicions and self-demystifications, potential dictators have only to play to public opinion the card, which is far more effective, of candour and courage in clearly revealing what they know the bad conscience of their opponents has already largely conceded and implicitly confessed' ('La vengeance de Spengler', in Bouveresse, *Le Temps de la réflexion*, vol. 4, Gallimard, Paris 1983, pp. 371–402).

62   See Daniel Bell, *The Cultural Contradictions of Capitalism*, Heinemann, London 1976.

63   See ibid.

64   This uncertainty revolves around the condition of entities, whether objects or people, and in particular their respective power, on which their place in the mechanisms that frame action depends. In a world where all powers were fixed once and for all, where objects were immutable (where, for example, they were not subject to usury), and where people acted in accordance with a stable programme that was universally known, tests would always be avoided, since their certain outcome would render them useless. It is because the potential of objects (as when one speaks of testing the potential of a vehicle) and the capacities of people are, by their very nature, uncertain (one never knows for sure what people are capable of) that beings enter into relations of comparison wherein their potential is revealed.

65   Given that it is organized not in some abstract universe but in a real world shot through with multiple forces, the most carefully organized test cannot guarantee that it does not admit forces that do not form part of its definition. Moreover, an absolutely irreproachable test is a logical impossibility, for it would presuppose establishing a specific procedure for each unique situation (and for each person) – which would no longer allow for judgement in terms of equivalence and the constitution of a justifiable order. A completely just world presupposes a kind of prior coding of each situation and a procedure for negotiation so that the actors could reach an agreement on the definition of the situation, which is materially impossible (the time devoted to negotiation prevailing over the time given to action) and logically impossible (for it would also be necessary to define the negotiating situations by means of negotiations, in an infinite specularity). In addition, there would be nothing to guarantee that the *ad hoc* coding thus obtained would be genuinely adequate to the situation, for the persons, in the absence of precedents and apprenticeship by trial and error, would find it impossible to pinpoint parasitic forces and correct the calibration of the test.

66   See Boltanski and Thévenot, *De la justification*.

67   In the case of recruitment tests, it is the firm that bears the direct cost, whereas the main beneficiaries are, for example, those with degrees from certain schools. In the case of the test for sharing value added, the beneficiaries are wage-earners and capitalists in proportions that are precisely the subject of the dispute, and the cost rests with firms, but also with the state inasmuch

as it has responsibility for seeing that the regulations are respected and operating controls to protect the relative rights of the parties.

68   We can speak of rounds of tests when, as is usually the case for the most established tests, access to a test is closed – i.e. conditional upon success in an earlier test – and in such a way as to standardize the properties of the competitors facing one another. This is one of the conditions for the creation of equivalence that the test is based on being deemed valid.

69   Jean Baechler, *Le Capitalisme*, vol. 2, Gallimard, Paris 1995, p. 268.

70   See Ève Chiapello, *Artistes versus managers. Le management culturel face à la critique artiste*, Métailié, Paris 1998.

71   See Luc Boltanski, *L'amour et la justice comme compétences*, Métailié, Paris 1990; and *Distant Suffering*.

72   See Heilbroner, *The Nature and Logic of Capitalism*.

73   As Furet has shown (*The Passing of an Illusion*, pp. 4–19), bourgeois values have provided a powerful lever for the critique of the bourgeoisie.

74   See Cesar Grana, *Bohemian versus Bourgeois: French Society and the French Man of Letters in the Nineteenth Century*, Basic Books, New York 1964; Pierre Bourdieu, *The Rules of Art*, trans. Susan Emanuel, Polity Press, Cambridge 1996; and Chiapello, *Artistes versus managers*.

75   See Jerrold Siegel, *Bohemian Paris: Culture, Politics and the Boundaries of Bourgeois Life, 1830–1930*, Penguin, New York 1986.

76   See Françoise Coblence, *Le Dandysme, obligation d'incertitude*, Presses Universitaires de France, Paris 1986. From an absence of ties there flows an idealization of a particular use of space and time. As the multiple glosses on the theme of the *passer-by* (the *passages* of Paris, etc.) in Baudelaire endlessly repeat, the artist is primarily one who is only passing through: one whose freedom is expressed by passing from one place to the next, one situation to another, one day a brothel and the next morning with the marquise, without lingering or becoming attached, without privileging one place over another and, above all, excluding any value judgement where some moral intention could peep through, in favour of a purely aesthetic judgement whose sole principle is the artist's *vision*. See Gerald Froidevaux, *Baudelaire. Représentation et modernité*, Corti, Paris 1989.

77   In Marx, as in most theorists of modernity, one finds both critiques – the artistic and the social. If the former is still very prevalent in the young Marx, it is clearly in retreat – but not wholly absent – in *Capital* compared with the social critique. The concepts of alienation and exploitation refer to two different sensibilities. What is denounced in alienation is, in the first instance, oppression, but also the way in which capitalist society prevents human beings from living an 'authentic' existence, a truly human existence, and renders them alien to themselves in a sense – that is to say, to their deepest humanity. The critique of alienation is therefore also a critique of the new world's lack of authenticity. For its part, exploitation makes the connection between the poverty of the poor and the wealth of the wealthy, since the rich are such only because they have impoverished the poor. Exploitation thus links the issue of poverty and inequality, and the issue of the egoism of the rich and their lack of solidarity.

78   See, for example, the way in Proudhon in particular condemns the mores of artists and denounces 'the minstrels of the ugly and squalid', combining 'moral ignominies', 'physical corruptions', and '[s]candalously perverse indulgence but also scandalously cynical indifference to infamy and scandal' (Bourdieu, *The Rules of Art*, p. 110).

79   On the literally mythical figure of Sade in the Bastille as a victim of oppression who openly confesses the crimes he is charged with, and hence as a symbol of transgression, in the left-wing literature of 1940–60 (especially in or around Bataille), see Boltanski, *Distant Suffering*.

80   See Chiapello, *Artistes versus managers*.

81   To take a recent example – Situationism – studied by Julien Coupat, from whom we borrow this contrast, such a tension led to the self-dissolution of the movement following the rupture between Debord (anti-modernist critique) and Vaneigem (modernist critique): see

Coupat, *Perspective et critique de la pensée situationniste*, DEA dissertation, École des hautes études en sciences sociales 1997.

82 On the use, particularly in social philosophy, of the metaphor of the 'iron cage', see Peter Wagner, *A Sociology of Modernity: Liberty and Discipline*, Routledge, London and New York 1994, pp. 64–5.

83 'In contrast [to the social forms that preceded it], capitalism is built upon an inherent contradiction – a genuine contradiction in the literal sense of the term. The capitalist organization of society is contradictory in the rigorous sense that a neurotic individual is: it can attempt to realize its intentions only through acts that constantly thwart them. To locate ourselves at the fundamental level – that of production – the capitalist system can live only by continually trying to reduce wage-earners to mere *executants* and it can only function to the extent that this reduction does not occur. Capitalism is compelled constantly to solicit the *participation* of wage-earners in the process of production – a participation that it itself tends to make impossible': Cornelius Castoriadis, *Capitalisme moderne et révolution*, vol. 2, Union générale d'édition, Paris 1979, p. 106 (see also Castoriadis, *L'expérience du mouvement ouvrier*, vol. 2, Union générale d'édition, Paris 1974, pp. 15 ff.). The concept of spirit of capitalism is grounded in this contradiction, in the sense that it involves mobilizing initiative for a process that cannot mobilize by itself. And capitalism is permanently tempted to destroy the spirit that serves it, since it can serve it only by curbing it.

84 Michael Walzer's works (especially *The Company of Critics*, Halban, London 1989) precisely challenge the representation of a critique based on absolute exteriority and, conversely, makes critics' rootedness in their society the condition of possibility for critical activity and its effectiveness.

85 See Hirschman, *Économie comme science morale et politique*.

86 In his pages on the 1795 Speenhamland law, Polanyi already stressed, in connection with much earlier events than those we are concerned with in this book, the grandeur, the snares and the impossibility of terminating critical labour and reformist measures. This law, which aimed to guarantee a minimum subsistence income for everyone, combined with a certain state of society and legislation (in particular, the Anti-Combination laws), 'led to the ironical result that the financially implemented "right to live" eventually ruined the people whom it was ostensibly designed to succour' (*Origins of Our Time*, p. 86). The abrogation of the law in 1834 was accompanied by significant suffering, with the abandonment of indoor relief, and made possible the creation of the labour market, which had become inevitable. The disastrous effects of the operation of the labour market would subsequently become apparent, and lead to new measures of protection, notably the authorization of trade unions in 1870, intended to limit its violence without seeking to abrogate it (ibid., pp. 82 ff.).

87 Ibid., pp. 44–5.

88 Let us nevertheless stress that it goes without saying that democratic societies which guarantee freedom of expression, access to the media, and the chance for critical social movements to exist are those most likely to develop in accordance with the dynamic we have outlined.

89 See Hirschman, *Exit, Voice and Loyalty*.

PART I

THE EMERGENCE OF A NEW IDEOLOGICAL CONFIGURATION

I

MANAGEMENT DISCOURSE
IN THE 1990s

Our intention here is to bring out the profound transformation in the spirit of capitalism over the last thirty years: the abandonment of the specific ideological features characteristic of its second embodiment, and the emergence of a new image of firms and economic processes. The aim of this transformation was to provide those whose commitment is indispensable for the expansion of capitalism – the successors to *cadres* – with self-evident reasons for the 'right actions' (markedly different, as we shall see, from the recommendations made in the 1960s); a discourse legitimating these actions; encouraging prospects for individual development; the chance for people to project themselves into a future that was restructured in line with the new rules of the game; and the suggestion of new modes of reproduction for the children of the bourgeoisie, and upward social mobility for others.

I. SOURCES OF INFORMATION ON THE SPIRIT OF CAPITALISM

Management literature as prescription for capitalism

In order to carry out this project, we shall use management literature addressed to *cadres*.[1] This literature, whose main objective is to inform *cadres* of the latest developments in running firms and managing human beings, emerges as one of the main sites in which the spirit of capitalism is inscribed.

As the dominant ideology, the spirit of capitalism theoretically has the ability to permeate the whole set of mental representations specific to a given era, infiltrating political and trade-union discourse, and furnishing legitimate representations and conceptual schemas to journalists and researchers, to the point where its presence is simultaneously diffuse and general. From among its possible expressions, we have selected management literature as a medium offering the most direct access to the representations associated with the spirit of capitalism in a given era. Within this literature we have, moreover, restricted ourselves to non-technical writings that aim to offer general new managerial mechanisms of a sort to inspire a firm's operations as a whole. We have therefore excluded specialist literature dealing only, for example, with marketing, production management or accounting, in order to concern ourselves with what might be called 'management in general', whose boundaries with the discipline of entrepreneurial policy and strategy on the one hand, and human resources management on the other, are sometimes very tenuous.

Following the example of the spirit of capitalism, which presents two faces – one turned towards capital accumulation, the other towards legitimating principles – management literature can be read on two different levels. We certainly find in it a source of new methods of profit-making and novel recommendations to managers for creating firms that are more efficient and more competitive. But management literature is not purely technical. It is not composed only of practical recipes for improving the productivity of organizations as one improves the performance of a machine. It simultaneously has a high moral tone, if only because it is a normative literature stating what should be the case, not what is the case. Consequently, we may legitimately pose the question of the realism of this literature, and hence how believable it is when it comes to what 'really' happens in firms. And it is true that, although they are usually packed with numerous examples and based on case studies, management texts cannot replace survey materials, whether monographs on firms or statistical surveys. They make no claim to be exhaustive. Their orientation is not constative, but prescriptive. In the manner of edifying books or manuals of moral instruction, they practise the *exemplum*, select the cases employed according to their demonstrative power – what is to be done as opposed to what is not to be done – and take from reality only such of its aspects as confirm the orientation to which they wish to give some impetus. But it is precisely in so far as they constitute one of the main vehicles for the diffusion and popularization of normative models in the world of enterprise that they are of interest to us here.

As a public literature intended to elicit support for the precepts it states and the engagement of a large number of actors – first and foremost *cadres*, whose zeal and conviction are decisive in the smooth running of firms – management literature cannot be exclusively orientated towards the pursuit of profit. It must also justify the way profit is obtained, give *cadres* arguments with which to resist the criticisms that are bound to arise if they seek to implement its abundant recommendations, and to answer the demands for justification they will face from their subordinates or in other social arenas. Management literature must therefore demonstrate how the prescribed way of making profit might be desirable, interesting, exciting, innovative or commendable. It cannot stop at economic motives and incentives. It must also be based on normative aims, taking into account not only personal aspirations to security and autonomy, but also the way these aspirations can be attached to a more general orientation to the common good. Were it not for this, it would be impossible to understand why the transmission of operational modes for organizing firms is, in the work of some authors, glorified by a lyrical, even heroic style, or defended by numerous, heteroclite references to noble and ancient sources such as Buddhism, the Bible and Plato, or to contemporary moral philosophy (Habermas in particular).

It is likewise important for our subject to recall that the birth of management literature coincided, at the beginning of the century,[2] with the emergence of the new social body of salaried managers and administrators (later referred to by the term 'manager' or, in France, *cadre*). The operational management of large firms was progressively transferred to them, as owners withdrew to the role of shareholders, except where they themselves became salaried senior management.[3] From the outset management was thus intended for those who, following the crisis of the 1930s, were to become the new heroes of the economy and the principal addressees of the second spirit of capitalism. Management, which is presented as the systematization of practices within firms and their inscription in general rules of behaviour, gradually enabled a professionalization of supervision. Regarded as one of the founding fathers of the discipline, Henri Fayol wanted to perfect an 'administrative doctrine' that made it possible on the one hand to claim that management was a profession with its own rules, thus consummating the break with leadership whose legitimacy derived from ownership, and on the other to pave the way for a professional education. It is not surprising that *cadres* recognized their own aspirations in this eulogy to professionalism and competence (against the legitimacy of patrimony that was the reference-point for the first spirit of capitalism), as in the importance assigned to education. Hence the second spirit of capitalism finds its most natural expression in management literature. Consequently, it is reasonable to suppose that such literature will likewise register changes and a trend towards other representations, or at least that it will echo the breakdown of the spirit of which it was the main vehicle.

Our choice is, moreover, consistent with that of Werner Sombart or Max Weber. Sombart refers to the books of Leon Battista Alberti, whom he considers the perfect exemplar of the bourgeois of the *Quattrocento*, on 'family government'.[4] And Weber supplies a preliminary description of the spirit of capitalism by citing the writings of Benjamin Franklin ('Necessary Hints to Those That Would Be Rich', 'Advice to a Young Tradesman', 'Memoirs').[5] These texts and the management literature we use belong to one and the same literary genre: works of advice and edification concerning the conduct of business (or the family economy).

The choices of Weber and Sombart are also explained by the impact of the works they used, and this refers us today to the question of the impact of management literature on practice. Granted that realism is not a major feature of the texts studied – since their aim is to state what should be, not what is – it is nevertheless of some relevance to know to what extent they are read, are influential, and are thereby able to influence practices in the way intended by their authors. Failing this, they would not constitute an adequate object for studying the establishment of a new dominant ideology. To do things properly, we would have to know the figures for the diffusion, reading, and utilization in teaching of the texts concerned. In the absence of institutional sources, however, this represents an extremely onerous task. We have skirted round this problem by not choosing a limited number of texts, like our illustrious predecessors, but constructing corpora with many more authors, which afford a representative panorama of the writings of a given period. Moreover, a reading of these texts discloses a high degree of homogeneity in the discourse and, in each of the periods considered, its general organization around a limited number of themes – to the extent that it might be wondered, faced with the marginal variation in the texts, whether such a profusion of texts is justified. This is doubtless the best indication of their ideological character with a vocation to become dominant. Their ideas are taken up, repeated, conveyed by various examples, pass nimbly from one relay to another (from one management journal to the next, from one author or editor to another, from management literature to the professional press for *cadres*, from the written word to lessons and specialist radio broadcasts). The upshot is that it is extremely difficult to attribute paternity of these bodies of rhetoric to authorial authorities. Their differences, which are often minimal, have the effect of offering various actors different ways of getting a handle on the orientations the authors seek to communicate, and identifying with them. As is no doubt the case with any body of texts that is performative in intent, particularly when the number and diversity of persons to be convinced are great, variation on a few mandatory themes constitutes a condition for effectively transmitting a message that can be broadcast only by being adjusted appropriately.

We have therefore constituted two corpora comprising sixty texts each. The first corpus appeared in the 1960s (1959–69), the second in the 1990s (1989–94); and both deal, in whole or part, with the question of *cadres*, even if the latter are sometimes referred to by different terms (*manager, directeur, chef, dirigeant*, etc.). For each of the periods under consideration, these two corpora make it possible to bring out a typical image of what was recommended to firms as regards the type of *cadre* to employ, the way they should ideally be treated, and the kind of work that might appropriately be asked of them. Appendix 1 sets out the characteristics of the texts analysed, while Appendix 2 presents a bibliography of each corpus. The corpora thus constructed (more than a thousand pages) have been processed in two phases. In the first instance, we submitted them to a traditional analysis based on an extensive reading that aimed at an initial location of their authors' concerns, the solutions they proposed to the problems of their period, the image they offered of the inherited forms they declared to be outdated, and the various arguments advanced to effect the conversion of their readers. In a second phase, we used the analytical software Prospero@ (see Appendix 3) to corroborate our hypotheses and confirm, by means of specific indicators running through the body of texts, that our analysis did indeed reflect the general state of the corpus (not a personal bias with respect to certain themes that risked exaggerating their importance), and hence the general state of management literature in the relevant years.

The option adopted is basically comparative. Emphasis has been placed on the differences between the two corpora, whereas constants have been paid less attention.[6] Dumont observed that the comparative method is the most effective one in the study of ideologies, especially when they pertain to the world the analyst is immersed in, and their salient elements are difficult to identify without an external point of comparison.[7] Here that point will be provided by historical distance. Besides, the image of their era reflected by the 1960s texts is decidedly different from what the 1990s texts have to say about it. Once again, we should not ask this kind of literature to afford us a balanced panorama of the past, since its aim is to suggest improvements, and hence to break up some of the mechanisms derived from established practices. It selects, and consequently magnifies, the factors it is rebelling against, ignoring features that might be more enduring and no less important.

Analysing a change that is in the process of being effected, and in some respects remains embryonic, exposes one to the risk of being accused of naivety, even of complicity with one's object. It is true that in its modern forms – social evolutionism, prediction, futurology – prophecy has often been a powerful tool of mobilization and action. It can help to bring about what it describes (the self-fulfilling prophecy) or, in the case of certain prophecies of calamity, support reactionary opposition to reforms.[8] From this viewpoint, one unmasks the 'ideological' character (in the sense of illusion, even deception) of some analysis of change, where those who promote it are simply taking their own desires or anxieties for reality. Positivist versions of this challenge often rely on a statistical description of reality. Descriptions of change are supposedly based on an illusion that takes the part for the whole and extrapolates from deliberately selected, unrepresentative cases, to impose a vision of the future for which serious empirical study of the current reality offers not the slightest confirmation.

Thus, it will perhaps be objected that what we describe on the basis of management literature greatly exaggerates features that only marginally affect the operation of firms. The series of indicators assembled in Chapter 4, however, shows that there has already been considerable implementation of the mechanisms described in the literature. Moreover, it will be seen there that we do not possess all the requisite statistical data to bring out the relevant changes. The apparatus of statistical description rests, in fact, on equivalents that are homologous to those used in the established tests on which social selection mainly depended in the previous state. Hence – structurally, as it were – it does not constitute the most adequate tool for recording and counting the new forms of test, particularly when they are established gradually, under the impact of micro-displacements.

In addition, there is a mass of historical examples of descriptions of change that cannot, a posteriori, be said to have been without foundation, even though they were based on fragmentary, partial evidence – which furnished reasons for discrediting them in the name of factual realism. Thus, as Pierre Ansart has shown, Proudhon, spokesman for the artisans – who were a large majority in mid-nineteenth-century France – was statistically right against Marx, whose proletarian utopia seemed to be grounded in circumstances that were not prevalent at the time.[9] Criticizing Peter Laslett for slighting the role played by the English East India Company and the Bank of England prior to the eighteenth century, Fernand Braudel writes as follows:

> [t]hese are familiar arguments: every time the volume of a leading sector is compared to the total volume of the whole economy, the larger picture reduces the exception to more modest or even insignificant proportions. I am not entirely convinced. The important things are those that have consequences and when these consequences amount to the modernizing of the economy, the 'business model' of the future, the accelerated pace of capital formation and the dawn of colonization, we should think more than once about them.[10]

When it is read for the purpose of deriving ideal types of the spirit of capitalism in the two periods, one of the striking features of management literature is a persistent concern with mobilizing and motivating personnel, especially *cadres*. 'How can we give work in firms some meaning?' is one of the central questions for the two generations, albeit in different ways. This signal fact is all we need to confirm us in our choice of sources for identifying transformations in the spirit of capitalism.

Texts focused on the mobilization of *cadres*

In the 1960s, what concerned our authors was motivating *cadres*, whereas in the 1990s, knowing how to engage them is treated as only one particular instance of the problems involved in mobilizing all employees.

In the 1960s, there were various grounds for anxiety about the engagement of *cadres*. People wondered how the finest offspring of the bourgeoisie were to be enrolled in the service of capitalism: for example, the directors of business schools expressed concern over the 'weak attraction of business to elites', states Marvin Bower, director of the consultancy firm McKinsey and former president of the Harvard Business School (Bower, 1966). There was also a desire to obtain their unqualified positive involvement,[i] or to avoid

---

i 'You can buy someone's time, you can buy their physical presence in a given place, you can even buy a certain number of muscular movements an hour or a day. But you cannot buy loyalty – the devotion of hearts and minds. These things have to be earned', explains Fernand Borne (1966).

people of 'talent' and 'great value' resigning to go to other firms that satisfied their aspirations better. A majority of the management texts dealing with *cadres* in the 1960s seeks solutions to involving the personnel whom 'the value of firms' consists in. It is said that their aspirations are not satisfied,[ii] that they 'expect more from their work', that 'through their work they want to play a useful role in society, to develop, to progress', and that 'the question is whether firms, with their traditional managerial style, are responding properly to these aspirations, and whether *cadres* feel that they can make a success of their life and not waste it' (Froissart, 1969). The pervasiveness in the texts of the time of works on motivation by the human relations school (with such mascot authors as Maslow, Herzberg or McClelland) bears witness to this general concern.

Thirty years later, it seems that the problems have not changed much ('[e]very organization is in competition for its most essential resource: qualified, knowledgeable people': Drucker, 1992). But the problems of mobilization have increased as a result of redundancies or restructurings that are painful for the workforce.[iii]

In both periods, it is recognized that profit is not a very inspiring goal.[iv] *Cadres* initially, in the 1960s, and then the workforce as a whole in the 1990s, wanted 'genuine reasons' for engaged commitment. 'If it is to attract high-caliber men from the colleges and graduate schools – let alone develop them into productive executives – every business leader must somehow demonstrate that his company and others *do* contribute to society – that business does more than just make money', we can read in Bower's work of 1966. In 1990, it is noted that '[i]n contrast to previous generations, [people] feel that a salary alone is small compensation if they have a sense that their work isn't contributing to the greater good' (Waterman, 1990). Thus, the firm must be 'a site for creating meaning, for shared goals, where everyone can simultaneously develop their personal autonomy and contribute to the collective project' (Genelot, 1992). For 'as Jean Giono said, "the main thing isn't to live, but to have a reason for living". However, he added: "and that isn't easy"' (Bellenger, 1992).

ii 'The role they want to play exceeds what they are offered. ... This factual discrepancy, perhaps this time lag between declaration and aspiration, this ambiguity and discrepancy would appear to explain the discomfort of their current situation. ... Hence the difficulties currently being experienced by management: *cadres* are a problem' (Aumont, 1963).

iii 'The attempt to reduce the workforce through productivity increases, the outsourcing of jobs and the relocation of manpower lead to a social fragmentation of economic actors and the risk of a rupture in the traditional socio-affective relationship between a firm and its wage-earners' (HEC, 1994).

'The same strategies executed unwisely and without concern for the organizational and human consequences will not produce continuing business benefits – especially if people withhold effort and commitment for fear of being displaced or to hedge their own bets against change' (Moss Kanter, 1992).

iv 'It no longer goes without saying, for example, that the workforce conceives profit as the legitimate goal of the organization' (Blake and Mouton, 1964).

Thus giving a meaning to wage-labour, a spirit to capitalism, does indeed constitute an important concern on the part of management authors. We shall now examine what they proposed by way of response in each period.

2. THE DEVELOPMENT OF THE MANAGEMENT PROBLEMATIC FROM THE 1960S TO THE 1990S

To bring out the changes in the spirit of capitalism over the last thirty years, we shall tackle the following points for each period in turn: (a) What problems do the authors pose? These indicate the way that problems are broached and analysed in a given period, and the implicit a prioris that underly them. (b) What responses and solutions do they offer? (c) What aspects of the situation they are dealing with do they reject? In fact, the imposition of a new managerial norm is nearly always accompanied by criticism of a prior state of capitalism and a previous way of making profit, both of which must be abandoned to make way for a new model. We shall thus see that the management texts of the 1960s explicitly or implicitly criticize familial capitalism, whereas the principal foil of the 1990s texts is large, hierarchized, planned organizations. Criticism of the old *savoir faire* and habits, which are presented as outmoded, is the way in which the relation between past and present functions in this literature bereft of historical memory.

The 1960s: Pleas for target management

In the management literature of the 1960s, two problems are tackled as a matter of priority: on the one hand, *strong dissatisfaction on the part of cadres*; and on the other, *managerial problems bound up with the giant size of firms*.

Cadres, who (it is tirelessly repeated) are what a firm's value consists in, are not happy confined to the roles they play: first, that of technical expert – the typical *cadre* of the period was an engineer – and second, that of management relay, transmitting orders from above and taking up problems from below. They aspire to share decision-making power, to be more autonomous, to understand managerial policies, to be informed of the progress of business. This theme is present in numerous 1960s texts.[v]

---

v 'Recognized in their role as a technical relay, *cadres* demand much more ... they feel unduly inserted into a rigid context: they feel that they are regimented and that they are suffocating ... they often complain about the narrowness of their room for initiative; they find it difficult to tolerate not being extended broad trust' (Aumont, 1963).

'*Cadres* aspire more to "co-management". ... They suffer from not "knowing more about the situations on the basis of which objectives are fixed" and from not having "more real contact with the employer". ... They think that the authority of their [bosses] would remain intact and even be strengthened if, rather than operating mysteriously, they acted in such a way as to elicit from their subordinates the maximum number of "voluntary acts conducive to the execution of decisions taken at the top"' (Bloch-Lainé, 1963).

The history narrated to us refers to the emergence of *cadres* as a new social body accompanying the growth of firms. The separation of ownership and management was a veritable commonplace at the time, but there is still a need to refer to it, whereas the theme would be completely absent thirty years later. This was also because the desire for a detachment from family capitalism had been fulfilled by then, and it was no longer necessary to define what, by comparison with the owner-manager, was the still relatively novel category in postwar France of salaried managers.

In the 1960s, *cadres* have a sense of embodying modernity, but feel cramped – especially the young, more academically qualified among them – by structures that have developed without a change in the centralized, quasi-autocratic managerial mode characteristic of small and medium-sized firms. Managers have simply added further levels of hierarchy, without conceding one iota of power. This analysis explains why the demand for autonomy by *cadres* is often accompanied by a description of the perverse effects of large bureaucratic machines.[vi]

In addition, large firms inspire fear. They are presented as an enclave threatening freedom in democratic countries. If the rule of the small firm could seem like the realm of freedom, observers ponder the effects of bureaucratization on the distinctive value of the West in contrast to the communist bloc.[vii] From this point of view, the capitalist firm seems to share the same drawbacks as the collectivized or fascist firm.[viii]

The solutions to such problems are termed *decentralization, meritocracy* and *management by objectives*. The essential goal of the battle conducted by the 1960s

---

vi 'In large firms, the boss maintains contact with departmental heads, but loses contact with those who carry out orders: his orders follow the hierarchical route; they are communicated and recommunicated many times, and are sometimes distorted in the process – or get held up, at any rate. Since individual initiative is not welcome, orders from on high must be numerous and detailed: paper rules. ... The atttitude of the workforce becomes passive. ... The individual is now only a cog in an anonymous whole, subject not to human beings but to regulations' (Borne, 1966).

'Gigantism always entails greater formality in relationships, from regulated formulas to a profusion of printed forms. It is even the case in some departments that individuals are known, represented and handled only via the numbered and encoded punched holes of a rectangle of cardboard. ... At this point, it obviously becomes difficult for them to keep their eyes fixed on the firm's ultimate goal' (Colin, 1964).

vii 'As our business organizations have grown in size, limitations on individual freedom have become a matter of national concern. As John Garner says: "Every thoughtful man today worries about the novel and subtle restraints placed on the individual by modern large-scale organization.... . A modern society is – and must be – characterized by complex organization. It is not a matter of choice. We must cope as best we can with the pressures that large-scale organization places on the individual"' (Bower, 1966).

viii 'But all these methods are merely "techniques" that have little effect if they are not inspired by a "democratic" mentality on the part of managers. Moreover, this serious problem is as prevalent in collectivist-style firms as in capitalist firms' (Borne, 1966).

'These financial, mechanical and productivist mentalities have been reproduced in different doctrines by different political regimes. I do not need to remind you of national socialism, or refer you to Stakhanovism, for you to recognize in Berlin or Moscow what Detroit, with Ford, had already taught' (Devaux, 1959).

authors is to impose these new managerial methods. Management by objectives emerges as an especially effective mechanism for giving *cadres* the autonomy they desire, and for decentralizing decision-making in such a way as to limit the disadvantages of bureaucratic gigantism, since decisions will then be taken close to those concerned. All *cadres* find themselves granted autonomy, but this remains firmly controlled: on the one hand, by job descriptions that permit detailed specification of the margin of autonomy conceded; on the other, by fixing targets for them in line with the firm's general policy. *Cadres* will henceforth be appraised by their realization of these targets – that is to say, by the degree of success in their work, not by kowtowing to superiors. They will be given a certain autonomy in organization, resources will be allocated to them, and they will be monitored on the basis not of each individual decision, but of the overall outcome. Thanks to this ingenious mechanism, employers retain control while implementing the reforms deemed necessary by consultants. *Cadres* thereby gain autonomy, and firms will be able to profit from a workforce that is motivated once again.[ix]

Management by objectives has the further advantage of furnishing clear and reliable criteria for measuring performance, on which career management can then be based. Promotion will be given to those who meet their targets – that is to say, are effective – and not according to 'subjective criteria' that are deemed unjust. Management literature in the 1960s wants to sound the death knell of arbitrariness in personnel management. This is bound to motivate *cadres*, who will feel that they are being treated fairly.[x]

The subsequent extension of management by objectives in large firms, and the wealth of detail and practical advice given by management authors, indicate that the stylized images and models of excellence that feature in management literature cannot be reduced to ideology, in the sense of a merely superficial discourse aiming – in order, for example, to satisfy the expectations of a new public – to present a mode of organization and management in a new light, while concealing its reproduction in identical form. The new managerial norm accompanies a set of measures intended to establish new mechanisms in firms. Even though, at the time these texts were written, such mechanisms were not as prevalent as some of their authors claimed, they were nevertheless in place, to varying degrees, in enough enterprises, and represented a sufficient break with old habits, to make this intense effort to

ix 'There is presumably no business executive who works harder or more effectively than the successful individual proprietor of his own business in a free enterprise economy. He works with zest and determination. … The payoff comes in accomplishment, not in effort … the challenge to large-scale enterprise is to create the work situation that puts every executive on his own as much as possible … the most successful companies achieve this by making every executive responsible and accountable for his own decisions and actions' (Bower, 1966).

x 'The system of sanctions must help to instil a rational order in firms, by ensuring that the fate of the efficient person differs from that of the inefficient one. This difference of treatment plays a key role in creating and maintaining efforts towards good administration, the motivation to manage things well' (Gélinier, 1966).

explain and justify them necessary. As expressed in this literature, the spirit of capitalism is thus in a dialectical relationship with mechanisms whose implementation it accompanies and facilitates.

The operating models and styles that serve as *foils* in the 1960s all pertain, to varying extents, to the *logic of the 'domestic world'*. What is rejected is consideration of 'personal judgements' – an open invitation to nepotism – in decisions about promotion, in favour of 'impersonal judgement' on the basis of results.[xi] The new appraisal systems equally aim to abolish preferment on grounds of seniority, which rewards only loyalty – domestic value *par excellence* – not efficiency, and also to reduce the (unjust) role played by social relationships in career success.[xii]

Moreover, it is with these themes that discussion of the 'French case' becomes most specific. The elimination of forms of behaviour pertaining to a domestic logic is an urgent task in old Europe – particularly in France, which is still imbued with a feudal past of allegiances and privileges. Survivals of the Ancien Régime are ubiquitous, and the *coup de grâce* must be administered forthwith, emulating the example of the United States: the latter had the good fortune never to experience such constraints, and had been constructed as a society of equals from the outset. The adoption of American methods, which are more democratic but also more efficient, is felt to be a matter of survival in France, for the power of the United States is such that French authors fear being unable to resist an economic invasion (achieving 'American efficiency', but 'without colonization' [Froissart, 1969]. See also Jean-Jacques Servan-Schreiber's 1967 work, *Le défi américain*, which is entirely given over to this theme).[xiii]

xi 'In fact, it is too often the case that judgements of this kind are more a reflection of the idea one has of someone than an assessment of their results. And the great weakness of this formula lies in an absence of performance criteria linked to job responsibilities ... *cadres* are repelled by being treated on the basis of their superiors' opinion of them. They start off by suspecting them of favouritism and end up asking for their results to be measured by more tangible criteria and by quantifiable goals that are plausible and trustworthy' (Patton and Starcher, 1965).

'Potential review is particularly susceptible to the "halo effect" where the boss, sometimes quite unconsciously, overestimates a man's qualities because they have common interests, or "He's always been a good chap"'(Humble, 1968).

xii 'In France, a certain conservatism has long governed the pace of advance according to seniority, loyalty and, it must be said, social relationships (in which birth and class opinions weigh more than character)' (Bleton, 1967).

xiii 'This accounts for the difference in attitude between European and American workers. In a young society like that of the United States, the weight of traditions and "hereditary" privileges is less than in Europe. ... In an old society like Europe, social barriers are important, the persistence of privileges greater, and class conflict deeper' (De Woot, 1968).

'At this level, we observe in most traditional societies a tendency ... to classify human beings in stable categories (social or mandarin castes), to revere stability, to make each person's destiny dependent upon those of his characteristics that are deemed essential, rather than on his practical adaptation to efficient action' (Gélinier, 1966).

'Compared with European businesses, most American companies already have a large element of self-government. Perhaps this is because, as [Clement] Greenwalt indicated, our business methods incorporate in some measure the spirit of the American Revolution as reflected in the Declaration of Independence and the Constitution. ... In any event, European business practice typically calls for stricter control and more detailed instructions from the top' (Bower, 1966).

In the 1960s, the premium put on merit is coupled in those with the strongest convictions with a critique of academic qualifications when they procure lifelong advantages.[xiv] It must be noted that on this point at least, the reformists of the period failed, since the criticism has come down to us virtually unchanged.

Even if the point is not always dealt with explicitly in management literature, legitimation of *cadres* has as its negative converse the delegitimation of traditional employers, with criticism of their meanness, authoritarianism and irresponsibility. Especially denigrated are small employers, accused of abusing their property rights, confusing the firm's interests with those of their family, incompetent members of which are put in responsible positions,[xv] and endangering not only their own firm but society as a whole, by ignoring modern techniques for managing organizations and marketing products. This operation of symbolic separation between salaried *cadres* on the one side and patrimonial employers on the other – in conformity with the diffusion of theories of the firm opposing managers to owners – had, moreover, existed from the category's origin. Following the 1936 strikes, the first unions for *cadres*, derived from engineers' associations, had been compelled to exclude employers from their ranks and recognize the validity of a distinction that had hitherto been irrelevant for them. Management literature in the 1960s thus accompanies the transition from a patrimonial bourgeoisie centred on the personal firm to a bourgeoisie of managers, who are salaried, academically qualified, and integrated into large public or private managements.[11]

Comparison with the 1990s allows us to clarify this sketch. The 1960s project aimed at the liberation of *cadres* and relaxation of the bureaucracy that developed out of the centralization and growing integration of ever larger firms. The 1990s project was to present itself as a continuation of this process, taking up the themes of anti-bureaucratic struggle and autonomy. Even so, the 1960s proved respectful of the 'profession of boss'. Emancipation of *cadres* occurs against the background of a hierarchy that goes unchallenged. There are recommendations to clarify it,[xvi] not to add reactionary symbols of

xiv 'In practice, we have seen that employers, lacking objective criteria for assessing the abilities of *cadres*, and obliged to rely on their intuition as to individuals' personal worth, assign undue importance to academic qualifications – as if having one day succeeded in a competition were irrefutable proof of a capacity to hold senior positions in the hierarchy' (Froissart, 1969).

xv 'The unimpressive curriculum vitae of some employers' sons might be caricatured as follows: unexacting study – the father thinks his own case demonstrates that study is not of much use; after completing military service, the son enters Papa's firm and spends two years doing the rounds of the departments – three months in each department to see (like a tourist) what goes on there without assuming any responsibilities; then he is given an ill-defined managerial task (organization, supervision of administration), or – worse still – his father makes him take his place in his office, so as to be directly associated with management problems (whereas the young man lacks the requisite basic experience); given that his duties as a barely competent management assistant afford him free time, he is charged with various tasks representing the firm and ultimately, at the age of 35, unless he has a strong personality, he has been deformed rather than formed' (Gélinier, 1963).

xvi '[It is necessary] to determine *authority relationships* among positions. ... This will ensure that every person knows who his boss is, who his subordinates are, and what type and extent of authority he is subject to and can exercise' (Bower, 1966).

domination to it,[xvii] to avoid bypassing subordinates by addressing their teams directly.[xviii] But suppression or circumvention of hierarchy is never recommended. On the contrary, the point is to base it on merit and responsibility, and give it a new legitimacy by stripping it of the domestic ties that render it both inefficient and unjust.

It will likewise be observed that the project of the 1960s was largely realized, since the texts from those years that we have read frequently contain forms of deference and expressions of authority pertaining to the domestic world, which have subsequently disappeared from management literature. The difficulties of extricating oneself from the domestic world, even for advocates of change, once again clearly demonstrate the anchorage of management literature in a reality whose forms are to be transformed (it is not merely a matter of manipulating signs). Moreover, they confer sincerity on the authors in their reformist desire, since they carefully, more or less unconsciously, sift out what it is advisable to preserve, what they are attached to, and what it is important to reject in their domestic heritage.

Thus, for example, Octave Gélinier (1963), future director-general of the consultancy firm Cegos, where he has worked as trainer and engineering consultant since 1947, convinced liberal and tireless advocate in France of management by objectives, devotes several pages to the thorny question of 'making *cadres* redundant'. Ultimately, we are given to understand, it is important to make a *cadre* who has committed a few misappropriations, however minor, redundant, even if that *cadre* is competent and efficient; contrariwise, it is unjust to do the same thing to an 'old servant who has become inefficient'.[xix] These are two infringements of the principle of efficiency – one in the name of morality, the other in the name of loyalty. Gélinier nevertheless has every opportunity to conceal them afterwards by invoking the risk of demotivating other *cadres* in the firm and, consequently, referring to an efficiency constraint after all: the rhetorical argument that 'ethics pays'. This was to enjoy a vogue with the business ethics movement in the 1990s (in which Gélinier himself took a very active part), and is an indirect way, frequently employed in management texts, of introducing moral references without appearing to impede the profit imperative. What makes this text of Gélinier's strikingly dated is not the nature of the dilemmas faced, which remain

xvii 'The position held in the organization chart is sufficient indication of seniority ranking without such pointless symbols as different office furniture. To minimize these symbols is not to abolish the notion of hierarchical ranks, which is inherent in firms because some functions are more essential than others when it comes to realizing objectives or because some people contribute more than others to fixing these objectives' (Hughes, 1969).

xviii 'Having defined the remit and powers of his subordinates, the head must not interfere in these delegated domains' (Hugonnier, 1964).

xix 'Purely and simply dismissing this old servant, who is one of the firm's founders morally speaking, rejecting him like a tool that has become useless, is to perform a bad deed which, moreover, will create a disastrous climate of insecurity among *cadres*: it is therefore unacceptable' (Gélinier, 1963).

altogether current, but the fact that he devotes several pages to them. Making *cadres* redundant, which still represented a problem for this author, generally appears much more legitimate in management literature today. At the outset shocking, the 'major restructurings' of the 1980s ended up making redundancies accepted as 'normal' acts of management. And if the unemployment of *cadres* is present in the 1990s corpus, the question of redundancy is ignored.

As another indication of the pervasiveness of the domestic world even among those who struggle to be rid of it, we shall cite Louis Allen (1964), who peppers his plea for decentralization with remarks intended to preserve managerial power. Thus, a manager inspires and encourages, but can just as legitimately have recourse to power, and *cadres* must not be led to believe that they can decide everything and comment on everything just because they are permitted to 'participate'.[xx]

The 1990s: Towards a model of the firm as network

Depending on the angle they are considered from, the questions posed by authors in the 1990s appear different or identical. They are identical inasmuch as they take up the critique of bureaucracy begun in the 1960s and press it to a conclusion: hierarchy is a form of co-ordination to be excluded in that it is based on domination; it is now a question of liberating not only *cadres* but all wage-earners. They are different in so far as new themes, such as competitive pressures and consumer demand, become central.

The rejection in the 1990s of hierarchy (which, following economists of transaction costs, characterizes the 'organization' in so far as it differs from the 'market') is all the more striking in that the readership of the authors concerned basically consists of the *cadres* of large groups and multinationals, which, notwithstanding all their efforts, will have difficulty dispensing with hierarchies. The grounds invoked to justify this anti-hierarchical charge are often moral in character, and partake of a more general refusal of dominant–dominated relations.[xxi] They are also related to an ineluctable process of social evolution: human beings no longer want to be ordered about, or even to give orders.[xxii]

xx 'Don't create expectations! Not all decisions require participation. If your team cannot make a logical and rational contribution, do not ask for their ideas. People whose ideas are solicited often infer that their proposals will be automatically accepted and implemented. Do not arouse pointless expectations. Explain clearly how far you can go: it will be worth it' (Allen, 1964).

xxi 'The organization chart and the pyramidal hierarchy ... indicate those who know how to "manage" and those who can and must "manage", as opposed to those who do not know and who cannot. Even with the best will in the world, in such conditions a relationship of mutual contempt is bound to be established between the two categories of people, since those who "do not know how to and cannot" are, in fact, rendered inferior and infantilized from the outset' (Aktouf, 1989).

xxii 'The irresistible tendency towards freedom of choice in all domains fuels, together with a growing individualism, a demand for personal autonomy and its possibility. The era of

For others, a general rise in educational levels explains why hierarchy has become an outdated mode of organization.[xxiii]

If hierarchy is a favourite target, attacks are equally directed against planning, deemed to be rigid and based on coldly quantitative data that do not take account of the 'true reality'; and, against all instances, associated with authority (employers, bosses, orders, etc.). Pejorative comparisons with the army are sometimes used, preferably containing a reference to non-commissioned officers – objects of repulsion, symbols of authoritarian petty tyrants – whereas in the 1960s the military metaphor, which was very rare, pointed in the direction of the officer serving his country, in line with a theme that was very prevalent in the 1930s to 1950s (see, for example, Lamirand's *Le Rôle social de l'ingénieur*, modelled on Lyautey's *Le Rôle social de l'officier*). Never exclusively critical, the 1990s management authors imagine, as we shall see later, a number of new organizational forms that take the maximum distance from hierarchical principles, promising formal equality and respect for individual liberties.

Another striking feature of the 1990s is that the themes of competition and constant, ever more rapid technological change – already present in the 1960s – assume unprecedented salience. In virtually all the texts, we find advice on implementing the flexible, inventive organization that will be able to 'ride' all 'waves', adapt to all the changes, always have a workforce that is up to date with the most recent knowledge, and secure a permanent technological advantage over competitors. While the objective in the 1960s was to make bureaucracies more flexible, the literature refrained from challenging basic principles – for example, the unity of command so dear to Fayol. In the 1990s, subversion of the hierarchical principle refers instead to a 'big bang', in the words of the veteran guru Peter Drucker who, having been a highly esteemed promoter of management by objectives in the 1960s, now aims to turn organizations 'upside down'. Another key figure in management literature, Rosabeth Moss Kanter, explains to us that it is henceforth necessary to 'teach giants (the multinationals) to dance' (the title of her 1989 bestseller is *When Giants Learn to Dance* [Moss Kanter, 1990]).

This obsessive attention to adaptation, change, 'flexibility', is based upon a series of phenomena that left a deep impression on people's psyches from the end of the 1970s, and which the authors reintroduce, without any scrutiny,

---

adjutants is over. Not only do subordinates no longer accept authority, but superiors themselves are less and less capable of assuming it precisely when there is a need for more discipline to respond to the complexity of the environment's demands' (Crozier, 1989).

xxiii 'Because the modern organization consists of knowledge specialists, it has to be an organization of equals, of colleagues and associates. No knowledge ranks higher than another; each is judged by its contribution to the common task rather than by any inherent superiority or inferiority. Therefore, the modern organization cannot be an organization of boss and subordinate. It must be organized as a team' (Drucker, 1992).

under the theme of increased competition. However, it is important to recall them, since they are constitutive of the image of the world conveyed by our authors.

In the 1960s, management regarded as self-evident a representation of the world that can be schematically set out as follows: on one side there was the free, capitalist world – Western Europe and the United States, the other countries being largely absent from the picture – and on the other, there were the socialist countries with a planned economy. Within the free world, American domination was overwhelming, and Europe was scarcely emerging from a reconstruction that it was able to complete so rapidly only thanks to American aid. Thus, if we omit Jean-Jacques Servan-Schreiber's text, which contains a futurology on the economic development of all the world's countries at the dawn of 2000,[xxiv] we find not a single mention of a country in Africa, Latin America or Asia (not even Japan) in the 1960s corpus. France is the country cited most often, with 51 mentions (which is not surprising, given the character of the corpus), followed by the United States (19), Germany (5), the Soviet Union (3) and Italy (3). The other countries referred to are mentioned only once.

Things are different in the 1990s. On the new map of the world, we find the 'old capitalist countries' confronting the emergence of a third capitalist pole in Asia. First place here goes to Japan, whose success in penetrating the American market provoked genuine shock and fuelled a large number of managerial changes, followed by the four dragons (Taiwan, South Korea, Singapore and Hong Kong). In the mid-1980s, it was still possible to think that they would long remain the only newcomers. But although there is no trace of it in our corpus, which stops in 1994, added to them over the course of the 1990s were those Third World countries that abandoned the policy of development via import substitution in favour of competition with the developed countries and exports, thus imitating the successful formula of Japan and the four dragons. (This was the case in Asia to begin with, then Latin America, and, after the Berlin Wall came down, in ex-communist countries seemingly converted to capitalism.) The African continent remains absent from the dominant picture. Thus, in the 1990s corpus, Black Africa and Latin America are just as conspicuous by their absence (a single reference to Brazil). Contrariwise, Asia enters in force with 24 mentions (14 of them for Japan), and the countries of Western Europe have a greater presence: Germany (13),

---

xxiv 'The *post-industrial* societies will be, in this order: the United States, Japan, Canada, Sweden. That is all. The *advanced industrial* societies that have the potential to become post-industrial include: Western Europe, the Soviet Union, Israel, East Germany, Poland, Czechoslovakia, Australia and New Zealand. The following nations will become *consumer societies*: Mexico, Argentina, Venezuela, Chile, Colombia, South Korea, Malaysia, Formosa, and the other countries of Europe. The rest of the world – China, India, most of South America, the Arab countries, and Black Africa – will not even have reached the industrial stage' (Servan-Schreiber, 1967).

Italy (6), Switzerland (5), Spain, Ireland and Sweden (3 each), the other countries being mentioned only once. France with 84 mentions, and the United States with 24, have likewise increased their presence. The Soviet Union (or the countries descended from it) and the ex-Eastern bloc countries have disappeared. The development of the references to countries in the two corpora furnishes a good gauge of 'globalization' (quite relative) in the image management authors construct of it.

The active participants in the capitalist mechanism of competition, so we are told, will soon no longer number some hundreds of millions of people, but several billion.[12] With this image in the forefront, authors from the developed countries make competition a major part of their argument – all the more so because slower growth over the last twenty-five years, and the rise in unemployment, reinforce their conviction that economic development has become more difficult and economic struggle ruthless.

Furthermore, the constant progress in information technology, sound and image (the 'virtual') is frequently invoked, and represents the standard example to which technological development in its entirety supposedly conforms.

The mechanisms proposed by authors in the 1990s to face the challenges they identify comprise an impressive miscellany of managerial innovations. We may nevertheless attempt to articulate them around some key ideas: *lean* firms working as *networks* with a multitude of participants, organizing work in the form of teams or *projects*, intent on customer satisfaction, and a general mobilization of workers thanks to their leaders' *vision*.

We have transposed the term 'lean firm' from 'lean production', which was invented at the start of the 1990s to encapsulate a set of new production methods, partially drawn from observation of Japanese firms – Toyota, in particular.[13] Among these methods we may cite organizational principles like just-in-time, total quality, the process of continual improvement (Kaizen), autonomous production teams; and a series of tools to implement them, such as quality circles, which represent the oldest of the principles popularized in the West, quality assurance of suppliers, SMED, TPM, KanBan, 5S, proposals for improvement, and so on.[14] The lean, 'streamlined', 'slimmed-down' firm has lost most of its hierarchical grades, retaining between three and five only, and consigning whole layers of hierarchy to unemployment.[xxv] It has also parted with a large number of operations and tasks by subcontracting anything that does not form part of its core business[xxvi] – sometimes to former employ-

xxv 'There is a whole arsenal of techniques for streamlining managerial structures. The most frequently employed is "de-layering", which involves simply abolishing one or more hierarchical layers. One also finds, and often in tandem with the first approach, increasing the span of control, which comes down to assigning more people to the management of a smaller number of *cadres*, moving from the traditional ratio of 1 *cadre* for between 6 and 10 employees to a ratio, regarded as acceptable today, of 1 *cadre* for 20 or even 30 employees' (Aubrey, 1993).

xxvi '[Companies] contract out for some services, turning to suppliers that are specialists in that area and reducing the need for the company to manage activities largely unrelated to their ees who have set up their own firms (hiving off). As for its investments, increasingly it makes them in collaboration with other firms by means of 'alliances' and 'joint ventures'.[xxvii] So prevalent is this that the standard image of the modern firm today is of a slim core surrounded by a conglomeration of suppliers, subcontractors, service providers, temporary personnel making it possible to vary the workforce according to the level of business, and allied firms. It is then said to operate as a network.[xxviii]

The workers themselves, we are told, must be organized in small, multi-tasked teams (for they are more skilled, more flexible, more inventive and more autonomous than the specialist departments of the 1960s). Their real employer is the customer, and they have a co-ordinator, not a boss.[xxix]

The process of transforming the old organization to align it with this model is called *re-engineering* (Hammer and Champy, 1993). In addition, the teams are not exclusively composed of the firm's permanent workforce. In them are also to be found suppliers, clients, consultants and outside experts. And the members of a team do not necessarily operate together physically, for progress in telecommunications allows them to work at a distance.[xxx] Here again work is said to occur in a *network*, for the firm's boundaries become blurred, with the organization now seeming to comprise nothing more than a mass of more

---

core business competence; and they convert some service departments into "businesses" that compete with external suppliers to sell their wares both inside and outside the company. Such organizational changes allow post-entrepreneurial companies to do more with less, because their staffs are smaller, their fixed costs are lower' (Moss Kanter, 1990).

xxvii 'Some organizations are turning themselves nearly inside out – buying formerly internal services from outside suppliers, forming strategic alliances and supplier–customer partnerships that bring external relationships inside' (Moss Kanter, 1989).

xxviii 'Organizations are evolving towards a model made up of three series of elements: a permanent central core composed of managerial personnel and possessors of what is called strategic *savoir faire* (i.e. which cannot be delegated outside); a network form of organization, rather than one with the traditional hierarchies; and a series of satellite supplier subsystems (firms or individuals working from a distance), with varying certainty of business (and employment)' (HEC, 1994).

xxix 'An upside-down view of the organization chart will be used, where customers are at the top, those who work with customers are next, and those who work for those who provide service to customers are at the bottom. ... The role of management is to support those who are dealing directly with customers' (Tapscott and Caston, 1993).

'Process teams, consisting of one person or many, don't need bosses; they need *coaches*. ... Traditional bosses design and allocate work. Teams do that for themselves. Traditional bosses have little to do in a reengineered environment. Managers have to switch from supervisory roles to acting as facilitators, as enablers and as people whose jobs are the development of people and their skills so that those people will be able to perform value-adding processes themselves' (Hammer and Champy, 1993).

xxx 'Information and data communications technologies separate the site and moment of production of the face-to-face service from support, preparation and back-office activities. Thus people will work less and less "in the office". Working in the factory on a permanent basis will be a borderline case. Here again there is no reason for the legacy of the industrial and technological age to become permanently established. Plenty of *cadres*, representatives, servicing agents, teachers work far removed from their employer. The "virtual" firm has arrived' (Morin, 1994).

or less enduring contractual links. The development of new products thanks to simultaneous engineering (Midler [1993] refers to 'co-operative' engineering) is the stock example of the ideal team, which by definition is innovative, multiple, open to the outside world, and focused on the customer's desires. Teams are a locus of self-organization and self-monitoring.

Thanks to these new mechanisms, the hierarchical principle is demolished and organizations become *flexible*, *innovative* and highly *proficient*. Compared with integrated hierarchical organizations, organization in networks, which allows firms to be rid of a costly hierarchy that served merely as a management 'relay', and contributed no 'value added to the customer', is also thought to procure an economic advantage bound up with specialization. The integrated large firm undertakes a very broad set of functions. It cannot improve its performance in all tasks simultaneously. It must therefore keep in-house only those operations where it possesses a competitive advantage – its core business – and outsource the other operations to subcontractors who are better placed to optimize them. It maintains close and enduring ties with these subcontractors, continually negotiating terms and conditions, and exercising control over production (for example, by the regular presence on the subcontractor's premises of personnel from the firm placing the orders). The more rapid circulation of information and innovation facilitated by specialization is bound to be universally profitable. In fact, whereas in the integrated large enterprise each department works exclusively for the firm of which it is a unit, the subcontractor (at least when it is not subject to a single principal) must resolve the various problems posed by the demands of different customers. With the learning effects and transfer of information between different (and potentially) competing firms it induces, this enhances the general level of information and *savoir faire*. In very general terms, these analyses foreground the importance of information as a source of productivity and profit. They therefore present themselves as particularly well suited to an economic universe where the main source of value added is no longer the exploitation of geographically located resources (like mines, or especially fertile land), or the exploitation of a labour force at work, but the ability to take full advantage of the most diverse kinds of knowledge, to interpret and combine them, to make or circulate innovations, and, more generally, to 'manipulate symbols', as Reich puts it (1991).

But the thorny problem of management remains unresolved, for our authors do not abandon the idea that firms still exist. Firms have not been completely dissolved into networks. They develop strategies of competitive struggle opposing them to other multinationals (in those markets where they do not collaborate). All the *self-organized*, *creative* beings on whom performance now depends must be guided in a direction decided only by a few, but without reverting to the 'hierarchical bosses' of yesteryear. This is where *leaders* and their *visions* come into the picture. Vision has the same virtues as the spirit of capitalism, for it guarantees the workers' commitment without recourse to compulsion, by making everyone's work meaningful.[xxxi]

Thanks to this shared *meaning*, to which all subscribe, everyone knows what they must do without having to be told. Firm direction is given without resorting to orders, and employees can continue to organize themselves. Nothing is imposed on them since they subscribe to the project. The key point in this mechanism is the *leader*, who is precisely the one with a capacity for *vision*, who knows how to communicate it and get others to support it.[xxxii] This is doubtless the weakest link in the new mechanisms, for everything rests on the shoulders of an exceptional being; and it is not always clear how to train or even recruit such beings, especially in sufficient numbers, since every firm needs them. More broadly, neo-management is filled with exceptional beings: proficient at numerous tasks, constantly educating themselves, adaptable, with a capacity for self-organization and working with very different people. And in the final analysis, we are not told very much about the contribution of firms to the development of such a class of workers: firms are going to become 'learners', skills management is going to become a key issue, and some new professions are conjured into existence, like the 'coach', whose role is to supply personalized support, making it possible for everyone to develop their full potential. In the version that strives hardest to give 'coaches' an institutional position, the latter are responsible for training.[xxxiii]

Given the set of reforms proposed by management authors, it is hardly surprising that we find *cadres*, as the 1960s conceived them, largely on the way out. The very term *cadre*, which suggests hierarchy and status, is rejected. *Cadres* are now regarded as agents of the very bureaucracies that are to be dismantled. In these discourses, the status of *cadre* is treated, either explicitly or (invariably) implicitly, as an archaism whose rigidity obstructs the developments under way.[xxxiv]

xxxi 'The richest, most inspiring visions are those that possess meaning, that respond to aspirations' (Bellenger, 1992).
'Vision confers meaning; it points to the future; it transcends short-term objectives by integrating them into a whole. Filling people with enthusiasm, vision is not only a mission, but also a powerful magnet. Like major challenges, vision revitalizes collective capacity' (Crozier and Sérieyx, 1994).

xxxii 'The leader is the person who is invested in by the group, the person in whom, whether consciously or unconsciously, everyone recognizes themselves. Thanks to his influence, capacity for vision and guidance, he creates an atmosphere that invites everyone to confront new challenges, to have confidence and take the initiative' (Cruellas, 1993).
'Good leaders can inspire others with the power and excitement of their vision and give people a sense of purpose and pride in their work' (Moss Kanter, 1989).

xxxiii 'All the forms of apprenticeship mentioned above must be administered and a training department dependent on a personnel department is not what is required. Thus, a limited number of managers will be responsible for the apprenticeship processes useful for the firm. The responsibility of these manager-trainers is to support employees' development' (Aubrey, 1993).

xxxiv 'The notion of a specific and separate managerial staff in the organization of work is no longer useful. There is no justification for retaining the status of *cadre* in France. In most of the developed countries, such a status does not exist. There are many firms in France where the

A comparison between the uses of the term *cadre* in the two corpora underscores the developments of the last thirty years. Highly esteemed in the 1960s, *cadres* were the main agents of progress. In the management literature of the 1990s, reference to *cadres* is instead combined with criticism of a category deemed obsolete. The word *cadre* is surrounded by a whole set of terms which, employed pejoratively, are used to characterize the old organizational forms, regarded as outmoded. These are terms that convey rigidity and stability, but also self-interest and an attempt to control the future (e.g. structure, functions, career, administration, plans, objectives); and, secondly, terms referring to hierarchy, to statutory power defined as authoritarianism, to obedience (hierarchy, status, the army, subordinates). In the 1960s, the term *cadre* was employed in a sufficiently broad and vague way to point towards a principle of unity that transcended hierarchical divisions by associating executives or directors and middle managers or immediate supervisory staff. The literature of the 1990s, by contrast, alludes to *cadres* only to designate intermediate, subordinate employees (compared with non-commissioned officers in the army), and goes so far – an act of sacrilege inconceivable in the previous period – as to combine *cadres*, supervisors, technicians, white-collar workers, and even blue-collar workers in a single list.

As a substitute for the French term *cadre*, we witness the emergence of *manager*, transferred directly into French. Manager is relatively recent in the French-speaking world. In the 1960s, it referred predominantly to the American *cadre*. In other cases, it was translated by *cadre*, *directeur* or *organisateur*, and hence rarely featured as such in the texts. The term *manager* spread and assumed its current meaning in France in the course of the 1980s. Initially used to designate the management *cadres* in the head offices of large firms (in contrast to the mass of ordinary *cadres*), it began to be used at the end of the 1980s to refer to those who display their excellence in team leadership, in handling people, in contrast to engineers focused on technology. Similarly, *management* came to be contrasted with *gestion* (administration), distinguishing effective employment of people's abilities from a rational processing of objects and figures. Authors in the 1990s thus employ the term *manager*, in contrast to *cadre*, to define those qualities of human beings that are most appropriate to the present state of capitalism and the 'uncertain', 'complex' environment firms have been plunged into. *Managers* do not seek to supervise or give orders; they do not await instructions from management before applying them. They have understood that such roles are outmoded. They become 'team leaders', 'catalysts', 'visionaries', 'coaches', 'sources of inspiration'. This last appellation

---

level of *cadres* is more than half the workforce; in some it even reaches 80 per cent. It is clear that in these firms *cadres* are not paid to lay down how other people must work. Indeed, often they do not supervise anyone, for many *cadres* are secretaries, accountants and technicians' (Aubrey, 1993).

is specific to Hervé Sérieyx (1993). Like other authors in the 1990s, in the absence of a terminology to refer to the new entrepreneurial heroes, he was led to coin an expression of his own. Rosabeth Moss Kanter, for her part, talks about 'business athletes',[xxxv] Meryem Le Saget about the 'intuitive manager', and Lionel Bellenger about the 'pros'. Other terms, like coach, leader or 'midwife', are adopted by several authors.

Managers can no longer rely on hierarchical legitimacy, or, as in the past, manipulate career expectations, for with the reduction in the height of organizational pyramids, there are far fewer opportunities to 'rise' in-house; and in the framework of their projects, they must get all sorts of people to work over whom they have little formal power. Consequently, they are supposed to assert themselves by means of their 'skills' and 'charisma', define actors thanks to the effectiveness of their 'network of personal relations', which provides them with information and aid, and galvanize people by the power of their 'vision' and their skills as 'midwives' of other people's 'talent' and developers of potential. They derive the authority that makes them 'leaders' from their personal qualities, not from some official position. Moreover, they refuse the 'signs of power' (such as numerous secretaries, private lifts or dining-rooms, lavish offices). The authority they acquire over their teams is bound up with the 'trust' that is placed in them on account of their 'communication' and 'listening' skills, which are exhibited in direct contact with others.

Managers are in fact distinguished from *cadres* in terms of a contrast between creative intuition and cold, calculating administrative rationality. This opposition recycles a thematic initiated, in a wide variety of forms, around the mid-nineteenth century, in a large number of taxonomic contrasts – for example, between forms of intelligence (left brain/right brain) or the sexes;[xxxvi] between social groups (artists/engineers or financiers);[15] even between countries (France counterposed to Germany in the nineteenth century,[16] the Latin countries contrasted with the Anglo-Saxon countries today, etc.). *Managers* are 'intuitive', 'humanist', 'inspired', 'visionaries', 'generalists' (as opposed to narrow specialists), and 'creative'. The universe of the *manager* is opposed to that of the *cadre* as the reticular is opposed to the categorial. The *manager* is

---

xxxv 'We don't even have good words to describe the new relationships. "Superiors" and "subordinates" hardly seem accurate, and even "bosses" and "their people" imply more control and ownership than managers today actually possess' (Moss Kanter, 1989).

xxxvi 'When it comes to strategy, the best results are often to be found among people who are by nature right-brained, and who employ what is called an "integrated" process of decision-making – that is to say, one that brings the two hemispheres of the brain into play in balanced fashion' (Sicard, 1994).

'Those in charge are required to be efficient, enterprising, daring; they are expected to decide and realize their objectives, control their results, and succeed. These are dynamic, masculine qualities. But the world is changing rapidly. The firm must anticipate, pinpoint changes, and adapt itself. To do that, it needs a quite different register of skills: attentiveness, intuition, observation, communication, workforce participation, creativity, a sense of service, motivation.... These are instead qualities of openness and receptiveness' (Le Saget, 1994).

network man. His principal quality is his mobility, his ability to move around without letting himself be impeded by boundaries, whether geographical or derived from professional or cultural affiliations, by hierarchical distances, by differences of status, role, origin, group, and to establish personal contact with other actors, who are often far removed socially or spatially.

Besides the *manager* ('project head', 'team co-ordinator' or, according to an older term, the person responsible for a 'profit centre'), we have seen some authors identify another character. This is the 'coach' (when the *manager* is not also charged with this duty), whose task is to develop the skills and potential of the people in an organization. But we also come across a third striking figure in 1990s management: the 'expert'. Experts are necessary, for they possess the information about innovation and the highly specialist knowledge that must be mastered to embark on technological competition. They can be internal to the firm – a full-time researcher, for example, or a specialist in computer systems or in administrative control. They can also be external, belonging to an agency, an independent research centre or a university, and may be consulted on a selective basis. They are not asked to manage teams, for that is the role of the *manager*. In order for each of them to develop their specific skill in the most productive fashion – the *manager*, workforce motivation and the expert, technical performance – management authors completely separate the two profiles. In the 1960s, by contrast, there was still the hope that every competent engineer could be made a *manager* by dint of a good 'management system' (good planning and a good process of target fixing).[xxxvii]

Among the forms of technical knowledge that are useful for running firms, when it comes to controlling and supervising the human factor *management* is the equivalent of the engineer's science as regards machines and things. But it is important to highlight the way in which 'neo-management' definitely remains 'management' in the sense that we have just defined it. In other words, it still contains control mechanisms, even if they are different from those associated with the second spirit of capitalism.

The history of 'management' can in fact be conceived as involving constant refinement of methods for controlling what occurs in the firm and its environment. For Taylor and Fayol, regarded as the founders of management as a discipline, human beings are the main focus for the implementation of controls (the man–machine coupling in Taylor; general organization in Fayol). Subsequently, with certain subdisciplines of management, the will to control was to be extended beyond machines and workforce. With business strategy, control of markets and competition has developed; with marketing, control

---

xxxvii 'Traditionally, in the course of his career the young engineer could expect successive promotions – section head, departmental head, and perhaps even director. ... This was how merit was recognized and it was the symbol of success. ... A good expert does not necessarily become a good manager. ... Some highly successful firms thus adopt a different approach, which consists in clearly distinguishing a promotion path for experts and a promotion path specifically designed for the generalists responsible for people management' (Landier, 1991).

of the distribution circuit, customers and their purchasing habits; with purchase management, control of suppliers; with public relations, control of the press and political authorities. Similarly, within the workforce, each category has been subjected to specific mechanisms: Taylorism was invented to control workers, and management by objectives to supervise *cadres*. In our time, the mechanisms of 'corporate governance' are aimed at controlling the most senior managers of large firms.

In the sequel to this history, we must ask what are the *modalities of control contained in neo-management*. This question is central because, within firms, *cadres* are principally those agents who perform tasks of control over technical mechanisms, sales, and other wage-earners, this function being vital for profit creation. Furthermore, the history of managerial practices is very often bound up with the emergence of new control problems caused by the advent of new types of actors, the setting to work of whom requires a change in methods: *cadres* are not controlled in the same way as blue-collar workers; blue-collar workers who have gone through the education system are not controlled in the same way as workers who are first-generation immigrants or of rural origin, and so on.

Like their predecessors, the 1990s authors place the question of control at the centre of their concerns. One of their main problems is controlling a 'liberated firm' (to use Tom Peters's expression [1993]), composed of self-organized teams working in a network that is not unified in time or space. 'Controlling the uncontrollable' is not something with an infinite number of solutions: in fact, the only solution is for people to *control themselves*, which involves transferring constraints from external organizational mechanisms to people's internal dispositions, and for the powers of control they exercise to be consistent with the firm's general project.[17] This explains the importance given to such notions as 'workforce participation' or 'intrinsic motivations', which are motivations bound up with a desire to perform the work and the pleasure of doing it, and not with some system of sanctions–rewards tacked on externally and capable of yielding nothing more than 'extrinsic motivations'.[xxxviii] Moreover, the 1990s authors are suspicious of the term 'motivation', which connotes a form of control they endeavour to reject, and prefer 'mobilization', which refers to an attempt at motivation supposedly devoid of any manipulation.[xxxix]

The firm's culture and values, its project, the leader's vision, the ability of the firm's head to 'share his dream' – these are so many stimulants that are

xxxviii 'The manager of the future does not "motivate" his collaborators. By means of his daily care and attention, he reawakens their inherent motivation – something that everyone carries deep within them and which is made up of a desire to understand, to progress and to give life a meaning' (Le Saget, 1994).

xxxix 'The leader's role is no longer to motivate, but to mobilize. According to Omar Aktouf, to rely on motivation is to continue to accept the idea that employees and workers are "objects" which can be shaped at will, incapable of discovering inspiration in themselves. Motivation is an infantilizing concept that no longer has any purchase on highly educated people. If they are mobilized, employees mobilize themselves' (Sérieyx, 1994).

supposed to encourage the convergence of forms of individual self-control, since the controls voluntarily exercised by everyone over themselves are more likely to remain consistent with one another if their original source of inspiration is identical.

Moreover, the stress laid on the customer by management authors in the 1990s is a way of getting their readers to agree that customer satisfaction must be a supreme value, to which it is mandatory to subscribe ('the customer is king'). This dogma has a twofold advantage: on the one hand, it inflects self-control in a direction conducive to profit, given that a firm's differential ability to satisfy its customers is an essential ingredient of success in a competitive economy; and on the other, it transfers some of the control exercised by superiors in the 1960s to customers.

Oversimplifying, the transition from control to self-control, and the externalization of control costs formerly met by organizations on to wage-earners and customers, may be regarded as the most significant features of the evolution of management in the last thirty years. Why vest control in a hierarchy of *cadres*, who are all the more costly in that they subordinate their own adhesion to a stable career, if wage-earners can be induced to control themselves? From this viewpoint, hierarchical *cadres* are simply unproductive workers. Thus it is that the new mechanisms, combined with a reduction in the number of levels of hierarchy, aim to increase the autonomy of people and teams, leading them to take responsibility for some of the supervisory tasks once assumed by higher grades or managerial departments. This development is especially striking in the case of factories, which were more marked than any other enterprise site by a Taylorist form of organization involving a separation between design, control and execution. This is one of the most important principles undermined by Toyotism, which in the 1980s served as a fulcrum for rejecting Fordism and (in the words of Benjamin Coriat) rethinking production methods 'from top to bottom'.[18] Workers, henceforth called *operatives*, gradually found themselves charged with quality control and certain maintenance tasks.

The increase in automation and robotics has, in addition, significantly raised the loss of earnings entailed by stoppages to machines and industrial plant, which are often more expensive than the workforce operating them, and whose cost, above all, cannot be varied. As Michel Aglietta explains, the new mode of regulation, which has replaced the Fordist regulation associated with the second spirit of capitalism, is based upon an increase in the productivity of investments:

> Fordism weighed capitalism down ... but the gains in labour productivity were sufficient to maintain profit rates. This logic came up against its limits at the end of the 1960s, when the increase in income from wages outstripped productivity, triggering an inflationary process. The technological progress used to overcome these problems aimed to save on fixed – or constant – capital. This made it possible to turn around the productivity of capital in overall terms.[19]

In managerial terms, in particular, this translates into pursuing maximum employment of technical resources twenty-four hours a day, with a minimum of stoppages and faulty work, the latter representing not only a waste of materials and manpower, but also a waste of machine time. It therefore becomes crucial to train operatives to provide emergency maintenance, anticipate and diagnose breakdowns, and rapidly call on technicians where necessary. Making workers aware of their responsibilities for the 'good health' of machines has thus become economically important.

Similarly, considerable effort is made to organize them into 'autonomous teams' responsible for the whole of some output as regards quantity and quality. The requisite skills levels are therefore markedly higher for new entrants – a professional diploma is often demanded – with internal training programmes to advance established workers and redundancy for those deemed (by criteria such as inadequate written and oral skills, or a low capacity for initiative and autonomy) incapable of keeping up, who can consequently be declared 'unable to adapt'. Blue-collar workers are supposed to emerge as winners from these organizational changes, less 'alienated' than before, because they become wholly responsible for some output, their work is thereby 'enriched', they are freed from authoritarian petty tyrants, and it is easier for them to obtain adjustments that facilitate the performance of their tasks.

For its part, the outsourcing of a large number of operations, either by recourse to subcontracting or through the autonomization of sectors of large firms, which are treated as autonomous profit centres competing with the outside, has made it possible to replace hierarchical control by a *market type of control*. This is less directly associated with the dominant–dominated couple, rejected by contemporary authors, for it seems to refer to a contractually free relation between two formally equal parties. Creating competition has replaced control of work by the directors of these units, who in return can rely on customer demand to exercise control that seems to issue no longer from them, but from the market. At factory level, the suppression of stocks – a key mechanism of Toyotism – in addition to reducing the costs bound up with storage, has the effect above all of relaying the pressure of demand directly to the production unit. Production must be carried out as and when customers demand it, in the quantity and of the quality they expect. Concealing mistakes, faults and breakdowns becomes impossible, since it can no longer be disguised by drawing on reserve stocks. The slightest faults entail a production stoppage, and therewith become evident. Stock suppression reveals problems and compels their resolution, because the customer is waiting. Control, then, is exercised by the transmission of the customer's order, which everyone must face up to, *cadres* and non-*cadres* alike, as a single team united in adversity. Planning, which belongs to the control mechanisms of the 1960s, is no longer used in so rigid or long-term a fashion as previously. Employed in the short and medium term, it essentially makes it possible to establish capacity within which the volume and quality produced can vary depending on customer demand. For what is above all at stake is responding to orders when they arrive – hence the authors' insistence not on planning, but on an ability to react and organizational flexibility as the only things that can meet new specifications.

With the decline of close monitoring by superiors, we witness the rapid development in management literature (as in microeconomics) of the theme of *trust*. Trust is what unites the members of a team, a firm with its leader, the coach with the person he supports, or the partners in an alliance.[xl] Trust is a sign that the situation is under control, since people only place it in someone who they know will not abuse it, who is predictable, who says what he means and means what he says.[xli] Neo-management lays great stress on the need to develop this type of relationship, on the need for people to be worthy of trust themselves, and on the need to dismiss those who betray it. Trust is in fact the other term for self-control, since it designates a trustworthy relationship where the only mechanism that exists is the pledged word and moral contract. Besides, it is moral in character, whereas third-party control is simply the expression of a relation of domination.[xlii]

Finally, the reference to trust suggests that the new modes of organization are not simply the product of the market's entry into firms in force. Certainly, contracts are increasingly substituted for hierarchy, but this does not always involve traditional commercial contracts. The sales contract for goods is, moreover, one of the most simple and standardized that jurists have to handle, and they are generally agreed that the development of contractualism, or what they often call the 'contractual society', cannot be reduced to the expansion of market society. Whereas the purely commercial transaction is punctual, taking no account of duration, organizing collaboration and exchanges in network form assumes the creation of relations between the partners which, while not stabilized by plans or regulations, nevertheless possess a relatively enduring character. For if firms are more flexible and more reactive, they have not stopped being large and powerful. They are more so today than ever. Large

xl 'For mobilization around a vision to be effective, the leader must also inspire trust and inspire it absolutely' (Crozier and Sérieyx, 1994).

'A capacity for autonomy is required, just as a capacity for friendship is required. To support someone is to be at once very close to him, taking an interest in his story, and sufficiently distant to leave him room for freedom: he is the person who chooses to be helped and this aid must be based on a genuine climate of trust' (Aubrey, 1990).

'The doing-more-with-less strategies put an even greater premium on trust than did the adversarial-protective business practices of the traditional corporation. Business collaborations, joint ventures, labor–management partnerships, and other stakeholder alliances all involve the element of trust – a commitment of strategic information or key resources to the partners. But the partners have to rely on one another not to violate or misuse their trust' (Moss Kanter, 1990).

xli 'In fact, individuals are increasingly sceptical. They see statements for what they are: intentions. … This growing mistrust obliges employers to be exemplary, but also to be consistent and coherent even in the smallest details of everyday behaviour. Trust can only be won at this price' (Crozier and Sérieyx, 1994).

xlii 'The balance of power is out of place when it comes to winning support, creating a feeling of satisfaction and trust in other people' (Aktouf, 1989).

firms have not been dissolved into a set of commercial contracts between small units competing in a pure, perfect atomized market (even if it is always possible to model any organizational arrangement as a network of contracts). For large firms to retain an identifiable form, and the power associated with their name, some links must remain more enduring than others, without necessarily having the inflexibility of established hierarchical relations. The solution envisaged by management authors therefore consists, on the one hand, in relaxing and streamlining institutional mechanisms, which are invariably suspected of harbouring the threat of renewed rigidity; and, on the other, in conferring an important role in economic mechanisms on personal relations and the trust people place in one another. These, it is anticipated, will facilitate co-ordination of the various resources that go into the creation of value added. As a considerable literature inspired by the theory of transaction costs, and referring to Williamson, has endlessly repeated over the last ten years, networks constitute a specific form inbetween hierarchies and markets.[20]

The answers proposed by 1990s management literature to the two questions of most concern to it – anti-authoritarianism, and an obsession with flexibility and the ability to react – are conveniently assembled by the authors under the *metaphor of the network*, which is deployed in all sorts of contexts. These include the generalization of work in autonomous teams, which are not unified in space or time, operating 'as a network' (i.e. in part from a distance, with partners who are internal or external to the firm, with some stable full-time members and others who are part-time and/or occasional); the development of partnership relations where trust plays a major role (strategic alliances); analysis of the possibilities for long-distance work offered by 'computer networks'; or the establishment of 'networks of firms', as in the case of 'industrial parks'. The latter, especially with the recurrent example in the socioeconomics of work and neo-management of the 'third Italy' studied by A. Bagnasco, have served as models for generalizing the possibility of economic development based on types of relationship that are partially geographical, administrative and political and partially personal.[21/xliii]

To promote these new organizational forms, the authors must also, as in the 1960s, criticize and delegitimate certain aspects of the organizations contemporaneous with them, which are deemed obsolete from the standpoint of efficiency and outmoded as regards human relations. But this time the critique is no longer directed at arrangements that are accused of transposing the

---

xliii The small town of Prato, some kilometres from Florence, is still today the world capital for the manufacture of carded woollen fabric. ... The efficiency of the system, in terms of competitiveness and adaptability, is based on the intermeshing that exists between multiple artisanal workshops. This intermeshing is guaranteed by Prato's industrial union – which in particular manages the computer system that makes it possible to know what the available productive capacities are at any given time – by the local bank – which ensures the redistribution of financial resources – and by the supervision of the manufacturers of the wool-carding machines' (Landier, 1991).

domestic universe into the firm. It focuses on the type of organization advocated in the earlier period for purposes of ensuring a radical separation
between the private world of the family and personal relations on the one
hand, and that of professional relations and work on the other. In the 1960s,
this separation was intended to make competence the sole criterion of professional success – to the point, indeed, where some authors were concerned
about the balance between time devoted to the family and rest, and time spent
at work. In the 1990s, management authors rebel against this separation, which
is deemed deleterious inasmuch as it separates dimensions of life that are indis-
soluble, inhuman because it leaves no room for affectivity, and at the same
time inefficient because it runs counter to flexibility and inhibits the multiple
skills that must be employed to learn to 'live in a network'.[xliv]

To characterize the large impersonal organizations inherited from the
previous period, 1990s management adopts a term derived from Weberian
sociology, but popularized in the 1940s–1960s by the Trotskyist critique of
the state apparatus in totalitarian regimes: *bureaucracy*. This term connotes
authoritarianism and arbitrariness, the impersonal, blind violence of cold
monsters, but also inefficiency and squandering of resources. Not only are
bureaucracies inhuman, they are also unviable. The struggle conducted in the
1990s thus has as its objective largely *eliminating the model of firms constructed in
the previous period*, on the one hand by delegitimating hierarchy, planning, formal
authority, Taylorism, the grade of *cadre* and lifetime careers in the same firm;[xlv]
and on the other by reintroducing criteria of personality and the use of
personal relations that had been eliminated from firms. Even so, we are not
dealing with an attempt to return to the first spirit of capitalism, since firms
are larger than ever, managers are professionals not small-scale owners, and
life at work is inscribed in networks, not in a domestic framework.

xliv 'Professional life represents the domain of rationality *par excellence*; thus it is distinguished
from private life, which by contrast represents the domain of emotions, the search for meaning,
the expression of personal values. There is a watertight compartment between these two dimensions of existence. ... Any consideration of personal elements in the judgements made of someone
by a firm is a priori regarded as an intrusion into one's private life. It is clear that such a schema
... has become totally obsolete today. Developing a vision of the firm's future, conceiving a strategy,
leading work teams, creating a network of relations – these demand qualities that go far beyond
mere technical competence and mobilize the whole personality' (Landier, 1991).

'It requires us to give up the division between the professional person and the private person,
between rationality and intuition, between the natural and the artificial, between head and heart'
(Sérieyx, 1993).

xlv 'If the organization of the future only contains a few hierarchical levels – between three
and four, for example, rather than a dozen – there will remain few rungs for the candidate for
honours to climb. Career advancement will have to be pursued laterally rather than vertically: by
accepting new spheres of activity or a different type of responsibility; and hence by apprenticeship and an expansion of experience, as opposed to attaining a higher rung. Moreover, progress
of this kind will not systematically translate into higher pay. Different times, different rules. Given
that the paths are no longer all mapped out, successfully managing one's career in this new world
will signify being the agent of one's own evolution, taking control of one's future, since no one
else can do it for you' (Le Saget, 1994).

As we said at the beginning of this chapter, we used a textual analysis software program to compare the two corpora systematically. In Appendix 3, readers will find a presentation of this work, offering statistical confirmation of the interpretation of their content we have just presented .

Having identified the concerns, projects, hopes and enemies on which management literature in the 1960s and 1990s focuses, it still remains for us to verify to what extent these bodies of ideology do indeed contain two different expressions of the spirit of capitalism. To do that, we must examine whether their proposals do in fact offer those whom capitalism needs, and who must be persuaded by these texts, not only a list of 'good practices' for the purpose of making profits for the firm, but a series of arguments capable of mobilizing them. Let us reiterate that, in order to meet the constraints of the test to which we are subjecting them, these texts must present engagement in reformation as a personally exciting venture, demonstrate that the measures proposed are justifiable in terms of the common good, and, finally, explain how they will deliver to those who invest in them a certain form of security for themselves and their children.

3. THE CHANGE IN FORMS OF MOBILIZATION

The 1960s: The exhilaration of progress and job security

The *attractive dimension* of 1960s management is provided by the project of decentralization, and by the autonomy held out to *cadres*. They are finally going to be able to use the means put at their disposal as they see fit, and will be controlled exclusively on the basis of results. And those who are identified as efficient managers through this mechanism will have career opportunities, and rise in the hierarchy.

The new system will be more just, and hence more conducive to everyone's benefit, because people in firms will be assessed according to objective criteria, and there will be an end to nepotism, favours, 'string-pulling', 'the grapevine'. As for society as a whole, the 'rational management' proposed here, by making firms more efficient, serves economic and social progress, the two terms not being dissociated at the time.[xlvi] This is one of the essential features of the spirit of capitalism in the 1960s. Firms are at the heart of a societal project, and all are agreed in assigning them a prominent role with respect to general well-being – not only on account of the economic wealth they create, but also because of the way they organize work and the kind of opportunities they

---

xlvi 'Man is not only a productive animal. As the domination of nature creates new needs, work must procure him an increasingly fulfilled existence: the continuous rise in living standards must put this increased wealth within reach of ever larger masses of people. ... This need for an improvement in the physical, moral and social conditions of people's existence outside work is now felt in all milieux' (Borne, 1966).

offer.[xlvii] Certain texts from the 1960s indicate very clearly how the role allotted to firms in social progress is connected directly with the Marxist critique, which was pervasive at the time, and with the shadow cast over the 'free world' by the communist countries. There is no better illustration of the impact of critique on capitalism and the partial incorporation of its demands into the spirit of a particular period.[xlviii] The still recent memory of the fascist regimes, as well as the survival of dictatorships in Europe, is a further reason for urging firms to respond to people's aspirations, to divert them from totalitarian temptations.[xlix] Management is thus especially legitimate in that it serves the cause of democracy. Generalizing the use of rational criteria in the operation of firms, which marks the 1960s project, is presented as the best safeguard against the irrational assaults that threaten liberties.[l] For management in the 1960s, the association of reason and freedom, in opposition to passion and barbarism, goes without saying.

The 1990s hark back to this idea in order to counter it: the endeavour relentlessly to rationalize the way firms are run has created inhuman machines. The 'peculiarity of human beings' has changed: reason in the 1960s versus feelings, emotion and creativity in the 1990s. Despite everything, the irrational phenomena that people wanted to eradicate have succeeded in taking over the machinery, with bureaucracy proving to be the worst system imaginable.

As far as *demands for security* are concerned, management in the 1960s counted on the advantage enjoyed by large organizations in offering *cadres* career guarantees. This mechanism was perfectly suited to the various questions posed by management consultants at the time. It can be justified from the standpoint of justice (careers are meritocratic, and offer everyone development opportunities) and control of the future (it enables firms to hold on to the valuable individuals they need). Management works of the time are full of advice about how to guard against the risk of a lack of *cadres*: planning requirements, careful

xlvii 'Playing a key role in the phenomenon of industrialization, for those who work in them our firms increasingly represent a human environment that their fulfilment depends on. Without sacrificing any of their economic and social objectives, they must help their members in today's world to play the freely chosen personal role that has fallen to them' (Paul Huvelin, Chairman and Managing Director of Établissements Kléber-Colombes, quoted in Drancourt, 1964).

xlviii 'These facts lead us to think that ... in order to survive – and after all, the prize of freedom is worth it – private firms will have to become increasingly democratic in the diffusion of their capital, and increasingly concerned to promote more justice and real freedom for the people whom they employ' (Devaux, 1959).

xlix 'If we want social progress to go in tandem with material progress, minds must be improved at the same time as living conditions. People have to learn to live. The first countries to take an interest in the organization of leisure were the totalitarian ones. The movement first emerged in Italy, then Russia, and then in the Third Reich with the *Kraft durch Freude*' (Borne, 1966).

l 'Some critics, today, keep worrying that our democratic, free societies are becoming over-managed. The real truth is precisely the opposite ... the real threat to democracy comes from under-management. ... The under-organization, the undermanagement of a society is not the respect of liberty. It is simply to let some force other than reason shape reality' (Robert McNamara quoted in Servan-Schreiber, 1967).

recruitment, and the establishment of career profiles making it possible gradually to raise beginners up to the level of competence attaching to posts with significant responsibilities.[li] Careers motivate *cadres*, who feel appreciated for their abilities. The possibility of changing the post of someone who does not make the grade is mentioned; redundancy, never (except in the case of those guilty of embezzlement).

The career, which involves a guarantee of regular salary increases, also represents a mode of redistribution between the generations: young *cadres* are underpaid at the age when they are at their most effective, but recover the advance made to the firm at the end of their career, when their salary is higher even though their skills are tending to become obsolete. This way of organizing the life-cycle has as its corollary the development of credit – mortgages and consumer credit – which is required to finance investments at the start of family life, and which people are assured of being able to pay back thanks to salary increases. A meritocratic dimension is nevertheless maintained in that the most efficient will receive higher-than-average income growth. In this way, security and emulation are reconciled.[lii] The future is radiant.

The diffusion of Abraham Maslow's theory of needs, postulating a hierarchy of human needs such that certain needs cannot be satisfied unless other, lower needs have been, imparted self-evidence to the belief that security needs are essential because they rest at the base of the pyramid, immediately after physiological needs like food or sleep. As soon as one seeks to manipulate the needs of *cadres* for fulfilment through management by objectives, it becomes obvious that this cannot be achieved unless security is guaranteed.[liii]

Security forms part of the implicit, but universally accepted, definition of the work contract. It is one of the central arguments in defence of capitalism, to the point where some authors reject anti-capitalist demands to entrust the management of firms to workers on the grounds that they would thereby risk losing the security they enjoy in exchange for their subordination.[liv]

---

li 'Job rotation ... can provide a series of planned experiences which can help a manager to broaden in knowledge and skills' (Humble, 1968).
'Work promotion allows the wage-earner to accede to more refined, better paid tasks: it must allow everyone, depending on their abilities, to try their luck in life. For a firm, internal promotion is thus both an economic and a social necessity' (Borne, 1966).
lii 'In a firm, career development is essential, because if the wage must answer to the virtue of justice, career development answers to hope and there is no balanced human society without hope' (Devaux, 1959).
liii 'The first requirement for fulfilling oneself and making a success of one's life is a minimum of security, so that one's mind is not utterly consumed by anxiety about tomorrow and people can devote themselves completely to their work. It can be said that most French firms offer great security to their *cadres* in the sense that the chance of being made redundant and finding oneself without work is tiny; dismissing a *cadre* is not part of the tradition – except in the quite exceptional instance of serious embezzlement' (Froissart, 1969).
liv 'Finally, the decisive argument against any total or partial transfer of authority in firms to trade unions is that this operation involves transforming a contract for the hire of services into a contract of partnership. This cannot occur without major disadvantages. It assumes

The final security mechanism management authors count on is none other than the welfare state, which is regarded as the requisite complement to economic existence.[lv] The corpus of the 1960s thus contains several defences of the effectiveness of public policies and the central importance of the state.[lvi] Servan-Schreiber (1967) will seek to promote the principle of a modern economy based, on the one hand, on firms employing the most recent management techniques (American) and, on the other, on a state that practises a flexible form of planning.[lvii] Firms produce wealth and forge technical progress, while the state ensures that everyone gains from these benefits. The distribution of roles is clear and the state is not at issue. Alone among our authors, Octave Gélinier proves slightly critical when he worries about the freedom granted firms by the state. But what he proposes is that the state should enforce competition between firms, put an end to monopolies and forms of protection, while being responsible for offering the indispensable complement of security that workers need, and firms cannot fully satisfy.

The texts from the 1960s thus echo very strong concerns over security, with firms, which create redundancies only in exceptional cases, and offer jobs for life, and the state, which provides insurance against other types of risk and unemployment in the event of firms closing down, taking it in turns. In the 1990s, by contrast, we witness a *simultaneous* challenge to these two forms of protection, which is paradoxical, since one would have thought that any reduction in one of the two mechanisms would have led to greater intervention by the other. We may advance the hypothesis that the authors have in mind the financial difficulties of the welfare state, inhibiting them from turning to this ready-made solution. An apologia for change, risk and mobility replaces the high premium put on the idea of security.

As we shall now see, this is without a doubt one of the points where the new spirit of capitalism is at its weakest, even if management authors are not wanting in imaginative attempts to hit upon forms of security that are compatible with the currently dominant requirement of flexibility.

---

accepting serious risks: capital and job losses without any compensation if problems arise. Obviously, the wage-earner can lose his job in the event of the firm closing. But unlike the partner, he enjoys legal or conventional guarantees such as compensation for notice and, in most cases, redundancy, as well as insurance against unemployment' (Malterre, 1969).

lv '[The need for] security ... has been solved, at least partially, in most developed countries through a more or less sophisticated social security system. ... It has considerably altered – some would say revolutionized – everyday life by dispelling the misery and anxiety that resulted from blows of fate for those who work' (Borne, 1966).

lvi 'After a certain level of technical development, the opinion seems to be that the means exist to guarantee the right to work and a certain sum of income. ... It is less and less acceptable for employees in rapidly expanding sectors to be the only ones to benefit from progress, whether it involves wages or guarantees of every sort (illness, retirement, etc.). The same goes for the right to work' (Armand and Drancourt, 1961).

lvii 'It goes without saying that there is no end of difficult reconciliation to make between the freedom of individuals and the strategy of the government. But experience denies that there is a fundamental antagonism between the two' (Servan-Schreiber, 1967).

The 1990s: Personal fulfilment through a multitude of projects

Before broaching the way in which issues of security are treated in the 1990s corpus, let us examine the proposals by neo-management intended to galvanize those whose engagement is to be stimulated, and the justifications that are given for them in terms of the common good.

As was already the case in the 1960s, one of the main attractions of the proposals formulated in the 1990s is that they adumbrate a certain liberation. But it is no longer merely a question of obtaining the supervised freedom of management by objectives, which in any case is open exclusively to *cadres*. In the new world, anything is possible, since creativity, reactivity and flexibility are the new watchwords.[lviii] Now no one is restricted by belonging to a department or wholly subject to the boss's authority, for all boundaries may be transgressed through the power of projects. Lemaire (1994) dreams of abolishing bosses completely, in particular by introducing a principle of symmetry that allows the person in charge of a project to have as their basic collaborator the head of another project in which one is oneself merely a participant.[lix] With new organizations, the bureaucratic prison explodes; one works with people at the other end of the world, different firms, other cultures. Discovery and enrichment can be constant. And the new 'electronic relations' at a distance prove to be more sincere and freer than face-to-face relations.[lx]

Another seductive aspect of neo-management is the proposal that everyone should develop themselves personally. The new organizations are supposed to appeal to all the capacities of human beings, who will thus be in a position fully to blossom.[lxi] 'Coaches' will support people in this endeavour, and everything will be done to ensure that they attain a better knowledge of themselves, and discover what they are capable of.[lxii] The new model proposes, so we are told, 'genuine autonomy', based on self-knowledge and personal fulfilment, not the false autonomy, framed by the career paths, job descriptions, and systems of sanctions–rewards, proposed by the 1960s.[lxiii]

lviii 'To be effective, the firm must in fact increasingly count on the capacity for initiative of each of the wage-earners it employs. To call upon their initiative is to call upon their autonomy and freedom' (Landier, 1991).

lix 'The only way to avoid such conflicts is not to have hierarchical superiors!'(Lemaire, 1994).

lx 'Electronic nomads, relieved of symbols of power and "social conformism", express themselves more freely via networks than face to face' (Ettighoffer, 1992).

lxi 'However essential, administration constitutes a rustic domain pertaining exclusively to rationality; it is therefore readily communicable by a trainer. But giving dynamism and life to an organization brings into play the eyes, listening, the desire to extend one's own field of consciousness, a capacity for empathy, imagination, the ability to switch logics, courage in choices and in action. ... Administration deals with what is certain, leadership confronts what is fluid' (Sérieyx, 1993).

lxii 'Through questioning one can – according to Socrates, one should – help others to discover the values and truths they possess' (Aubrey, 1990).

lxiii 'The race for promotion fuels the illusion of autonomy that it seems to promise. Discovery of the illusion reinforces the need to dominate by way of compensation – which then

To conclude, let us recall that the 1990s authors also entrust leaders and the power of their vision with responsibility for helping human beings to advance themselves. What in theory is equally attractive in neo-management is the prospect of working on an interesting project, which is 'worth the effort', led by an 'exceptional' person whose 'dream' one is going to 'share'. And since management literature urges everyone, and especially *cadres*, to be 'charismatic leaders' and 'visionaries' who give meaning to people's lives, the implicit suggestion is that those to whom these proposals are addressed – the readers – could themselves – why not? – very well be among those who, with the help of their firms, will realize their dreams and share them with others.

As we have seen, in order to confront critiques that challenge the unjust character of capitalism, at enterprise level, management in the 1960s insisted on the meritocratic aspect of the mechanisms proposed, while at a more general level it stressed the necessity of sound economic management to defend democracy and the 'free world', and spur social progress. Justification through economic growth, assumed to be bound up with social progress, as well as the alliance of capitalism and democracy, are among the most stable justifications of capitalism, as we mentioned in the introduction. But we also observed that these very general justifications are insufficient in themselves to legitimate local action, in the absence of supporting evidence pointing towards *local justice*, to adopt Jon Elster's terminology.[22] Moreover, the possibility of rooting major principles in mechanisms attuned to the specific characteristics of the firms into which they were integrated was precisely what meritocracy, based on measurement by results, supposedly offered in the framework of the second spirit of capitalism.

In the 1990s, the classical arguments invoked in defence of capitalism are still deployed: the theme of liberties is obviously the most pervasive of them. Now combined with it is another, no less traditional argument, which asserts that firms serve consumers (it has always been more legitimate to say that firms served their customers than that they made their owners wealthy). This increase in generality is readily ensured in the 1990s, given the focus on customers proposed by the new mechanisms. Contrariwise, the theme of economic progress – a third classical justification – is less in evidence, doubtless because most management authors in our day are too embarrassed to invoke it with confidence, given the rise in unemployment. They therefore fall back on the theme of surviving in a situation of increased competition (the changes proposed are justified by necessity) – which does indeed represent a justification, but one that is rather too meagre to engage people and elicit their enthusiasm.

---

further intensifies the race for promotion. Here we have a vicious circle, or interminable "game", of power as described by Simone Weil. It is always people at the bottom who believe in the enviable freedom of the higher level of the organization and the further one ascends, the more this desirable objective recedes' (Orgogozo and Sérieyx, 1989).

It remains for us to spell out the forms of local justice presented by contemporary authors, without which support for the current changes in capitalism risks being insufficient. In the 1960s, the idea was to reward people according to their results or efficiency. In contrast, the 1990s enhance the status of those who know how to work on a project, whether as leader or simple contributor. From this perspective, valuable members of staff are those who succeed in working with very different people, prove themselves open and flexible when it comes to switching project, and always manage to adapt to new circumstances.[lxiv]

This way of appraising people, which is conveyed in most of the 1990s texts, contrasts sharply with the precepts of justice formulated in earlier periods. But it remains decidedly unconvincing on account of its still imprecise character, and its vagueness about how it might give rise to convincing tests. Our hypothesis is that we are witnessing *the emergence of a new ordinary sense of justice*, which should eventually be amenable to codification in line with the architecture of political cities as described in *De la justification*, whose main lines we recalled in the introduction.[23] For judgements corresponding to this new expression of the sense of justice to be made explicit, and embodied in tests with a claim to general validity, we still lack an elaborated grammar based on a clearly stated anthropology and political philosophy. (This was the case, for example, with the commercial order, whose syntax can be derived from reading Adam Smith; or with the industrial order, resting on a principle of efficiency – central in the justifications of the 1960s – which was clearly formulated by Saint-Simon.) The next chapter is devoted to this labour of clarifying and grammaticizing forms of judgement corresponding to the sense of justice contained in neo-management, deriving this new form by comparing the texts in our corpus. We have dubbed this new 'city' the *projective city* with reference to the flexible world, composed of multiple projects conducted by autonomous persons, whose picture is painted by management authors.

The question of what guarantees of *security* are contained in contemporary management texts exposes us to other problems, above all because security is not a dominant value in the 1990s, when it is associated with status, hierarchy, bureaucracy – all of them things that are insistently denounced, in contrast to what we observed for the previous period.

The most combative author in this respect is Bob Aubrey, who recalls that Maslow's pyramid is a false scientific law.[lxv] More troubled by this lack of

---

lxiv 'In future, those who can master the greatest variety of professional situations, and who integrate into teams of different configurations without posing demands, will have an incontestable advantage in their professional advancement' (Le Saget, 1994).

lxv 'Today's organizations must assimilate the new reality by treating each wage-earner as an enterprise. This change dictates abandoning a number of assumptions that dominated industrial society, the first of them being that individuals seek job security – an idea generated in the 1950s by Abraham Maslow's famous "pyramid of needs", which posited as a rule that basic needs must be satisfied before thinking about fulfilment. Not only is this thesis debatable theoretically (how interest in security, Rosabeth Moss Kanter weighs the reduction in guarantees for the future against the freedom that has been won, and hopes that the excitement generated by greater autonomy will prove stronger than fears for the morrow.[lxvi]

Even so, management authors also know that without new forms of security, their proposals will not tempt many people.[lxvii] The first problem they have to resolve is to suggest some alternative to the hierarchical careers whose importance in the second spirit of capitalism we have seen. The suggestion is to replace them by a succession of projects. Henceforth people will not make a career, but will pass from one project to another, their success on a given project allowing them access to different, more interesting projects. Since each project is the occasion for many encounters, it offers an opportunity to get oneself appreciated by others, and thus the chance of being called upon for some other project. Being by definition different, novel, innovatory, each project presents itself as an opportunity to learn and to develop one's skills, which are so many assets for finding other engagements.[lxviii]

The key idea in this conception of life at work is _employability_, which refers to the capacity people must be equipped with if they are to be called upon for projects. The transition from one project to the next is the opportunity to increase one's employability. This is the personal capital that everyone must manage, comprising the total set of skills people can mobilize. While it is not

can we then explain someone who risks their security to become an artist or to embark on a new career?), but the interpretation of it in the management sphere – firms must guarantee security first of all and only then fulfilment – is hardly justified' (Aubrey, 1994).

lxvi '[T]he new business forms are accompanied by insecurity and overload at the same time that they generate more exciting and involving workplaces and give more people more chances to operate like entrepreneurs, even from within the corporate fold' (Moss Kanter, 1990).

lxvii 'The post-entrepreneurial principles I have identified clearly have both an upside and a downside. At their best, they create opportunity, giving people the chance to develop their ideas, pursue exciting projects, and be compensated directly for their contributions. At their best, they encourage collaboration across functions, across business units, and even across corporations. The business benefits from the use of these principles are lower fixed costs and increased entrepreneurial reach. But at their worst, the same strategies can lead to displacement instead of empowerment, rivalries instead of teamwork, and short-term asset-shuffling and one-night stands with the latest attractive deal instead of long-term commitments to build capacity. The same strategies executed unwisely and without concern for the organizational and human consequences will not produce continuing business benefits – especially if people withold effort and commitment for fear of being displaced or to hedge their bets against change' (Moss Kanter, 1990).

lxviii 'The post-entrepreneurial career is a constant race from one project to the next. The value added at each project signals so many successes. ... People's careers are more dependent on their own resources and less dependent on the fate of a particular company. This means that some people who know only bureaucratic ropes are cut adrift. It means that incomes are likely to fluctuate rather than increase in an orderly fashion each year. It means more risk and uncertainty. It does not necessarily mean lower productivity, for professional standards and concern for reputation may be sufficient incentives and also the best guarantee of continuity of employment even with the same corporation. No longer counting on the corporation to provide security and stature requires people to build those resources in themselves, which ultimately could result in more resourceful people' (Moss Kanter, 1990).

able to avoid redundancies, or promise careers, a firm will be regarded as offering a certain form of security when it does not destroy the employability of its wage-earners, but enhances it instead.[lxix] Thus, the 1990s authors do indeed have solutions to propose for the problem of security. But their proposals still lack comparable orchestration to that offered by the 1960s literature on managing *cadres*, which explained in detail how to recruit, appraise and advance human beings. In the texts that we have read, there are scarcely any mechanisms for appraising employability or confirming that it is increasing rather than diminishing. An optimistic explanation for this is that the 1960s texts offer a comparatively belated formulation of the second spirit of capitalism at a time when it is widely entrenched, whereas the 1990s texts are associated with a nascent new spirit of capitalism, which has not yet received its most bracing formulation.

Another risk, of a very new type, generated by flexible organizations is that it is much easier for actors in firms to be 'out for themselves', as popular language has it – to pursue their own interests, without taking into consideration those without whom their action would not have been crowned with success. The refusal of instrumentation, regulations and procedures, the rehabilitation of the affective and relational dimensions against which the 1960s consultants had struggled – these open up more space for this kind of behaviour than in the past. Such reprehensible forms of behaviour involve an opportunism in relationships that seizes on all the actually or potentially useful connections to which participation in the mechanisms surrounding daily life provides access (the mechanisms of a firm, training courses, academic, amicable, familial, romantic connections), in order to divert them to the end of personal profit. In a world 'without borders', in which the firm is 'fragmented', 'virtual', 'postmodern', where hierarchical constraints are very attenuated, where institutions no longer reveal their presence through tangible signs and, in particular, a symbolic system of power, how can one guarantee the loyalty of the manager both to the team and to the (often remote) profit centre he depends on?

Similarly, what guarantee is there that the integrity of persons will be respected in a context where they are called upon to bring to firms all their skills, including the most personal ones – not only their technical skills, but also their creativity, their sense of friendship, their emotionalism, and so on? The introduction of the 'coach', functioning as a psychologist in the firm's service, although charged with helping people to flourish, can be experienced by some as a danger of the firm encroaching on their private lives. Hence it is clear that, in order to be genuinely convincing in the eyes of those concerned, neo-management must comprise a minimum number of mechanisms aimed at controlling those risks that constitute other forms of attack on personal

---

lxix 'Job security cannot be guaranteed. On the other hand, firms can guarantee "employability" – that is to say, a level of skills and flexibility allowing each individual to find a new job inside or outside the firm' (Aubrey, 1993).

security. Management authors show that they are conscious of these risks to the extent of mentioning them, in particular when they tackle the question of 'coaching'. Yet they rapidly brush them aside, stressing that not just anyone can be a 'coach', and that those who play this role will have to possess personal qualities such that they will not intrude upon the subjects with whom they work, or oppress them, in line with a deontological approach akin to psychoanalysis.[lxx]

Generally speaking, the mechanisms of neo-management need to be used by people whose behaviour evinces a high level of ethical concern. The recent development of 'business ethics', as a specific management discipline, is no doubt related to these anxieties. Triggered by episodes of corruption to obtain procurement contracts, particularly abroad, this current of thought attests to the difficulty of supervising people's distant intrigues. And the problem is compounded by the generalization of new flexible mechanisms, since a very large number of wage-earners are now induced to move around and pursue 'network' activities that are less amenable to control. Once again the security of workers, as of the firm, can be guaranteed here only by a form of self-control that assumes the internalization of rules of behaviour safeguarding the integrity of persons, and avoiding a situation where their contribution is not acknowledged. Here we rediscover the theme of trust evoked in connection with new forms of control.[lxxi]

To meet these anxieties, management authors foreground the regulatory effect of mechanisms of reputation (which we also find in microeconomic modelling): actors in the world of business will police themselves, and will be keen in future not to work with those who have not observed the basic ethical rules. Reputational effects play a central role here. On the one hand, they are at the heart of employability – a good reputation being the surest means of continuous employment. On the other, they make it possible to exert especially effective normalizing pressure, since the persons with whom one is involved can seek to destroy one's reputation in the event of behaviour they deem harmful.[lxxii] What remains problematic in these proposals is that repu-

lxx 'His approach is basically amorous, oblatory; he creates lasting bonds; his collaborators are developing beings' (Cruellas, 1993).

'Administrator of a process that is, when all is said and done, an educative one, the coach is therefore very keen to watch over the different stages of autonomy that his support should lead to' (Lenhardt, 1992).

lxxi '[B]usiness athletes must *operate with the highest ethical standards*. While business ethics have always been important from a social and moral point of view, they also become a pragmatic requirement in the corporate Olympics. ... The trust required for all of these new business strategies is built and reinforced by a mutual understanding that each party to the relationship will behave ethically, taking the needs, interests, and concerns of all others into account' (Moss Kanter, 1990).

lxxii 'It will be observed that "highly ambitious individuals" are often solitary. When they seek to integrate into a group, they are very rapidly identified and rejected. We should be aware that a network has its own invisible "police" capable of getting the better of profiteers and usurers: "old school friends, regimental comrades, bridge club enthusiasts ... or those sharing a table at at a wedding very quickly identify those who are only there to exploit the situation". So much the better. It is because networks are anxious about their image. The better the image, the more effective the network is in influencing economic life and relationships' (Bellenger, 1992).

tation can also be taken hostage for less noble reasons, and be misappropriated to the advantage of the strongest. But this scenario, which doubtless
requires a perverse mind to be taken seriously, is not envisaged by management authors, who are rather inclined to optimism.

In the final analysis, the mobilizing capacity contained in the new spirit of
capitalism as displayed in 1990s management literature seems to us poor. The
proposals advanced certainly aim to sketch a world where life would genuinely
be very exciting. But they exhibit a deficit in terms of justice, in that they presuppose reference to a new value system which exists only in outline. As for
the security on offer, while there is no lack of ideas, they suffer from weak
orchestration. 'Employability', 'personal ethics', and 'holding reputations
hostage' – in management literature at least, these have yet to find any very
solid translation into mechanisms. It is nevertheless the case that the people
best adjusted to the new world, and best placed to take full advantage of it,
should not suffer from these absences and, consequently, should enthusiastically engage in reformation. The problem will be to persuade larger groups of
people – in particular, all those without a very high reputation or varied
resources, or whose possibilities of mobility are, for various reasons, restricted,
and who desire a more sheltered existence, even if it might be reckoned less
exciting according to the new criteria.

CONCLUSION: NEW MANAGEMENT AS A RESPONSE TO CRITIQUES

The management literature of the 1990s contains ideals, proposals for organizing human beings, ways of arranging objects, and forms of security so
different from those of the 1960s that it is difficult not to accept that the spirit
of capitalism has undergone a sea change over the last thirty years. And this
is so even though the new configuration does not possess the mobilizing power
achieved by its predecessor, because of its incompleteness at the level of justice
and security.

In so far as we have established that the critiques to which capitalism is vulnerable constitute one of the determining elements in the formation of the
spirit of capitalism peculiar to a period – changes in this domain invariably
being based upon the satisfaction of certain criticisms, whether of the
reformist variety that seeks to improve existing mechanisms, or the radical
variety that demands a transformation of the tests – we shall now seek to
identify the demands which the new spirit is capable of satisfying. In any event,
in order to take root, it must find sufficiently broad support and, to that end,
offer different kinds of satisfaction from those proposed by the previous spirit.
Otherwise, the change will be received in purely negative fashion. It must therefore be capable of meeting a demand that was not satisfied in the earlier period,
for whose duration it was probably predominantly expressed in the rhetoric

of critique. The pinpointing in the introduction of the four sources of indignation on which critiques of capitalism draw will help us to identify the
demands satisfied by the new spirit. It thus seems to us fairly obvious that
neo-management aims to respond to demands for authenticity and freedom,
which have historically been articulated in interrelated fashion by what we have
called the 'artistic critique'; and that it sets to one side the issues of egoism
and inequalities traditionally combined in the 'social critique'.

Challenging the hitherto dominant forms of hierarchical control and
affording greater freedom are thus presented in management literature, but
also by sociologists of work, as a response to demands for autonomy from
more highly qualified wage-workers, who on average have spent longer in the
education system (the percentage of autodidacts among *cadres* fell, for example,
in the 1980s), and especially from young *cadres*, engineers and technicians.
Trained in a more permissive familial and educational environment, such
people find it difficult to tolerate the discipline of the firm and close supervision by bosses, rebel against authoritarianism when they are subject to it, but
are also loath to exercise it over their subordinates.

It is not difficult to find an echo here of the denunciations of hierarchy
and aspirations to autonomy that were insistently expressed at the end of the
1960s and in the 1970s. Moreover, this filiation is claimed by some of the consultants who contributed to establishing neo-management mechanisms in the
1980s. Hailing from leftism, and especially the self-management movement,
they stress the continuity between the commitments of their youth and the
activities that they pursued in firms, following the political turning-point of
1983, with a view to making working conditions appealing, improving productivity, developing quality, and increasing profits. Thus, for example, the
qualities that are guarantees of success in this new spirit – autonomy, spontaneity, rhizomorphous capacity, multitasking (in contrast to the narrow
specialization of the old division of labour), conviviality, openness to others
and novelty, availability, creativity, visionary intuition, sensitivity to differences,
listening to lived experience and receptiveness to a whole range of experiences, being attracted to informality and the search for interpersonal contacts
– these are taken directly from the repertoire of May 1968.[24] But these themes,
which in the texts of the May movement were combined with a radical critique
of capitalism (particularly the critique of exploitation), and the proclamation
of its imminent end, are often to be found in the neo-management literature
autonomized, as it were – represented as objectives that are valid in their own
right, and placed in the service of forces whose destruction they were intended
to hasten. The critique of the division of labour, of hierarchy and supervision – that is to say, of the way industrial capitalism alienates freedom – is
thus detached from the critique of market alienation, of oppression by impersonal market forces, which invariably accompanied it in the oppositional
writings of the 1970s.

Similar remarks may be made about the critique of disenchantment, of the inauthenticity of daily life in the capitalist universe. At the level of organizing production, the stress in neo-management on interaction, on authentic human relations (in contrast to bureaucratic formalism), represents a response to critiques that condemned alienation in work and the mechanization of human relations. The discrediting of bureaucracy and its project of eliminating everything that is not 'rational' – that is, formalizable and calculable – should, we are told, facilitate a return to a 'more human' *modus operandi*, in which people can give full vent to their emotions, intuition and creativity. Does not neo-management propose that everyone should stop being an instrument, and instead 'realize their deep desires and flourish' (Le Saget, 1994)?

More generally, in stressing versatility, job flexibility and the ability to learn and adapt to new duties, rather than possession of an occupation and established qualifications, but also the capacity for engagement, communication and relational qualities, neo-management looks to what are increasingly called 'life skills', as opposed to knowledge and *savoir faire*. Recruitment is now based on an assessment of a person's most generic qualities – those that are just as valid in justifying the pairings of private life, whether amicable or emotional – rather than on objective qualifications. Accordingly, it becomes difficult to distinguish between engaging collaborators to perform a particular task and attaching certain people to yourself because they suit you personally. These trends in neo-management are often, as we have seen, presented as an attempt to inflect the world of work in a 'more human' direction. But through a backlash they can create new risks of exploitation, on which we shall elaborate later. For now, let us simply observe that those of the new mechanisms which are justified not only by the reduced wage costs and increased productivity they entail, but also by the intention of breaking with Taylorist forms of work, legitimately considered inhuman (job enrichment, improvement in working conditions), are especially ambiguous in this respect. The Taylorization of work does indeed consist in treating human beings like machines. But precisely because they pertain to an automation of human beings, the rudimentary character of the methods employed does not allow the more human properties of human beings – their emotions, their moral sense, their honour, their inventive capacity – to be placed directly in the service of the pursuit of profit. Conversely, the new mechanisms, which demand greater commitment and rely on a more sophisticated ergonomics, integrating the contributions of post-behaviourist psychology and the cognitive sciences, precisely because they are more human in a way, also penetrate more deeply into people's inner selves – people are expected to 'give' themselves to their work – and facilitate an instrumentalization of human beings in their most specifically human dimensions.

Another form of reaction to the theme of disenchantment aims to answer critiques of the inauthenticity of daily life – the loss of uniqueness, the destruction of spontaneity, anxiety, the generalization of calculation, the will to total mastery, the proliferation of ossified things (as opposed to living entities), the creation of products or spectacles – which are rooted in the sphere of consumption. These denounce prefabricated needs, the ascendancy of advertising and marketing, the 'crumbling away of human values under the influence of exchange mechanisms',[25] the reign of the quantitative (as opposed to the qualitative), the standardization of goods in mass production, the domination of appearances, the tyranny of standing, the invasion of useless, ugly, ephemeral objects, and so on. The capitalist response to this modern variant of the artistic critique will to some extent take the form of seeking to develop the production and marketing of goods that are always new (the famous imperative of continual managerial innovation), whose novelty and limited distribution when they are first introduced temporarily assuages anxieties about massification. Furthermore, insistence on personalized service to customers, on the importance of careful attention to their wishes, and on the development of individualized relations[26] aims to introduce 'authenticity' into capitalist production in the form of the 'personalized'. On a wider scale, this same concern to return to personal desires as closely as possible inspires the transition from mass production to the limited series production of an ever greater variety of goods – the 'flexible production' characteristic of the 'second industrial divide'.[27]

Hence new-style management does indeed offer various responses to the critique of disenchantment by promoting the creation of products that are attuned to demand, personalized, and which satisfy 'genuine needs', as well as more personal, more human forms of organization. Similarly, it satisfies demands for liberation from the sway of bureaucracy associated with the critique of the second spirit of capitalism. These two dimensions help to give it salience and appeal, even if it proves to be somewhat lacking at the level of mechanisms of security and rests upon a form of justice which, while presenting characteristics that may be regarded as very specific, still remains largely implicit. The next chapter is devoted to bringing out that form of justice.

Notes

1 We distinguish between literature intended for *cadres* and research literature in management whose aim is not normative, and whose mode of composition in particular assumes a critical apparatus that is offputting for the average reader, meaning that it is intended primarily for instructors in management orientated towards research.

2 We date management not from the appearance of the various practices it comprises (in which case one could find examples of management, as some authors indeed do, even in antiquity – for example, in the organization of the building of the Egyptian pyramids), but from their codification. It is then that reference is made to the discipline of 'management', which is generally held to begin with the works of two emblematic figures: the Frenchman Henri Fayol (1841–1925) and the American F.W. Taylor (1856–1915). The founding works of the two authors date from the second decade of this century.

3 See Alfred D. Chandler, *The Visible Hand: The Managerial Revolution in American Business*, Harvard University Press, Cambridge (MA) 1977.

4 See Werner Sombart, *The Quintessence of Capitalism*, trans. M. Epstein and T. Fisher Unwin, London 1915, pp. 104–5. Weber is not in agreement with Sombart's choice, and considers that Alberti's writings lack essential elements of the spirit of capitalism, such as the fact that 'time is money': Max Weber, *The Protestant Ethic and the Spirit of Capitalism*, trans. Stephen Kalberg, Fitzroy Dearborn, Chicago and London 2002, pp. 170–71 n. 12.

5 See ibid.

6 Our way of constructing the two images of management in the two epochs is thus similar to that employed by Weber: 'If one can discover at all an object for which the phrase *spirit of capitalism* is meaningful, then it can only be a specific *historical case*. Such a singular entity is nothing more than a complex of relationships in historical reality. We join them together, from the vantage point of their *cultural significance*, into a conceptual unity. Such a historical concept, however, cannot be defined according to how it is "demarcated" vis-à-vis other concepts (*genus proximum, differentia specifaci*). This holds if only because the concept denotes a phenomenon that is of qualitative importance as a consequence of its individual *uniqueness*. Moreover, this concept must be gradually *put together* from its single component parts, each of which is taken out of historical reality' (*The Protestant Ethic and the Spirit of Capitalism*, p. 13).

7 See Louis Dumont, *Homo aequalis*, Gallimard, Paris 1977.

8 See A.O. Hirschman, *The Rhetoric of Reaction*, Belnap Press, Cambridge (MA) 1991.

9 See Pierre Ansart, *Marx et l'anarchisme*, Presses Universitaires de France, Paris 1969.

10 Fernand Braudel, *The Wheels of Commerce*, trans. Sian Reynolds, Harper & Row, New York 1982, p. 453.

11 See Luc Boltanski, *The Making of a Class: Cadres in French Society*, trans. Arthur Goldhammer, Cambridge University Press/Éditions de la Maison des Sciences de l'Homme, Cambridge 1987.

12 See Lester Thurow, *Head to Head: The Coming Economic Battle among Japan, Europe and America*, Nicholas Brealey, London 1993.

13 See James Womack, Daniel Jones and Daniel Roos, *The Machine that Changed the World*, Rawson, New York 1990.

14 SMED (Single Minute Exchange of Die) is a means of rapidly changing tool or reference that makes it possible to multiply changes of series without increasing the time machines have to run in order to produce; TPM means Total Productive Maintenance and aims to organize the set of relations to machines (preventive maintenance, avoidance of errors by the operator, training of the latter to detect signs of impending breakdowns, etc.) in such a way that the machines are never out of order; KanBan, which is a method allowing for prior communication of the requirements of the following stage of production (for example, by sending a car ferry to load up), is the main tool for organizing production on a just-in-time basis; 5S, from the name of the five Japanese words beginning with S, aims to organize a workspace visually so that it becomes, as it were, 'obvious' (that each thing has a place and one place only, that it is always returned there after use, etc.).

15 See Ève Chiapello, *Artistes versus managers. Le management culturel face à la critique artiste*, Métailié, Paris 1998.

16 See Luc Boltanski, 'Pouvoir et impuissance. Project intellectuel et sexualité dans le Journal d'Amiel', *Actes de la recherche en sciences sociales*, 1 (5–6), 1975, pp. 171–99.

17 See Ève Chiapello, 'Les typologies des modes de contrôle et leurs facteurs de contingence – un essai d'organisation de la littérature', *Comptabilité–Contrôle–Audit*, vol. 2, no. 2, September 1996, pp. 77–114; and 'Les organisations et le travail artistique sont-ils contrôlables?', *Réseaux*, November–December 1997, pp. 77–114.

18 Benjamin Coriat, *Penser à l'envers – Travail et organisation dans la firme japonaise*, Christian Bourgois, Paris 1991.

19 Michel Aglietta, 'Nouveau régime de croissance et progrès social' (interview), *Esprit*, November 1998, p. 147.

20 See Oliver Williamson, *The Economic Institutions of Capitalism*, Free Press, New York 1985; Walter Powell, 'Neither Market nor Hierarchy: Network Forms of Organization', *Research in Organizational Behavior*, vol. 12, 1990, pp. 295–336.

21 See Michael Piore and Charles Sabel, *The Second Industrial Divide*, Basic Books, New York 1984; Georges Benko and Alain Lipietz, eds, *Les Régions qui gagnent. Districts et réseaux: les nouveaux paradigmes de la géographie économique*, Presses Universitaires de France, Paris 1992.

22 Jon Elster, *Local Justice: How Institutions Allocate Scarce Goods and Necessary Burdens*, Russel Sage, New York 1992.

23 Luc Boltanski and Laurent Thévenot, *De la justification. Les économies de la grandeur*, Gallimard, Paris 1991.

24 Take, to give only one example, these passages, chosen almost at random from Vaneigem's book, which could feature in the corpus of neo-management (Raoul Vaneigem, *The Revolution of Everyday Life*, trans. Donald Nicholson-Smith, Left Bank Books and Rebel Press, London 1983):

'Has anyone bothered to study the approaches to work of primitive peoples, the importance of play and creativity, the incredible yield obtained by methods which the application of modern technology would make a hundred times more efficient?' (p. 39.)

'What people do officially is nothing compared with what they do in secret. People usually associate creativity with works of art, but what are works of art alongside the creative energy displayed by everyone a thousand times a day: seething unsatisfied desires, daydreams in search of a foothold in reality, feelings at once confused and luminously clear, ideas and gestures presaging nameless upheavals' (p. 147).

'Once the light of the qualitative is shed upon them, the most varied kinds of knowledge combine and form a magnetic bridge powerful enough to overthrow the weightiest traditions. The force of plain spontaneous creativity increases knowledge at an exponential rate. Using makeshift equipment and negligible funds, a German engineer recently built an apparatus able to replace the cyclotron. If individual creativity can achieve such results with such meagre stimulation, what marvels of energy must be expected from the qualitative shock waves and chain reactions that will occur when the spirit of freedom still alive in the individual re-merges in collective form to celebrate the great social fête, with its joyful breaking of all taboos' (p. 153).

'But in the end the disgust aroused by this world of inauthenticity revives an insatiable desire for human contact' (p. 194).

'The problem then is how to organize, without creating a hierarchy; in other words, how to make sure that the leader of the game doesn't become just "the Leader". The only safeguard against authority and rigidity setting in is a playful attitude' (p. 202).

25 Ibid., p. 59.

26 In the new customer-orientated organizations, customers must, for example, always deal with the same person whatever their requirements, this person being charged with mobilizing the resources required to satisfy the customer. In Taylorist organizations, by contrast, the counters or services that customers inquire at vary according to their demands, and they may end up having several interlocutors and having to discover the route to be followed to receive satisfaction. In the second case, customers are themselves Taylorized.

27 Piore and Sabel, *The Second Industrial Divide*.

2

THE FORMATION OF
THE PROJECTIVE CITY

The 1990s management texts reflect the image of a world that has been largely reorganized by comparison with the 1960s. This process took shape gradually, with successive organizational innovations, technological inventions and managerial modes since the 1980s. One by one, all the mechanisms derived from the second spirit of capitalism have been questioned, modified, transformed, abolished, replaced. As a result, the need for some new general representation of the economic world has become pressing. The texts we have studied are presented as attempts to unify the small-scale alterations that have occurred over more than a decade into a comprehensive vision.

In effect, there comes a time when it is very difficult for actors in firms to continue to work, to project themselves into the future, if their only support is a kaleidoscopic image of economic existence and forms of economic success, composed of a mixture of queries and fragmented mechanisms. Those who run firms, those who advise them, and those who train the *cadres* destined to join them (or in retraining) need to be able to invoke some plain, self-evident truths that make the world intelligible. Young *cadres* in particular feel a need clearly to identify the new forms of success and the new rules of the game in the economic world, in order to know how to conduct themselves and prepare their children. This demand for intelligibility exerts significant pressure for greater explanation and formalization of the rules of conduct, which will then guide action. In fact, people tend to conform to these emergent new rules, if only because they confer meaning on what would otherwise merely seem like an arbitrary proliferation of *ad hoc* mechanisms and locally convenient improvisations.

There is no doubt that the term 'network' is, as we suggested in Chapter 1, the term most frequently used to connect up elements that are in fact highly disparate – not only in management literature but also, for example, in microeconomics and sociology.[1] So pervasive is this in management literature that it can lead people to take their distance from it. We witness this in the case of the 'futurologist' Alvin Toffler (1990), one of the authors in our corpus. Noting the fad for 'reticular' forms, which are in the process of becoming the new 'one best way', he counterposes the proliferation of forms recommended by him.

Not so long ago, the term 'network' was associated either with technical distribution networks (water, electricity, etc.) – a usage that was extended to the distribution of other goods (e.g. banking networks) – or with organizations of a secret character (resistance networks). The latter invariably possessed a negative connotation (trafficking networks), their members being accused of seeking illicit advantages and profits through this type of association, obtained without going through the usual meritocratic mediations, thanks to favours (the Freemasons) and sometimes by resorting to patently illegal methods (the Mafia).

The term has been rehabilitated owing to a particular historical conjunction, characterized by the development of computer networks opening up possibilities of long-distance work and collaboration in real time, and by the search in the social sciences (see below) for concepts with which to identify structures that are minimally hierarchical (if at all so), flexible, and not restricted by boundaries marked out a priori. As an existing concept, constructed around contemporary ideas, technologies and research, associated with a specific vocabulary, models of causality and mathematical models, and formed to offer an alternative to hierarchical algorithms, 'network' naturally enough finds itself mobilized by capitalism. Employed in academic works in economics and the sociology of work – disciplines that helped to provide management with its theoretical foundations – it was almost bound to invade the literature addressed to *cadres* that we have studied. This is how the forms of capitalist production accede to representation in each epoch, by mobilizing concepts and tools that were initially developed largely autonomously in the theoretical sphere or the domain of basic scientific research. This is the case with neurology and computer science today. In the past, it was true of such notions as system, structure, technostructure, energy, entropy, evolution, dynamics and exponential growth.[2]

Social life today is no longer presented in the form of a series of rights and duties towards an extended familial community, as in a domestic world; or in the form of the wage-earning class within a hierarchical body whose rungs one climbs, where one spends one's whole career, and where professional activity is clearly separated from the private sphere, as in an industrial world. In a reticular world, social life is composed of a proliferation of encounters and temporary, but reactivatable connections with various groups, operated at potentially considerable social, professional, geographical and cultural distance. The *project* is the occasion and reason for the connection. It temporarily assembles a very disparate group of people, and presents itself as a *highly activated section of network* for a period of time that is relatively short, but allows for the construction of more enduring links that will be put on hold while remaining available. Projects make production and accumulation possible in a world which, were it to be purely connexionist, would simply contain flows, where nothing could be stabilized, accumulated or crystallized. Everything would be carried off in an endless stream of ephemeral associations which, given their capacity to put everything in communication, constantly distribute and dissolve whatever gels in them. The project is precisely a mass of active connections apt to create forms – that is to say, bring objects and subjects into existence – by stabilizing certain connections and making them irreversible. It is thus a temporary *pocket of accumulation* which, creating value, provides a base for the requirement of extending the network by furthering connections.

New maxims for success accompany the establishment of such a world, and a new system of values is constructed on which people can rely to make judgements; to discriminate between behaviour that is satisfactory and behaviour that leads to exclusion; to put a value on qualities and attitudes that had not hitherto been identified as distinctive; to legitimate new positions of power; and to select those who are to enjoy them.

We have endeavoured to bring out this new system of values by identifying anything in the management literature that seemed to us specific and unprecedented, particularly compared with the dominant values of the 1960s. In order to put this in relief, and reveal its systematic character, we have codified it using the grammar of cities presented in *De la justification*.[3] This has led us to construct a seventh city – the *projective city* – a sketch of which will be found below. Obviously, the 1990s texts do not contain only the rhetoric of projects. In them, though to very different degrees, we find references to other logics of action – for example, commercial, industrial or reputational logics. In accordance with the methodology of ideal types, however, we have tried to extract from the most recent management texts whatever marked them out as singular, without stressing the more familiar features – for example, all those referring to an industrial logic – which are still present.

For reasons it is advisable to explain, given that the term might seem unwieldy and rather unclear, we have chosen to call the new apparatus of justification that seems to us to be being formed the 'projective city'. It is in fact modelled on a term that frequently crops up in management literature: project organization. This refers to a firm whose structure comprises a multiplicity of projects associating a variety of people, some of whom participate in several projects. Since the very nature of this type of project is to have a beginning and an end, projects succeed and take over from one another, reconstructing work groups or teams in accordance with priorities or needs. By analogy, we shall refer to a social structure in project form or a general organization of society in project form.[4]

What is more, the term designating the city which codifies the forms to which justice must conform in a reticular world could not simply refer directly to 'networks', as would have been the case had we spoken, for example, of the 'connexionist city' or the 'reticular city'. For a certain number of constraints must weigh on the operation of the network if it is to be characterized as just, in the sense that the relative status accorded to beings in it appears to be justified and legitimate. For this it is imperative that various tests can be identified, in the course of which beings confront one another in a relationship that creates equivalence between them. Now, we shall see that in such a world these tests are quintessentially the moments marking the end of a project, when people are in search of a new engagement, their ability to integrate themselves into a new project constituting one of the palpable signs of status.

Fairness in the distribution of status, according to people's contribution, also presupposes closing the list of the relevant parties at any given moment. Now, in a completely networked world, no such closure is possible. The network is continually extended and altered, with the result that there exists no apposite principle for finalizing, at a given point in time, the list of those between whom scales of justice may be established. It follows that in a world so constructed as to be entirely subject to a network logic, there is no reason to pose the question of justice, because those of low status (who, as we shall see, can be very precisely characterized in such a framework as *excluded*) tend to disappear without trace. Not only is there no equipment with which to establish the equivalences required to weigh justice, but there is not even that co-presence in the same space which makes it possible, through simple comparison, to inquire into the relationship between the misery of some and the happiness of others.

This is why the network cannot in itself represent the support for a city. Given that membership of the network remains largely indeterminate, the very notion of the common good is problematic in the topic of the network because it is not known *between whom* a 'good' might be placed in 'common' and also, for that reason, *between whom* a scale of justice might be established. In fact, a demand for justice cannot wholly dispense with units conceived on the basis of a spatial metaphor (representable units), wherein people's claim to have access to material or symbolic goods in accordance with their comparative value might be assessed. The notion of 'project', in the sense we intend it, can thus be understood as a compromise formation between exigencies that at first sight appear antagonistic: those that follow from representation in networks and those inherent in the design of providing a form which makes it possible to venture judgements and generate justified orders. In the seamless fabric of the network, projects delineate a multitude of mini-spaces of calculation, wherein orders can be generated and justified.

Finally – as we shall see later in this chapter, when we investigate the support that these new reticular representations of the world have found in recent developments in political philosophy – the ontology of the network has been largely established in such a way as to liberate human beings from the constraints of justification placed on action by metaphysics at two levels – the one occupied by scattered beings; the other by conventions making it possible to compare them as equivalents, and thus subject them to judgement. These mark the political philosophies of the common good from which the concept of city has been derived. Against these two-tiered constructs, the network is presented as a 'plane of immanence' – to use Gilles Deleuze's expression – in which the test is wholly defined as a 'test of strength', or simply as a 'structure of relations', or again as an 'encounter'. This dispenses with the loops of reflexivity that take the form of a moral judgement.[5] This is why the composite notion of 'project', which is taking root in the common sense of members of our society, involves loans from at least two different sets of paradigms: paradigms of the network and paradigms that, while likewise stressing communication and relation, include the requirement of reflexivity and convergence on shared judgements – for example, in Habermas – via the medium of exchanges regulated by communicative reason.

The projective city thus presents itself as a system of constraints placed upon a network world that encourages people to forge links and extend its ramifications, while respecting only those maxims of justifiable action that are specific to projects. Projects are a fetter on absolute circulation, for they demand a certain engagement, albeit temporary and partial, and presuppose monitoring by the other participants of the qualities that everyone brings into play. As we suggested in the introduction to this work, reference to justice presupposes that force is shackled in such a way that relations of force can be redefined as relations of status. Cities thus present themselves as constraining forms, restricting the possibilities of action in a certain world whose logic they embrace and also legitimate. The projective city is no exception. It constrains the network, subjecting it to a form of justice that nevertheless safeguards its content and puts a premium on the qualities of the network creator – something none of the established cities was able to do.

I. THE PROJECTIVE CITY

This city is founded on the *mediating* activity employed in the creation of networks, making it valuable in its own right, independently of the goals pursued or the substantive properties of the entities between which the mediation is conducted. From this standpoint, mediation is a value in itself, or rather, in the conceptual framework employed here, a specific *status* of which each actor is liable to take advantage when 'putting people in contact', 'making connections', thereby helping to 'construct networks'.

But let us be quite clear. Entertaining the hypothesis that we are witnessing the formation of a new city, where the tests that matter involve constructing or loosening connections in a network world, obviously does not mean that the establishment of networks represents a radical new departure. This is what is sometimes suggested by the writings devoted to them, whose current proliferation precisely contributes to establishing the world *vis-à-vis* which such a city might be pertinent. Our position is different. The formation of more or less extensive networks is no more novel than commercial activity was when Adam Smith wrote *The Wealth of Nations*. But it is as if we had to wait until the last third of the twentieth century for the activity of mediating, the art of making and using the most diverse and remote kinds of connection, to be autonomized – separated from the other forms of activity it had hitherto been bound up with – and identified and valued for itself. This is the process that seems to us to be a novel development deserving of attention.

We shall now seek to paint a full picture of the projective city without any critical distance, as if we were entering it with the determination and natural-ness expected of those to whom these new normative requirements are furnished as an exemplum. The architecture of the 'projective city' is illus-trated in the main by extracts from our 1990s corpus, and secondarily by other social science works employing the metaphor of the network. We present it in three stages. (a) The first is devoted to highlighting the principle of equiv-alence that makes it possible to order things and persons, and to deliver a judgement as to their 'superior' or 'inferior' status. (b) The second is centred on the forms of justice employed in the projective city, and thus bears on the preconditions that must be satisfied for the hierarchy of conditions, in accor-dance with the principle of equivalence established in (a), to be transmuted into a justifiable order. (c) The third stage of our exposition concerns the rooting of the projective city in a definition of nature: the nature of society, in order to confer a universal vocation on the city; and human nature – an indispensable specification for grounding the equal potential of all human beings to attain the status that corresponds to the logic of this city and, con-sequently, a precondition for the realization of justice in the world corresponding to it.

Principle of judgement and hierarchy of beings in the projective city

According to the grammar employed by us, the <common superior principle>* is the principle in accordance with which acts, things and persons are judged in a given city. In the industrial city, for example, the common superior prin-ciple is efficiency. It represents the convention that creates equivalence between entities – in the sense, for example, that it can be said: 'In terms of efficiency, X is equivalent to Y'. Similarly, using this same convention, it can be said that 'Z is superior or inferior to X'. Thus, identification of the common superior principle in a city leads us straight to the <condition of great man>, the great man being the one who embodies the city's values, as well as to the <condition of little person>, defined by the absence of such values. The

* In this section, we place the grammatical terms derived from *De la justification* between [acute] square brackets and the key terms that describe the projective city in italics.

<decline of the city>, like the <condition of little person>, refers to situations where behaviour is deemed unsatisfactory by the city's values. But it also makes reference to general configurations which, while claiming to be inspired by the relevant status, fall down in such fundamental aspects that they embody nothing but a perverted status. If the <condition of little person> in the new city applies to bad (individual) behaviour in a world of projects, the <decline of the city> involves unsatisfactory rhizomorphous forms, 'bad networks'.

The description of what counts in this world is based on categories of things – the <repertoire of objects and mechanisms> – of human beings – the <repertoire of subjects> – or of verbs – <the natural relations between beings> – referring to figures, objects and modes of relations, specific to a given form of status. Each of these value spheres thus tends to encompass a specific vocabulary, referring to the categories that embody status according to the city's criteria. The presence of these categories of things, beings, qualities or actions in an argument is an index of the justificatory register adopted by the speaker. Thus, someone situated in an 'industrial' world will readily refer to 'instruments', 'methods', 'measures' or 'procedures', invoke 'engineers' and 'specialists', and list 'controlling' or 'organizing' as among the actions worth performing. On the other hand, it would be incongruous to find them evoking 'opinion leaders' or 'press attachés', who are subjects of the reputational world; 'propriety' and 'good manners', which are domestic mechanisms; or to hear them using the verbs 'dream' and 'imagine', which point to inspirational status. To facilitate the city's insertion into concrete situations and impart substance, as it were, to the value hierarchy measured by the 'common superior principle', we shall now present these different categories of words.

Activity, Projects,
Extension of the network,
Proliferation of connections
<Common superior principle>

In a projective city, the general equivalent – what the status of persons and things is measured by – is *activity*. But in contrast to what we observe in the industrial city, where activity merges with work and the active are quintessentially those who have stable, productive waged work, activity in the projective city surmounts the oppositions between work and non-work, the stable and the unstable, wage-earning class and non-wage-earning class, paid work and voluntary work, that which may be assessed in terms of productivity and that which, not being measurable, eludes calculable assessment.

Management authors take up the idea floated by their English colleague Charles Handy, in his book *The Age of Unreason*, when he proposes to replace the traditional notion of a job by the concept of a port-folio of activities that everyone manages for themselves. At least five categories of work are listed: waged work, remunerated in line with the time spent on it; work for oneself, remunerated by the results obtained; domestic work, performed for the upkeep and maintenance of a home; voluntary work, performed for charitable organizations, the community, friends, family, or neighbours; educational work, which makes it possible to learn, to develop skills, to read, and to educate oneself. (Aubrey, 1994).[6]

The suggestion is to avoid being dependent on a single category, especially the first, given that after the age of forty many people will have to reconstruct their portfolio completely. '[Simultaneous] development of all the categories in the portfolio' is therefore indicated: 'Thanks to the multiplicity of clients, work for fees offers a certain guarantee of activity. Self-educational work helps improve the chances of remaining active and voluntary work makes it possible to construct social networks outside work, to participate actively in progress towards a better world and to transmit wisdom to others' (Aubrey, 1994).

Activity aims to generate *projects*, or to achieve integration into projects initiated by others. But the project does not exist outside of the *encounter* (not being integrated once and for all into an institution or environment, it presents itself as an action to be performed, not as something that is already there). Hence the activity *par excellence* is integrating oneself into *networks* and exploring them, so as to put an end to isolation, and have opportunities for meeting people or associating with things proximity to which is liable to generate a project.

Activity expresses itself in the multiplicity of projects *of all kinds* that may be pursued concurrently and which, no what matter what happens, must be elaborated successively, since the project represents a transient mechanism in this logic. Life is conceived as a *succession* of projects; and the more they differ from one another, the more valuable they are. Characterization of these projects according to categories that are apposite in other cities (whether familial, affective, educative, artistic, religious, charitable, etc.), and above all their classification according to the distinction between that which pertains to leisure and that which relates to work, is not what matters in this city's logic, except in a very subsidiary fashion. What matters is to develop activity – that is to say, never to be short of a project, bereft of an idea, always to have something in mind, in the pipeline, with other people whom one meets out of a desire to do something.

When they engage in a project, everyone concerned knows that the undertaking to which they are about to contribute is destined to last for a limited period of time – that it not only can, but must, come to an end. The prospect of an inevitable, desirable endpoint thus accompanies *engagement* without affecting enthusiasm. This is why engagement is conceived as voluntary. Having the option not to engage in a given project, and hence choice over one's projects, is a condition for the city's harmonious functioning; and this condition is guaranteed by the multiple activities everyone develops. Furthermore, awareness that the project will come to an end is accompanied by the hope that a new project will follow, that it is already in gestation in the fabric of current connections, even if it is not yet known what form it will take. Accordingly, tension between the requisite commitment and the indicated outcome appears surmountable.

Anything can attain the status of a *project*, including ventures hostile to capitalism. Describing every accomplishment with a nominal grammar that is the grammar of the project erases the differences between a capitalist project and a humdrum creation (a Sunday club). Capitalism and anti-capitalist critique alike are masked. Utterly different things can be assimilated to the term 'project': opening a new factory, closing one, carrying out a re-engineering project, putting on a play. Each of them is a project, and they all involve the same heroism. This is one of the ways in which the projective city can win over forces hostile to capitalism: by proposing a grammar that transcends it, which they in turn will use to describe their own activity while remaining oblivious of the fact that capitalism, too, can slip into it.

It is precisely because the project is a transient form that it is adjusted to a network world: by *multiplying connections* and *proliferating links*, the *succession of projects* has the effect of *extending networks*.

The extension of the network is life itself, whereas any halt to its extension is comparable to death: 'the network spontaneously tends to develop, but it is constantly threatened by the risks of internal ossification or degeneration that can result in death, which might consist in its transformation into a pyramidal organization' (Landier, 1991). Those without a project who no longer explore networks are threatened with *exclusion* – that is to say, in effect, with death in a reticular universe. They risk not finding a way to attach themselves to projects, and ceasing to exist. The *development of oneself* and one's *employability* ('being the agent of one's own evolution, taking control of one's future' [Le Saget, 1994]), which is the long-term personal project underlying all the others, will not be successfully accomplished.

Connection
<Natural relations between beings>
Connecting,
Communicating,
Co-ordinating,
Adjusting to others,
Trusting

In a connexionist world, a natural preoccupation of human beings is the desire to *connect* with others, *to make contact*, to make *connections*, so as not to remain *isolated.* To succeed, they must *trust* and be *trusted,* know how to *communicate, discuss* openly, and also be capable of *adjusting* to other people and situations, depending on what the latter demand of them, without being held back by timidity, rigidity or mistrust. This is the price of *co-ordinating* themselves in mechanisms and projects.

Engaged, Engaging,
Mobile
<Condition of great man>
Enthusiastic, Involved,
Flexible, Adaptable,
Versatile, Having potential,
Employable, Autonomous,
Not prescriptive, Knows how to engage others,
In touch, Tolerant,
Employability
(providing)

Knowing how to *engage* in a project, to get fully involved in it, is the mark of the <condition of great man>. To engage, one must be capable of *enthusiasm.* Furthermore, given that the project is a complex, uncertain process, which cannot be confined within the limits of invariably incomplete contracts, one must know how to *trust* those with whom connections are formed – connections that are destined to develop as the project develops. But since projects are by their very nature temporary, the ability to disengage from a project in order to be *available* for new connections counts as much as the capacity for engagement. Even at the peak of engagement, enthusiasm, involvement in a project, people at ease in a network world remain '*adaptable,* physically and intellectually *mobile*' (HEC, 1994), prepared for change and capable of new investments, in order to increase their 'ability to respond to a changing world' (Crozier and Sérieyx, 1994).

Far from being attached to an occupation or clinging to a qualification, the great man proves *adaptable* and *flexible,* able to switch from one situation to a very different one, and adjust to it; and *versatile,* capable of changing activity or tools, depending on the nature of the relationship entered into with others or with objects. It is precisely this *adaptability* and *versatility* that make him employable – that is to say, in the world of firms, in a position to attach himself to new projects.

Flexibility and adaptability here are qualities that do not derive from obedience. The great man in a connexionist world is active and *autonomous.* He is 'his own leader, leader in his relations with those above and those below, leader in his networks' (Sérieyx, 1993). The great man in the projective city retains the initiative in his projects, and knows how to *take risks* in order to make connections, to be forever making new contacts that are full of possibilities: 'Thus, the idea of a link seems to pros rather like a vein or seam to exploit, in the manner of a gold prospecter. You never quite know what is at the end of it. It is sometimes necessary to turn round and go back, give up *en route*, go and look elsewhere' (Bellenger, 1992). Always on the lookout, great men refuse to be impeded by rigid plans, for to follow such plans could result in squandering the opportunity for interesting connections. Plans and strategies would diminish their capacity for local action.[7] But they know how to take full advantage of each situation in its uniqueness.[8] For the same reasons they appear spontaneous, in contrast to strategists, whose manoeuvres are overly conspicuous, and frighten people.

They know how to locate *sources of information* ('being a radar' [Bellenger, 1992]), and to select between connections with a lot of new potential and those that revert to routine existing links. They are capable of optimizing the use they make of their scarcest resource – time - by selecting their relationships with discrimination and, in particular, by avoiding linking up with people who occupy kindred positions, and are thus likely to contribute superfluous information and connections: 'Given that one can't do everything, what should one concentrate on? This is a question pros are familiar with' (Bellenger, 1992).

In this city, the great man is a 'plunderer of ideas' (Sérieyx, 1993). For that, he must possess *intuition* and *talent* (in the sense in which we speak of an artist's talent). He 'scans the world around him in search of novel signs' (Sicard, 1994), and knows how to anticipate, sense, sniff out the links worth pursuing.

This is to say that in a network world there is a close correlation between the importance of social capital and of information capital. Information is at once the result and the condition of multiplying connections, so that inequalities of information are cumulative. To succeed in discovering good connections, such information must be integrated into a representation of the universe to be explored. In a network world, however, there can be no question of an overarching representation. Useful representations are local, singular, circumstantial, able to be deployed from one person to the next, and bound up with a kind of knowledge deriving from *personal experience*.

But those of high status in the projective city do not merely identify connections. They must also show themselves capable of becoming established in them, by forging links that last as long as is necessary. Given that links presuppose the engagement of at least two people, they must avoid being rejected; on the contrary, they must attract the attention and sympathy of others – *interest* them.[9] To this end they must not be timid, or – which boils down to the same thing – so proud as not to take the first step for fear of rejection. They write to people in the public eye to express their admiration and request advice or a meeting. They regard everyone as contactable and any contact as possible and natural; they treat well-known and obscure people in identical fashion. They tend to ignore the differences between separate spheres – for example, the private, professional, and media, etc., universes. For them the world is a network of potential connections. In respect of links, it's all one.

The great man in the projective city is not a nowhere man. At ease wherever he finds himself, he also knows how to be local. In fact, since the network has no overarching representation, actions in it are always embedded in the contingency of a present situation.[10] To adapt to the situations that crop up, while preserving something unfamiliar that makes him interesting, connexionist man relies on his *communication* skills, his *convivial* temperament, his *open* and *inquiring* mind. But he knows also how to *give of himself*, to be there as and when appropriate, to exploit his *presence* in personal relations, in face-to-face encounters: he is always available, even-tempered, self-assured without being arrogant, familiar without overstepping the limits, obliging, with more to offer than he expects in return. Without his demanding information or going in search of it, others give him the information he needs.[11] He knows how to listen, to give answers that are to the point, to echo people, to ask good questions. As Bellenger (1992) develops the point, he possesses 'a strategy for conducting relationships, a kind of *self-monitoring* that results in an aptitude for producing signs which can *facilitate contacts*'. He knows how to '*be attentive to others* in order to identify signs that will make it possible to intervene advisedly in uncertain situations'; he possesses 'the ability to control and *alter self-presentation*, which can extend to a capacity for improvizing appropriately, even for "lying without qualms" if necessary', as well as the 'desire and ability to adjust his own actions with ease, in order to *adapt to different people*'. Great men, past masters when it comes to self-monitoring, know how to judge 'other people's emotional states more lucidly and are perceived in their turn as more *friendly*, *open*, less uneasy, less anxious, less nervous in their relationships'. Basically, they have 'a *good manner with people* ... [an] adroitness in the way they conduct themselves in the world, in making connections, in acting in such a way as to get what they want' (Bellenger, 1992). They also possess 'charm', in the sense that they depart from the stereotyped image one might have had of them before getting to know them.[12] They make it clear (without this being attributable to strategy or calculation) that they are not reducible to the statutory properties defining them in their curriculum vitae. Face to face, they are real people, in the sense that, far from mechanically performing their social roles – in the way a programme is executed – they know how to step back and deviate from their role, which makes them captivating.

But these qualities do not suffice to define the condition of great man, because they can be employed in opportunistic fashion, as part of a purely individual strategy for success. In the logic of the city, the great are not only those who excel at exploiting the specific resources connected with a world, but also those who place the capacities disclosed in tests at the service of the common good. That is to say: in the projective city they are not only those who know how to engage, but also those who are *able to engage others*, to offer involvement, to make it desirable to follow them, because they inspire *trust*, they are *charismatic*, their *vision* generates enthusiasm. All these qualities make them leaders of teams that they manage not in authoritarian fashion, but by *listening* to others, with *tolerance*, recognizing and respecting *differences*.[13] They are not (hierarchical) bosses, but integrators, facilitators, an *inspiration*, unifiers of energies, *enhancers* of life, meaning and autonomy.

The team trusts them inasmuch as they prove to be *connectors, vectors*, who do not keep the information or contacts gleaned in networks to themselves, but redistribute them among the team members. 'Tomorrow's manager must ensure that information is shared, that it irrigates the firm thoroughly' (Le Saget, 1994).

In such a context, everyone can 'constantly and increasingly improve their employability, both through these technical skills and their ability for teamwork, even and especially when these teams are flexible, neural, and rarely made up of the same individuals' (Lemaire, 1994). The project head thus *provides employability*, and develops for others 'in the firm a network of personal relations that they can count on in the event of unforeseen problems' (Landier, 1991). In this way, 'employability [can be guaranteed] – that is to say, a level of skills and flexibility allowing each individual to find a new job inside or outside the firm' (Aubrey, 1993); employability is thus 'a gift in return from the firm to individuals who are aware of their responsibilities in it' (Aubrey, 1994).

Mediator, Project head
<Repertoire of subjects>
Coach,
Expert,
Customer, Supplier,
Innovator

If everyone possesses the capacity to relate, and thus to constitute a link in a network, some people realize this potential in their person in exemplary fashion. In very general terms, this is true of all those who, playing an active role in the expansion and *animation* of networks, act as *mediators*, whether characterized as *strategic brokers* able to 'make strategic exchanges outside of hierarchy and boundaries' (Aubrey, 1994), as *partners of the third kind* (Archier *et al.*, 1989), or as tangential contributors. They possess the art of reconciling opposites, and know how to bring very different people together, and put them in contact.

Such are, in the first instance, *project heads*, '*managers*' (in contrast to the old *cadres*), but also *coaches*, who *stimulate*, support the development of managers and practise 'the art of delivering minds' (Aubrey, 1990). But such equally are *customers, suppliers* and *subcontractors* when they enter into *relations of partnership*.

These *innovators* have scientists, and especially artists, as their models. 'The informal network is the preferred organizational mode of writers, scientific researchers and musicians, who develop in domains where knowledge is highly specialized, creative and personalized' (Aubrey, 1990). The *intuitive manager*, like the artist, 'is accompanied by disorder' (Le Saget, 1992), is 'in a permanent state of alert and doubt' (Vincent, 1990) and 'at ease in *fluid* situations' (Archier *et al.*, 1989).

But the intuitive manager, the source of inspiration and the coach are not the only models of excellence. We saw in Chapter 1 that another figure also lives on – the *expert*, whose 'leadership' is 'based upon competence and intelligence' (Arpin, 1994), on a 'highly specialized, creative and personalized knowledge' (Aubrey, 1994). Experts also enjoy high status in the projective city because their competence, which is indispensable, is composed not of standardized knowledge but of personal, integrated knowledge. It is the fruit of past experience – that is to say, of multiple connections, particularly with others possessing specific knowledge, formed during earlier projects, of which they preserve the memory. Dispensing with experts would require being in a position to repeat their careers. Experts are consulted. But their image is less heroic than that of the *project head*, because they are deemed less *adaptable*. The project head is precisely the one who proves capable of making connections between very different zones of expertise.

What all these exceptional beings have in common is that they are in a position to explore the links with the richest opportunities, those that will extend the network furthest, which are defined largely by the *distance* they surmount. Not all links are of equivalent worth. The status of a connection depends upon the extent to which it has established a *mediation* that makes it possible to abolish distance. In so doing, creators of links temporarily find themselves in the position of *keyholder*,[14] since all those who in turn want to cross the boundaries they have traversed will, for a certain period of time, have to go through them. The most interesting links often consist, in fact, in crossing zones where there were few, if any, mediations (*structural holes*, in the terminology of Ronald Burt).[15]

This distance, the crossing or gradual reduction of which defines the quality of the links created, can be referred to in different ways. It can be referred to *in temporal terms*, when old, dormant connections are reactivated. It can be alluded to *in spatial terms*, whenever there is co-ordination in real time with others who are spatially distant ('[t]he starting point will be to ignore geographical distances' [Tapscott and Caston, 1994]) – particularly by taking full advantage of modern means of communication (the Internet) – as we see in the example of the 'global laboratory', which is not geographically located and allows researchers in the same discipline, but scattered throughout the world, to collaborate in solving the same problem.[16] And above all, it can be evoked *in institutional or social terms*, when the beings between whom some transfer is established, and who are proximate in space and time, were hitherto separated by boundaries isolating institutions, disciplines, domains, or (in Pierre

Bourdieu's terminology) fields from one another. The forms in which a distance is overcome define different ways of possessing high status. Thus, whereas the expert is above all rich in links of the first (temporal) or second (spatial) types, the *project head* or *source of inspiration* excels in establishing connections between domains or fields: he establishes collaboration between people from different disciplines or professions, belonging to various departments, institutions or firms, and brings together, for example, two experts each of whom has experience, but in different domains.

In a network world, where the more unpredictable and remote connections are, the more likely they are to prove profitable, the class *habitus*, on which the spontaneous convergence of tastes relies in predominantly domestic social orders, is no longer a sufficient support for intuition or flair.[17] On the contrary, the great man is he who establishes links between beings who are not only removed from one another, located in different universes, but also distant from his social background and the circle of his immediate relations. This is why, unlike the old bourgeois society, a capitalism that incorporates connexionist justifications accepts those who, thanks to a rather erratic career path (at least in their youth), have a fund of experience and are acquainted with several worlds, endowing them with considerable adaptability.

The verdict delivered on the quality of a link does not take into account only the distance that it has made it possible to bridge – that is to say, its *ex-ante* probability (less likely links being more prized than very likely ones). It also takes account of the degree to which the link, once established, has proved fruitful (*ex-post*), in the sense that its result is to refocus and extend the network by prompting the emergence of new links. In this way, we can distinguish between (a) links that are highly probable but largely unproductive, such as those established between the members of a *clique*, where the connections are compact and within everyone's reach, but define a self-enclosed set; (b) very probable but nevertheless productive links, in the sense that they open on to the outside world, such as the links that popularizers or journalists make; (c) links that are very unlikely but also very unproductive, such as those established by the misunderstood forerunner or, worse, the crank or madman who, finding no one to follow him, cannot operate as a keyholder; and finally (d) links that are simultaneously unlikely and highly productive, which create the status of the *innovator* or audacious *project head*.

All the instruments of connection
<Repertoire of objects and mechanisms>
New technologies,
Informal relations,
Relations of trust,
Partnership, Agreements,
Alliances,

Subcontracting,
Networks of firms,
Network firms,
Link, Loop,
Synapses, Neurons,
Projects

In a world where the principal operation is establishing connections, it is thus normal to find a marked presence of new communication technologies based on *computer science* (Internet, interfaces, etc.). The characteristics of our corpus, composed exclusively of management texts, certainly entail an overrepresentation of instruments of industrial dimensions, to the detriment of more familiar devices for making contact (such as visiting cards or address books). Numerous in the domestic world, such objects are reinterpreted in other contexts, so that they can take their place in the connexionist world of the projective city.

The same may be said of the mechanisms, primarily entrepreneurial mechanisms here (*subcontracting, flexible specialization, out-sourcing, autonomous units, franchises*), which characterize the *postmodern, post-Fordist, 're-engineered', network,* etc., *firm*.

The descriptive terminology of the connexionist world is pulled in two different directions: either towards a thematic of action without a subject, where the only entity that counts is the network, where what occurs is of the anonymous order of the *id*, of *self-organization* ('the organization increases its capacity for self-organization' [Crozier and Sérieyx, 1994]); or towards a neo-personalism, which emphasizes not the system, but human beings in search of *meaning*. This second orientation is dominant because it is on it that the normative, *ethical* dimension of the projective city largely rests. Hence the importance accorded to *face-to-face* relations, to *taking responsibility*, to *trust*, to *situations experienced in common*, to *giving one's word* (which is worth all the contracts in the world), to *mutual aid*, to *co-operation* in establishing *partnerships*, in setting up *projects*, in constructing *networks*: 'trust is established in time through the consolidation of behaviour involving reciprocal understanding, through a whole learning process' (Weiss, 1994). Given that what matters most is *intangible, impalpable, informal* – a term that characterizes both *relations* and the *rules of the game*, which are invented as one goes along – the most appropriate organizational mechanisms are thus likewise *interpersonal*.[18] In numerous texts, these two dimensions – the systemic and the personalist – overlap to a great extent.

The general nature of the rhizomorphous form is declined by means of different metaphors, which refer either, in traditional fashion, to weaving (*stitch, loop, knot*); or to the devices in which fluids circulate (*flow, oil pipeline, channel, electric cables*); or, in more modern fashion, to the biology of the brain (*synapses, neurons*, etc.). This last register is employed in particular to emphasize the autonomy and even the volition of the network, which is stronger than that of the beings immersed in it, and whose properties are then described in the language of *self-organization, self-regulation*, and *spontaneous* morphogenesis.

Finally, the project is indeed the central mechanism of the city that bears its name. It 'has at its disposal unity of time, but not unity of place. It must optimize internal resources, compare them with external resources, and make the best use of experts organized in network strutures' (HEC, 1994).

Unemployable
<Condition of little person>

Unadaptable,
Does not inspire confidence,
Authoritarian, Rigid,
Intolerant,
Immobile, Local,
Rooted, Attached,
Status (has one), Security
(prefers)

In a projective city, the little people are those who cannot *be engaged*, who are not *employable* on a project, or who prove incapable of *changing* projects. Different grounds for non-engagement identify different types of little person.

Given that *trust* and *relational qualities* are the cement of projects, the unemployable ones are those who do not know how to *inspire trust*, or cannot be trusted because they do not deliver what is expected of them, or do not circulate the information they possess and are 'out for themselves' – which is a form of dishonesty in their engagement (opportunism). The basic rule is 'reciprocity: the best-intentioned are discouraged if they receive nothing in exchange for what they have given. Anyone who retains information that could be useful to others to himself is a killer of networks' (Orgogozo, 1991).

Likewise inferior are those who do not know how to *communicate*, because they are *impervious* or have *fixed ideas*, are *authoritarian* and *intolerant*, making them *incapable of compromise*. They resemble all 'the office "miseries", the sullen types, the individualists who withdraw into themselves, never go out, don't participate in the end-of-year drinks, shun cocktails, return to the hotel pronto, and plant themselves in front of the tele, that absolute "network-killer"' (Bellenger, 1992).

Rigidity, which, as the converse of *flexibility*, in this world constitutes the main failing of little people, can have different origins. It can derive from *attachment* to a single project that it is impossible to let go of when a new project comes along; or from attachment to a place which, by rendering them *immobile* and *rooting* them in what is *local*, confines little people to the existing circle of links, and prevents them making new connections. Finally, its origin can be found in a preference for *security* even at the expense of *autonomy*.

Thus, in a projective city someone who has a *status* is not *mobile*. Someone who has a status knows what to expect from life: what their duties are (what is expected of them) and what their rights are (what they can expect of others). If the disadvantages attaching to a status stem principally from the *limits* it imposes on people's activities, in the logic of the projective city statutory advantages are suspected of concealing injustices. For by establishing people in a situation of *continuity*, they make it possible to avoid the quintessential tests represented by the moments of transition from one project to another.

Closure of the network
\<Decline of the city>

Corruption, Privileges,
Buddy–buddy relationships, Mafia

The city falls when the network is no longer extended and, closing in on itself, benefits some people, but no longer serves the public good.

This is the case when the networker keeps information to himself, weaves connections in secret, unbeknownst to his team, in order not to share the links he has established and retain the benefits for himself, avoiding a situation where others can pursue them without going through him ('the most important adaptive function of a network consists in absorbing and redistributing information' [Landier, 1991]).

This monopolistic conduct leads fairly rapidly to the closure of the network on itself for two reasons. On the one hand, the activity of the networker, who acts alone and without others knowing it, is rather quickly restricted by his availability in time. On the other hand, maintaining his connections exclusively for himself, he has no incentive to construct new ones – unlike the major mediator of the projective city who, redistributing his links to place them in the service of the common good, must incessantly discover new contacts, and thus extend the network, in order to retain the comparative advantage on which his high status depends.

Closed networks permit privileges. In them the tests of connections are distorted: they are 'networks of privileges' that encourage 'string-pulling',[19] which predominantly benefit the members of corporate bodies closed in on themselves, to the detriment of others who are in fact better endowed with connexionist skills. This is the case with large bodies: 'For large bodies are today anti-networks inasmuch as they exercise authority over their members in order to further their own objectives' (Bellenger, 1992).

Closed networks that call a halt to their own extension, and which are appropriated for the exclusive benefit of 'those who are in on them', are also dangerous: 'It would be a mistake to think that every network automatically favours enterprise and development, as is clearly indicated by the dramatic events marking Italy's attempts to restructure an economy engulfed by networks of corruption. It is important to sweep away the networks of "buddies", bureaucracy or corruption that obstruct the path of progress' (Aubrey, 1994).

Forms of justice in the projective city

The elements of grammar we have just laid out clarify the principle of equivalence on which the projective city is based, and the way it can be employed to characterize persons and things, and to define the conditions of great man or little person. But we also know that in order to be robust in the face of critiques based on a sense of what is just, this specific order must be geared towards the common good, and submit to a certain number of constraints. We have already seen that great men are not only versatile, engaged and mobile themselves, but that they cause others to benefit from these qualities by striving to advance their employability at the same time as they develop their own. They do not keep what they garner via their connections for themselves, with the result that the good network remains open and expands continuously, to the maximum benefit of all. The <status relation> specifies precisely the nature of the relations between great men and little people and, in particular, the way in which the <condition of great man>, because it contributes to the common good, contains the <condition of little person>. In the civic city, for example, it is via political representation that the great man, elected by universal suffrage, represents all the little people.

Redistribution of connections
<Status relation>

Putting in contact,
Redistributing information,
Integrating into networks,
Providing employability

The relation between great man and little people is just when, in exchange for the trust that the little people place in them and their zeal for engaging in projects, great men enhance the value of the more humble, in order to increase their employability – that is to say, their capacity, once one project is finished, to integrate themselves into another. Terminating a project without worrying about what becomes of those who have participated in it is unworthy of a great man. 'In place of the traditional contract, which guaranteed security, promotion and development, it is now appropriate to make an agreement that creates a sense of belonging, which helps the individual to maintain his "employability" or the value of his labour, and which exploits the various opportunities to learn while at work' (Aubrey, 1994).

To that end, great men must redistribute the scarce goods they have access to – in the first place, information ('eliminating the restrictions that limit everyone's access to information'[Le Saget, 1994]), and integration into networks, 'whose collective function is to support and enrich each member's assignment' (Aubrey, 1990). They must 'publiciz[e] people outside their own departments, and … [plug] people into organizational and professional networks' (Moss Kanter, 1989).

More generally, great men must inspire in others their own dynamism, and awaken them to themselves, by liberating 'their taste for thinking and acting with their talents', by 'making them collaborators, authors' (Sérieyx, 1993), and by helping them to publicize their results in such a way as to enhance their reputation.

We still have to clarify two elements that are crucial for the implementation of justice in a rhizomorphous world – what the grammar we are employing calls the <formula of investment> as well as the <model test>.

The <formula of investment> is a major condition for the city's harmony, for by linking access to the <condition of great man> to a sacrifice, it arranges things so that benefits are 'balanced' by costs. High status procures benefits for the person who accedes to that condition. But the customary sense of justice also has it that 'you can't win on all counts': that people deserved access to high status on account of specific sacrifices which have, moreover, been of universal benefit or, more simply, useful to society as a whole. It is then just that someone who is so deserving, and who has done so much for the common good, should be recognized as great, and enjoy the advantages bound up with this condition.

Adaptability
<Formula of investment>

Being streamlined, Flexibility,
Tolerance, Renting

In a projective city, access to the condition of great man presupposes sacrificing anything that might impede availability – that is to say, the ability to engage in a new project. The great man renounces having a single project that lasts a lifetime (a vocation, a profession, a marriage, etc.). He is mobile. Nothing must hamper his movements. He is a 'nomad'.[20] In this sense, all the sacrifices that are made have the effect of enhancing the streamlined character of entities – of persons, but also of things – in order to favour their reorganization when the next project comes along. Thus, '[t]he leaner organization that contracts out for services depends on the suppliers of those services and therefore benefits from close co-operation with them' (Moss Kanter, 1990).

The requirement to be streamlined first of all assumes renouncing stability, rootedness, attachment to the local, the security of longstanding links. When it comes to links, to invest effort is to give up what one already has for an uncertain alternative: not to shut oneself away in pre-established links, so that one is available to try out new connections that might fail. In the knowledge that time is limited, it is in fact advisable to carve out the time to forge links with different persons and universes, rather than always remaining in the same circle of people: 'Being a pro means revising one's accessibility in quasi-strategic fashion. Time can't just be invented and so it is a question of making choices and daring to take decisions. A pro's appointments are handled with extreme care' (Bellenger, 1992). Extension of the network thus demands that people renounce friendship or, rather, that when assessing the quality of a link they abandon the distinction between disinterested bonds of friendship and professional or useful relations:

> [a] network is always based on strong interpersonal relations, situated beyond work in the strict sense. ... Depending on the case, such trust can be founded on situations that were experienced in common in the past, on belonging to the same institution, on the existence of a common objective or project, on relations of friendship or mutual respect, even on mere complicity derived from being connected to the same communications network. (Landier, 1991).

Thus, it can be said of 'social and family networks' that 'this capital represents relations which, in addition to satisfaction on a human level, offer a potential contribution to the enterprise envisaged' (Aubrey, 1994). But while connections with members of the extended family, assimilated to a network, can prove profitable, the restricted family, like the group of 'old mates' or the clique of 'office neighbours', preserves the tie to old, superseded connections, and by that token represents a burden, a handicap.

Great men in the projective city are also *streamlined* in that they are liberated from the burden of their own passions and values: open to differences (unlike rigid, absolutist personalities attached to the defence of universal values). For the same reasons, they are not critical (except when it comes to defending tolerance and difference). Nothing must get the upper hand over the imperative of adjustment, or hamper their movements. They are determined exclusively by factors deriving from the situation and connections they are caught up in, which completely define them.[21] The tolerance required to adjust to others can also be expressed in terms of emancipation from 'bourgeois morality'. The streamlined human being has learnt from psychoanalysis – and, more generally, from the diffusion of 'interpretation as exercise of suspicion'[22] – that one must know how to free oneself from moralism by casting suspicion on the hidden motives involved in moralizing ventures and acknowledging the validity of ambivalence. The numerous tools of analytical provenance integrated into the projective city thus aim to develop realism: they serve to look reality in the face – including (or especially) the reality of desire, treated as one datum among others – but also, by the same token, to recognize the limits placed on desire by reality. In a network world, it is thus realistic to be ambivalent (in contrast to the boss who is all of one piece in the hierarchical world), because the situations people have to confront are themselves complex and uncertain.

According to the same principle of eliminating anything that might hinder mobility, the streamlined human being must not be attached to a burdensome patrimony, and should prefer to ownership other formulas that provide access to the enjoyment of objects, such as renting. In this instance, distance with respect to ownership does not derive from some ascetic contempt for material goods, which it is perfectly licit to have at one's disposal and to enjoy, but is simply the result of the need to streamline oneself so that one can move around easily.

For the same reasons, connexionist man likewise tends not to let himself be trapped by institutions, with all the various obligations that entails, and not to allow himself to become entangled in a web of responsibilities towards the other people or organizations he has responsibility for. That is why he prefers to renounce official power in favour of network forms of power,[23] freed of the constraints of supervision, invigilation, management, representation, and respect for the state rules regulating the use of goods and the management of human beings. He leaves that to others. For he prefers autonomy to security.

Great men in the projective city likewise renounce exercising any form of domination over others by taking advantage of statutory or hierarchical properties that would vouchsafe them ready recognition. Their authority depends exclusively on their competence. They do not impose their rules or objectives, but agree to discuss their positions (principle of tolerance).

Underlying these different forms of renunciation we find a more basic sacrifice: that of personality, in the sense of a manner of being that expresses itself in similar attitudes and conduct whatever the circumstances. 'The image of the chameleon is a tempting one for describing the pro, who knows how to conduct his relationships in order to reach other people more easily … adaptability is the key to the network spirit (efforts have to be made to take the first step)' (Bellenger, 1992). Streamlined people sacrifice a certain interiority and fidelity to the self, the better to adjust to the people with whom they come into contact and to the ever-changing situations in which they are obliged to act (this also assumes renunciation of the hubris of calculation in favour of a limited rationality).

Consequently, streamlined people can root themselves only in themselves ('the self-enterprise') – the sole instance endowed with a certain permanency in a complex, uncertain and changing world. However, the quiddity that is recognizable is not the result of a pre-existing endowment, or even of a trajectory or experience. It derives from the constellation of established connections. They are themselves only because they are the links that constitute them.

<Model tests> are just as necessary for fulfilling the requirements of justice, and for their inscription in the fabric of everyday relations. These are situations when the status of persons and things is revealed with especial clarity. Disagreement over a claim to status can be resolved only through a test on which assessments can converge, and which for that purpose must be wholly uncontaminated – that is to say, directed towards measuring status and nothing else. This presupposes that any risk of contamination by forms of status pertaining to alternative worlds has been excluded. The test provides proof of status. It must be amenable to demands for renewal since, as a result of the ability formally accorded everyone to accede to conditions of high status and the non-attachment of a definitive status to persons (which would be at variance with the existence of a human community), people must be in a position to reveal changes in their condition and have them recognized.

As for the <way of expressing the judgement>, it characterizes the manner, different in each city, in which the outcome of the test is marked. The <form of self-evidence> is the mode of knowledge peculiar to the world under consideration. These categories aim to define the qualities and the acts of the persons engaged in a test. So-and-so will be adjudged great if he does some particular thing and inferior if he exhibits a particular kind of behaviour.

The end of a project and the beginning of another
<model test>

People cannot be judged on the basis of a single project, because their status reveals itself in the model test and this, as we already know, is the transition from one project to the next. It is when a project is finished that the keyholders are revealed and an appraisal is conducted. Appraisal is positive in the case of those who, having enhanced their reputation in the course of the project they are leaving, succeed in integrating themselves into a new one. Contrariwise, it is negative when an inability to maintain or develop links and to liaise with others disqualifies the applicant. In fact, links are a form of capital that does not belong to those who have the use of them. By way of sanction, links can always be unilaterally withdrawn by those with whom they are made.

If the moment of the transition from one project to another constitutes the test *par excellence*, in the logic of a projective city the world is the more testing – and hence also the more just – the shorter, the more numerous, and the more changeable projects are.

Being called on to participate
<Expression of judgement and forms of self-evidence>

Inserting, Causing to participate,
Speaking of,
Avoiding, Keeping at a distance,
Ignoring, Rejecting, Excluding

People are appreciated if others want to make their acquaintance, to meet them, call upon them, or work with them. Those from whom nothing is to be expected are avoided, kept at a distance or, more simply, ignored. One of the peculiarities of network forms is that, unlike what occurs in totalities defined by an inscription of spatial order in a territory (nations, districts, etc.), of temporal order in a history (lineage), or of legal order in an institution (administrations, churches, etc.), those who are depreciated lose all visibility and even, in a way, any existence. For in the logic of this world, existence itself is a relational attribute: every entity, and human persons by the same token as the rest, exists to a greater or lesser extent depending upon the number and value of the connections that pass via it.

This is why such a world has no sanctions other than rejection or exclusion, which, in depriving someone of their links ('disaffiliation', in Robert Castel's terminology),[24] expels them to the margins of the network, where connections are at once both sparse and worthless. The excluded person is someone who depends on others, but on whom no one any longer depends, who is not wanted by anyone, who is no longer sought after, no longer invited, who, even if his address book is full of names, has disappeared from other people's address books.

It follows that in such a world the mechanisms of justice are essentially preventive. They must anticipate the possibility of failure by relying on predictive indicators.

Anthropology and naturalness in the projective city

The question of a city's anchorage in a definition of nature is a crucial one. First of all, it is important on the level of justice that all human beings have the ability to achieve better conditions, and only a definition of human nature guarantees the sharing of this ability by the whole of humanity. The <dignity of persons> refers to this dimension in each city; it is what makes for equality and points towards the natural human properties that give everyone the same opportunity to achieve greatness if they do what is required – in particular, if they make the indicated sacrifices (compare the <formula of investment>).

The need to connect
<Dignity of persons>

All the active operators in a network can accede to better conditions, because they all possess the ability to connect with others. The desire to connect is a basic property of human nature. In this anthropology, all women and all men are beings of contacts and relations: 'attachment is not the result of a libidinal or learning process … it corresponds to a primary tendency – the need for others – which is stronger than hunger and earlier than sexuality' (Bellenger, 1992). This need for connection, which is so universal, is the reason why everyone can integrate themselves into networks and acquire employability. No one is excluded a priori.

Functioning in networks also satisfies the highly human characteristic of wanting to be *simultaneously* free and engaged: '[a]ll of us make commitments. They may erode our freedom to act autonomously, but in return they provide some meaning in our lives and on the job.' Our 'deep desire for autonomy and self-reliance [is] combined with an equally deep conviction that life has no meaning unless shared with others in the context of community' (Waterman, 1988). Without this radical duality that each of us bears within ourselves, the series of engagements and disengagements supposed by the projective city would seem absolutely inhuman.

Every city also presupposes the designation in nature – that is, in 'reality' - of an ideal form in which conditions are fairly distributed. If it is to be mobilized in everyday life, inspire action, or foster justifications, a city's logic must be embodied in some typical examples putting it within people's reach. In the case of the projective city, the <harmonious figure of natural order> is obviously the network, or rather, the networks that have always existed in the life of human beings.

The network
<Harmonious figure of natural order>

The most natural form is the network. It imposes itself on entities, whether human or non-human, even if actors are not conscious of it: 'Organization in networks is not something new; it has always existed, like the prose that Monsieur Jourdain composed unawares' (Landier, 1991).

We are also dealing with a quite universal form of organization: the 'example of the Silk Road' teaches us that 'networks are "primitive", universal things. The family, friends, old school mates, the members of all the associations that people belong to, are so many networks around each of us' (Aubrey, 1990).

All beings and all societies have their networks, and

[w]e normally think of them as the informal pathways along which informa-
tion and influences flow. Feminists complain [about] an 'old boys' network'.
… Homosexuals have networks that are particularly strong in certain indus-
tries like fashion and interior design. Ethnic minorities have strong networks
– the overseas Chinese throughout South-East Asia, Jews in Europe and
America, West Indians in Britain. Transplanted people in general – New
Yorkers in Texas, the so-called Georgia Mafia that came to Washington when
Jimmy Carter was President, the Ukrainians who came to Moscow with Leonid
Brezhnev – also form their own communication networks. In short, informal
networks of many kinds crop up in virtually all complex societies. To these
one must add formal networks – Masons, for example, Mormons, or members
of the Catholic order Opus Dei. (Toffler, 1990)

But the network form of organization was previously suspect in firms, and bore
the stamp of the clandestine. The moment for its rehabilitation has now arrived:

in the traditional firm, it had an unofficial, even clandestine character, which
was deemed subversive of the official hierarchical organization. For workers,
for example, it consisted in discovering tricks to reduce the unpleasantness of
their task. … Informal networks were thus directed against hierarchy; the
objective was to defend oneself against decisions that were resented as irrational or unjust. Such relationships were the breeding ground of trade-union
activity. The expression 'network management', by contrast, emerged only very
recently. (Landier, 1991)

The projective city as we have just described it allows us to underline the
main themes of justification in a world conceived as a network. With it we
have sought to grasp the new forms of justice for which the existing cities
could not account, but which nevertheless featured in 1990s management texts.

We shall now satisfy ourselves that the projective city does indeed constitute a specific form, not an unstable compromise between existing cities, by
rapidly comparing it with the other normative forms described in *De la justification* and, in particular, with those that seem closest to it – that is to say, the
commercial city and the domestic city.

2. THE ORIGINALITY OF THE PROJECTIVE CITY

Compared with the inspirational city

The projective city shares with the inspirational city the importance assigned to
creativity and innovation (as attested, for example, by the use made of the
paradigm of the network in the dominant currents of the sociology of innovation). Similarly, both these cities stress the uniqueness of beings and things,

whose very difference creates value (not their ability to merge into collective forms, as is the case, for example, in the industrial city). But these similarities are superficial, and even misleading. In effect, whereas in the inspirational city people are creative when they are separated from others, withdrawn into themselves as it were, into their internal being – the only place where they can enter into direct relation with a transcendent source of inspiration (the supernatural) – or buried in the depths of the psyche (the unconscious), in the projective city creativity is a function of the number and quality of links. Moreover, it is a matter of *recombination*,[25] rather than creation *ex nihilo*, and readily assumes a 'distributed' form (as one talks of 'distributed intelligence'), with responsibility for innovation being allocated between different actors. Accordingly, within the framework of this city it would be inappropriate to seek to specify the particular responsibility of each person in the process of innovation too closely, or, worse, to demand radical originality and accuse others of 'plagiarism'.

Compared with the commercial city

Network models have been developed over the last twenty years in the framework of classical microeconomics – in particular, to deal with market failures and account for market transactions in situations characterized by a marked asymmetry of information, in which the quality of goods (e.g. second-hand cars) or services (e.g. those of barristers) cannot be known a priori, and consequently remains uncertain for the purchaser, who will be able to test it only after consumption.[26] In these cases, it is important that a relationship of trust be established between vendors and purchasers, with the purchasers *trusting* the vendors – who, for their part, are supposed to know the true quality of the goods offered – so that they know they are not being misled about what they are buying. The weapon at the purchaser's disposal when it comes to committing the vendor to being trustworthy is the *reputation* that he can act on. Ultimately, business will go to vendors whose reputation is good – that is to say, vendors whose trustworthiness is regularly tested and just as regularly confirmed. On the basis of this research, we can bring out various aspects of the specificity of a network world, to which the projective city applies, compared with the ideal of a commercial world.

The first aspect is time. Whereas the purely market transaction is of the moment, and ignores time, organization of collaboration and exchanges in network form assumes establishing relations between partners which, without being stabilized by plans or regulations, nevertheless possess a relatively enduring character. Two partners (a supplier and his customer) operating in a network can thus envisage investing together – something that is not pertinent in a commercial world.

A second aspect is transparency. Whereas the market is assumed to be transparent for the purposes of price formation, networks can be known only on a person-by-person basis. No one is in a position to totalize them. They are not regulated by the projection of a general equivalent. Each connection, as well as the transactions conducted there, has a local character. If, in a network regulated by the projective city, information circulates from one person to the next and is not interrupted, it is accessible only at the point of connections. Information is not available to everyone simultaneously in its entirety, as in the ideal of pure and perfect information allowing all the participants in a market to be put on an equal footing. Moreover, it is this characteristic that renders networks so vulnerable to the strategic practices of withholding information, not circulating it, in order to derive an advantage that is unwarranted in terms of the projective city's values.[27]

The third aspect, which derives from the first two, concerns personal relations. The market functions anonymously, or with personal relations that are reduced to a minimum and conducted from a distance (close, enduring, local personal relations being assimilable in a market logic to a 'conspiracy against the public', to quote Adam Smith, hampering the operation of the market).[28] By contrast, exploitation of the network form presupposes an ability to establish relations of interdependence and trust, and consolidate them, over the long term.

Relations of this type offer different advantages. What they have in common is that they rest on the utilization of fine-grained, open information, rather than on possession of minimal information about prices and, when standards exist, quality, as is the case with the market. Take trust, for example – leitmotiv of partisans of networks. It can be described as a prop for selective, specific information that is difficult to confirm (or unverifiable in the case of a promise), with the help of tacit, diffuse information, bound up with a syncretic estimation of persons, past experience, or an impression of reputation. One of the most important things about relations of trust in market relations is, as we have seen, that they facilitate the exchange of goods and services which are difficult to format in a contract that is intended to be reasonably comprehensive. They also lie behind two other types of advantages. The first is the possibility of sharing or exchanging fine-grained information. A mere 'it is said' when separated from a human medium, such information can circulate only from person to person, because it is credible and interpretable only in the light of the implicit knowledge mobilized by the recipient about the character of the person communicating it. The second is the possibility of restricting the pursuit of selective, purely selfish gains by sharing solutions (on condition of reciprocation), allowing a more rapid adaptation to the changes affecting technologies or markets.[29]

A fourth aspect concerns the description of the products included in the transactions. Whereas, in a commercial world, the product is separated from persons and stabilized by conventions or standards guaranteeing its quality – this, in particular, is the role of brands[30] – in a connexionist world the product, which circulates with difficulty when separated from persons, is transformed by the relation. In a commercial world, the transaction sees a price formed, but it does not alter the qualities of the product, or of those supplying and demanding, which predate the market encounter.

In a connexionist world, by contrast, links are useful and enriching when they have the power to change the beings who enter into relations.[31] Obviously, this is especially true of work, whose autonomization with respect to persons constitutes the essential legal fiction on which the operation of the labour market is based. To be able to talk about a market where the price of labour is formed at the intersection of supply and demand, there are two prerequisites: both the work qualifications people offer, and the job descriptions they are capable of filling, must be stabilized and predefined independently of one another. By contrast, in a network organization the qualities of persons and the qualities of jobs are mutually defined in the relationship (what François Eymard-Duvernay and Emmanuelle Marchal call 'negotiated competence').[32] But in such a set-up, labour can no longer be treated as a commodity separable from the person of those performing it.

It is, in particular, by changing their information that the connection alters the beings who enter into a relationship. The transmission of information plays a key role in establishing the link in all those sectors where the value added is cognitive in kind – as is the case, for example, with scientific research.[33] Each partner can hope to access the information held by the other – either by supplying information in exchange, or, if the relation is asymmetrical, by obtaining information without reciprocation, so to speak, from the connection itself. In the latter instance, little people spontaneously present great men with useful information, in order to make themselves interesting – that is to say, both in order to be noticed and identified and so that great men find it advantageous to remain in contact with them. The information released by the connection can also focus on the beings between whom a link is established. The relationship alters the information each of the partners possesses concerning the other, and can thereby change their image of the other. It is to an unfolding process of this kind that people refer when they speak of earning (or losing) someone's trust – something that consequently opens up or shuts off access to resources (the use of goods or services, credit, reputation).

It follows that in a connexionist world, products (especially products without a material medium) are not – contrary to what occurs in market exchange – clearly identified and distinctly separated from persons. Consequently, it is understandable that the issue of whether the relationship is advantageous or costly, symmetrical or asymmetrical, can remain unresolved for rather a long time. No one knows straight off what they have to gain or to lose (if only a waste of time) from the relationship. The forms of calculation specific to the commercial world encounter their limits here.

This set of characteristics specific to the connexionist world constitutes so many checks on the harmonious functioning of competition, which is the common superior principle of the commercial city. Yet without guaranteed competition, no commercial justice is possible. But the partisans of a network world do not set much store by this central value of the commercial city, and argue instead for 'co-opetition', to employ the neologism used of late to designate a relationship comprising a mixture of co-operation and competition.[34]

The connexionist world is therefore distinguished from the commercial world and calls for different mechanisms of justice. This prompts some reservations about interpretations that describe recent changes as a mere strengthening of economic liberalism. It would seem, in fact, that in a number of cases the activity of those who succeed in a network world is relatively free of commercial tests. It could even be that their ventures, their *projects*, would have been subject to negative market sanctions and, consequently, would have failed on a strictly commercial basis. But such failures do not affect their status, or the reputation they have acquired.

Compared with the reputational city

At first sight, the world in which the projective city is inscribed seems to have a great deal in common with the reputational world. As Ronald Burt emphasizes,[35] the extension of relations in a connexionist world is also profitable inasmuch as it makes it possible to enhance the reputation of those who form them and who, incapable of being everywhere at once, must rely on others talking about them, pronouncing their name at opportune moments (e.g. when a new project is being set up), in arenas from which they are absent. To exist in this world, one must exist in the memory (largely focused on the name) and the habits of those who might 'call upon you'.

But the network world of the projective city does not possess the transparency that is one of the dimensions of the reputational world. Each link in it is established independently of the others, without visibility, and without there existing a point from which the quantity of links amassed could be assessed in the way, for example, that the popularity of a particular politician or TV star is measured by opinion polls.

If the reputational world is today associated with mass communications in the first instance, the world of the projective city privileges personal communication, by two people alone together or in a small group. Reputations spread by word of mouth more than by media hype: lobbying replaces advertising campaigns.[36] It can even happen that accusations are levelled against the reputational world from a normative position favouring networks, by invoking its asymmetrical character: famous people ignore the little people who admire them, whereas in the projective city great men 'know how to listen'.[37]

Compared with the domestic city

Considered superficially, the projective city appears to have a lot in common with the domestic city – so much so that it might be asked whether it does not simply represent its contemporary form. In fact, in both cases we find a strong emphasis on personal relations, direct dealings and trust, particularly in work relations.

Furthermore, celebration of the advantages of family organization is by no means absent from the writings of 1990s management authors, who see in it the original source for the construction of networks: 'if links can be created in the name of friendship, work, fraternity, they remain of a kinship type in the first instance. To live a highly pro life, the best thing is a well-constructed family universe. For the family represents a primary network that is less outmoded than people think and which, on the contrary, is undergoing massive changes' (Bellenger, 1992). Alvin Toffler goes so far as to foresee a major return of family organization in the business world, but not in the 'superseded' form of the independent small firm. On the contrary, family organizations should, in his view, develop within large firms or in close collaboration with them: '[I]t is clear ... that in the economy of tomorrow huge firms will become more dependent than in the past on a vast substructure of tiny but high-powered and flexible suppliers. And many of these firms will be family-run. Today's resurrection of small business and the family firm brings with it an ideology, an ethic, and an information system that is profoundly antibureaucratic' (Toffler, 1990).

But this apparent similarity does not withstand closer examination of the way links are formed in a domestic world and in a connexionist world. The domestic city presents forms of control, gratification and sanction that are very different from those proposed by a projective city.

In a domestic world, personal relations are largely defined in advance by the properties attaching to persons and, in particular, according to the position occupied in the family hierarchy, or the position of the family in the community. Links, the cost of access to which is high, are enduring and rarely elective (thus, marriage is in part prescribed). On the other hand, relations are subject to community control that is made possible by the co-presence of persons in one and the same space. It is very difficult for people to escape from this space, inasmuch as it is in the community, defined by spatial proximity, and not in their individuality that the resources they need to be what they are, or simply to survive, are to be found.[38] Communitarian rootedness and local presence play a not insignificant role in the tests of status. Consequently, links at work are controlled largely through the medium of links outside work and, in particular, family links, as we can see, for example, in the case of apprenticeship. The apprentice master is not merely a substitute for the father in the workplace. He also derives his authority from the possibility that is open to him of appealing to the apprentice's family to reinforce his own sanctions.[39] In a domestic world, the level of information everyone has about others is high,[40] although this does not mean that such a universe is subject to the exigency of transparency (as is the case in a civic world for the public sphere). Disclosure of what everyone knows about others cannot occur freely (except in the form of gossip), and the transfer of information is, in common with all transfers, controlled and subordinated to hierarchical relations. Thus, for example, in the predominantly domestic system of academic patronage as it operated in France until the middle of the twentieth century or thereabouts, students remained attached to their supervisor during the often very extended period in which they worked on their doctorates, without being able either to publish freely, or to move around as they wished and circulate information between different centres of intellectual power.[41] This high level of social control and personal dependency was compensated for by guaranteeing the subordinate a certain security, their loyalty to their superiors presupposing the their superiors' loyalty to them in return.

In terms of the different relations that we have just mentioned, the world of the projective city is opposed at every point to the domestic world. In the first place, relations are not prescribed – something management authors do not fail to stress in contrast to the restriction of freedom in the family model: 'people nostalgic for the family of yesteryear ignore the restrictions it actually imposed on the individual's autonomy and freedom of choice, as well as the limited opportunities for escaping the framework of family origins' (Aubrey, 1994).

In a network world, everyone seeks to establish links that interest them, and with people of their choice. Relations, including those not involving the world of work directly but the family sphere, are 'elective'.[42] What is more, the distant and relatively unpredictable character of a contact is precisely what enhances its value. The links of no interest are those that are maintained within the narrow group of mutual acquaintances (strong links in the sense of Mark Granovetter),[43] whereas interesting links are the ones established with new people or objects from which one is separated by several levels of mediation. Spatial distance is not relevant. Nothing exists resembling a territory where displacements could be subject to control. The circulation of information is very difficult to control. No one can totalize the network, which is more or less opaque to everyone as soon as they deviate from paths that have already been opened up.

Finally, in contrast to what we observe in a domestic world, mobility and instability are very important elements in the stuff a person is made of, and constitute a condition of access to high status. It follows that personal relations assume a very great importance, even though no one can be sure of the loyalty of those with whom the links are established. They are not only free to move around; they are stimulated by the very logic of the network to form different links, with other people or mechanisms.

We can even venture the hypothesis that the formation of a connexionist world, to which the projective city applies, is correlated with the disintegration of the domestic world. The latter's particular form of status has, over the last twenty years, been excluded from most situations in social existence and, in particular, from professional life, retaining validity only in the narrow field of family relations in the strict sense. This is to say that if the projective city borrows some of the vocabulary with which it describes itself from the domestic world (personal relations, trust, face-to-face, etc.), actions or mechanisms with the same name (friendship, affinities, dinners) have a quite different character in the two cases. The preservation and even revaluation of a domestic way of being (against the impersonality of industrial relations, and especially the regulatory constraints of the civic world) have, in fact, been accompanied by a withering away of the modes of control, gratification and sanction associated with the domestic city, whose formulas of investment (loyalty, employment for life, security, dependency) were becoming unacceptable to the various actors on more than one account.

Compared with the industrial city

The attraction exercised by the network model over 1990s management authors is based in large measure on the fact that it is opposed precisely to the 'industrial' world of the 1960s. In the industrial world, people are respected only to the extent that they perform certain duties and occupy certain pre-existent posts in an organizational structure designed in specialist departments. They are judged on their functional character – that is to say, the efficiency with which they perform their job. Work relations are prescribed by the structure, and the same goes on the whole for methods, supervised by regulations and procedures.

In a connexionist world, people are called upon to move around, to forge the links they use in their work themselves – links that cannot, by definition, be pre-established in advance – and to distrust any structure and post designed in advance, which risk confining them to an overfamiliar universe. Their flexibility, their ability to adapt and learn continuously, become major advantages, which take precedence over their technical expertise (knowledge changes so quickly) and their experience. Personality make-up, the qualities of communication, listening and openness to differences, thus count for more than efficiency as measured by the ability to achieve predefined objectives. Work methods are developed in line with constantly changing needs: people organize themselves and invent local rules that are not amenable to totalization and comprehensive rationalization by some putative organization department.[44]

The analyses above lead us to believe that what we have called the projective city does indeed constitute an original mode of justification, whose architecture is based on a world of objects and mechanisms whose formation is relatively recent. We can also confirm it by demonstrating, with the aid of the textual analysis program Prospero, that the projective city definitely specifies the 1990s corpus.

The specification of the 1990s corpus by the projective city

We have entered into the interpretative apparatus in which the program gives access to the grammars of the six previously identified worlds (inspirational, domestic, reputational, civic, industrial, commercial), as well as that of the projective city. The grammars are represented in their computerized form by groups or categories of words associated with one or other world. It is then possible to compare the two corpora with respect to the presence or absence of the different categories. The presence of a city will be measured here by the sum total of all occurrences in a given corpus of the members of the category created to represent it (see Table 2.1).

Table 2.1 The presence of the seven worlds in each corpus

1960s		1990s	
Industrial logic	6,764	Industrial logic	4,972
Domestic logic	2,033	Network logic	3,996
Commercial logic	1,841	Commercial logic	2,207
Civic logic	1,216	Domestic logic	1,404
Network logic	1,114	Inspirational logic	1,366
Inspirational logic	774	Civic logic	793
Reputational logic	479	Reputational logic	768

A first observation, which is scarcely surprising given the nature of our two corpora (whose subject matter is improving the organization of work), is that industrial logic is dominant in both periods (although the references are generally positive in the 1960s and frequently critical in the 1990s). But this pre-eminence is virtually uncontested in the 1960s (see the relation between the number of occurrences of the industrial world and of what immediately follows it in the two cases), whereas it is qualified in the 1990s by the position occupied by the entities of the projective city (whose numbers are nearly double those pertaining to the logic ranked second in the 1960s). If the second-ranking logic in the 1990s is that of the network, domestic logic occupies this position in the 1960s – which would tend to confirm the hypothesis of a substitution, or rather an absorption, of domestic by connexionist logic. The maintenance of commercial logic in third place, albeit with a slightly higher number of occurrences, is a further indicator suggesting that the changes affecting the world of work over thirty years do not so much take the form of an increase in popularity of market mechanisms as of restructuring described by reference to networks. This tends to invalidate analyses that seek to reduce current tendencies in the spirit of capitalism solely to the extension of market justifications.

Two other phenomena should be emphasized: on the one hand, the eclipse in the 1990s of the civic world, which can be straightforwardly related to the important association that obtained in 1960s discourse between the action of firms and that of the state, which has subsequently disappeared; and on the other hand, an increase in popularity of the inspirational city, which should be connected with the stress laid in the 1990s on innovation, risk, the constant search for new solutions, and highly personal qualities. Appendix 4 offers supplementary analysis of the relative presence of the different justificatory registers in the two corpora.

The programme of textual analysis that we have employed thus makes it possible to bring out a major transformation in the space of thirty years in the registers of justification on which management literature bases itself, and an increase in the popularity of the network logic to top position. Further changes of smaller magnitude also occurred: a redistribution of commercial references (see Appendix 4); a significant decline in domestic references; and the disappearance of civic logic, replaced by inspirational logic. The projective city – which, we argue, is the basis for the local justifications used to account for the new mechanisms over and above the classical theoretical justifications of capitalism – equally describes what distinguishes the 1990s from the 1960s. For the emergence of the register that corresponds to it proves to be the most striking phenomenon when one uses the grid for analysing cities. Hence this tends to confirm the hypothesis that the construction we have extracted from texts does indeed represent, in stylized and concentrated form, what characterizes the new spirit of capitalism in a highly original fashion.

Certainly, the list of words used by the program to make an inventory of appearances of the projective city includes numerous new terms that were by no means common in 1960s management literature, and which precisely correspond to the new mechanisms – words such as 'alliance', 'partnership', 'coaching', and so on. But this observation does not invalidate our results, for every change of significance brings in its wake a new terminology and new ways of thinking. And one of the analyst's roles is to extract what is new in a given situation. The cities were not all unfurled in the same period, and just as there was a time when the notions of 'objectives', 'planning', 'organization chart', and 'optimization', which characterized industrial status, did not exist, so there was a time when the network could on no account claim to serve as a general model for organizing societies.

For one of the most striking aspects of the emergence of this new system of values, of which we have sought to offer an initial description by applying to recent management texts a grid previously used to describe the worlds associated with the cities, is that this phenomenon is in no way restricted to the domain of management, or even to the sphere of firms. On the contrary, various indications suggest that the metaphor of the network is gradually taking on the task of a new general representation of societies. Thus, the problematic of the link, the relationship, the encounter, of rupture, loss, isolation and separation as a prelude to the establishment of new links, the formation of new projects, and insistence on a constantly reactivated tension between the demand for autonomy and the desire for security – these are also at the heart of current changes in personal life, relations between friends, and especially family life. Such changes have been analysed in recent works on the sociology of the family,[45] but equally – and this is perhaps even more relevant for our purposes – redescribed in TV dramas which, via imaginary variations, put this stock theme to work, as it were, by setting its various facets in motion.[46] As disclosed by novelistic, cinematic or TV fiction, an investment of the imagination by the *social* in the shape of dramas, tensions, complexes or dilemmas associated with the question of class and social origins – which was very marked in the 1960s and 1970s, and was doubtless in keeping with the sensibility of generations that had experienced high social mobility – thus tends to be replaced today by a focus on the question of bonds, which are grasped as invariably problematic, fragile, to be created or re-created. The focus is on a representation of the lived world in terms of connection and disconnection, inclusion and exclusion, of closure in collectivities that are closed in on themselves ('sects'), or of openness to a hazardous world of encounters, mutual aid, losses and, ultimately, solitude.

3. THE GENERALIZATION OF THE NETWORK FORM OF REPRESENTATION

One cannot fail to be struck by the protean, heterogeneous character of the references that can be mobilized from numerous domains of research and thought, in the construction of a new everyday morality. Below we offer a general survey of the enormous conceptual brew that such a construction presupposes.

The proliferation of texts on networks

The connexionist genre, whose formalization we have sketched, does not constitute a form which is, as it were, *sui generis* – which has a meaning only by reference to developments internal to the literature intended for firms.

Even a rapid overview of various highly active currents during the last twenty years, in both philosophy and the social sciences (which in certain respects today perform the role once assigned to political philosophy), is enough to demonstrate the opposite. The notion of network – which, until approximately the 1970s, was a relatively specialist or marginal usage – has since become the object of much attention and is now to be found at the heart of a large, fairly diverse number of theoretical or empirical works in several disciplines – so much so that promoters of these developments readily talk about a new paradigm.[47] The ease with which the reference to networks has spread, the speed of diffusion of specialist research and the new usages it has given rise to, further makes any attempt to trace a clear line of demarcation between a 'scientific' and an 'ideological' use of reticular themes hazardous.[48]

However, although a large number of the terms or notions drawn from management texts where network logic predominates have their equivalent in writings from the human sciences, direct references to these works are rather rare in our corpus, and pretty much concentrated under the signatures of a few authors. These authors associate management in network form with three terms: first, communication (represented by references to Habermas, Bateson and Watzlawick); secondly, complexity (J.-P. Dupuy, Edgar Morin); and, finally, disorder, chaos and self-organization (represented by references to Prigogine, Stengers, Atlan, Heisenberg, Hofstadter and Varela).[49] As a general rule, the authors of our corpus predominantly cite other management authors, and frequently one another; this accords with the existence of management as a specific discipline.[50]

In other respects, we find in the writings of the main authors from whom we have extracted the outline of the projective city traces of a reading of Ivan Illich's works in the 1970s. Their anti-authoritarian emphasis, critique of centralization, stress on autonomy and on what might, with a certain anachronism, be called self-organization, and also their technological humanism – placing tools in the service of humanity, not vice versa – were to be taken up in the thematic of the projective city. It remains the case that Illich is rarely, if ever, cited by the management authors, at least in their writings (this does not exclude acknowledgement when speaking, in the course of discussions, of a youthful debt or enthusiasm). And this is because the extent to which he pushed the critique of industrial society, his critique of commodification and the power of capital, are not readily compatible with managerial tasks.[51]

In order to outline the interface between management literature and literature from the natural or social sciences capable of supporting a representation of the world based on a minimal grammar of the link – that is to say, to construct sets containing both management texts (in particular, some of the texts we have relied on to model the projective city) and texts frequently cited in works published in social science journals – we must turn to a different source. The works of interest to us here have as their objective, in a more generalist perspective, to get a broad public to understand that in order to decipher the world we are entering into we must, whatever the sphere concerned, call upon the notion of the network. Take, for example, *La Planète relationnelle*, published in 1995 by two consultants (A. Bressand and C. Distler). Products of the *grandes écoles* (Bressand is an ex-student of the École polytechnique, Distler an ex-student of the École normale), they composed a work mediating between the spaces of academia and enterprise. Thus, in this work we find references to: (1) the administration of firms in network mode – and particularly to a large number of management texts included in our corpus (Georges Archier, Hervé Sérieyx, Alvin Toffler, etc.); (2) classics of communication (Marshal McLuhan, Régis Debray); (3) information economists (for example, Alfred Chandler, O. Williamson and J. Tirole); (4) works on cyberspace, the virtual, 'Internet culture' and, more generally, information technology (S. Papert, Shelly Turkle, M. Cronin); (5) theories of self-organization (J.-P. Dupuy, F. Varela); (6) works connected with the American sociology of network analysis (R. Eccles, R. Nollan and Mark Granovetter); (7) the new sociology of science and technology (Bruno Latour and Michel Serres).[52]

The rather heterogeneous character of these references should not surprise us. In the formation of cities, the assimilation as equivalents of a multiplicity of objects, hitherto perceived as belonging to distinct spheres or logics, is accompanied by an intensive collective effort of homogenization to exhibit the potentialities of a world and also to test its moral consistency, to test its compatibility with the requirements of justice, so that action in this world can be adjudged legitimate.

So self-evident is it that there is no need to stress the way that significant development in the technical mechanisms of communication and transport has stimulated the connexionist imagination. In particular, it has had the effect of making universally tangible a phenomenon that is not in itself novel: the way that the bonds and constraints consequent upon belonging to a territory (including national territories) are challenged by links that are established at a distance. Today, it is a commonplace that long-distance communication in real time, even more than transport facilities, tends to diminish the importance of neighbourhood solidarities compared with links deriving from despatialized affinities.[53] Take, for example, the model of the scientific researcher who is connected with people who share his interests throughout the world, but has no relationship with colleagues in adjoining offices. More generally, for a significant number of wage-earners the development of the media, and especially of computer tools in workplaces, has conferred concrete existence on the abstract notion of network. The accumulation of specifically technical changes, combined with an appreciable, regular reduction in the cost of using them, has helped to attenuate the boundaries between units. Combined with obvious political responsibility for deregulation or the absence of legislation,[54] it has equally rendered obsolete a number of forms of legal protection that were secured through prolonged, costly effort. It has thereby opened up space for possible connections, and given unprecedented impetus both to the activity of networking and to the theoretical work of redefining the social bond and, more profoundly, establishing a new anthropology grounded not, for example, in a universal propensity to exchange objects (the case of the commercial city), but in a propensity, described as no less universal, to form links.

The network: From the illegitimate to the legitimate

The establishment of a projective city, by conferring an exigency of justice on the network form, constitutes it as a legitimate political form. This legitimating operation is observed every time the establishment of a city gives salience to a way of seeing and constructing the world that was hitherto either absorbed into other forms and not identified as such, or criticized. In the case to hand, it is all the more striking in that, but a short while ago, the term 'network' was used uncritically only in approximately technical senses (the electricity or telephone network).

Thus, in the 1960s management literature, where the word is still rare (21 occurrences in the 1960s corpus as against 450 in the 1990s corpus), reference to networks is made in passages dealing with communication, mainly to evoke vertical and horizontal relations within the firm.[55] Hence it is used in a sense that is quite different from the sense given to it today, when the network is associated with the idea of transgressing all boundaries – in particular, those of the firm and the channels of communication and subordination inscribed in organization charts. The word network is thus used in the 1960s to refer to constraints, meshes being associated with those of a net hemming the individual in, rather than representing the activity of connecting. Thus, the French 'are protected from "others" by a complicated network of laws' (Servan-Schreiber, 1967); *cadres* are caught up in 'networks of obligation' (Gabrysiak *et al.*, 1968); bureaucracy 'maintains a whole network of authority, dependency and subordination' (De Woot, 1968). Similarly, in order to ground a negative appraisal of someone factually, it is necessary 'to close around the person concerned the network of policies, objectives, programmes and budgets that he was unable to realize' (Gélinier, 1963). The rarest usage, and the one closest to the current sense, employs the word to distinguish the informal dimension of life in firms from formal structures.[56] But the authors then turn out to be embarrassed when it comes to assessing the phenomenon negatively or positively, for in one respect the emergence of processes that are not controlled by the structure is problematic for management, while in another the authors are sensitive to the support that is often afforded by informal relations.

Research into the uses of the word 'network' in dictionaries from earlier decades likewise indicates that this term, until the 1980s when it was used to refer to human organizations, was nearly always employed pejoratively to characterize clandestine, illegitimate and/or illegal forms of links. Practically the only exception is 'resistance networks', which were distinctive in being simultaneously illegal (with respect to Vichy and the Occupation authorities), and hence clandestine, but legitimate. But even in this case, unlike what we observe today, network is always associated with secrecy, in contrast to the transparency of public relationships that are legal. Finally, unlike the tight-knit gang, a criminal conspiracy, the network is not only opaque in relation to the outside, it is also opaque from within: those involved in it do not know the identity of all the others. Consequently, network conjures up conspiracy or what Rousseau, to designate forms of private association contrary to the general interest, calls *intrigues* in the *Social Contract*. In this essentially pejorative sense, network could refer either to dealing (arms, drugs, stolen property, moonlighting), which was simultaneously illegitimate and illegal. Or it could refer to groups of people who, while dispersed in space and mixed with other populations, secretly maintain a private bond and aid each other, to the detriment of others, without their actions necessarily possessing an illegal character (the term 'mafia', often combined with network, serving as a bridge between these two variants).

In a recent work by two journalists, *Les bonnes fréquentations, histoire secrète des réseaux d'influence*,[57] we still find this older use of the reference to networks. This book, which is presented as a 'secret history of networks', aims to expose 'the covert solidarities' that 'swarm around the power of money and knowledge'. Moreover, in their introduction the authors take the trouble to differentiate themselves from the new, positive conception of networks developed in management literature: 'This charming rediscovery of the warm, reassuring collective restores a rather idyllic image of networks.'[58] For our two authors, by contrast, networks are neither 'lobbies, because they go beyond a strict, conjunctural alliance of interests', nor 'community structures, because they carefully avoid any institutionalization'. Rather, they are 'fluid' links aiming at 'mutual aid', 'influence', 'money', 'power', forged by people who, unbeknownst to others, recognize each other by the fact that they possess an identical original quality, which is not emphasized in public life. The list of networks that the two authors follow closely gives a good enough idea of the groups traditionally suspected of serving hidden interests at the expense of the public good. What unites them might be regional, particularly when they come from peripheral or poor regions (Corsicans, Corréziens, Savoyards, Bretons and Auvergnats: pp. 23–49); ethnic, religious or communitarian (Jews, pp. 67–9; Protestants, pp. 79–86; Freemasons, pp. 163–74; Catholics, pp. 327–55); sexual (gays, pp. 53–60); political (former Trotskyists, pp. 146–52; ex-members of Occident, pp. 152–61); financial (the networks around the Lazard group, pp. 213–15); administrative (technocrats, pp. 216–17); intellectual (pp. 235–50); or fashionable (pp. 109–15).

The use of the term network in sociology has, over the last twenty years, undergone the same changes of connotation as we observe in its ordinary usage. Predominantly used in the 1960s to expose privileges, particularly in education and the labour market, which people advantaged by their social origin were able to exploit discreetly, network is today employed neutrally, as a tool. It is even presented, at least implicitly, as a more efficient and just social form than formal relations based on criteria, making possible gradual, nego-tiated integration into employment. Consequently, sociology makes its contribution to the delegitimation of conventions resting upon a compromise between the civic and industrial cities, and to the enhanced legitimacy of the projective city.

But we cannot really understand why the metaphor of the network has been chosen to the represent the world that is in the process of emerging, and its increased legitimacy, if we limit ourselves to registering its compatibility with the development of new technical instruments of connections, transport and communication, or its concomitance with the proliferation of associated concepts in other fields. It is also important to show, through a rapid sketch of the origins of the notion of network, how it was itself constructed to counter conceptions bound up with the old world. Hence it was fairly natu-rally pressed into service for its transformation.

Remarks on the origin of works on networks

Such is the number and profusion of currents contributing to the develop-ment of the network paradigm over the last thirty years that it is impossible to retrace their history – something which would demand a book in itself. On the other hand, we can present some of the main outlines.

The formation of the network paradigm was bound up in a very general way with a growing interest in *relational properties* (and relational ontologies), as opposed to properties substantially attached to entities they supposedly defined in themselves. On to this central perspective, common to approaches pertaining to different disciplines that are fairly diverse at first sight, other rep-resentations were then grafted (sometimes to the point of masking or obscuring it). They found support, for example, in the persistence since the nineteenth century of an organicist conception of society as a living body irri-gated by flows, whether material (communication routes or systems for distributing energy sources) or immaterial (financial flows, flows of informa-tion, or movements of symbolic diffusion).[59] Or they could find a prop in the development (ensured by computer programs making it possible to automate the representation of relations in the form of graphs) of sociometric tech-niques perfected in social psychology, particularly by J.L. Moreno, in the 1930s and 1940s, to describe by means of diagrams ('sociograms') the way individ-uals in small groups are connected by directed communication flows.[60] This latter current, in particular, was to ensure the success of network analyses, first of all in social anthropology,[61] and then in sociology and history – a domain where their employment poses particular problems that we shall underline shortly. Finally, as a last example we may take the formation over the last twenty years, in the framework of the cognitive sciences seeking to bring together computer science and brain biology, of models of distributed intelligence of a connexionist type, intent on conceiving theoretical devices for simulating intelligence without appealing to hierarchical algorithms.[62]

If we can assimilate these very diverse expressions of interest in networks to a shared epistemological orientation – that is, the privileging of relational properties over properties attached to entities – it remains the case that the routes leading to the formation of this paradigm assumed different courses in the Anglophone countries, especially the United States, and in France.

In France, interest in the field of the human sciences for representations in network terms emerged in the course of the 1960s from philosophy – in particular, philosophical enterprises that helped to renew the philosophy of science by rejecting the boundary established by the dominant epistemologies between scientific activities and other types of practice of knowledge, in order to set this discipline on non-reductionist paths.

References to networks were combined with a search for modes of totalization that would introduce minimal distortion into the particularity of the relations identified and the entities they connect. This was contrasted with reductionist approaches that totalize by relating entities and relations to original types, classes, structures, in such a way as to assemble them into groups amenable to becoming objects of calculation in their turn. Consequently, approaches based on a representation in terms of networks have a complex relationship with structuralism. They share with it the fact that they stress relational properties, not substances: as is well known, since Saussure the game of chess, where each move displacing a piece alters the positional value of all the pieces in play, has constituted the quintessential metaphor for the structural approach. However, unlike structuralism, whose project is to identify the original structures on the basis of which transformations occur, and which therefore sets off 'in search of the "logical structure of the world"',[63] the network approach is identified with a radical empiricism. Rather than assuming a world organized according to basic structures (even if they remain hidden and must be unveiled by a scientific labour reducing them to elementary constituents), it presents a world where everything potentially reflects everything else: a world, often conceived as 'fluid, continuous, chaotic',[64] where anything can be connected with anything else, which must therefore be tackled without any reductionist apriorism. Recourse to the notion of network thus derives from an aspiration to furnish very general formulations and models capable of combining any kind of entity, without necessarily specifying their nature, treated as an emergent property of the network itself. Yet this reticular world is not posited as a chaos. Analysis will be able to detect some relations that are more stable than others, preferential paths, crossing points.

However, as Michel Serres explains,[65] this requires the support of a schema that makes it possible for us to understand how this generalized connexity can be realized. In his work, this schema is 'communication', 'elective site of innovation', which makes it possible to 'take up the challenge of the multiple',[66] by furnishing instruments of totalization that encompass sensitivity to differences. Here the reference to communication is clearly associated from the outset with the project of replacing essentialist ontologies with open spaces, without borders, centres or fixed points, where entities are constituted by the relations they enter into and alter in line with the flows, transfers, exchanges, permutations, and displacements that are the relevant events in this space.[67] The ontological primacy accorded to the event of connection with respect to entities related to one another is much more radical than in American versions of the network paradigm, which we shall examine shortly. The moment of connection (the 'encounter' in Gilles Deleuze[68]) is the moment of constitution of the identity of the entities that enter into a certain relation. In such a world, nothing is thus a priori reducible to anything else from a standpoint which would be that of an outside observer, since 'reduction' (one element assimilates, translates, or expresses another element with which it comes into contact) is precisely the operation whereby the links are created and stabilized within the network. To describe the network is to observe and report these operations of reduction which, in the open space of interconnections, create relative irreversibility.

The utterly original kind of description made possible by this novel language helped in the 1980s to renew sociology, penetrating it via the new sociology of science developed by Bruno Latour and Michel Callon. In this current, representations in terms of networks are turned to good account to overcome the separation, hitherto dominant in the sociology of science, between that which supposedly pertains to 'science' proper (deemed 'objective') and that which belongs among its 'social uses' (involving interests that corrupt this alleged 'objectivity').[69]

But the same philosopheme is also involved in less specific trends. At least in France after May 1968, it was placed in the service of a critique (particularly by Deleuze) of the 'subject', in so far as the latter is defined with reference to a self-consciousness and an essence that could be anything but the trace of the relations in which it has been caught up in the course of its displacements. It was likewise deployed in a critique of anything that could be condemned as a 'fixed point' capable of acting as referent. This comprised, for example, the state, the family, churches and, more generally, all institutions; but also master thinkers, bureaucracies and traditions (because they are turned towards an origin treated as a fixed point); and eschatologies, religious or political, because they make beings dependent upon an essence projected into the future. During the 1970s, this critique was almost naturally directed at capitalism, which was conflated in one and the same denunciation with the bourgeois family and the state. These were condemned as closed, fixed, ossified worlds, whether by attachment to tradition (the family), legalism and bureaucracy (the state), or calculation and planning (the firm), as opposed to mobility, fluidity and 'nomads' able to circulate, at the cost of many metamorphoses, in open networks.[70] On the other hand, however, it also made it possible to have done with rigid separations between orders, spheres, fields, classes, apparatuses, instances, and so on, which had in the same period, particularly in sociological versions of Marxist structuralism, assumed the form of hypostases that were regarded as sacred, any querying of which was tantamount to blasphemy at the time.[71]

In so doing, and in part unbeknownst to itself, this critique also lent itself to an interpretation in terms of liberation: not only from the personal and institutional loyalties, now experienced as unjustified servitude, which characterized the old domestic order that was in the process of being marginalized, but also from all 'hierarchies' and 'apparatuses' – that is to say, both from the 'state apparatus' and from the 'apparatuses' which, like 'trade-union apparatuses', had contributed to the creation of labour law, the recognition of social classes, and the process leading to their representation in the state.[72]

In the Anglophone literature, the world-views (and not simply conceptions of society) based on network logics attached themselves to pragmatism and radical empiricism. In this case, too, the question of how a relationship is established between elements posited as different and separate (rather than being unified a priori by an observer who renders them equivalent by imposing predefined categories upon them) is primordial; and it directs attention towards processes of communication. It leads to representing the world in the form of a meshing of 'signs', each of which is capable of reflecting or representing the others according to its particular position (and not from some overarching standpoint, which does not feature in such a model). Hence the often implicit importance of semiotics, invented by C.S. Peirce, in the formation of a representation of the world conceived as a network. Indeed, in Peirce's work the sign is not only related to an object (as in the dyadic relation between signified and signifier). It must itself be interpreted in order to have a meaning (rather as a word is defined in a dictionary by a paraphrase composed of other terms, whose definition can in turn be sought, and so on). This triadic conception of the sign (sign, object, interpretant) makes it possible to represent the world, inasmuch as it can be invested with a meaning, as a 'network' with indeterminate contours constituted by a multiplicity of translations, since 'the sign is not a sign unless it can be translated into another sign in which it is more fully developed'.[73] The interpretant thus plays a role as translator or mediator, allowing the network to expand by connecting entities that would otherwise remain isolated, and hence devoid of meaning. The network thus makes it possible to conceptualize objects inbetween 'crystallized form', defined by stable but closed connections (representable in the concept of structures), and 'chaotic non-form', where no link makes it possible to cross several times from one element to another by the same path.

It was mainly in the American sociological currents which situate themselves in a straight line from pragmatism (such as the Chicago School or symbolic interactionism) that this problematic was to penetrate the field of the social sciences. Without for the most part resorting to the methodology of networks, these two currents posit a framework into which analyses in network terms integrated themselves without difficulty because, in a way, it presupposes and calls for them. The properties of this framework that interest us here are essentially of three sorts: first, the possibility of establishing causal links between highly diverse elements that coexist in the same space, whose uniqueness is respected (Park's 'social ecology'); secondly, a concern to grasp processes situated between what can be discovered by a purely individualist approach, criticized for its atomism, and, conversely, an institutional approach focused on the most formal organizations and macro-social phenomena; finally, a desire to start out from interactions within small groups, conceived essentially, according to the perspective established by G.H. Mead, as communicative activities through which people at once construct their own 'self' and produce the meanings operative in social life, defined by its symbolic nature. In this logic, people are inseparably 'actors', who perform actions, and 'interpreters', who elaborate social meanings by exchanging 'signs', which are the form action takes when it is caught up in flows of relations on which people seek to confer meaning. From this angle, the seemingly most stable properties of individuals – for example, sex or profession – are themselves signs subject to interpretation in interaction. Rather than treating them as substantial properties, it is therefore appropriate to regard them as relational properties: it is in interactions, where they are subject to interpretation, that these qualities are invested with meanings; and meanings, depending on the relation as they do, vary as we pass from one relation to another. It is therefore not possible to define individuals, as in structuralist-influenced constructions, by a bundle of properties that derive mechanically from membership of groups, institutions, organizations, and so on.

The radicalization of these positions led, in the 1960s and 1970s, in two different directions. The first – of which ethnomethodology, which does not directly concern us here, constitutes the consummate expression – consisted in laying stress exclusively on the processes of interpretation whereby actors seek to impart meaning to social accomplishments in the course of action itself. It is stymied by the problem of totalization, since the meaning of the words on which the work of interpretation depends is itself tied to these situations; and these situations are, hypothetically, quite unique. The second radicalization likewise consisted in abandoning the idea that there exist stable properties of persons, individual or collective, which permit totalization. But rather than focusing on the work of interpretation in interaction, it would endeavour – redeveloping the old Morenian sociometry, and employing a language derived from the theory of graphs – to reconstruct mechanisms of totalization by fixing exclusively on relations in a network, which were hypothetically open-ended (even if the aim of totalization presupposes closing the list of the relations considered at any given point). In this perspective, individuals are always less pertinent than the relations linking them.[74] They can be treated as 'nodes' at the intersection of bundles of relations, so that it becomes possible to populate this empty space with highly diverse entities.

Together with those of Mark Granovetter,[75] it is without doubt the works of Harrison White and his team that have played a predominant role in the development of this current, by proposing algorithms amenable to automated treatment in order to construct networks of relations on a much grander scale than did Moreno, whose works were concerned with small groups. The innovation was not simply technological. It also aimed to free sociology from 'old' ideas of 'categories', 'groups', 'classes' which, presented as valid for earlier, status-based societies, were no longer suitable for open, fluid (liberal) societies where 'chance' plays a preponderant role.[76] The much-heralded methodological revolution thus contained, in embryo, the promise of liberation from 'old' institutions enclosed within their boundaries, 'rigid' organizations, comprising registers of 'roles' and 'statuses' that were fixed once and for all, treated as constraining and outmoded. As with the most radical versions of the paradigm, this orientation was to lead to discounting the properties of the elements between which a relation is established – that is to say, people, whose characteristics, for example, of being a woman, a black, a youth, a worker, and so on, were no longer treated as relevant – and considering only the relational properties – that is to say, the number, frequency and direction of connections.

It is only in the last ten or so years that the American sociology of networks has become solidly rooted in France, through the medium of surveys focused on sociability,[77] and taking directions which, in the majority of cases, do not overlap with those whereby the network paradigm was diffused – via French philosophical currents in the 1960s and 1970s, which we have cursorily recalled, to the new sociology of science and technology.

We have sought to demonstrate that it is possible to derive both from schemas which are ultimately fairly cognate, and can evidently be deployed to undertake a delegitimation of the world associated with the second spirit of capitalism, with its bureaucracies, states, bourgeois families and social classes, in favour of a new reticular world on which the third spirit of capitalism helps to confer meaning. Even so, we do indeed find ourselves in the presence of two 'schools', whose intersection, measured by the frequency of personal contacts in seminars, colloquia, and so on, or by citations, would turn out to be limited, if not nonexistent.

Why have we not used one of these seminal texts to delineate the features of an order founded on the construction of the network, following the approach tried and tested in *De la justification*, which proceeds from canonical texts to manuals of practical application? Because, as far as we know, there is no key text that attempts to establish the possibility of a harmonious, just world based on the network. The connexionist type of order whose formalization we have sketched has not – in the same way as the domestic, civic or commercial orders, for example – been the object of a systematic construction in the tradition of political philosophy. This, no doubt, is because the contemporary currents in which the concept of network was elaborated were constructed precisely against the metaphysical structures underlying the political philosophies of the common good (put to work in *De la justification* to establish the architectonics of the cities). And in some cases they were constructed as philosophies of immanence in such a way as to avoid, bypass or absorb the position occupied by a moral instance whence legitimate judgements referring to justice might derive. This is why these philosophies have, as we shall see later, borrowed from psychoanalysis notions such as 'force' or 'displacement' (which we ourselves shall employ, but conjugating them with those of the common good and justice), in such a way as to absorb the two-tiered space of Western political metaphysics into a 'plane of immanence', as Deleuze puts it.

This is also why attempts to reconcile representations in terms of networks and concerns expressed in moral terms, containing a reference to justice, which thus approximate most closely to what we have called the projective city, have been composed by grafting elements derived from quite different currents on to reticular themes. These currents, while likewise stressing communication, elaborated a new problematic of the subject, formulated with the aid of a pragmatics, and, adopting a Kantian legacy that reticular ontologies had jettisoned, more or less explicitly assigned themselves the task of refounding the possibility of judgements cast in terms of truth and/or moral correctness.[78]

The naturalization of networks in the social sciences

The contribution of the social sciences to describing a connexionist world with the coherence and immediacy of something natural, where action can be justified if it is inscribed in projects, stems ultimately from their capacity for naturalization, which itself derives from their conception of science. For, in the final analysis, to state what the world is composed of is always to confer a nature upon it. Obviously, the naturalization effect is especially powerful in those disciplines which, aiming to connect biology and society, derive the social bond from implantation in the order of living organisms; or construct their representation of society on the basis of a physiological metaphor – not, as in the old organicism, cellular differentiation, but instead today the metaphor of the neuron, with its networks and flows. But naturalizing effects are equally brought to bear in less hardline paradigms, especially when they are orchestrated by a specific technology. Thus, the ambition, inscribed in the strong programme of the sociology of networks, of describing all social processes solely in terms of the number, form and orientation of connections (regardless of any characteristics attaching to those between whom these links are established, or any specification of the regime in which these links are formed, or of the logic wherein they can be justified) – this ambition does indeed aim, in a reductionist spirit, to give the social sciences a genuinely scientific foundation by basing them on analysis of fundamental components, or the connections that supposedly constitute the 'cement' of societies (as Jon Elster puts it in a different context).

The wish to construct an authentically scientific sociology on the basis of network analysis has been expressed in two different fashions. Schematically, the first might be characterized as *historicist*, the second as *naturalistic*.

The first, historicist approach has consisted in defending the idea that network analyses are especially suitable for describing contemporary societies, because the development of networking activities is characteristic of these societies. This first point of view would appear to be that adopted by White, Boorman and Breiger.[79]

However, with the development of specific technologies applicable to any object whatsoever, and the formation of a veritable school, network analysis has increasingly been employed to re-examine and reinterpret historical data, in an approach that we would characterize as naturalistic. These redescriptions replace earlier explanations – in terms of conflicts between classes, groups, political cultures, for example, or symbolic exchanges – by analyses that aim to describe historical changes taking account solely of the structure of networks. Typical in this respect is the interpretation of the rise of the Medicis in Florence between 1400 and 1434 proposed, on the basis of previous data, by John Padgett and Christopher Ansell. Against earlier interpretations that invoke the rise of new groups and class conflicts, they stress the way in which Cosimo de Medici succeeded in positioning himself at the junction of different networks, whose structural holes he exploited judiciously.[80] Similarly, we can read Fernand Braudel emphasizing that in his description of the origin and development of capitalism he stressed, not competition and the market, but the social networks that served as a support for long-distance trade.[81]

From the viewpoint of elaborating a projective city, each of these two positions presents advantages and disadvantages. The first – historicist – position is good because it underscores the novelty of the network world and the suitability of the description of networks to the current world, the one we inhabit and are seeking to understand. It chimes well with the assertion, which accompanies the description of a connexionist world, that this form is characteristic of the world being constructed before our eyes. But the second – naturalistic – position possesses the advantage of basing the network form more solidly on the naturalness of the world.

The researchers who are active in these two currents could reply that debates on networks revolve not around the world but around modes of description; and thus that it is purely a matter of methodological discussion. But over and above the fact that the validity of the description cannot be separated from the properties of the object being described, the critiques they direct at categorial approaches do indeed tend to establish the image of a world whose meaning is disclosed only to those who have understood that networks constitute its main armature.

However, the tension between a historicist position (the network is the form that suits our age) and a naturalistic position (the network is the texture constitutive of any social world, even of nature in its entirety) can be reduced if one accepts that in the order of knowledge, reticular organization constitutes the form that is best adjusted to the global vision of the world from the viewpoint of a city founded upon a connexionist logic. To take the example of the commercial city: the market had to be placed at the heart of a political philosophy at the end of the eighteenth century for the market dimensions of past societies in their turn to be apprehended as such – that is to say, with the vocabulary and concepts of the commercial city. Similarly, the network possibly constitutes an appropriate form for describing the way in which, according to Braudel, the bankers of London or Amsterdam realized surplus-values greatly in excess of the opportunities offered by local markets. But they did not describe their own actions on the basis of the network form and, above all, did not appeal to the network or project to deliver value judgements or construct justifications.

The historicist and naturalistic approaches commit the same error, which consists in believing that states of things and modes of description can be treated independently of the normative positions from which a value judgement on events can be made. We believe that if something new has come to pass in the respect that concerns us here, it is precisely the formation of a mode of judgement which, taking it for granted that the world is a network (and not, for example, a system, a structure, a market or a community), offers fulcra for appraising and ordering the relative value of beings in such a world.

CONCLUSION: THE CHANGES WROUGHT BY THE NEW SPIRIT OF CAPITALISM AT THE LEVEL OF ETHICS

The development of what we have called a connexionist world, and the gradual formation of a projective city that subjects it to a demand for justice, comprise the main normative fulcra on which the new spirit of capitalism rests. Now that we have largely set out the projective city, we can extend the comparison between the new spirit of capitalism and those that preceded it, endeavouring to bring out their differences at the level of ethics. Whereas the first spirit of capitalism gave more than its due to an ethic of saving, and the second to an ethic of work and competence, the new spirit is marked by a change in terms of the relation to both money and work.

The change in the relation to money and possessions

In the form of the spirit of capitalism that dominated the nineteenth century and the first third of the twentieth, saving constituted the main means of access to the world of capital and the instrument of social advancement. It was, in large part, by means of inculcating an ethic of saving that the values of self-control, moderation, restraint, hard work, regularity, perseverance, and stability prized by firms were transmitted.

In a network world, the significance of saving has not disappeared, but it applies to a different kind of goods. As Gary Becker anticipated more than thirty years ago,[82] the main scarcity in our societies – at least among categories like *cadres*, who do not face immediate necessity – concerns time, not material goods. In this world, to save is thus in the first instance to prove sparing with one's time and judicious in the way one allocates it. Obviously, this applies in the first instance to the time one devotes to others: not wasting time involves reserving it for establishing and maintaining the most profitable connections – that is, the most improbable or the most long-distance connections – as opposed to squandering it in relations with intimates or people with whom social intercourse brings only pleasure of an affective or ludic variety. But a suitable allocation of free time also concerns access to information and money (the two often go together). People must not be prodigal with their time, or reserve it for themselves – save it up to no purpose. They should devote their time to seeking information about good projects and, if they have saved up time, not squander it on useless things, but keep it in reserve to exploit opportunities to invest in a new project, which is unexpected but potentially interesting. Time represents the basic resource for connecting the actors who control access to money, and on whom the project budget depends. Given that time is a resource that cannot be stored, however, this type of saving cannot remain dormant, and must be constantly reinvested. The imperative to make the resource on which one is dependent work, which also applies to money, is rendered more exacting in this instance by its personal character. Whereas the management of monetary savings can be entrusted to others, optimum investment of one's time must be handled personally.

More generally, in a network world the everyday relationship to money and property differs from bourgeois custom as traditionally defined. But it also differs from the new forms of relationship to property that marked the rise of an elite of university-educated, qualified, salaried managers, integrated into large bureaucracies, in the 1940s. The modes of activity best adjusted to a connexionist world signal a turning-point in the history of capitalism, because they contribute to making a Western definition of property operative. Kiyokazu Washida has devoted a remarkable article to this definition, on which the remarks below draw.[83]

The constitution of the category of managers was marked in the first instance by a fragmentation of the various components contained in the notion of property, in the form of a separation of ownership and control. Managers, who do not own what they control, are counterposed to owners, who are often numerous and whose power is limited or nonexistent. To a certain extent, this separation may be regarded as the basis for the formation of one of the principal modern conceptions of power (and its critique) – bureaucratic power (which, once defined, can obviously be identified in other societies and different periods). It is pure in the sense that it is severed from the characteristics it possessed by dint of its association with property (e.g. wealth or personal enjoyment of worldly goods). Construed thus, however, power retained an essential feature of property, analysis of which, present in Hegel, was popularized by Marx: just as the possessor is possessed by his possession,[84] the man of power is dependent on what his power is exercised over. Hence two temptations, both of which aim to dispose of the constraints of possession or power: absolute power and radical divestment.

However, a third possibility exists, whose current development is remarkable: renting or borrowing/loaning. Renting isolates a third component of property: *availability*, which is total but temporary. Now, it is precisely this component, and it alone, that people should be concerned with in a connexionist world. Rather than property-owners absorbed by the things they possess, or managers dependent upon the objects whose reproduction they ensure, there is another option privileging things that are loaned, which are used as one pleases at a convenient moment. Thus is isolated in the relation of property to objects the component that corresponds to the mode of existence in the world of the projective city: availability, without the constraints of property or those of power. Human beings adjusted to a connexionist world will thus prefer, for example, to rent their main residence, since they often have to change it, or the cars they drive. This, in particular, is what distinguishes the streamlined human being of the projective city from the traditional figure of the bourgeois, who is always associated with heaviness, with weight (caricatures invariably represent him as fat). Renting is the form suitable to the project, to *arrangements* for a temporary operation. In fact, given the comparatively unpredictable character of fruitful projects, it is difficult to anticipate the kind of assets one might need. To full, outright ownership, it is therefore reasonable to prefer ready, temporary access to resources that are borrowed, employed or expended in the framework of the project, while maintaining sufficient flexibility to refund them when required.

But this kind of relationship to property is not restricted to the world of objects. It is just as valid in the sphere of information, where the optimal strategy consists in borrowing elements that can be recombined without having to become the exclusive owner of the ensembles to which they pertain. In some respects, intellectual rights may be treated as rental contracts. The main issues then concern the form that information must take if it is to have the characteristics of a property – that is to say, be subject to identification and, consequently, to protection such that borrowing is no longing possible without taking the form of renting. This presupposes, on the one hand, some form of objectification (we know that ideas, which are common goods, can be protected as such only if they are objectified in a patent, a process, or a work); and, on the other, a definition of the level starting from which protection is guaranteed (as we see, for example, in 'copyright' law, which restricts the extent of permissible quotations).

Does this mean that the anthropology underlying the projective city is indifferent to ownership? On the contrary, it takes an element at the origin of the liberal conception of property to its ultimate conclusion: connexionist human beings are the owners of themselves – not by natural right, but inasmuch as they are the product of a labour of self-fashioning. The advent of the projective city is thus closely bound up with another striking feature associated with the current change in conceptions of ownership and, in particular, the ownership we have over bodies, whether our own or those of others (e.g. in the case of organ transplants). This is the very significant growth in industries whose purpose is the exhibition of a self-image, from fashion, health, dietetics or cosmetics, through to the rapidly expanding personal development industry which, as we have seen, accompanied the reorganization of firms with the emergence of new professions, like that of coach. In this logic, property is dissociated from responsibility to others (which represented an additional constraint in the case of bureaucratic power, not to mention traditional patrimonial property). It is now defined exclusively as a responsibility towards the self: in so far as they are the producers of themselves, everyone is responsible for their bodies, their image, their success, their destiny.

The change in the relationship to work

As Max Weber insistently stressed, the formation of capitalism was accompanied by a growing separation between the domestic and professional spheres, in terms of both the modes of subordination and the accounting methods used in the home and the firm. Separation between the domestic unit and the firm was the corollary, in the property regime and for employers, of a separation between the person of the worker and the labour-power he sells on the market, for the wage-earning class. These two dynamics – which, according to many observers helped to define the very essence of capitalism – culminated in the organization of a capitalism of bureaucratized large firms, managed by competent, academically qualified salaried staff, distinct from the owners. For the second spirit of capitalism, the separation between family life and professional life, the family and the office or the factory, personal opinions and professional competence – a separation laid down in law in various forms (e.g. the offence of misusing company property, which aims to protect the firm's property in particular from the misappropriation of funds for the direct benefit of owners) – seems to be an established thing, if not always *de facto*, then at least in principle. Evidence of this is to be found in the fact that during this period a number of the critiques directed at capitalism, particularly by academically qualified personnel, focused on its failure to respect the distinction. Such, for example, was the case when employers were criticized for favouring their intimates, confusing the firm's interests with that of those of their families, or taking account, when it came to hiring or appraising people, of their employees' private lives, the morality imputed to their family or sexual life, or again of their political opinions.

In a connexionist world, the distinction between private life and professional life tends to diminish under the impact of a dual confusion: on the one hand, between the qualities of the person and the properties of their labour-power (inseparably combined in the notion of *skill*); and on the other, between personal ownership and, above all else, self-ownership and social property, lodged in the organization. It then becomes difficult to make a distinction between the time of private life and the time of professional life, between dinners with friends and business lunches, between affective bonds and useful relationships, and so on (see Chapter 7).

Erasure of the separation between private life and professional life goes together with a change in working conditions and rhythms, as well as methods of remuneration. The full-time salaried *cadre*, holding a stable job in a large firm, who embodies the second spirit of capitalism, is replaced by the periodic contributor, whose activity can be remunerated in different ways: wage, honoraria, author royalties, royalties on patents, and so on. This tends to blur the difference between capital revenues and labour incomes.

At the same time, the whole work ethic or, as Weber put it, the ethic of toil, which had permeated the spirit of capitalism in various forms, was affected. Associated in the first state of capitalism with rational asceticism and then, in the mid-twentieth century, with responsibility and knowledge, it tends to make way for a premium on *activity*, without any clear distinction between personal or even leisure activity and professional activity. To be doing something, to move, to change – this is what enjoys prestige, as against stability, which is often regarded as synonymous with inaction.

The transformation of everyday morality as regards money, work, assets and relations to the self supposed by the new spirit of capitalism is thus not tantamount to a mere adjustment or alteration at the margins, if we take seriously the new form of normativity underlying it, to which this chapter has been devoted. We are indeed witnessing a profound change in the type of normativity that permeated the second spirit of capitalism, not its continuation in partially transformed external forms.

The mystery we must now resolve is why such a change seemed to transpire without encountering any pronounced hostility. A priori, it is hard to imagine so significant a change in normativity provoking no significant struggle, critique, or reaction. Apart from the denunciation of exclusion, however, which is precisely a condemnation of the new connexionist world in terms of disaffiliation – that is to say, disconnection – which appeared at the beginning of the 1990s but remained largely unconnected with the new mechanisms of capitalism, at least until recently, it must be said that the new world became firmly established without a fuss. It was as if it had been covered up by the clamour surrounding the slowdown in growth and rising unemployment, which no public policies succeeded in curbing. Similarly powerless, critique was unable to analyse the transformation beyond exposing the new forms of social suffering. Quite the reverse, those in the vanguard of critique in the 1970s often emerged as promoters of the transformation. The following chapter is devoted to the history of the establishment of this new world and to the roles – active in certain respects, passive in others – played by critique in the years when it emerged and established itself.

Notes

1 Thus, for example, the sociologist Manuel Castells assembles the numerous transformations that have affected capitalist countries in the last two decades under this term: *The Rise of the Network Society*, Blackwell, Oxford 1996.

2 See Pierre Bourdieu and Luc Boltanski, 'La production de l'idéologie dominante', *Actes de la recherché en sciences sociales*, nos 2–3, June 1976, pp. 4–73.

3 Luc Boltanski and Laurent Thévenot, *De la justification*, Gallimard, Paris 1991.

4 Such a correspondence would have been impossible with a 'city of projects', for the organization '*of* projects' or the structure '*of* projects' refers to each project taken individually, not to the form that they confer, taken all together, on the social world. Let us make it clear that the term 'project' is to be understood in the management literature, largely inspired by Anglo-American authors, as referring to a process consisting in co-ordinating diverse resources with a precise aim and for a limited period of time (people speak, e.g., of a 'housing project'), without indexing to the same extent as the French term *projet* either the ideas of plan and planning, or the existential project's embodiment in a person and an indefinite temporal horizon.

5 Gilles Deleuze provides the genealogy of the modern concept of test – in the sense of test of strength – in his interpretation of Spinoza and Nietzsche. From Spinoza he takes the notions of 'composition between bodies' and 'encounter'. He uses them to coincide with Nietzsche in replacing the moral notions of good and evil with those of good and bad: 'That individual will be called *good* (or free, or rational, or strong) who strives, insofar as he is capable, to organize his encounters, to join with whatever agrees with his nature, to combine his relation with relations that are compatible with his, and thereby to increase his power' (*Spinoza: Practical Philosophy*, trans. Robert Hurley, City Lights Books, San Francisco 1988, pp. 22–3). What Deleuze calls here 'encounters' or 'combinations of relations' is the event that brings forces together and puts them to the test of one another. In this logic, forces precede bodies whose existence, purely relational, is the trace or inscription of their relation. It is the relation of forces, inherent in the encounter, that constitutes bodies, and hence states of the world. The displacement of ontology on to the test of strength unifies the natural order and the social order, and makes it possible to be free of morality: 'In this way, Ethics, which is to say, a typology of immanent modes of existence, replaces Morality, which always refers existence to transcendent values.' What is at stake here for Deleuze are the questions of consciousness and judgements that invoke reasons for acting, which must be reduced to illusions in order to vouchsafe a world stripped of

normative supports ('[t]he illusion of values is indistinguishable from the illusion of conscious-ness': p. 23).

6   One finds references to Handy in other authors – for example, Peters (1993); HEC (1994).

7   See Eric Leifer, 'Interaction Preludes to Role Setting: Exploratory Local Action', *American Sociological Review*, vol. 53, December 1988, pp. 865–78.

8   See Harrison C. White, 'Agency as Control in Formal Networks', in N. Nohria and R. Eccles, eds, *Network Organizations: Structure, Form, and Action*, Harvard University Press, Cambridge (MA) 1992, pp. 92–117.

9   See Michel Callon, ed., *Ces réseaux que la raison ignore*, L'Harmattan, Paris 1993.

10   See Mark Granovetter, *Getting a Job*, Harvard University Press, Cambridge (MA) 1974; and 'Economic Action and Social Structure: The Problem of Embeddedness', *American Journal of Sociology*, vol. 91, no. 3, November 1985, pp. 481–510.

11   See John F. Padgett and Christopher K. Ansell, 'Robust Action and the Rise of the Medici, 1400–1434', *American Journal of Sociology*, vol. 98, no. 6, May 1993, pp. 1259–1319.

12   See Cyril Lemieux, *Le Devoir et la grâce*, Cerf, Paris 1999.

13   'Thanks to his influence, his capacity for vision and guidance, he creates an atmosphere that invites everyone to confront new challenges, to have confidence and take the initiative' (Cruellas, 1993). 'This power tends to be replaced by a power consisting in influence, based on a capacity to listen, to understand situations, strength of conviction and moral authority' (Landier, 1991).

14   Callon, ed., *Ces réseaux que la raison ignore*.

15   Ronald S. Burt, *Structural Holes*, Harvard University Press, Cambridge (MA) 1992.

16   '"Where I happen to be physically has strictly no significance, as long as I am in western Europe". Then, I preferred France", he confides. In a traditional structure, Patrick would doubt-less be at the head of a fine lifeless laboratory. Instead, he directs a fragmented laboratory that is pursuing a hundred projects' (Ettighoffer, 1992).

17   See Pierre Bourdieu, *Distinction*, trans. Richard Nice, Routledge, London 1989; Bonnie H. Erickson, 'Culture, Class and Connections', *American Journal of Sociology*, vol. 102, no. 1, 1996, pp. 217–51.

18   '[A] *network* organization whose rules, based on relations that are both *informal* and *inter-personal*, are known only through the *experience*, which is difficult to communicate, of the actual people concerned' (Landier, 1991).

19   '[P]eople demand … more equality and justice when privileges form an increasingly subtle network in the organization' (Girard, 1994). 'String-pulling is the hidden or hypocritical side of networks, a contagious disease which, if not restricted, can endanger social cohesion' (Bellenger, 1992).

20   See Gilles Deleuze and Félix Guattari, *A Thousand Plateaus*, trans. Brian Massumi, Athlone Press, London 1988.

21   See Ronald S. Burt, 'Models of Network Structure', *Annual Review of Sociology*, vol. 6, 1980, pp. 79–141.

22   Paul Ricœur, *Freud and Philosophy*, trans. Denis Savage, Yale University Press, New Haven and London 1970, pp. 32–6.

23   See Noah Friedkin, 'Structural Bases of Interpersonal Influence in Groups: A Longitudinal Case Study', *American Sociological Review*, vol. 58, December 1993, pp. 861–72.

24   Robert Castel, *Les Métamorphoses de la question sociale*, Fayard, Paris 1994.

25   See David Stark, 'Recombinant Property in East European Capitalism', *American Journal of Sociology*, no. 101, 1996, pp. 993–1027.

26   See George Akerlof, 'The Market for "Lemons": Quality, Uncertainty and the Market Mechanism', *Quarterly Journal of Economics*, vol. 84, 1970, pp. 488–500; and *An Economic Theorist's Book of Tales*, Cambridge University Press, Cambridge 1984; L. Karpik, 'L'économie de la qualité', *Revue française de sociologie*, vol. 30, 1989, pp. 187–210.

27   Liberal analyses of corruption and illegal transactions thus show how they are made possible by obstacles, particularly of a regulatory or state order, curbing the formation of a transparent market: see Jean Cartier-Bresson, 'De la définition d'un marché de la corruption à l'étude des ses formes organisationnelles: un premier bilan des analyses économiques de la corruption', communication to the seminar on 'La corruption dans les systèmes pluralistes', Poitier, November 1993.

28   Adam Smith, *The Wealth of Nations*, Penguin edition, Harmondsworth 1976, pp. 232–3.

29   See Brian Uzzi, 'The Sources and Consequences of Embeddedness for the Economic Performance of Organizations: The Network Effect', *American Sociological Review*, vol. 61, August 1996, pp. 674–98.

30   See François Eymard-Duvernay, 'Conventions de qualité et pluralité des formes de coordination', *Revue économique*, no. 2, March 1989, pp. 329–59.

31   This is the kind of change that the concept of translation relates to in Michel Callon, 'Éléments pour une sociologie de la traduction. La domestication des coquilles Saint-Jacques et des marin-pêcheurs dans la baie de Saint-Brieuc', *L'Année sociologique*, no. 36, 1986, pp. 169–208.

32   See François Eymard-Duvernay and Emmanuelle Marchal, *Façons de recruter. Le jugement des competences sur le marché du travail*, Métailié, Paris 1996.

33   Not knowing exactly what they are searching for, left to themselves innovators are faced with a corpus of texts, articles, works, patents that is often vast and far removed from their own competences, where the selection of potentially useful information for some recombination demands knowledge and, more precisely, a sense of orientation that is acquired only through long experience. Why explore one direction rather than another? And select one work in library catalogues rather than another? The information transmitted in a personal relationship with someone trustworthy can entail a very significant economy in terms of time and effort. But there is more. It is in the relationship and personal exchange – in conversation – that information is conveyed with the determinations or, by analogy with music, the harmonics that give it meaning (this is the quality that justifies the existence of teachers). That is to say, more precisely, that it orientates it in the direction of the expectations and interests of the person receiving it, who, without this formating, would not be able to 'intuit' how it might be of use.

34   'Even with competitors, it seems indispensable to create opportunities and zones for co-operation that make it possible to learn from one another. In this way, possibilities for development in a wider system will be offered, without thereby eliminating or even reducing competiton, but directing it towards a non-zero-sum game' (Crozier, 1989). '[B]usiness athletes must *know how to "compete" in a way that enhances rather than undercuts cooperation.* They must be oriented to achieving the highest standard of excellence rather than to wiping out the competition. In the new game, today's competitors may find themselves on the same team tomorrow, and competitors in one sphere may also be collaborators in another' (Moss Kanter, 1990).

35   Burt, *Structural Holes*.

36   '[O]ne of the characteristics of a network existence is that it privileges individual communication or proximity and ignores mass communication' (Bellenger, 1992). 'Patagonia, which does not do publicity or promotion, uses lobbying. Thanks to its activities in defence of forests and endangered species, it has a network of some 250 ecological associations, which are sometimes very active, to develop its 350 sales points' (Ettighoffer, 1992).

37   'Our elites are trained not to hear. But the development of ever more complex totalities, the decline of traditional humanist constraints and reference points, and lastly the acceleration of the media whirlwind tend increasingly to obscure reality as it is experienced' (Crozier, 1989).

38   See Élisabeth Claverie and Pierre Lamaison, *L'impossible mariage. Violence et parenté en Gévaudan, xviie, xviiie, xixe siècles*, Hachette, Paris 1982.

39   See Bernard Urlacher, *La Protestation dans l'usine et ses modes d'objectivation: des graffiti aux tracts*, Sociology DEA, École des hautes études en sciences sociales, Paris 1984.

40 'In a family firm nobody kids anyone. Too much is known by all about all' (Toffler, 1990).

41 See Pierre Bourdieu, Luc Boltanski and Pascale Maldidier, 'La défense du corps', *Information sur les sciences sociales*, vol. X, no. 4, 1971, pp. 45–86.

42 Sabine Chalvon-Demersay, 'Une société elective. Scénarios pour un monde de relations choisies', *Terrain*, no. 27, September 1996, pp. 81–100.

43 Mark Granovetter, 'The Strength of Weak Ties', *American Journal of Sociology*, vol. 78, 1973, pp. 1360–80.

44 The following list of the changes that have to occur according to Sérieyx (1993) is sufficient indication of how the network world contrasts with the industrial world: 'from quantity production to quality production, from pyramid to network, from territory to flow, from simple delegation to the principle of subsidiarity, from centralized organization to self-organization … from personnel to persons … from reduction to order at any cost to recognition of the dynamic virtues of the paradoxical, the contradictory, the ambiguous, from regulations to the rule'.

45 See Irène Théry, *Le Démariage*, Odile Jacob, Paris 1994.

46 See Chalvon-Demersay, 'Une société élective'.

47 See Burt, 'Models of Network Structure'; Callon, ed., *Ces Réseaux que la raison ignore*; Alain Degenne and Michel Forsé, *Les Réseaux sociaux*, Armand Colin, Paris 1994; and Stanley Wasserman and Katherine Faust, *Social Network Analysis*, Cambridge University Press, Cambridge 1994.

48 It is thus, for example, that the model from *De la justification* that we have used here to give shape to the projective city, and whose original, purely descriptive aim was to contribute to an anthropology of justice, can be misappropriated to support a moral orientation tailored to the activity of networkers, if one regards the possibility – with which this model endows people – of changing ethical principles and legitimacy depending on the situations or worlds experienced as a mark of human excellence or the basis for a new morality: the 'best' are not 'rigid'; they know both how to engage and to alter their engagements; to adjust to the situation and to adapt to new situations, and so on. As a further example of the rapidity with which the new model is vulgarized, we shall cite the advice proffered by a family specialist recently explaining, on the airwaves of a national channel, that contrary to what had hitherto been believed, the new families of divorcees were far from being unfavourable for children's education, because they developed their capacity for adaptation in a complex universe, for adjustment, and for the construction of diversified links, which is precisely the capacity they will need to make their way in life and, in particular, to submit to the operations of the labour market.

49 The following management authors are the only ones to deploy comparatively recent references from the human sciences: Hervé Sérieyx, Omar Aktouf, Lionel Bellenger, Philippe Cruellas, Isabelle Orgogozo, Hubert Landier, Edmond Adam, covering only 11 text-files out of 66. As for references to contemporary scientists, they are used in two-thirds of cases by the same authors: Hubert Landier, Bob Aubrey, Philippe Cruellas, Hervé Sérieyx, Claude-Pierre Vincent and Lionel Bellenger, involving 3 text-files out of 66. It will nevertheless be observed that the 1990s authors are more open to the scientific works of their time than those from the 1960s, who confined themselves to a few management authors when they felt the need to cite.

50 Thus, for example, Aktouf cites Crozier, Peters and Sérieyx; Aubrey cites Landier, Sérieyx and Peters; Landier cites Aubrey and Sérieyx; Orgogozo cites Aubrey; Sérieyx cites Aubrey, Crozier, Genelot, Landier, Le Saget, Orgogozo, and so on. The network of citations nevertheless extends beyond the authors of the corpus since, of the 63 management authors cited, only 15 belong to our corpus. For the most part, the others involve writings predating our corpus or untranslated Anglo-American authors, who for this reason do not feature in the corpus.

51 The particular genius of Ivan Illich arguably consists in shifting the angle of vision in order to adopt a viewpoint on the most effective and most modern arrangements – those on which capitalism seems most justified in priding itself – which is that of those for whom these arrangements were not made, who are invariably still excluded or impoverished by them: that is

to say, the standpoint of the poor. Thus, for example, he observes the motorway from the viewpoint of the Mexican peasant who has to go to sell his pig at market, and assesses the speed of the journey (very low, in the event) entailed by this technical instrument examined from this angle (*Tools for Conviviality*, Calder & Boyars, London 1973). It is the effect of this switch of vision that might indeed be declared revolutionary. But for the same reasons, it cannot be recuperated by management literature.

52   Thus, we could take as an example Daniel Parrocchia's book *Philosophie des réseaux* (Presses Universitaires de France, Paris 1993), which, coinciding to a considerable extent with authors cited in *La Planète relationnelle* (Prigogine, Varela, Bateson, etc.), allows us to complete the standard list of references associated with the constitution of this paradigm by extending it on the side of philosophy (Wittgenstein, Deleuze, Lyotard), or the disciplines of communication and the cognitive sciences (Weaver and Shannon, Wiener, Turner, etc.), or mathematical modelling (Benzécri, Mandelbrot, Thom), or finally towards geography and the study of communication systems.

53   'Expatriate workforces that find themselves in the most cosmopolitan stopovers and places in the world are already familiar with this feeling: a feeling that sometimes distances them from their original community in favour of a very strong relationship with one another' (Ettighoffer, 1992).

54   The role of the United States and Great Britain in the creation of international financial markets eluding the legislation and financial controls developed after the great crisis of 1929 needs no further demonstration. Allowing British banks from the 1960s to develop the market in eurodollars, which grew very strongly especially after 1973, when the Americans lifted certain regulatory restrictions, the governments of the two countries unleashed a process that rapidly became uncontrollable. All financial centres have progressively had gradually to deregulate and lift any controls in order to withstand the competition of the City of London. See François Chesnais, *La Mondialisation du capital*, Syros, Paris 1994.

The Internet was initially conceived as a medium of absolute freedom, which obviously encouraged its very rapid development in the United States before it conquered the planet. Once the worldwide web was spun, and the anarchic creation of sites erected into a system, it was much more difficult to exercise any control whatsoever over the network, with the consequent abuses that we are aware of today (terrorist and Nazi sites, sites for trafficking of children, prostitution, etc.).

55   '[J]ams in the communication networks' (Blake and Mouton, 1969); '[t]he duality of circuits, functional and operational, means that the wires are joined only at the summit of the transmission networks. ... The functional network is no more subordinate to the operational network than it is superior to it' (Bloch-Lainé, 1963); 'the horizontal and vertical communications characteristic of work in a "network" develop' (Maurice *et al.*, 1967).

56   'Rather than regarding formal organization as an instrument for realizing the firm's objectives, they stress the informal relationships that intersect with the formal structure of the organization ... in such a way that this network can serve as a support for the organization's goals' (Monsen, Saxberg and Sutermeister, 1966). 'Networks that are *de jure* informal, but which are closely connected with realities, are constructed' (Aumont, 1963).

57   Sophie Coignard and Marie-Thérèse Guichard, *Les bonnes fréquentations: histoire secrète des réseaux d'influence*, Grasset, Paris 1997.

58   Their target is an article published in *Le Monde*, 14 May 1996, in which Mike Burke, 'a sociologist who studies *cadres*', declares that networks are no longer 'old-style clans, closed, exclusive, with systems of string-pulling', but 'laterally [unite] people from different departments in centres of common interest'.

59   See Parrochia, *Philosophie des réseaux*.

60   See Jacob Levy Moreno, *Who Shall Survive? A New Approach to the Problem of Human Interrelations*, Beacon House, New York 1934; and 'La méthode sociométrique en sociologie',

Cahiers internationaux de sociologie, vol. 2, 1947, pp. 88–101. It is to these works, focused on the issue of 'influence' and 'leadership' deemed central in a period marked by the mobilization of the masses behind the words of a leader, that we owe notions which are still at the heart of the contemporary sociology of social networks, like those of *clique* (individuals connected in a more or less stable fashion, forming a subsystem of communication within the general system); of bridges (individuals who, while belonging to one clique, make links with another clique); of *connections* (individuals who also build bridges, but without belonging to any clique); and so on.

61   An anthropologist pupil of Gluckmann, Jeremy Boissevain (*Friends of Friends: Networks, Manipulations and Coalitions*, Blackwell, Oxford 1974) has systematized the approach to the study of Mediterranean societies in terms of networks, on the basis of the seminal works of the Manchester School, particularly those of Barnes and Mitchell (see James Clyde Mitchell, ed., *Social Networks in Urban Situations*, Manchester University Press, Manchester 1969). His research has been particularly focused on phenomena of clientelism in southern Italy and then the island of Malta. He has brought out the importance of what he calls *brokers*, intermediaries and go-betweens between different networks. This term and the descriptions with which it is associated have since been widely adopted, especially by historians.

62   These models are often transposed today, more or less metaphorically, to the study of human societies. Moreover, it is this reference, implicit but frequent, that justifies the use we make of the adjective *connexionist*, in order to refer to some of the most specific characteristics of the new spirit of capitalism with one word.

63   Vincent Descombes, *Philosophie par gros temps*, Minuit, Paris 1989, p. 169. As a result, structuralism may indeed, as Descombes indicates, be regarded as the 'latest manifestation' of the modernist project: that of a 'unified science' which 'succumbs to the temptation of the grandiose programme', a phrase which (according to Descombes) Putnam uses to define the project of Carnap and the Vienna Circle. 'With identical enthusiasm Carnap believed in *Esperanto*, socialist planning and the ideal language of science, which is like a *cité 'radieuse* of the spirit [an allusion to the radiant city built by Le Corbusier, an expression of the modernist project in architecture]. ... That is why he and the Vienna Circle never stopped developing vast programmes or provocative manifestoes: soon, human knowledge would be reduced to physics, soon physics would be translated into purely factual observations connected by purely logical relations.' Similarly, for structuralism, 'it would one day be shown that the structures of representation are those of the mind, that the structures of the mind are those of the brain, and finally that the structures of the brain, which is a material system, are those of matter' (ibid., pp. 165, 169). Such programmes are *reductionist* in that they aim to transcend phenomenal appearances in order to unveil the underlying forms (structures) which are simultaneously deeper, more original and more real than the phenomena, *vis-à-vis* which they play the role of generating matrix.

64   Ibid., p. 170.

65   See Michel Serres, *Hermès ou la communication*, Minuit, Paris 1968.

66   Michel Serres, *Hermès II. L'interférence*, Minuit, Paris 1972, p. 128; Parrochia, *Philosophie des réseaux*, p. 59.

67   'In these points of connexion, it is a question of receiving a multiplicity of channels, whatever they might be, of flows, whatever they carry, of messages, whatever their content, of objects, whatever their nature, etc., and redistributing this multiplicity in any fashion. In the totality of exchanges that flow in the network, such and such a node, specific crest, starred centre or pole, performs the role of a receiver and redistributor, synthesizes and analyses, mixes, classifies and sorts, selects and emits. It imports and exports': Serres, *Hermès II*, pp. 130–31.

68   See Deleuze, *Spinoza*.

69   They make it possible to describe 'socio-technical networks', composed of collections of 'human' and 'non-human' beings (natural entities, animals, technical or legal constructs, etc.), wherein the connexions – defined as so many 'tests' where what is at stake is the possibility of one network being speaking for or representing another (being its 'spokesperson' or 'translating'

it) – would lead to the creation of more or less stabilized associations no longer subject to inter-pretation or controversy ('black boxes'). In particular, this is the case with 'scientific truths', which are presented as true statements once they have been accepted and no longer arouse con-troversy. See, for example, Michel Callon, 'Réseaux technico-économiques et irréversibilité', in Robert Boyer, ed., *Réversibilité et irréversibilité en économie*, EHESS, Paris 1991, pp. 195–230; and *Ces réseaux que la raison ignore*; Bruno Latour, *Les Microbes, guerre et paix, suivi de Irréductions*, Métailié, Paris 1984; and *Science in Action*, Open University Press, Milton Keynes 1987.

70   Chapter 12, 'Treatise on Nomadology: The War Machine', of Deleuze and Guattari's *A Thousand Plateaus* thus opens with a contrast between the game of chess and the game of go. The image of chess – which, as we have seen, was used by structuralism to underscore the rela-tional character of the relevant constructions – is still too ponderous from this standpoint, because the chess pieces have a fixed, legal identity, since it is written into the rules of the game. This restricts their movements and gives them the ponderousness of a *subject* endowed with a substantial identity. Contrariwise, the pieces in the game of go are empty units, which are filled or characterized only by their position in an arrangement of a reticular kind.

71   Here we are thinking in particular of the versions of Althusserianism that invaded soci-ological thought in the first half of the 1970s – for example, in an author like Nicos Poulantzas, whose influence was for some years considerable, before the sudden oblivion of the 1980s.

72   Without subscribing to the *marxisant* oversimplification of base versus superstructure, we cannot ignore the obvious analogy between these two forms of dualism: the critique in man-agement of hierarchical, planned organizations in the name of the fluidity of networks, and the critique in epistemology of systems in the name of multiplicity and chaos to which Jacques Bouveresse refers: 'The secret of success seems to consist in the consistent application of pro-cedures of the following kind: on one side, a series of notions that are connoted negatively – such as reason, system, order, unity, uniformity, law, determinism, necessity, repetition, etc.; on the other hand, their opposites connoted positively – (poetic) intuition, fragmentation, chaos, multiplicity, polymorphism, anomaly, chance, accident, invention, etc. It will be taken as estab-lished that the concepts of the first category, which have obviously served their time, have always been dominant and that those of the second category have been scandalously undervalued, neg-lected, ignored, suppressed, concealed, repressed, etc. Fortunately, the moment of revenge and reparation, which opens limitless perspectives for science, thought and humanity, has finally arrived' ('La vengeance de Spengler', in *Le Temps de la réflexion*, vol. 4, Gallimard, Paris 1983, pp. 387–8).

73   Oswald Ducrot and Jean-Marie Schaeffer, *Nouveau dictionnaire encyclopédique des sciences du langage*, Seuil, Paris 1995, pp. 180–81.

74   'In social network analysis … [r]elational ties among actors are primary and attributes of actors are secondary. Employing a network perspective, one can also study patterns of relational structures directly without reference to attributes of the individuals involved': Wasserman and Faust, *Social Network Analysis*, p. 8.

75   Granovetter, 'The Strength of Weak Ties'.

76   Very explicit in this respect is the founding article, now some twenty years old, published in 1976 by White, Boorman and Breiger. Sociology, they say in the preamble to this long method-ological work published in two successive issues of the *American Journal of Sociology*, continues to articulate notions like 'category' or 'class' that are legacies of the nineteenth century, whence they convey the archaic vision of a compartmentalized, closed world. It is time, they add, to dispense with this outmoded image in order to fashion new descriptive tools attuned to the open character of modern societies: '[a]ll sociologists' discourse rests on primitive terms – "status," "role," "group," "social control," "interaction," and "society" do not begin to exhaust the list – which *require* an aggregation principle in that their referents are aggregates of persons, collec-tivities, interrelated "positions," or "generalized actors." However, sociologists have been largely content to aggregate in only two ways: either by positing categorical aggregates (e.g., "functional

subsystems," "classes") whose relation to concrete social structure has been tenuous; or by cross-tabulating individuals according to their attributes (e.g., lower-middle-class Protestants who live in inner-city areas and vote Democrat). ... In contrast to the standard wisdom, there is a growing list of empirical findings regarding the effect (and frequency) of "accidents" and "luck" in the actual functioning of societies [i.e. the distance between the categorical model, which aims to identify the specific effect of "variables", and reality]' (Harrison C. White, Scott A. Boorman and Ronald L. Breiger, 'Social Structure from Multiple Networks. 1. Blockmodels of Roles and Positions', *American Journal of Sociology*, vol. 81, no. 4, 1976, p. 733).

77   See Degenne and Forsé, *Les Réseaux sociaux*.

78   The most influential of these works as regards our subject has doubtless been Jürgen Habermas's *The Theory of Communicative Action* (published in 1981 and in French translation in 1987). A bulky and not readily accessible work, its diffusion was facilitated by numerous commentaries. In our 1990s corpus, it is referred to by Orgogozo (1991).

79   See White, Boorman and Breiger, 'Social Structure from Multiple Networks'.

80   See Padgett and Ansell, 'Robust Action and the Rise of the Medici, 1400–1434'.

81   Our management authors do not miss the opportunity to mobilize this very reference to demonstrate that business has always been conducted with networks: 'Organization into networks in fact largely coincides with the history of economic development. We speak of "trading networks", "banking networks" and, more recently, of "television networks". The transition in the West from the feudal period, dominated by warlords, to the market economy in which we live today occurred gradually, through a continual effort to create new links. It was necessary to transport merchandise from far-off lands, and that required reliable correspondents who could be entrusted with one's interests. A key word: trust. Such, moreover, is the origin of the bill of exchange. The description Fernand Braudel gives of sixteenth-century practices is striking in this regard' (Landier, 1991).

82   See Gary Becker, 'A Theory of the Allocation of Time', *The Economic Journal*, vol. LXXXV, no. 299, 1965, pp. 493–517.

83   See Kiyokazu Washida, 'Who Owns Me? Possessing the Body, or Current Theories of Ownership', *Iichiko Intercultural*, no. 7, 1995, pp. 88–101.

84   'In feudal landownership we already find the domination of the earth as of an alien power over men. The serf is an appurtenance of the land. Similarly the heir through primogeniture, the first-born son, belongs to the land. It inherits him. ... In the same way feudal landed property gives its name to its lord, as does a kingdom to its king. His family history, the history of his house, etc. – all this individualizes his estate for him, and formally turns it into his house, into a person': Karl Marx, 'Economic and Philosophical Manuscripts', in Marx, *Early Writings*, Penguin/NLR, Harmondsworth 1975, p. 318.

PART II

THE TRANSFORMATION OF CAPITALISM AND THE NEUTRALIZATION OF CRITIQUE

3

1968: CRISIS AND REVIVAL
OF CAPITALISM

How was the new spirit of capitalism, and the projective city from which it draws justifications in terms of justice, formed? We shall seek an answer to this question by starting out from the dynamic of the spirit of capitalism in so far as its mainspring is critique. We shall show how the opposition that capitalism had to face at the end of the 1960s and during the 1970s induced a transformation in its operation and mechanisms – either through a direct response to critique aiming to appease it by acknowledging its validity; or by attempts at circumvention and transformation, in order to elude it without having answered it. In a more complex fashion, as we shall demonstrate, evading a certain type of critique often occurs at the cost of satisfying criticisms of a different kind, so that opponents find themselves disorientated, even making common cause with a capitalism they earlier claimed to be contesting. One of our objectives will also be to understand how the large-scale social mobilization that embodied critique at the end of the 1960s and in the 1970s could, in the space of a few years, disappear without a major crisis at the beginning of the 1980s.

In fact, one cannot fail to be struck by the contrast between the decade 1968–78 and the decade 1985–95. The former was marked by a social movement on the offensive, extending significantly beyond the boundaries of the working class; a highly active trade unionism; ubiquitous references to social class, including in political and sociological discourse and, more generally, that of intellectuals who developed interpretations of the social world in terms of relations of force and regarded violence as ubiquitous; a distribution of value added that shifted in favour of wage-earners, who also benefited from legislation affording greater security; and, at the same time, a reduction in the quality of products and a fall in productivity gains that were attributable, at least in part, to the inability of employers, directorates and management to control labour-power.

The second period has been characterized by a social movement that expresses itself almost exclusively in the form of humanitarian aid; a disorientated trade unionism that has lost any initiative for action; a quasi-obliteration of reference to social class (including in sociological discourse), and especially the working class, whose representation is no longer guaranteed, to the extent that some famous social analysts can seriously assert that it no longer exists; increased casualization of the condition of wage-earners; growth in income inequality and a distribution of value added that is once again favourable to capital; and a reassertion of control over labour-power, marked by a very significant reduction in disputes and strikes, a decline in absenteeism and turnover, and an improvement in the quality of manufactured goods.

Order reigns everywhere. The main objective of political action in Europe since the first crisis of modernity at the end of the nineteenth century[1] – the construction of a political order in which the capitalist economy could expand without encountering too much resistance or bringing too much violence in its train – seems finally to have been achieved. And this has been done without having to compromise with social classes represented at the political level, unlike the solution negotiated between the end of the 1930s and the beginning of the 1950s.

How could such a change have come about in such a short time-span? It is difficult to answer this question inasmuch as the period under consideration is not marked by any sharp political breaks – a change of political power in an authoritarian direction (like a military *coup d'état* with the proscription of unions and imprisonment of militants), for example, or an ultra-liberal turn (as with Thatcherism in Great Britain) – but, on the contrary, by comparative continuity. This was assured, in particular, by the arrival of the Socialists in government in 1981, which seemed to extend and entrench the May '68 movement politically. Nor can we evoke clearly defined economic events of major significance, like the Wall Street crash of 1929, for example. And the term 'crisis', used to refer to the years that followed the first oil shock, proves inapposite if, as is sometimes the case, one seeks to apply it to an entire period that was in fact marked by a massive redeployment of capitalism.

Our interpretation takes the revolt of May '68 and its sequels seriously (rather than stressing the symbolic aspects of what a number of commentators have treated as a 'psychodrama'); and we shall regard it as a major phenomenon from two contrasting angles. On the one hand, we are dealing, if not with a revolution in the sense that it did not lead to a seizure of political power, then at least with a profound crisis that imperilled the operation of capitalism and which, at all events, was interpreted as such by the bodies, national (CNPF) or international (OECD), charged with its defence. On the other hand, however, it was by recuperating some of the oppositional themes articulated during the May events that capitalism was to disarm critique, regain the initiative, and discover a new dynamism. The history of the years after 1968 offers further evidence that the relations between the economic and the social – to adopt the established categories – are not reducible to the domination of the second by the first. On the contrary, capitalism is obliged to offer forms of engagement that are compatible with the state of the social world it is integrated into, and with the aspirations of those of its members who are able to express themselves most forcefully.

I. THE CRITICAL YEARS

The worldwide conflicts that marked the year 1968 were the expression of a very significant rise in the level of critique directed at Western societies. Forms of capitalist organization, and the functioning of firms in particular, were the targets of the protesters and, as we shall show, this critique was not merely verbal but accompanied by actions that entailed a not insignificant disruption of production. A crude indicator of the level of critique, at least in terms of work, can be found in the statistics for the number of strike days, which averaged four million in the years 1971–75. By comparison, this number was to fall below half a million in 1992.

The combination of the social critique and the artistic critique

An important feature of the period around 1968 is that the critique of the time developed from the four sources of indignation we identified in the Introduction. The first two sources are at the heart of what can be called the *artistic critique*, while the last two are characteristic of the *social critique*. These two types of critique (which, as we have seen, are not automatically compatible) are frequently combined in the revolutionary movements of the second half of the nineteenth century and the first half of the twentieth, especially in France. But whereas the artistic critique had hitherto played a relatively marginal role because its investigators – intellectuals and artists – were few in number and performed virtually no role in the sphere of production, it was to find itself placed at the centre of protest by the May movement. The French crisis of May had the dual character of a student revolt and a working-class revolt. The revolt by students and young intellectuals was in fact extended to *cadres* or engineers who had recently left the university system, and served as a trigger for a very widespread working-class revolt.[2]

The workers, mobilized against the threats posed to them – especially wage-earners in traditional sectors (mines, shipyards, the iron and steel industry) – by the restructuring and modernization of the productive apparatus undertaken in the 1960s, would speak the language of *capitalist exploitation*, 'struggle against the government of the monopolies', and the *egoism* of an 'oligarchy' that 'confiscates the fruits of progress', in the tradition of social critique.[3] The working-class revolt can thus be interpreted as the result of the economic policy pursued since the arrival of the Gaullists in power, and as a response to the prolonged exclusion of unskilled and semi-skilled workers from the benefits of growth, and to an unequal distribution of the costs of growth borne by different categories.[4] Moreover, the employers' report of 1971 on the problem of semi- and unskilled workers would recognize the exceptional character of the French situation when it came to the wage inequalities suffered by blue-collar workers.[5]

Students (and young wage-earners recently graduated from universities or the *grandes écoles*), who had seen their numbers increase significantly during the previous decade marked by the university explosion (the number of students enrolled in faculties virtually quintupled between 1946 and 1971, from 123,313 to 596,141),[6] but had simultaneously seen their conditions deteriorate and their expectations of obtaining autonomous, creative jobs diminish,[7] instead developed a critique of *alienation*. It adopted the main themes of the artistic critique (already pervasive in the United States in the hippie movement): on the one hand, the disenchantment, the inauthenticity, the 'poverty of everyday life', the dehumanization of the world under the sway of technicization and technocratization; on the other hand, the loss of autonomy,[8] the absence of creativity, and the different forms of oppression in the modern world. Evidence of this in the family sphere was the importance of demands aimed at emancipation from traditional forms of domestic control ('patriarchal control') – that is to say, in the first instance, women's liberation and youth emancipation. In the sphere of work and production more directly of interest to us, the dominant themes were denunciation of 'hierarchical power', paternalism, authoritarianism, compulsory work schedules, prescribed tasks, the Taylorist separation between design and execution, and, more generally, the division of labour.[9] Their positive counterpoint was demands for autonomy and self-management, and the promise of an unbounded liberation of human creativity.

The forms of expression of this critique were often borrowed from the repertoire of the festival, play, the 'liberation of speech', and Surrealism.[10] It was interpreted by commentators as 'an irruption of youth' (Edgar Morin), as the manifestation of 'a desire to live, to express oneself, to be free',[11] of a 'spiritual demand' (Maurice Clavel), of a 'rejection of authority' (Gérard Mendel), of contestation of the bourgeois family and, more generally, of domestic forms of subordination.

These themes, which revived the old artistic critique by translating it into an idiom inspired by Marx, Freud and Nietzsche, as well as Surrealism, were developed in the small political and artistic avant-gardes of the 1950s (one thinks in particular of *Socialisme ou barbarie* and *Internationale situationniste*),[12] long before exploding into broad daylight in the student revolt of May '68, which was to give them an unprecedented audience, inconceivable ten years earlier. They answered to the expectations and anxieties of new generations of students and *cadres*, and spoke to the discrepancy between their aspirations to intellectual freedom and the forms of work organization to which they had to submit in order to be integrated socially.[13]

Nevertheless, we must guard against inflating the divergences between the student contestation and the forms of protest expressed in firms into an outright opposition. Themes pertaining to both critiques – the social and the artistic – were developed conjointly in the world of production, particularly by technicians, *cadres* or engineers in hi-tech industries and by the CFDT. The latter, competing with a CGT that was firmly implanted among manual workers and skilled workers, sought to mobilize both intellectual workers and semi- and unskilled workers.

In the context of firms in the 1970s, the two critiques were formulated primarily in terms of a demand for security (as regards the social critique) and a demand for autonomy (as regards the artistic critique).

In those of its aspects directly related to work at least, the critical movement in effect challenged two types of division. The first focused on power and, more particularly, the distribution of the legitimate power of judgement. Who has the right to judge whom? According to what criteria? Who is to give the orders, and who is to obey? Its point of attack was most of the tests that involve the faculty of appraisal and decision-making at work, especially making decisions for others. It was expressed in a challenge to those in command and to hierarchy and by a demand for autonomy in the tradition of the artistic critique.

The second division concerned the distribution of risks and, more specifically, of the ups and downs in life experience directly or indirectly connected with market developments. The critical movement aimed to increase the security of wage-earners and, in the first instance, of those who, possessing neither savings nor an inheritance, were highly vulnerable to the impact of changed economic circumstances or modes of consumption on the productive apparatus. In particular, it applied to tests involving time and, more especially, those that define the kind and degree of solidarity linking the present to the past and future: for example, in cases where it is agreed to make holding a certain type of post dependent on obtaining a particular educational qualification, paying on a monthly basis, calculating a pension, or defining a level of unemployment benefit. The construction of stable intertemporal links (if I possess a particular qualification, I will be entitled to some particular post; if I occupy that post for so many years, I will be entitled to a particular level of pension) must ensure people's continuity between their current condition and potential future conditions. People at work being eminently changeable (they age, their capacities diminish or, on the contrary, grow with their experience), this operation can be performed only by stabilizing identity with categorial instruments (a category by definition including a number of individuals, collectively), hence guaranteeing people an *official status* that is itself dependent on their attachment to a category. Challenging the just character of tests assumes a different meaning depending on whether we are dealing with a test of performance or statute. In the first case, 'it isn't just' signifies that the relative reward, or the ranking of status, is not aligned with relative performance. In the second, 'it isn't just' signifies that people have not been treated in accordance with their statute (there was some special dispensation, privilege, etc.). Furthermore, we usually refer to 'justice' in the first instance and 'social justice' in the second.

The way in which tests are resolved concerning power and distribution of the capacity to deliver legitimate judgements on the one hand, security and the distribution of risks originating in the market on the other, affects the capitalist test *par excellence*: profit. Where the former is concerned, an increase in demands for autonomy, in the refusal to obey, in rebellion in all its forms, disrupts production and has repercussions on labour productivity. Where the the latter is concerned, protecting wage-earners against risks originating in markets has the effect of increasing firms' vulnerability to market fluctuations and increasing labour costs.

The demands for autonomy and security, which originally derived from different sources, converged in the years after 1968 and were often embodied by the same actors. On the one hand, it was obviously in sectors where protection was best guaranteed, and where the need for averagely or highly academically qualified personnel was great, that demands for autonomy could be expressed with most vigour – that is to say, in study or research services, teaching or training, belonging to the public sector, the nationalized sector, or large hi-tech firms where the CFDT happened to be particularly well implanted. On the other hand, those who did not have a statute often backed up their demands for autonomy with equivalent demands for protection. The young graduates who, faced with what they called the 'proletarianization' of their positions, demanded more autonomous, more interesting, more creative, more responsible work, did not thereby envisage quitting the wage-earning class. They wanted more autonomy, but within the framework of large organizations that could offer them job and career guarantees.

The conjunction of these two types of critique, simultaneously aiming for more autonomy and more security, posed problems. In effect, critiques focused on the fact that judging for others is unjust, contesting the command structure, and demanding autonomy – these lead to an emphasis on individual performance (people must be as autonomous as their ability permits). Contrariwise, critiques centred on the unequal distribution of market risk, which demand a strengthening of security, incline towards tests of a statutory variety. To press these two types of demands simultaneously, and radically, can pretty rapidly lead to demanding a world without tests – without professional tests in the usual sense, at least – which has some features in common with the communist stage in Marx (which, as we know, assumed a society of abundance). In such a world, security would be guaranteed to completely autonomous producers whose appraisal by a third party would never be legitimate (as we see, for example, in the dual demand for a student wage and the abolition of examinations).

The disruption of production

In May 1971, a meeting of employment experts from various West European countries, the United States and Japan was held in Paris under the auspices of the OECD. The rapporteur was Professor R.W. Revans, adviser to the Belgian Industry/University Foundation. This group conference was prompted by the 'phenomenon of a deterioration in workers' behaviour today', by a 'hardening of attitudes' and 'flagging motivation in industry'. The 'industrial economies … are undergoing a revolution' that 'crosses all cultural boundaries'. Occurring simultaneously in all the OECD countries, it 'is not restricted to workers', but is also 'influencing the conceptions and reactions of *cadres*'. This 'revolution' takes the form of a 'challenge to authority'. It is prevalent, so the report informs us, 'even in nations where the Protestant ethic was expressed with the greatest moral vigour and material success' (for example, Germany, the Netherlands, Great Britain or the United States, where some young people 'go so far as to prefer poverty or begging to factory work'). The crisis of capitalism was deemed especially acute in 'industrial France', which 'endlessly debates the need to construct a society "without classes, hierarchy, authority or regulations"'; and in Italy, a country where 'the effects of industrial conflicts and social malaise are constantly combined', and 'minor details of technical progress in workplaces … provoke conflicts whose violence is out of all proportion to their causes'. In these two countries, but also in Germany, 'established authority has been demolished in an organized, deliberate manner that sometimes takes the form of outright physical violence'.[14]

The crisis referred to by these experts was not imaginary; their concerns were justified. The very high number of strike days provides only a limited idea of a protest movement that equally found expression in a stepping up of the level of disputes, often accompanied by violence, and also (or above all) daily guerrilla warfare in the workplace.[15] If interprofessional national strikes remained within legal bounds, the same was not true of strikes in individual factories, 'where recourse to illegal and even violent action was frequent', signalling a clear break with the previous period.[16] In their work on 123 conflicts in 1971, Claude Durand and Pierre Dubois find instances of verbal violence (threats of violence, abuse, jeering at management) in 32 per cent of cases; heavy picketing (preventing wage-earners who wanted to work from entering company premises) in 25 per cent of cases; occupations in 20 per cent of cases; physical violence against the employer, *cadres*, supervisory staff, illegal confinements, or deliberate clashes with the police in 20 per cent of cases. Resort to some form of 'significant illegality' affected one in two strikes. Participation in illegal action extended to something like a third of workers.[17]

Strikes and open conflicts were not the only indicators of a crisis that manifested itself in many forms in firms' everyday operations: absenteeism; turnover, reaching 'a disturbing level for [the] normal functioning' of many firms and betokening 'an escape from the situation of work'; a 'quality of work and service' that 'increasingly suffers because of the workers' lack of interest', occasioning 'problems of delays and obstruction', and leading firms to include in their costs 'scrap and defects connected with a decline in the quality of work, the wastage of raw materials and the social costs of the climate of discontent'; 'go-slows remain as widespread as ever' and 'instances of sabotage are far from rare'; 'a working-class capacity to control output has crystallized in firms', and wage-earners are developing 'a kind of passive resistance that is expressed in a variety of forms', such as 'workers' resistance to timing, interprofessional pressures on the group not to exceed norms, concerted slowing down of the pace of work, refusal to apply the operating methods that have been laid down'. The same author, one of the most acute observers of the disruption of work in the 1970s, stresses 'the crisis of authority' and 'opposition to hierarchies' that exacerbate 'tensions inside workshops and offices' and lead to a 'risk of paralysis' in 'large production units', where 'young workers have made certain workshops ungovernable for supervisors', and 'monthly paid staff' – employees, typists, and so on – rebel against the 'work rhythms', 'harassment' and 'impoliteness of managerial staff'.[18]

The extension of these forms of resistance had direct and indirect consequences on production costs. On the one hand, writes Benjamin Coriat, 'difficulty in ensuring the pursuit of increases in labour productivity during this period' can at least in part be attributed to it. On the other, management sought to restore control over the workforce by 'overloading their apparatuses of supervision and control', significantly increasing control costs that were not directly productive. 'New categories of controllers, retouchers, repairers, etc., rapidly emerged. Thus repair workshops in manufacturing units had to review an increasing number of products for tests and various kinds of repair, even before they were delivered to the public.'[19]

The demands

Three sets of demands, associated with three different social groups but closely linked in commentaries, attracted particular attention from socioeconomists of work: the refusal of work by the *young*; the strikes and crisis of *semi- and unskilled workers*; finally, demands which, especially among *cadres*, express a need for autonomy, a demand for greater participation in control of the firm or, in its most radical forms, for self-management.

The refusal of work by the *young* – the 'allergy to work', as Jean Rousselet put it[20] – was the subject of a very large number of commentaries: the young no longer wished to work; above all, they no longer wanted to work in industry, and many of them were opting for 'marginalization'. In 1975, the recently created Centre d'études de l'emploi (CEE) devoted a notebook to what the authors called 'marginalism'.[21] The number of young people under the age of twenty-five who had a marginal, occasional activity was estimated by Rousselet to be of the order of 600,000–800,000 in 1975. The fact that they were not integrated into an occupation and regular work was attributed not by the youth specialists questioned in the CEE investigation to a shortage of jobs, but to a form of deliberate avoidance of wage-labour, the pursuit of 'a different lifestyle', working conditions that offered greater flexibility in hours and rhythm, transient 'schemes' that made it possible to maintain 'a stance that was detached, distanced from work', to be autonomous, free, without having to put up with the authority of a boss. The authors of the CEE research justifiably observe that the 'marginal activities' cited by the 'youth specialists' surveyed are not fundamentally different, in their content, from the jobs offered to young people on the labour market (for example, unskilled jobs in the service sector). What is different is the irregular, transient character of the activities dubbed 'marginal'; and one cannot fail to be struck by the similarity between the attitudes of the young denigrated at the beginning of the 1970s as betokening a 'refusal of work', and those that were to be extolled in the second half of the 1980s in so far as they supposedly displayed a spirit of resourcefulness and flexibility in the search for 'odd jobs'.[22]

The beginning of the 1970s was marked by a series of serious, long strikes: among the most notable of these disputes we might mention Rhodiaceta in 1967, Ferodo in 1970, Leclerc-Fougères (in the last two conflicts the management was illegally confined), Sommer-Sedan, Batignolles and Moulinex in 1971, the strikes by semi- and unskilled Renault workers at Mans and Sandouville in 1969–72, the bank strikes from 1971 to 1974, Lip in 1973, and Radiotechnique in 1974. In a number of cases, the initiative lay with *semi- and unskilled workers*,[23] not with skilled workers or craft workers, who had a longer and stronger record of unionization. Involved 'in the front line of social struggles' were 'immigrant workers, semi- and unskilled workers in automobile firms, unskilled workers in the electronic and textile industries, bank and insurance company employees, girocheque employees, packers at sorting centres, shop assistants in hypermarkets'.[24] As we shall see, the role played in these disputes by young, unqualified workers – sometimes, as in the west, newly urbanized workers – prompted numerous commentators – sociologists of work or 'employment experts' – to regard strikes by the semi- and unskilled as an indirect expression of rejection of the working conditions and forms of authority that obtained in mass production industries or in highly standardized services.

As Olivier Pastré has shown, the 1960s and the beginning of the 1970s were marked in France by an acceleration in the process of rationalization and Taylorization of work, which went together with a growth in the size of firms and increased concentration of capital.[25] Yet whereas in the 1950s work rationalization was accompanied by significant productivity gains, the relationship was inverted in the 1970s, characterized by 'pursuit of the process of

Taylorization' and a conjoint 'collapse in productivity gains'.[26] To explain this paradoxical relationship, Pastré invokes the 'crisis of work' in the 1970s, whose scope he seeks to measure by means of a number of quantitative indicators – absenteeism and turnover, in particular – which increased in different but invariably significant proportions in the main industrialized countries between the mid-1960s and mid-1970s. Without possessing the statistical series, the author amasses the indices of a no less significant rise in other manifestations of the crisis of work, such as obstruction, defective products, or even sabotage. As this study indicates, this phenomenon, far from affecting only assembly-line workers – something that would be insufficient to give it the requisite explanatory value, since they remained a minority despite the increase in Taylorization during the period – affected most categories of young wage-earners, including 'white-collar' staff, office employees, technicians or *cadres*.

The 'decline in the quality of work' was, according to Pastré, bound up with 'the improvement in the quality of workers that occurred at the same time'. Like many commentators on the crisis, in particular those belonging to employers' circles, Pastré regards the increase in educational levels accompanying the development of Taylorization as the main reason for the 'rejection of work': higher aspirations generated by a higher level of studies came into conflict with the generalization of work fragmented into individual operations.

The challenge to hitherto predominant forms of authority in firms, which constitutes one of the principles of the interpretation of strikes by semi- and unskilled workers, is quite explicit among *engineers and technicians*, who joined in the wave of protest at the beginning of the 1970s. A minority of *cadres* participated in the movement: it seems that they were basically young, university-educated *cadres*, still closely related to students, like young engineers in research centres or leading firms in high-tech sectors (aeronautics, electronics, etc.).[27] Even though they were a minority, the mere fact that they entered into open rebellion, unionized, and expressed their solidarity with blue-collar workers constituted an especially troubling sign for the management of firms. Did not the very existence of the category of *cadres*, albeit very heterogeneous in many respects, primarily mark a break with the working-class world and solidarity with the firm's design and supervision departments?

Among *cadres*, two demands were especially clear. First of all, a demand for security. It was bound up, especially among junior, self-taught *cadres*, with fear of unemployment and a loss of status following the restructurings and fusions of the mid-1960s. The expression of such fears was evident above all among CGT *cadres*, who included a majority of the highest-ranking *cadres*, promoted and self-taught.[28] Among graduate *cadres*, and especially young *cadres* belonging to the CFDT, the security dimension found expression predominantly in anxieties about the future, which were closely akin to the question – very important in student discourse – of 'prospects'. It was linked with fears about a devaluation of degrees as a result of the increase in the number of graduates during the period and the theme (associated with that of the 'new working class') of the proletarianization of students and *cadres*.

The second demand advanced by engineers and *cadres*, which was much more insistent than the demand for security, concerned autonomy. Moreover, this demand was not really new, *cadres* having taken a lead over other wage-earners in demanding autonomy. The management literature of the late 1960s that we have studied already suggested some solutions, with the generalized establishment of management by objectives. What was new in the demands of the 1970s was the challenge to the hierarchical principle itself, which was particularly worrying when it involved those who embodied that principle in firms; and an extension of the demand for autonomy beyond managerial *cadres* to all the occupations using graduate personnel. In its most radical versions, the demands extended as far as laying claim to 'democratic' control over firms.

In the CFDT, the demand for self-management and democracy in firms played a key role in *cadres'* participation in the 1970s movement.[29] It was accompanied by a critique of traditional forms of representation ('the existence of workers' committees in workshops means that there is no longer any reason for staff representatives') and traditional trade unionism ('we cannot demand democracy in the firm if the unions themselves are not democratic').[30] The self-management proposals of the CFDT, wholly unacceptable to the employers, would nevertheless inspire the renewal of managerial methods some years later.

2. REACTIONS AND RESPONSES TO THE CRITIQUES

Initially, the employers (active members of the CNPF, directors of large firms), in collaboration with the Chaban-Delmas government, interpreted the crisis *in terms of social critique*; they sought to calm things down by negotiating benefits in terms of wages or security with union federations at the national level, without conceding anything on points which, like demands for autonomy or creativity, were bound up with the artistic critique. Management of the crisis was situated on the terrain of employers–state–unions industrial relations, where tests of strength had been gradually codified and established since the 1930s, thereby assuming the form of legitimate tests. Contrariwise, demands for which no established framework existed (self-management, power relations, respect for people's dignity, etc.) were ignored or foiled.

In a second phase, confronted with what the employers regarded as the failure of this strategy, which proved costly and did not succeed in halting the protest or reasserting control over behaviour at work by either management or unions – disruption to production did not decrease significantly – innovative fractions among the employer class adopted a new interpretation of the crisis. From this there flowed a second strategy: the crisis would be construed *in terms of the artistic critique* – as a revolt against oppressive working conditions and traditional forms of authority. Employers would no longer anticipate a restoration of social peace from action by union federations, would stop negotiating social benefits with them, and would instead endeavour to circumvent them at a local level and in the workplace.

But the order of response to the two critiques – the social critique in the first instance, then the artistic critique – derived not only from an evolution in employers' thinking and opportunities, but also from a transformation of critique itself. In fact, at the end of the 1960s and the beginning of the 1970s, social critique in its most classical form, articulated by the working-class movement (for instance, the wave of adhesions to the CGT in autumn 1968), but also in Trotskyist and Maoist far-left activism, underwent a revival to the point of eclipsing the artistic critique, which had unquestionably been more in evidence during the May events. The artistic critique was to have its revenge in the second half of the 1970s, when the social critique seemed to be exhausted. This period was in fact marked by the flowering of 'new social movements'[31] (feminist, homosexual, ecological and anti-nuclear); by the progressive domination on the left of the ideas of its non-Communist, self-management fraction; and, throughout the 1980s, by a very harsh critique of communism, to which the analytical categories of totalitarianism were applied, without encountering the same resistance as in the 1950s or 1960s.[32] Given the especially strong association in France between social critique and the Communist movement, the discrediting of the latter was accompanied by a temporary but very pronounced abandonment of the economic terrain by critique. Under fire from the artistic critique, the firm was reduced to the function of oppressive institution on a par with the state, the army, the school or the family; and the anti-bureaucratic struggle for autonomy at work supplanted concerns about economic equality and the security of the most deprived. As was said at the time, 'qualitative' demands seemed more crucial, but also more revolutionary, than 'quantitative' demands, in that they attacked the very forms of capitalist accumulation.

We are now going to elaborate on the history of capitalism's two responses to the critiques of 1968 in greater detail. The first response accounts for the majority of initiatives between the Grenelle agreements and 1973, but extends beyond that date. The second response, whose effects are conspicuous above all from 1975 on, was in gestation among certain employers' groups as early as 1971 (year of the appearance of the CNPF's report on semi- and unskilled workers, which attests to an already advanced state of reflection on work organization and conditions).

A first response in terms of social critique

Characteristic of the first response was that it did not go beyond the solutions proposed by the second spirit of capitalism. It represented an attempt to improve its security mechanisms, as well as the sources of motivation, the latter being reduced to questions of pay on which employers gave way more readily, since the context of inflation made it possible rapidly to recoup what had been conceded. At issue was restoring an acceptable level of motivation at work, but without stepping outside the usual solutions and without conceding on demands for a transformation of work itself.

The disruption of production, the breakdown in work routines, challenges to the disciplinary forms obtaining in firms that rested largely on a compromise between industrial logic (compulsory working hours, performance measurement, etc.) and domestic logic (close control, respect for hierarchy, for the authority of senior figures, etc.) – these resulted in a significant increase in the number and intensity (including emotional intensity) of tests in the workplace. But because they were rooted in new kinds of conflict (often, for example, personal disputes with a line manager), and because they involved situations that had not hitherto been deemed problematic enough to require a high degree of formalization and control, these tests had difficulty arriving at an acceptable outcome of a procedural type, in local negotiation or the mobilization, for example, of staff representatives or union groups. However, given the risks of further degeneration involved in such uncertain situations, which demanded a rapid response, the actors who retained most control over the situation – that is to say, representatives of the employers' organizations and of the major union federations – agreed to reduce the multitude of local tests, which were difficult to interpret, without an obvious resolution, and often on the verge of violence, to the arena of identified, recognized, established and legally framed tests.

Here, no doubt, the *initiative* reverted to the *unions*, who were concerned to obtain tangible, cumulative results – something that was easier in the case of old demands, dubbed 'quantitative' at the time. Whereas local disputes were often characterized by the fact that they were not staged on the initiative of the unions (which caught up with movements arising from the base as they went), and sometimes broke out over individual conflicts (rebellion against a supervisory agent deemed abusive, for example), the work of transformation and translation performed by unions during them led to the emergence of 'economic' demands. Simultaneously of interest to the unions, because they could be extended to a statutory or categorial base, and regarded as negotiable by the employers, they involved such demands as the catching up of wages, monthly payment, and raising menial categories.[33] This attitude derived directly from the Grenelle agreements of May 1968, which had nevertheless not halted the strikes in the short term and had been rejected by the membership, which precisely found them too 'quantitative'.[34] As Durand and Dubois show, the prioritization of new 'qualitative' demands was slowly worked at by union federations. Whereas these demands were statistically very much in the minority when it came to official grounds for strike action, the disputes identified with them attracted comparatively more interest in the trade-union and general press. It was a question of learning to identify such 'new demands' and prioritizing them in disputes, rather than translating them into wage demands, thereby distorting them. But this learning process remained slow, and the majority of reasons for dissatisfaction continued to boil down to economic issues.

The way the unions understood the crisis in practice, by directing local, confused, emotionally charged tests, conveying a multiplicity of grievances, towards tests with a higher degree of formalization and generality, concerning wages first and foremost, coincided to a certain extent with *employers' expectations*. At least this was true of their most enlightened fraction, which regarded the concession of economic benefits, and even an institutionalization of relations with the unions, as a lesser evil. It is true that in 1968 France looked very different from other Western countries (the United States, Great Britain or Germany in particular). Its wage-labour trade unionism was highly fragmented, disunited in fact; and it had weak practical experience of negotiating agreements with employers, whether at national, sector or firm level – agreements that did not penetrate into the life of firms to any appreciable extent, and were invariably signed under pressure from the state. French employers could therefore certainly entertain the belief that strengthening one of the weakest Western industrial relations systems would not be very dangerous.

Employers' attitudes towards unions and predispositions to negotiation nevertheless differed between traditional employers – who, as ever, blocked union activity, and especially recognition of union groups in firms that had been obtained during the Grenelle agreements – and 'progressive' employers, who formed the majority in the team directing the CNPF after 1969.[35] Like the promoters of the 'new society' – Jacques Chaban-Delmas, and especially Jacques Delors – and like the sociologists of work close to the CFDT, these employers interpreted the forms that the May crisis had assumed in firms, and the agitation that followed, as the result of inadequate institutionalization of social relations between employers and unions, and a lack of negotiating practices at enterprise level.[36] Powerful but reasonable unions, in firm control of their membership, while not abolishing social conflict, would make it possible to establish institutionalized tests for solutions at all levels, and were regarded as an important factor in social peace and economic progress.[37]

At enterprise level, this policy came up against the hostility of a large number of company heads and also the weakness of unions, whose local implantation had always been contested (except in the public sector and major nationalized industries), and whose representatives had enjoyed legal protection only since the Grenelle agreements. The 'new society' therefore turned instead to negotiating agreements with the major union federations at national level – something that paradoxically, but in line with the history of French industrial relations, strengthened the role of the state in industrial relations, whereas Delors wanted to establish regular negotiations at enterprise level in order to disengage the state and depoliticize employer/union relations.[38] The employers' conversion to negotiations rested upon two convictions. The first was that the unions were more responsible, trustworthy, 'serious' than the working-class membership, or even union groups in firms.[39] There was a constant fear of unions being outflanked by their membership.[40] It was therefore advisable to strengthen national bodies by making interprofessional agreements with them. The second was that wild-cat manifestations of the new libertarian spirit, the multiple challenges to authority and hierarchy, the demands for autonomy and democratic control of the firm, and, more generally, the troubling symptoms of a 'rejection of work' (particularly among the young), these would be damped down by concessions on wages and, above all, by measures strengthening stability and security – that is to say, by agreements guaranteeing a *statute* to wage-earners in firms. At the time, the CNPF regarded 'continuous dialogue with the social partners', and the establishment of a 'joint policy', as means – so François Ceyrac declared in 1971[41] – 'of combining economic expansion and an improvement in people's condition in a single pursuit', and preserving economic development of the capitalist type against its detractors.[42] In this way, a 'model of society' was mapped out that would have its political translation in Chaban-Delmas and Delors's 'new society', which aimed to sustain the industrialization effort (the objective was 6 per cent growth in GNP a year) in a free exchange framework, by 'strengthening the cohesion of the firm' through a social policy based on categorial measures. This policy included raising low wages, reducing wage differentials, forward-looking personnel management, continuous training, the development of collective facilities, and so on.

This negotiating strategy on the part of the public authorities and employers was subordinated to the economic policy of the period,[43] and thus corresponded to what could be conceded in a context not yet marked by the 'crisis' that set in in 1974 (an economic crisis this time, not a crisis of governability as in 1968). With the opening of borders consequent upon France's entry into the Common Market, stress was insistently laid on industrialization – foremost objective of the Sixth Plan – and the competitiveness of firms – the result of the adoption of new techniques, concentration and internal reorganization. It was necessary to avoid social convulsions that would inflict damage on the entire system, and make concessions primarily on things that were conducive to this policy. (These included improvement in the quality of the workforce through continuous training and monthly paid status, which improved the working-class condition and made it possible to attract higher-quality personnel; and participation mechanisms for wage-earners, which sought to get them to collaborate in strategies for expansion.) Contrariwise, the brakes had to be applied in other areas (retirement age amid a shortage of manual labour, union rights in the firm challenging undivided authority).[44] The favourable economic climate (strong growth in output, inflation close to that of France's trading partners, full employment, equilibrium in the balance of payments) allowed room for supplementary concessions on the guaranteed minimum wage and purchasing power. The inflation situation, aggravated since 1968, was also suitable for negotiation, since employers can afford to be more 'relaxed' about wages when they can increase prices.

This corporatist policy issued in the *signature of a large number* of interprofessional national agreements, giving rise to the promulgation of laws and decrees, and was pursued by contractual negotiations at branch and professional levels. It would significantly enhance wage-earners' security, and contribute to establishing a statute for the wage-earning class. Among these agreements, which involved between five and nine million wage-earners, we may recall, in particular, the interprofessional national agreement on job security, obliging professions to create interprofessional regional committees (1969); four weeks' paid holiday (1969); introduction of a guaranteed minimum wage or SMIC (1970); the joint declaration on monthly payment (1970); the agreement on daily maternity payments (1970); the interprofessional national agreement on the right to continuous training (concluded in 1970 under pressure from Delors); the amended framework of the agreement on training and professional development (1971); the law on maximum working hours (1971); the agreement on early retirement and guarantees of resources, giving those entitled 70 per cent of their previous wage (1972); the law on the participation of immigrants in occupational elections (1972); the law providing for tougher penalties in instances of infraction of labour law (1972); the law proscribing illegal work (1972); the law generalizing supplementary pensions (1972); the agreement of guarantees in the event of compulsory liquidation (1973); the agreement on full unemployment payment (90 per cent of gross salary) for a year.[45]

The main trade unions participated in this policy of compromise, even if the CGT and the CFDT persisted with the logic of class struggle, and regarded it simply as a step on the road to an exit from capitalism. Evidence for this is their rejection of any law or agreement 'that would link improvement in the lot of workers to the prosperity of the capitalist system'.[46] The significance of these agreements should not be underestimated (as it was by most leftist movements in the 1970s which, in a spirit of fatalism about worst-case scenarios, regarded them as a mere ruse of capitalist reason). The post-May '68 years were marked in France by the most important social advances since the Liberation. The agreements concluded, and the laws and rulings promulgated, could henceforth serve as a contractual fulcrum from which to challenge the justice of the tests at work that capitalist accumulation depends on. Ways of making profits could more frequently be criticized not simply as unjust, but as illegal. The fact that the security or protection thus established were often of a categorial or statutory kind prevented employers from excessive manipulation of individual differences to set wage-earners in competition with one another.[47] If access to a statute is genuinely subject to a test, the categorial character of agreements reduces uncertainty and creates stable conditions such that 'everyone covered by the agreement considers *a priori* that the others conform to the indicated condition and does not demand proof of it'.[48] The negative converse is nothing other than what was not yet called the 'flexibility' but, for example, the 'fluidity of manual labour', which means that the vagaries from which the statute offers protection fall on individuals.

The agreements concluded in 1968–73 altered the distribution of value added to the advantage of wage-earners,[49] and enhanced their security in significant measure. They thus substantiated and terminated an initial definition of the crisis of capitalism in terms of demands for greater social justice – that is to say, benefits granted not to individuals on the basis of merit, but to collectives with reference to their overall contribution to the production of value added. As Delors clearly expressed the point in a book of interviews from 1974, social justice in the sense it was used in during this period is clearly distinguished from remuneration according to individual performance, which was rejected under the label of meritocracy.[50] Unlike meritocracy, which divides – since it ranks people according to their level of competence – and is by definition unstable – since the test of performance, to be legitimate, must be reversible – social justice is achieved when benefits are collectively obtained and are guaranteed, protected against any challenge, by a statute underpinned by a legal document.

In the period we are concerned with, however, these benefits or 'entitlements' were secured at the cost of maintaining the status quo as regards power in firms and autonomy.

In fact, the employers were less fearful of a test of strength with the unions over wages at a national level, than disruption of production and progressive loss of control at workshop and enterprise level. The example of the latent Italian May served as a foil and a warning. The disputes in the Fiat factories at Mirafiori offered an especially troubling example. It was during these conflicts in 1969 that the 'shop stewards' movement' was established, with its assemblies, representatives and factory councils. This was to spread to one hundred firms and, at the beginning of the 1970s, ended up assuming a significant degree of control over working methods at Fiat: overtime, assignments, transfers, grade promotions (so as to obstruct individual promotions and the divisions they create among wage-earners), and so on.[51]

Via the CNPF, the employers evinced strong opposition to any sharing of power at enterprise level. This opposition was maintained throughout the period, and was equally evident in the Lip dispute in 1973,[52] and, two years later, on the occasion of the Sudreau report on reforming firms. Proposals to grant 'each wage-earner a right of individual and collective expression', and 'to integrate representatives of the wage-earners with voting rights into administrative or supervisory committees', were singled out for criticism.[53] Employers' opposition to anything that closely or even remotely resembled self-management was equally apparent in the case of *cadres* and engineers, whose demands for autonomy did not for the most part, however, have the radical character of workers' councils.

At the end of the 1960s and the beginning of the 1970s, the CNPF – which, alongside the directors of large firms whose opinions were primarily expressed through the Centre des jeunes dirigeants, still contained a large number of employers from small and medium-sized firms – initially responded to the crisis of authority in traditional terms. They regarded any demand for control as 'dangerous and intolerable interference', to be condemned in the name of the 'natural laws of economics'. In 1968, the employers' federation thus reiterated the positions it had held prior to the crisis, as expressed, for example, in the common declaration issued by the general assembly of the CNPF in January 1965: 'When it comes to the managing firms, authority cannot be shared; experience consistently demonstrates that any other formula leads to impotence. And it is the presence of a man in charge at the head of the firm that is most conducive to authority being exercised in a humane manner and to guaranteeing the requisite dialogue with wage-earners.' On 21 May 1968, the CNPF's offices were occupied by a group of *cadres*. The following day, the CNPF released a statement condemning the strike and summarizing its earlier themes. In particular, in this declaration the CNPF expressed its reservations over 'participation', watchword of left-Gaullism, proposed by the government to respond to the crisis: 'Participation in firms can be a factor of efficiency only if it is based on a strengthening of structures, not on their destruction; on respect for hierarchy, whose authority must not be undermined by it.' As Catherine Gadjos writes: 'whereas talk about relaxing existing structures was ubiquitous, the CNPF spoke of reinforcing the old structures; whereas the authority of those who held the levers of command was everywhere under challenge, the CNPF demanded a strengthening of hierarchy and measures to guarantee the exercise of this authority, whose rationale lay in "the economic facts of life" that imposed themselves on firms or "natural economic laws"'.[54] The demand for participation was in fact to be translated into the language of involving wage-earners in profit-sharing and the development of employee shareholding. Rather than conceding power in the workplace, employers preferred to share the status of shareholder at a financial level.[55]

A second response in terms of the artistic critique

The first oil shock and the recession of 1974–75 accelerated challenges to the policy of corporatism. The employers developed a different social policy, and effected a series of changes. These changes, which were based on a second interpretation of the crisis of capitalism in the latter half of the 1970s, were implemented not *on the initiative* of the unions, but by *advanced sections of the employers*. A particular role was played by Entreprise et Progrès, which took the advice of 'experts', consultants, human relations specialists and sociologists seriously, and realized that the 'ideas of '68' were not to be rejected in their entirety.

According to this second interpretation, which had been formulated at the end of the 1960s, particularly by sociologists of work, the crisis of capitalism was not rooted in a demand for higher wages, still less in demands for greater job security. It was the expression of *rebellion against working conditions*, and especially Taylorism. Interest in working conditions, the critique of assembly-line work, consciousness of the relationship between job satisfaction and the performance of more complex tasks, executed more autonomously – these were so many themes that had appeared in employers' literature from 1970 to 1971. They were paths to be explored to confront the challenge to authority and, above all, to prevent future revolts,[56] strikes by semi- and unskilled workers in these years having seemingly triggered such reflections.

But explanations in terms of a rejection of Taylorism, credible enough in the case of semi- and unskilled workers, were insufficient either to understand why the revolt was only now manifesting itself, or to account for the significance of the crisis and its extension to the far more numerous categories of wage-earners who did not work on assembly lines. The rebellion was then interpreted by a number of observers as the product of the chance encounter of two independent causal series: the ongoing rationalization of work and – in the same period but for different reasons – a very significant increase in educational levels. This dual development thus brought together increasingly deskilled work, whose quality was ever more degraded, and increasingly skilled workers, whose quality was much higher than in the past. According to this interpretation, the upshot, especially among the young, was a feeling of *frustration*: their aspirations met with disappointment, since the test of work did not allow them to do the things that would have displayed their abilities, and to demonstrate their skills.[57]

This second interpretation contained a potential change of analytical perspective, which would become fully apparent only in the 1980s: the transition from a representation of social relations in terms of collectives, establishing an equitable relationship between whom was a matter of social justice, to an individualizing representation combined with a demand for justice – but this time in the meritocratic sense of differentiated remuneration of particular contributions and individual performance.[58]

The new way of interpreting the crisis did not emanate directly from actors on the ground – local employers, factory managers, or wage-earners and union representatives.[59] In fact, the stress on working conditions initially derived from reflection by work specialists – factory inspectors[60] or sociologists of work. It was only subsequently that the union federations, like the innovative employers' organizations, took up this theme as they sought to formulate 'new demands'. It was to be transformed by the CNPF into a slogan that was widely diffused by an extensive press campaign, and adopted by the political spokesmen of the government majority in 1973–1976. Improvement in working conditions and job enhancement, watchwords launched at the end of 1973, were to constitute major themes under the presidency of Valéry Giscard d'Estaing.[61]

There were many causes and reasons for this altered response. In addition to the 1974–75 recession, which, by reducing turnover and margins, functioned as a revelation and brought out the costs of the policy pursued since 1968, mention must be made of other sets of factors involving the employers and the critical forces respectively. As far as employers were concerned, as we shall see, it was clearly in their interest to switch policy. As for critique, its own evolution in the second half of the 1970s, partially isolated from what was happening inside firms, prompted it to alter the focus of its protest and the issues it concentrated on.

The corporatist policy pursued since 1968 had proved comparatively costly for the employers. Witness the shift in the wages/profits share of value added in favour of wage-earners during these years. In the previous period (1945–65), wage increases had accompanied productivity gains (in accordance with the principles of a Keynesian policy seeking not to repeat the mistakes of 1929–30, when significant productivity gains had not been passed on in wages, helping to precipitate the crisis). But from the beginning of the 1970s, what was observed in France and other developed countries was an appreciable decrease in productivity gains. In the second half of the 1970s, the periodic reports of the CERC thus indicated that the purchasing power of wage-earners was outstripping progress in productivity, and income distribution was hobbling returns to capital.[62] The gains in terms of job security also involved a significant cost, corresponding to greater socialization of risks and an enhancement of firms' responsibility for the consequences of job insecurity.

But the main problem facing employers was that, despite its cost, the corporatist policy had not produced the anticipated results. It had neither restored social peace, nor – above all – halted the process of disruption of production. On the one hand, the major union federations, while negotiating important national agreements, were reluctant to help establish the new contractual forms of professional relations at which the social policy of the 'new society' was aimed, and retained the achievement of socialism as their objective, even though the term had very different meanings for the CGT and the CFDT. On the other hand, on the ground spontaneous strikes proliferated, over which the unions could no longer guarantee control. As a result, Jean-Marie Clerc wrote on the basis of the daily reports by factory inspectors, 'we can speak of a new type of dispute, whose main characteristic is that it is unexpected, disconcerting throughout its duration and hence unpredictable'. The same author referred to a hardening in employers' responses, 'increasingly tough reactions' involving frequent recourse to lockouts.[63] Something else was needed to reassert the control over firms that appeared doubly imperative – on the one hand because work was constantly disrupted; on the other because the costs of such disruption were very high, doubtless even higher than the costs of the new gains that had been secured.

We find in Olivier Pastré's article an attempt to calculate, on the basis of disparate indicators, the costs entailed by absenteeism, delays, turnover, obstruction, defective work, below-average productivity, strikes and criticisms, protests or temporary stoppages in the workplace.[64] Drawing on various sources (the Commissariat au Plan, the Heilbroner Report of the Inspection générale des Finances, statistics supplied by the UIMM, and a study by Anthony Hopwood dating from 1979), Pastré concludes that factoring in these costs requires doubling or tripling the wages bill; or, according to other estimates, that they represent between 8.5 and 10.6 per cent of firms' turnover, or around 60 billion francs corresponding to more than 4 per cent of GDP. To the costs attributable to the disruption of work must be added the increase in costs of control, which are difficult to quantify but no doubt appreciable.

Employers' interest in working conditions also derived from a simple, realistic analysis: repetitive tasks, bereft of responsibility or autonomy, timesheets, and the scientific organization of work were no longer accepted to a young, highly educated workforce. In addition to a rebellion by the young, already mentioned, employers feared a manpower shortage in these years of full employment, with young French people refusing to do the hardest, most thankless jobs, and having to resort to immigrant labour. Like political officials, employers operated on the assumption of a reduction in or halt to immigration.[65] We find this issue clearly set out in a CNPF report of November 1971 on 'The Problem of Semi- and Unskilled Workers'. The author's starting-point is the idea that 'it is not unreasonable to suppose that in a few years there will be jobs which it will be impossible to find anyone to do'. Certainly, it is possible to call on women, 'whose natural adaptation to repetitive, simple tasks' is superior to that of men. But with women one encounters 'a prejudice on the part of managerial staff, who reckon that female employment is too expensive, particularly on account of absenteeism'. 'Has thought ever been given to the possibility – retorts the author of the report – that a fuller economic calculation would doubtless demonstrate that when the problems of adaptation, the alterations necessitated by the poor quality of the work, and the irregularity of output are factored in, employing a sometimes highly uneducated foreign workforce is infinitely more costly?'[66]

If nothing can be expected from the unions, who have proved incapable of channelling discontent, reject 'class collaboration', and push for the signature of costly agreements, the solution is to bypass them and abolish their mediation. The new social policy, declared François Ceyrac in 1978 during an interview with economics journalists, should not 'pile on new social benefits … but reform structures to give firms more flexibility and freedom'.[67]

The CNPF called this new policy 'competitive management of social progress'. The term 'competitive' refers not to increased competition between firms, or to setting wage-earners against one another, but to the competition that management must undertake with the unions to recover the social initiative. Firms must 'manage the social', and take care of the 'aspirations' and 'demands' of wage-earners. At enterprise level, the hierarchy, and especially supervisory staff, must seek to understand and, as far as possible, satisfy – even anticipate – the individual demands of wage-earners, leaving only collective demands to the unions.[68] This switch in social policy consisted in regaining control of the workforce from the unions and returning it to management.[69] Thus attempts to construct a strong system of industrial relations, after the fashion of France's commercial partners, did not last long, and French employers quickly reverted to their ancestral habits of independence and undivided authority. The more modernist among them even believed that such a withdrawal would bring more creativity, leaving everyone free to experiment in their own firm, whereas fears of seeing measures imposed in collective negotiations led those in charge to be far from innovative when it came to national agreements. At the end of the 1970s, the same CNPF leadership team that had promoted national negotiations admitted that it had been wrong: 'We have now understood that the old utopias had to be abandoned and the impossibility of reaching agreement with trade unions on a definition of the purpose of firms acknowledged.'[70]

This new policy chimed with developments in the thinking being done in international economic and political co-ordinating bodies. Thus, for example, the Trilateral Commission, which expressed the positions of financial organizations and multinationals seeking to promote an internationalization of capital,[71] proved favourable to collaboration with 'responsible union leaders' enjoying 'real authority over their members' in their 1975 report. But in a new report, published in 1978, the authors opted for the development of forms of direct participation in the workplace:

Recognition of the deficiencies of authoritarian management on the one hand and the limitations of representative systems on the other has led to the development of what Professor Trist calls 'work-linked' democracy. The focus of this approach is on replacing authoritarian management with semi-autonomous work groups, which have the responsibility to manage the jobs carried out by the group. The manager at all levels becomes much more of an examplar and supplier of technical expertise, more of a democratic leader than a dictator. The principles of work-linked democracy may be applied right through an organization and indeed often have been the method by which management is carried on at the upper levels of the managerial hierarchy. They are a central element in the Japanese *ringi seido* method of decision-making.[72]

Such a switch in strategy would not, however, have been possible without *a concomitant alteration in the critical forces themselves*, albeit for largely independent reasons. In particular, the weakening of the CGT in the second half of the 1970s, with the closure of a number of industrial sites where it was the most strongly established union – a development that was not offset by equivalent progress in new occupations in the tertiary sector – reduced the intensity of the critical pressure of 'quantitative' demands, to which the CGT was more committed than the CFDT. And it freed up a space for discussion of 'qualitative demands' at the very moment when the employers themselves began to think that their interests lay in displacing the social question on to the problem of working conditions. This switch in orientation was encouraged by the concomitant decline of the PCF, whose full extent is not conveyed by its gradual electoral erosion in favour of the PS in these years.[73] Simultaneously faced with a Leninist critique from the ultra-left, which accused it of revisionism, and intensified denunciation by other sections of the far left of its Stalinist past and ongoing compromises with the CPSU[74] – from the liquidation of the Prague Spring to the invasion of Afghanistan – the CP, torn apart by internal conflicts between the 'orthodox' and 'reformers' (at the time called 'Eurocommunists'), wavered between incompatible positions. One day it abandoned the 'dictatorship of the proletariat' in favour of a 'union of the French people', only to seek to maintain its revolutionary identity the next by multiplying attacks against the Socialist Party, to which it was bound in 1972 by the signature of the Common Programme, according to a political line that made 'union' 'a struggle that was to benefit the PCF in its endeavour to conquer power'.[75] The years of the Common Programme (1972–77) were not bad for the PCF: it took advantage of the protest wave initiated by the leftists, while presenting itself as more serious and reasonable than the 'irresponsible groupuscules' (which also allowed it to make up for the failures and ambiguities of its strategy in May '68).[76] It won new members, and retained a large part of its electorate. But the incoherence of its political positions simultaneously had the effect of disorientating numerous militants who – less well controlled than in the past and themselves sensitive to the critique of totalitarian institutions – increasingly took their distance from official Communist values, and a party that had remained Stalinist to the end.

The rupture of the Union of the Left on the initiative of the CP in 1977, attributed by the PS to the CP's tougher stance (under the influence of Moscow, which looked kindly on Giscard d'Estaing's presidency and did not want a left-wing victory), and by the CP to a rightist drift by the PS intended to break up the Union without taking responsibility for the rupture, would lead to defeat in the legislative elections in 1978. This defeat was to be attributed wholly to the PCF's intransigent attitude, and to hasten its downfall. From 1980 onwards, the internal decomposition of the Party was patent.[77] The trade unions connected with the Union of the Left were profoundly shaken by it. Unity of action between the CGT and the CFDT was broken off in 1979 – all the more so since the CGT vigorously supported the Soviet intervention in Afghanistan. The CFDT then adopted a strategy of reorientation, abandoning political engagement to devote itself exclusively to union demands. The dispute between the formations of the left and the increasing popularity of self-management ideas, against a Communist Party that was in the process of scuppering itself, sanctioned a transformation of critical sensibility on work issues. At the same time, there emerged a new kind of protest grouping, prioritizing rejection of totalitarianism. Itself especially sensitive to the artistic critique of capitalism, with its demands for liberation (particularly sexual), and a 'truly' authentic existence (feminist, homosexual, anti-nuclear and ecological movements), it was going to ally with the dominant new forces on the left. The change firms were working towards, which was to lead to the creation of new, direct forms of wage-earner expression and representation (quality circles, discussion groups, etc.), thus benefited from the critique of hierarchies developed in particular by the CFDT, the works of sociologists close to the self-management movement,[78] and leftist experiments in direct representation aimed against both employers and established unions.

It was on the terrain of working conditions that this new politics would assert itself. The attention paid to improving working conditions, 'making work more rewarding', or flexible hours had two effects. On the one hand, it won the support of a section of wage-earners by securing personalized benefits that collective action could not offer. On the other, however, by individualizing working conditions and remuneration, it handed the initiative back to employers.[79]

But the principal new departure consisted in recognizing the validity of the demand for autonomy, and even making it an absolutely central value of the new industrial order. This applied not only to those who were demanding it – academically qualified engineers and *cadres* in large firms – but also to those who were not demanding it, at least not explicitly – that is to say, blue-collar workers who had conducted most of the social struggles of the previous ten years. Measures aimed at giving wage-earners greater security were replaced by measures directed towards relaxing hierarchical control and taking account of individual 'potential'. *In a political reversal, autonomy was, as it were, exchanged for security.* The struggle against the unions, and the concession of more autonomy and individualized benefits, were pursued with the same methods – that is, by changing work organization and altering productive processes. This affected the very structure of firms and, in particular, had the effect of dismantling organizational units (firms, plants, sections, departments) and categories of persons (occupational groups, holders of the same type of post, social classes) – that is to say, the set of collectives on which critical bodies, particularly the unions, were based. As with the interpretation of the demand for student autonomy by Edgar Faure, autonomy was construed here in the sense both of autonomy of persons (less directly hierarchically controlled in their work) and autonomy of organizations (departments treated as independent units and autonomous profit-centres, or the development of subcontracting).[80] The world of work now contained only individual instances connected in a network.

Restoring control over firms – employers' key objective in this period – was not achieved by increasing the power of the hierarchy, the length of hierarchical lines, and the number of accounting tools or bureaucratic directives. It was secured thanks to a break with previous modes of control and an assimilation of demands for autonomy and responsibility hitherto regarded as subversive. To oversimplify, we can say that this change consisted in substituting *self-control* for *control* and, consequently, in externalizing the very high costs of control by shifting the burden from organizations on to wage-earners. A proven capacity for autonomy and responsibility constituted one of the new tests that made it possible to part simultaneously with oppositional workers and abusive petty tyrants, whom the new method of control, relying mainly on self-control, henceforth rendered redundant.

The series of changes in job organization and classification equally made it possible to render work sufficiently attractive for a young, French and educated workforce to adapt to it.

We find an inventory of the changes effected in a series of writings that attest to the intense intellectual effort undertaken by 'employer experts', and to the vast number of experiments in firms.

The *4ᵉˢ Assises nationales des entreprises d'octobre 1977*, which presented in the form of index cards several hundred 'innovations' introduced over the course of the decade in firms, medium or large, marked the first large-scale public manifestation of the spirit of '68 in the world of the employers. In his preface, François Ceyrac sketched a liberal interpretation (for which Michel Crozier had paved the way as early as 1970)[81] of the leftist criticisms directed at both the rigidity of industrial-style planning and the hierarchical forms of the domestic world: the 'reality of firms' was 'diverse, fluid, differentiated ... refractory by its very nature to rigid, abstract organizational formulas, to pre-established schemas'; and the firm was the privileged site of 'social innovation, creative imagination, free initiative'. The two thick volumes were divided into six chapters (communication in firms, training, improvement in working conditions, reform of working hours, role of managerial staff, appraisal of social administration).

Thus, for example, in the chapter on *improvement in working conditions* we find an experiment conducted in a Rouen metallurgy firm from 1974 onwards, consisting in the abolition of assembly-line work in the assembly of electronic terminals, in order to 'afford everyone greater autonomy'; or again, the establishment of 'assembly units' at Peugeot from 1973, accompanied by a 'modification of hierarchical structures in order to reduce the number of levels of command and enhance workshop autonomy'.[82] A firm making industrial fans explained how it had been able to 'restore a taste for technical progress, in an improved social climate, to a workshop that was in a bad technical condition and socially unstable', by constituting 'work groups' led by an outside consultant.

The chapter on *reform of working hours* is especially informative, indicating the strategically crucial character of hours both for winning over wage-earners and for paving the way for greater flexibility, despite union reservations. In this chapter, we find numerous experiments in variable hours, part-time work, the 'flexible week', the staggering of holidays, 'adjusted retirement', and so on. An electronics firm employing 650 people describes an experiment in 'free time and autonomous teams'; a pharmaceutical laboratory outlines an experiment in flexible hours begun in 1973; the personnel management of a large store explains how part-time work has been developed; an insurance company explains the organization of systems of 'early retirement and end-of-career leave'.[83]

The CNPF's 1971 report on semi- and unskilled workers had already suggested some significant alterations in the organization of work itself, but did not have so many examples of successful experimentation to hand as in 1977, and called for an 'empirical ... and experimental approach, that is to say, engaging in appraisal of the results, examining trial runs, stepping back if necessary'.[84]

To start off with, the report stresses the necessity of *making hours more flexible*: 'The duration of work will always have to possess a certain flexibility and in practice this is the only way of adjusting production to the market'. It is necessary to move towards 'flexible hours, that is to say, accepting certain differences for part of the workforce. ... Over and above the fact that they can facilitate recruitment, such systems of flexible hours possess the advantage of giving those who benefit from them a sense of freedom, of autonomy, which satisfies an increasingly profound desire.' In addition, the author advocates the development of part-time work, particularly for mothers.[85]

It then commits those in charge of firms to exerting themselves on *conditions of security*:

> The emphasis of recent years on the problems of security (in connection with road traffic) and pollution will increasingly render industrial workers sensitive to the way in which these problems are resolved in the workplace. Heads of firms are therefore going to be subject to ever more intense pressures for an improvement in working conditions, security and hygiene. In fact – adds the author of this report – the solutions are so obviously conducive to good production that one sometimes wonders why such efforts were not made sooner.[86]

Finally, the essence of the innovations revolves around the *restructuring of work posts*. It is necessary to 'create a situation in which workers are intrinsically motivated by the work they perform', by assigning 'the worker a set of tasks adding elements of responsibility and participation. This will be the case when the functions of adjustment, control and maintenance of the material, even an improvement in methods, are added to specific tasks of execution.'

This restructuring requires '*a new conception of the role of managerial staff*, with supervisors playing not so much the role of boss as of adviser to autonomous groups, who are called on to participate in the manufacture of part of the finished product'. The main obstacles to the diffusion of this innovation will derive – so the reporter predicts – from managerial staff, whose behaviour it would be advisable to alter through 'the method of group work'. In fact, 'an evolution in methods of command is an indispensable condition for altering the image of industry'. *Cadres* could 'formulate a problem and ask the workforce for solutions'. The final phase, which is still largely hypothetical, consists in wage-earners themselves 'identifying the problems, discussing possible solutions, and then arriving at shared decisions'. To achieve such outcomes, the best thing 'is perhaps to create an entirely new climate, based upon new norms'. The best way of achieving that is to 'construct a new factory, with new employees, and a new group of *cadres* disposed to implementing new managerial systems in this virgin environment. Once the new factory has been constructed, all efforts will focus on the creation of more efficient teams of workers'.[87]

Finally, we find similar proposals in the *report of the 'employer's experts' of the OECD* (1972), already referred to, with a still greater insistence upon the crisis of authority and the necessity of developing responsibility, autonomy and creativity to confront it. 'The criterion used for measuring individual success', we read in the report, 'consists less and less in technical skill, and greater emphasis is placed on a *constant ability to acquire new qualifications* and perform new tasks: thus social maturity will find expression in creative imagination and not in mastery of an age-old occupation.' 'Most of the ideas that have inspired these discussions', adds the rapporteur, 'assumed that a *more active role would be allowed workers* at all levels, whether that of the workshop or junior *cadres*, in the conception, organization and control of their work.' There follows the example of a Japanese firm that has had to struggle not against 'anarchy', but 'against its opposite – hyper-organization and rigid structures'. In order 'to create a situation where everyone is as involved as possible in their work', the firm organized 'small work groups that enjoy a high degree of autonomy and are also organized in such a way as to allow their members to improve their individual and social qualifications in their everyday work'.[88]

Thus, as early as 1971, on the occasion of this reflection on working conditions, most of the mechanisms whose diffusion was generalized during the second half of the 1980s were conceived, and then tested out. And this process was accompanied, as we shall see in subsequent chapters, by an increase in both the flexibility and the role of the unions.

This strategy (and in this sense the word is inapposite)[89] was pursued without an overall plan and without challenging the main 'social entitlements' of the previous period head-on or outright – which might have provoked violent reactions. The deregulation of the 1980s and reduction in the security of wage-earners, more and more of whom were threatened with job insecurity, was not the result of a brutal 'deregulation',[90] which would have been the case had most of the measures adopted at the beginning of the 1970s simply been abrogated. Reassertion of control over firms was achieved through a multiplicity of partial or local measures – of 'innovations', in consultants' terminology – co-ordinated by means of trial and error. More generally, it was effected by manipulating a series of displacements, whose character was morphological (e.g. relocation and the development of subcontracting), organizational (just-in-time, versatility, or reduction in the length of hierarchical lines), or legal (e.g. the use of managerial staff on more flexible contracts as regards salary, the greater importance of commercial law as opposed to labour law). Among these displacements was the transition from 'social justice' to 'justice'. These multiple shifts changed the nature of the stakes, the terrain on which tests were staged, the characteristics of the persons confronting each other in them, and the forms of selection that resulted from them. In other words, it changed the character of the whole society without a *coup d'état*, revolution or commotion, without wide-ranging legislative measures, and virtually without debate – or, in retrospect at least, without a debate commensurate with the upheaval that occurred.[91]

The many transformations initiated during the 1970s would be co-ordinated, assimilated and labelled with a single term in the following decade: *flexibility*. In the first instance, flexibility is the possibility firms have of adapting their productive apparatus, and particularly their employment levels, to variations in demand without delay. It would equally be associated with a move towards greater autonomy in work, synonymous with more rapid adaptation on the ground to local circumstances, without awaiting orders from an inefficient bureaucracy. The term was simultaneously adopted by management and the employers, and by certain socioeconomists of work hailing from leftist traditions (like Benjamin Coriat). Abandoning their erstwhile critical stance, these socioeconomists proceed as if the necessity of 'flexibility, characterized as dynamic', as a 'new form of totalization', imposed itself as self-evident.[92] For a decade – that is to say, until the re-emergence of a large-scale critical movement at the end of 1995 – flexibility was pressed in a narrative that would ossify with time, conferring a simultaneously anonymous and inevitable character on the developments of the last twenty years, in accordance with an organicist or Darwinian vision of history. This process without a subject, willed by no one, was supposedly the product of a collective reflex of adaptation in a situation whose external causes imposed themselves on agents – or, rather, on 'structures' – that were condemned to change or disappear. Oil shocks, globalization, the opening of markets, the growing strength of the newly industrializing countries, new technologies, changes in consumer habits, diversification of demand, increasing rapidity of the life-cycle of products – these had brought about an exponential increase in uncertainties of all sorts. And they condemned the ponderous, rigid industrial systems inherited from the Taylorist era, with its concentrations of workers, its smoking, polluting factory chimneys, its unions and welfare states, to inevitable decline. What disappeared from general commentaries on the evolution of society was something that seemed obvious to a number of analysts in the second half of the 1970s: the way changes in work organization and the condition of wage-labour made it possible to reverse a balance of power which was relatively unfavourable to the employers at the start of the period, and to increase control over work without a commensurate increase in supervision costs.[93]

Paradoxically, the consensus on flexibility was furthered by the Socialists' arrival in government and the integration of new economic experts into the state. On the one hand, these experts established a compromise between the demand for flexibility and themes derived from the left or the extreme left. On the other, they lent greater legitimacy to employers' demands by offering the backing of the most advanced sectors of economic science. Accordingly, we shall conclude this summary of capitalism's responses to the critiques of 1968 with a rapid overview of the 1980s. These years witnessed extensive implementation of the 'second response', thanks in part to the support of partisans of the artistic critique from the class of '68, who regarded the developments under way as marking a certain progress compared with the oppressive world of the 1960s.

The class of '68 in power: The Socialists and flexibility

There is no doubt that there was a rapid increase in labour flexibility and, correlatively, of casualization after the arrival in power of the Socialists (who had been elected on a programme that assigned a significant role to the protection of labour legislation). Abandonment of the index-linking of wages to prices – particularly of the minimum wage – and the possibility of 'catching up' at the end of the year, depending on negotiations firm by firm and the 'actual situation of the firm', were especially significant contributory factors. Paradoxically, the dismantling of collectives that developed especially under the Fabius government, after the turn of 1983, relied on legislative measures implemented during the first Socialist government by the Labour Minister Jean Auroux, with the opposite intention of 'reunifying the work community'. To take another example: the 1982 edicts aiming to restrict atypical work contracts by defining instances where they could be authorized had the effect of conferring a kind of official recognition on them. More profoundly, the important Auroux laws of 1982–83 (a third of labour laws were rewritten in these years), aiming to strengthen the role of the unions by guaranteeing them official recognition in the workplace, had an unforeseen result, which was certainly alien to the wishes of their promoters and initially unnoticed by employers, who were very hostile to them. They favoured casualization and individualization of working conditions, by displacing negotiations to enterprise level. By giving consultative powers to works councils and making the holding of annual negotiations at enterprise level obligatory, the Auroux laws had the unintended effect of wrecking the hitherto centralized character of the industrial relations system. Between 1982 and 1986, the number of agreements reached at branch level fell by half, while the number reached at enterprise level more than doubled.[94] However, the unions, relatively powerful in national negotiating bodies, were often very weak locally; and this was even truer as one moves from the public or nationalized sector to large firms and, above all, small and medium-sized firms. Back in power after 1986, the right pursued the deregulatory work of the Socialists, notably with the introduction by the new Labour Minister, Philippe Séguin, of additional facilities as regards the organization of working hours and the abolition of administrative authorization of redundancy. Moreover, the effectiveness of the latter had always been more symbolic than real, given the very limited character of the obstacles the clause put in the way of redundancies.[95] We shall elaborate on these different issues in the next two chapters.

The support paradoxically given by the left in government to moves leading to reduced security for wage-earners, and to a drastic cut in the power of its traditional union allies, is obviously explained by the economic and social circumstances of France in the 1980s. Acknowledging that social measures were insufficient to deal with unemployment amid a continuous rise in the number of those seeking work, and having to confront the impossibility of the state itself taking people on – which would have aggravated the budget deficit – politicians gradually became accustomed to the idea that only firms could solve the problem, by creating jobs. Logically enough, not being able to force them to do this, the government listened to the demands from heads of firms, who claimed that greater flexibility would enable them to hire.[96] At the same time, employment difficulties restricted the bargaining power of the unions, which were less confident of mobilizing their membership bases. The reversal in the balance of forces between employers and unions was thus inscribed in the economic situation.

But this analysis neglects the role of the *new elites won over to the artistic critique* and distrustful of the old social critique, which was too closely associated with Communism in France. In actual fact, the policy of flexibility was not simply pursued in desperation, but also found numerous champions within the left-wing government.

Between 1981 and 1983, numerous left-wing or extreme-left militants, self-taught trade unionists, or, most often, statisticians, sociologists and economists trained in universities or the *grandes écoles* attained official positions in the state or public bodies: ministerial advisers, research departments answerable to the Labour Ministry, committees of experts, Commissariat au plan, advisers to mayors of large towns, laboratories linked by constantly renewed contracts to regional authorities, and so on. A significant percentage of these new experts in the socioeconomics of work had supported the CFDT's reorientation in 1978 – that is to say, the transition from an aggressive policy (notably in the maximum use of existing law to expand the field of demands), characteristic of the 1970s, to a policy that made negotiation, contractual agreements and realistic compromises its main objective. The CFDT's switch in attitude also focused on the reform of working hours, which could be submitted to local negotiation in exchange for a reduction in working time.[97]

Now in office, close to political power, these left-wing experts assimilated employers' demands into their culture with remarkable rapidity – in particular, demands for flexibility. To understand this conversion, in addition to the change in attitude that frequently accompanies the transition from a critical stance to a position of responsibility – often described by the actors in terms of the test of reality – we must doubtless also take account of the way themes and postures derived from the oppositional left could be reinterpreted in such a way as to conform to new managerial requirements. This was particularly true of the leftist theme of self-management. Central since the 1950s among those fractions of the extreme left most opposed to the Communist Party and statism – notably Trotskyists (with Yugoslavia as a model) – but also to the inhuman character of Taylorism, this theme had been massively adopted by the new left, the CFDT and the PSU. In the event, expectations about self-management were, at least in part, able to be reinvested at the beginning of the 1980s in flexibility, the decentralization of industrial relations, and new forms of management. Japan replaced China in the Western imaginary as a Far Eastern model of humanism, something to rely on to mitigate the inhumanity of Western industrial societies.[98]

But this transfer of leftist skills to management was not restricted to the research consultancies associated with defining government social policy. It also affected firms. In their formative years, the *new consultants*, who in particular established local discussion mechanisms in the second half of the 1980s, had often participated very actively in the effervescence that followed May '68. In becoming professionalized, often after very eventful careers, they invested a specific skill in their work on behalf of firms – a skill acquired not in the form of a technical apprenticeship, but through their life experience. Their professional value was now sustained by their very person, their experience in its most personal dimension – even, in the case of those for whom spiritual commitment had come to take precedence over political commitment, its most intimate dimension.[99] They had become experts in the Foucauldian critique of power, the denunciation of union usurpation, and the rejection of authoritarianism in all its forms, above all that of petty tyrants. Contrariwise, they specialized in humanist exaltation of the extraordinary potential secreted in each person, if only they were given consideration and allowed to express themselves; in the supreme value of direct encounters, personal relations, particular exchanges; and in the proselytizing adoption of an attitude of openness, optimism and confidence in the face of life's ups and downs, which were invariably beneficial.

Finally, we must mention the rise of another group of experts, whose profile differed from that of the former *soixante-huitards*, but whose entry into dominant positions in administration and circles close to political power facilitated the socialists' turn in 1983–84, and the institution of the policy of competitive deflation. As Bruno Jobert and Bernard Théret observe,[100] the second half of the 1970s had been marked by the advent of a new politico-administrative elite, issued from the École nationale d'administration, the Polytechnique and ENSAE, ready to replace the old 'community of planners' around Claude Gruson, which had dominated the Plan and the Institut national de la statistique et des études économiques, especially its forecasting department, during the 1950s and 1960s. This group, composed of top-level economists, rooted the legitimacy of its expertise in its acknowledged authority in the international field of econometrics and microeconomics, dominated by Anglo-American academics. Starting from the mid-1980s, marked by the decline of the Plan, which was transformed into research departments with uncertain assignments, they invaded the forecasting department, profoundly altered the orientation of training at ENSAE, and acquired a preponderant influence over the budget department in the Finance Ministry. More generally, they concentrated most of the state centres of economic expertise in their hands (with the notable exception of the CERC) and, given the quasi-absence of centres of expertise independent of the state (linked, for example, to the unions, as in Germany), monopolized economic information and diagnosis. Witness, as an example of this change, the relative marginalization in terms of power and prestige of the departments within the INSEE responsible for statistical surveys, in favour of econometrics and theoretical microeconomics. The abandonment of the Keynesian policy of Prime Minister Mauroy (still marked by the influence of the 1960s planners), which followed the surge in American interest rates, capital flight and the sudden deterioration in the balance of payments in 1982, gave this group the opportunity to promote a different image of the state's economic activity. Whereas planners emphasized the state's redistributive function, and its role as arbiter between social groups, the new economic elites concurred in 'reducing public intervention as much as possible', and 'drastically reorienting its activities to make it compatible with the market'.[101]

CONCLUSION: THE ROLE OF CRITIQUE IN
THE REVIVAL OF CAPITALISM

The history of the years following the events of May 1968 demonstrate the real but sometimes paradoxical impact of critique on capitalism.

The first response by the employers to the crisis of governability was, so to speak, traditional. It consisted in conceding benefits in terms of wages and security, agreeing to negotiate with the wage-earners' unions, using the formula of industrial relations to damp down class struggle – which also meant acknowledging its reality. In so doing, the employers were simply observing the rules of the game fixed after the great strikes of 1936, which suggested a way out of the crisis via negotiations with the unions under state pressure. Focusing mainly on the issue of economic inequalities and the security of those who live exclusively from their labour-power, this first reaction was presented as a response to the social critique and an attempt to silence it by satisfying it. It must be said that the social advances of these years were very real, and hence that critique was effective.

Even so, it is also clear that the additional costs entailed by these benefits, combined with a more difficult economic situation, prompted those in charge of firms to look for new solutions – all the more so in that the level of criticism they had to face did not seem to drop despite the concessions. They then gradually introduced a series of innovations in the organization of work, with the dual objective of meeting another series of demands and bypassing the unions, which were patently unable to channel such demands, and were often outflanked by them. The effect of these new operational methods, which took the form of a mass of micro-developments and micro-displacements, was to render many of the provisions of labour law null and void in practice, even though they had not been repealed. This process was widely encouraged by a significant number of the protesters of the era, who were especially sensitive to the themes of the artistic critique – that is to say, the everyday oppression and sterilization of each person's creative, unique powers produced by industrial, bourgeois society. The transformation in working methods was thus effected in large part to respond to their aspirations, and they themselves contributed to it, especially after the left's accession to government in the 1980s. Once again, one cannot fail to stress the fact that critique was effective.

Correlatively, however, at the level of security and wages various gains of the previous period were clawed back – not directly, but via new mechanisms that were much less supervised and protective than the old full-time, permanent contract which was the standard norm in the 1960s. Autonomy was exchanged for security, opening the way for a new spirit of capitalism extolling the virtues of mobility and adaptability, whereas the previous spirit was unquestionably more concerned with security than with liberty.

The displacements operated by capitalism allowed it to escape the constraints that had gradually been constructed in response to the social critique, and were possible without provoking large-scale resistance because they seemed to satisfy demands issuing from a different critical current.

The PCF's central position in the vanguard of French social critique no doubt also explains the incredible reduction in its vigilance over its favoured issues while the displacements were under way. The non-Communist left's insistence on the themes of the artistic critique would possibly not have been so great had it not been for the PCF's monopolization of the theme of class struggle. Those who wanted to construct a different left, and found the PCF unconvincing because of its stubborn attachment to the Soviet model, could nevertheless not really attack the Communists head-on given their strong position in the working class, and the fact that they were (or had been) their brothers in the anti-capitalist struggle.[102] The desire to create a different model of society and organization from that offered by the Communists thus led to mobilizing different critical forces on the left and abandoning social critique to the PCF and CGT. Social critique would thus accompany communism in its downfall, and no one (or next to no one) would agitate in the short term to revive it, out of undue fear on the right – but also no doubt on the left – of seeming to want to give a new lease of life to a party that most people wanted to be shot of. This abandonment of the social terrain by a significant component of critique, and its occupation by a movement that was deemed more archaic with every passing day, and increasingly discredited, certainly facilitated recouping on this terrain what had been conceded on the front of the artistic critique.

The fact that some successes were simultaneously achieved by the artistic critique, with the shift in the focus of protest on to questions of mores or ecological-type problems, helped to conceal the growing disaffection with the bodies on which decades of conflicts had conferred a sort of legitimate authority, for the level of contestation generally remained high. The fact that critique focused on new areas did not seem to endanger the advances made on the old front.

Thus there is another way of explaining the transformation of capitalism and the emergence of a new set of values intended to justify it besides discourses on the inexorability of adaptation to new competitive conditions. Just as likely to inform us about the springs of change is an analysis of the critiques capitalism faced – which are more or less vigorous depending on the period, more or less focused on certain themes while neglecting others, more or less internally constrained by their own history – combined with research into the solutions advanced to silence them, without formally quitting the rules of the democratic game.[103]

What we have observed of the role of critique in the improvement, but also the displacements and transformations, of capitalism – which are not

always conducive to greater social well-being – leads us to underscore the inad-
equacies of critical activity, as well as the incredible flexibility of the capitalist
process. This process is capable of conforming to societies with aspirations
that vary greatly over time (but also in space, though that is not our subject),
and of recuperating the ideas of those who were its enemies in a previous
phase.[104]

Thus the second spirit of capitalism, which emerged at the end of the 1930s
crisis and was subject to the critique of mass communist and socialist parties,
was constructed in response to critiques denouncing the egoism of private
interests and the exploitation of workers. It evinced a modernist enthusiasm
for integrated, planned organizations concerned with social justice. Shaped
through contact with the social critique, in return it inspired the compromise
between the civic values of the collective and industrial necessities that
underlay the establishment of the welfare state.

By contrast, it was by opposing a social capitalism planned and supervised
by the state – treated as obsolete, cramped and constraining – and leaning on
the artistic critique (autonomy and creativity) that the new spirit of capitalism
gradually took shape at the end of the crisis of the 1960s and 1970s, and
undertook to restore the prestige of capitalism. Turning its back on the social
demands that had dominated the first half of the 1970s, the new spirit was
receptive to the critiques of the period that denounced the mechanization of
the world (post-industrial society against industrial society) – the destruction
of forms of life conducive to the fulfilment of specifically human potential
and, in particular, creativity – and stressed the intolerable character of the
modes of oppression which, without necessarily deriving directly from historical capitalism, had been exploited by capitalist mechanisms for organizing
work.

By adapting these sets of demands to the description of a new, liberated,
and even libertarian way of making profit – which was also said to allow for
realization of the self and its most personal aspirations – the new spirit could
be conceived in the initial stages of its formulation as transcending capitalism, thereby transcending anti-capitalism as well.

The presence within it of the themes of emancipation and the free association of creators brought together by an identical passion and united, on an
equal footing, in pursuit of the same project, distinguishes it from a simple
reversion to liberalism, after the parenthesis of the 'planist' constructs,
whether fascism or the welfare state, derived from the crisis of the 1930s.
(These 'planist' solutions had taken as their ideal state supervision of capitalism, even its incorporation into the state, with a view to progress and social
justice.) In fact, the new spirit of capitalism, at least in the initial years of its
formation, did not lay stress on what constituted the core of historical
economic liberalism – notably the requirement of competition in a self-sufficient market between separate individuals whose actions are co-ordinated

exclusively by prices. On the contrary, it emphasized the necessity of inventing different modes of co-ordination and, to that end, of developing ways of connecting with others integrated into ordinary social relations that had hitherto been neglected by liberalism, founded upon proximity, elective affinity, mutual trust, and even a shared past of activism or rebellion.

Similarly, the relationship to the state is not that of liberalism. If the new spirit of capitalism shares an often virulent anti-statism with liberalism, this has its origins in the critique of the state developed by the ultra-left in the 1960s and 1970s. Having started out from a denunciation of the compromise between capitalism and the state ('state monopoly capitalism'), this critique, linking up with the critique of the socialist state in the countries of 'real socialism', developed a radical critique of the state as an apparatus of domination and oppression, in so far as it possessed a 'monopoly of legitimate violence' (army, police, justice, etc.), and of the 'symbolic violence' practised by 'ideological state apparatuses' – that is to say, schools in the first instance, but also all the rapidly expanding cultural institutions. Formulated in a libertarian rhetoric, the critique of the state in the 1970s was apt not to perceive its proximity to liberalism: it was, as it were, liberal without knowing it. Thus, subscription to a violent denunciation of the state did not necessarily presuppose renouncing the benefits of the welfare state, which were regarded as so many legal entitlements. The critique of the state (like that, from a different angle, of the union bureaucracies) was one of the mediums for expressing rejection of the second spirit of capitalism and hopes, not formulated as such, of an original construct, reconciling opposites: a leftist capitalism.

The next stage of our analysis will consist in further exploring the displacements in capitalism during the second half of the 1970s and especially the 1980s, seeking to understand what has been dismantled – and how – in the course of these displacements. We aim to roll the rock of Sisyphus back up the slope once more, and revive critique, which, as we have shown, can never really claim victory. The following two chapters are therefore devoted to the socially negative effects of the transformation of capitalism over the last twenty years, in the knowledge that we are not unaware of its genuine contribution to autonomy at work and the opportunity for more people to make more of their abilities.

Notes

1 See Peter Wagner, *A Sociology of Modernity: Liberty and Discipline*, Routledge, London and New York 1994.

2 See Alain Schnapp and Pierre Vidal-Naquet, *Journal de la commune étudiante. Textes et documents, novembre 1967–juin 1968*, Seuil, Paris 1988.

3 Quoted in Philippe Bénéton and Jean Touchard, 'The Interpretations of the Crisis of May/June 1968', translated in Keith A. Reader, *The May 1968 Events in France: Reproductions and Interpretations*, Macmillan, Basingstoke and London 1993, pp. 20–47.

4 See Chris Howell, *Regulating Labor: The State and Industrial Relations Reform in Postwar France*, Princeton University Press, Princeton 1992, p. 61.

5 'The technical institute of wages has published a study that compares the unskilled or semi-skilled blue-collar worker with the fully qualified engineer, and tends to show that the hierarchy is decidedly more open in France than in Germany and other countries. In this study, it emerges that the wages hierarchy in Germany, England and the United States is of the order of 2.5, while in France it is of the order of 4. Moreover, in a certain number of industries, for the reference period, and sticking to Germany, which is the closest to France in its structure, the French *cadre* has a purchasing power 11 per cent greater that of the German *cadre*, and the French blue-collar worker a purchasing power 16 per cent lower that of the German blue-collar worker' (CNPF, *Le problème des OS*, CNPF, Paris 1971, p. 4). Similarly, Piketty shows that France is the Western country where wage inequalities were greatest in 1970, surpassing even those of the United States at the time (Thomas Piketty, *L'économie des inégalités*, La Découverte, Paris 1997, p. 19).

6 Pierre Bourdieu, Luc Boltanski and Monique de Saint Martin, 'Les stratégies de reconversion. Les classes sociales et le système d'enseignement', *Information sur les sciences sociales*, 12 (5), 1973, pp. 61–113.

7 The theme of the proletarianization of intellectual workers, introduced in 1963 by Serge Mallet (*The New Working Class*, trans. Andrée and Bob Shepherd, Spokesman Books, Nottingham, 1975) and Pierre Belleville (*Une nouvelle classe ouvrière*, Julliard, Paris 1963),was associated by the student movement with inequality of opportunity to complete university studies, and especially to capitalize on degrees in the labour market depending upon social inheritance – a theme given wide echo by Pierre Bourdieu and Jean-Claude Passeron's 1964 book *The Inheritors: French Students and their Relation to Culture* (trans. Richard Nice, University of Chicago Press, Chicago and London 1979). In the discourse of the student movement, the proletarian condition intellectual workers were destined for was characterized primarily by an absence of autonomy and subjection to tasks of execution, as opposed to creative work.

8 The rejection of the 'ideology of output and progress': S. Zegel, *Les Idées de mai*, Gallimard, Paris 1968, p. 93.

9 See, among many examples, the work published in 1973 under the editorship of André Gorz, *The Division of Labour: The Labour Process and Class in Modern Capitalism* (Harvester Press, Hassocks 1976). In Gorz's preface, we read: 'the fragmentation and specialization of jobs, the divorce between intellectual and manual labour, the monopolization of science by élites, the gigantism of industrial plant and the centralization of power that results ... none of this is a necessary prerequisite for efficient production. It is necessary only for the perpetuation of capitalist domination. For capital, all organization of work must be inextricably a technique of production and a technique of dominating those who are producing, because the goal of capitalist production can only be the growth of capital itself, and this goal, alien to the workers, can be realized through them only by constraint (direct or disguised)' (p. viii).

10 See Épistémon, *Ces idées qui ont ébranlé la France*, Fayard, Paris 1968; Michel de Certeau, *The Capture of Speech and Other Political Writings*, trans. Tom Conley, University of Minnesota Press, Minneapolis 1997; Alfred Willener, *L'image-action de la société et la politisation culturelle*, Seuil, Paris 1970.

11 Jean-Marie Domenach, quoted in Bénéton and Touchard, 'The Interpretation of the Crisis of May/June 1968'.

12 Raoul Vaneigem's book *Traité de savoir-vivre à l'usage des jeunes générations* (trans. Donald Nicholson-Smith as *The Revolution of Everyday Life*, Left Bank Books and Rebel Press, London 1983), which was written between 1963 and 1965 and published in 1967, unquestionably contains the most concentrated version of the themes of the artistic critique.

13 With respect to the development of management forms that we have sought to bring out, the students significantly took as their foil the representation of the *cadre* predominant in the 1960s. When alluding to '*cadres*', their spokesmen inextricably refer to the holders of

'technocratic power' and supervisors in the 'major capitalist firms'; to the 'petty tyrants' who 'tyrannize' the workers, or the 'intellectual workers', 'new proletarians', compelled to perform 'fragmented tasks' (Luc Boltanski, *The Making of a Class: Cadres in French Society*, trans. Arthur Goldhammer, Cambridge University Press/Éditions de la Maison des Sciences de l'Homme, Cambridge 1987, p. 219). A column by Maurice Clavel published on 12 January 1972 in *Le Nouvel Observateur* is sufficiently eloquent as to the disgust inspired by the figure of the *cadre*: 'Big *Hexagon* programme on *cadres*.... There were lots of *cadres* in it, young *cadres*, apprentice *cadres*. Living standards, retirement, salary scale, taxes, promotion, hierarchy, career – it had everything. This world is absolutely terrible, though the people themselves aren't to blame. ... Humour is out of the question. Things are too dismal. ... How can one avoid a kind of absolute hatred for these young elites. ... *Cadres* ... they'll be the enemy, since we definitely need one, alas! And there will be a fight.'

14 See OECD, *Les nouvelles attitudes et motivations des travailleurs*, Direction de la main-d'oeuvre et des affaires sociales, Paris 1972, pp. 11–12, 17, 18, 20, 23.

15 The wave of protest in firms at the end of the 1960s and beginning of the 1970s affected most countries in Western Europe. Readers can refer to the comparisons made by Pierre Dubois between France, Belgium, Italy, the United Kingdom and West Germany. In these five countries, the number of strikes and strikers and the number of days lost increased significantly in the period 1968–73. Much more so than previously, these strikes were often spontaneous, initiated by the rank and file even in countries like West Germany or Great Britain, where unofficial strikes are illegal. In addition, a radicalization of forms of action was observed in these countries during the period, such as occupations, expulsion of management, sequestrations, go-slows, sabotage, illegal sale of products by striking wage-earners, increased workers' control over apprenticeship, security (in Great Britain), hours, the organization of work (in Italy), and so on (Dubois, 'New Forms of Industrial Conflict', in Colin Crouch and Alessandro Pizzorno, eds, *The Resurgence of Class Conflict in Western Europe since 1968*, vol. 2, Holmes & Meier, New York 1978, pp. 1–34). The intensification of struggle equally, and perhaps even more enduringly and precociously, affected the United States, which saw the development of forms of open struggle (wild-cat strikes, sabotage, rejection by the rank and file of agreements negotiated by the unions, etc.) and latent struggle (absenteeism, turnover) (Gilles Margirier, 'Crise et nouvelle organization du travail', *Travail et emploi*, no. 22, December 1984, pp. 33–44). In these years, the journal of the Association national des directeurs et chefs du personnel (ANDCP), *Personnel*, devoted numerous articles to the 'crisis of authority in firms', to the 'more open indiscipline', the 'refusal to carry out orders or follow instructions', the 'concerted challenge to certain disciplinary rules', to campaigns of denigration against 'supervisors, derisively dubbed "petty tyrants"', and so on.

16 One can get an idea of the variety and creativity of the forms of action that developed in the 1970s by reading the description of 183 actions recorded by Claude Durand in his study of the iron and steel dispute at Usinor-Longwy between December 1978 and August 1979: occupations, demonstrations, blocking of roads and rail tracks, disrupting trains, the mass arrival of workers at work on a day when they had been laid off, occupying the Banque de France, occupation of the telephone exchange, blocking of the works council, ransacking of the Union partronale de la métallurgie, sequestration of the manager of the Chiers factory, attack on the police station, occupation of the office of the head of personnel at Usinor, unloading of a train laden with iron ore, assaults on temporary staff, occupation of the magistrates' court, overturning lorries, cutting a gas pipeline supplying the factory, blocking the supplying of oxygen factories, creation of a radio station, 'Lorraine Coeur d'Acier', march by 120,000 demonstrators on Paris, banners on the towers of Notre-Dame, etc. (Durand, *Chômage et violence. Longwy en lutte*, Galilée, Paris 1981). Readers will find an ethnographic description of critical attitudes in the everyday relationship to work, from go-slows to challenges to the organization of the line and supervision, in Philippe Bernoux, Dominique Motte and Jean Saglio, *Trois ateliers d'O.S*, Les Éditions ouvrières, Paris 1973, esp. pp. 33–7.

17 Claude Durand and Pierre Dubois, *La Grève. Enquête sociologique*, FNSP–Armand Colin, Paris 1975, pp. 221–2.

18 Claude Durand, *Le Travail enchaîné. Organisation du travail et domination sociale*, Seuil, Paris 1978, pp. 7–8, 69–81.

19 Benjamin Coriat, *L'atelier et le chronomètre*, Christian Bourgois, Paris 1979, pp. 197, 218. See also Olivier Pastré, 'Taylorisme, productivité et crise du travail', *Travail et emploi*, no. 18, October/December 1983, pp. 43–70.

20 Jean Rousselet, *L'allergie au travail*, Seuil, Paris 1974.

21 Gabrielle Balazs and Catherine Mathey, 'Opinions sur le marginalisme: analyse d'interviews de spécialistes de la jeunesse', in Jean Rousselet *et al.*, *Les Jeunes et l'emploi*, Cahiers du CEE no. 7, Presses Universitaires de France, Paris 1975.

22 The ANDCP's journal *Personnel* devoted numerous articles in 1972 to changes in youth and its refusal to 'work in industry' (the title of an article by J. Dupront, rapporteur of the Commission de l'emploi du VIe Plan). Take also these remarks by the employers: 'To genuinely unemployed people, who are not mobile or who are at any rate encountering serious problems despite a real desire to work, we must also add to some 30,000 registered young job-seekers a contingent of unregistered youth, which is often assessed at approximately 150,000. And it is a fact that attention generally focuses predominantly on this impressive mass of young people, their arms crossed and not working, it is true – but whether they are unemployed is a lot less obvious (at least if by unemployed one means someone who is actually looking for work but cannot find any)': UPRP (Union des organisations patronales de la région parisienne), *Combien de chômeurs?*, CNPF, Paris 1969, p. 10.

23 The fact that the number of strike days in the car sector – by far the most Taylorized – was in the region of 478,000 in 1971 and 330,500 in 1974, and represents between 10 and 12 per cent of all recorded strike days (compared with between 5 and 8 per cent from 1975 to 1980), is a good indication of the rebellion against fragmented work at the beginning of the 1970s. See Daniel Furjot, 'Conflits collectifs: les conditions de travail en mauvaise posture', *Travail et emploi*, no. 61, 1994, pp. 92–5.

24 Durand, *Le Travail enchaîné*, p. 7.

25 See Pastré, 'Taylorisme, productivité et crise du travail'.

26 The same phenomenon is observed in the United States in the automobile industry, where productivity rose by 4.5 per cent a year between 1960 and 1965, and by only 1.5 per cent a year from 1965 to 1970 (Emma Rothschild, 'Automation et O.S. à la General Motors', *Les Temps modernes*, nos 314–15, September/October 1974, pp. 467–86). The decline in productivity was perpetuated by a snowball effect: the reduction in productivity brought about increased Taylorization and an increase in the pace of work in order to expand output and enhance productivity as cheaply as possible, which in turn led to working-class resistance that caused productivity to drop.

27 See Renaud Dulong, 'Les cadres et le mouvement ouvrier', in *Grèves revendicatives ou grèves politiques?*, Éditions Anthropos, Paris 1971, pp. 161–326.

28 Marc Maurice and Roger Cornu, *Les Cadres en mai–juin 68 dans la région d'Aix-Marseille*, report of the Commissariat général au plan, LEST, Paris 1970.

29 We find a faithful echo of it in no. 82 of *La Revue du militant* (March/April 1969), published by the CFDT and providing an account of the five commissions that assembled 80 CFDT activists on 7 and 8 December 1968 to 'identify the experiments practised in May–June'. The first reported on the 'establishment of strike committees and commissions'; in some firms, these were not simply deliberative structures (an example: at the Clermont hospital the permanent action committee was the decision-making body, the staff having decided to run some of the hospital's services). The second commission cited the case of firms where 'the workers took charge of the instrument of production. In these instances, production was carried out whatever people's position in the hierarchy, whether the hierarchy was "in on it" or replaced by the workers

(the case of Pechiney: Lacq), who then proceeded to establish a much more streamlined structure, whose role was predominantly technical and where the allocation of responsibilities was
very flexible: collective decisions wherever possible, decision taken by the relevant party when
it was a matter of urgency. In this framework, a spirit of initiative allowed for expression of the
ingenuity of workers, who managed to solve problems the engineers had considered insoluble.'
'An initial observation' – writes the rapporteur of the third commission – is that 'taking power
in firms is possible: the outside, the context can be a stimulant, but the essential lies in the firm
and depends on us.' The members of the fourth commission state that in two cases out of six
they demanded powers (Rhône-Poulenc, Centre hospitalier of Nantes). They 'demonstrated
workers' managerial capacity in limited technical spheres', and the possibility of 'constructing
an experiment in a non-hierarchical organization of work'. Finally, the rapporteur of the fifth
commission reports demands aimed at 'a certain power over the organization of work and
training'. See CFDT, 'Pour la démocratie dans l'entreprise. Mai–juin 68, des expériences, des
documents, des faits', *La Revue du militant*, no. 82, March/April 1969.

30 Ibid.

31 The expression was coined to underscore the fact that what was involved was not 'class'
movements and, in particular, to signal their differences from the model of social movement
represented by the workers' movement at the time. The student movement was regarded as the
precursor of this type of grouping partially transcending class differences, even though it found
itself discredited as 'petit-bourgeois' – that is to say, reassimilated to the conceptual categories
of class struggle. Furthermore, this specific characteristic of the student movement was one of
the reasons advanced to explain the incomprehension of the events of 1968 displayed by the
CGT and PCF. Since the students did not constitute a 'class', they could not in any serious sense
be at the forefront of the challenge to capitalist society.

32 François Furet, *The Passing of an Illusion*, trans. Deborah Furet, University of Chicago
Press, Chicago 1999, p. 494. The 'new philosophers' (André Glucksmann, *La Cuisinière et le
mangeur d'hommes*, Seuil, Paris 1975; Bernard-Henri Lévy, *Barbarism with a Human Face*, trans. George
Holoch, Harper & Row, New York 1979) signal the turn from anti-capitalist *gauchisme* to the
critique of communism. Jean-Pierre Le Goff, *Mai 1968. L'héritage impossible* (La Découverte, Paris
1998) devotes a whole chapter – a very critical one – to the 'new philosophy', and makes it one
of the key turning-points in the permeation of the ideas of 1968.

33 See Michelle Durand, 'La grève: conflit structurel, système de relations industrielles ou
facteur de changement social', *Sociologie du travail*, no. 3, July/September 1979, pp. 274–96.

34 André Barjonet (*La CGT*, Seuil, Paris 1968), who, after twenty years as secretary of the
CGT's Centre d'études économiques et sociales, resigned in 1968, thus recounts how the CGT
reduced the vast protest movement that shook the country to a set of traditional demands, to
the great relief of the employers. 'On 20 May, in a speech to the Renault workers, George Séguy
vigorously asserted the strictly trade-union character of the strike. A request for contact ensued
from the president of the CNPF, M. Huvelin, who wanted to know whether this speech was a
snare or whether the CGT really was only pursuing economic goals, and who made it known
that, were that to be the case, negotiations could begin.' The CGT and PCF, in not pressing at
any stage for rioting or for the ousting of the Gaullist government (for which Raymond Aron
congratulated them in *Le Figaro* on 4 June 1968), demonstrated that they were the government's
best allies when it came to maintaining order. Furthermore, by agreeing to elections they had
no hope of winning, they likewise accepted recourse to established means of conflict resolution and an uninnovative end to the crisis.

35 See Jean Bunel and Jean Saglio, 'La redéfinition de la politique sociale du patronat
français', *Droit social*, no. 12, December 1980, pp. 489–98.

36 See Dubois, 'New Forms of Industrial Conflict'.

37 A declaration by the president of Alfa Romeo, published in *Il Giorno* on 11 May 1970,
sufficiently conveys the state of mind of European employers at the time: 'Wages are not the

real problem, and Italian industry can absorb the increases. But on condition that work can be organized and that production proceeds. Italy has accomplished its economic miracle because it has worked with creativity and enthusiasm. But today a spirit of continual rebellion, of making things worse to achieve one's ends, of reckless agitation seems to prevail' (quoted in Yves Bénot, *L'autre Italie, 1968–1976*, Maspero, Paris 1977, p. 113).

38 Howell, *Regulating Labor*, p. 85.

39 In the 1970s, a strengthening of 'responsible' trade unions was very widely regarded as one way to combat the risk of anarchy created by the excesses of democracy and egalitarianism in developed countries. See, for example, the 1975 report of the Trilateral Commission (Michel Crozier, Samuel P. Huntington and Joji Watanuki, *The Governability of Democracies*, Mimeo, The Trilateral Commission, 1975), which argued that the governability of a society at a national level depends on the extent to which it is effectively governed at the subnational, regional, local, administrative and industrial levels. In the modern state, for example, the existence of strong bosses at the head of trade unions is often regarded as a threat to the power of the state. Today, however, to have responsible union leaders with real authority over their members is not so much a challenge to the authority of political leaders as a prerequisite for the exercise of that authority (p. 7).

40 Thus, we read in the already cited 1972 OECD report, '[i]n France ... the agreements concluded following collective negotiations have been widely ignored in many cases and have been very vulnerable to attack from young activists': *Les nouvelles attitudes et motivations des travailleurs*, p. 20.

41 François Ceyrac was the manager on the employers' side of the social policy known as the 'corporatist policy'. The employers' conversion to negotiations was recent (Bunel and Saglio, 'La redéfinition de la politique sociale du patronat français'), and those in charge of firms were very concerned to maintain their autonomy, traditionally looking unfavourably on any delegation of power to the CNPF that might commit them to national or sectoral agreements, as well as on state legislation regarded as a fetter upon their freedom as employers. Although it was advocated from the beginning of the 1960s by the Centre des Jeunes Dirigeants, the switch to a strategy of nego-tiation occurred between 1965 and 1968, in all likelihood with the accession of François Ceyrac to the social vice-presidency of the CNPF at the end of 1967. Prior to the May events, this ori-entation was to be confirmed, and the rebellion seemed to vindicate the new leadership team, marked by Ceyrac's accession to the presidency of the CNPF in 1972. Although no CNPF leader ever said that he was negotiating 'because, faced with heightened social struggle, he considered it the only way of maintaining a capitalist form of development', employers' discourse in these years strongly suggests that this was the case (Durand and Dubois, La Grève, p. 180).

42 Ibid.

43 Ibid., pp. 187 f.

44 'The most expensive reforms (continuous professional training, monthly payment, profit-sharing) derived from initiatives by employers and government in the absence of genuine union pressure. They were part of the logic of the economic policy followed. The other reforms, which did not directly pertain to this logic (SMIC or the index-linked minimum wage, pensions), had less financial impact. ... Here are some examples of cost. Continuous professional training: in 1972, the year it was implemented, around 1.5 billion; starting from 1976, more than 4 billion a year. Monthly payment: approximate overall cost between 5 and 8 billion, essentially distrib-uted over four years from 1970 to 1973. Profit-sharing: provision for profit-sharing for 1968 (year of implementation) 0.7 billion; for 1973, more than 2 billion. SMIC: incidence of the more rapid raising of SMIC (relative to the average hourly wage) in 1971, 0.1 billion; in 1972, 0.26 billion. Pensions: cost of the December 1971 law, 1.9 billion over four years' (ibid., p. 189).

45 See Annette Jobert, 'Vers un nouveau style de relations professionnelles?', *Droit social*, nos 9–10, September/October 1974, pp. 397–410.

46 Durand and Dubois, *La Grève*, p. 183.

47 In offering statutory – i.e. lasting – guarantees that were not revisable depending upon economic performance, whether local or general, these agreements helped to shelter wage-earners from the vagaries due to market uncertainty, which were transferred on to other actors (managers of firms, shareholders, potentially the state, by means of incentives and subsidies). The definition of a statute tends to diminish the number, intensity and unpredictable character of the tests confronting workers. Take, for example, the case of monthly payment. In the mid-1960s, depending on the estimates, between approximately 7 and 11 per cent of blue-collar workers in processing industries were paid monthly. But access to monthly-paid status was invariably subject to foremen's judgement, and had the effect of provoking hostility towards those who enjoyed it, separating them from their peer group, whose working conditions they continued to share. For this reason it was sometimes the case that workers who had been selected by the management refused monthly payment. The generalization of monthly-paid status and legislation providing for the conditions of access to this category mean that it is no longer possible to hold out the promise of changed status in everyday work tests so readily (see Jean Bunel, *La Mensualisation. Une réforme tranquille?*, Les Éditions ouvrières, Paris 1973, pp. 60–63).

48 Francis Chateauraynaud, *La Faute professionnelle. Une sociologie des conflits de responsabilité*, Métailié, Paris 1991, pp. 166–7.

49 In view of the fact that the division between profits and wages in value added is a fairly stable ratio (around 1/3 – 2/3), one cannot but register the extent of the alteration of this rate in France during the 1970s: the share of wages (including social expenses), which was 66.4 per cent in 1970s, rose continuously to reach 71.8 per cent in 1981, the share accruing to capital being its complement measured by the gross surplus of exploitation. More than 5 per cent of national income was redistributed from capital to labour between 1970 and 1982 (Piketty, *L'économie des inégalités*).

50 'According to it [meritocracy], there is only one criterion of success and society is essentially based on a certain hierarchy. In our societies today, a benchmark model flourishes that allows a minority to accumulate all the advantages: power, money, interesting work, the lifestyle offering the most freedom. … The meritocratic temptation in fact exists in all societies. It nevertheless takes more acute forms in our country and is in profound contradiction with the aspiration to equality…. We are forgetting one of the major axes of socialism: collective advancement' (Jacques Delors, *Changer*, Stock, Paris 1975, pp. 138–9).

51 See Adriano Sofri, 'Sur les conseils de délégués: autonomie ouvrière, conseils de délégués et syndicats en 1969–1970', *Les Temps modernes*, no. 335, June 1974, pp. 2194–2223; Bénot, *L'autre Italie*, pp. 162–6; and G. Santilli, 'L'évolution des relations industrielles chez Fiat, 1969–1985', *Travail et emploi*, no. 31, March 1987, pp. 27–36.

52 'Ambroise Roux thought that Charles Piaget [the trade-union leader in the Lip dispute] was going to be prosecuted and convicted for theft, and that one could not support his intrigues if the idea was to avoid him gaining ground' (Henri Weber, *Le parti des patrons. Le CNPF 1946–1986*, Seuil, Paris 1987, p. 211). The Lip workers' struggle to save their firm, placed in liquidation in 1973, which would last three years, will remain the symbolic dispute of the turn of 1974. It represents one of the rare examples of self-management in France, for in 1973 the wage-earners decided to restart a production line for watches, market them, and pay themselves on an egalitarian basis. Enjoying very wide support among anti-capitalist associations and personalities, and highly favourable public opinion, the struggle embodied the attempt by wage-earners to defend their firms and jobs before such closures came to be regarded in the 1980s – including by their victims – as the inevitable result of economic determinism. The history of the Lip workers is recounted in Gaston Bordet and Claude Neuschwander, *Lip 20 ans après*, Syros, Paris 1993.

53 Weber, *Le parti des patrons*, p. 226.

54 Quoted in Alfred Willener, Catherine Gadjos and Georges Benguigui, *Les Cadres en mouvement*, Éditions de l'Épi, Paris 1969, pp. 15–16.

55   Employers' profit-sharing initiatives began before 1968. The first edict dates from 1959 and a second was issued in August 1967. But the movement continued after 1968 (February 1970: law on shareholding at Renault; December 1970: law on share options in limited companies; January 1973: law on shareholding in banks and SNIAS; December 1973: law on shareholding and profit-sharing [decrees in April and May 1974]).

56   See Durand and Dubois, *La Grève*, p. 365.

57   This is the thesis defended, notably, by Olivier Pastré ('Taylorisme, productivité et crise du travail') and certain Regulationists. In retrospect, it seems to us that these interpretations, offered at the moment of the crisis, conflate different causes that are valid for different groups. The rebellion of unskilled and semi-skilled workers cannot be attributed to a rise in their level of education. On the contrary, in France as in Italy, the second half of the 1960s and the beginning of the 1970s correspond to a period of rapid industrialization and an increase in unskilled jobs, which employers met by calling on workers of rural origin, newly urbanized workers, foreign workers, migrants from the south into the industries of northern Italy, and so on. As Charles Sabel puts it, these peasant workers had a very low educational level. They possessed neither work experience nor political or trade-union experience. They were not rebels against Taylorism, but aspired to a decent standard of living and wanted to be treated in a way that did not offend their dignity, their 'social honour'. According to this interpretation, the rebellions of unskilled and semi-skilled workers at the beginning of the 1970s were essentially the result either of a rise in the cost of living such that it no longer seemed possible to live decently, or of poor treatment by employers or petty tyrants impugning the social honour of the migrants. This would explain the fact that the major strikes by unskilled and semi-skilled workers often began with a local, apparently minor 'incident' – an insult, a personal confrontation in the workshop, and so on (Sabel, *Work and Politics: The Division of Labor in Industry*, Cambridge University Press, Cambridge 1982, pp. 132–3). By contrast, the interpretation in terms of rising educational level is certainly valid for young *cadres*.

58   See Alain Ehrenberg, *Le Culte de la performance*, Calmann-Lévy, Paris 1991.

59   A limited number of disputes – 7 per cent in 1971, for example – had working conditions as their main *official* demand (Michelle Durand and Yvette Harff, 'Panorama statistique des grèves', *Sociologie du travail*, no. 4, 1973), whereas a study of strikes at the beginning of the 1970s carried out by Durand and Dubois in 1975 (*La Grève*) shows that in 62 per cent of cases, union activists acknowledged that demands for wage increases were bound up with frustration at hierarchical relations and dissatisfaction over working conditions (Pierre Dubois, Claude Durand and Sabine Erbès-Séguin, 'The Contradiction of French Trade Unionism', in Colin Crouch and Alessandro Pizzorno, eds, *The Resurgence of Class Conflict in Western Europe since 1968*, vol. 1, Holmes & Meier, New York 1978, pp. 53–100).

60   Jean-Marie Clerc cites the following report written in 1971 by the regional directors of labour: 'To begin with, this discontent is expressed by demands over wages or related issues, demands that are poorly formulated, imprecise, and which in reality invariably express deeper dissatisfaction, sometimes of an unconscious kind, bound up with the conditions for performing work (repetitive tasks, uninteresting work, work rhythm, hours, resentment of hierarchy ...). This discontent often manifests itself in workshops employing numerous young people, of unskilled or semi-skilled grade, but also sometimes in workshops containing a large number of young professionals: too high a proportion of youth precludes any hope of promotion and makes the burden of everyday constraints impact more heavily. The expression of this discontent is sudden' (quoted in Clerc, 'Les conflits sociaux en France en 1970 and 1971', *Droit social*, no. 1, January 1973, pp. 19–26).

61   At the end of 1973, several study groups on improving working conditions were set up by the Labour Ministry. A brief on the technical, economic and financial aspects of the changes that might be introduced was given to the sociologist Jean-Daniel Reynaud. On 4 October, a bill for the improvement of working conditions was adopted by the National Assembly. It provided

for an expansion in the remit of the works council with the creation in firms of more than 300 wage-earners of a committee charged with studying these questions. Finally, at the national level an agency for the improvement of working conditions was created (Guy Caire, 'La France est-elle encore à l'heure de Lip?', *Droit social*, no. 11, November 1973, pp. 522–9). It seems that the creation of ANACT played a predominantly promotional role, at least at the outset. Thus, in the report of the National Assembly on the 1976 finance law, we read that 'nearly two years after its creation, the Agency has not really got off the ground' – something the report's authors excuse by reference to the very modest character of its means.

62 See Bruno Jobert and Bernard Théret, 'France: La consécration républicaine du néo-libéralisme', in Jobert, ed., *Le Tournant néo-libéral en Europe*, L'Harmattan, Paris 1994.

63 Clerc, 'Les conflits sociaux en France en 1970 et 1971'.

64 Pastré, 'Taylorisme, productivité et crise du travail', pp. 66–9.

65 In theTrilateral Commission report we have already cited, we find expressed the fear that an increase in the rate of immigration into Europe will lead to similar racial problems to those experienced by the United States in the period. According to Crozier *et al.*, prioritizing problems of work and work organization was the only way to reduce the new tensions affecting post-industrial society, which would otherwise risk fuelling irresponsible blackmail and new inflationary pressures. It was simultaneously necessary to restore the status and dignity of manual labour. This would help resolve the increasingly acute problem of immigrant workers in Western Europe, which would otherwise become the equivalent to the problem of racial minorities in the USA (Crozier, Huntington and Watanuki, *The Governability of Democracies*, p. 38).

66 CNPF, *Le problème des OS*, pp. 3, 11.

67 Quoted in Weber, *Le Parti des patrons*, p. 233.

68 See ibid., pp. 232–7.

69 Howell, *Regulating Labor*, p. 116.

70 Yvon Chotard, quoted in Bunel and Saglio, 'La redéfinition de la politique sociale du patronat français'.

71 Holly Sklar, ed., *Trilateralism: The Trilateral Commission and Elite Planning for World Management*, South End Press, Boston 1980, p. 73; Crozier, Huntington and Watanuki, p. 7.

72 Benjamin C. Roberts, Hideaki Okamoto and George C. Lodge, 'Collective Bargaining and Employee Participation in Western Europe, North America and Japan', Trilateral task force on industrial relations (1979), in Trilateral Commission, *Task Force Reports: 15–19*, New York University Press, New York 1981, p. 231.

73 Until 1978, the PCF's electoral position remained good, despite a gradual erosion in the Parisian region, while the PS made regular advances (thus the cantonal elections of 1976 marked a reversal in the balance of electoral forces between the PCF and the PS, with the Communist Party losing its rank as the principal formation of the left for the first time since the war). But over the next five years, the PCF lost half its voters, dropping below the 10 per cent mark in 1986.

74 Well-documented, reliable information on the terror that reigned in the communist countries was available from the end of the 1940s. But it required a denunciation – and a very partial one at that – from within the system, Khrushchev's 1956 Report, for French Communists to recognize the *personal* crimes of Stalin, without thereby acknowledging the criminal character of the Soviet regime. Restoring some vigour to the Marxist–Leninist ideal, the 1960s saw the pro-liferation of other communist models (Trotskyism, Maoism, Castroism, Titoism), but this was already a sign of the declining hold of communist structures on French critique (see Furet, *The Passing of an Illusion*). As for the second half of the 1970s, it was marked by the appearance in 1974 of Solzhenitsyn's *Gulag Archipelago*, which had a print run of over a million in France.

75 Stéphane Courtois and Marc Lazar, *Histoire du Parti communiste français*, Presses Universitaires de France, Paris 1995, p. 353.

76 Initially very critical of the student demonstrations (Georges Marchais attacked these 'pseudo-revolutionaries', 'sons of the bourgeoisie', in *L'Humanité*, 3 May 1968), from 17 May

the PCF was to adopt a strategy that seemed to point in the direction of taking political power. While condemning ultra-leftism and those features of the May movement that were deemed unacceptable because they led to a liberation regarded by the Communists as unacceptable 'disorder', the PCF rapidly abandoned the purely negative attitude it had initially adopted. Through the CGT, it initiated or followed the strike movement (six million strikers by 20 May, ten million a week later), demanded a 'change of political regime', and set up 'committees for a popular government of democratic union' that were to organize the base with a view to a potential assumption of power. But this strategy was not carried through to a conclusion: Communist action was self-limiting out of a fear of civil war after de Gaulle's journey to Germany, by warnings from the Soviets, who were content with Gaullist positions in foreign policy, and by a constant fear throughout the crisis of seeing the movement escape their control. But having engaged in an explicit strategy of taking power without giving itself the means, if only by sketching out its realization, the PCF proved its comparative impotence in the course of this test, despite its size and seeming strength. Henceforth, *it no longer inspired fear*, or at least not as much as it had done in the past. In the eyes of the most enlightened among the employers, it would even appear in some circumstances as a perfectly acceptable ally for confronting the danger of the moment: ultra-leftist agitation.

77   In her 1987 book on Communist intellectuals between 1956 and 1985, Jeanine Verdès-Leroux deems the decline of the PCF irreversible, and maintains that it 'became blindingly obvious *at least* from the spring of 1978', for the disintegration of the organization, which was clear then, was to be translated at the electoral level – as was evident in 1981. By reference to opinion polls from the beginning of the 1980s, she shows that the discredit of the party, particularly among the young, stemmed above all from its relationship with the USSR, especially shocking at the moment of the invasion of Afghanistan; but also from its lack of internal democracy and, more profoundly, from 'its being cut off from the evolution of society', 'an absence of analyses and proposals to confront the problems that developed at the beginning of the 1980s': 'The degeneration of the party was thus inscribed in the narrowness, provincialism and limits of Communist intellectual culture.' But Verdès-Leroux also shows that in the same period these criticisms were widely shared by a number of intellectuals who were still members of the Party, whom she questioned, and who no longer 'believed' in the principles on which the adhesion of their elders was based: the 'working class' (become a 'myth'); Marxism, of which activists had a poor knowledge; the USSR, 'a paradise that had turned into a nightmare'; the leadership, formerly venerated but increasingly discredited and scorned, with their head, secretary-general Georges Marchais, at the top of the list (*Le Réveil des somnambules. Le parti communiste, les intellectuels et la culture (1956–1985)*, Fayard–Minuit, Paris 1987, pp. 11–31). Hence the PCF imploded from within. But the effects of the collapse of a critical instance which, as a result of the fear it inspired in its glory days, offered an effective incentive to capitalism to social reforms, would all find expression on the outside, on the living conditions of wage-earners in general, whether or not they were 'on the left'.

78   Thus, for example, in 1977–78 the Centre de sociologie des organisations, with financing from CORDES (i.e. from the Plan), conducted a study of 'the functioning of work collectives' that aimed to understand the operational logic of communitarian work groups whose 'purpose has certainly been to survive and produce, but whose most profound results have also aimed at the search for new human relations in the community' ('monastic communities of mental and manual labour', village communities of land-clearers and artisans in the America of the pioneers, but also in Israel's kibbutzim and mochavim, Chinese communes, self-managed farms in Algeria, workers' production co-operatives in the industrial societies created under socialism, and self-managed firms in Yugoslavia'). The report relied in particular on an investigation of twenty-one organizations where experiments in self-management had developed: four production co-operatives, five experimental health institutions, four artisanal firms in arts and crafts, two experiments in improving living conditions and semi-autonomous teams in a metallurgical factory and

an insurance company in the public sector, and so on (Marie-Odile Marty, Rosa Nehmy, Renaud Sainsaulieu and Pierre-Eric Tixier, *Les Fonctionnements collectifs de travail*, 3 vols, mimeo, CSO, Paris 1978). The second volume of this important report (signed by Rosa Nehmy) was devoted to 'project organizations'. It developed 'the notion of project in the organization', in its functional but also 'socio-affective' dimensions, and by this token constitutes an important document in what might be called the 'archaeology' of the projective. In the third volume ('From the Experimental to the Durable'), Sainsaulieu and Tixier ponder how these experiments might contribute to the management of large firms in their efforts at creativity and imagination, in order to meet a new 'craving for community' in modern firms.

79 We can see it, for example, in the case of flexible or 'tailor-made' hours. It is undeniable that they have advantages for wage-earners and, in particular, for women with families. Presented, legitimately, as a common-sense reform (why demand that all the members of the workforce in a firm are present at the same time on the premises, when it is enough that they are there for a limited period of the day and certain hours of the week?), flexible hours were the subject of experiments encouraged by the Labour Ministry as early as 1972 (a bill was discussed in 1973 in the Conseil économique et social). From 42 in 1972, the number of firms experimenting with flexible hours rose to 400 in 1974; according to some estimates, it reached 20,000 in 1980. These measures put the trade unions in an awkward position, since they could not oppose a change that was favoured by numerous wage-earners outright, even though they sensed the risks of a dismantling of labour regulations in the legalization of flexible hours. In fact, the question of the length of the working day and week was central in the formation of labour law. Yet flexible hours were to allow a transfer of working hours from one day to the next and one week to the next (working, for example, thirty-six hours one week and forty-four hours the following week). In addition to the problem posed by harmonization with the 1946 law on the obligation to pay overtime, the transfer of working hours opens the way to 'flexibility' – that is to say, to the transfer of the constraint deriving from market uncertainties onto wage-earners. For, as Philippe Lamour and Jacques de Chalendar justly remark, 'the employer can also have an interest, in order to finish some important piece of work, in his employees working forty-four hours one week, even if it means them coming in for only thirty-six hours the following week – and this without paying the four additional hours at a higher rate in the first week. How to know who is behind these forty-four hours? The employee, for personal reasons, or the employer, in the interests of the firm? Is it a question of a surplus hour or a genuine hour of overtime? This is not always easy to untangle, above all in the small and medium-sized firms where the risks of pressure are not inconsiderable' (*Prendre le temps de vivre. Travail, vacances et retraite à la carte*, Seuil, Paris 1974, pp. 42–3).

80 We might inquire whether the employers' conversion to autonomy was not aided by the example afforded after a few years by the blueprint law on higher education presented by Edgar Faure in autumn 1968. This law (which adopted numerous themes developed during the crisis months, and had benefited from the work of committees set up by students and some professors) aimed to introduce greater autonomy into universities, understood both as an autonomy of persons (students with respect to teachers, assistant lecturers with respect to professors), and as an autonomy of units: competing universities, divided into faculties with committees with representation for students, assistant lecturers and professors, themselves broken up into teaching and research units. This new organization, which had made more conservative professors shudder, in fact proved to be an excellent device for integrating, channelling and sapping the energy of the protesters.

81 Michel Crozier – and he was unquestionably the first to do so – had sensed that the anti-institutional critiques developed by the May movement, once detached from their revolutionary references, could pave the way for a more liberal society, making much greater room for the market than in the past. This is why, while opposing the egalitarian tendencies of the movement, he approved of the critique of the *grandes écoles* in such a fashion as to break down the barriers to the formation of a large, unified skills market. See Crozier, *La Société bloquée*, Seuil, Paris 1970.

82 CNPF, *L'amélioration des conditions de vie dans l'entreprise*, 2 vols, Paris 1977, pp. 327, 329.

83 Ibid.

84 CNPF, *Le problème des OS*, p. 25.

85 Ibid., p. 14.

86 Ibid., p. 16.

87 Ibid., pp. 20, 22, 24, 21.

88 OECD, *Les nouvelles attitudes et motivations des travailleurs*, pp. 23, 25, 32.

89 Obviously, the employers are not a single actor and the managers of firms do not universally subscribe to the slogans launched by the employers' organizations. To speak of a strategy – in the sense of a planned project – on the part of the CNPF during these years is excessive, which does not mean that the transformations of the 1970s can be turned into the automatic result of some process without a subject. As Chris Howell remarks, the CNPF and other employers' bodies (for example, the Centre des Jeunes Dirigeants), if they did not orchestrate the employers' response to the crisis, at least played a very significant role: on the one hand, by putting pressure on the state, and on the other by playing the role of laboratory for deliberation and innovation in the invention, and especially the diffusion – via conferences, seminars, symposia – of new managerial forms and practices (Howell, *Regulating Labor*, p. 115). The same could be said of a body like the OECD. Employers' associations can in this sense be assimilated to 'clubs' (Bernd Marin, 'Qu'est-ce que le patronat? Enjeux théoriques et résultats empiriques', *Sociologie du travail*, no. 4, 1988, pp. 515–44). As Marin further remarks, it remains the case that although the employers' associations have no problems with membership (they contain almost all the members of a sector), they have the utmost difficulty co-ordinating the action of their members: 'whatever is advantageous for the *totality* of businessmen in one sector (high price levels, good professional training of skilled blue-collar workers and technicians, for example), each of the firms taken *individually* has an interest in undermining it (and in lowering prices, not contributing to the training of apprentices, etc.)'.

90 See François Gaudu, 'Les notions d'emploi en droit', *Droit social*, no. 6, June 1996, pp. 569–76.

91 This is to indicate how unrealistic it would be to seek to make a distinction between the characteristics of the 'context' and the properties of the 'actors', in the manner of an evolutionistic and neo-Darwinian theory of change, and especially economic change, wherein 'actors' 'react' to 'contextual constraints' and succeed, or fail, in 'adapting' to them. On the contrary, it is the way in which interacting actors construct their identity according to the strategies they deploy that tends to alter and continually redefine the contextual constraints, in such a way that the action constitutes the context as much as it is inflected by it. For a critique of economic change conceived as a process of adaptation guided by the defence of vital interests and neo-Darwinian analogies, popularized by Richard Nelson and Sidney Winter (*An Evolutionary Theory of Economic Change*, Harvard University Press, Cambridge (MA) 1982), see the excellent introduction by Charles Sabel and Jonathan Zeitlin to the collective volume they published recently on the historical alternatives to mass production, *World of Possibilities: Flexibility and Mass Production in Western Civilization* (Cambridge University Press and Éditions de la Maison des Sciences de l'Homme, Cambridge and Paris 1997).

92 Chateauraynaud, *La faute professionnelle*, pp. 149–52.

93 In retrospect, we can in fact assign different functions to the emphasis laid on flexibility in the mid-1980s. The first, and most conspicuous, was to make it possible for firms to confront market uncertainties by modulating their wage costs in accordance with short-term demand. For that, it was necessary to lift restrictions on hiring, redundancy, working hours, the nature and especially length of work contracts, access to temporary work, and so on. But flexibility also incorporates a social policy that tends towards tightening of supervision over wage-earners.

94 See Howell, *Regulating Labor*.

95   Administrative authorization of redundancies was established by law in 1975. Prior to its abrogation in 1986, however, it was granted in 90 per cent of cases. If, immediately after the repeal of the law at the end of 1986 and beginning of 1987, economic redundancies rose by 17 and 19 per cent, the figures thereafter returned to their earlier level (François Guéroult, 'Faut-il rétablir l'autorisation de licenciement?', *Alternatives économiques*, no. 140, September 1996).

96   Nevertheless, being highly conscious of the paradox of a left-wing government supporting measures in favour of flexibility, the government wanted an agreement between employers and unions. The negotiations broke down in 1984. While present at them, the CGT had never been enthusiastic, but the other unions (CFDT, FO, CFTC and CGC) had agreed to discussions and had ended up with a protocol with the employers, although they could not sign it as a result of rumbling discontent within their respective apparatuses. This failure was widely interpreted in the press as the sign of the unions' inability to 'adapt to modernity', and reinforced their crisis of representation (Raymond Soubie, 'Après les négociations sur la flexibilité', *Droit social*, no. 3, March 1985, pp. 221–7). For its part, the government had to start all over again, now obliged to proceed openly. But it found itself in a more legitimate position to do so, given media dismay at the failure of the negotiations.

97   One can only be struck after the event by the similarity between the positions expressed in two texts published the same year – 1986 – which both had the defence of jobs as their main argument: the first signed by Yvon Gattaz, representative of the CNPF; the second by Edmond Maire of the CFDT. As one might expect, Gattaz criticizes the 'rigidity, regulation and irreversibility of established benefits', which 'block' employment. He demands an increase in flexibility and, more precisely, the possibility of 'modulating workforces', making redundancies freely, developing 'wage flexibility', in such a way as 'to take account of individual merit and reward the qualities of those who put their skills and their energy in the service of the firm', against the 'egalitarianism that has been extolled for so long', and 'social envy', the 'flexibility of working conditions' and 'hours', and 'flexibility in the minimum number of employees required to establish works councils' (Gattaz, 'L'emploi, l'emploi, l'emploi', *La Revue des entreprises*, no. 477, March 1986, pp. 15–18). While criticizing the 'liberal policy of the employers', Maire wonders how to improve the profitability of firms, whose main handicap consists – he says – 'in an archaic, centralized management, which squanders the potentialities of wage-earners and ossifies their qualifications'. What he proposes by way of remedy can readily enough be reinterpreted in terms of flexibility: 'To give our firms the quality, flexibility, and capacity to adapt and innovate they urgently require, we must perfect forms of organization of work that are flexible and enhance skills, of types of management which call on the active participation of wage-earners in firms and public services. And the necessary adaptations in social benefits must be defined contractually…. The reduction of working hours will then assume its full meaning' ('Le chômage peut être vaincu', *Le Monde*, 20 August 1986).

98   In order to resolve the problem of the rejection of work by young people, the ANDCP thus undertook to look for models elsewhere. The journal devoted an issue to 'Japanese Management' and, in particular, to the way in which firms in Japan accommodated the young (no. 149, February 1972). The Association even sent a mission to Yugoslavia to study self-management there, which gave rise to a special issue of the journal (no. 156, November/December 1972). Far from being negative, the account of this mission noted numerous positive features of self-management – features that were to be exploited when, after the turn of 1974, the question of 'self-management' was taken seriously in French firms. Thus, we learn that 'self-management is concerned with human beings, whom it regards as the only factor in collective progress'; that 'self-management is a system in which orders are to be avoided and instead people are to be persuaded'; and that 'this point is particularly important when we know the problems of supervision in some firms in France, which has not yet realized that it is no longer a matter of ordering (in the literal sense of the term), but of inducing collaborators to participate by obtaining their consensus'. Other 'positive points' noted were 'information within the firm, the

linchpin of self-management', and the 'creation of work units, which has made it possible to restore work to a more human scale. In fact, the work unit is a small firm with its own trading account, existing autonomously of management.'

99 See Paolo Virno, *Opportunisme, cynisme et peur*, Éditions de l'Éclat, Combas 1991. Thus, Virno has shown how Italian capitalism reintegrated and set to work the skills acquired by the young protesters of the 1970s in militant or ludic activities, pertaining to 'the invention of new lifestyles' or the 'counter-culture'. The same thing occurred in France. Thus, for example, artistic directors in light-music record companies, one of whose tasks consists in spotting and selecting new talent that may please the public, are often renegades into capitalist organizations from the marginal worlds they frequented in their youth (Antoine Hennion, *La Passion musicale*, Métailié, Paris 1995).

100 Jobert and Théret, 'France'.

101 Ibid., p. 45.

102 As Furet (*The Passing of an Illusion*) observes, the condemnation of anti-Communism on the left, which continues beyond the Soviet collapse, is what survives of this party's sway over critique in France.

103 It must nevertheless be reckoned that supporters of the 'inexorable movement' were not altogether wrong inasmuch as the search for social innovations, intended to resolve the problems facing capitalism – as a result particularly, but not exclusively, of critique – actually results in the invention of new, more profitable mechanisms. Once these are discovered, especially if they do not clash with ordinary morality, it is virtually impossible without legislating to avoid them spreading, for those in charge of firms know that they are obliged to adopt them if their competitors adopt them.

104 As Marshall Berman emphasizes, commenting on Marx in the work that he has devoted to the critical experience of modernity from Goethe to the 1970s new left, one of the basic contradictions of the bourgeoisie, inasmuch as its fate is associated with that of capitalism, is to mean to serve the party of order while constantly, and without qualms, shattering the concrete conditions of existence so as to ensure the survival of the accumulation process, going so far as to reappropriate the most radical critiques, in some cases transforming them into commodity products (*All That Is Solid Melts into Air*, Verso, London 1983, esp. pp. 98–114).

4

DISMANTLING
THE WORLD OF WORK

What were the effects of the displacements effected in the period under study? It may be said that they made it possible to redirect the wages/profit share of value added in favour of capital-holders, and to restore order in production.[1] Restoration of control over firms was furthered by the co-operation of wage-earners, treated as so many separate individuals, capable of different, unequal performances. Thanks to a mixture of differential benefits and fear of unemployment, they were induced to engage freely and fully in the work tasks assigned them. Most of these displacements thus helped to restore the initiative to capital and management. Securing the collaboration of wage-earners in the realization of capitalist profits remained the issue. But whereas in the previous period, notably under pressure from the workers' movement, this had been sought through the collective, political integration of workers into the social order, and by a form of the spirit of capitalism that yoked economic and technological progress to the aim of social justice, it could now be achieved by developing a project of self-realization, linking the cult of individual performance and extolment of mobility to reticular conceptions of the social bond. However, for many people, especially new arrivals on the labour market by comparison with their elders, this was accompanied by a marked deterioration in economic situation, job stability and social position.

That is why, after trying to identify the scale of the changes that occurred in firms, in this chapter we shall examine the different ways in which these changes acted on the world of work, creating the problems we are familiar with today. As for effects that may be deemed positive, if we take the critique of the Taylorism and mass production of 1930–70 as our reference-point, for example, these have been brought out during our analysis of the arguments developed to elicit workers' mobilization in the new spirit of capitalism (see Chapter 1).

I. ON THE RANGE OF THE TRANSFORMATIONS INVOLVED

One of the main targets of firms' new strategy was, as we have seen, a significant increase in what from the 1980s onwards was called *flexibility*. In particular, this makes it possible to transfer the burden of market uncertainty onto wage-earners, but also subcontractors and other service providers. It breaks down into *internal flexibility*, based upon a profound transformation in the organization of work and the techniques employed (multitasking, self-control, development of autonomy, etc.), and *external flexibility*. The latter presupposes a so-called network organization of work, wherein 'lean' firms seek the resources they lack from among a profusion of subcontractors, as well as a labour force that is malleable in terms of employment (casual jobs, temping, self-employed workers), working hours, or the duration of work (part-timers, variable hours).[2]

Changes in the internal organization of work

As we have seen, interpretation of the crisis of capitalism as a crisis of Taylorism had, since the beginning of the 1970s, prompted a number of initiatives by employers to change the organization of work. These changes continued and accelerated during the 1980s. If it is more than likely that dispositions and practices did not evolve as rapidly as the management works featuring in our corpus assume, particularly when it comes to the importance of the principle of hierarchy and the ability to introduce wage-earner participation and discussion, experiments and initiatives nevertheless abounded.[3] But as with the introduction of Taylorism into France and the spread of assembly-line work – the moment and pace of which are still the subject of debate among historians of work – it is not very easy to assess the scale of these changes, which affected firms very unevenly, depending upon their size and their sector of activity.

Thus, small firms often remained pre-Taylorist, whereas medium-sized industrial firms could seek to make good their discrepancy by introducing methods of rational work organization of a Taylorist type – methods that were already under challenge or being altered in large firms in these years.[4]

According to Danièle Linhart, it is in processing industries (cement works, petrochemicals, iron and steel, etc.) that the most significant break with Taylorism has occurred: 'There we find examples of multiskilling organization in which multiskilled groups are set in place on the basis of an expansion in the scope and level of skills and incorporating genuinely technical tasks.' Contrariwise, other sectors, like clothing or building, are noteworthy for their reinforcement of Taylorization. But the dominant tendency is the reproduction of previous Taylorist forms of organization: 'The role of the workshop is not really reassessed, and the division between design and organization of work on the one hand, execution on the other, is largely maintained in its existing state. The field of occupational intervention of operatives is not significantly expanded.' One nevertheless finds a number of developments in these cases, like 'the assignment of tasks of an initial level of maintenance and quality control to manufacturing operatives', as well as 'the proliferation of participatory formulas such as quality circles, exchange and progress groups'.[5]

The available figures in fact reveal a mixed picture. In support of those who emphasize the pursuit or preservation of Taylorization, we may underline the fact that assembly-line work did not decline, and even extended beyond 40–45-year-olds, where it had hitherto been far from common. Rigid constraints incorporated into machinery also affected a growing proportion of blue-collar workers, and some sectors, like the meat industry, were characterized by rapid mechanization.[6] Moreover, Taylorization advanced in the service sector.

Data indicating a large-scale transformation in other aspects of the organization of work are not lacking either. As a sign of the greater *autonomy* of wage-earners, we shall concentrate on developments in working hours up to 1991.[7] Fixed hours (the same hours every day) were in decline: they affected 65 per cent of wage-earners in 1978, 59 per cent in 1984, 52 per cent in 1991;[8] and this development was entirely due to the progression in free hours and flexitime, which went up from 16 per cent in 1984 to 23 per cent in 1991. This freeing-up of hours affected all socioprofessional categories, but was more wide-ranging the more highly placed in the hierarchy people were. Free or flexible hours progressed by only 4 points (from 6 to 10 per cent) for blue-collar workers between 1984 and 1991, whereas 13 per cent more *cadres* benefited from them (from 44 to 57 per cent), 8 per cent more of those in intermediate professions (from 24 to 32 per cent), and 6 per cent more white-collar workers (from 13 to 19 per cent). As for the development of workers' multitasking, the proportion of workers undertaking tasks of maintenance and quality control progressed, respectively, from 56 to 66 per cent and from 41 to 58 per cent between 1987 and 1993.[9] *Continuous training* also increased: in 1989, one firm in two sent a wage-earner on a training course, compared with one in three in 1977.[10]

The survey conducted by Thomas Coutrot[11] enables us to estimate that in 1992, around 20 per cent of plants had largely implemented the organizational innovations associated with the third spirit of capitalism, which means that it was already a far-from-marginal phenomenon. Twenty-three per cent were organized in just-in-time mode;[12] 34 per cent used quality circles; 27 per cent had abolished a level of hierarchy; 11 per cent employed quality norms of an International Standardization Organization (ISO) variety;[13] and as many had autonomous groups. It is still only a question of methods, some sectors being very affected by certain techniques and less so by others.[14] *Overall, in fact, 61 per cent of plants adopted at least one organizational innovation, while 20 per cent adopted three or more.*[15] Given that innovations were adopted in greater proportion by large plants, the percentage of wage-earners directly or indirectly affected by such reorganization is higher than the figures above suggest. We may also assume that since 1992 the rate of penetration and impact on firms of these 'innovations' has further increased.[16]

Over and above the changes to work within plants just mentioned, we must now stress the scale of the displacements affecting the productive fabric. This fabric was profoundly restructured under the impact of measures of outsourcing, reduction in plant size, creation of subsidiaries, and concentration on core business in which a competitive advantage was sought.

Changes in the productive fabric

The development of *subcontracting* has been appreciable, going from 5.1 per cent of industrial turnover in 1974 to 8.9 per cent in 1991, and remaining at this level thereafter.[17] This involves only direct subcontracting of turnover, whereby the principal leaves to others the creation of all or part of a product that it will sell and whose specifications it determines. It must therefore be distinguished from other purchases from suppliers of parts, subsets, or services (caretaking, catering, etc.). Only recently has an Industry Ministry survey of manufacturing firms with more than twenty wage-earners sought to measure 'expanded subcontracting', in order to take account of the development of subcontracting from simple manufacturing (with material supplied by the principal) to 'industrial partnerships'.[18] The figures then turn out to be higher, since we obtain a volume of expanded subcontracting of the order of 21 per cent of industrial production.[19] With the development of closer, durable subcontracting relations, firms seek to reduce the number of those they liaise with, so that what we are witnessing is the organization of subcontracting at several levels, large firms calling upon first-level subcontractors, who subcontract to second-level subcontractors, and so on. The more complex the final product is, the longer the chain. Subcontracting thus generates highly ramified networks, often involving hundreds of firms.

Temping has likewise undergone very significant growth, making this branch of services one of the leaders in job creation. In 1997, the rate of recourse to temping, or the number of posts occupied by temps compared with the total number of posts, was 5.1 per cent in construction and 4.3 per cent in industry, but only 0.9 per cent in the tertiary sector, which prefers to use fixed- and/or part-time contracts to secure flexibility. Given that around 85 per cent of assignments involve blue-collar jobs, rates when it comes to this kind of employment are therefore a lot higher.[20]

The rise in market services is the major phenomenon of recent years. In 1990, they 'weighed in' almost as heavily as manufacturing in terms of both value added and workforce, whereas twenty years earlier they represented only half of both. Among them, it is services to firms that have fuelled the sector's growth: in 1990, they accounted for 21 per cent of tertiary-sector employment as against 14 per cent in 1975; in 1970, households were consuming approximately as many services as firms, whereas the latter consumed 50 per cent more in 1990. In addition to the case of temporary work already referred to, another significant section of expanding services results from the outsourcing of functions of execution (cleaning, caretaking, laundry, catering, transport, etc.), and hence constitutes a shift of activities from industry towards services rather than genuinely new activities, with the possible exception of some workplace catering, whose requirements have developed.[21] The occupation of cleaner is thus one of the rare jobs for unqualified workers to have experienced sustained growth (3.2 per cent a year between 1982 and 1990).[22] In 1978, cleaning firms had 25 per cent of the market, the remainder going to 'in-house cleaning'. In 1988, they held 40 per cent, and this share has gone on increasing since.[23] Two other categories of services profit from the move to outsourcing: on the one hand, 'conceptual services' (consultancies, studies, research, computer, legal and accountancy services, etc.), partially replacing in-house teams and allowing the customers to benefit from high concentrations of expertise; on the other hand, services for rental goods, freeing firms of the burden of owning fixed assets or forming a new source of financing (long-term rentals grew by 7 per cent a year, and leasing activity by 10 per cent a year, in the period 1970 to 1990).[24]

This general move to outsourcing helps to explain the growing share of small establishments in employment. Breaking, in fact, with a time-honoured tendency towards a growth in the size of firms, the share of small and medium-sized enterprises in employment has expanded since the mid-1970s. Establishments with more than 500 wage-earners accounted for 21 per cent of the workforce at the end of 1975, against 11 per cent in 1996. Those with fewer than 10 wage-earners, on the other hand, went up from 18 per cent to 26 per cent in the same period.[25] Many firms without wage-earners – that is to say, involving no one but the head of the firm – have been set up, accounting for a large proportion of the increase in the number of firms (they represent half of the two million registered firms). This is especially true of the building industry, where the trend was effectively to transform wage-earners into subcontractors.[26] Industrial employment, which lost a million people overall between 1980 and 1989, has above all declined in firms with more than 500 wage-earners (- 40 per cent), whereas in firms with between 20 and 499 people it only fell by 10 per cent. In 1989, small and medium-sized firms together accounted for 51 per cent of industrial employment, compared with 42 per cent in 1980.[27]

But this general decrease in the size of firms masks the growing importance of groups in the productive fabric to the extent that the reduction is only apparent, and leads to locating jobs that were formerly grouped together in distinct legal structures. We have in fact witnessed the birth of new enterprise structures, closer to networks than the large firms of the industrial age. The number of groups thus went up from 1,300 at the end of 1980 to 6,700 at the end of 1995; the number of firms in the survey went from 9,200 to 44,700, representing only 2 per cent of the two million firms but one wage-earner in two, more than 60 per cent of value added, three-quarters of corporate assets, and 87 per cent of personal capital. Groups of more than 10,000 people – whose number has shown less variation over the period, rising from 73 to 84 – have likewise increased the number of their subsidiaries, which grew from 40 in 1980 to 125 in 1995; while the average workforce in each of them dropped from 310 to 210 people. These large groups alone account for a quarter of the labour force, half of fixed capital, and half of gross operating profits. In fact, one in three jobs in small and medium-sized firms depends upon a group.[28] The lesser concentration of the productive fabric is thus only apparent, in the sense that it disappears when the issue is formulated in terms of groups.[29] Moreover, the market share of the leader has grown in all sectors, rising on average from 16 to 22 per cent between 1980 and 1987.[30] This general restructuring was accompanied by an alteration in business portfolios, with each group concentrating on a few activities where it seeks a position of strength on the market and purchasing from new service groups whatever does not pertain to its core business. Thus, between 1980 and 1987, groups lost 13 per cent of their workforce in activities that disappeared or were abandoned and 11 per cent in activities that they retained, while they increased their workforce by 17 per cent via activities that were new to them.[31]

The share of groups varies from sector to sector. It appears notably weak in construction, services to private individuals, and stores, contributing to only 30 per cent of value added.[32] These sectors, however, have undergone significant concentration in recent years. In the public buildings and work sector, the share of the four first groups in total sector output had already gone up from 11 to 20 per cent between 1980 and 1987,[33] while at the other end of the scale, craftsman builders proliferated and were counted as so many firms without wage-earners. In the case of the retail sector, the development of hypermarkets is a major phenomenon, affecting independent small shopkeepers,[34] who organized their own form of resistance by grouping in networks, in the manner of certain networks of hypermarkets like Leclerc and Intermarché. In particular, they share a central buying office, a shop sign and intangible investments of the advertising variety. Such creations of networks have something in common with a form of concentration, but they are virtually impossible to identity in the national statistics, except by conducting sectoral studies specifically designed to reconstruct them.[35] The pioneering study conducted in 1995 by the retailing department of the INSEE on the clothing trade allows us to calculate that 'genuinely' independent retailing specializing in clothing accounts for only 31 per cent of volume sales, which calls into question the idea of low concentration in the sector. This is even more the case given that the functions performed by the heads of networks of specialist shops (which account for 34 per cent of sales) are often so extensive (equipping shops, training retailers, deciding 'recommended' sales price, sign advertising or own brand, tracking sales via a computer system, purchase, stocking, referencing and/or design, manufacture or subcontracting of manufacture, quality control of manufacture) that the networks can actually be regarded as quasi-firms.[36] The market share of the independents, as well as of trade fairs and markets, is in decline in a stagnant market, the advance of networks being the strongest of the different channels of distribution.[37] Networks are also common in the 'services for private individuals' sector – launderettes, dry-cleaning, hairdressing salons, property sales, hotels, car rentals, fast food, and so on. In the event of a specific study, this would lead us to adjudge the sector rather more concentrated than it appears from the size of firms alone, or the professed presence of groups.

The convergence between these various pieces of evidence makes it possible to assess the influence of large-scale, co-ordinated economic bodies (large firms, groups, independents organized into a network, partnerships between firms, alliances, etc.) as being greater than ever in the French productive fabric, despite the seemingly increasing importance of medium-sized and small firms. This is why describing neo-capitalism as a development of the market economy misses the major phenomenon of a strengthening in the power of large or allied firms, with all markets gradually conforming to oligopolies, the largest units fighting each other at a global level and extending their implantation and network of partners beyond national borders. A market economy in the sense of partisans of liberalism, who make it the very model of efficient functioning, would presuppose a genuine proliferation of average-sized independent firms. The network image used by management authors seems better suited to the new situation: more numerous groups, composed of a large number of small units, resorting to subcontractors that are not necessarily more numerous in each instance, but are more integrated into the running of the head firm, and in more diversified sectors, with the development of network forms making it possible to combine a position of market strength with flexibility.

The impact of these new practices of work and enterprise organization on the condition of wage-earners is rarely studied. The most accessible figures concerning, for example, casual jobs are related to the number of jobs (thus we know that in March 1995 one wage-earner in eleven was employed in the form of an 'exceptional' job);[38] or to socioprofessional category (blue-collar workers are more insecure than *cadres*). But the sectors, the size of establishment involved, and the development of practices are less often indicated, which comes down to saying that analysts who work on the national statistics do not systematically connect job insecurity with the practices of firms, and that it then becomes fairly easy to present it as an inevitable consequence of occupation, age, class or education. In particular, this is attributable to the fact that in the INSEE, as in the ministries, firms and work are not studied by the same departments; and also that statisticians experience the utmost difficulty obtaining representative images of the new structures of firms and markets.[39]

By contrast, our intention in the rest of this exposition is going to be to try to make the link between the displacements introduced into organizations since the 1970s and developments in the condition of wage-labour.

2. THE CHANGES IN WORK

Implementation of the displacements described above has led first and foremost to job insecurity.

The casualization of employment

We owe to Thomas Coutrot's article cited above an attempt to link 'organizational innovations' to the employment policy of the organizations concerned. Thus he notes that the adoption of innovations goes together with 'greater selectivity in personnel management': 23 per cent of the most innovative establishments have both laid off and recruited personnel of the same category, compared with 16 per cent for all establishments. Even so, the turnover rate that measures the renewal of personnel as a percentage of total workforce, which Coutrot analyses as the result of a more or less strong desire on the part of employers to create loyalty, appears to be lower in innovative establishments – with the exception of those that practise just-in-time – than in the sum total of establishments. One way of resolving the apparent contradiction between these two tendencies is to suggest the hypothesis that 'innovative establishments' operate with a permanent group of casual workers alongside personnel for whom policies aimed at developing loyalty are implemented.

Displacements aimed at giving firms more flexibility have in fact had the consequence of producing job insecurity at the margins of the working population. It is connected with either the nature of the job (temping, fixed-term contracts, part-time or variable hours), or its location in subcontracting firms that are the first to suffer from variations in economic circumstances, and heavy users of casual labour for that very reason. However, this casualization is not incompatible, for example, with increased expenditure on training for those who are not subject to such insecurity.

The current practice of employing the meticulously calculated minimum number of people to occupy permanent jobs, and using 'outside labour' to fill the rest, has made possible, at the same time as a development of subcontracting, the development of *temporary work*: the number of temping establishments went up from 600 in 1968 to 1,500 in 1980, and then 4,883 in 1996.[40] In 1997 – a year when the volume of temping activity increased by 23 per cent – 1,438,000 people were reckoned to have performed at least one temping assignment; this represents the equivalent of 359,000 full-time jobs.[41] The temporary work enterprise Adecco thus became the premier private employer in France in 1997.

Generally speaking, *forms of temporary work* developed appreciably in the second half of the 1980s: the total of temps, trainees and fixed-term contracts increased from approximately 500,000 in 1978 to around 1,200,000 in 1989.[42] In March 1995, they stood at more than 1,600,000, or a little under 9 per cent of wage-earners.[43] In 1997, their number increased still further. By mainly hiring staff for limited periods, employers establish a 'mobile' manpower reserve: in 1992, temporary contracts represented nearly 8 per cent of the waged workforce, or almost twice as many as in 1985. In the event of a changed economic climate, firms can henceforth rely on this greater 'external' flexibility: as early as 1991, they replaced nearly 20 per cent of their personnel, compared with 12 per cent in the mid-1980s.[44]

Part-time work – a female phenomenon in 82 per cent of cases – is also a form of job insecurity when it is imposed, which was the case with 54 per cent of men and 37 per cent of women working part-time in 1995.[45] It has developed significantly in recent years (9.2 of the workforce in 1982; 15.6 in 1995).[46] And since a sizeable number of temporary contracts are also part-time, the two forms of vulnerability compound one another.[47] Part-time work is a key tool of flexibility. It makes it possible to increase workforce presence during peak hours, and hence is especially common in services that cannot be stored. The service must be supplied when the customer wants it, and it is impossible to smooth out the workload. Consequently, it is very common in domestic services, whether these involve cleaning ladies or child-minders. For the same reasons, it is also highly developed in the case of office cleaners, who can operate only outside the occupants' working hours, in catering and retailing. 'The search for greater flexibility and increased productivity have prompted firms to generalize short-term work contracts, inferior to half-time. This is the best way for them to adjust the volume of hours worked to variations in the workload. In peak periods, firms resort to extra hours which, unlike overtime, are not paid at a higher rate.'[48]

The use of working hours to create flexibility does not necessarily take the form of part-time work. The mechanism can equally operate in the opposite direction, and take the form of an increase in workloads beyond the legal schedule. Thus, while the working day was becoming shorter for some (the percentage of people working fewer than six hours a day went up from 7.8 per cent in 1984 to 9.3 per cent in 1991), it increased for others (the percentage of those working more than ten hours increased in the same period from 17.9 per cent to 20.4 per cent).[49] Similarly, the proportion of those working five days a week was in decline, in favour of those who worked fewer – or more – than five days.

As early as 1980, Gérard Lyon-Caen demonstrated that the proliferation of casual workers was the result of new strategies on the part of firms. These strategies were structured around two points: a new employment policy, making it possible for the employer to 'maintain a free hand', and a new 'policy of enterprise structures', such that employers – by outsourcing manpower, for example – could 'shield themselves as employer'. In addition to the proliferation of 'job transfers' and subcontracting, these strategies involve using the possibilities offered by company law in order to circumvent the constraints of labour law.[50] These new ways of operating were thus established by avoiding the 'normal job form' (i.e., in Lyon-Caen's definition, employment on a permanent full-time contract in a specified, stable workplace, with career prospects, social security, and a trade-union presence in the workplace). He analyses in detail the series of processes that make it possible to achieve such a result:

(a) the employer 'endeavours to restrict his commitments in advance', the advantage of this being that it 'exempts him from offering severance pay';

(b) the employer seeks to pay only an 'irregular' wage, which makes casual (holiday) work possible, rendering the 'distinction between the self-employed and wage-earners' increasingly problematic;

(c) the employer can take advantage of the possibilities opened up by new legal situations (training periods, job-training contracts, etc.), in which he is simultaneously employer and trainer;

(d) the employer can call upon a temping agency. The legislation governing these companies, 'originally conceived for the purposes of replacing absent workers' (law of 1972), was outflanked as follows. French law (unlike German law) allows the payment of temps only for the duration of their assignment (not between two assignments); temps receive compensation for job insecurity which, even if the length of their assignment is more than six months, deprives them of any right to notice. Temps thus represent a 'mobile labour force that is cheap, lacking social benefits, whether contractual or statutory, offering firms an opportunity to reduce the number of their wage-earners with entitlements';

(e) the employer resorts to 'creating subsidiaries', to 'service provision' and 'subcontracting', or 'making personnel available', which affords him the opportunity to locate his workforce 'outside the firm', as it were. In addition, some large firms create service-provider firms with whom they will contract for loaning individual wage-earners or teams, and which in fact operate as their temporary labour agencies. In covert fashion, this represents illicit renting of manpower (illegal subcontracting of labour).[51]

Armelle Gorgeu and René Mathieu provide an exemplary description of various new practices in a monograph on the new, on-hand plants of car parts manufacturers.[52] This involves production units created between 1988 and 1994 and set up in close proximity to the manufacturers' assembly units, so as to service them more easily on a just-in-time basis. These plants carry out assembly and finishing operations previously performed by the manufacturers, and deliver a finished product (exhaust system, set of seats, bumpers fitted with headlights, dashboard planks incorporating different elements of the dashboard). Often entirely dedicated to the nearby factory customer, these plants, although they belong to legally and financially independent groups, are in fact annexes of the manufacturers' assembly units. Born out of the move towards outsourcing (purchases now represent between 65 and 75 per cent of the cost price of a vehicle), they have allowed the manufacturers to reduce the number of unskilled jobs in their plants by outsourcing them, and to raise their requirements beyond what they could have imposed upon their own workforce.[53] Employment in these new plants is characterized by a very large reserve of casual personnel (temporary and fixed-term contracts). At certain points in the year, and in certain plants, the proportion of temps can reach 55 per cent. 'In the course of a year, the percentage of casual personnel relative to those on permanent contracts varies between 10 and 30 per cent in the sum total of the units created.[54] ... The use on a quasi-permanent basis of temporary staff is one of the key characteristics of most of the plants studied.' So far as is possible, the same people work every day on a temporary basis, the firms taking care not to part with the highest-performing individuals. The use of temporary personnel not only makes it possible to deal with the variations in volume of the manufacturers' orders. It also acts as a mechanism for selecting people and putting them under pressure. 'When they can hire production workers on a permanent basis, because they have growth prospects or because they have too high a proportion of casual jobs compared with permanent personnel, plants that have been established for several years always "make permanent" temporary workers who have been around for a long time, or former temps whom they know well and recall.' 'A fixed-term contract or a skills contract can come in between temporary status and being made permanent. Thus the probation period for "best temps" is often very extended.'[55] For the duration of the casual job, temps must demonstrate constant engagement in their work. Thus it is that, concealed behind the imperative of flexibility, we also discover a development of employment practices with a very marked preference for casual hires.

Grégoire Philonenko's narrative of his years at Carrefour suggests that subcontracting in the automobile industry does not have a monopoly on these practices. Thus, on 31 December 1991, ten months after its opening, the employment track record of the Montreuil hypermarket where he worked indicated a turnover of 100 per cent (or 349 persons present for 692 taken on), departures being divided between redundancies (34), resignations (121), and the termination of contracts or probation periods (184). The author analyses these figures as indicating a deliberate intention to put people under pressure, rather than betokening incompetence on the part of the recruitment department. The people concerned invested body and soul in the hope of being promoted, but most were dismissed on various pretexts, many of them being pressurized into resigning. The upshot was twofold: on the one hand, employment was in effect on a casual basis; on the other, these mechanisms served as a method of selecting the few 'chosen ones' who were to be promoted or hired on permanent contracts.[56]

The available statistics indicate that these practices spread far beyond the two cases that have been cited above, which might otherwise seem very specific. Among the newly employed in March 1995 (i.e. those who on that date had held their job for less than a year), 19 per cent were on fixed-term contracts (13 per cent in 1990), 8 per cent were temporary (5 per cent in 1990), and 10 per cent benefited from a subsidized contract (7 per cent in 1990). Between 1990 and 1994, the share of permanent contracts had fallen by 9 points (from 53 to 44 per cent), and that of part-time contracts had increased by 10 points (from 29 to 39 per cent).[57]

In the context of employment policies justified by the pursuit of lower unemployment, the public authorities, while distancing themselves from the most radical forms of deregulation advocated in some quarters (e.g. abolition of the guaranteed minimum wage), embarked on the path of creating labour flexibility from the end of the 1970s:

> Abolition of administrative control of employment; withdrawal of the law in favour of negotiated agreements (notably as regards working hours); facilitatation of a (downward) revision in wage-earners' individual and collective rights; reduction in workforce representation (single delegation); proliferation of derogations from the principle of permanent employment; encouragement of part-time or occasional work;[58] presumption of non-wage-earning status (the Madelin law).[59]

In 1982, the reforms introduced into regulations concerning permanent contracts and temporary jobs aimed to reduce recourse to forms that were legitimately accused of marginalizing those who held them, and were scarcely compatible with the democratizing project contained in the Auroux laws. But 'government policy gradually reverted to a doctrine less hostile to temporary hiring: in the unchanged legislative framework of 1982, various regulatory texts first of all extended the possibility of recourse to fixed-term contracts, and then the law of 25 July 1985 deliberately increased instances of resort to this form of casual employment as well as to temporary work'.[60]

In addition to these developments, inspired by the 'liberal critique' that regards 'labour law [*droit du travail*] as the main obstacle to respect for the right to work [*droit au travail*]', came measures of a very different inspiration, aiming to intervene in the labour market: measures for subsidizing employment, which in part helped make labour more flexible, since subsidized jobs represent 'the archetype of low-cost labour enjoying weak protection';[61] measures for reducing the demand for jobs through early retirement, which in return facilitated making older workers redundant. The 'social treatment of unemployment' and measures in support of restructuring likewise had the unforeseen effect of putting firms in the clear: 'They opened the way to effective tactics from the moment that they guaranteed a kind of immunity to decisions to axe jobs.'[62] There is no question here of us deploying the reactionary argument of the 'perverse effect' – subjected to critical analysis by A.O. Hirschman[63] – according to which reformism is pointless, since reforms will have unanticipated, 'perverse' effects that lead to a worse situation than obtained before the measures were taken. The sincerity of lawmakers' concerns about jobs is evident and, unless we engage in political fiction, we cannot know what would have happened had these interventions not occurred. Nevertheless, it must be said that in one respect they sanctioned and facilitated certain practices of exclusion and casualization implemented by firms, and that in another respect they registered the changed balance of forces on the job market.

But if we consider their impact on the social structure as a whole, the casualization of certain jobs was not the only consequence of the displacements effected. Casualization also led to a segmentation of the wage-earning class and a fragmentation of the labour market, with the formation of a dual market: on one side, a stable, qualified workforce, enjoying a relatively high wage level and invariably unionized in large firms; on the other, an unstable, minimally qualified, underpaid and weakly protected labour force in small firms, dispensing subsidiary services.[64] In addition, the fact that the enduring handicaps produced by this casualization were concentrated on certain sections of the population accelerated the process of exclusion.

The segmentation of the wage-earning class

The combined effects of the new entrepreneurial practices produced extreme diversity in the condition of wage-labour, including among personnel employed on the same site, whose members may have a large number of employers and be managed according to different rules as regards wages, hours, and so on.

The first work to bring out the divisive effects bound up with the development of subcontracting and casual jobs was the historic article by Jacques Magaud.[65] He takes the example of an establishment whose 500 wage-earners come under ten different employers: the office personnel depended directly on an economic interest group; the maintenance staff on a service company; the wage-earners on the production line on the company itself; the canteen staff on a specialist catering company; the caretakers on a security company; the cleaning was carried out by a specialist company; thirty-five people came from two temping agencies; six *cadres* were waged employees of a sizeable group with which the firm had made financial agreements. The author shows that such a situation was recent: ten years earlier, the firm's 400 wage-workers were employed by a single employer; and the transition had occurred 'imperceptibly', without 'anyone noticing anything'.

Drawing on J. Broda's work on the Fos-sur-Mer zone in the mid-1970s, Guy Caire makes the following distinctions as regards the nature of the employee link and the character of the employer: (a) workers assigned on a permanent basis by service provision firms; (b) workers assigned on a temporary basis by a subcontracting establishment in a principal establishment; (c) temporary workers assigned by temping agencies; (d) workers on fixed-term contracts directly hired by the establishment. J. Freyssinet demonstrates that on this same site of Solmer at Fos, no fewer than 223 different firms could be identified at the end of the 1970s.[66]

'The outsourcing of employment' thus leads to the 'coexistence within one and the same establishment of a mosaic of workforces, to which as many statutes apply as there are companies represented in the workplace' – and this 'despite identical working conditions, despite the similarity of professional qualifications and the tasks performed, and despite unified real managerial power'.[67]

The most favourable statutes (permanent contracts in large firms) seem to be reserved increasingly for wage-earners with a comparatively rare qualification, or with particular responsibilities. For other categories of wage-earners, a more casual statute (temporary, fixed-term) is appropriate, or a less favourable one (wage-earners in subcontracting or subsidiary firms).[68]

Thus, in Gorgeu and Mathieu's study,[69] a certain number of blue-collar workers' jobs are deemed 'strategic', since customer satisfaction as regards quality and delivery depends on them (e.g. painting jobs in the plastic material processing industries). These jobs are held by personnel on permanent contracts, and the firm always has replacements. Those who hold them enjoy better grades and pay than the others, who must make do with the legal minimum wage and temporary contracts that are at best regularly renewed.

State policies 'targeting' categories eligible for subsidized employment, which attempt to manipulate 'queues' (the average time taken to find a job) to aid the categories in greatest difficulty, contribute to this phenomenon of labour-market fragmentation. For they discriminate between 'job-seekers who find themselves more or less highly valued depending upon their age, sex, qualifications, or the length of their unemployment'.[70] More broadly, because policies geared to flexibility and intervention in the labour market have proceeded in tandem with 'continual reinforcement of the rights attaching to the "typical" work contract (training, special leave, regrading, etc.)', the development of labour law has led to a profound 'segmentation within the wage-earning class between those who have a real job and those who are relegated to hire-and-fire and social security'.[71] According to Alain Supiot's analysis, the new employment law

establishes several job markets: that of managerial *cadres*, who combine the benefits of the wage-earning class and those of employers; that of ordinary wage-earners (full-time permanent work), who in principle benefit from the wage-earning status in full; that of casual jobs (fixed-term, temporary), which are *de jure* or *de facto* deprived of the rights attached to long-standing presence in the firm (training, representation, etc.); and finally that of subsidized jobs (the integration market). Furthermore, this compartmentalization is self-reinforcing, with firms hesitant to transfer wage-earners from one category to another, and wage-earners nervous about changing jobs and risking losing the benefits of a permanent contract or large firms.[72]

Christophe Dejours mentions extreme situations that sometimes constitute a total departure from labour law: subcontracting firms which undertake the tasks previously performed by fully integrated wage-earners taking on foreign workers without residence or work permits, workers who suffer from ill-health, workers who do not possess the requisite qualifications, or do not speak French.[73] This may apply, for example, to the public buildings and works sector, companies that carry out the maintenance of nuclear power stations or chemical factories, or, to take another example, cleaning firms:

> The spate of subcontracting leads to the constitution of a 'reserve army' of workers condemned to permanent insecurity, to underpayment and to a staggering job flexibility, obliging them to rush from one firm to the next, one building site to the next, living in makeshift accommodation, groups of huts some distance from the firm, caravans, etc. ... These workers, whom the personnel of the firm legally responsible for work supervision and monitoring come across, in turn elicit mistrust, disgust, even moral condemnation.[74]

The process of social discrimination compounds that of job discrimination, and encloses these workers ever more tightly in their 'poverty trap'.

Without going so far as to regard such extreme conditions as representative of all instances of job insecurity, we cannot fail to register the accumulation of handicaps by those who arrive on the labour market already in possession of the fewest qualifications. Unqualified blue-collar workers are thus most affected by unemployment and job insecurity. When they do eventually find a stable job, it is invariably at the end of several years of casual jobs, involving temping, skills contracts, or fixed-term contracts. The situation is scarcely better for other blue- and white-collar workers. How could such a difficult, harrowing existence not affect their physical and psychological health, and erode their productive capacity? How could it give them the opportunity to develop their skills, when they have less ready access than other wage-earners to training courses, are less frequently trusted with new technologies, and the jobs they perform do not lead to an acquisition of skills?[75] How could it permit them to create a family that will be a source of support, when their prospects are utterly uncertain and, even when they have a stable job, their firms do not allow them to be with their family, or do not care about their future?[76] More generally, how could it enable them to have long-term projects in a society where they can make only short-term plans?[77] Because of the pitfalls and problems that accumulate on it, the path they are obliged to follow renders them likely to be unable to escape their condition but, on the contrary, to sink into it, sometimes to the point of exclusion. The figures supplied by Brigitte Belloc and Christine Lagarenne substantiate the theory that it is increasingly difficult to escape a casual work situation.[78] In 1990, 43 per cent of those on fixed-term contracts the previous year had succeeded in securing a permanent contract. In 1995, the rate had fallen to 33 per cent. In 1990, 30 per cent of temporary workers the previous year had obtained a permanent contract, and 11 per cent a fixed-term contract; the respective numbers in 1995 were 27 per cent and 9 per cent. The deterioration was most marked in the case of trainees and subsidized contracts: 29 per cent held a permanent contract one year later in 1990, as opposed to 15 per cent in 1995. These contracts have in fact ended up being substituted for fixed-term contracts in the least qualified positions and, as Alain Supiot suspects, have possibly reinforced the stigmatization of those on them and the problems they face escaping from their 'segment'.[79]

Finally, concerns about the development of workers' employability, echoed by management, relate especially to those who have the chance of obtaining the best paid and best-protected jobs (permanent contracts in large firms). Their enhanced importance in productive processes and, more simply, their continuous presence in the organization prompt those in charge to concern themselves with their future in the firm, and even outside it, by offering them training or increasing their versatility. But these genuine efforts conceal a much less positive reality for all those consigned to the margins, who appear in workplaces only fleetingly or at times when others are not present, or responsibility for whom falls to subcontractors, who are not necessarily in a position to offer the same opportunities as the central firm. Hence words and deeds about employability simultaneously mark a *de facto* exclusion of the 'unemployable'. The managerial innovations and vulgate we have studied are addressed principally to *cadres* in large multinational firms, and it remains possible for the latter to satisfy their sense of justice by concentrating on 'their' employees, whose potential they will seek to develop, and whom they will even strive not to make redundant. But in order to avoid redundancies, they are also going to avoid recruiting those who are most 'interchangeable', so as not to give them 'false hopes', not to mislead them about the rules of the game – especially the fact that tomorrow they will possibly no longer be needed. At the end of their temporary contract, they will leave; the firm will have abided by the contract and will not have mistreated them. This situation – which in many respects appears to be the result of a rational economic decision, since it makes it possible to avoid the expense and upset of terminating permanent contracts – is also a lot less difficult to live with than making people redundant. We may therefore consider the development of casual jobs as constituting psychological protection for *cadres*, who would otherwise have to undertake tasks that are much more traumatic, as they know from previous experience. The fact that access to more stable situations and training has become significantly difficult is thus the result of a dual ethical imperative: that of continuing to offer opportunities to those one is responsible for, and who are on the 'inside'; and that of not arousing false expectations in those whom one needs only from time to time, and who are on the 'outside'. As with public initiatives to help certain categories of the unemployed, *cadres'* desire to offer employability can thus also help to reinforce the segmentation of the wage-earning class.

Nevertheless, our hypothesis about the current behaviour of those in charge of firms, which contributes to segmenting the wage-earning class, assumes that firms have been 'emptied' of their least productive and 'adaptable' personnel, following more than twenty years of reforms and restructuring. These people find themselves consigned to casual labour markets, and kept there. This is what we now wish to demonstrate.

The result of a process of selection/exclusion

The curse that seems to have descended upon the least-qualified population groups, and been compounded over time, is the result of a process of selection/exclusion that has been going on for more than twenty years, and has its roots in the new practices of personnel management in firms. Gradually, the least competent, the weakest physically or psychologically, and the least malleable have been 'externalized' and 'casualized' – something that, in a familiar cumulative process, could only add to their handicaps in the competition for employment. We know that those on the 'outside' can participate only sporadically, but it remains for us to show that barring them from entry was not enough: in the first instance, they were actually cast out.

At this point in the analysis, we must clarify our position on the question of who is responsible for this phenomenon. Querying the practices of firms rapidly leads, in effect, to pointing the finger at those who implement them – first and foremost, the *cadres* and managers.[80] Yet it cannot be argued that the outcome was planned, thought through and deliberated, in order to exclude from stable employment, and even from access to employability, a certain number of people who were already the least well-equipped. Rather, it would appear that the processes of exclusion we are about to describe emerged at the end of an accumulation of micro-alterations, micro-displacements, involving an abundance of goodwill, with people who often believed that what they were doing was for the best. Obviously, one can accuse those who organized redundancy plans, but these plans were frequently drawn up in a context of considerable economic difficulty for their firms. By sacrificing some jobs, they could entertain the belief that they were safeguarding others; and despite the personal dramas, it was less obvious than it is today, in a period of rising unemployment, that those redundancies meant consignment to almost certain job insecurity.[81] But we must also take into account those in the state who encouraged the departure of older workers or created subsidized underemployment; those who did not re-employ people, or did so only on a casual contract, in order to escape the constraints of permanent contracts when different, more flexible mechanisms were available, to create the illusion that unskilled jobs were no longer threatened, or in order not to have to create more redundancies; those who offered the two training courses that they were able to allocate in the year to the wage-earners who would get the most out of them; those who preferred to call upon less costly, more efficient subcontracting firms to improve the performance of their companies; those who exchanged a reduction in working time for greatly flexibility in the hours and days worked; those employed in recruitment agencies who dealt with the flood of cv's by making a rapid initial selection according to age or university degree, or who, wishing to satisfy their customers, presented only white-skinned people for the available post, thus contravening anti-discrimination legislation.[82] Although it is not possible to impute some perverse desire to them, in their various ways they all contributed to the growth in unemployment and job insecurity, under duress from forces that presented themselves as if 'from without'. And this is the result: through their cumulative effects over more than twenty years, the new enterprise practices have indeed fragmented the wage-earning class, and created a two-tier French society. Facilitated by new organizational mechanisms, a massive selection of wage-earners occurred, without ever having been conceived, still less planned, as such.

Developments in this direction were, however, foreseeable from the beginning of the 1970s. In the article already cited on the social conflicts of 1970–71, based on reports from the factory inspectorate, Jean-Marie Clerc writes:

> Some observers have simply forecast that firms would compensate for this effort by increasing profitability and being more exacting in the selection of their workforce, thereby increasing the number of those 'rejected', unemployed, because they are too old or very slightly handicapped. Only a few years ago, and in greater numbers than is generally believed, firms kept on workers whose 'productivity' was mediocre, and sometimes hired them; humanitarian concerns could often be found among heads of personnel. It is likely that firms will be less and less able to afford such considerations, which they will happily offload on to the state. Certain factories employ young girls or young women exclusively between the ages of 16 and 30, their sharpness of vision or manual dexterity declining thereafter. Are we not moving towards a future situation of more 'rejects', categorized as handicapped simply because their 'productivity' is inferior to that of young people? An abundance of information provides reasons to fear so, and this risks becoming a serious problem in the near future.[83]

Highlighting the selection process that has gradually made it possible to exclude from stable employment the least-qualified, the least 'adaptable', in the sense that they seem capable of performing only a limited number of jobs, and the least adjusted to the new ways of organizing work, makes it possible to pave the way for a search for policies to counteract exclusion. For it reveals the multitude of actions, each of them fragmentary, that feed into the process we are dealing with. Responsibility for such a process cannot be imputed to a single, Machiavellian subject. But by the same token, it cannot be made the result of a 'mutation' that imposed itself automatically – from without, as it were on the volition of human beings, condemned to 'adapt' or die. This social Darwinism secretes an unduly mechanistic interpretation of the phenomenon. Globalization, exposure to international competition, and the destruction of protected pockets of employment where incompetent workers were 'buried away' – these are supposed to determine a selection process, dubbed 'natural', and hence without a 'selector', that affects not only firms but also people. According to such Darwinian interpretations, the 'fittest' (even the genetically best-endowed) seize their opportunities, whereas the least fit, the weakest, find themselves excluded from the economic universe.

How can we explain the fact that the likelihood of job insecurity, and possibly social exclusion, varies depending upon a person's attributes,[84] if not by a process of selection which, far from being blind, does not reserve the same fate for everyone? The fact that there are fewer unskilled jobs than unskilled workers can certainly be cited. But this argument, based upon a 'market' logic,[85] no longer works when the characteristic feature of those casualized is sexual (are there fewer 'jobs-for-women' than women?); connected with age (fewer 'jobs-for-the-over-fifties' than people over fifty?); the place where people live (fewer 'jobs-for-those-who-live-in-cities' than people who live in cities?); or with national origin (fewer 'jobs-for-descendants-of-non-EU-immigrants' than children of non-EU immigrants?). In fact, just as it is perfectly plausible that employers prefer a man, someone aged between twenty-five and forty, or of French descent – and hence by the same token that they exclude a woman, a worker who is younger or older, or the child of an Algerian immigrant – it is also plausible that unskilled jobs have been abolished in order to restrict the recruitment of unqualified people, whom it is more difficult to get to change, switch job, or adapt to new duties;[86] and that employers prefer to recruit relatively overqualified people to the remaining positions. In a situation where 'there isn't a job for everyone',[87] it is always the same people who are not selected – which can only aggravate their handicaps, and erect barriers that are increasingly difficult to surmount between the different 'segments' of the wage-earning class.

There are many routes to selection, starting with *mass redundancies*, whose massive character seems to contradict the idea of a personal selection, wage-earner by wage-earner. When a factory is closed, the objection might run, all the jobs are destroyed, not only those held by the 'least employable'. But the distinction between collective redundancies on economic grounds and individual redundancy for personal reasons is not as clear, or as easy to establish, as it might appear. In the first place, in cases of mass redundancy the employer must define the criteria used to determine the order of redundancies. Yet these criteria (people with family responsibilities, seniority, professional qualities, being a single mother, social characteristics that make reintegration difficult, etc.) refer 'to the individual as a *person*, not merely as a wage-earner'. Furthermore, when a job is subject to alteration or abolition for technical reasons (related to economic grounds), while being replaced by another job, access to training and appraisal during training constitute filters for personal selection, and discussion will revolve around the abilities of the person concerned. It is then very difficult for the judge to give the 'grounds inhering, and those not inhering, in the person of the wage-earner' their respective due.[88] Despite the non-discrimination provisions to which they are supposed to conform (which, moreover, are regularly violated by incentives to those over fifty to leave), mass redundancies have thus in practice been equivalent to a sum of redundancies on personal grounds. Moreover, it remains the case that differences in people's lot, which are slight enough at the outset (all the jobs are abolished), have entailed a very marked diversification in subsequent destinies. The first to leave threatened firms, prior to mass redundancies but when rumours began to evoke their possibility, were those with the best chances of finding work elsewhere – either by dint of specific skills, or because they could access socially and spatially more extensive networks, or simply because they were less rooted locally (single as opposed to married people, renters rather than owners of property, etc.), and hence the cost of changing location was less risky and less high. We know, moreover, that the chances of those involved in mass redundancies finding new work are highly unequal. For a second exclusion – from *being taken on* this time – supervenes to sift people on a criterial basis (notably by age, sex, French or foreign – especially North African – patronymic), and according to their ability to engage and make the most of the many mechanisms (support from the redundancy plan, training, etc.) offered them, which operate as so many detailed selection mechanisms.

The process of redesigning the firm's contours and *outsourcing* certain tasks has also turned out to be an opportunity to *push unskilled jobs into less advantageous statutes*, into subcontractors and/or insecure contracts. Fine-grained analysis of the changes in blue-collar work indicates that they are not in fact reducible to the loss of a million jobs since 1975, and to massive job reductions in sectors that were traditionally heavy employers.[89] Certainly, we observe advances in automation leading to a marked reduction in certain kinds of job, like those of metalworkers, fitters, or panel-beaters, while at the same time creating occupations for mechanics specializing in machine maintenance.[90]

But technical progress, which for the sake of medium-term national competitiveness it would scarcely be reasonable to seek to fetter seriously, is not the only cause of these changes. The transfer of unskilled jobs to lower-wage countries has likewise played a role of the first importance. In fact, from the end of the 1960s large firms initiated a process of relocating segments of production, and a search for subcontracting, in countries where wage levels and the capacity for collective defence of wage-earners were lower than in the major developed countries. The available studies demonstrate that the increase in international trade tends to destroy unskilled jobs and to create skilled jobs in the developed countries.[91] If, in the final analysis, the job losses were not extensive, with some studies even indicating that the balance was positive for France when account is taken of all the effects generated,[92] and did not affect all sectors to the same extent (clothing, footwear and the assembly of electrical goods were the main ones affected), it is nevertheless the case that this translated into a net destruction of unskilled jobs in our country. Here again, it is difficult to regret the general shift towards more qualified jobs. But even so, this dynamic, by liberating a great mass of workers, transformed the balance of forces with the employers as regards less skilled work. It allowed employers to impose harsher contractual conditions on those who took such jobs,[93] and facilitated reconstruction of the profile of blue-collar employment around less advantageous statuses.[94] Indeed, blue-collar employment has not disappeared, since some of it is wholly unamenable to relocation – for example, cleaning, catering, sales work, factories for which the proximity of the final customer is vital, and so on. But it has experienced an overall shift towards services, towards jobs coded as 'white-collar' in the nomenclatures,[95] and to smaller firms in the grip of outsourcing practices. Now, this general evolution in working-class employment has contributed to significantly casualizing it: blue-collar workers, like employees in the service sector and/or small structures, are in fact more insecure than those in industry and/or large concerns.[96] Moreover, in addition to instances of outsourcing of various entire tasks (cleaning, caretaking), frequent recourse to subcontracting or temping was aimed at eliminating the hardest, least-skilled tasks from large firms – tasks that were proving to be sources of disputes and problems in managing the workforce. Thus, Francis Ginsbourger cites the example of the Solmer factory in Fos-sur-Mer, which systematically entrusted dangerous tasks to Somafer, often characterized locally as a 'meat-dealer'. Similarly, during a strike in November 1974, workers on the blast-furnace floor, who were demanding a revision of their grades, and the abolition of the category of labourer in particular, obtained satisfaction, but the corresponding duties were simply handed over to outside firms.[97]

Selection also operates through *access to training*, which is initially offered to those whose disposition is deemed sufficiently promising to justify the investment.[98] We encounter the same inequalities in access to new technologies.

Finally, as a last site of selection, we shall mention the *new mechanisms* and, in particular, *local discussion groups*, but also *training periods and courses*, which make it possible to put people to the test and select them on the basis of their ability to engage in the available work situations. The way actors conduct themselves in these instances indicates their goodwill and their ability to integrate into the new organization of work. In everyone's presence, and under the noses of supervisory staff, such internalized dispositions as the ability to transmit knowledge, team spirit, enthusiasm, inventiveness or commitment are exhibited. The involvement of temporary workers in these bodies is thus a good indicator, making it possible to identify those who deserve to be made permanent should the opportunity arise.[99]

Obviously, as we have already suggested, the *state of the labour market* and the pressure of unemployment are strong incentives to 'cream off', since firms 'have the option'. Thus, in Gorgeu and Mathieu's study the factories are established in job pools, allowing them to 'sift', to be exacting about job experience, and to achieve selection rates of 3 to 5 per cent relative to the number of candidates.[100] In addition, the *general increase in the level of education* has made access to a qualified, competent workforce easier. From the second half of the 1970s onwards, for example, large firms, even in advanced sectors, no longer had to 'stock up on' young *cadres*, engineers or qualified technicians, and promise them a career – as was still the case in the mid-1960s – in order to have them on hand, and deprive the competition of their services. Now abundant, young *cadres* offer their services on a vast market where they can be called upon, or are occupied in smaller firms offering less protection, while the quality of this category of personnel is superior to what it was.[101] In addition, in so far as the number of skilled jobs did not increase as rapidly as the number of university graduates, the latter have tended to cut in on less skilled jobs, thus aggravating the situation of those most lacking in qualifications and adversely affecting their position in the balance of forces with the employers accordingly. The question of the criteria governing selection is thus sharply posed.

Selection according to *age, national origin* and *sex* is the best-documented. Historically, the selection of the employable in the context of 'redundancy schemes' or economic redundancies affected wage-earners *over fifty* in the first instance, and was facilitated by the establishment of early retirement schemes and bonuses for leaving during the 1970s and 1980s.[102] Contrary to the rules that prevailed in the type of capitalism associated with the 'second spirit', seniority has become a factor less of security than of insecurity. Transformation of the practices of remuneration according to stages of life has helped to set up competition between the generations, which did not exist in the previous period. It is characterized, on the one hand, by enhanced remuneration throughout one's career, marked at the outset and slowing down thereafter; and, on the other, by the hiring of new, more educated generations on wages higher than those of their elders, so that wage-earners aged forty found themselves better paid than those of fifty, while the latter found themselves better paid than they had ever been. Today, in contrast, if remuneration still increases throughout the course of a career, starting salaries have declined, while the level of academic qualification among the young continues to increase, so that the wage-earner becomes exorbitant at fifty and the young person cheaper than ever. Hence the temptation to part with older workers, in the absence of downgrading them – a practice that is current in Japan, but not in France. In addition, these practices fuel strong hostility between the generations, the young increasing the vigour of their age with the energy that comes from the will to prove that they are more successful, and rectify the injustices that have been done to them.[103] This development is in part explained by a reduction in the relative share distributed to wage-earners, which means that it is no longer possible to offer both increases in the course of a career and increases for younger generations. The line of least resistance is to privilege those who are already inside the economic system, even if this means rejecting them at the age of fifty and reducing wages for newcomers. Furthermore, various studies indicate the central role of new generations in the spread of the new forms of organization.[104]

The second priority target was *immigrant workers*. In the automobile sector, which had called on them in massive quantities from 1965 to 1973, the reorganizations of the late 1970s and the beginning of the 1980s were associated with new employment policies. Combining a bonus on leaving and on being taken on, these policies led to a massive reduction in the number of immigrants (and semi- and unskilled workers), and to the recruitment of educated young people,[105] regarded as more capable of dealing with new forms of tests at work that demanded greater capacity for initiative (in the case of breakdowns), versatility, adjustment to different manufacturing programmes, and communication.[106] Most industrial sectors seem, in fact, to have privileged a national workforce:

> The concentration of foreign manpower in sectors in difficulty is insufficient to explain the loss of nearly 100,000 unskilled jobs and 20,000 skilled jobs between 1982 and 1990: if the decline had been identical for French people and foreigners in each sector and for each level of qualification, the latter would have lost 50 per cent fewer jobs (60,000 unskilled; 10,000 skilled). In other words, the destruction of jobs entailed a much more rapid fall for foreigners than for nationals.[107]

Sexual discrimination has taken a different course from direct exclusion from employment, inasmuch as the period was characterized by the arrival of very large numbers of women on the labour market. This is indicated by the increase in the rate of paid female employment between the ages of twenty-five and fifty, which rose from 74 per cent to nearly 79 per cent between 1990 and 1998.[108] As in the case of the generations, a new form of competition among wage-earners has been established between the sexes. Employers use women's search for part-time work to generalize underemployment contracts that subsequently become the norm in certain occupations. In addition, women suffer significant discrimination when it comes to being hired.[109]

Besides these familiar criteria, we may suggest the hypothesis that selection has to a large extent also been conducted according to people's *medical and psychological characteristics* (whose distribution is not independent of more readily objectifiable characteristics or situations, such as hierarchical status, age, educational level, etc.). Take, first of all, *state of health*. Studies of long-term unemployed people have in numerous cases identified a professional accident or illness at the root of their exclusion from the labour market, this principle of selection being operative above all in the case of less qualified workers.[110] In the CERC study of 'Job Insecurity and the Risk of Exclusion', those who considered their own state of health to be 'bad' accounted for 4.4 per cent of the sample, but for 10.3 per cent of those who had been unemployed for more than two years, and 5.9 per cent of those who had been unemployed for at least two years.[111] Moreover, if people with 'bad' or 'mediocre' health are not especially numerous among those holding an 'unstable' job (which assumes that they are recent recruits), they are overrepresented among those who say that they hold a 'stable but threatened' job – that is to say, according to the definition of the category, among those who think that they will lose their job in two years.

More extensive no doubt, but also more difficult to assess, have been the effects of *psychological selection*. In the first instance, it has affected those whose predispositions were least attuned to the new mechanisms of local negotiations, in particular *'yesterday's enemies'*. These consist, on the one hand, in junior *cadres*, 'petty tyrants', who have often risen to senior positions, but whose ineradicable authoritarianism justified their exclusion (through redundancy or early retirement), which was further rendered desirable by the reduction of lines of hierarchy and measures to rejuvenate the population pyramid; and, on the other hand, in wage-earners, often union members, who around May 1968 had developed a critical culture in firms and invested a lot in activism. Thus, in Gorgeu and Mathieu's investigation, those not selected live in towns reputed to be 'oppositional', or have worked in firms known for their high wages, their frequent disputes, or strong CGT representation.[112] A young, rural workforce, without any experience of industry, is preferred for its presumed docility. Moreover, the choice of site for setting up a factory takes account of these different criteria. For Christophe Dejours, the exclusion of older workers pertains to the same principle of excluding sources of opposition.[113]

But other dispositions (in part bound up with the level of education), like an *ability to relate* and a *capacity to communicate*, have also played a role in selection.

The new work mechanisms in fact require adequate access to written culture on the part of wage-earners (in order to read instructions and write short reports);[114] and forms of collectivization of skills (progress groups, quality circles) demand sufficient discursive ability to give an oral progress report in public. Finally, transverse modes of co-ordination (teams, projects, etc.) place greater weight not only on specifically linguistic mastery, but also on qualities that might be called more 'personal', more clearly bound up with the 'charac-ter' of the person – for example, openness, self-control, availability, good humour, composure – which were by no means so highly prized in the old work culture. The techniques of enterprise psychology (interviews, graphol-ogy, etc.) are used to pinpoint these propensities in candidates for a job. And this applies to applicants not only for jobs as *cadres*, but equally for blue-collar jobs.[115] An ability to adjust to face-to-face situations in the course of a psy-chological interview in fact already represents a form of self-testing.

Capacities for commitment and adaptation, which can be assessed according to the same mechanisms, have also served as selection criteria. These capacities, which are essential in a logic of 'flexibility' presupposing a series of engage-ments in, and disengagements from, various tasks and different jobs, require the selection of people who can prove themselves capable of flexibility. One of Gorgeu and Mathieu's interlocutors details the qualities of a good recruit as follows: 'There is sharing and communication, you don't cover up a defect, you do not let a customer down, you take on an even less skilled post in the immediate interests of the site. You do extra work even if the working day is over, you agree to come in on Saturday morning if required, you are mentally adaptable.'[116] Thus, for example, in a firm that makes soldering instruments studied by Christian Bessy, economic redundancies, numerous in the second half of the 1980s, were made on the basis of a selection whose main criteria were 'wage-earners' personal commitment' and 'versatility'.[117] The role accorded to the possession of academic qualifications has, it seems, never been so important[118] – for example, certificates of general education are demanded for blue-collar jobs. Over and above the technical skills they sometimes certify, this is explained by the fact that such qualifications presuppose a minimum capacity to engage in a task, to see a project through to a successful conclu-sion over a period of time – that is to say, to pursue studies to the point of obtaining a qualification, and to prove oneself sufficiently malleable to conform to the examiners' assessment standards.[119]

Wage-earners with *restricted mobility*, especially women with children, are especially vulnerable. They can be forced to resign following compulsory trans-fers, or changes in hours, or simply as a result of the abolition of the school bus.[120]

In a work devoted to the reorganization of an arms factory, Thomas Périlleux conducts a very precise analysis of the forms of selection accompa-nying the transition from the old manufacturing workshop – a hall in which

800 female machine operators worked – to the new workshop, comprising a pool of versatile, digitally controlled machines.[121] This process, which was spread over five years, saw the firm's workforce go down from 10,000 to 1,400 wage-earners. The female workers were made redundant, and the 'operatives' who work in the new workshop are all former adjusters. The levels of hierarchy have been reduced from nine to four. The new organization is supposed to allow for 'involvement' and the 'development of a sense of responsibility' on the part of the 'operatives'. Tests that personalize selection have been established for access to the new workshop. Selection is made on the basis of a technical exam and a test in an assessment centre in the firm's employment department. The technical exam focuses on mathematical knowledge, draughtsmanship and machinery. The psychological test focuses on people placed in group situations. Its role is to confirm an 'aptitude for working in a team, an ability to transmit knowledge, possession of an analytical mind, a capacity to assimilate new knowledge'. These tests aim to assess the malleability of the operatives, their capacity for enthusiastic engagement, but also for 'intervening without getting emotional', 'being open to others', and 'avoiding irritability'. Previous criteria of selection and promotion, such as seniority, are denounced and formally abandoned. New criteria emerge: autonomy, communication skills, malleability, openness to others. Selection on the basis of these new criteria produces irreversible effects of exclusion from the organization, notably with a rash of early retirements.

The list of the criteria used in the case we have already cited of the recruitment accompanying the opening of a new on-hand factory in automobile subcontracting is likewise illuminating. In addition to the first sifting by criteria of age, sex, academic qualification and place of residence, the candidates underwent psycho-technical tests designed to measure their adaptability, dexterity and memory, their capacity to distinguish colours and to pass from theory to its practical application. Next, an interview with a psychologist was designed to assess the candidates' real motivation, their emotional equilibrium – especially their ability to withstand the stress of just-in-time and versatility – their capacity for teamwork and sense of responsibility. Finally, candidates who had survived these stages were put to the test in a 'normal' work situation during a seven-week training period for the job, as precursors to a possible permanent contract.[122]

Thus, twenty years of systematic selection during which, every time the opportunity for such a choice arose, the least 'mobile', the least 'adaptable', the least 'qualified', the 'too old', the 'too young', those 'from' North Africa, Black Africa, and so on, were excluded, have led to the current situation. As we have seen, it is characterized by an increasingly clear segmentation of work situations between those who enjoy a certain amount of security – even if it can be put in doubt by the closure of their establishment or workforce reductions – and those who, condemned to job insecurity and poor wages, witness their chances of getting a regular job recede that little bit more every day, and who are driven to despair and violence.[123] This increasing segmentation helps to divide wage-earners: those with a stable position are often represented to 'casuals' as 'privileged', while the latter may in turn regard casual work as a kind of disloyal competition impacting on wages and working conditions. And it is accompanied by a social regression and a reduction in protection affecting all workers, even those who hold what are considered to be protected jobs.

The reduction in the protection of workers and social regression

The form of enterprise organization that replaces the work contract by a commercial contract with a service provider makes it possible largely to *brush aside the constraints of labour law* – in the first instance, by rendering a number of legislative and regulatory texts stipulating a minimum number of staff inapplicable.[124] Thus, smaller units, especially when they have the legal status of companies in their own right (while being highly dependent on their principals), do not have a works council, and are scarcely unionized. The risks of the non-application of labour law in small firms are likewise increased by the fact that there is less chance of those in charge of them knowing about the rules, whereas large groups have a legal department. In this way, a *de facto* circumvention of certain measures is organized, which are not applied out of ignorance. The public prosecutor's department of Colmar, faced with the proliferation of excuses from small employers invoking their ignorance and denouncing the law's complexity, thus decided to oblige the guilty parties to undertake training courses in labour law, for which they had to pay themselves.[125] The Labour Ministry, for its part, wanted to transform the brief of the factory inspectorate from controlling implementation of the law to acting as consultants to small and medium-sized firms.[126]

With the increase in unemployment and the intensification of competition on the labour market, the often very isolated workers in subcontracting – some on casual contracts, others made psychologically insecure by dint of the very fact that they do the same work as their temporary colleagues – do not have sufficient resources to put pressure on their employers, or to resist them. This is particularly true of demands that fall outside the legal framework. The workforce in subcontracting firms, which in a different epoch would have been employed by the firm passing on the orders, is likewise excluded from the often more advantageous statute provided for by collective agreements or a local agreement. Finally, the central firm also sees outsourcing as an opportunity partially to divest itself of responsibility in the event of professional accident or illness. (These are more common in service-providing firms than in the stable core, as has been demonstrated, for example, in the case of temporary staff in the nuclear industry – wage-earners in service firms responsible for the maintenance and upkeep of the power stations.)

One result of these various displacements is revealed by the 1991 inquiry into 'Working Conditions', which demonstrates a contrast between large firms (more than a thousand personnel), where 'risk and hardship are developing in a rather positive direction', and smaller firms, 'where the situation is deteriorating'.[127] 'The results of the investigation chime with the observations of certain factory inspectors. For some years, many of them have been drawing attention to frequent breaches of labour legislation, particularly in small and medium-sized firms. Pointing in the same direction is the recorded upsurge in accidents at work, particularly in the public buildings and works sector.'[128] Temporary staff are obviously more vulnerable to hardship and injuries than other wage-earners, for they invariably hold blue-collar jobs, and frequently the most dangerous such jobs.[129]

A less familiar but nevertheless well-documented aspect of the situation is that the difficulties of the job market have not affected only the working conditions of people holding less skilled jobs. They have equally fuelled a process of social regression in the case of positions that are more stable, or in stronger firms. The novelty to be underscored is that collective agreements, formerly required to improve the conditions of wage-earners, can now just as easily make them worse: 'Thus French legislators in 1982 ... came down in favour of the right for the parties [employer and unions] to make working conditions worse, a decision that was expressly confirmed five years later.' The parties 'can, as regards both working hours and wages – i.e. the two most important spheres of labour legislation – lower the threshold of the requirements formulated by the legal provisions and the relevant extensive conventions'. This development 'leads to collective agreements contravening the hitherto accepted limits and deviating from a conception of the rules which, in the worst-case scenario, accepted stagnation, but never a collectively agreed regression'.[130] By encouraging recourse to negotiations, notably at enterprise level, the law offered employers an opportunity to press their own demands. As a result, traditional negotiations, intended to improve the rights and benefits of wage-earners with respect to the legal minima, have gradually been replaced by negotiations aiming at 'give-and-take' agreements. The balance of forces in these negotiations, which is unfavourable to the wage-earners, led to outcomes whereby the latter might hope to protect jobs, while employers achieved tangible advantages, such as revised methods for increasing or determining wages, or a reform of working hours.[131] The increase in the proportion of 'negotiated rights' *vis-à-vis* 'legislated rights' has thus itself accentuated the disparity in rights between workers (which already existed, but not on such a scale, because of the device of staff thresholds). Variations from one branch to the next, one firm to the next, even from one group of wage-earners to the next in the same firm, are more frequently recorded than in the past. The fragmentation of labour law under this pressure does not really seem to bode well for an improvement in the 'real' condition of wage-labour, which is increasingly excluded from the legal provisions that accompany the so-called 'normal' work contract (full-time, permanent contract).

Another effect of the new enterprise mechanisms is a significant increase in the intensity of work for an equivalent wage. Certainly, productivity gains are involved here. But achieving them has more to do with methods resembling increased exploitation of the workers – who, to put it schematically, 'work more to earn less' – than with gains realized thanks to technological or organizational changes that benefit wage-earners and firms alike.[132]

The increase in work intensity for the same wage

First and foremost, the casualization of labour and the development of subcontracting make it possible to *pay only the time actually worked*, and to subtract from paid time all slack periods, training time and breaks that used to be partially included in the definition of the fair working day. As often implemented, the development of part-time work aims to get the workforce to adjust to demand almost in real time, with an hour's overtime not costing more than the normal hour.

In Damien Cartron's narrative of his job at McDonald's,[133] the firm gives him an indicative schedule of the hours at which he is obliged to present himself for work. But the clocking-in and clocking-off hours are administered by the person in charge of the branch, who, depending on the day, can urge him to work less, but especially more, the schedule being planned to a minimum.[134] The hours actually provided for are in fact respected only to the tune of about 50 per cent, the compensation being that the wage-earner occasionally has opportunities to deviate from the stipulated schedule for personal reasons – which, in this particular case, accounts for roughly one-quarter of departures from the schedule. The shortest working week of the eleven concerned was 11.5 hours, the longest 27.3, with an average of 20.2 hours for a part-time contract providing for 10 hours.

In the case of subcontracting, it has been noted that the requirements of the firms passing on the orders 'to their suppliers are always greater than what they can possess in-house, and these requirements have had uncompensated repercussions for the latter's workforces'.[135] Generally speaking, outsourcing makes it possible to increase the intensity of work by using the pressure of the market, which appears to be an uncontrollable external factor, and to exonerate the local managerial staff, who are equally subject to it. This mode of external control is more potent and more legitimate than that which the principals could exercise over their own workforce. Equally conducive to it are the 'availability clauses' that have proliferated in recent years, whereby 'the employer ensures the continuous availability of wage-earners while being obliged to pay only for periods that have actually been worked'. This brings the 'constraints of self-employed work (irregular income) and subordination (submission to the firm passing on the orders)' to bear upon wage-earners.[136]

Increased work intensity is also obtained in-house as a result of new managerial methods. A subtle accounting division of cost centres makes it possible, for example, to make each person in charge of a department, an 'autonomous team', or a workshop branch accountable. In the first instance, it has led to the optimal use of personnel, wage costs frequently representing the majority of the costs of these minor 'accounting centres'.[137] Mechanisms for invoicing working time between departments encourage attempts to verify that the hours paid are hours that have actually been worked on identifiable projects, and hence invoicable in terms of analytical accounting, which tends to reduce intervening periods, waiting time, slack periods, 'breaks' in the working day or week to a minimum, and to develop an external manpower reserve.[138] Given that they pay, internal customers are also going to seek to pack as much into the hours used as possible, by continually increasing their specifications. Where this is possible, the firm's departments and subcontractors are set in competition with one another. The creation of 'internal markets', via managerial control techniques (extension of budgetary monitoring to ever smaller units and the establishment of internal invoicing), thus has the same kind of results as the development of subcontracting or temporary contracts. Anything that is not directly productive is discarded as non-working time, and the costs of maintaining the workforce are transferred on to the workers or, in the event of unemployment or occupational disability, the state.[139]

The *new forms of work organization*, particularly those inspired by Toyotism, likewise facilitate 'the trend towards a situation in which the workforce will never be unproductive and will be able to be discarded as soon as orders decline'.[140] Thus, Shimizu explains that a continual decline in cost price (more familiar under the name of *Kaizen* or 'continual improvement') – an essential aim of the Toyota firm that is today regarded as a model by the largest groups – was achieved mainly by pursuing workforce economies. This implied the use of technical and organizational mechanisms, but also the abolition of all slack periods and the maximum increase in work tempos. Workers went along with this in so far as their pay was directly linked to the labour savings made.[141]

The 1991 'Working Conditions' inquiry (confirmed by 'Techniques and Organization of Work' in 1993) demonstrated that more and more wage-earners were finding themselves subject to tempo constraints in their work. This phenomenon affects all social categories, from *cadre* to worker, and all sectors, including the tertiary sector, which might have been thought to be less vulnerable than industry. Between 1984 and 1993, the percentage of wage-earners experiencing tempo constraints due to the automatic displacement of a component or a product went up from 3 to 6 per cent; due to the automatic rhythm of a machine, from 4 to 7 per cent; due to norms or tight deadlines, from 19 to 44 per cent; due to the demands of customers or the public, from 39 to 58 per cent; and due to constant control by superiors, from 17 to 24 per cent.[142] The mental responsibility of workers is likewise everywhere on the rise, as is indicated by the trend in the percentage of wage-earners who claim that they cannot take their eyes off their work, which progressed from 16 to 26 per cent between 1984 and 1991.[143] Like others, *cadres* have seen the demands on their work increase. They complain about a lack of time, and about colleagues.[144] Their working hours have gone up: between 1984 and 1991, the percentage whose working day was longer than 11 hours rose from 14 to 18 per cent, and between 10 and 11 hours from 19 to 20 per cent.[145] 'Exercising hierarchical responsibilities even increases the risk of being caught in a pincer between the market and the organization. If managerial *cadres* are well shielded, the intermediate hierarchy is struggling against deadlines'.[146] In Toyotism, daily, hourly adaptation by the labour force to the ups and downs of production plays the buffer role that stocks used to perform. The result, as has been demonstrated in particular by studies of Japanese transplants to the United States, is an increase in people exceeding working hours, and in health risks related to fatigue and anxiety.[147] A great many observations of the same sort can be found in the work by Y. Clot, J.-Y. Rochex and Yves Schwartz on the reorganization of work in the PSA group.

In addition to deadlines, exacting standards are imposed – this is the case, for example, with the ISO 9000 rating. A typical case is that of 'subcontractors working in concentrated flows who must simultaneously meet customer demand but also respect very strict quality standards, since there is neither space, nor time, nor money to correct mistakes. Wage-earners are thus in a position where they suffer a dual constraint: that generated by variations in demand, and that generated by consistency of standards.'[148] As François Eymard-Duvernay explains, when they can, firms overwhelmingly transfer on to wage-earners and subcontractors responsibility for the quality assurance demanded by consumers, who are desirous of obtaining 'flawless' products and services.[149]

The use of *new technologies* is also an opportunity to increase the pressure on wage-earners: on an equivalent socioprofessional grade, workers who use information technology have a cleaner and physically less punishing job, but they experience the pressure of demand, especially when they are blue- or white-collar workers. Other workers are more autonomous and better paid, but see the deadlines to which they are subject play a growing role.[150] Computerization is thus accompanied by 'a greater degree of psychological obligation', with an increase in 'demands for attention, vigilance, availability and concentration'.[151]

The new information technologies can now organize a very strict control over workers' performance, gradually abolishing 'uncontrolled' spaces. Grégoire Philonenko cites the Anabel system used at Carrefour which, in addition to its functional importance for stock and order management, facilitates a precise knowledge of the performance of each stock manager; or the camera system installed in the shop that makes it possible both to prevent shoplifting by customers and to monitor the work of staff, while other cameras are installed in the storerooms.[152]

In the arms factory studied by Périlleux, the new production mechanisms assign a significant role to the 'versatility' and 'autonomy' of 'operatives'. But as an informant explains, the 'log' of the software program for managing digitally commanded tools 'makes it possible to follow all the operations performed since 1988 in chronological order, almost to the second'.[153] Thus, new computer mechanisms make it possible, on the one hand, to impose a monitoring that abolishes slack periods and, on the other, to ensure a record of deeds and gestures facilitating remote control in real time or a review of old operations – for example, in the case of a lawsuit. Moreover, these two operations can be largely fused when standardized systems for receiving information tend to direct and format behaviour, if only in so far as they necessitate a detailed encoding of the task to be performed.

In his study of the management of subcontracting networks in the clothing industry in the Cholet region, Francis Ginsbourger shows that a new type of asymmetry has accompanied the development of information technologies as a result of the use of a program that makes it possible to calculate times for the various processes and impose them on workshops.[154] One of the most obvious results of the computerization of work has thus been to equip management with many more, much more sensitive instruments of control than in the past, capable of calculating value added at the level not only of the firm or plant, but also of the team, or even the individual – and this, as it were, *from a distance*. At the same time, this allows a reduction in the number of supervisors (reduction in the length of lines of hierarchy) who, no longer having to be *in the presence* of the workers, looking over their shoulders, can make themselves unobtrusive, even quasi-invisible.

Finally, we shall cite the current rapid implementation ERP (Enterprise Resources Planning), under the impetus particularly of the millennium bug. Presenting itself as an opportunity to renew computer systems, this leads to considerably reinforcing remote control, by making it possible, for example, for headquarters to know the exact performance of each employee in real time, and to assemble in record time all the available information on that employee held on the firm's previously disconnected databases. Occupations previously characterized by a high degree of independence, like those of sales representatives, are today put under pressure as a result of the complete computerization of customer records, the portability of computers, techniques of transmission from a distance, and the obligation to key in data after or during each visit. *Cadres* are beginning to be asked to make their diaries freely accessible on networks so that available slots for meetings involving numerous people can rapidly be found, by compiling information on the various ways in which they use their time. On each occasion, the gain in terms of speed, and the reliability of transmission and data processing, is coupled with an extension in control, and tends to reduce slack periods.

Another way of increasing work intensity, which is less conspicuous than upping tempos, is the *development of multitasking on the same wage*. Gorgeu and Mathieu show that the qualities looked for in candidates during recruitment are never aligned with qualification scales and hence are not paid. Semi- and unskilled workers are recruited on the guaranteed minimum wage even when they perform 'tasks of quality control, adjustment, maintenance, production management, which were all considered skilled when they fell to staff not directly involved in production, but are no longer deemed so when performed by an agent of production'.[155] The new ways of organizing work have made it possible to expand the tasks and develop the autonomy of blue-collar workers, who can show more initiative than in the most Taylorized organizations. The career profiles of operatives are different – they are more qualified, more competent – but wages have remained at the same level. So in order to earn a minimum wage, one must do more, and be better qualified, than in the past. Whereas at the beginning of the 1970s employers' attempts to restructure jobs had come up against strong unions demanding compensation in the form of wages, the low combativeness of recent years has made it possible to push through changes in work without having to pay more for a workforce that has, however, seen its work intensified.[156]

The wish to use *new layers of skills* among workers hitherto subject to fragmented work, by encouraging their engagement, likewise leads to greater exploitation. Exploitation is in fact intensified by setting to work human abilities (relating to people, receptiveness, flexibility, emotional involvement, commitment, etc.), which Taylorism, precisely because it treated human beings like machines, did not seek and was not able to reach. Yet this subjection of human qualities challenges the separation, inscribed in law, between work and the worker. What the worker brings to the job depends increasingly upon generic capacities or skills developed outside the firm, and is thus less and less measurable in terms of working hours; and this applies to an ever higher number of wage-earners. In the words of a consultant who was one of the first to establish quality circles, 'the employers couldn't get over what a worker was able to do'.[157] With the new mechanisms for discussing and resolving problems, much more was demanded of people than before, in terms of deploying their intelligence, their capacity for observation, and their shrewdness for the firm's benefit. If this development is not in itself negative – no one could wish work to be restricted to a series of mechanical gestures – it is likely that the workforce's additional contribution has been remunerated only by retention for those who proved capable of it and exclusion for the rest. Given the state of the labour market, and methods of managing remuneration according to generation, employers can also *recruit overqualified people whom they will pay at the rate of someone less qualified*, affecting not to register the actual contribution of this overqualification.[158] Thus, paradoxically, corresponding to a move in the direction of an ever deeper exploitation of the layers of skills possessed by workers as people, there is a tendency to reduce wage costs.

Finally, the move towards an *individualization of work situations*,[159] and especially *remuneration*, has made it possible to have a much firmer grip on wage-earners individually, and thus to put them under pressure much more effectively. The years 1950 to 1970 were marked by a relative autonomization of remuneration with respect to individual performance (which was often difficult to measure in the dominant organizational forms of the time, especially in the case of assembly-line work); by collective increases in wages according to productivity increases assessed at aggregate level; and by a standardization of remuneration (reduction in remuneration by output, generalization of monthly payment, etc.).[160] During the 1980s, the growing automation of work went in tandem with increased differentiation and individualization of remuneration, which was much more directly linked to individual performance (performance-related pay), or the results of the unit to which the wage-earner was attached. Hitherto fixed to posts, remuneration was now increasingly linked to the personal properties of those holding them, and to appraisal of their results by managerial authority.[161] In 1985, of the firms that had implemented wage increases, two out of ten practised the individualization of basic wages. Between 1985 and 1990 this proportion doubled, and the proportion of wage-earners affected went up from 45 to 60 per cent. The percentage of workers affected by individualization measures rose from 43 to 51 per cent between 1985 and 1990. The process started in large firms: from 1985, 85 per cent of firms with more than a thousand wage-earners practised the individualization of wages.[162] Such practices have since been extended to smaller firms.[163] The individualization of skills, bonuses and sanctions had a further pernicious effect by tending to make individuals exclusively responsible for their own successes and failures.

As we have already seen, this set of transformations has made it possible to restore a degree of order in firms that was compromised at the beginning of the 1970s, and to generate significant productivity increases, to the extent that today, French firms involved in direct opposition on foreign markets are, by and large, competitive.[164] Such an outcome can in no way be deemed worthless. Nevertheless, it looks as if wage-earners have paid a high price for these changes. For everything would appear to suggest that simply in order to maintain their standard of living, they must work more intensively; and, by the same token, that those regarded as incapable of keeping up, and as 'unadaptable', have been pushed into less skilled jobs, or even out of the labour market. *Part of the current job shortage must thus be clearly attributed to the practices that have removed any dead time from paid worked time, just as a percentage of firms' profits must be related to the extraction of more value added from human labour for an unchanged wage.*[165]

The question that those who defend the results of these transformations in terms of 'economic progress' neglect to pose, while making do with lamenting the unbalanced character of a labour market biased in favour of firms, concerns the nature of what is actually exchanged on such a market. As we know, labour is a legal fiction when it is regarded as a commodity that can be separated from the person who performs it.[166] 'Human resources' cannot be consumed like other resources, for they presuppose a maintenance and reproduction cost that ought to be inseparable from the cost of their utilization. Someone who buys a tomato in principle pays for the cost of its production, from the generation of the seed through to the earth, fertilizer and attention lavished on it.[167] He does not simply rent the time that it spends between his plate and his stomach. This, however, is the kind of situation that is becoming ever more frequent as regards labour, since the costs that arise prior to employment (education, training, maintenance during periods of inactivity and rest), or after it (rebuilding strength, wear and tear, ageing), are increasingly excluded from the wages paid. And this is not to take account of the negative impact of the intensification of work on physical and mental health. This situation is all the more problematic in that 'human resources' take a long time to 'produce', like the wood of certain trees planted long before it can be gathered; and the effects of the current situation are therefore going to be felt over several decades. The costs of maintaining and reproducing labour have thus been transferred largely on to private individuals and public systems. This has reinforced income-related inequalities among the former – the poorest being able neither to maintain nor to reproduce themselves unaided – and aggravated the crisis of the welfare state in the case of the latter. The state is forced to operate new compulsory levies, allowing firms to evade their responsibilities still further, in the kind of vicious circle of which socioeconomic phenomena offer numerous examples.

Transfering the costs of putting people to work on to the state

As Alain Supiot argues:

> there is no general mechanism (adjustment of contributions) that makes it possible to attribute to a firm part of the cost (surcharge) or the saving (bonus) that its managerial options (internal or external flexibility) entail for unemployment insurance and hence for other firms.[168] Today, no doubt, this question could be usefully tackled from the perspective of equality of treatment between firms, rather than from that of the firm's social responsibility. For, from the standpoint of the operation of the labour market, what matters is less the share of social costs borne by firms than equal treatment of the firms facing these costs. Yet this equality is not guaranteed, to the detriment of the firms most respectful of 'human resources'. Rather than creating

more wealth, it becomes easier, in order to increase profits, to get the community to bear these costs.[169]

But the state has been and remains in agreement with the socialization of costs formerly borne by firms,[170] like the costs relating to older workers or those regarded as less productive. Subsidizing the employment of certain categories (young people, the long-term unemployed, the unskilled, etc.) is already an accepted practice. So is the assumption, notably via the special allowances from the Fonds National pour l'Emploi (FNE), affecting 56,000 people in 1994, of part of the cost of older workers who have been excluded from employment.[171] Thus, when 940 jobs were lost at Peugeot in 1991, the state and the Union nationale pour l'emploi dans l'industrie et le commerce (UNEDIC) paid 210 million francs for them to be covered by unemployment insurance or the FNE (403 people), as against the firm's 32 million francs.[172]

The number of people benefiting from employment policy (which covers only job subsidies, training courses, and early retirement from work) has thus gone up from 100,000 in 1973 to 1.5 million in 1990, and then to 2.85 million in 1997, or 10.7 per cent of the working population. The level of expenditure is almost ten times what it was in 1973; relative to GDP, it has multiplied seven-fold, to reach 1.5 per cent in 1996 (or 118 billion francs). To this must be added, since 1993, general measures exempting employers from their costs for wage-earners close to the guaranteed minimum wage, which cost around 40 billion francs in 1997 and applied to more than 5 million jobs.[173] These figures do not take into account the payment either of unemployment benefits,[174] or of the RMI (paid to a million people as of 31 December 1997). The RMI is looking more and more like a kind of social integration allowance for those who are seeking their first stable job, and an allowance for those who are not entitled to receive unemployment benefit, who are all the more numerous because the eligibility criteria have been tightened up in recent years.[175] Certain allowances relating to family policy but also employment, like the APE (*Allocation parentale d'éducation*), which encourages mothers with two children, the younger of whom is under three, to withdraw from employment, could equally feature here.[176] So could the various measures 'condoning moonlighting', like AGED (*Allocation de garde d'enfants à domicile*) and AFEAMA (*garde d'enfants chez les assistantes maternelles*), which cover the related social contributions under certain conditions, or again the reduction in taxes for family jobs. We could almost add a percentage of the cost of retirements between the ages of sixty and sixty-five, which place a significant strain on the public accounts,[177] had the lowering of the retirement age in 1981 not been regarded as a social entitlement, rather than as a way of reducing the working population. Finally, these items do not include the subsidies offered by local communities: grants and tax breaks for setting up in certain regions, part of the social budget of regional councils (which are in particular supposed to come within the RMI mechanism).

But let us confine ourselves to the targeted devices of employment policy, costing 118 billion francs in 1996, which made it possible for people to stop work early (early retirement, exemption from job-seeking for unemployed people over fifty-five, etc.); which allowed for occupational training (AFPA or the adult professional education association, training courses for integration, retraining agreements, etc.); and which have subsidized market jobs (the *Contrat initiative emploi*, part-time allowances, training contracts, etc.), or non-market jobs (youth employment schemes, the *Contrat emploi-solidarité*, etc.). Between 1973 and 1997, the potentially active population increased by 4.2 million (people in jobs, the unemployed, or those who have withdrawn from the labour market), whereas the supply of jobs went up by only a million. Thus 2.6 million people have arrived to swell the unemployment figures, and 0.6 million have been withdrawn from the market thanks to employment policies, one-third of them by training measures and two-thirds of them by stopping work early. Given that at the same time, 2.1 million market and non-market jobs were subsidized, and the number of jobs has not increased by more than a million, this means that the number of 'ordinary' – that is, unsubsidized – jobs has fallen by a million in twenty-five years.[178] Nevertheless, these figures do not mean that without subsidized jobs, employment would have fallen by a million. The job total would have grown, but by a little under one million (an additional 140,000 unemployed are mentioned), given the importance of windfall effects (the employer pockets the subsidy without changing his decision) and substitution (the employer opts for someone who belongs to the target population without changing his decision to hire as such).[179] Furthermore, contrary to certain generally accepted ideas, in the main subsidies go to market jobs, whose share in the overall total is increasing. Reducing employers' social security contributions when they hire wage-earners on a part-time basis, or convert full-time posts into part-time ones, has become the principal measure of public action in the market sector in terms of volume. Thus, between 1992 and 1994, the number of jobs partially exempted from social costs went up from 32,000 to 200,000.[180] *What has been organized in this fashion is a general subsidy to the private sector.*

Over the period 1973 to 1995, industry and market services have each received 37 per cent of the beneficiaries. Industry is thus overrepresented relative to its weight in employment. It has predominantly resorted to early retirement (67 per cent of beneficiaries were in industry), whereas market services, on the whole, used employment subsidies (56 per cent of beneficiaries). Similarly, early retirement has been overwhelmingly used by large establishments (78 per cent of beneficiaries), whereas establishments with fewer than ten wage-earners received 63 per cent of those with subsidized jobs.[181] So this means that the transfer of employment towards smaller units most often belonging to the service sector – part of which, we should remember, derives from the development of enterprise strategies (outsourcing, creation of subsidiaries, and reorientation towards core business) – has occurred with grants from the community at both ends: both during the elimination of jobs in the large industrial concerns and during their creation (which is often more of a re-creation) in a small tertiary structure. Similarly, analysis of the agreements signed following the Robien law of 11 June 1996, which allowed for a reduction of social contributions in the event of a reduction in working time in exchange either for recruitment (the positive plank), or for avoidance of redundancies (defensive plank) indicates that the positive agreements tend to involve small service firms, while the defensive ones relate to larger units that tend to be industrial.[182] These figures draw our attention to a phenomenon that is familiar to those who follow redundancy schemes: subsidies are given to support restructuring and, simultaneously, others are given to subcontractors to create jobs. If the overall result cannot be regarded as the product of a systematic intent to exploit the welfare state, and if the co-ordination of the subsidies at the two ends of the chain is not always as simultaneous and tailored as the example used indicates, it is nevertheless the fact that the costs of the change in strategy by firms have been paid for largely by the community – something which those in revolt against the rates of compulsory tax levies fail to mention.

At the very least, it might be argued, progress is real when it comes to the behaviour of the hierarchies whose 'petty tyrants' have been abolished, and attempts to enrich the work experience and enhance autonomy in work have borne fruit. People are freer in their working hours, and the development of part-time work has satisfied numerous aspirations. None of this is untrue. Yet greater autonomy also conceals more constraints.

As far as work is concerned, the balance-sheet of the changes in capitalism over recent decades cannot, by any stretch of the imagination, be called gloriously favourable. There is no doubt that young wage-earners, who have no experience of previous methods of organizing work, would not tolerate the hierarchies of the 1960s, with their authoritarianism and moralism, any better than their elders, who rebelled against such mechanisms in 1968; and that in numerous instances job enrichment, the development of responsibilities at work, and merit-based remuneration have satisfied some important aspirations on the part of wage-earners. At the same time, however, we can only underline the many reverses that have marked the evolution in the condition of wage-labour over the last twenty years.

It is obvious that regression on such a scale would not have been possible had it not been for a difficult labour market fuelling a widespread fear of unemployment and favouring the docility of wage-earners – so much so that the latter have partially participated in what might be described as their self-exploitation. Likewise, it would certainly have been checked by strong social critique and unions. Yet the displacements of capitalism have also contributed to deunionization and the quelling of social critique. The next chapter is devoted to these issues.

Notes

1 The share of value added accruing to capital, measured by the gross surplus of exploitation, which had settled around 29 per cent in the second half of the 1970s, rose to nearly 40 per cent in 1995. The share of wages, which had risen in the 1970s to reach 71.8 per cent in 1981, gradually fell from 1982–83, to 62.4 per cent in 1990 and 60.3 per cent in 1995. Whereas more than 5 per cent of national income had been redistributed from capital to labour from 1970–82, now 10 per cent of national income was redistributed in the opposite direction, from labour to capital, between 1983 and 1995. In order to assess the extent of these variations, Thomas Piketty observes, to provide a point of comparison, that the measures of fiscal redistribution decided by the Socialist government upon its arrival in power in 1981 (denounced by the right as a 'fiscal mugging') led to a redistribution corresponding to 0.3 per cent of the then national income (*L'économie des inégalités*, La Découverte, Paris 1997).

2 See Jennifer Bué, 'Les différentes formes de flexibilité', *Travail et emploi*, no. 41, 3, 1989, pp. 29–35.

3 See Danièle Linhart, 'À propos du post-taylorisme', *Sociologie du travail*, no. 1, 1993, pp. 63–73.

4 Frédéric de Coninck, 'Évolutions post-tayloriennes et nouveaux clivages sociaux', *Travail et emploi*, no. 49, 1991, pp. 40–49.

5 Linhart, 'À propos de post-taylorisme', pp. 69–71.

6 Valérie Aquain *et al.*, 'Vingt ans d'évolution des conditions de travail', *Travail et emploi*, no. 61, April 1994, p. 87.

7 Source: Ministère du Travail, de l'Emploi et de la Formation professionnelle, 'Horaires de travail en 1991. Résultats de l'enquête Conditions de travail', *Dossiers statistiques du travail et de l'emploi*, nos 98–99, October 1993.

8 The percentage of people with the same hours every day increased to 49 per cent in 1998: Catherine Bloch-London and Pierre Boisard, 'L'aménagement et la réduction du temps de travail', *Données sociales 1999*, INSEE, Paris 1999, p. 212.

9 Michel Cézard and Lydie Vinck, 'Contraintes et marges d'initiative des salariés dans leur travail', *Données sociales 1996*, p. 224.

10 See Paul Jansolin, 'Une formation à deux vitesses', *L'Entreprise*, special issue, 'La France des entreprises', in collaboration with INSEE, no. 2518, 1992, pp. 162–3.

11 Thomas Coutrot, 'Les nouveaux modes d'organisation de la production: quels effets sur l'emploi, la formation, l'organisation du travail?', *Données sociales 1996*, p. 210.

12 Firms' stocks were sharply reduced in line with the recommendations of just-in-time. From 1985 to 1990, the value of the stocks of manufacturing industry as a whole grew by 4 per cent, while the volume in value of production increased by 32 per cent: Michel Amar, 'Les effets du "flux tendu"', *L'Entreprise*, special issue on 'La France des entreprises', no. 2518, 1992, pp. 234–5.

13 The ISO quality standardization, which has developed even more strongly since 1992, might seem to accord with the second spirit of capitalism, given its normative character. Nevertheless, its approach to quality (total quality and not simply manufacturing quality), and some of the questions it takes up, like the employment of a simultaneous engineering process for the development of new products, make it a managerial tool marked by the conceptions of the third spirit.

14 The implementation of just-in-time principles affects 36 per cent of establishments belonging to the agricultural and food industry sector. The figure is 49 per cent for the energy and intermediate goods sector, 43 per cent for household goods, 56 per cent for consumer goods, and 27 per cent for the public buildings and works sector. Services, rather less affected by this practice, which was initially developed for industry (20 per cent for retailing and the transport and telecommunications sector, 17 per cent for commercial services, but only 9 per cent for the health sector, and 3 per cent for banking and insurance), are more affected by other innovations,

such as quality circles (41 per cent in banking and insurance), multidisciplinary groups (42 per cent of establishments in the market services sector and 49 per cent in the health sector), or the abolition of a level of hierarchy (30 per cent in the banking and insurance sector). See Coutrot, 'Les nouveaux modes d'organisation de la production'.

15 Ibid., p. 211.

16 To those who wish to point an accusing finger at the relative slowness of the transformations in the organization of work, since it has taken nearly twenty years to arrive at the current stage, it should be recalled that there is nothing exceptional about this if we compare it with the pace of the implementation of Taylorist principles (see Gilles Margirier, 'Crise et nouvelle organisation du travail', *Travail et emploi*, no. 22, December 1984, pp. 33–44). Organizational innovations take time to become established and, to the extent that the precepts of the third spirit of capitalism presuppose, as we have seen, a profound transformation in habits and attitudes anchored in education, it may even be held that their diffusion assumes a turnover of generations at work. Thus, the role of those under the age of forty appears very significant in that they are the bearers of new behaviour and new values, as Frédéric de Coninck's study ('Évolutions post-tayloriennes et nouveaux clivages sociaux') has shown.

17 INSEE, *Annuaire statistique de la France*, INSEE, Paris 1998 (CD-ROM version). Nearly one in two firms was subcontracting in 1988. The sectors most engaged in subcontracting in 1988 were the auxiliaries of transport and travel agencies (41 per cent of turnover), aircraft construction (28 per cent), building and civil engineering (15 per cent), industries processing non-ferrous metals (14 per cent), and road transport (13 per cent): Yves Bournique and Chantal de Barry, 'Donneurs d'ordres et sous-traitants', *L'Entreprise*, special issue on 'La France des entreprises', no. 2518, 1992, pp. 224–5.

18 The 1995 investigation 'Liaisons industrielles' used eight categories, the first four of which can be characterized as 'industrial partnership' or 'expanded subcontracting': customized work, production to specification, supply of design and production, supply of design, production under licence, production on demand under the brand of a distributor, autonomous production, supply of services.

19 See Michel Hannoun, 'Présentation d'une investigation', *INSEE Méthodes*, nos 67–68, 'Les réseaux d'entreprises: des collectifs singuliers', 20 November 1996, pp. 155–60.

20 See Colette Jourdain, 'L'intérim, une voie d'accès à l'emploi', *Données sociales 1999*, INSEE, Paris 1999, pp. 169–76.

21 See Jean-Luc Bricout, 'La montée des services', *L'Entreprise*, special issue on 'La France des entreprises', no. 2518, 1992, pp. 38–41; Michel Lacroix, 'Les services aux entreprises', in ibid., pp. 56–8.

22 See Alain Chenu, 'Une classe ouvrière en crise', *Données sociales 1993*, INSEE, Paris 1993, pp. 473–85.

23 See Philippe Trogan, 'Nettoyage et sécurité', *L'Entreprise*, no. 2518, 1992, pp. 240–41.

24 See Lacroix, 'Les services aux entreprises'.

25 See Olivier Marchand, 'Population active, emploi, chômage au cours des années 90', *Données sociales 1999*, INSEE, Paris 1999, pp. 100–16.

26 See Philippe Pommier, 'Le monde des entreprises', *L'Entreprise*, no. 2518, 1992, pp. 12–13.

27 See Patrick Crosnier, 'Les PMI dans le sillage des groupes', *L'Entreprise*, no. 2518, 1992, pp. 22–3.

28 See Éric Vergeau and Nicole Chabanas, 'Le nombre des groupes d'entreprise a explosé en 15 ans', *INSEE Première*, no. 533, November 1997.

29 The growth in the number of groups is unquestionably attributable in large part to the growth in 'micro-groups' of fewer than 500 wage-earners, which rose from 1,966 in 1980 to 5,279 in 1995; then of 'small groups' (between 500 and 2,000 wage-earners), which went up from 383 to 1,027, while 'medium groups' (between 2,000 and 10,000 people) only increased from 223 to 292, and large groups of more than 10,000 from 73 to 84. On the other hand,

ignoring this reality distorts perceptions of the productive fabric: what, for example, twenty years ago would have been a single firm of 150 people is today perceived in the first instance as a set of four firms of fewer than 150 people. It might seem as if the employment share of small firms has genuinely increased, but this is not altogether certain. Moreover, the number of large groups has itself increased. Hence there is no less concentration today (see Vergeau and Chabanas, 'Le nombres des groupes d'entreprise a explosé en 15 ans').

30   See Michel Amar and Jean-Luc Bricout, 'La concentration financière', *L'Entreprise*, special issue on 'La France des entreprises', no. 2518, 1992, pp. 70–71.

31   See Vincent Thollon-Pommerol, 'L'armature des groupes', in ibid., pp. 18–19.

32   Conversely, groups predominate in the car, energy or financial business sectors. In the sector of services to firms, the share of groups is around two-thirds of value added, as in industry excluding energy (Vergeau and Chabanas, 'Le nombre des groupes d'entreprise a explosé').

33   See Amar and Bricout, 'La concentration financière'.

34   At the end of 1990, hypermarkets and supermarkets together accounted for 52 per cent of the food market, as against 31 per cent in 1980 and 13 per cent in 1970. Their share in the market for 'personal amenities' went up between 1980 and 1990 from 18 to 26 per cent; for 'household appliances' from 23 to 31 per cent; and for 'hygiene–culture–leisure–sport' from 9 to 14 per cent. In the course of the 1980s, hypermarkets specializing in things other than food also developed (furniture, DIY, clothing, sport). Finally, the hypermarkets have conquered an important share of the market in the distribution of car fuels (more than a third in 1990), accelerating the closure of independent petrol stations (see Francis Amand, 'Petit et grand commerce', *L'Entreprise*, no. 2518, 1992, pp. 61–2).

35   Since the end of the 1970s, INSEE has annually inventoried the ownership links of capital, which makes it possible today to observe the development of groups of firms. Likewise, since the mid-1970s the SESSI of the Industry Ministry has sought to identify the volume of industrial subcontracting, which does not account for all subcontracting, as we have seen, leading to the 'liaisons industrielles' survey being set up only in 1995. But the observation of other forms of network organization, which take the form neither of subcontracting in the strict sense, nor of significant financial links, is very difficult. The first problem is to find a point of entry in order to untangle the web; conversely, when the network is complex, it is important to know where to stop, so as to confer an identity on a network and make calculations on the basis of this group of firms otherwise perceived as independent (turnover, staff, value added, etc.). (See Benjamin Camus, 'Les débuts de la mesure', *INSEE Méthodes*, nos 67–68, 'Les réseaux d'entreprises: des collectifs singuliers', 20 November 1996, pp. 139–41.) An additional difficulty derives from the fact that network heads, although intervening in the same markets, belong to very different sectors, which prevents the creation of a clear statistical picture. Thus, in the specialist clothing business the network heads belong to services (advertising, training), or to industry (when it is responsible for a large percentage of the manufacture of the clothes, for example), or to wholesale trade, or to retail trade. In addition, the characteristic accounting flows (subscriptions to bulk-buying organizations, franchise rights) are not isolated in the accounting information traditionally collected (see Maryvonne Lemaire, 'Les réseaux d'enseigne. Le cas de la distribution des articles d'habillement', *INSEE Méthodes*, nos 67–68, 20 November 1996, pp. 161–72).

36   See ibid.

37   See Jérôme Philippe, 'Réseaux de commercialisation de l'habillement: l'imbrication des logiques de distribution et de production', *Économie et statistique*, no. 314, 1998.

38   See Brigitte Belloc and Christine Lagarenne, 'Emplois temporaires et emplois aidés', *Données sociales 1996*, INSEE, Paris 1996, pp. 124–30.

39   'The basic tools of economic statistics in France – the SIRENE index and *Enquête annuelle d'entreprise* – take as their units of observation firms in the sense of legal units. Groupings of firms are not subject to systematic observation, with the notable exception of groups ... as

things stand, most networks of firms are transparent for statistics. ... The problems to be solved in order to overcome this gap are obvious: the interfirm connections that would have to be taken into account are extremely diverse. Numerous informal co-operative links, such as those revolving around research or the exchange of services, are difficult to detect, and still more so to classify and measure. In addition, networks that go beyond the area of metropolitan France are far from rare, and hence the strategy of firms cannot be accurately assessed simply by observing the units investigated on the national territory' (INSEE, *L'économie française. Édition 1998–1999*, Livre de Poche, Paris 1998). These problems are encountered once again at the level of international statistics for monitoring the movements of international firms. It is more or less possible to know the sums of direct foreign investment of different countries, but these take into account only the actual outflows of capital from territories, not the reinvestment of profits on the spot, or calls upon international financial markets or foreign banking systems. An estimate indicates that in 1990, American direct foreign investment was financed to the tune of 44 per cent by capital outflows from parent companies to foreign subsidiaries; to that of 31 per cent by the reinvested profits of these; and to 25 per cent by loans from subsidiaries on the spot. Direct foreign investment is thus very significantly underestimated. In addition, what the experts call 'new forms of investment', which are not participation links but connections of a 'network' type (grants of licences, technical assistance, franchising, international subcontracting, industrial co-operation, etc.), are not subject to any assessment, which once again tends to underrate the power of global firms (Wladimir Andreff, *Les Multinationales globales*, La Découverte, Paris 1995, pp. 8–9).

40 See, respectively, Guy Caire, 'Précarisation des emplois et régulation du marché du travail', communication to the *IIes Journées d'économie sociales*, faculty of economic science of Dijon, 24–25 September 1981; INSEE, *Annuaire statistique de la France*, INSEE, Paris 1998 (CD-ROM version).

41 See Jourdain, 'L'intérim, une voie d'accès à l'emploi'.

42 See Aquain *et al.*, 'Vingt ans d'évolution des conditions de travail'.

43 See Belloc and Lagarenne, 'Emplois temporaires et emplois aidés'.

44 See Dominique Goux and Éric Maurin, 'La mobilité est plus forte, mais le chômage de longue durée ne se résorbe pas', *Données sociales 1993*, INSEE, Paris 1993, pp. 170–75.

45 A larger number of the new employees on these forms of contracts nevertheless want to work more. Among those on part-time for less than a year, 67 per cent in 1995 wanted to work more, compared with 33 per cent among those who had more than a year's service, which means that acceptance of a part-time contract today is temporary, for want of something better, in 67 per cent of cases (Sophie Audric and Gérard Forgeot, 'Le développement du travail à temps partiel', *Données sociales 1999*, INSEE, Paris 1999, pp. 177–81).

46 See Laurent Bisault *et al.*, 'Le développement du travail à temps partiel', *Données sociales 1996*, INSEE, Paris 1996, pp. 225–33.

47 Seventy-four per cent of those on a subsidized contract in the public sector were in a situation of underemployment in March 1995 (i.e. 'against their own wishes they worked less than the normal length of work in their job and were looking for additional work or available for such work'). This was also the case with 36 per cent of holders of subsidized contracts in the private sector, with 9 per cent of temps, and 17 per cent of wage-earners on fixed-term contracts, but with only 5 per cent of wage-earners holding a stable job (Belloc and Lagarenne, 'Emplois temporaires et emplois aidés', p. 130).

48 Bisault *et al.*, 'Le développement du travail à temps partiel', pp. 227–28.

49 Source: Ministère du Travail, de l'Emploi et de la Formation professionnelle, 'Horaires de travail en 1991. Résultats de l'enquête Conditions de travail', *Dossiers statistiques du travail et de l'emploi*, nos 98–99, October 1993, Table III.3.1c, p. 102.

50 See Gérard Lyon-Caen, 'Plasticité du capital et nouvelles formes d'emploi', *Droit social*, nos 9–10, September/October 1980, pp. 8–18. And see also Michèle Voisset, 'Droit du travail et crise', *Droit social*, no. 6, June 1980, pp. 287–98. Labour law, which was based on the notions

of firm and employer, has been circumvented particularly by using legal techniques from commercial law to restructure firms.

51 See Jean de Maillard *et al.*, 'L'éclatement de la collectivité de travail: observations sur les phénomènes d'extériorisation de l'emploi', *Droit social*, nos 9–10, September/October 1979, pp. 322–38.

52 See Armelle Gorgeu and René Mathieu, 'Recrutement et production au plus juste. Les nouvelles usines d'équipement automobile en France', *Dossiers du CEE*, new series, no. 7, 1995; and 'Les ambiguïtés de la proximité. Les nouveaux établissements d'équipement automobile', *Actes de la recherche en sciences sociales*, 1996, pp. 44–53.

53 Gorgeu and Mathieu, 'Recrutement et production au plus juste', p. 55. The elimination of jobs at PSA and Renault, which was considerable from 1990–92 (loss of 12,575 people), continued in 1993 and 1994, albeit at a reduced rate. In the first instance, it affected older and less skilled workers (ibid., p. 69). The new jobs created among subcontractors involved different people, since components manufacturers are wary of recruiting their manufacturer's former workers and prefer a young, more educated workforce without industrial experience, which is more malleable, more productive, and less expensive.

54 It would appear that the situation is not very different among manufacturers. The employment of operatives on permanent contracts has become rare (opening of Sevelnord by PSA and creation of a third work team at Renault-Flins), for PSA and Renault continue to draw up redundancy plans, and use a lot of temporary workers: of the order of 30–40 per cent of the productive workforce in certain factories at certain times (Gorgeu and Mathieu, 'Recrutement et production au plus juste', p. 69).

55 Ibid., pp. 72, 74.

56 Grégoire Philonenko and Véronique Guienne, *Au carrefour de l'exploitation*, Desclée de Brouwer, Paris 1997.

57 See Christine Lagarenne and Emmanuelle Marchal, 'Les recutements sur le marché du travail de 1990 à 1994', *Lettres du CEE*, no. 9, May 1995; and Belloc and Lagarenne, 'Emplois temporaires et emplois aidés'.

58 Prior to 1981, part-time work was regarded as an exception, and was subject to a set of rules restricting its use (designation of beneficiaries, duration of work, pay, agreement of the social partners). In 1981 and 1982, most of the restrictions were lifted: notably, no lower limit as regards the number of hours and the possibility of hiring directly on a part-time basis. From 1992 onwards, a policy of exempting employers from social contributions in order to encourage the development of part-time work was even initiated (see Audric and Forgeot, 'Le développement du travail à temps partiel', p. 177).

As for the adjustment of working hours, it was not until the édict of 16 January 1982 that it was possible to adjust the collective duration of work. Up to 1982, firms were able to vary the duration of work only by recourse to overtime, subject to the authorization of the factory inspectorate and by means of partial unemployment. From 1982, they were allowed to resort to overtime without authorization, within an annual quota, to vary in certain conditions the length of the working week within the framework of the year, and, by means of negotiation, to adjust collective working hours. This dynamic was encouraged by the Auroux law of November 1982, which made obligatory an annual negotiation in firms on the actual duration and organization of work, when union representatives existed. The quinquennial law of 20 December 1993 established annualized part-time work by making temporary work a particular mode of part-time work (Bloch-London and Boisnard, 'L'aménagement et la réduction du temps de travail', p. 208). The implementation today of the thirty-five hours, allowing for a reduction in working time in exchange for adjustments in it, does not always translate into an improvement in the condition of wage-earners either, particularly when it is necessary to work hours that are scarcely compatible with family life or leisure activities. Certain wage-earners, notably women, particularly suffer from the irregularity of working hours, above all when it frequently involves serious alterations in individuals' arrangements (child-care, in particular), often at very short notice (ibid., p. 212).

59 Alain Supiot, 'Du bon usage des lois en matière d'emploi', *Droit social*, no. 3, March 1997, p. 231.

60 Antoine Lyon-Caen and Antoine Jeammaud, 'France', in Lyon-Caen and Jeammaud, eds, *Droit du travail, démocratie et crise*, Actes Sud, Arles 1986, p. 37. In 1990, nevertheless, the regulatory framework was once again restricted by returning to a closed list of grounds and limiting the number of possible renewals of assignments.

61 Supiot, 'Du bon usage des lois en matière d'emploi', p. 231.

62 Lyon-Caen and Jeammaud, 'France', p. 33.

63 See A.O. Hirschman, *The Rhetoric of Reaction*, Belnap Press, Cambridge (MA) 1991.

64 See Susan Berger and Michael Piore, *Dualism and Discontinuity in Industrial Societies*, Cambridge University Press, New York 1980.

65 Jacques Magaud, 'L'éclatement juridique de la collectivité de travail', *Droit social*, no. 12, December 1975, pp. 525–30.

66 See Caire, 'Précarisation des emplois et regulation du marché du travail'.

67 See de Maillard *et al.*, 'L'éclatement de la collectivité de travail'.

68 See Patrick Broudic and Jean-Michel Espinasse, 'Les politiques de gestion de la main-d'oeuvre', *Travail et emploi*, October 1980, pp. 10–25.

69 Gorgeu and Mathieu, 'Recrutement et production au plus juste'.

70 Supiot, 'Du bon usage des lois en matière d'emploi', p. 231.

71 Ibid., p. 232. Moreover, it is these multiple rights attached to permanent contracts that are the target of those who wax indignant about the lack of flexibility permitted by French law. In particular, they criticize the cost of redundancies (compensation to be paid, obligation to construct a redundancy scheme for more than ten redundancies, etc.), which is alleged to be too high, as well as the administrative control exercised over them, the judge being able potentially to amend a redundancy as 'without genuine and serious reason', and to demand either reinstatement or the payment of additional money. Firms, now able to avail themselves of many other contracts that are more flexible than the permanent contract, prefer wherever possible solutions that are possibly less expensive, since temporary and fixed-term contracts presuppose recompense for job security that increases the payment received, while leaving their hands completely free and, for small and medium-sized firms, avoiding suddenly straining their accounts in the event of economic problems that involve redundancies. The proliferation of flexible contracts reveals the lesser flexibility of the 'normal' contract, the rights attaching to which have gone on being strengthened without changing the opportunity for access to less advantageous contracts, thereby prompting firms to continue casualizing employment.

72 Moreover, the low fluidity of the labour market is the reason advanced by Daniel Cohen (*Richesse du monde, pauvreté des nations*, Flammarion, Paris 1997) to account for the differences between the United States and France; according to him, it is much more significant than the impact of the cost of less skilled labour. American workers are said to change work more readily (hence in greater number and more frequently), and firms hire and fire more easily, which by comparison with France translates into a greatly reduced period of time spent seeking work. The shorter amount of time spent in unemployment than in France would explain the divergence in the two unemployment rates.

73 See Christophe Dejours, *Souffrance en France. La banalisation de l'injustice sociale*, Seuil, Paris 1998.

74 Ibid., pp. 114–15.

75 Francis Ginsbourger quite correctly stresses that 'the work content of jobs that are "outsourced" is rarely equivalent to what prevailed in earlier organizational and statutory forms. ... Casual jobs are most often jobs of abbreviated apprenticeship time, consumers of established skills and unproductive of new skills. They hardly offer a prospect of professional advance to

those who hold them. They are occupied in conditions that allow little opportunity to influence the content of work, to appropriate it and become professionalized in it' (*La Gestion contre l'entreprise. Réduire le coût du travail ou organiser sa mise en valeur*, La Découverte, Paris 1998, p. 64). On access to new technologies, see Michel Cézard, F. Dussert and Michel Gollac, 'Taylor va au marché. Organisation du travail et informatique', *La Lettre d'information du CEE*, no. 26, December 1992. As for access to training, the following figures say it all: in 1989, 51 per cent of technicians and supervisors, 47 per cent of engineers and *cadres*, did a training course, as against 27 per cent of white-collar workers and 22 per cent of skilled blue-collar workers. For their part, unskilled blue-collar workers only had little more than a one in ten chance of pursuing continuous training. Moreover, the wage-earners of small firms were disadvantaged compared with those of large ones: in 1989, firms of between 10 and 50 wage-earners had a financial interest per capita (1,600 F per wage-earner) that was four times smaller than those with 2,000 wage-earners (6,300 F). In addition, they finance much of the training expenses of the large firms. In fact, not achieving the minimum budget imposed, many small firms had to return unused funds to the public revenue department, or to the administrative bodies they belonged to. In this case, the funds were used for training in other firms, which were often larger (Jansolin, 'Une formation à deux vitesses').

76   The correlation between economic insecurity and family insecurity is brought out by the 1993 CERC report on *Précarité et risque d'exclusion*. Either people delay the moment of starting a family or hesitate to settle down, or unemployment has a very destructive impact on people, especially males, and couples do not survive it in the medium term, even if break-ups often occur several years after the episode of unemployment (Serge Paugam, ed., *Précarité et risque d'exclusion en France*, La Documentation française, Paris 1993). Grégoire Philonenko relates several occasions when he wittingly let his family down in what for it were exceptional situations (a birth, a gas explosion in his building), so concerned was he to satisfy his employer. A six-day working week is the norm for *cadres*, and night work for filling shelves is frequent, with 'normal' working weeks always adding up to between 65 and 70 hours, and sometimes much more in seasonal periods that can lead to them being at work for 24 hours solid. Since 80 per cent of the work of departmental heads is done in storehouses, their status as *cadres* seems to be bound up more with the possibility of demanding permanent work without overtime payments than anything else (Philonenko and Guienne, *Au carrefour de l'exploitation*).

In the local establishments of car components manufacturers studied by Gorgeu and Mathieu, 'prospects are never long-term and the ageing of the workforce is not envisaged. It is as if the investment in selection and training is very rapidly recouped, and as if a certain turnover of personnel, making it possible always to have a young workforce, is, in the last analysis, desirable' ('Recrutement et production au plus juste', p. 107).

77   Richard Sennet, *The Corrosion of Character: The Personal Consequences of Work in the New Capitalism*, Norton & Company, New York 1998, p. 26.

78   See Belloc and Lagarenne, 'Emplois temporaires et emplois aidés'.

79   Similarly, it is much more difficult to integrate into a large firm when one has come from a small firm than from another large one. In 1991, for every 100 people who changed job during the year to join a firm of more than 500 wage-earners, 62 already worked for a firm of this size. Yet the wage-earners of large firms represent only 22 per cent of the total of those who change firms in the course of a year (Goux and Maurin, 'La mobilité est plus forte, mais le chômage de longue durée ne se résorbe pas').

80   This is a step taken by Dejours (*Souffrance en France*), whose work is devoted wholly to the search for the mechanisms through which *cadres*, although possessed of a moral sense, can participate in an abject process of social destruction, improperly (in our view) assimilating this enigma to that of the participation of many Germans in the process of exterminating the Jews. To answer this question, he develops three-stage responses. At the very top of the scale, those who give the orders are depraved elements who also organize a systematic distortion of

information so that 'this is not known'. The intermediate hierarchy that performs the 'dirty work' is manipulated by means of extolling virility, the proof of which, always to be demonstrated anew, consists in being able to do evil. Finally, the least implicated survive thanks to a system of blinkers. Despite the interesting information it supplies on the psychic processes which can be mobilized when implementing redundancies, this interpretation seems to us to be inadequate precisely on account of its desire to unmask the way that all the actors are radically in the grip of evil and ready to do anything. It assumes that people are perfectly conscious, without any ambiguity, that they are performing 'bad deeds', even if this consciousness is repressed. Yet such a presupposition seems to be rather simplistic and, incidentally, far from certain (and not simply because the information is manipulated in such a way as to conceal the abjectness of the system).

81   Ravi Baktavatsalou shows that people who are made economically redundant experience greater difficulty finding a new job than other job-seekers. At the end of 1995, the average duration of unemployment was 505 days for those who had become unemployed following redundancy, compared with 361 days for the rest. These figures had deteriorated by comparison with the end of 1993, when they stood at 420 and 350 days respectively. Among those who found a new job, the period of unemployment was longer for those made redundant than for the rest ('Licenciements économiques et mesures d'accompagnement au début des années 90', *Données sociales 1996*, INSEE, Paris 1996, pp. 150–56).

82   See François Eymard-Duvernay and Emmanuelle Marchal, *Façons de recruter. Le jugement des compétences sur le marché du travail*, Métailié, Paris 1996; and Christian Bessy, 'Cabinets de recrutement et formes d'intermédiation sur le marché du travail', in Bessy and Eymard-Duvernay, eds, *Les Intermédiaires du marché du travail*, Cahiers du CEE, Presses Universitaires de France, Paris 1997, pp. 103–42.

83   Jean-Marie Clerc, 'Les conflits sociaux en France en 1970 and 1971', *Droit social*, no. 1, January 1973, pp. 19–26.

84   See Serge Paugam, ed., *L'exclusion. L'état des savoirs*, La Découverte, Paris 1993.

85   As Ginsbourger (*La Gestion contre l'entreprise*, p. 94) observes, if one judges the low qualification of a person at his or her initial level of training, it must be reckoned that there are always more unskilled workers than unskilled jobs. The population census for 1982 indicated that at the time, more than half of the working population (56 per cent) possessed neither CAP [vocational training certificate] nor BEP [technical school certificate] nor BEPC [equivalent of GCSE]. This 'low qualification' was notably the case for 56 per cent of blue-collar workers classified as 'skilled' in industry.

86   'The components manufacturers hive off manufacture requiring manual work that is difficult to enhance, because they do not want to retain jobs of unskilled and semi-skilled grade, which are often hard, especially for older workers' (Gorgeu and Mathieu, 'Recrutement et production au plus juste', p. 113). In fact, the components manufacturers know from experience that workers, unskilled and semi-skilled blue-collar workers in particular, age, and that one cannot bank on everyone developing. Hence there is eventually a problem, when they can no longer perform their work like young people. The best thing is therefore to be free of such jobs in order to steer clear of such manpower.

87   This is all the more the case, as we shall see later, in that employers refuse to create 'full jobs' so as to pay only for directly productive time, to the point where the definition of what a job is has altered greatly over the last two decades.

88   See Françoise Favennec-Héry, 'Le droit et la gestion des départs', *Droit social*, no. 6, June 1992, pp. 581–89.

89   Between the last two censuses (1982 and 1990), blue-collar employment has declined at the rate of 11 per cent a year in collieries and by 8 per cent a year in iron and steel and iron mines (- 53, 000 jobs), or at a faster rate than the reduction in farmers, which has only exceptionally exceeded the rate of - 5 per cent a year. Building lost 122,000 blue-collar jobs, textiles

and clothing 108,000, cars 62,000, and mechanical engineering 55,000 (Chenu, 'Une classe ouvrière en crise').

90 See ibid.

91 For a review, see Jean-Louis Mucchielli, *Multinationales et mondialisation*, Seuil, Paris 1998; Dominique Welcomme, 'Mondialisation et emploi: les éléments du débat', *Lettre du CEE*, no. 24, November 1997; and Pierre-Noël Giraud, *L'inégalité du monde. Économie du monde contemporain*, Gallimard, Paris 1996.

92 For his part, Giraud (*L'inégalité*) tends to think that the real job losses are higher than indicated by all the studies: 'there are, however, very good reasons for thinking that the indirect effect of the competition of low-wage countries – i.e. its effects *via* the competition between industrialized countries – is far from insignificant. To illustrate the point, it is enough to indicate that an IBM-PC computer, accounted in Europe as an American import, contained only 24 per cent of value added in the United States, 46 per cent in Japan, 30 per cent in Singapore and Korea. Another example: the booking software program "Socrate" bought by the SNCF from the American company Amris, subsidiary of American Airlines, whose registered office is in Houston, was in fact developed largely by teams of programmers in Barbados and the Dominican Republic. It is a service import from low-wage countries that is not accounted as such. Thus, the undoubted intensification of price competition by global firms from wealthy countries, which, as we have seen was characteristic of the 1980s, was certainly also in part due to the increased importance of the first newly industrialized countries. Today, competition between territories does not come down to direct exports from one to the other. It is global firms that set territories in competition with one another. These indirect effects are very difficult, in truth impossible, to measure. To take account of them, Wood multiplies by four the figures obtained by assessing the jobs content of direct trade, but this assessment is very tenuous' (pp. 295–6).

93 A good example of the disequilibrium in the balance of forces is the comparison recurrent in most of the media between the cost of the least skilled labour in France and in certain countries of the East or South, fuelling downward pressure on wages and a constant debate on the level of the French minimum wage, which is alleged to be at the root of unemployment difficulties, whereas the American minimum wage, having fallen, has permitted the creation of jobs in much greater proportions. The idea that one day the wages of French blue-collar workers will be determined in Bangkok is growing, and definitely furthers an increase on the same territory of wage inequalities which, after narrowing for some years, started to rise again in most Western countries during the 1980s, and sometimes much earlier, as in the United States (Piketty, *L'économie des inégalités*). It is self-evident that decisions to relocate do not depend upon a single criterion – the level of the hourly wage for blue-collar workers. Yet this explanation is simple, easy to get people to understand and diffuse, and in addition it serves the interests of firms, which are therefore not going to deny or qualify it.

94 This is all the more true in that genuinely unskilled workers suffer competition from more qualified workers, notably students who agree to work part-time for modest wages in unskilled jobs, and prove more inclined to co-operate in that for them it is simply casual work. Thus, employers benefit from a workforce that is generally more qualified without paying it more, and do not have to bother about upgrading it, since the pursuit of their studies will lead the students to leave the job of their own accord. Thus, students represent 21 per cent of temporary workers (Jourdain, 'L'intérim, une voie d'accès à l'emploi'), and in the service sector firms like McDonald's recruit almost exclusively from this kind of population (Damien Cartron, 'Autonomie et contrôle dans un restaurant McDonald's', working paper discussed in Luc Boltanski's seminar at the École des hautes études en sciences sociales, 1998). In this latter case, contracts are permanent, since the majority of departures will occur through resignation; the firm will pay little by way of severance pay, but will save on the value of allowances paid to compensate for lack of job security on contracts that were conceived as casual from the outset.

95   Cleaners, like cooks – two job categories that are markedly on the increase – are 'blue-collar working-class' jobs, and involve industry largely as a result of subcontracting. But they are classified under services, since they fall within companies that supply services. Moreover, packers in shops, waiters and waitresses in catering, sales staff and cashiers, which are also so many rapidly expanding jobs, are recorded among white-collar employees even though they have many features in common with blue-collar workers.

96   Some figures illustrate the point. In 1991, 23 per cent of blue-collar workers in the tertiary sector had less than one year's length of service, as against 15 per cent for industrial blue-collar workers (Chenu, 'Une classe ouvrière en crise'). The higher rates of turnover of personnel in the tertiary sector are also those in small firms. In 1991, the rate of turnover in small firms was 23 per cent, compared with 15 per cent in medium-sized firms and 13 per cent in large ones (Goux and Marin, 'La mobilité est plus forte').

97   Ginsbourger, *La Gestion contre l'entreprise*, pp. 46–8.

98   See Dominique Goux and Éric Maurin, 'Les entreprises, les salariés et la formation continue', *Économie et statistiques*, no. 306, 1997, pp. 27–40.

99   Gorgeu and Mathieu, 'Recrutement et production au plus juste', p. 57.

100   The researchers cite the example of recruitment linked to the opening of a new establishment in 1993. More than 3,200 application letters were first of all graded on a criterial basis. For blue-collar workers, this sifting was carried out according to sex (male), age (under thirty-five), qualifications (holder of a CAP or BEP), and residential address (under thirty-six kilometres from the factory). Fewer than 50 per cent of applications were retained at this stage. A pre-selection interview of half an hour then made it possible to reject a further 20 per cent of people. A recruitment agency then came into the picture, staging psychotechnical tests (for three or four hours) and interviews that made it possible to reject another 50 per cent of candidates. A further interview with a psychologist (three-quarters of an hour for blue-collar workers) made it possible to exclude another 50 per cent. Those who managed to get through all these stages were not then hired. Production workers were sent on a training course for access to work (financed and run in part by the ANPE) for seven weeks prior to definitive recruitment. In April 1994, there were thirty-six production workers on permanent contracts and seventeen in training. The 'non-productive' personnel comprised thirty-three people (baccalauréat level + 2, the minimum for secretaries, supervisors and maintenance staff), all on permanent contracts. See Gorgeu and Mathieu, 'Recrutement et production au plus juste', pp. 81–2.

101   Let us nevertheless note that the very rapid expansion in the number of graduates from higher education and of young *cadres* in the 1970s complicated the perpetuation of a mode of relations between generations based on the domestic principle of succession. In effect, the rapid increase in the number of young graduates and young *cadres* unbalanced the ratio between the occupants of higher posts and those who were applying to replace them, and hence provoked veritable wars of succession. In the university system between 1960 and 1970, the same process had unbalanced the relationship of subordination in expectations of succession between assistant lecturers and professors (see Pierre Bourdieu, Luc Boltanski and Pascale Maldidier, 'La défense du corps', *Information sur les sciences sociales*, vol. X, no. 4, 1971, pp. 45–86). From this perspective, the choice by firms to limit career prospects, and their growing recourse to the external labour market (as opposed to the market internal to the firm), might seem reasonable.

102   See, for example, the special issue of *Travail et emploi* devoted to early retirement from working life (Xavier Gaullier and Maryvonne Gognalons-Nicolet, 'Crise économique et mutations sociales: les cessations anticipées d'activité (50–65 ans)', *Travail et emploi*, no. 15, Janary/March 1983). Between 1968 and 1975, the percentage of working people in the population of those over the age of fifty-five fell from 31.5 per cent to 15 per cent. Among men of fifty-five to fifty-nine, the share of those working fell from 82.5 per cent to 68.9 per cent (Anne-Marie Guillemard, 'Attitudes et opinions des entreprises à l'égard des salariés âgés et du vieillissement de la main-d'oeuvre', in *Emploi et vieillissement*, La Documentation française, Paris 1994, pp. 57–70). The rates

of inactivity among those over the age of fifty-five rose in all the OECD countries from 1975 (with the exception of Japan), but it was in France that the increase was most significant (from 31 per cent in 1975 to 58.5 per cent in 1993), stimulated by mechanisms for stopping work early. These mechanisms were all the better received, particularly by *cadres*, in that the norm of increases with seniority which had prevailed in this category was replaced by a tacit norm devaluing the performance of older people and hence their wage: thus 49 per cent of highly qualified men over fifty who had found work again after a period of unemployment experienced a drop in wages, compared with 19 per cent of minimally qualified men (Robert Castel, Jean-Paul Fitoussi and Jacques Freyssinet, *Chômage: le cas français*, La Documentation française, Paris 1997).

103 See Michel Gollac, *À marches forcées? Contribution à l'étude des changements du travail*, University of Paris VIII, 1998; Christian Baudelot and Gollac, 'Le salaire du trentenaire: question d'âge ou de génération', *Économie et statistique*, nos 304–305, April 1997.

'On average, one job in seven is held by a young person under twenty-five, but one entrant out of two and more than one leaver out of three involved establishments of more than fifty wage-earners in 1993': Olivier Marchand and Liliane Salzberg, 'La gestion des âges à la française, un handicap pour l'avenir?', *Données sociales 1996*, INSEE, Paris 1996, pp. 165–73. Particularly striking in this respect is the imperceptible transition at the turn of the 1970s from a situation where a significant number of young people were – as we saw in Chapter 3 – accused of deliberately avoiding work in firms, of delaying embarking on a stable adult life, and of hijacking the mechanisms of the welfare state by alternating between temporary posts and periods of subsidized unemployment, to the current situation. Now members of the same age group are presented as fervently desiring work that has become scarce or inaccessible – any work – and are induced, notably by state mechanisms of job incentives, to accept the training courses or little jobs, whatever they may be, which are offered to them. The portrayal of youth, particularly young people from the popular classes, as preferring a life of hedonism (François Dubet, *La Galère. Jeunes en survie*, Fayard, Paris 1987) to the work ethic drummed into them in the framework of family socialization, is thus replaced by that of youth forced into inactivity and a desperate search for any job whatsoever.

104 De Coninck, 'Évolutions post-tayloriennes et nouveaux clivages sociaux'.

105 See Odile Merckling, 'Transformation des emplois et substitution travailleurs français-travailleurs immigrés: le cas de l'automobile', *Sociologie du travail*, no. 1, 1986, pp. 58–74.

106 Between 1973 and 1979, the employment of immigrants in the car industry declined by 27,000, while that of French people rose by 40,000. Even more so than in the past, the immigrant workforce found itself consigned to peripheral, unstable and frequently dangerous jobs (Paugam, *L'exclusion*). A particularly spectacular instance of substitution was the replacement in the second half of the 1970s of immigrant refuse collectors by national refuse collectors. Thus, for example, a refuse collection firm in the Lyon region, in which 95 per cent of the refuse collectors were North Africans (but French people were drivers), made 130 immigrants redundant in 1976 following a strike, and set about reorganizing its administration in such a way as to call on only young French people in future (less unpleasant work, possibility of promotion from refuse collector to driver). (See Anne Mayere, 'Revalorisation qualitative des emplois et substitution de jeunes travailleurs français à des travailleurs immigrés. Le cas d'une entreprise de collecte des ordures', *Travail et emploi*, no. 17, July/September 1983, pp. 41–7.) At the beginning of the 1970s, it was also in particular in order not to have to resort to immigrant manpower that Volvo tried out a reorganization of tasks with the experimental factory of Uddevala, which was to serve as a model for many to the generalization of Toyotism (Margirier, 'Crise et nouvelle organisation du travail').

107 Annick Échardour and Éric Maurin, 'La main-d'oeuvre étrangère', *Données sociales 1993*, INSEE, Paris 1993, p. 506. Total employment went up by 3 per cent between the last two censuses (1982 and 1990). Yet foreigners held 40,000 fewer jobs (-3 per cent) and 100,000 more of them of were unemployed (a rise of 48 per cent, compared with 36 per cent for the whole population). However, the proportion of foreigners in the working population did not change. If a

general slowdown of entries since 1974 is observable, these primarily involved family reunification, foreigners having brought over their family for fear of not being able to return if they left, as well as requests for asylum. 'The chance of being without a job is nearly twice as great for a North African as for a Portuguese (or French) person of the same age, the same level of education, working in the same sector with the same qualifications. Yet North African immigration predates that of the Portuguese and its links with the French language are closer' (ibid., pp. 505–11).

108 See Olivier Marchand, 'Population active, emploi, chômage au cours des années 90', *Données sociales 1999*, INSEE, Paris 1999, pp. 100–16.

109 At the level of the total working population, the rate of unemployment for men in March 1998 was 10.2 per cent, compared with 13.8 per cent for women – a difference that is in part bound up with the occupation of posts that are generally less skilled. Measurement of the rate of female unemployment is made difficult by deterrent effects (when the job market is too difficult, some prefer to withdraw from it, and these effects are furthered by measures allowing young mothers to remain at home while receiving a monthly allowance in certain conditions). But it may be reckoned as being approximately 50 per cent higher than that of men (see Daniel Teman, 'L'inégalité devant le chômage', *Alternatives économiques*, special issue no. 21, July 1994; Louis Maurin, 'Le travail des femmes', *Alternatives économiques*, no. 127, May 1995; and Marchand, 'Population active').

110 Numerous works have likewise shown that in the case of economic redundancy the first people to be affected had a medical or psychological handicap (for example, difficulties sleeping attributed to night work or variable working hours – on which see Dominique Meurs and Pascal Charpentier, 'Horaires atypiques et vie quotidienne des salariés', *Travail et emploi*, no. 32, June 1987, pp. 47–56). See also, for example, Dominique Dessors, Jean Schram and Serge Volkoff, 'Du handicap de "situation" à la sélection-exclusion: une étude des conditions de travail antérieures aux licenciements économiques', *Travail et emploi*, no. 2, 1991, pp. 31–47; Nathalie Frigul *et al.*, 'Atteintes à la santé et exclusion professionnelle: une enquête auprès de 86 femmes au chômage de longue durée', *Travail et emploi*, no. 56, 1993, pp. 34–44.

111 Paugam, *Précarité et risque d'exclusion en France*.

112 See Gorgeu and Mathieu, 'Recrutement et production au plus juste'.

113 Dejours, *Souffrance en France*. In particular, he refers to an operation under way in social security that aims to exclude women aged between thirty-five and forty who have 'a memory of practices of social assistance in times past', and who 'massively resist pressures from managerial staff to make economies by cheating those who have paid their contributions of the benefit and services they are entitled to' (ibid., p. 79).

114 The works of F. Mottay cited by Gollac in *À marches forcées?* indicate that the new forms of organization at work are heavily reliant on the skills acquired in the course of educational socialization, for the new structures are not only more 'communicative' but also more formalized, to the point where written communication is increasing most. These factors have doubtless played their part in the relatively greater exclusion of immigrants, around a third of whom are reckoned to have a poor command of the French language (Échardour and Maurin, 'La main-d'oeuvre étrangère').

115 Gorgeu and Mathieu, 'Recrutement et production au plus juste', p. 81.

116 Ibid., p. 54.

117 See Christian Bessy, 'La selection des salaries licenciés: économie d'une réglementation', *Travail et emploi*, no. 58, 1994, pp. 38–54.

118 See Pascale Poulet, 'Allongement de la scolarisation et insertion des jeunes: une liaison délicate', *Économie et statistique*, no. 300, 1996, pp. 71–82.

119 Starting from a sample group of 'enquêtes Emploi' (1990–94) and the FQP investigation, Goux and Maurin have brought out a specific effect of diplomas: 'Uncertified years of education (of which no diploma marks successful completion) do not involve the same wage-

earners as certified years. Conversely, graduates who have repeated a year have careers that are comparable to those graduates who have experienced no problem with education' ('Éducation, expérience et salaire. Tendances récentes et évolutions à long terme', *Documents d'études*, no. 4, DARES, Paris 1994, pp. 17–18).

120 See Danièle Linhart and Margaret Maruani, 'Précarisation et destabilisation des emplois ouvriers', *Travail et emploi*, no. 11, January/March 1982, pp. 27–36.

121 See Thomas Périlleux, *La Travail des épreuves. Dispositifs de production et formes de souffrance dans une entreprise industrielle*, thesis at the École des hautes études en sciences sociales, Paris 1997.

122 Gorgeu and Mathieu, 'Recrutement et production au plus juste', pp. 81–2.

123 While believing that 'the crime statistics must be treated with caution', if only because not all incidents are reported, and they simultaneously measure variations in crime and variations in the activity of the forces of law and order responsible for curbing it, the authors publishing under the name of Louis Dirn believe that a marked increase in offences against property since the 1970s is undeniable (*La Société française en tendances, 1975–1995*, Presses Universitaires de France, Paris 1998, p. 358). Offences against the person have remained stable since the Second World War. But thefts have risen appreciably, as have damage to buildings, etc., cases involving cheques, and 'petty crime' in general. Thefts rose from fewer than 200,000 in 1951 to more than 2.3 million in 1985; 235,000 cases of damage to public or private property were recorded in 1984. But it is in the case of drugs-related offences that the increase in crime has been most marked: the recorded incidents rose from a few hundred in the years to 1968 to 49,500 in 1987. Claude Chiaramonti interprets this increase as the sign of a 'non-integration into consumer society', or rather, if one follows his commentary, a tension between the adoption of the values of the consumer society and, more generally, the capitalist world and the impossibility of procuring sufficient income by legal means to permit access to consumption. The prison population has undergone uninterrupted growth since 1975, increasing as an average population from 27,000 at that date to 46,500 in 1987 (Chiaramonti, 'L'asocialité dénoncée par ses victimes', *Données sociales 1990*, INSEE, Paris 1990, pp. 434–7), and then to 54,269 on 1 January 1997 (Odile Timbart, 'La délinquance mesurée par l'institution judiciaire', *Données sociales 1999*, INSEE, Paris 1999, pp. 373–7).

124 The legal rules concerning thresholds for numbers of workers make the exercise of certain rights (workforce representation and trade union activity, in particular), or enjoying certain guarantees, dependent on the firm employing a particular number of wage-earners.

125 See L. Van Eckhourt's article in *Le Monde*, 2 March 1999, 'En Alsace des patrons "sauvageons" écopent de leçons de droit du travail'.

126 See Dominique Sicot, 'Cents ans de galère pour l'inspection du travail', *Alternatives économiques*, no. 104, February 1993.

127 It is also deteriorating in the public sector. We omit the public sector from our analysis because it does not directly form part of 'capitalism'. But its development cannot be disconnected from the development of the private sector. The lack of resources, shift work (mandatory for the police and medical services), the degradation of the social condition that social workers, medical personnel, teachers, the representatives of law and order, and so on, directly experience, have thus contributed to a significant increase in the difficulties of public work – a phenomenon that is doubtless unduly obscured on the grounds that these workers possess job security. But this is also to forget that the public sector is an important supplier of 'subsidized little jobs' – certainly a way of helping those without work, but also a means of filling-public service assignments on the cheap. The interaction between the condition of the public sector and the capitalist sector, and investigation of the causes of the problems of the public sector, deserve a book in their own right. We shall have to content ourselves with simply highlighting a few aspects.

128 See Michel Cézard, F. Dussert and Michel Gollac, 'Conditions, organisation du travail et nouvelles technologies', *Dossiers statistiques du travail et de l'emploi*, DARES, nos 90–91–92, 1993, p. 10; Aquain *et al.*, 'Vingt ans d'évolution des conditions de travail'.

129   In the intermediate goods industry, 48 per cent of temporary staff state that they breathe in smoke and 41 per cent toxins, compared with 36 per cent and 32 per cent for the sum total of wage-earners in this industry (Cézard, Dussert and Gollac, 'Conditions, organization du travail et nouvelles technologies', p. 90). See also the examples given by Ginsbourger, *La Gestion contre l'entreprise*.

130   Spiros Simitis, 'Le droit du travail a-t-il encore un avenir?', *Droit social*, nos 7–8, July/August 1997, p. 660.

131   Lyon-Caen and Jeammaud, 'France', p. 38. See also Alain Supiot (*Critique du droit du travail*, Presses Universitaires de France, Paris 1994, pp. 173 f.) on the development of dispensatory collective agreements. There even exists an employers' project, presented by such associations as 'Entreprise et progrès' or 'ETHIC', for a 'collective firm contract' that would make it possible to legislate locally on a very large number of subjects, with the exception of a 'hard core' of strictly public matters, and whose validity would consist in its signature by two responsible partners – management on the one hand, representatives elected by the wage-earners on the other, who do not necessarily belong to a trade union. It would allow derogation from legislative, regulatory and sector agreement provisions, if the parties so agreed on such a measure. 'Given the weakness of union implantation in most French firms, such projects, were they to see the light of day, would be tantamount to self-regulation by the employers' (ibid., p. 175).

132   We are not claiming here that *all* the productivity gains have been achieved by greater exploitation of the workforce, which is most certainly not the case. On the other hand, that many wage-earners are subjected to more intensive work for wages that are sometimes in decline is a reality which must be highlighted.

133   Cartron, 'Autonomie et contrôle dans un restaurant McDonald's'.

134   It forms part of the implicit agreement that the wage-earner must be ready to work at least one additional hour, since the person in charge is in the habit of asking the wage-earners if they can stay longer only starting from the second excess hour. Wishing to earn more, most of the wage-earners are inclined to extend their working hours.

135   Gorgeu and Mathieu, 'Recrutement et production au plus juste', p. 55.

136   Alain Supiot, 'Du bon usage des lois en matière d'emploi', *Droit social*, no. 3, March 1997, pp. 229–42.

137   The latest advance in accounting, the 'activity accounting' that developed widely from 1989 onwards, was intended in particular to improve the supervision of staff management departments. For these departments, reputed to be uncontrollable, it sought performance indicators linked to the services rendered and combined with 'cost indicators' that were supposed to express the quantity of resources required depending on the performance levels attained (see Thomas Johnson and Robert Kaplan, *Relevance Lost: The Rise and Fall of Management Accounting*, John Wiley & Sons, New York 1987; John Shank and Vijay Govindarajan, *La Gestion stratégique des coûts*, Éditions d'organisation, Paris 1995; and Philippe Lorino, *Comptes et récits de la performance. Essai sur le pilotage des entreprises*, Éditions d'organisation, Paris 1995). The breaking up of the firm into a group of smaller firms similarly makes it possible to define smaller zones for delivering accounts, allowing greater pressure to be brought to bear. Research into the supervision of administration was thus not inconsequential in enhancing the supervision and evaluation of activities that had hitherto escaped control (see Véronique Malleret, 'Méthode d'évaluation des performances des services fonctionnels', *Revue française de comptabilité*, no. 259, September 1994, pp. 44–53; and 'Les évaluations des situations complexes: des processus à maîtriser', in L. Collins, ed., *Questions de contrôle*, Presses Universitaires de France, Paris 1999, pp. 149–72; Ève Chiapello, 'Art, innovation et management: quand le travail artistique interroge le contrôle', in Collins, *Questions de contrôle*, pp. 194–218).

138   When the task to be performed does not seem to require a full-time wage-earner, or is subject to significant temporal variations, those in charge of cost centres are led to resort to temporary staff, or to hire on fixed-term contracts.

139   See Caire, 'Précarisation des emplois et régulation du marché du travail'.

140   See Gérard Lyon-Caen, 'Plasticité du capital et nouvelles formes d'emploi', *Droit social*, nos 9–10, September/October 1980, pp. 8–18.

141   See Koichi Shimizu, 'Kaizen et gestion du travail chez Toyota Motor et Toyota Motor Kyushu: un problème dans la trajectoire de Toyota', *Actes du GERPISA*, no. 13, March 1995, pp. 14–42. The mechanism functioned well for nearly forty years, until the emergence of a 'crisis of work' led firms to humanize production unit work (ibid., p. 31).

142   See Valérie Aquain, Jennifer Bué and Lydie Vinck, 'L'évolution en 2 ans de l'organisation du travail: plus de contraintes mais aussi plus d'autonomie pour les salariés', *Premières synthèses*, no. 54, 16 June 1994, DARES.

143   See Cézard, Dussert and Gollac, 'Conditions, organisation du travail et nouvelles technologies'.

144   Ibid. Obviously, *cadres* are not subject to the tempo constraints built into machines or bound up with the automatic displacement of a product or component, and only minimally so to constant supervision by superiors (11 per cent in 1993, but nevertheless on the increase). But the fact of being subject to pressure as a result of norms or tight deadlines rose from 8 to 28 per cent, and as a result of demands from customers or the public from 51 to 66 per cent, between 1984 and 1993 (Aquain, Bué and Vinck, 'L'évolution en 2 ans de l'organisation du travail').

145   Source: Ministère du Travail, de l'Emploi et de la Formation professionnelle, 'Horaires de travail en 1991'.

146   Gollac, *À marches forcées?*, p. 62.

147   See Christian Berggren, 'Lean Production: The End of History?', *Actes du GERPISA*, no. 6, February 1993, pp. 15–36.

148   Yves Clot, Jean-Yves Rochex and Yves Schwartz, *Les Caprices du flux. Les mutations technologiques du point de vue de ceux qui les vivent*, Éditions Matrice, Vigneux 1992, p. 59.

149   François Eymard-Duvernay, 'Les marchés du travail: une approche institutionnaliste pluraliste', communication to 'Politique économique' seminar, FORUM, University of Paris X, Nanterre, 1998, p. 16.

150   See Michel Cézard, F. Dussert and Michel Gollac, 'Taylor va au marché. Organisation du travail et informatique', *La Lettre d'information du CEE*, no. 26, December 1992.

151   See Michel Gollac and Serge Volkoff, 'Citius, altius, fortius. L'intensification du travail', *Actes de la recherche en sciences sociales*, no. 114, September 1996, pp. 54–67.

152   Philonenko and Guienne, *Au carrefour de l'exploitation*, pp. 26–8.

153   Périlleux, *Le Travail des épreuves*, p. 268.

154   See Francis Ginsbourger, 'Marie-Thérèse, le rendement et le Lectra', *Travail*, no. 10, November 1985, pp. 30–39.

155   Gorgeu and Mathieu, 'Recrutement et production au plus juste', p. 99.

156   See Margirier, 'Crise et nouvelle organisation du travail'.

157   However, Shimizu ('Kaizen et gestion du travail chez Toyota Motor et Toyota Motor Kyushu') indicates that there is not a single instance of Toyota's directors anticipating very significant productivity improvements from the ideas emanating from workers' quality circles (because engineers' offices have a much greater opportunity to act and control a greater number of variables, they generally invent the most profitable mechanisms). On the other hand, the role of the circles is to make it possible to maintain a certain satisfaction at work on the part of wage-earners, who have the satisfaction of resolving problems and improving their workplace. They also make it possible to reduce critical distance from a system in whose service people must involve themselves.

158   The classificatory grids contained in the collective agreements that guarantee minimum wages hierarchically differentiated according to skills cannot take into account people's real skills, only those demanded by the different work posts. Firms are therefore not obliged to overpay

someone who is overqualified for a particular job (see Michèle Bonnechère, *Le Droit du travail*, La Découverte, Paris 1997, p. 67). We have already cited the case of student employment. But students do not compete only with those less qualified than them, they directly compete with themselves as they will be once they have graduated. With the accumulation of difficulties faced by young people integrating into work at the end of their studies, education centres thus seek, in order to aid them in the medium term, to multiply the training courses and the duration of professional experience of their future graduates over the course of their education. Thus, for example, business schools tend to generalize long training courses of up to a year for those of their students who are close to leaving, and the posts of 'young recruits', like those of assistant product manager in marketing, are progressively being filled by students in the course of studies who are paid less, and for whom the social charges are reduced.

159   The move towards the individualization of working conditions goes together with great diversity in work contracts, working hours and the management of working time. See Linhart and Maruani, 'Précarisation et déstabilisation des emplois ouvriers'.

160   See Robert Boyer, 'L'introduction du taylorisme en France à la lumière de recherches récentes', *Travail et emploi*, no. 18, October/December 1983, pp. 17–41; Dominique Eustache, 'Individualisation des salaires et flexibilité. Le cas des entreprises chimiques et de leurs ouvriers de production au début des années quatre-vingt', *Travail et emploi*, no. 29, September 1986, pp. 17–35.

161   Moreover, this development occurred in accordance with demands from a section of wage-earners: in firms where uniform increases were the rule (banks, food-processing), more than 70 per cent were interested in the establishment of more individualized remuneration; among the young, supervisory staff and managerial staff, the percentage exceeded 80 per cent (Thomas Coutrot and Sylvie Mabile, 'Le développement des politiques salariales incitatives', *Données sociales 1993*, INSEE, Paris 1993, pp. 218–24). It was accompanied, as we saw in Chapter 3, by a profound change in conceptions of justice, with the transition from a conception of justice centred on a fair distribution of benefits between socioprofessional categories ('social justice') to a conception of justice centred on fair remuneration of individual performance.

162   See Coutrot and Mabile, 'Le développement des politiques salariales incitatives'.

163   Olivier Barrat, Thomas Coutrot and Sylvie Mabile, 'La négociation salariale en France: des marges de manoeuvre réduites au début des années 90', *Données sociales 1996*, INSEE, Paris 1996, p. 207.

164   Economic profitability, which measures the yield of the capitals employed (gross surplus of exploitation/fixed assets + requirements in circulating funds) increased sharply between 1979 and 1988, rising from 9 to 18.3 per cent. As for financial profitability (current pre-tax profits/equity capital), it went up in the same period by 6 per cent (Jean-Luc Bricout and M. Dietsche, 'Un bilan de santé favorable', *L'Entreprise*, special issue on 'La France des entreprises', no. 2518, 1992, pp. 172–74).

165   We have already referred to the evolution of the distribution of value added in favour of firms during the 1980s. This was approximately maintained at the same level in the 1990s. It should also be indicated that wage-earners' purchasing power did not alter: 'Assuming an unchanged post at work (with a constant qualification structure), the purchasing power of the net wage had advanced by 4.2 per cent a year from 1951 to 1967 and by 3 per cent a year in the period 1967–78. Since 1978, it has fallen back slightly. The reduction in the purchasing power of the net wage attached to a given post, limited to 0.1 per cent a year from 1978 to 1994, rose to 0.8 per cent a year from 1994 to 1996' (Adrien Friez, 'Les salaires depuis 1950', *Données sociales 1999*, INSEE, Paris 1999, p. 156). Some of the problems must certainly be put down to a rise in social security contributions and hence to an increase in redistribution between wage-earners. But the increase also has to do with the transfer on to social bodies of various costs previously met by firms. Thus, the contributions intended to finance UNEDIC – the body for unemployment insurance – have regularly increased, with some rare exceptions. From 0.25 per cent of gross

salary, the rate of contribution rose to 3.6 per cent in 1979, 4.8 per cent in 1982, reaching 8.4 per cent in August 1993. Moreover, the division of this contribution between firms and wage-earners altered to the disadvantage of the latter. At the outset, employers bore 80 per cent of the cost; today, the figure is in the region of 62 per cent (source: *Alternatives économiques*, May 1994).

166 See Karl Polanyi, *Origins of Our Time: The Great Transformation*, Victor Gollancz, London 1945; Supiot, 'Du bon usage des lois en matière d'emploi'.

167 Although, listening to farmers, one might wonder if this is systematically true. Together with human labour, land forms part of those goods supplied by nature that will find themselves valued at market prices which are theoretically established by the interplay of supply and demand, and can be fixed at a level below their reproduction cost. See Polanyi, *Origins of Our Time*, on the fictive commodities of land, labour and money.

168 See Supiot, 'Du bon usage des lois en matière d'emploi'. A mechanism of this kind is, it seems, nevertheless being studied at the Employment Ministry today.

169 Ibid., p. 236.

170 The example of unemployment insurance for professions in the performing arts provides a good idea of what the general regime might become if the same route is pursued. According to the relevant mechanism, the artist, who works irregularly and thus belongs to the category of casual workers, must amass a certain number of stamps in a given period of time for unemployment insurance to be available. In balance at the outset, the scheme is now in deficit and financed by the general regime. In particular, this is explained by the fact that employers, counting on this source of income, come to an arrangement to supply a number of stamps and of a total value such that the artist is guaranteed a certain standard of living while the employer pays only the minimum. This mechanism, diverted from its initial purpose of offering guarantees to personnel in the performing arts, who were the original casual workers historically, now equally serves broadly to subsidize the employing establishments. See Pierre-Jean Benghozi, *Le Cinéma entre l'art et l'argent* (L'Harmattan, Paris 1989) for the effect of subsidizing cinema production; and for the overall mechanism and development of the balance of the scheme, see Pierre-Michel Menger, 'Marché du travail artistique et socialisation du risque. Le cas des arts du spectacle', *Revue française de sociologie*, vol. XXXII, 1991, pp. 61–74, 'Être artiste par intermittence. La flexibilité du travail et le risque professionnel dans les arts du spectacle', *Travail et emploi*, no. 60, 1995, pp. 4–22; and 'Les intermittents du spectacle: croissance de l'emploi et du chômage indemnisé', *Insee-Première*, no. 510, February 1997.

171 FNE (Fonds national pour l'emploi) agreements are signed between the state and the employer. The job situation in the region or profession must be marked by a serious imbalance making the redeployment of older workers impossible. The agreement is aimed at those over the age of fifty-seven, who up to retirement receive 65 per cent of their wage within the limits of a ceiling and 50 per cent of their wage for the remainder. The firm's contribution varies between 6 and 18 per cent. The figure of 56,000 derives from Christian Abrossimov and Didier Gelot, 'La politique de l'emploi de 1990 à 1994 entre croissance économique et action publique', *Données sociales 1996*, INSEE, Paris 1996, pp. 131–37.

172 See François Guéroult, 'Faut-il rétablir l'autorisation de licenciement?', *Alternatives économiques*, no. 140, September 1996.

173 See Norbert Holcblat, Pierre Marioni and Brigitte Roguet, 'Les politiques de l'emploi depuis 1973', *Données sociales 1999*, INSEE, Paris 1999, pp. 108–16.

174 If we add to the 118 billion of targeted employment policy schemes unemployment benefit and the functioning of the public employment service (ANPE, etc.), we arrive at 343 billion francs (ibid.). Unemployment contributions are in theory paid by the social partners, but in fact, given the level of UNEDIC's accumulated deficit, the state has been obliged to take over part of its expense. Thus, in 1984 responsibility for some of the people without work was transferred to the state and the state budget. Added to this on several occasions were grants and low-interest loans to bail out the system (4. 8 billion francs at the beginning of 1993, for example) (source: *Alternatives économiques*, May 1994).

175   See Cédric Afsa and Selma Amira, 'Le RMI: un dispositif en mutation', *Données sociales* 1999, INSEE, Paris 1999, pp. 406–12.

176   This mechanism, originally reserved for the parents of three or more children, has been extended to families with two children. The additional expenditure projected for this extension was 6.8 billion francs in 1994 during the drafting of the law. Such was the success of the measure that a further 2.5 billion must be added. The APE (*Allocation parentale d'éducation*) involved around 500,000 people in June 1997 (see ibid.).

177   See Gérard Abramovici, 'La protection sociale', *Données sociales 1999*, INSEE, Paris 1999, pp. 390–97.

178   See Holcblat, Marioni and Roguet, 'Les politiques de l'emploi depuis 1973'.

179   See Christine Charpail *et al.*, 'L'évaluation des politiques de l'emploi', *Données sociales* 1999, pp. 117–27. On the other hand, employment policy has been effective in reducing conjunctural rises in unemployment by absorbing the social effects of a sudden rise in redundancies: this was the case in the mid-1980s and at the beginning of the 1990s, when the increased unemployment thus avoided may have amounted to 500,000. It has thus played an important counter-cyclical role (see ibid.). It remains the case that with each increase the number of subsidized jobs rises, and it is subsequently very difficult to reduce their volume: it is as if jobs preserved by means of subsidies during difficult periods are maintained – although the same people are not necessarily involved – when the economic situation picks up again, resulting in a current figure of 2.1 million subsidized jobs. See the graph in ibid., p. 11.

180   See Abrossimov and Gelot, 'La politique de l'emploi de 1990 à 1994 entre croissance économique et action politique'.

181   See Holcblat, Marioni and Roguet, 'Les politiques de l'emploi depuis 1973'.

182   Bloch-London and Boisard, 'L'aménagement et la réduction du temps de travail', p. 213.

5

UNDERMINING THE DEFENCES OF THE WORLD OF WORK

The weakening of trade unionism and the reduction in the level of critique directed at capitalist firms, particularly from the beginning of the 1980s to the mid-1990s, are clear indications of the difficulties social critique encountered in checking a process that was especially damaging for those with the fewest resources of all kinds (economic, educational, social).

Changes in the world of work during this period continued to prompt complaints or indignation. But the institutions traditionally responsible for transforming complaint – a way of expressing discontent that remains attached to persons in their particularity – into a general condemnation and public protest were widely discredited and/or paralysed at the time. We shall confine ourselves to examining the position of the unions, which are very close to problems at work, the phenomenon of deunionization emerging as both symptom and cause of the crisis of the social critique.[1] An analysis of the development of political parties of the left (roughly sketched out in Chapter 3), but also of the right – since they, too, supported the construction of the postwar social state, and served as a reformist relay for a social critique of capitalism given more radical expression by left-wing movements – would be required to complete the analysis.

The difficulties experienced by unions and political parties must also be related to the lack of analytical models and solid, oppositional arguments that was one consequence of the decomposition of hitherto accepted ideological schemas, which relied largely on a representation of society in terms of social classes. Now, as we shall see in the second part of this chapter, the mechanisms of representation (in the sense of social, statistical, political and cognitive representations), which helped to give substance to social classes and endow them with an objective existence, tended to disintegrate, particularly under the impact of capitalism's displacements. This led many analysts to regard this principle of division as obsolete. If, in a sense, such challenges ultimately serve the reconstruction of critique, because they encourage attention to the features of the new world such as it is, their immediate effect was to delegitimate its traditional ideological organizations, and thus accentuate the crisis of critique.

I. DEUNIONIZATION

The weaker establishment of unions in firms and the decline in their audience among workers played a decisive role in the reduction in the level of critique to which the capitalist process was subject from the start of the 1980s.

It is in fact difficult to counterbalance firms' own analyses of business developments, whose content is geared towards concerns about profits, without advancing an alternative, equally well supported representation from the workers' standpoint. When unions are well established and active, work problems relating to a firm, to certain occupations, or to particular sectors of business activity can be referred upwards to the national level and aggregated. This makes it possible to establish data and general interpretations which form the basis for alternative assessments. But the imbalance in information greatly redounds today to the benefit of those who manage firms, who invest significant sums in information systems, whereas unions can only organize sketchy and partially clandestine data collection. Greater access to the information on the firm's system would constitute a first step towards greater equality between the parties (it exists to some extent in the case of works councils).[2] Yet it would not completely alter the situation, inasmuch as the system is basically formated to answer questions about profitability, leaving in the shade problems that a wage-earners' representative would be bound to raise. Without the relay of the union group at the base, the groups of affiliated unions representing wage-earners in national or branch negotiations, whose existence appears necessary both to firms and to employers who want interlocutors on certain subjects (or who are obliged by law to have them), are vulnerable to criticism for lack of realism, incompetence or narrow-mindedness. They have found it difficult to raise fundamental questions, and curb the most destructive developments before they have gone too far.

The factory inspectorate – to which wage-earners do not report because they do not know how to, or because they do not dare – is likewise largely powerless. Without an internal union relay exercising control on a daily basis, the likelihood that workers' rights will not be respected is strongly on the increase.[3] How are people to know what the employer is entitled to request by way of 'effort'? Are they obliged to accept it? What is the employer obliged to offer in exchange? Does he respect collective agreements? Training in labour law is not a requirement of employment. Who will inform wage-earners? Here again, as far as knowledge of workers' rights is concerned, as with access to the 'realities' of work, the playing field is not level.

From the standpoint we are concerned with, the union also has the advantage of providing points of support outside the firm – places for meeting, pooling information and reflecting, for the development of beliefs different from those put forward by the employers, work methods, a socialization of means of resistance, training in negotiating – to which an isolated union representative does not have access.

Through the blunting of critical tools and capacities it produces, the deunionization we have witnessed over the last twenty years, in a country where unions were already very weakly established and divided, has thus contributed significantly to the change in the balance of forces between employers and employees in a direction unfavourable to the latter, and facilitated the task of restructuring capitalism. But it would be incorrect to regard deunionization as a development independent of alterations in the process of realizing profit. Quite the reverse: the displacements of capitalism have had the effect of greatly weakening unions in part deliberately and premeditatedly, and in part through a combination of unintended consequences and the unions' poor handling of the new conditions they faced. The supposed rise of individualism and a culture of everyone-for-themselves, the crisis of confidence in political action, or the fear of unemployment, which are usually advanced to explain, for example, difficulties in establishing resistance to the growth in exclusion, thus cannot be disconnected from the dynamic of capitalism and its critiques.

The extent of deunionization

The first symptom of the crisis of unionism was the drop in membership levels. According to Pierre Rosanvallon, 'we may estimate that French trade unions saw the number of their members fall overall by more than 50 per cent between 1976 and 1988. The rate of unionization (the number of union members relative to the waged working population), which was 20 per cent in 1976, is thus currently in the order of 9 per cent. The collapse is sometimes spectacular. The CGT metal federation – the historic, symbolic core of this confederation – which claimed 420,000 members in 1974, now has no more than 80,000 working dues-payers.'[4] As was the case twenty years earlier, France in 1990 had the least well established unions of all the European countries; it was also one of the countries where the decline in membership was most significant (-12.5 points, or a fall of 56 per cent).[5] These data betoken the quasi-disappearance of trade unionism from workplaces. In a poll conducted by the Conseil supérieur de l'audiovisuel for the CGT in July 1993, 37 per cent of wage-earners in the private sector stated that they had never encountered a CGT trade unionist, and 25 per cent that they had, but did not any more – and this at a time when the CGT was the main wage-earners' union in numerical terms. Sixty-three per cent stated that they had never had any contact with trade unions.[6]

Deunionization can also be observed at the level of the *elections* for wage-earners' representatives in various bodies (industrial tribunals, works councils, mutual benefit societies, social security funds, etc.). Thus, abstention in the *assurés sociaux* college for social security elections rose from 28 per cent in 1947 to 31 per cent in 1962, reaching 47 per cent in 1983. In the industrial tribunal elections, the abstention rate among wage-earners was 65 per cent in 1997.[7]

The same process is evident in the case of works councils. This election takes place in firms, which limits the amount of travel, and involves representation in an institution that is normally known to those who vote. The weight of abstentions is nevertheless on the rise, increasing by nearly 10 points between 1970 and 1990.[8] In the votes cast, non-union candidates have made strong gains, from around 14 per cent to 28 per cent between 1967 and 1992, this advance coming mainly at the expense of the CGT, which received 50 per cent of votes at the beginning of the period as compared with roughly 22 per cent in 1992.[9] While works councils possess a considerable number of powers – for example, informing wage-earners about the firm's economic results and defending jobs (which has particular implications during redundancy schemes) – wage-earners experience them in the first instance through their social and cultural activities (libraries, holiday camps, various discounts, trips, etc.). In fact, this is the function declared most important by the largest number of voters. Only those elected on a union ticket identify some other function as their priority (economic results for 27 per cent, employment for 26 per cent, and only then social and cultural activities for 19 per cent).[10] Since 1945, works councils have had the right, further extended by the Auroux laws, to call upon outside experts to help them examine a firm's accounts, to analyse the validity of a redundancy plan, or the repercussions of the introduction of new technologies. Yet this right to expertise is very little used – by fewer than 9 per cent of central works councils and fewer than 4 per cent of plant councils. It is essentially used by councils comprising union members, with 55 per cent of them availing themselves of it.[11] In fact, it is virtually only works councils where unions are present that concern themselves with issues of jobs or wages.[12] The decline of the unions in elective structures is thus also accompanied by a redefinition of their positive role at the expense of social vigilance and the protection of workers, since the role of existing institutions is being altered without having to change the legal rules.

Observing that unions have always been weakly established, certain analysts have sought to construe unions as structures whose legitimacy is elective, with the elector/client relationship supplanting activist commitment.[13] But the rise in abstentions and the decline in the votes cast for unions reveal the weaknesses of this interpretation: without a union presence in the workplace, elections on their own lose some of their meaning and effectiveness. The loss of audience measured by votes is in fact directly bound up with the collapse in establishment, for union groups can obtain votes only where they present candidates and, except in the case of the CGT, their audience has scarcely fallen in establishments where they are present.[14]

The crisis in trade unionism, which has gone on deepening whatever indicators are used, would appear difficult to counter. Younger generations have never experienced very high levels of combativeness, and often do not know what a trade unionist looks like. Yet they are among the first victims of the problems afflicting the world of work. In the 1991 poll already cited, wage-earners reveal a low level of optimism about a trade-union revival, since 54 per cent of those in the private sector think that unions will go on declining.[15] Even if confidence in trade-union activity has been somewhat on the increase in recent years (up from 40 to 47 per cent of wage-earners between 1990 and 1997),[16] this does not extend to the youngest (under twenty-five). To the question 'to prepare for your future and society's, whom do you most rely on?', 8 per cent of young people mentioned unions, which came far behind the family (40 per cent), heads of firms (31 per cent), friendships (27 per cent), elected officials – mayors and deputies – (16 per cent), and the President of the Republic (13 per cent).[17]

Social conflicts have hit a historical low point against a background of growing social problems. Whereas the number of strike days averaged four million between 1971 and 1975, the figure fell to an annual average of three million between 1976 and 1980. The 1980s were marked by a much more significant ebb: an annual average of 1.5 million strike days between 1981 and 1985. This number fell below one million over the next five years, and even below half a million in 1992. Fewer than 700,000 were registered in 1990 – a low that had not been hit since 1946. Since then, the ebb has continued. The recovery of 1995, with two million days, should not engender illusions. Fewer than 500,000 days were lost in 1996, and fewer than 360,000 in 1997 – a year when scarcely 110,000 people went on strike.[18] This lower level of conflict is part and parcel of a reduced union presence. In fact:

> the presence of union representatives has the strongest influence on the likelihood of a dispute, which is lower when the representatives on the works council or workforce representatives have been elected without a union label. The impact is especially clear in the case of a CGT branch where this confederation is in the majority (this then involves disputes launched on its initiative), the impact of the CFDT being significantly less. It is more conspicuous when at least two unions are established, particularly if a CGT-CFDT duo is involved.[19]

Refusal of overtime certainly constitutes a somewhat more frequent form of resistance in firms without a union presence. But this kind of protest is in any case not at all widespread and, even in non-unionized firms, less frequent than strikes and petitions.[20] The only ways of refusing to work that then remain are absenteeism and resignation, but interpreting these is difficult.

The cumulative effect of these various phenomena is obvious. Weakly established unions see their role diminished and their ability to operate as a countervailing power greatly reduced; for these very reasons, their credit with wage-earners declines. Becoming less and less representative of wage-earners in elections as a result, they find themselves that little bit more discredited, accused of forming a new 'nomenklatura' benefiting from perks in the social security funds and unjustified hours for union work, as well as no longer knowing anything about hardship at work because of their insufficient presence on the ground. Lacking recruits, branches also tend to put more pressure on the rare union members to be active, increasing the insider–outsider divide.[21] Union representatives thus find themselves ever more isolated in performing tasks that have been expanded by law-makers in this period: they have less and less contact with wage-earners and no longer have the time to develop membership, or even to concern themselves with members, which further aggravates deunionization.

Analysis of the many causes of this cumulative process faces two questions about the evolution of French trade unionism since 1968. How is it that France is one of the countries where the decline in unions has been most marked, when their powers and protection have been enhanced? In 1968, significant weaknesses in French unionism were corrected, with a considerable strengthening of legal rights and protections in favour of local branches. The law of December 1968 thus offered offices and additional hours off for union duties, and increased the possibilities of action within plants. In 1982, the Auroux laws marked a second significant advance for union rights: for example, they required management to submit internal regulations to workforce representatives, strengthened the protections and powers of union branches, made the election of workforce representatives in all establishments mandatory, established an obligation to negotiate, and so on.

The second question concerns a certain tacit consensus between wage-earner confederations, the employers and the state to mask the scale of the erosion and not to take account of its real implications.[22] For 'people continue to characterize the unions as "representative" and to believe that a "social dialogue" exists in France, because they discuss with government and employers' "representatives" whose actual representativeness is no longer clear'.[23] Does the existence of unions one can confer with in high places, which are laden with powers and prerogatives in theory, but have largely lost contact with workers of whose hardships and concerns they are not really aware, satisfy those in charge of firms and the state? For the latter are anxious to achieve a social peace that has every appearance of being agreed, not imposed. And for their part, are the confederations giving in to the fear of losing what they have if they reveal how difficult they find it to carry out their functions?

The analysis of the factors behind deunionization we are now going to undertake is all the more tricky in that the information to hand is by no means satisfactory. If we have a certain amount of information on the two unions that are best established in the private sector – the CGT and the CFDT – we are at a comparative loss when it comes to analysing the workings or organ-ization of the 'representative' unions described as reformist – the CFTC, the CFE–CGC and FO – whose role, at least when it comes to employers' strate-gies for dividing unions or renegotiating collective agreements, is unquestionably crucial. Consequently, and reluctantly, we have taken our examples essentially from the two largest confederations in the private sector.

Anti-union repression

Most works on deunionization do not make anti-union repression a basic cause of the phenomenon – no doubt because it has always existed without equiv-alent deunionization being recorded, but possibly also because we lack information as to the proportion of deunionization that should be attributed to such practices. For example, we do not know the precise scale of over-representation of unionized wage-earners or former union representatives among wage-earners who have been made redundant.[24]

It is nevertheless appropriate to recall the demonstrable existence of anti-union policies in firms, and employers' fairly widespread hostility towards trade unionism, all the more so because trade unionism in France was dominated for a long time by an influential oppositional union – the CGT – to which the CFDT was in no way inferior in this respect, at least during the 1970s.

The International Confederation of Free Trade Unions (ICFTU), which groups together the majority of European trade unions, has thus clearly iden-tified a certain number of multinationals, often American, which follow a policy that is sharply hostile to unions: in particular, Kodak, United Fruit, IBM. At IBM, for example, anyone who seeks to set up a union branch is rated poorly, and often obliged to hand in their resignation. Even the French CGC experiences major problems with this type of multinational. When wage-earners display too militant a temper, they are made redundant and new, more obedient applicants are recruited. Some firms also set up their own company unions, as did Citroën with the CFT (Confédération Française du Travail), in order to obtain a union's support. The repression of struggles by employers' militias supported by the CFT has been the subject of 'black books' published by the CGT and the CFDT.[25]

More subtle, but no doubt more effective as well, is the use of informal systems of sanctions and rewards. 'Hotheads' see their careers blocked, and receive only the remuneration stipulated in collective agreements, whereas those who display a 'good attitude' receive bonuses.[26] Michel Pialoux, who knows the Peugeot site at Sochaux well, thus cites the case of a CFDT militant who has never secured professional promotion and remained P2, whereas his mates at the Peugeot school have become supervisory staff, technicians, even department managers.[27] He likewise mentions the case of a former unskilled worker, who was offered promotion in the following terms: 'Either you continue to sound off in your corner, or you show more intelligence and come on board with us.' This was interpreted by the wage earner as follows: 'It was overalls or coat. I chose the coat.' Another significant example is that of a former CGT militant who went over to the FO for career reasons. In fairly general fashion, the firm 'offers promotions, opens up a space for interaction and makes it understood, directly or otherwise, but often cynically, that at this point it is necessary to shelve one's political sympathies'.[28]

In Dominique Labbé, Maurice Croisat and Antoine Bevort's investigation into why union members have left the CFDT, several militants referred to managerial repression. Some left thinking that they had 'suffered enough'. Half a dozen said they had been made redundant or compelled to resign. This kind of withdrawal from the union on account of recognized disciplinary elimination of the job is ultimately rare (between one and two per cent in the survey cited). Yet these cases serve employers in stressing another possible outcome to union members: leaving the union for the sake of promotion – something that is far more frequent. 'It is remarkable to observe that the skilled worker who becomes the head of a team, the foreman who becomes the head of a workshop, the *cadre* promoted to taking charge of a section – all these people feel morally obliged to quit the union and often do so reluctantly … in the French tradition it seems clear that disciplinary power is incompatible with union membership'. Moreover, other union members, fearing compromises with the hierarchy, equally desire these resignations, thus doing management's work for it.[29]

A method of intimidation that is likewise more or less consciously used by management consists in evincing contempt and irony for workers' interpersonal skills, so that stating their case in public proves especially difficult; this eventually leads to a shortage of candidates for certain elective duties.[30] How can an elected blue-collar representative, who does not enjoy the backing and support of a union, pass the test except by remaining silent or supporting the employer's line?

When several unions are represented, we might also mention systematic endeavours to divide their representatives; or attempts, which sometimes succeed, to 'buy' silence of representatives by manipulating the benefits attaching to their function, like hours for union work; or again, insinuations to wage-earners about collaboration between their representatives and management because of the advantages enjoyed by the former. Florence Weber recounts that at Dambront, where she was investigating, 'a CGT representative worked "overlapping hours" (a normal hourly schedule from 8 to 17 hours), whereas nearly all the blue-collar posts were on 2 x 8. He experienced this as a punishment, which cut him off from other workers; the others accused him of having better hours, a foreman's hours.'[31] The suspicion directed at activists who take their hours off for union work at the point of the 'rush to finish', leaving the responsibility for the work to their mates, or who systematically favour their 'comrades', are so many rumours creating 'a climate of distrust or hostility that is very unfavourable to unionization'.[32] Such suspicions can also be inspired by management. Faced with the reduction in membership, unions themselves agree to accept 'anyone', the 'least competent', the 'lazy', those 'who want to benefit personally', and have thus given some purchase to these condemnations, and fuelled the loss of confidence.

The repertoire of anti-union practices is thus vast, from harassment to intimidation of all varieties, via an insidious process of undermining 'union status' among the wage-earners. The lesser visibility of these practices to today's observers no doubt stems largely from their lesser utility since the restructuring, which has had a more radical effect: with the establishment of new mechanisms in firms, restructuring has made it possible to be shot of unions.

There are even cases where it is impossible to know what motivates the change of organization in the first instance – anti-union struggle[33] or the pursuit of productivity gains – given that the two are inseparable, since more docile workers are often also more productive. Factory closures by multinationals, which can be justified on grounds of overcapacity, thus tend in the first instance to hit unionized sites where strikes are more frequent. And the manufacturing that firms seek to subcontract or outsource is often predominantly that performed by the best-organized workers. Not so long ago, temporary workers appeared to be strike-breakers.[34] Now blue-collar workers see their children form part of that contingent, and be subjected to such difficult conditions at the start of their working lives that they even condone them carrying on working while they themselves are on strike.[35]

Restructuring as a source of deunionization

The first consequence of restructuring that analysts of deunionization think of is the development of *unemployment* and *casual jobs*. The casualization of work status, and the fear of unemployment that accompanies it, have the effect of weakening workers' fighting spirit and their propensity to join a union. The rate of unionization of casual workers is below three per cent,[36] and being made unemployed often translates into withdrawal from the union.

> Starting from a certain threshold of unemployment, we observe that contact with unions is less regular among workers. It is difficult to fix a threshold, but it seems that starting from 8 per cent the rate of unemployment entails a fall in the rate of unionization. ... Employers exploit unemployment to be more demanding about the 'social references' of job candidates. A non-trade unionist will be preferred to an activist. Even those who keep their job experience the

pressure against trade unionism. A sizeable number of wage-earners seek to leave unions in order to keep their job.[37]

We must also take into account the 'despondency' effects induced by employment problems, particularly for those in the least skilled jobs, who see their future and often also that of their children 'blocked'.[38] Thus, 5 per cent of the ex-trade unionists studied by Labbé, Croizat and Bevort say that they left the union out of a sense of powerlessness, which the researchers analyse primarily as professional demoralization.[39]

The closure of numerous 'great bastions' of trade unionism (coal mines, iron and steel, iron deposits, shipyards, automobiles, etc.), or their subjection to severe job cutbacks, and the exclusion in the first instance of older wage-earners – that is to say, those most likely to have experience of unionized workplaces – are legitimately cited as related sources of the rise in unemployment and deunionization.[40]

Nevertheless, the relation between unemployment rates and unionization levels is not one-to-one. On the contrary, analysis of the comparative situation of European countries in 1981 reveals the diversity of cases.[41] 'It is wrong to think that the higher the rate of unemployment, the weaker trade unionism is. It is equally mistaken to believe that the unemployment rate is low when unions are powerful. To reason in this fashion is to ignore a middle term, which is the political instance. It is not simply a question of the political complexion of the governing group, but of the political, or rather political-social, structures inherited from the more distant past.'[42] On its own, the rise in the unemployment rate, which now affects 12 per cent of the working population, seems equally insufficient to explain a halving of union membership – a decline whose magnitude has, as we have seen, been especially pronounced in France.

This is why, over and above the mere statistics for job insecurity and unemployment, it seems to us that it is necessary to take the measure of the impact on unionization of the *reconstruction of the economic fabric* (outsourcing, the creation of subsidiaries, relocation, etc.).

The transfer of jobs towards services and small and medium-sized firms – which, as we have seen, derives largely from a reconstruction of ways of producing, and only in part from the emergence of new needs – has had the consequence of locating wage-earners in structures that are weakly unionized, without a tradition of opposition, and where increased job insecurity militates against any potential desire for organization. We know that the existence of representative institutions and unions grows with the size of the firm. Thus, in 1992, 83 per cent of wage-earners employed in establishments with fewer than twenty workers had no representative. The figure is still of the order of 48 per cent for wage-earners in establishments containing between twenty and fifty. These people had neither a union representative, nor a workforce representative, nor obviously a works council, since these are only mandatory above fifty personnel.[43] The level of conflict is likewise largely correlated with business sector and size of firm,[44] which explains the motive firms may have for splitting up large structures into a flotilla of small and medium-sized firms and outsourcing previously industrial functions to services. In addition, we know that, so far as is possible, employers avoid establishing new structures in towns that are too 'red' or close to former 'bastions', because the risks of a strongly oppositional political culture there are demonstrable.[45]

Workforce mobility, whether encouraged or forced, contributes in large measure to deunionization.[46] People arrive in workplaces where there is no local branch, and links with the union have disintegrated. The departure of a particularly effective union representative can be enough to bring about the death of a branch. Dominique Labbé's writings have revealed the importance of the trade-union fabric for unionization, which is the result of an intense presence of representatives among union members and the creation of an atmosphere conducive to joining. Thus, in large firms we note that membership occurs in bunches: one sector is heavily unionized, while another is not unionized at all, or affiliated to a different federation. Each weakening of the branch through the mobility of union members results in the disappearance of the network it helped to maintain. It can be shown that new union members (post-1978) lead a professional existence characterized by mobility: only 40 per cent of them have not changed jobs, whereas the rate was double for members of the previous trade-union generation. Consequently, the time they spend in the union is shorter and professional problems constitute part of the explanation for their departure. The evolution of the wage-earning class thus involves greater difficulties for unions when it comes to consolidating branch activity and developing the loyalty of new members. The mobility of enterprise structures is a similar issue. In all large firms, quasi-constant concentrations, takeovers, transfers and rationalizations tend regularly to alter the organizational structure, to move the unions' interlocutors around frequently, and to make access to the 'real decision-makers' difficult.[47] They prevent the establishment of settled professional relations, and thus hamper trade-union development.

Breaking up the work community, by employing people with different job statuses belonging to different firms on the same site, also helps to disarm and disorientate collective action. In an article devoted to the jurisprudential success of formulas for 'making personnel available', Antoine Lyon-Caen and Jean de Maillard write:

> We shall presuppose related companies, whose activities are complementary. They proceed to exchange personnel with one another. But their establishments are clearly distinct, as is the collective status of their workforce. Thus, wage-earners attached to different companies and, consequently, subject to

different statutes will work on the same site. How can organized representation of the workforce be established? If the practice making personnel available is simply routinized, it is a strong bet that the judge will decline to accept the existence of an economic and social unit. Possibly he will accept the presence of an economic group, but it is hard, notwithstanding pressing intuition, to imagine him accepting 'the existence of a community of workers constituting a social unit'.[48]

The separation between what Jacques Magaud calls 'legal ownership' (those who pay) and 'real ownership' (those with the power to organize wage-earners' work in the framework of the production collective) tends to separate wage-earners' demands (addressed to those who pay) from 'challenges to the organization of work', which are directed to those who 'assign duties'. It thereby hampers the establishment of house agreements or collective agreements. It helps to make the issue of who is to receive the demand problematic (who is the real employer?), to reduce the negotiating capacity of the wage-earners very severely, and to restore a 'margin of initiative' to firms compared with a situation where all the wage-earners belong to a 'single entity'.[49] By making it difficult to identify the employer, it hampers the exercise of wage-earners' collective rights. Membership of one and the same work community by all is dismantled by the new forms of organization, severely handicaping mobilizations.[50] Francis Ginsbourger and Jean-Yves Potel's analysis leads to the same conclusions: from the mid-1970s onwards, there was a decline in collective negotiations, attributed by the authors in particular to the 'socioeconomic restructuring that shattered the erstwhile unity of work collectives and brought about a decline in collective trade-union strength'.[51]

Together with increased productivity and a reduction in the cost of operations requiring a minimally skilled workforce, the new ways of structuring firms have thus facilitated a widespread destruction of union opposition. The new forms of personnel management (involvement, individualization, participation, etc.) have had the same kind of effect.

The circumvention of trade unions by neo-management

At the beginning of the 1980s, in most firms where it was practised, the *individualization of wages* took the form of an enhanced role for immediate superiors (or, later, project heads) in appraising wage-earners. Once or twice a year, each wage-earner 'reviews their situation' with their superior, leading to a 'general appraisal'.[52] For firms, this method of determining wages has the advantage of engaging the maximum number of wage-earners in situations where they have to make judgements about colleagues and also, in a sense, about themselves. But wage-earners obliged to appraise one another can also find it more difficult to forge a common front against central management. The development of additional pay based on meeting targets, whether these are individual or specific to a small group, has equally had the result of increasing the spirit of competition between groups and wage-earners, as well as involvement in work, reducing the possibilities of combining or rebelling accordingly. The representative interviewed by Michel Pialoux thus identifies the development of bonuses as a basic element in the loss of solidarity among blue-collar workers.[53] The introduction at the end of the 1970s – first of all in large firms, then in medium-sized firms, and, from the mid-1980s, in the public services – *of workers' discussion groups*, 'quality circles', and a whole sophisticated panoply of human-relations tools has permitted greater control by managers, who are now much better informed than the unions about the workers' demands and discontents.[54] The purely local character of these bodies also makes it possible rapidly to avert the risks of any diffusion to other firms (or other units of the same group) of information, discontent, or – when they exist – forms of resistance. Unions have seen their role diminish in proportion to the development of direct attention to demands; wage-earners today more often trust the hierarchies of firms to defend their interests than unions.[55] If there is no doubting the improvements facilitated by the establishment of more frequent communication, and the increased satisfaction of numerous wage-earners at work, whose advice is now taken into account, it also turns out that in a fair number of cases demands have quite simply been nipped in the bud by intensive workplace control.

Finally, a multiplicity of mechanisms, including the individualization of wages just referred to, have aimed to develop *people's involvement in work*, to encourage them to assume responsibility and exercise self-control. Preserving jobs or gaining access to new, more flexible and versatile ways of organizing work, which are gradually replacing the old Taylorist methods, has provided an opportunity to secure greater commitment in the work situation and a reduction in critical distance from it. A particularly striking example is the opening of the new Peugeot bodywork factory at Sochaux, called HC1. The blue-collar workers intended for the new factory were sent on a training course for three weeks in a château usually reserved for training *cadres*. And they were obliged on this occasion to make a formal commitment, in front of witnesses, to observe the new organization's 'Ten Commandments'.[56] During one of these training periods, a worker who refused was requested to leave the course and sent back to his old job, despite the illegal character of the commitment demanded.[57]

The new ways of managing human relations have had the effect of sharply reducing the level of conflict in firms, and circumventing trade unions. However, for those who argue in favour of professional relations of a new, less hostile kind, with a trade unionism that is more involved in business, as in countries with a strong social-democratic tradition, these developments were not necessarily negative. Similarly, numerous innovations by employers have met with wage-earners' approval. Here it is the ambiguity of the mechanisms, whose validity and risks are equally evident, which has tended to paralyse or defuse the critique formulated by trade unionists, and to accelerate a loss of confidence in them.

The paralysing ambiguity of the new mechanisms

The new enterprise mechanisms caught the unions on the hop, as it were. They often had no idea what to make of them.[58] Sometimes they took refuge in an oppositional attitude in principle to any initiative by the employers, deemed bad a priori. Sometimes they regarded such initiatives as echoing their own proposals, as was especially the case with the adoption of ideas about self-management initially developed by the CFDT. Similarly, the reorientation of the CFDT, whereby in 1978–79 it retreated to concrete issues, local problems and negotiation at enterprise level, privileging working conditions, innovation and lived experience ('action must start out as closely as possible from everyday concerns') can, in retrospect, be seen as in harmony with the evolution of employers' attitudes from the late 1970s.[59]

For example, the unions did not know what position to adopt when they were faced with quality circles. Thus, the CFDT branch in a large firm noted that there was no common view among its members: some were hostile, believing that the organization of work 'isn't the job' of the workers; others wanted to wait and see; a final group internalized the firm's problems and wanted to achieve productivity increases to safeguard jobs. Nor were union labels decisive when it came to predicting people's attitudes, which ranged randomly within each union from violent denunciation to active support.[60]

On other subjects, such as reduction and reform of working hours as well as flexibility, the positions of the various confederations were clearer-cut but different, shattering the possibility of a united front among wage-earners.[61] If French trade unionism had always been characterized by pluralism – and never more so than at the end of the 1970s, with the CFDT's reorientation – quarrels had not been as frequent or, above all, so demobilizing for trade unionists, who found themselves hostage to them. Previously, despite their ideological differences, agreements for unified action had obtained between the CFDT and the CGT, and it was rare for the confederations to compete for the same members, since in firms where several branches existed a certain allocation was evident (a particular workshop to the CFDT, a particular office to the CGT, etc.).[62] Conflict between the confederations, much of it attributable to the CGT's dependence on the PCF, was also exacerbated by the issue of how to interpret the crisis. The CFDT in particular did not share the CGT's purely 'economic' viewpoint, believing that the crisis was as much cultural and political as social and economic. It was not enough, 'according to its leaders, to go on about the need for jobs in order to revive growth'. It was important to '"take advantage" of the crisis, as it were, to "envisage" another kind of growth, which would be of a different kind from that which made the success of the *trente glorieuses* possible'.[63] In the first half of the 1970s, the conflict between the CGT and the CFDT thus revolved around the hierarchical or egalitarian character of wage increases. The CGT was in favour of increases proportional to level of seniority, respecting classifications and qualifications, against the capitalist tendency to deskill workers. In contrast, the CFDT regarded wage hierarchies as signs of the ascendancy of capitalism within the world of work, which ought therefore not to be taken into consideration.[64]

The impossibility of reaching a straightforward decision about workers' interests in the new mechanisms made the unions uncertain about their position. It also divided them from one another, generating a process of politicization that their members overwhelmingly rejected.

More or less active participation in restructuring almost systematically discredited the action of branch membership. According to Labbé, Croziat and Bevort, none of the union branches they studied emerged unscathed from a confrontation with 'redundancy plans', regardless of the attitude they adopted, for this varied considerably from one place to the next, from quasi-co-management of the question to rejection of redundancies in principle.[65] In the French tradition, the unions qualified as 'representative' in fact have the ability to commit wage-earners, but this becomes a source of self-disqualification when it no longer involves negotiating improvements and distributing them, but instead arbitrating in the distribution of sacrifices.[66] On their side, the confederations' official positions sometimes seemed to contradict the convictions of their members, or what they were experiencing in their firms.[67] The CFDT's attitude during the 1984 negotiations on flexibility, when it accepted the principle alongside organizations traditionally held in low esteem by its militants like FO or the CGC, thus appeared to be a veritable 'betrayal' and, it seems, lay behind numerous resignations.[68]

Contrariwise, it might be that wage-earners were favourable to certain provisions, and that union opposition to them risked becoming a further source of loss of confidence. Thus it was, in the first half of the 1980s, that agreements containing individualized increases were signed by unions in many firms, despite their fundamental opposition to this formula. But these agreements too obviously satisfied the expectations of many wage-earners for the unions to risk weakening themselves still further by opposing them.

In the 1970s, a whole generation of new graduates rejected the forms of personal dependence characteristic of the domestic world, which were deemed humiliating – and, in the case of young *cadres*, refused to exercise this kind of close authority. It equally rejected bureaucratic forms of impersonal control, which were regarded as inefficient and inhuman. They no longer wanted to be treated either as 'domestics' or as 'machines'. Critiques were also formulated by women, who held paid jobs in increasing numbers, and were less and less disposed to accept the often abusive power, frequently accompanied by sexual harassment, brought to bear on them by 'petty tyrants' – adjusters, foremen, head clerks, and so on.[69] They also wanted to see an increase in part-time work, in order to achieve a more balanced existence. These demands for liberation, the focal point of what we have called the artistic critique, were heard and partially satisfied. But their satisfaction had the effect of dividing wage-earners and unions over their interpretation of the developments under way. As Pialoux stresses, young semi- and unskilled workers recruited to Peugeot were comparatively won over by certain aspects of the new mechanisms: competition, the prioritization of individual success, the competitive spirit.[70] Branches consequently found themselves shot through with a generational conflict, and experienced the utmost difficulty uniting wage-earners.

At least with the arrival of the left in government, the unions – the CFDT at their head, since it was very closely associated with the elaboration of the Auroux laws – had the opportunity to pass on numerous ideas, and achieved an improvement in their status and prerogatives. But the legislative balance-sheet was not as favourable as a mere reading of the laws' content might lead one to suppose. For the way in which they were implemented, the tricks hit upon by employers to take advantage of them, and the weaknesses of the unions themselves resulted in a series of unforeseen consequences that some analysts identify as major causes of deunionization.

The unforeseen consequences of legislative advances

In fact, it seems that in many respects these conquests did not bear the fruit expected of them, starting with the development of negotiations between social partners that was to give unions a prime position. The Auroux laws thus sought to step up negotiation at enterprise level,[71] but the displacement of arbitration from the national level, where the unions were conspicuous and comparatively strong, to the local level, where they were generally weak, rendered them pretty much incapable of offering resistance to the employers' will. This deficiency in effectiveness worked in favour of deunionization.

Yet at the outset, the Auroux laws had seemed to employers to be very unfavourable to them. Witness the brochure published by CNPF in April 1983 (*Les Applications des lois Auroux. Recommandations du CNPF*), which warned employers against laws that 'risked seriously compromising the efficiency of firms to the detriment of those who work in them and the whole national community'. In particular, they feared – wrongly, it can be said in retrospect – that the Auroux laws would strengthen the position of the unions as the sole interlocutors of firms, and thus compromise the restoration of managerial control and the establishment of discussion groups inspired by quality circles. The alteration in employers' attitudes to forms of negotiation was in fact well-nigh complete: in the 1960s, they preferred sectoral negotiations, in order to avoid 'the best-placed firms economically becoming a reference-point for the demands of wage-earners from other firms'; in the 1980s, by contrast, employers found it in their 'interest to negotiate at enterprise level, so as to be able to take more effective account of the constraints of the economic situation'.[72]

Moreover, at the same time as these laws presented unions as the natural interlocutors in negotiations, they legitimated consultation outside union structures, with 'wage-earners' right of expression' – something that was doubtless not irrelevant in the unions losing their audience. In fact, the modalities of the exercise of 'wage-earners' right of expression' had to be settled by means of collective negotiations. Yet if numerous agreements were made, they often assigned immediate superiors a leading role in the meetings,[73] turning the right of expression into an ordinary tool in the panoply of participatory management.

As for the principle of equality of treatment for all the confederations, practised since the war for democratic reasons (to allow for representation of wage-earners' diversity), but also out of motives that were less democratic (to restrict the power of the CGT, which enjoyed a strong majority for a long time), it was not transformed, even though it furthered the fragmentation and weakening of union representation and, above all, prevented the development of genuine collective negotiations, which were nevertheless at the heart of the Auroux laws. 'Majority representation of wage-earners is only very rarely taken into consideration by the right to collective negotiations, and in conditions that are so restrictive that they seem designed never to be fulfilled. Hence it is lawful for employers to conclude agreements with a union organization that in fact represents only a small minority of wage-earners. In such a system ... continuous state intervention remains inevitable.'[74] Some, like Ginsbourger, even believe that by issuing, before the Auroux laws had even been voted, seven edicts between January and March 1982 fixing the prescriptive content of what henceforth fell outside negotiation (reduction of the working week to thirty-nine hours, a fifth week of paid holidays, restriction of the possibility of recourse to temporary labour and fixed-term contracts, the regulation of part-time work, and retirement at sixty), the intended revival of negotiations was strangled at birth. For the partners most often made do with writing the new legal provisions into collective agreements.[75] This is typical of the dominant forms of social regulation in France, which assign the state a key role. In view of the unions' weakness – itself bound up with a regulatory framework that does not encourage unionization, and maintains competition between confederations – it is clear that they would not by themselves have been able to obtain from employers the social advances decreed in the 1982 edicts. As a result, the state must intervene, and is the real motor of social progress, which in turn helps to discredit the unions.

Other double-edged conquests involved an extension in the scope of union activities and an increase in the means put at their disposal, notably through hours allowed for union work. These measures facilitated the emergence of full-time trade unionists accumulating hours for union duties from several representative bodies (union representatives, workforce representatives, works council, health and safety committee), and spending their time in meetings. Professionalized and technicized, by the same token they lost contact with members and no longer had the time to collect stamps, recruit members, and so on. From the standpoint of firms and wage-earners, the French system of representation is top-heavy and scarcely intelligible, characterized by the coexistence of numerous bodies with different spheres of activity. But although this multiplicity impedes effective action, the unions are attached to it because of the powers it involves and the many opportunities it offers for 'protecting' certain wage-earners. The passage on 20 December 1993 of the Giraud law, relating to firms with fewer than two hundred wage-earners, sought to remedy this situation by giving heads of firms the right to decide unilaterally that workforce representatives were also the wage-earners' representatives on works councils. If these provisions did indeed simplify things somewhat, it is to be feared that they were primarily used to reduce the union presence in the small and medium-sized firms that had a union, not to create hitherto nonexistent representative bodies.[76] From this example it is perfectly clear that, in order to be effective, a simplification of the mechanism would have to be combined with incentives to unionization; and it is easy to understand why, in the absence of such a political project, unions cling on to what some denounce as 'established benefits' and 'perks'.

Unions have thus become a matter for professionals, rather than activists. It even seems as if members have in some ways become a burden: they must be listened and attended to, while the law has entrusted numerous duties to trade unionists that can be fulfilled without any need for members. Moreover, since various powers are bound up with the electoral success of the different confederations (posts in the social security funds, secretaryship of the works council, etc.), and elections follow one another in rapid succession, most of the effort *vis-à-vis* the workforce was invested in electoral campaigns. The focus on elections contributed to members being neglected that little bit more, until the realization dawned that too extensive a loss of union presence was leading to electoral regression and the staging of elections which were pointless given abstentions, once again fuelling the process of discrediting the unions.[77]

Thus, the conquests made possible by the 1970s movement, many of whose ideas were implemented with the left's arrival in government, generated numerous perverse effects that it would have been the role of critique to block, for the employers did not take the risk of rebelling against the loss of influence on the part of the unions, which they were fighting with other weapons. But for a long time, the sense of conquest and satisfaction prevented people perceiving the weakness of the new mechanisms. These factors are further indication that satisfying critiques, which is always desirable if their demands are deemed valid, represents a danger for critique itself, which is then slow to put the world to the test once more.

By another rebound effect of critique against itself, the artistic critique not only encouraged the dismantling of bureaucracies in firms, but also berated the state, political parties and, in terms of what interests us here, trade unions. Moreover, the latter – albeit to different extents, depending upon the confederation, the sector, and so on – assimilated it, and thus fuelled forces that had no hesitation in targeting them for reform.

Trade unionism as a semi-willing victim of the artistic critique

The critique of trade unions reached a peak towards the mid-1980s, but it did not come only from employers. It was also rooted in leftist opposition (which the Maoists, however few in number, had succeeded in make highly conspicuous) to the union bureaucracies (the CGT being the particular target of these accusations), and to the union power which, in some sectors, was often conflated with that of petty tyrants.[78] At the same time, the very violent attacks to which unions were subject, and which, as in the works of François de Closet published at the beginning of the 1980s, inverted their image – from defenders of the oppressed into defenders of the categorial privileges of protected minorities – met with conditions conducive to their diffusion.[79] This was all the more true in that unions, which had never been well established in small firms, maintained an active presence predominantly in the public sector, nationalized firms, and the core concerns of large firms that had escaped the wave of outsourcing of the least specific tasks. Trade-union bodies (like political parties) belonged to the hierarchical and bureaucratic world the class of 1968 had wanted to destroy, and which they finally saw in retreat. Failing to renew their own forms of opposition with sufficient speed to adjust to the new aspirations[80] – a task that capitalism seemed to acquit better than them – the parties and unions on which critique was based attracted fewer and fewer activists – when they were not accused of having become retrograde and sectarian, falling back on serving various unfairly privileged corporative minorities. For example, the CGT was very hesitant about self-management, which it rightly regarded as a critique of the traditional forms of representation and trade unionism it had adopted.

The ambiguity of this critique of trade unions stemmed from the fact that the accusation of corporatism had purchase on the inside, among activists who dreamt of a union of the whole working class (or of all wage-earners around the working class), transcending all particularistic interests, and hence especially those associated with occupations and firms. It had purchase among another section of activists inspired by a radical egalitarianism that rejected all hierarchies, including those of occupation or skill, denounced as sources of oppression. Thus, it is astonishing to observe that even before reaching a broad public at the beginning of the 1980s, the accusation of corporatism had been wielded within, prompting numerous organizational changes that may retrospectively be reckoned to have been one source of deunionization.

For a long time the confederations had long been organized by sector and geographical subdivision, rather than by occupation or firm. But the structures remained loose. Subsequently, this form of organization was imposed on all the federated unions: 'Starting from the 1960s, in the name of broad solidarity and the unity of wage-earners in the face of their employer, the confederations abolished categorial divisions and proceeded to dismantle the national unions that were the natural extension of the corporative principle.' In a 1974 circular, the CFDT thus recalled that a nurse or social worker in a factory could not be attached to the health services federation but must, for example, belong to the HaCuiTex federation if a textile factory was involved. The same thing happened with social workers in the CGT. In 1969, the confederation asked its national union to dissolve itself and to distribute members into federations corresponding to their respective employers. This kind of requirement led to certain 'transverse' occupations like social workers, but also computer scientists, trainers, marketing personnel and so on, not having representation.[81]

Accordingly, a tendency set in to suppress the different social categories coexisting in firms: thus, the CFDT set up single-union sections that were supposed to combine all categories of the workforce. But this noble idea was not a success, because members wanted somewhere where their specific professional problems could be addressed.[82] In the same years, the CGT had the utmost difficulty taking account of the particularities of certain groups, notably *cadres*, who – despite the UGICT's existence – found it difficult to get a hearing.[83]

Finally, the union leaderships also wanted to transcend occupational divisions between sectors by strengthening geographical, local and departmental combines, which led to a proliferation of organs, committees, and decision-making sites at a time when activist numbers were in decline; this had the result of absorbing them still further into the union machinery, and reinforcing their distance from the base and the membership.

'In the past, French trade unionism derived its strength from its corporative dimension and its ability to deal with individuals' problems in the workplace itself. Consequently, in claiming to "transcend corporatism" and organize "broad solidarity", were the unions not destroying the bases on which they were constructed? ... In many cases, "restructuring" resulted in the disappearance plain and simple of union members and the union branch.'[84] At the beginning of the 1980s, there unquestionably remained various bastions of corporatism that had not been dismantled by internal union efforts (for example, railworkers, teachers, and workers in book publishing). But if they were so conspicuous and so strong, it was also because their corporative form had enabled them to shed fewer members.

Here the artistic critique, articulated in the name of freedom that is deemed unduly restricted in a categorial framework assuming rights and duties relative to the group people belong to, formed an alliance with the egalitarian dream of the social critique. Together they worked on union structures in an attempt to eliminate sites where members could have constructed unity of action on the basis of sharing a more concrete common lot than the mere fact of being a wage-earner.

The artistic critique also attacked all institutions (familial, religious and political, particularly the Communist Party) deemed oppressive. Their prescriptive, controlling character was challenged and ways of rendering them more flexible had to be found. But the freedom wrested also led union recruitment to dry up. The critique of religion as an ally of bourgeois morality helped exacerbate the crisis of activism with a religious origin and of the Catholic movements, whereas these had been a significant source of recruitment for the CFDT up until the 1970s.[85] The critique of the dirigiste methods of the Communist Party and countries of 'real socialism' contributed to the drying-up of recruitment to the CGT. French trade unionism was a unionism of activists, whose numbers were very small, but who were inspired by strong convictions, whether the Christian faith or socialism. The drying-up of traditional sources of recruitment at precisely the time when, for the reasons referred to above, the creation of a more professional, less ideological mass trade unionism proved especially difficult, likewise contributed to deunionization.[86] As for the critique of the family, it ran through each union branch in the form of a generational conflict that cannot be separated from two other processes – the rejection of traditional Catholic morality and the rejection of parents' working-class culture – or from the state of the labour market and the practice of remunerating and managing wage-earners according to their age which, as we have seen, had the effect of intensifying the competition between young people and their elders.[87]

Among the factors involved in deunionization, it remains for us to enumerate those for which union bodies are almost totally responsible. Here we are not dealing with manoeuvres by the employers, which directly (anti-union repression) or indirectly (restructuring, neo-management) weakened branch cells, or with the unintended consequences of legislative progress or the critical successes of the 1970s. What is at issue is malfunctioning of the unions. Although it is not directly connected with capitalism's displacements and the changes in critiques of capitalism, we must briefly consider it in the framework of this study, since there is no question that played a role in weakening critique, and hence helped to brush aside the resistance that endeavours to restructure capitalism might have encountered.

Union malfunctions not conducive to unionization

A first malfunction is to be found in the blindness that the unions displayed, incapable as they often were of getting the measure of the concerns of wage-earners, and hence of defending them, in their manifest lack of understanding of the problems of certain occupations, or certain categories of wage-earner. We have already mentioned the difficulty finding a place in the union movement faced by people in 'transverse' occupations, by *cadres* and engineers (outside the CGC), or by the young. Christophe Dejours also accuses the union movement of refusing to consider the risks for mental health entailed by work.[88]

A second accusation that is frequently made, and is linked to the first, is that of having abandoned members. As Labbé stresses, '[m]ore than a third of the membership did not leave of its own accord; rather, it was the union that left them. In fact, we met a lot of people who did not regard themselves as having resigned: people were no longer coming to ask them to pay their subs, the branch was not meeting or they were not summoned to meetings, there was no longer anyone on duty, no one answered the phone. The end of the unions was, in the first instance, the end of activism'.[89] In addition to the reasons already adduced for this transformation of trade unionism (professionalization, emergence of full-time trade unionists, shortage of breeding-grounds for traditional recruitment of activists, etc.), we must also mention a trade-union ideology, fairly widespread at the time, derived from the 'myth of the glorious day' or the 'general crisis of capitalism'. According to this conception, there is no point seeking to adapt to changes in society; it is sufficient to await the moment when the 'contradictions of the system' will provoke a kind of general uprising. 'The job of trade unionists is not to resolve problems; on the contrary, they must help the contradictions to "mature" and explode.'[90] This kind of ideological blockage – which is also mentioned by Dejours and all those who construe obstinate workerism, especially in the CGT, as one of the factors in the crisis of trade unionism – is part and parcel of the difficulty in developing social critique to tailor it to the new world. On some points, the unions evolved rapidly, as is indicated by the development of a professional trade unionism; on others, they exhibited dreadful inertia, proving incapable, for example, of renewing their doctrines and analyses at a time when the world of work was being profoundly transformed. It was as if the instances that supported social critique no longer possessed the requisite intellectual tools to understand what was being implemented, having in fact been constructed by a kind of isomorphism in close proximity to the industrial world ideologically, if not numerically, dominated by the planned large firm, which employers were precisely in the process of revolutionizing. Why they were unable to renew themselves ideologically with sufficient speed – whether because they had lost contact with their members, or because their previous analyses prevented them from realizing what was happening – is difficult to determine. No doubt the two phenomena were mutually reinforcing.

Dominique Labbé finally invokes the co-option practices of the union confederations. Whatever the confederation, officials at each level are chosen by
the higher level, never by the members. Hence it is the local or departmental
union, not the branch, that appoints union representatives, who in order to
keep their post must please their union superiors, not their base. A common
feature of the current leaders of confederations (CGT, FO, CFDT, to cite
only the largest of them) is that they have spent the bulk of their working life
in union apparatuses, far removed from their original work environment.

To conclude, we must mention a final critique directed at politicization and
its excesses, which in fact covers numerous grievances: the link between the
CGT and the PCF, which became increasingly burdensome as French
Communism immured itself in support for the Soviet Union; the less solid
but nevertheless real link between the CFDT and the PS,[91] which brought discredit on the CFDT during the political switch of 1983; the turf war conducted
by CFDT and CGT branches after years of joint action. What seemed normal
in the 1970s – that is, union support for a political project (Union of the Left,
the call by confederations to vote for certain candidates, etc.) – which, at the
time, attracted numerous members – rebounded on the union movement in
the 1980s, when political perspectives became blurred, giving free rein to the
accusation of politicization.

Trade unionism should have been the premier force attempting to curb or
correct the dismantling of the world of work induced by capitalism's displacements. It should likewise have mobilized to prevent its own rout, which was
in part inscribed in the new enterprise practices. But the successes scored by
the bilateral critique whose vehicle it had been – the gains achieved by the
social critique as regards union institutionalization, or the adoption of certain
proposals from the artistic critique – made the assessment of novel developments difficult, and delayed realization of the unintended consequences they
might entail. The world having in part changed under the impact of critique,
the critique was slow to reconstruct itself, and confront the new tasks that fell
to it.

One reason for this slow response lies in the deconstruction of the forms
and methods for establishing equivalence, which on the one hand permitted
comparison between situations – and, consequently, stimulated a sense of solidarity, and favoured collective mobilization – and on the other supplied tools
for interpreting management measures and initiatives. Among the equivalences
that were deconstructed, particular significance must be accorded to one
which, far from being limited to the space of the firm, had for a century and
a half played a central role in the ordinary interpretation of society and which,
since the war, had in a sense been integrated into the very structure of the
state: social classes. These classes delimit groups of people in the social arena
occupying different positions in the division of labour, property relations and
the distribution of resources that might yield a profit. The space of social

classes – which, until the 1980s, had constituted a common framework of reference that was both practical and cognitive, particularly in the form given them in the 1950s by the INSEE's classification of socioprofessional categories – had in fact become blurred, and was no longer self-evident.

2. CALLING SOCIAL CLASSES INTO QUESTION

As in the case of deunionization, changes in capitalism must be regarded as one of the causes of the crisis in the model of social classes. Displacements towards new forms of test during the 1970s and 1980s not only affected the selection of the employable and unemployable and, for those who kept their jobs, routes to success or marginalization. They not only helped to reduce the unions' presence and audience. They also altered the frameworks in which society was conceived in discourses about the social world and scholarly analyses. In talking about *society*, people were at least tacitly agreed in a very general way, in previous decades, in referring to a nation-state where the main divisions were represented by classifications of social classes, or socioprofessional groups at any rate.

The representation of society as a set of social classes in the framework of a nation-state

From the mid-1930s onwards, the existence of social classes and the need to accord them official recognition was the subject of almost general agreement, even if the nature of these classes, and especially their conflictual or complementary character, continued to fuel often violent disputes between Marxists on one side and corporatists, neo-socialists or social Catholics on the other.[92] A conception of society became established: a society is a set of socioprofessional groups in the framework of a nation-state. This society is a good one when the relations between the groups who compose it can be justified by reference to an approximately equal share of private and public goods and, where these exist, the fruits of growth calculated on a national basis. The state is the arbiter of this balance and, consequently, of social peace. It therefore plays a preponderant role in the system of social regulation, and particularly in the system regulating industrial relations, as is attested by the fact that the economic organizations – wage-earners' trade unions and employers' organizations – negotiate at national level under state auspices.

The slow progress in establishing this conception – which, in France at least, took more than a century – is explained by the fact that it had to be constructed *against the conception of national representation derived from the French Revolution* (largely Rousseauist in inspiration). According to this conception, the nation is composed of citizens whose political qualification presupposes that they are separated from all local or professional attachments referring to private interests (intrigues, in *The Social Contract*), so that they can address themselves to the general interest. There is no room for the representation of interests and, consequently, no room for the recognition, institutionalization and representation of socioprofessional groups. In this political design, the citizen is a man *without properties*, qualified solely by dint of belonging to the nation.

We must look elsewhere for the political origins of the conception of society as a whole divided into social classes. As Jean-Philippe Parrot has shown, the gradual introduction from the mid-1930s and postwar years of a representation of professional interests in the state through institutions like the Plan, the Conseil économique et social, the national accounts office, and the INSEE's socioprofessional categories, and also of a system of professional relations where the state is the guarantor of the negotiations between employers and unions, derived from the conjunction of three currents of political ideas: corporatism, one of whose main components was social Catholicism; the trade-union movement; and a technocratic, planning current that was Saint-Simonian in origin.[93]

From the 1950s onwards, the classification of *socioprofessional categories* was to represent a powerful tool for unifying and representing social classes, in the different senses of political or administrative representation, statistical representation, social representation, and mental representation.[94] Created for the 1954 census and revised in 1982, this nomenclature rapidly emerged as a remarkable instrument for gathering knowledge about the social structure, as is attested by the large number of studies conducted over forty years using its classification system, both in public research centres and in private polling institutes. Once this became available, it was a particularly useful tool for systematic analysis of the correlations between social position, academic qualification, income and social origin, which had been at the centre of the meritocratic conception of society since the war, and also at the heart of the second spirit of capitalism.

Now, this nomenclature did not spring fully equipped from the head of its creator (Jean Porte). It was the product of a social history of the definition of relevant classificatory criteria. Alain Desrosières describes the three steps required for the production of the 1954 nomenclature.[95] The first was marked by the organization into professions that obtained under the Ancien Régime, whose persistence is evident throughout the nineteenth century despite the abolition of guilds by the Le Chapelier law of 1791. This made possible an enumeration of 'professions'. Within each profession, no distinction was as yet made between masters and journeymen, contrary to the future separation between employers and employees; and 'hands' were separated from 'professionals' (they were negatively defined as 'without a profession'), unlike another categorization that was to become established later, in which 'unskilled workers' (ex-labourers) were assimilated to 'skilled workers' (ex-journeymen) to constitute a 'working class'. The second step consisted in the separation of employers from wage-earners, non-wage-earners from wage-earners. But this became possible only with the advent of labour law and the clearly codified definition of the wage-earning class towards the end of the nineteenth century. The third step leading to the nomenclature of socioprofessional categories was characterized by the codification of a hierarchy within the wage-earning class, according to levels that were bound up with the duration and type of training. The distinction between workers and employees constructed around the manual/non-manual dichotomy was already in use, but the sets of workers and employees were not hierarchically organized in the way we are familiar with today: that is to say, where workers are concerned, the series 'labourers', 'semi- and unskilled workers' and 'skilled workers'; and where employees are concerned, the series 'employees', 'intermediate professions', and '*cadres* and higher intellectual professions'.

This third step extended from the 1930s to the 1950s, relying on the Parodi agreements and the framework of the classifications written into collective agreements. These agreements, established by law in 1919, issued in results only after the Matignon agreements in 1936,[96] and became one of the main institutions on which social relations were based after the war. In 1946, the Parodi–Croizat decrees established classifications for calculating wages, partly in order to ensure that the 'sacrifices' entailed by reconstruction 'will be fairly distributed'. Thus, they extended to all sectors levels of blue-collar skills inspired by the 1920s collective agreement in metallurgy (labourers, OS1, OS2, P1, P2, P3). Each sector was to append lists of occupations to each skill level. The postwar period equally saw the creation of works councils, whose representatives were elected by wage-earners divided into three colleges (workers, employees–technicians–supervisors, and *cadres*), once again crystallizing boundaries between groups of wage-earners. The public services statute was established in the same years, introducing a distinction between A and B categories of *cadres* that was to serve as a model for separating 'middle *cadres*' ('intermediate professions' in the 1982 nomenclature) and 'senior *cadres*'. The nomenclature of socioprofessional categories was thus directly bound up with the appearance over the course of history of rules of job segmentation used by firms, but largely established by the state. This unique history explains the original form assumed by French socioprofessional categories compared with stratifications elsewhere. It also accounts for their robustness for analysing data.

The classifications carried out with the aid of the nomenclature are all the more reliable in that the professions are well represented by professional groups, and established by laws and regulations. Thus, it has been shown how the most salient groups and classes of the 1970s – those whose existence was simultaneously acknowledged by political partners, professional representatives, statisticians or sociologists, and ordinary people – were the object of a prolonged labour of construction and institutionalization. Take, for example, the category of *cadres*, which is very heterogeneous in most respects (occupations performed, income levels, size of patrimony, academic qualifications, etc.): its existence is due in the first instance to the creation of representative institutions (associations, unions, journals, etc.), which obtained the definition of an official status and the implementation of regulatory mechanisms,[97] whose legislative character guaranteed their enforcement in each firm and over the whole national territory.[98] By analysing the coding operations carried out within the INSEE, it has also been demonstrated, for example, that errors of classification regarding doctors in the nomenclature are extremely rare, despite the wide variety of professional titles they may use. For the requirement that one must be a doctor of medicine in order to practise is a powerful instrument for determining the contours of the profession.[99]

Collective agreements represent a crucial link between the socioprofessional categories, aiding statistical work and offering a representation of society in terms of social classes,[100] and enterprise practices, because in a sense they are guarantors of the soundness of statistical classifications within the wage-earning class. Contracts developed and signed in professional life between professional organizations representing the employers (or employers themselves) and wage-earners represented by trade unions, their purpose is to deal with the whole set of conditions of employment and work (conditions for hiring, working hours, overtime, part-time work, holidays, training, means of promotion, resignation, redundancies, retirement). In particular, they use *classificatory grids* (called Parodi classifications), and categorize the different jobs and occupations of the firm or sector, according to a division and a minute specification of the tasks and duties of wage-earners. They distinguish different conventional regimes according to a division in terms of categories (semi- and unskilled workers, employees, technicians, supervisory staff, *cadres*), within which skill levels are differentiated (level, group, scale, degree). Skill levels pertain to posts, not to the people who occupy them, even if reference may be made to academic qualifications in their definition. Collective agreements mention a wage coefficient that corresponds to a minimum wage depending on the wage-earner's position in the scale. They thus establish categorial divisions in firms correlated with types of training and wage levels. Collective agreements do not quite cover the whole wage-earning class in the private sector, despite repeated attempts by the public authorities to encourage their extension. In 1993, there were 13.5 million wage-earners in the private sector, and it was estimated at the time that around 800,000 of them were not covered by any agreement.[101]

The resonance of this model in ways of thinking is clear. On the one hand, socioprofessional categories constitute the largely implicit format on which what might be called the ordinary sense of the social structure rests.[102] On the other hand, French sociology of social class, which flourished in the 1960s and 1970s, employs and theorizes the implications of this analytical framework. Thus, for example, the emphasis in work by sociologists of social mobility on the distinction between the space of social positions (the *structure*) and the properties of their potential occupants (the *qualities of the agents*) reproduces, at a theoretical level, the distinction to be found in collective agreements between the specification of 'work posts' and the professional 'qualification' of those fit to hold them. Similarly, a notion like 'social trajectory' generalizes the modes of promotion or career that were extended in the same period from the public sector to large firms, where they feature in collective agreements.

The crisis of the model of social classes

Whereas social classes were highly pervasive in the 1970s – not only in the social sciences, where they were the subject of a large number of works, but also in literature, the media or cinema – they gradually faded from the field of representation. In the second half of the 1980s, respected, esteemed analysts could seriously believe and claim that they no longer existed.

The rise in blue-collar workers' living standards since the war, their access to certain consumer goods like cars or televisions, the improvement in the comfort of housing, together with the regular decline since 1975 in the number of such workers, paved the way for a theory of the absorption of all classes – especially the working class – into a vast middle class. Opinion polls conveyed the idea that class consciousness was declining: comparison between a 1966 Ifop survey and several Sofres surveys (1982, 1983, 1985, 1993 and 1994) demonstrates a rise in the sense of *not* belonging to a class,[103] with 'those who state that they do belong to a social class' increasingly referring 'to the middle class, which can in a way be interpreted as the negation of class consciousness, since there is no opposition to another class'.[104] The phenomenon seems all the more striking in that the percentage of blue-collar workers who say that they belong to the middle classes rose from 13 per cent in 1966 to 30 per cent in 1994.[105] In this way, the Louis Dirn study group was also able to question the vision of a society divided into social classes in its 1990 publication.[106]

Pierre Rosanvallon, for his part, endeavours to show that classes have been dissolved, and that society is no longer composed of anything more than a collection of individuals who can no longer be aggregated into classes, or who all belong to the same middle class.[107] To demonstrate the inadequacy of the nomenclature of socioprofessional categories, he cites, for example, income statistics for the 'intermediate professions', and observes that 21 per cent of *cadres* are situated below the median wage level of 'intermediates', while 14 per cent of blue-collar workers exceed it.[108] Rosanvallon's position is radical in that his goal is not to encourage a reconstruction of statistical categories, but quite simply to dispense with them: 'Income level, cultural capital and socioprofessional category are no longer as clearly correlated as in the past, making society less easy to read. ... It is no longer collective identities that have to be described, but individual trajectories. ... When the cognitive returns of imposing statistical machinery are diminishing, it is time to revert to a new use of monographs, in order to arrive at a sensitive appreciation what might be called the grain of the social.'[109] Now the only thing that is thought to count is individual trajectories, which cannot be grouped into a category – the 'excluded', for example, in fact being nothing more than a collection of individuals who have experienced 'failures' in their lives, without it being possible to construct a homogeneous class out of them.[110]

In the work of de-representing social classes, sociology's role was at once passive and active. It was passive in the sense that, less autonomous than it often claims to be, it gradually ceased to be interested in classes as they, in their traditional contours, came to be less represented in society. It was active in the sense that sociology makes its own contribution to the task of selecting and representing what matters socially. By ceasing to offer a representation of classes, it thus contributed to their erosion.

In this respect, the case of sociology – which, as a discipline claiming scientific validity, should be under an obligation to account for the changes that affect it – is exemplary. In the years 1960 to 1980, analyses in terms of classes, categories, socioprofessional groups, and so on, played a key role in the rapid development of French sociology. The nomenclature of socioprofessional categories formed the framework on to which were grafted masses of data accumulated by public or private research bodies that fed into sociological interpretations. Yet analyses in class terms have become much rarer since the early or mid-1980s – that is to say, paradoxically, during a period when the highly significant changes affecting economic activity posed the issue of their impact on classes and class relations.[111] The abundant literature that has accumulated over the last ten years on organizations, work and, to a lesser extent, poverty, unemployment and employment, invariably ignore this issue. We have in fact witnessed a transformation in social debate: structured around the theme of inequalities up until the end of the 1970s, it has gradually shifted to exclusion. Yet whereas the first approach 'leaves room for antagonism between social groups, the second establishes the idea of a broad consensus, a vast standardization which is scarcely impeded by a few extreme situations'.[112]

The disappearance of social classes is even more palpable in social philosophy, not to mention the media or political discourse – particularly that of the Socialist Party, which was in power for most of the 1980s. By broadly developing subsidies for 'targeted' employment, public policy has in effect aided this process, for it is less and less concerned with the distribution of effort and profit between social groups, and focuses its action instead on 'those most in need'.

The role of capitalism's displacements in the process
of deconstruction of social classes

If we accept that social classes are not formations which derive from external causes, by a process that is, as it were, natural, but that their institution is dependent upon a labour which forms and represents them – especially, in France, in the state – it will readily be accepted that the transformation of capitalism referred to above has contributed, to an extent that is still difficult to gauge, to blurring the focal points around which class identities were constructed, and to challenging the validity of the equivalences on which perceived similarities in condition were based.

Despite their comparative weakness at the beginning of the period, unions played a significant part in the work of representing different classes or socio-professional groups. They did so by ensuring their representation in the negotiating bodies umpired by the state, but also by contributing to the formation of social representations by highlighting the similarities associated with membership of a group. Deunionization thus also means that unions have gradually lost their ability to preserve identities which were largely bound up with the hitherto tacitly acknowledged isomorphism between representatives and represented.

As for the individualization of employment conditions associated in many firms with a reconstruction of work situations, this has had the effect of suddenly rendering obsolete the unspoken equivalences on which perception of social identities rested. The fading of institutional boundaries, the division into smaller, more temporary units with less consolidated relations between them – these have helped to obscure comparisons between conditions that were based on established classifications. Nor should we underestimate the role played in the erosion of social identities by the new sensitivity to differences, stimulated by increased competition on the labour market.

But the effects of capitalism's displacements on social classes do not operate only by increasing the difficulties that unions experience representing classes, or by an evolution in work situations such that 'class consciousness' dwindles. A large number of employer initiatives have equally contributed to directly transforming the analytical framework.

To start with, let us mention the work done by those in charge of firms on the *terminology used*. Has not the recent transformation of the CNPF into the Mouvement des Entreprises de France resulted in eliminating 'employers' from the legitimate field of representation, since it no longer recognizes itself in this term, so that use of it will increasingly be associated with critique, and its connotation will become yet more negative? The CNPF now presents itself as the representative of firms, and hence – why not? – also of their wage-earners, erasing the conflict of interests between shareholders and wage-earners. Thus the previously established separation is denied, and only critique can revive it.

The substitution of the term 'operative' for 'manual worker', recommended as early as 1971 in the employers' report on semi- and unskilled workers (analysed in Chapter 3), represents another symbolic sleight of hand, one of whose results is to make the 'working class' disappear by insisting on the novelty of working-class posts, and erasing a significant continuity in conditions.

These kinds of practices make it easier to break up the 'typical examples' with which each category was traditionally associated. In fact, when they are read in the margin of a diagonal table, for example, or heard in radio commentary on a poll, the categories of the nomenclature speak to people, as they say, only in so far as it is possible to fill each of the items with representations whose origin has nothing statistical about it (hence covering effects, with the word *cadre*, for example, being filled by representations associated with key examples of the category at the expense of its peripheral members).[113] How is it now possible to place a representation under the category of 'worker' when heads of firms, indicating the number of workers employed in their firm, hasten to add 'workers in the sense of the INSEE', and abandon the use of the term in-house, replacing it with 'operative', which is absent from the nomenclature?

Action on the classifications used in collective agreements, whose crucial importance in the representation of social classes in France we have noted, has also been very sustained since the mid-1970s, gradually breaking down the hierarchies and categories used previously.

From the mid-1970s and in the 1980s, various initiatives helped to *circumvent* these classifications, regarded by a section of the employers as one of the main obstacles to flexibility.[114]

From the beginning of the 1970s, the usual classification grids, which prompted a series of demands and, consequently, collective increases, were regarded as an obstacle to the individualization of pay, and hence as an obstacle to justice. But practices of individualized management of the workforce would in turn bring about large wage disparities between comparable posts and qualifications within a group of firms governed by the same sectoral collective agreement.[115] The flagging of collective bargaining with the implementation of the employers' second response to the crisis of governability gradually facilitated a separation of remuneration practices from the minima written into the agreements, by simultaneously exploiting agreed minima inferior to the guaranteed minimum wage,[116] and a bonus mechanism making it possible to minimize the role of official grids. Thus, in the 1971 CNPF report on semi- and unskilled workers, there is a recommendation to 'make the law of supply and demand operate' by raising their wages 'relative to employees and certain professionals', 'on condition, obviously, that pay increases for these categories are not automatically applied to other jobs'. But the classifications derived from the Parodi agreements represent an obstacle to this project, because they entail excessive rigidity in the relations between pay and membership of a category: 'It must indeed be observed that in our country, above all since the application of the 1945 Parodi classifications, we confront a certain tendency to "assimilation to the state sector". ... It is extremely difficult to alter the conditions of remuneration of a job without affecting the whole scale. ... The rigidity of the system extends to the national level.' To escape this rigidity, 'as a first step' the author advises 'separating the notion of wage from that of classification' by means of 'allowances' and 'additional pay'; and then reconstructing the classification by introducing new criteria – 'responsibility', for example, or 'nervous tension'.

Action on the actual grading of posts in the classifications is another way of bypassing the regulatory framework laid down by them. Thus, according to François Jeger-Madiot, the distinction between 'skilled workers' and 'unskilled workers' reflects not so much a difference in skills as a categorization in the collective agreements which may, with an equivalent skill level, depend upon the state of the labour market.[117] This is particularly clear for young people with a CAP (vocational training certificate) or BEP (technical school certificate), who are now systematically hired for the posts of unskilled workers, whereas the CAP remains widely associated in agreements with skilled workers' jobs.[118]

François Eyraud et al.'s study of the relations between the classifications and the wages actually paid on the basis of twenty-seven establishments in four industrial sectors shows that the correlation between classifications and wages remains strong (of the order of 0.8). On the other hand, the way the grids are used varies with firms, which combine pay policy and classification policy differently.[119] They identify three types of practice: (a) the type mentioned here, which consists in actively neutralizing the grid; (b) the type which takes the grid as a management tool, simply adapting it at the margins; and finally (c) the type which assigns classifications an active role in a desired organizational change, involving a significant renegotiation of criteria and hierarchies.[120]

Let us touch on precisely those practices that consist in working to *transform the grids*, rather than trying to bypass them. The history of the classificatory grids is marked by the signature in the metallurgy sector in 1975 of a new kind of grid, called 'weighted criteria'. Agreements of this kind have multiplied since, to the point where such grids are well on the way to gradually replacing the Parodi grids. They contribute significantly to blurring the division into social classes since, although they represent approximately half of the collective agreements in force today, they no longer allow the direct coding of socioprofessional categories.[121]

The grids negotiated during the postwar years in accordance with the Parodi decrees were characterized by an exhaustive enumeration of hierarchized tasks and work posts within the career paths of distinct jobs. Thus the road haulage agreement, for example, indicates that group one of employees contains cleaning personnel, caretakers who do not undertake rounds, and nightwatchmen who do not do rounds. In group two, we find cleaning staff (big jobs), concierges, caretakers with rounds, nightwatchmen with rounds, guards on the gates, messengers, cyclists and office assistants.

In the grids with weighted criteria that have been negotiated since the mid-1970s, the hierarchy is established on the basis of a combination of criteria on which the negotiators have reached agreement (technical nature of the job, level of knowledge, initiative, responsibility). The metallurgy agreement, which is similar to 'grading criteria', defines level one, grade one of administrative and technical staff (the same level as the groups in road haulage mentioned above) as follows: 'Performance of simple, repetitive or similar tasks, in accordance with simple instructions and indicated procedures, under the direct supervision of a more highly qualified official'. This straightforward example is sufficient illustration of the room for manoeuvre introduced with the new classifications. It is now up to each firm in the signatory sector to grade its jobs itself, within the framework defined by the agreement, whereas with the Parodi grids the classification was already fixed and laid down. The grid in the metallurgy agreement still retains a certain subdivision between categories, distinguishing different hierarchies for blue-collar workers, white-collar workers, technicians and supervisory staff, and *cadres*. But other grids, like those in pharmaceutical industries, make do with setting out a continuum from manual labour to managerial *cadre*, which gradually leads to the disappearance of specific arrangements by workforce grouping.

As with the other displacements that have occurred, assessment of the new grids is not straightforward. The organization of a continuum may appear more conducive to equality and restriction of the hierarchical principle. More general formulations seem less subject to limitation periods and easily adjustable in the event of new occupations emerging. They also seem appropriate in sectors that negotiate for firms with very different occupations. But it is equally clear that systems with weighted criteria, by restoring room for manoeuvre in job classification, also offer fewer guarantees of classification and treatment for wage-earners. These are not insignificant issues, since collective agreements retain a role of the greatest importance in managing jobs, especially in small and medium-sized firms which, as we have seen, are seeing their weight in the distribution of wage-earners increase. The INSEE's 1992 survey *Structure des salaires* indicated that virtually one firm in three with between twenty and two hundred wage-earners had 'assigned paramount importance' to the recommendations of sectors when it came to adjusting wages in the period 1988 to 1992. (For firms with fewer than twenty wage-earners, financial results played a major role, whereas larger firms produced their own directives.) Moreover, the role of sectoral collective agreements is predominant when it comes to deciding basic wages, the hierarchical distribution of jobs, and calculation of seniority bonuses.[122] We must therefore reckon that the impact of alterations to collective agreements may be considerable.

It is also relevant here to point out that the 1975 metallurgy agreement, which inaugurated these kinds of practices, was signed only by the FO, the CFTC and the CGC, while the CGT and the CFDT, the two most representative federations in metallurgy, abstained.[123] Nevertheless, by virtue of the French rules of trade-union representativeness, the agreement was considered valid. This constitutes a good example of the inextricable link between capitalism's displacements, reduced protection for workers, the development of flexibility, the discrediting of the unions, and the rules of French law where political responsibilities are concerned.

According to Annette Jobert and Michèle Tallard, the 1990s marked the advent of grids that were even more flexible than the former weighted criteria:

> framework-grids that break new ground … by supplying firms with a method of classification rather than an already constructed system, which leads firms (or subsectors), on the basis of the criteria and within the limits fixed by the sector, to elaborate their own job hierarchy. … The conception of a framework agreement is most explicit when it comes to forms of insurance. The role of the sector is to define seven classes on the basis of five criteria. Its role virtually ends there, since it is then up to the firm to fill the classes with the duties that it has inventoried and appraised on the basis of a weighting of the criteria. … By agreement, firms can determine intermediate classes and they assign the duties names of their own choosing. The number of duties is not limited. Indeed, at the end of the two-year period for implementing the new system, one will be dealing with very different classificatory grids depending on the firm, according to the number of duties identified and their mode of appraisal.[124]

The role traditionally assigned to collective agreements – equalizing the conditions of competition between firms in the same sector – breaks down at the same time as guarantees of fairness for workers crumble.

The relaxation or neutralization of qualification grids has the direct effect of multiplying particular situations, and creates variation from one firm to the next in the rules for organizing wage-earners into a hierarchy. This gradually amounts to deconstructing collectives and progressively voiding the statistical categories used to account for the social structure that relied on the earlier form of organization.

Attempts at deconstruction are sometimes still more direct, as in the case of the category of *cadre*, which has for some time been subject to a certain amount of pressure from employers, aimed at eliminating its specificity. This challenge is another striking example of the growing discrediting of the model of social classes. In appearance, nothing has changed. The statute of *cadre*, with the benefits (notably in terms of retirement) and constraints (e.g. non-payment of overtime) attached to it, is still in place and, as in the past, transition to the status of '*cadre*' represents a desirable crossing of a social boundary.

Cadres still feature in the INSEE's nomenclature, and the Institute's periodical publications still regularly present figures that demonstrate the continuous expansion of the category. Nevertheless, its validity is increasingly subject to challenge, particularly in high-tech sectors and by some more innovative employers. Thus, Entreprise et progrès devoted a dossier to the subject of *cadres* published in 1992 and entitled *Cadre/non-cadre, a superseded boundary*, which presents a set of arguments for the abolition of the statute of *cadre*, for the disappearance of this social category and, more generally, for questioning a 'system of socioprofessional categories that proved its worth in the past, but which no longer makes it possible to prepare for the future'.[125] The arguments, which take up themes already encountered in the neo-management literature, are worth enumerating, since they offer an almost complete picture of the grounds invoked for abolishing the statute of *cadre*.

A first set of arguments stresses the historical character of a category institutionalized in the 1930s and 1950s (what history has done, history can undo); and also the fact that it is a fluid category ('as sociologists have demonstrated'), subject to a multiplicity of definitions and, hence, statistical evaluations. Useful and 'motivating' as late as the 1970s, today its existence plays a harmful role for the following reasons: (a) because social environments have become homogeneous and there are no longer, as formerly, notable differences in lifestyles and social attitudes between *cadres* and non-*cadres* (all alike belong to a large middle class); (b) because, with the development of the service sector, the number of *cadres* has increased significantly, whereas the number of blue-collar workers has declined; (c) because the number of students has likewise considerably increased, and it is dangerous to encourage the hope that they will all become *cadres*; (d) because the title of *cadre* is specifically French and hence an impediment to the internationalization of French firms.

Other arguments refer to changes in modes of organization and the transition from Taylorism to 'flexible', 'modular' or 'projective' organization: (e) *cadres* no longer perform a supervisory function and the volume of the category increased considerably at a time when the number of hierarchical levels was diminishing; (f) the title of *cadre* emphasizes hierarchy, centralization, compartmentalization, vertical communication – features of superseded modes of pyramidal organization to which infexible collective agreements correspond; (g) the title of *cadre* assumes a clear division between the tasks of conception and execution, yet this Taylorist distinction no longer exists. Differentiating *cadres* from non-*cadres* impedes autonomy, individual initiative and creativity at all levels; (h) the title of *cadre* assigns too much importance to academic qualifications, and is a brake on the prioritization of experience and skills. 'It runs counter to the recognition of real skills and responsibilities', so that, where once it was 'motivating', it is now perceived as a 'factor of exclusion'.

The last argument is especially relevant for our purposes. It revolves around the issue of working hours and manner of remuneration: (i) previously, we are told, there was a real difference between the duties required of *cadres*, which demanded 'total devotion', translated into 'objectives', and could not be quantified in terms of time (hence the non-payment of overtime), and tasks that were adequately defined by the working time devoted to them and which pertained to other wage-earners, whose relation to their firm was also (so we are told) 'more distant'. This difference went together with different methods of appraisal, satisfaction and stimulation, which were individual in the former instance, collective in the latter: whereas *cadres*, whose appraisal was conducted by 'regular interviews', were 'paid on merit', other wage-earners were paid on the basis of 'the same general trend'.[126] Yet now, in the new organizations, 'numerous occupations exist among non-*cadres* whose productivity is only secondarily bound up with the time spent on them' and, since technology is becoming ever more sophisticated, one finds skilled workers whose 'responsibilities' are greater than those of *cadres*.

This challenge to the category issued in proposals that sought to unify conditions by simultaneously treating former *cadres* as ordinary wage-earners and by applying managerial methods hitherto reserved for *cadres* to other wage-earners. Thus, for example, the authors of this dossier propose to stop taking official differences in status (especially those connected with academic qualifications) into consideration during induction periods for new employees; and, on the other hand, 'to extend the methods for appraising performance and potential applied to *cadres* to all levels, so as to create "relations based on trust and recognition of skills", and to "prioritize a dynamic conception of hierarchy grounded in capacities for organization, delegation and promotion of talent wherever it manifests itself"'.[127]

But the proposals do not concern only the internal management of firms. They equally demand 'the revision, even abolition, of certain collective rules that are conventional, regulatory or legal'. In particular, they seek: (a) revision of 'statutory differentiations in territorial sectoral collective agreeements'; (b) 'relaxation of the rules of categorial collective representation featuring in the labour code', with, in particular, the opportunity for firms that so wish to set up a single electoral college for the whole workforce; (c) 'challenging the *cadre*/non-*cadre* distinction when it comes to supplementary contributory pension schemes' (concretely, the progressive merging of ARRCO and AGIRC [Confederation of Executive Pension Funds]) and, more generally, a standardization of modes of compensation for retirement, redundancy and contingencies. The authors of this text display a preference for a formula that privileges the direct wage, leaving wage-earners to arrange supplements for contingencies and retirement.[128]

These proposals are not utopian. They have begun to be implemented, and there is manifest pressure on state institutions to alter the regulations and procedures currently in force. Witness, for example, a letter sent in October 1996 to the INSEE by the Syndicat national de l'industrie pharmaceutique (SNIP), informing it that the pharmaceutical industry would not in future be able to respond to the mandatory surveys and declarations based upon socioprofessional categories (e.g. the survey of the structure of employment). It based its argument on the fact that the industry had revised its system for classifying jobs in June 1994, and now no longer referred to the socioprofessional categories, 'estimating that these notions no longer reflect current realities and prepare firms and wage-earners poorly for the economic developments that are under way'. In the note accompanying this letter, the existence of the official status is presented as not only detrimental to firms, but also as dangerous for wage-earners themselves, whose chances of 'finding another job' in 'an unstable world' depend upon 'the value added the wage-earner has been able to acquire with the aid of his firm', not on their 'former job title and socioprofessional category, however flattering'. The report of a subsequent meeting on the issue explained that the SNIP's initiative aimed 'to promote in the sector new modes of managing and recognizing qualifications more in tune with the new realities. In sum, it is a question of moving from collective modes of management basically centred on status to collective and individual modes of management basically centred on managing skills'. And it concluded that 'administrative contingencies must not constitute an obstacle to the emergence of the new values desired by the sector. Thus, reconstructing the previous logic of statuses solely for the purposes of statistical or administrative processing is something to be avoided.' The importance of the battle emerges in these last phrases, for the INSEE's experts were able to establish that the job nomenclature established by the federation made it easy enough to code the jobs in the industry according to the nomenclature of socioprofessional categories. Accordingly, the technical difficulty involved in presenting the statistics in the format expected by public bodies emerges as a pretext for carrying through an ideological reform.

The documents we have just examined indicate that the possibility of an imminent fragmentation of the category of *cadres* must be taken seriously. Twenty years ago, efforts were made to deconstruct the category, by showing that far from possessing the unicity and natural character imputed to it at the time, it was heterogeneous, shot through with relations of interests and power, and the product of an economic and political history. (In short, at least in the most schematic versions of this paradigm, the category was simply the embodiment of an ideology.) Today, employers are endeavouring to demolish it, on the basis of arguments often drawn from the critically inspired sociological literature whose relevance they previously contested. Thus, maintaining a high degree of solidarity, of unity, between managers and *cadres* charged with tasks of execution, which seemed crucial in large, integrated firms with their heavy concentrations of workers and combative trade unions, is no longer a priority.

The validity of the categories employed by the nomenclature of socioprofessional categories, which the image of French society as a set of social classes largely rested on, was heavily dependent upon their adequacy to the divisions operative in the social world. But the sharpness of these divisions itself resulted in large measure from the objectification of the regulatory mechanisms and modes of organization of work, of which the nomenclature was itself the product. Ultimately, it was the overlapping confirmation provided by the divisions of the nomenclature and the divisions observable in the world that gave the nomenclature its credibility. As in the case of the currency, however, the confidence people had in its soundness and, more profoundly, the integration of the nomenclature's categories into their own mental categories contributed in large measure to maintaining this adequacy and, consequently, to maintaining confidence in the nomenclature and the analyses in class terms based on it. The effect of the challenge to the regulatory mechanisms and modes of organization aligned with the nomenclature has been to estrange it from the world, detach it from its object and, as a result, to shatter tacit adherence to it. Moreover, over and above the actual content of the nomenclature, credence in its validity was based on the possibility of crediting the social world with a minimum of stability. The nomenclature's details could be amended without invalidating the possibility of describing the socioprofessional world by means of a taxonomy. Conversely, challenging the even comparatively stable character of the social world, in favour of a vision foregrounding uncertainty and complexity, had the effect of reducing confidence in the descriptions it made possible.[129]

However, there is nothing more naive than contrasting the particularity of real conditions with the supposed uniformity of class membership. This is what is done today by those who, basing themselves on the monographic or statistical techniques associated with micro-history, or those who take their inspiration from them,[130] rediscover the diversity of working conditions, social trajectories, migration paths, acknowledged identities or networks of relations, and make as if the phenomena they highlight, which are perfectly real, cast radical doubt upon descriptions in terms of categories, groups or classes. As numerous works have demonstrated,[131] this is to forget that the formation of groups and classes always assumes a long, arduous and often conflictual labour to establish equivalence. Against the background of a greater or lesser diversity of conditions, this is required to bring out the properties, adjudged common, that will be foregrounded in order to highlight similarities. But establishing equivalence does not in any sense erases the particularity of conditions, which can always be emphasized so as to impede the constitution of equivalences or undo established equivalences that, as Michel Callon and Bruno Latour have shown,[132] are never irreversible. It follows that all the measures which help undo established equivalences – whether measures in the administrative sense or measures in the sense of sociography and statistics – restore the salience of particularities, in the view of observers as in the view of the actors themselves. More generally, they construct a world sensitive to differences, which, without thereby being less real, could be regarded as minor when systems of equivalence were in place. With the deconstruction of the representation of social classes, numerous particularities have resurfaced wherever they had been obscured under the homogenizing impact of the equivalences inscribed in established forms (classifications, organizational mechanisms, etc.), as well as integrated into the cognitive competences of social actors. The often schematic – and hence readily criticizable – representation of a social world divided into homogeneous groups or categories has thus been replaced by the no less perfunctory vision of a confused, fragmented universe, composed solely of a juxtaposition of individual destinies – a representation on which sociologists recording or announcing the 'disappearance of society' as a 'very particular representation of social life' have relied.[133]

The impact on critique of the challenge to social classes

The social critique is the one most directly affected by the fading of the model of social classes in so far as, for more than a century, it was based on highlighting all kinds of inequalities between classes of individuals, and endeavoured to promote a fair distribution of the hardships and profits associated with the participation of these different groups in the same productive process. The negation of the existence of different classes, with interests that were construed as completely or partially contradictory, and the focus of analysis on an aggregate – the 'excluded' – defined precisely by its lack of participation in the productive process, invalidate the discourse of traditional social critique virtually from the word go. For example, it would adduce increased inequalities among the 'included', whereas, according to the currently dominant analytical schemas, this characteristic makes them the new 'privileged'. Or again, reconstructing the 'working class' by adding an appreciable percentage of new employees to manual workers, it would show that it has by no means disappeared, and that its demographic weight is even quite imposing.

The artistic critique is also affected by the deconstruction of social categories inasmuch as this likewise blurs another opposition that has played an altogether central role in France since the mid-nineteenth century: the opposition between intellectuals and artists on one side, and economic elites on the other. Various indicators suggest that this is well on the way, if not to losing all relevance, then at least to fading rapidly.[134]

The way in which the figure of the manager is today assuming the qualities of the artist and intellectual tends to blur the distance, established since Romanticism, between the realism of those in business and the idealism of cultured people. And this is all the more the case in that the changes affecting the system of cultural production lead artists and intellectuals, in order to bring their projects to fruition, to work very hard at making connections with the most diverse people and bodies, exploring networks, establishing partnerships, arranging – especially financially – projects (particularly, but not exclusively, in the domain of research or live entertainment, theatre, music, etc.). Thus, for example, artistic life, as described in Pierre-Michel Menger's recent writings on the entertainment professions,[135] constitutes the limit – which is real, for all that – towards which the ideal of the 'manager', as outlined in the works of consultants, seems to be headed. Artists respond to a very changeable and uncertain professional world by spreading the risks and equipping themselves with 'portfolios of activities and resources containing different risks', which confers on 'the individual organization of artistic work certain properties of a mini-firm'. For them, irregular work represents the most widespread form of employment, with a succession of short periods in work and more or less prolonged periods out of work. A career consists not in filling 'vacancies', but in engaging in a multitude of often very heterogeneous projects (an average of five a year in 1988, and more than ten for 10 per cent of entertainment artists). The optimal strategy consists in accumulating relatively stable jobs (which in particular guarantee the right to draw unemployment insurance) and very short, diverse contracts that make it possible 'to explore new, rich working environments', to augment the number of non-recurrent contacts, to acquire new skills and information, and to benefit from the effects of 'reputation'. These are so many factors that enhance 'employability', which is highly dependent upon the 'visible reputation' and weight derived from earlier involvement in projects that have attracted attention. When the ideal of the manager without ties is substituted for the figure of the owner – possessed by his possessions – or that of the manager – weighed down with the planning and rational administration of production – the tension between the mobility of the artist and the obsessive fixity of those who prosper in the business world tends to diminish. Is not the neo-manager, like the artist, a creative figure, a person of intuition, invention, contacts, chance encounters, someone who is always on the move, passing from one project to the next, one world to another? Like the artist, is he not freed of the burdens of possession and the constraints of hierarchical attachments, of the signs of power – office or tie – and also, consequently, of the hypocrisies of bourgeois morality? Conversely, however, is not today's artist, even today's intellectual or researcher, likewise a network creature in search of producers, the realization of whose projects demands costly, heterogeneous and complex arrangements, an ability to arrive at an understanding with distant, multiple actors who hold very different positions – from the local elected official, to the head of a firm, via an attaché from the ministry – and whom he must interest, persuade, win over?

As a result, the whole conflictual balance within ruling elites is compromised, with the former antagonisms governed by the interplay of critical traditions making room for an alternation between fusion, where each of the partners risks losing their identity, and savage competition, practically on the same terrain. One effect of these changes has been to make the adoption of a critical stance – which since the mid-eighteenth century and, more sharply still, since the Dreyfus affair, has helped to define the artist or intellectual as such – at once more necessary than ever and largely ineffectual. It is necessary for intellectuals, because it represents the last marker capable of preserving their specificity or identity in the face of businessmen and men of power. But the critique developed by intellectuals or artists is rapidly hailed as 'biting', 'disturbing' or 'radical' by the major media and adversaries whom it was supposed to scandalize. And the latter, turning out instead to be partners – even replicas – hasten to adopt the critique on their own account, so that critique loses its point of application, and is condemned to constant modification or vain overstatement.

We can also relate this phenomenon of osmosis to the considerable development in the last thirty years of a public educated in secondary schools and universities, whose members are equipped with cultural schemas transmitted to them by the previous generation. In particular, this group comprises cultural instructors and mediators – journalists, presenters, theatre people, and so on – who were themselves students around May 1968, and who today hold positions of cultural power in the academy, publishing or the media. These intellectual guides have widely diffused the forms and expressions of the artistic critique that characterized the avant-gardes in the first half of the century – Cubist, Dadaist, Surrealist, and so on – on which they themselves were raised. They have thus contributed to a market demand for products labelled 'transgressive', even if the 'taboos' now under challenge have only the remotest connection with the real content of the censorship, the unspoken or prohibited things which today hang over the power to think and speak.

Inasmuch as it is connected with the relaxation of statistical formats for registering workers and the classifications used by firms, the deconstruction of social categories has also helped to disrupt work relations, and particularly the tests governing access to employment, promotion, certain levels of remuneration, and so on.

The impact of decategorization on work tests

When we set up the concept of test in the introduction to this work, we maintained that a society (or a state of society) may be defined by the nature of the tests it sets – tests through which social selection is performed – and by disputes over the more or less just character of these tests. Now, in this respect, the transformation that this book seeks to explain is radical. Tests connected with work (selection, promotion, matching of people and posts, determination of pay, etc.) were strongly institutionalized in the 1960s around the organization of long careers; and these were framed by relatively constraining collective agreements and a significant trade-union presence capable of enforcing compliance with them. The distribution of income between wage-earners was administered within large collectives where only wage-earners attached to the same employer worked. This simultaneously made it possible to bring out commonalities of condition and interest, and to establish a formalized, negotiated justice associating an income with a level of qualification. The only employment contract possible was the permanent contract, the others being subject to very tight restrictions.

Thirty years on, this edifice has been dismantled. The determination of pay occurs largely via an unbalanced relation of forces on the market, which brings face to face an individualized wage-earner who needs work in order to live and a highly structured firm that is capable of seizing all the opportunities afforded by the deregulation of labour law. With careers much less organized, people are compelled to keep returning to the market, where their value is assessed at different stages of their working life. The transformation of large collectives into flotillas of small structures, and the proliferation of different conditions for wage-earners (types of contract, types of employer, hours, applicable collective agreements, etc.), have shattered a unified space of calculation into a multiplicity of particular situations that can no longer be easily aggregated to obtain an overall image. The proliferation of local calculation eclipses the main distributions in the network, which are difficult to totalize. In fact, the technical obstacles in the way of aggregating disparate data are considerable. But over and above this problem, the information is quite simply unavailable. The mechanisms for representing wage-earners and collecting information are in fact based on the legal entity of the 'firm' and, in certain conditions, on the smaller unit of the establishment as a work collective attached to a single firm, to the exclusion of workers who come under other structures (temping, service companies, subcontractors). Or, at a higher level of aggregation, they are based on the larger unit of the group of firms linked by majority interests, but strictly defined by the territory of the nation-state, despite recent progress towards the creation of 'European group committees' in some multinationals.[136] As a result, they do not permit access to data that are international in scope.

Capitalism's displacements have contributed to dismantling tests which, under the impact of decades of active social critique, were highly supervised and very strict in terms of justice. In the terminology used in this work, they could be presented as 'tests of status'. Once they have been dismantled, only 'tests of strength' remain.

3. THE IMPACT OF DISPLACEMENTS ON THE ESTABLISHED TESTS

The ongoing impact of displacements on the established tests is brought out in particular by their role in the disintegration of the analytical categories that made it possible for tests to strive for justice.

Our intention here is to set to work in tandem two logics, elaborated in different intellectual traditions, which underlie descriptions of the social world that are invariably presented as incompatible, even antagonistic – that is to say, a logic of *categorization* on the one hand, and a logic of *displacement* on the other. In the first, a discourse is formed referring to justice, right, legitimacy, generality. In the language of the second, descriptions in terms of forces, strategies, positions and networks are elaborated. In our view, analysis of the way in which these two logics are articulated is imperative for understanding the strength of critique, but also the difficulties it encounters getting a grip on the world.

The role of categorization in the orientation of tests towards justice

We have defined tests as always being a test of strength (Introduction). But we have also brought out a continuum between, at one end, so-called tests of 'status' where the strengths involved and measured are specified to the exclusion of others, and formating of the test ensures that these strengths do not intervene to disrupt the results; and, at the other end, what are simply called tests of 'strength', characterized by the fact that they are neither specified nor supervised.

A test of status – that is, conforming to a model of justice – thus first of all presupposes establishing mechanisms intended to control the nature and number of the strengths that may be engaged in it. This process of organizing social competition can be illustrated in numerous ways. Take, for example, the history of the development of the education system, with the introduction of anonymity in competitive examinations or the list of schools restricting the choice of establishment; or economic history, with anti-trust laws or the establishment of commissions to oversee stock-market operations; or, to take another example, the institution of electoral democracy with the ban on including members of the same family on the same municipal list, which aims to protect civic status from parasitic behaviour by forces from the domestic world. But we can also find examples in the case of sporting tests which, as Alain Ehrenberg has spotted,[137] is certainly of the paradigms underlying our own conception of the fair test.

Georges Vigarello has outlined the process of regulation in the case of sporting tests.[138] It was initially bound up with the progressive autonomization of the different sports, or the achievement by a practice independently developed by amateurs – each with its own means and hence, in a variety of ways, involving diverse, weakly qualified strengths – of the status of an autonomous discipline that could participate as such in international competitions. 'The history of each sport is thus, basically, the history of a body of rules, which are increasingly detailed and precise, imposing a single code on ways of playing or competing that were previously strictly local or regional.'[139]

In this instance, the rules aim to specify the kind of strength that may be committed to the test, and the way the test is to be organized so that it is this strength which is exhibited, not some other kind. The aim is to prevent the competitors employing strengths of a different kind and thus to give the different parties an equal chance, so that success or failure is attributable solely to their merits.

But the work of regulation does not cease once the sport is established in its specificity. The efforts made by sportsmen and women to win lead them to introduce modifications, often of a minor kind, into the techniques deployed, whether in the way they use their bodies, or the way in which the material instruments they employ (poles, cycles, javelins, etc.) are constructed. For a time, these modifications may pass unnoticed and favour victory. They may then be subject to regulation under the pressure of opponents who, not having had the benefit of them, have lost in a way that they consider unfair, in the sense that the conditions of the test have been unilaterally altered. Hence they can argue that they and their more fortunate opponents have not in fact been facing one another in the same test pertaining to the same sport.

Let us take a few examples. In 1956, a Spanish athlete, Erausquin, introduced a new method of javelin-throwing, the so-called 'rotating' method, derived from a traditional Basque sport that consisted of throwing tree-trunks. It was a resounding success. However, the technique was banned fifteen days before the Melbourne Olympics on the grounds that it was 'dangerous' (the javelin can easily deviate from its path and hit spectators), but also because it radically altered the 'physical qualities hitherto required' of a thrower. A new regulation was brought in in 1986, this time following a modification of the javelin itself, two years after the introduction by Held of a more effective javelin whose centre of gravity had been altered. We might also take the example of the high jump. In this instance, changes in the use of the body perfected by certain athletes led to a change in the rules and the technical characteristics of the material used. Horine had invented a very horizontal, costal jump in 1910. Osborn imitated him in 1922, but – in a new move – added 'a light supporting touch on the fixed post'. After this modification, the rules were changed in order to 'alter the position of the supports so that the jump posts could not, in any circumstances, prevent the bar falling'. As Vigarello quite correctly notes, the rule change – which, in the analytical framework proposed here, is of the order of categorization – was the more or less belated outcome of the modification effected. It thus involves a 'reactive mechanism'.

The development of sports regulation is thus largely the product of a meritocratic requirement for equality of opportunity. The conditions of the test must be arranged in such a way as to bring out the competitors' merit in its most personal dimension, by limiting, so far as is possible, inequalities attributable to chance or luck. This is also why the contestants must be of approximately equivalent strength prior to the test. In sports where unalterable physical characteristics – for example, size or weight – are a decisive factor, this is achieved by establishing categories (as in the case of boxing) and, more generally, through qualifying rounds, comprising an organized sequence of tests to which only those who were ranked highest in the preceding tests are admitted. As for the social selection process in general, the existence of an ordered course of tests likewise plays a central role, notably by limiting the number of candidates in each test so that the bodies required to exercise judgement are not overwhelmed by the presence of a multitude of candidates between whom it is not materially possible, whether for reasons of mental overload or sheer lack of time, to make a justifiable choice.

For the test to be considered legitimate, it must therefore have been subject to a formalization that specifies its objective and aim. But its conduct must also be supervised in such a way as to avert infiltration by unknown or, at any rate, illegitimate forces. A test may formally be governed in such a way as to bring only the same kind of forces together, and yet in practice let in a mixture of forces. This is one of the reasons why no test, not even the most impeccable in formal terms, is immune from criticism.

In addition to its more or less specified and supervised – that is to say, legitimate – character, the test can be characterized in two further respects.

The first has to do with the extent of the expression of a change in condition that it discloses, and hence concerns the *level of reflexivity* of the beings engaged in the test. Any change in the condition of a being in the world leaves a trace, but this trace can go virtually unnoticed or, alternatively, be displayed by someone who seizes upon it to reveal that something has changed. Demonstration of the change of condition can thus take diverse forms, of very uneven intensity. At one extreme, we have tests whose trace is weakly registered (it may be a passing anxiety: 'Why did X turn away from me when I spoke to him in the lift? Why wasn't I invited to the leaving drinks for that colleague seconded to another department?'). At the other extreme, there are tests where the possibility of a change in condition is expressed in such a way as to be heard by anyone – which assumes a number of conditions satisfying criteria of impartiality and stability (as with exams or recruitment tests).

The second dimension concerns the *comparative stability of the being engaged in the tests*. A world where all beings were constantly faced with the uncertainty of tests would be chaotic. Nothing could be said about it. For the expression of a test 'to have a meaning, there must exist at least one being whose condition remains certain'.[140] In this context, we may trace an axis contrasting two extremes. At one extreme, we have situations where the condition of a large number of beings is uncertain, subject to numerous disputes, and where it is even impossible to achieve the slightest understanding about the object of the test under way or, as people say, about its 'stakes'. At the other extreme, we have situations where, on the one hand, judgements concur as to the condition of most of the beings present, so that uncertainty focuses exclusively on one, or a limited number, of them (e.g. uncertainty about the value of the students who pass the exam, but not that of the examiners); and, on the other hand, where there is agreement on what is uncertain in the condition of this being or small number of beings (e.g. one is seeking to test the student's knowledge of Latin, not the degree of her affection for her parents).

These three continua in tests – according to the degree of legitimacy, reflexivity or relative stability of the beings involved – which it is useful to distinguish analytically, are not independent of one another. In effect, the stabilization of a large number of beings surrounding the test presupposes a fairly formalized expression of conditions (reflexivity). As for reference to a principle of legitimacy (justice), it requires precise definition of the respect in which the beings engaged in a test are being compared with one another. In general, the greater the degree of conventionalization of a test, the more it is subject to regulatory or legal supervision, and the more these different parameters are specified. We may then talk about *established* tests (such as political elections, academic exams, sporting tests, equal negotiations between social partners), which are defined and recognized as such. Those involved in them, in one way or another, cannot ignore the fact that their judgements and actions in such situations will have enduring effects. This contrasts with situations where at least one of the participants has the sense of being put to the test and subject to judgement, but such situations, not having been subject to a collective labour of qualification, are not universally recognized. In this second instance, those who explain what has occurred by redefining it as a test situation may meet with scepticism from other participants, or even be disqualified as 'paranoid'.

By comparison with conflicts in everyday life, these highly formalized tests have advantages, but also costs. The advantage is that they facilitate the exclusion of violence, the end of conflict, and the restoration of agreement, by restricting the number of uncertain beings facing one another, and by obliging actors to reach agreement on the stakes and standpoint from which these beings may be assessed. But in consequence, they have the cost of obliging people to clarify and limit the grounds for their conflicts and, as a result, of requiring them to sacrifice ambiguity, vagueness, uncertainty, that which is displaced in favour of that which is stabilized through a process of categorization.

For categorizing processes intervene at all levels in the transformation of a test into a test of status: the classes of beings who may participate in the test (compare weight or age categories in sport), and the classes of strengths that may be engaged and those that are excluded, are specified. Assessing the test's outcome itself assumes using categories of judgement.

The change in the tests we observed where the world of work is concerned amounts to a general disruption of the former established tests and a deinstitutionalization along the three axes we have referred to (specification and supervision, reflexivity, stability).

The nature of what is being judged in recruitment and promotion tests (actual skill of the personnel? Market shortage? Access to information on job vacancies? Reputation? Malleability? Long-term employability? Degree of collective organization of the workers?) seems especially unclear and variable depending on the mechanism adopted. (Thus François Eymard-Duvernay and Emmanuelle Marchal have shown that the 'skills conventions' used in recruitment depend more on the recruitment channel used – small advertisements, personal acquaintances, headhunting – than on the person assessed.)[141] Selection rounds no longer seem to function, the number of candidates presenting themselves at tests being out of all proportion to the number of people capable of passing them. Thus, consultants charged with recruitment via small advertisements regularly find themselves faced with such quantities of CVs that they subject them to an initial sifting based on discriminatory demographic variables, such as age, sex or place of residence. As is generally accepted, these have only limited relevance to people's skills and suitability for a given position, but on the other hand they do reinforce the exclusion of the 'too young', the 'too old', women or immigrants.[142] People find it more difficult than ever to decide which tests they may present themselves for – for example, to assess whether they have a reasonable chance of succeeding because the distance between the strengths of the various candidates does not seem too great (otherwise the test is unjust), and to obtain a stable definition of the selection criteria that will be used, or, more generally, to get an idea of the qualifications and education that will make it possible to find work. The number of people who are uncertain of their 'value' on the labour market or within their firm is very much on the increase, despite the proliferation of individual appraisals organized by firms which, far from stabilizing appraisal levels, help to diffuse a belief that the value of each person is patently changing, so that the test is a daily one. If everything is a test; if all tests are daily; if identification of the most important tests is non-existent, or changes from one day to the next; if the criteria of judgement are multiple, variable and sometimes not formalized, then it is not at all clear how selections may be deemed just, and how judgements about access to work, quality of the contract offered or remuneration may be said to be a function of people's relative merit. A universe whose rules are not reliable for anyone is a universe that allows the strong, endowed with various, unspecified strengths, to take advantage of the weak, whose weakness is also difficult to define. For, in the absence of great men and little persons, what we have is indeed the strong and the weak – that is to say, winners and losers at the end of a series of tests which were largely invisible, barely specified, poorly supervised and far from stable.

Displacements and decategorization:
From tests of status to tests of strength

Categorization presupposes comparison between particular elements in a form that makes equivalence possible. Establishing equivalence makes it possible to absorb distinct elements, compared with one another in a certain predefined respect, into a common type (as we observe in coding operations). Categorization thus involves a two-tier space – that of the particular elements and that occupied by conventions of equivalence with the characteristic of generality. Relating these two levels is a reflexive kind of operation, requiring description and relying on language, which tends to inflect it towards legal constructions.

In contrast to categorization, displacement dispenses with reference to conventions, and assumes neither exteriority nor generality. The logic of displacement has only one level. Displacement is therefore always a matter of the local, the factual, the circumstantial. It is easily confused with chance, and makes do with a limited reflexivity. It escapes the constraint of justification of a wholly general kind, which assumes reference to a second level – precisely where, in a logic of categorization, the convention of equivalence is situated. In the examples of sporting tests we have cited, displacement takes the form of an innovation within the framework of the official rules one day by some sportsman. But the issue of the displacement's justification is posed only if the innovation is related not to the rules, but to the principles underlying the rules – that is to say, to second-level structures that make it possible to judge things, compare particular situations, to classify them into at least two groups: those that are permitted, and those that are precluded, by the test. Without this increased level of generality, if we remain at the level of the rules – that is to say, the former analytical categories – without undertaking a phase of recategorization, the displacement is invisible.

Situated on a single level – that is, without reference to conventions of justice – displacement concerns beings who, from each other's perspective, are all different, heterogeneous. From the confluence of these differences proceeds displacement, which goes from difference to difference, from one person to the next, or – by analogy with the Freudian use of the term – according to associative chains. Thus, for example, employers began by introducing bonuses in order to loosen the shackles of pay classifications. They then refined and extended their systems of individual appraisal so that they were in a position to allocate merit bonuses. Finally, they sought to casualize those who, in the light of the appraisals, appeared the least productive. These actions are very different from the highly visible activities of renegotiating collective agreements and classification grids, which present themselves as changes in categorization, and whose transformation follows practices more than it precedes them.

In test regimes based on categorization – i.e. tests of status – beings do not find themselves engaged in all respects in the test. As a result, their permanency can be guaranteed during their passage through successive tests. In this instance, the test is *par excellence* the moment for establishing correspondence between an activity and a qualification, with a view to a justification that can claim general validity.

Tests assume a different form in a regime of displacement. They take the shape of an encounter where beings confront one another in an unlimited number of respects, without the strength employed being qualified. As a result, during each test their permanency and potential for persisting are at stake. In this regime, tests may be defined as moments when beings, upon encountering resistance, seek to persevere by altering themselves – that is to say, displacing their energy in order to come to terms with other beings, in such a way as to profit from a difference, however minimal, which confers an advantage. The balance of forces, which is altered, is thus the outcome of the test. Since tests in the displacement regime are tests of strength, every displacement within the framework of an established test to circumvent it, or prevail in it, by taking advantage of unacknowledged strengths, pulls it in the direction of a test of strength. This is all the more irremediable to the extent that displacements accumulate without the test being recategorized to take account of them.

In a categorization regime, change, which is equivalent to a rule change, cannot but make itself visible, since it involves using a public language and engages all the beings whom the category assimilates and assembles. But as was observed by Freud, for whom displacement constituted the main means of unconscious functioning, in the absence of an overarching point of view displacement is at best manifested locally, momentarily, circumstantially. The extra strength provided by displacement is thus enhanced by the effect of surprise it enjoys.

Up to now, we have used the term 'strength' without clarifying it. But examination of the conditions for a test of status makes it possible better to appreciate what we understand by it. When we refer to 'strength' or 'status', we are not referring in substantive fashion to entities that are different in kind, but to different test regimes. By 'status' we mean a quality of beings demonstrated in tests whose employment rests upon categorization. By 'strength' we mean a quality of beings expressed in tests whose sudden appearance relies upon a displacement. We shall therefore say that in a regime of displacement, strengths are the result of an interaction of differences, which guarantees the success of the tests without having been subject to a labour of identification or generalization. Or, more briefly, strengths are what are displaced in the absence of constraints of a normative, conventional or legal kind – that is to say, doing without categorization.

The identification of new tests and reconstruction of the categories of judgement

To be in a position to subject tests that have been transformed by displacements to the exigency of justice once more, we must begin by identifying these displacements and giving them a *meaning*. In other words, we must determine their significance for the set of pre-existing relations by comparing them with other displacements, which (we intend to show) are proceeding in the same direction. This presupposes connecting them in a sequence, and hence the transition to a regime of categorization. In effect, in order to compare these displacements – that is, to constitute a class,[143] or establish a temporal series – we must quit the logic of displacement, equip ourselves with the possibility of an external viewpoint and, consequently, switch into categorization.

Any reflexive review of the test thus tends to induce a change of regime. For in order retrospectively to identify the causes of success or failure, it is necessary to switch into categorization. But if it is to have lasting effects, a reflexive review must lead to the constitution of classes of tests or, at least, to the identification of precedents. This operation has a rationale only if one is seeking to avoid the repetition of failure, or to achieve the pursuit of success – something that would be pointless if all tests were regarded as utterly particular or, if you like, circumstantial.

This is also to say that while the transition to categorization is initially made by those who, faced with repeated failure, are seeking to understand what has occurred, in order to back up a critique of the tests that have been disadvantageous to them, it is also performed by those whose displacements have brought success. They make the transition when they realize that their good fortune is not down to luck, but to something that they have done, without clearly understanding which of their actions has advantaged them, and hence without being in a position to repeat their success. But in so doing, they lose the advantage of ignorance (innocence), which, in a displacement regime, formed part of their strength.

The transition to categorization is one of the tasks incumbent upon critique in so far as it seeks to improve the justice of tests, which leads, as we have seen, to 'tightening' them up. The paradox of critique is thus that in the mode of categorization it has to confront alterations that are invariably of the order of displacement. It speaks in the name of those who, in the logic of displacement, decline in strength with each test and, consequently, lose purchase on the world. Powerless to increase the strength of each of the losers taken separately, which would presuppose its inscription in the multiple mechanisms that make up the lived world, its main resource is to make suffering visible in a discursive form that orchestrates a single protest out of a multiplicity of complaints. It must therefore compare individual situations and, in order to constitute them as injustices, measure them by a general equivalence. This immediately situates it in a regime of categorization, orientated towards the legal aim of defining rules or even constructing rights that are universally valid and, consequently, open to all. For what purpose do rules and rights serve? How do they increase the strength of the weak? They set constraints on tests in such a way as to limit the displacement of strengths, and make visible – hence controllable (or punishable) – alterations which, induced by a multiplicity of local displacements, modify the field of forces.

But the temporality of categorial changes is not that of alterations in a displacement regime. Precisely because it is local, circumstantial and multiple, and occurs through differential variations on a single level without seeking to be assembled under a common name, displacement proceeds rapidly. *Critique always arrives behind displacement.* To it falls the work of assembling the heterogeneous in order to make what disparate local situations have in common visible – that is to say, to give them meaning. On it lies the burden of proof that something has indeed changed, even if the categories of law and everyday thinking have not (or not yet) registered the change. Its temporality consists in doing this work. And the world has already changed to such an extent that critique, whose normative reference, because it relies on existing categories, is inscribed in the past, often finds itself, when it finally succeeds in making itself heard, without any purchase on a world that is already different.

In Chapter 4, which sought to provide a synthetic picture of the reality of work today, we had on various occasions to note the difficulties of critique when its categories no longer apply to the world it has to interpret. Thus, we saw that it is very difficult to know the level of concentration of economic power in France, for the new network mechanisms are not easy to categorize. We likewise saw that it is no longer clear where the boundaries between employers are to be situated; or how to redraw the contours of the working class since it has partially been transferred to the service sector; or, once again, whether casual workers are to be regarded as the reincarnation of a class that was thought to be well on the way to disappearing during the *trente glorieuses*: the sub-proletariat. The separation between researchers who study firms and those who study work is another example of ineffective classification. The regulatory and legislative mechanisms that contributed to creating categories of workforce or firm have been dismantled; and the individualization of workers and firms has continued at the very least in the respects that once made it possible to compare them. In order to resume its course, however, critique must go beyond recording the re-emergence of particularities once what connected situations has unraveled, and search for new principles that will enable it to order the world so as once again to have some purchase on it.

Conclusion: The End of Critique?

The moment of disenchantment with the hopes placed by some in a leftist version of capitalism in the 1970s and 1980s arrived soon enough. While the reformulation of capitalism in terms of what was exciting, creative, protean, innovative and 'liberating' about it initially allowed a reconstruction of grounds for commitment, these were essentially individual. As we have seen, the opportunities offered for the flourishing of the self went together with the exclusion of those individuals or groups that did not possess the requisite resources to seize those opportunities and, consequently, with an increase in poverty and inequality.

Throughout the process, over the last twenty years, capitalism has benefited from the enfeeblement of critique. What are the prospects today of seeing critique reconstructed with sufficient self-confidence not only to compel acceptance of the institution of minimal security mechanisms, but also to impose stricter limits on the development of a destructive capitalism? In order to outline a response to this question, we must recall that one of the peculiarities of the crisis of critique is that it has simultaneously affected the social critique and the artistic critique, but for different reasons.

In the case of the *social critique*, capitalism's displacements have produced a world that is hard to interpret, one which it is difficult to oppose with the tools forged by oppositional movements over the previous century. Ideologically, these were based on the taxonomy of social classes that became established after the Second World War. Practically, they were based upon political and trade-union movements which were capable of getting a hearing for a different interpretation of society from the one that originated with economic elites. These difficulties were compounded by the implosion of communist regimes throughout the world and, in Western Europe, by the problems encountered by the welfare state. These problems were in large part the consequence of strategies developed by an aggressive capitalism which, with the collapse of communism, no longer needed the alliance forged with the social state after the crisis of the 1930s in order to strengthen its legitimacy, or simply to ensure its survival.

In the second half of the 1980s, with the end of the Cold War, capitalism found itself on its own again, without any apparent credible alternative. This belief did not become established only among the managers of a triumphant capitalism. It was widely shared by sympathizers and activists of the old left-wing parties. In order to preserve a legitimacy that was less and less readily accorded them, the great majority of these activists, even when they came from communist parties in rapid decline, were keen to show that they had abandoned revolutionary violence, the project of radical social change, the future projection of a new society and a new humanity, a radiant future – things which full acknowledgement of the horrors that had accompanied the building of Soviet society, obvious to anyone willing to see them for more than fifty years, rendered at once odious, chimerical and ridiculous.

In various parts of the periphery of the world system, movements of different degrees of importance did indeed pursue a critique, often accompanied by violence, which was presented as an alternative to capitalism or, more generally, to Western liberal society or even modernity – 'anti-systemic' movements, to adopt Immanuel Wallerstein's term,[144] or Islamist movements. But in the core zones of capitalism these forms of protest, operating as a pole of repulsion, tended instead to reinforce its ideological domination.

The deletion of a positive alternative likewise accounts for the specific character of attempts in France since the mid-1990s to reconstruct a radical critique. The novelty of these attempts which have erased any direct reference to communism – and often even to Marxism – is that they are *purely critical*, without ever disclosing the normative fulcrum that serves as a basis for the critique, or proposing alternative mechanisms or ideologies.

The lack of an alternative has had two results – one practical, the other theoretical – that chime with one another. The practical result has been to displace the wish to act, prompted by indignation in the face of poverty, on to a charitable or humanitarian position, centred on direct encounters, the present situation (as opposed to some remote future), and direct action aimed at alleviating the sufferings of the needy. On the theoretical level, this has corresponded to the abandonment of macro-sociological and macro-historical approaches, and to a retreat into micro-analysis of actions or judgements *en situation*, often interpreted as indicating 'the end of critique'. This move was itself largely subordinate to the crisis of forms of totalization relying on philosophies of history which, in increasingly discreet, shamefaced fashion over the last thirty years, sustained 'macro' approaches – grand narratives and descriptions – in history and sociology. The classical authors of the nineteenth century and the first half of the twentieth, from whom contemporary sociology still takes its inspiration, had all grounded their descriptions in a historical tendency: the succession of modes of production in Marx; the transition from mechanical solidarity to organic solidarity in Durkheim; the development of rationality in Weber. In sociology even more than in history, the possibility of projecting a point in time in the future and taking up position there, in a kind of thought-experiment, was a precondition for macro-descriptions: sociology, a history of the present, needed to anticipate the future in order to select what was relevant in the present – that is to say, in this perspective, the vector of the future.

The problems of the social critique, which have only worsened over recent decades, were already evident in the 1950s and 1960s, with the critique of communism that took the form of *gauchisme* on the left – that is to say, an alliance between the artistic critique and the social critique. The social character of the second spirit of capitalism, its tactical alliance with the welfare state, were thus subject to violent denunciation, especially from intellectuals. Radicalization of the social critique occurred largely through adopting and intensifying various themes from the artistic critique. The social state associated with capitalism and social democracy was accused of inducing the 'embourgeoisement' of the working class, its 'integration', its curbing and, by obscuring the revolutionary horizon, ultimately serving the purposes of capitalism itself – an accusation that was by no means false, incidentally, since the role of the second spirit of capitalism in its alliance with the social state did indeed involve increasing legitimation by a self-limitation of the level of exploitation.

As for the *artistic critique*, its crisis was, rather, the result of its seeming success and the ease with which it found itself recuperated and exploited by capitalism. This recuperation has taken several forms.

The demand for *autonomy*, integrated into the new enterprise mechanisms, has made it possible to re-engage workers in productive processes and reduce supervision costs by substituting self-control, combining autonomy and a sense of responsibility *vis-à-vis* customer demands or tight deadlines.

The demand for *creativity*, voiced primarily by highly qualified wage-earners, engineers or *cadres*, has received greater recognition than could have been hoped for thirty years earlier, when it became obvious that an ever growing share of profits derived from the exploitation of resources of inventiveness, imagination and innovation developed in the new technologies, and especially in the rapidly expanding sectors of services and cultural production. Among other effects, this has led to a fading of the opposition, on which the artistic critique had been based for a century, between intellectuals and businessmen and production, between artists and bourgeois.[145]

The demand for *authenticity*, which was focused on the critique of the industrial universe, mass production, homogenization of lifestyles and standardization, has been placated by the proliferation and diversification of commodity goods. This has been made possible by flexible production in short series,[146] in tandem with the development, especially in the fashion, leisure and service sectors, of higher quality (even semi-luxury) products, which the reduction in costs due to new forms of production[147] suddenly put within reach of social categories that – like the intellectuals – had hitherto displayed a certain contempt for luxury brands.

Finally, the demand for *liberation* – which, particularly in the moral sphere, was constructed in opposition to bourgeois morality, and could present itself as going hand in glove with the critique of capitalism by reference to an earlier, already superseded spirit of capitalism centred on thrift, family virtues and prudishness – found itself emptied of oppositional charge, when the lifting of former prohibitions proved conducive to opening up new markets. The expanding market in sex-related goods and services (films, videos, chat lines, objects) is a particularly striking example of this.

The recuperation of the artistic critique by capitalism did not bring about a transfer to the social critique, which, as we have seen, was itself in crisis. A majority of intellectuals made as if it was nothing, and continued to display the hallmarks (notably sartorial) of an opposition to the business world and enterprise, and to regard as transgressive moral and aesthetic positions that were now incorporated into commodity goods, and offered without restrictions to the public at large. The kind of disquiet that this more or less conscious bad faith was bound to provoke found an outlet in the critique of the media and mediatization as the derealization and falsification of a world where they remained the exclusive guardians of authenticity. Among a minority it led to the adoption of the only course that was still available: public silence, aristocratic withdrawal, individual resistance, and an eschatological anticipation of the implosion of capitalism (in the manner of communism) or the collapse of modernity upon itself. In this case, too, it was not unrealistic to diagnose the end of critique.

Notes

1 Although it is not the exclusive vehicle, trade unionism is the vector of social critique in theory and practice. Moreover, the artistic critique is not absent from its ranks, as is indicated by the example of the CFDT, which combined the artistic and social critiques in an original fashion with the project of self-management, simultaneously geared towards the resolution of the problems of alienation and exploitation in work.

2 In comparison with the laws of bordering countries, French law is characterized by provisions that are especially favourable in terms of the right to information. However, contrary to what we observe in Germany, for example, this right does not assume participation in decision-making. Moreover, French trade unionism's traditional rejection of 'class collaboration' has never really been conducive to the latter, to the point where the real power of works' councils to inflect things depends on local union membership at the base. In addition, the considerable access to information extended to French works councils allow the employer considerable room for manoeuvre when it comes to determining the format and degree of detail of the documents transmitted.

3 Deunionization is a source of significant disruption for the factory inspectorate and industrial tribunals. The abolition of any intermediary between employers and wage-earners leads to a situation in which problems arrive directly in front of tribunals and in the offices of the inspectorate. For the latter, the clogging-up of the system is all the more unwelcome in that understaffing is chronic and the problems of employment, like the increasing complexity of labour law, make the inspectors' task at once more urgent and more arduous (see Dominique Sicot, 'Cent ans de galère pour l'inspection du travail', *Alternatives économiques*, no. 104, February 1993).

4 Pierre Rosanvallon, *La Question syndicale*, Calmann-Lévy, Paris 1988, p.14.

5 Only four countries have lost more in absolute value (Austria -16 points; Netherlands -13.5 points; Portugal -29 points; Spain -16.4 points). But in relative value, Spain has experienced a sharper fall (of 60 per cent), yielding a unionization rate of 11 per cent, Portugal having lost 48 per cent with a unionization rate that still stood at 31.8 per cent in 1990. Unions in the United Kingdom, which were subject to significant repression during Margaret Thatcher's terms of office, lost barely 4.3 points, and maintained a unionization rate of 39 per cent of wage-earners. Some countries have even seen their unionization increase (Belgium, Denmark, Finland, Iceland,

Italy, Luxembourg, Norway, Sweden). See René Mouriaux, *Analyse de la crise syndicale en 1995*, working document no. 68, 1995, p. 5.

6 Françoise Duchesne, 'Le syndicalisme à venir', in J.-P. Durand, ed., *Syndicalisme au futur*, Syros, Paris 1996, p. 229.

7 Mouriaux, *Analyse de la crise syndicale en 1995*, p. 23; Louis Dirn, *La Société française en tendances, 1975–1995*, Presses Universitaires de France, Paris 1998, p. 277.

8 Valérie Aquain *et al.*, 'Vingt ans d'évolution des conditions de travail', *Travail et emploi*, no. 61, April 1994, p. 86.

9 Dirn, *La Société française en tendances*, p. 277.

10 Source: DARES, quoted in ibid., p. 217.

11 See Christian Dufour, 'Comités d'entreprise: le savoir sans le pouvoir', *Alternatives économiques*, no. 142, November 1996.

12 See Christian Dufour, 'Le repli sur soi des comités d'entreprise', *Alternatives économiques*, no. 125, March 1995.

13 See Gérard Adam, *Le Pouvoir syndical*, Dunod, Paris 1983; and Rosanvallon, *La Question syndicale*.

14 Michel Cézard and Jean-Louis Dayan, 'Les relations professionnelles en mutation', *Données sociales 1999*, INSEE, Paris 1999, p. 192.

15 Duchesne, 'Le synicalisme à venir', p. 223.

16 Sofres-Liaisons sociales poll, cited by Guy Groux, *Vers un renouveau du conflit social*, Bayard Éditions, Paris 1998, p. 18.

17 Ibid., p. 19.

18 Aquain *et al.*, 'Vingt ans d'évolution des conditions de travail'; Groux, *Vers un renouveau du conflit social*, p. 23; and Bruno Herault and Didier Lapeyronnie, 'Le statut et l'identité. Les conflits et la protestation collective', in O. Galland and Y. Lemel, eds, *La nouvelle société française. Trente années de mutation*, Armand Colin, Paris 1998, p. 183.

19 Cézard and Dayan, 'Les relations professionnelles en mutation', p. 195.

20 Questioned in a survey in 1993, 17 per cent of employers of more than 50 wage-earners mentioned at least one strike in their firm during the three years 1990–92, 13 per cent mentioned petitions, 10 per cent rallies and demonstrations, 6 per cent a refusal of overtime, 3 per cent go-slows and 'pilfering of goods' (ibid., p. 195). As an indication of the current hierarchy of forms of combativity, we might also cite the CGT survey that has already been referred to: 78 per cent of wage-earners in the private sector declared themselves ready, in order to defend their interests, to sign a petition, but only 57 per cent were ready to demonstrate, 48 per cent to strike, 40 per cent to join a union, and 30 per cent to occupy their firm (Duchesne, 'Le syndicalisme à venir', p. 229).

21 Dominique Labbé, Maurice Croizat and Antoine Bevort, *La Désyndicalisation. Le cas de la CFDT*, Institut des études politiques de Grenoble, 1989, p. 71.

22 Maryline Baumard and Michel Blanchot, *Crise du syndicalisme*, Hatier, Paris 1994, p. 11.

23 Dominique Labbé, *Synicats et syndiqués en France depuis 1945*, L'Harmattan, Paris 1996, p. 7.

24 Baumard and Blanchot (*Crise du syndicalisme*, p. 20) certainly state that the number of union representatives made redundant has undergone such an increase since 1986 that the federations are worried about it. But we know nothing more. Given that factory inspectors must give their agreement in the case of redundancy for a 'protected wage earner', some information on this issue could probably be obtained, but we have not found a statistical source for it.

25 Michel Launay, *Le Syndicalisme en Europe*, Imprimerie nationale, Paris 1990, pp. 454–5. The list of forms of repressions of strikers and 'strike leaders' given by Robert Linhart in his testimony as a former *établi* in Citroën is a pretty good example: individual summoning of immigrant strikers (i.e., at the time, the majority of manual workers), who are informed that strikes are illegal and punishable by redundancy without warning; intimidation by mentioning some

workers' accommodation in the Citroën hostel; reference to France's generosity in providing them with work; notifying each striker that he is being individually targeted and put on file by management; implementation of threats and the expulsion without formalities of twenty strikers from the hostel, who found their suitcases on the doorstep in the evening; transfer during the strike of Linhart himself, one of its leaders, to a warehouse where he could be in contact with the strikers only in the evening after work; concerted wearing down of the last to hold out (a dozen), by means of harassment, surveillance, blackmail, demands to redo work many times over, driving them to resignation; provocation and insults on the part of a CFT member, provoking the injured party to throw a punch and be instantly dismissed for it. As for Linhart, he was subsequently assigned to tasks designed to 'give him a hard time' physically and then, on the last working day before the holidays, when no one could be mobilized, he was made redundant and exempted from working his notice. These events date from 1969, but there is no reason to suppose that such practices are no longer current, at least in firms where the workforce has retained a certain fighting spirit. See Linhart, *The Assembly Line*, trans. Margaret Crosland, John Calder, London 1981.

26   Launay, *Le Syndicalisme en Europe*, pp. 454–5.

27   Michel Pialoux, Florence Weber and Stéphane Beaud, 'Crise du syndicalisme et dignité ouvrière', *Politis*, no. 14, 1991, pp. 7–18.

28   Ibid., p. 13. One of the employers' successes in this regard is to have transformed the act of joining a union, which would once have been deemed 'normal', into a declaration of war, which is obviously a good way of contributing to deunionization. It might be thought that pretty much the same would apply to membership of a 'discussion group on work problems', unless the group is hosted by an employers' organization. Only the charitable sphere, because the role it claims is more caring than preventive, because it often works more in emergencies than on reforming the causes of distress, seems capable of escaping management suspicion, which doubtless explains its dynamism at a time when other groupings are disappearing. In it wage-earners concerned with the social situation discover the only investment that they can make without fearing, rightly or wrongly, reprisals or a loss of trust on the part of their employer, were they to end up finding out about it.

29   Labbé, Croisat and Bevort, *La Désyndicalisation*, pp. 57, 58.

30   'It is significant that it is a lot more difficult to find candidates among unskilled and semi-skilled blue-collar workers for elections to the works council, whose meetings (which occur approximately every two months) involve a confrontation in a situation that is official, formal (everyone speaks in turn, proposals are recorded, the 'bosses' give free rein to their irony, etc.), than for the election of staff representatives, where very violent confrontations sometimes occur with junior *cadres*, whom one has known a long time, who can be countered, with whom one shares a common language. ... In the narrative recounted to us by an experienced activist of the way works council meetings operate, he first of all stressed the contempt shown by *cadres* for the linguistic habits, the ready-made rhetorical formulas used on these occasions by CGT and CFDT representatives, and their inability to conform to the rules of legitimate public speaking. ... The effort involved in such confrontations with *cadres* is greatly underrated. Several former representatives told me – this was stated only after the event – that a lot of representatives "booze" before going to meetings. Several of us drink together – it's a way of getting up courage': Pialoux, Weber and Beaud, 'Crise du syndicalisme et dignité ouvrière', pp. 8–9.

31   See ibid.

32   Labbé, Croizat and Bevort, *La Désyndicalisation*, pp. 59, 63.

33   Francis Ginsbourger's analysis (*La Gestion contre l'entreprise. Réduire le coût du travail ou organiser sa mise en valeur*, La Découverte, Paris 1998, p. 58) of the changes in production that have affected the clothing industry in the Cholet region attributes the breaking up of large units, the dispersion of production and the creation of workshops of subcontracting manufacturers to a desire on the employers' part to 'avoid social contagion'. The same author cites other examples:

the Solmer site at Fos-sur-Mer (p. 48), the Compagnie marseillaise de réparation (naval ship-yards) (p. 53), a laundry firm in the Paris region (p. 80), all of which adopted modes of organization that made it possible for them to be exempt from union pressure.

34 Ibid., p. 49.

35 See Michel Pialoux and Stéphane Beaud, 'Permanent and Temporary Workers', in Pierre Bourdieu *et al.*, *The Weight of the World*, trans. P. P. Ferguson *et al.*, Polity Press, Cambridge 1999, pp. 257–66; Pialoux, Weber and Beaud, 'Crise du syndicalisme et dignité ouvrière', p. 10).

36 Groux, *Vers un renouveau du conflit social*, p. 20.

37 Launay, *Le Syndicalisme en Europe*, p. 449.

38 Under the impact of the 'pedagogy of the crisis' and the endless reiteration that only improved skills can bring down unemployment rates, working-class families instead seek a way out in their children's scholarly success, everything else seeming doomed to failure (Pialoux, Weber and Beaud, 'Crise du syndicalisme et dignité ouvrière').

39 See Labbé, Croizat and Bevort, *La Désyndicalisation*. They are guided by remarks such as the following: 'In the factory, the fighter has nothing but problems and slanging matches. I'll end my life as a blue-collar worker. So I do my 8 hours. That's it' (ibid., p. 59).

40 In a study of union membership numbers from 1912 to the 1980s, Huguette Bouzonnie demonstrates the importance of factors that stabilize or destabilize work communities. Periods of decline in union membership in the interwar period were in part bound up with 'crises that destabilized work communities'. Contrariwise, the consolidation of union implantation in the years 1945–60 appears to be consequent upon 'the stabilization of industrial bastions constructed before the war' ('L'évolution des effectifs syndicaux depuis 1912: un essai d'interprétation', *Revue française des affaires sociales*, vol. 41, no. 4, October/December 1987, pp. 59–82).

41 To start off with, we can distinguish a first group of small, highly unionized countries, with a low unemployment rate, legislation that affords workers significant protection, a social-democratic politics implemented over a very long period, and close collaboration between political leaderships and union headquarters (Austria, Greece, Iceland, Luxembourg, Norway, Sweden and Switzerland). A second group is composed of countries that had an average unemployment rate in 1981 (between 4 and 9 per cent), where the law offers less protection to workers and government policies are more liberal (Denmark, Finland, France, Italy, the Netherlands and the Federal Republic of Germany). A third group contains countries with high unemployment rates (above 9 per cent), some of which possess industrial sectors in serious crisis (mines, metallurgy, shipyards in Belgium or the United Kingdom), or a very significant demographic burden (Portugal, Spain). Countries in this third group are marked by a strong and very militant trade unionism: Launay, *Le Syndicalisme en Europe*, pp. 444–6.

42 Ibid., p. 447. The trade-union realities of the different countries are in fact difficult to compare. The notion of membership and the meaning of holding a union card cannot be transposed from one country to another. Rates of unionization notably reflect different degrees of incentive and social support: Joëlle Visser, 'Tendances de la syndicalisation', *Perspectives de l'emploi*, OECD, Paris 1991, pp. 103–5, quoted in Michel Lallement, *Sociologie des relations professionnelles*, La Découverte, Paris 1996, p. 47.

43 Olivier Barrat, Thomas Coutrot and Sylvie Mabile, 'Le négociation salariale en France: des marges de manoeuvre réduites au début des années 90', *Données sociales 1996*, INSEE, Paris 1996, pp. 199–268. These data concern firms in the non-agricultural retail sector with more than 50 wage-earners. We may assume that the union situation of their *establishments* of fewer than 20 people is more favourable than that of *firms* with fewer than 20 people. Among establishments which possess a works council (or only 80 per cent of those with more than 50 wage-earners), 58 per cent had a union presence in 1995 (Cézard and Dayan, 'Les relations professionnelles en mutation').

44 Between 1983 and 1995, industry accounted for 70 per cent of strike days, although it represents only a third of the total number of wage-earners. The fall in industrial employment

is thus a factor in the decline in strikes. Moreover, strikes and stoppages are especially rare in retail services and shops. As regards the sizes of establishment, it will be noted that only 14 per cent of those with between 50 and 100 wage-earners had to face a strike in three years (1990–92), compared with 73 per cent of those employing more than 1,000 people (ibid., p. 195).

45 See Armelle Gorgeu and René Mathieu, 'Recrutement et production au plus juste. Les nouvelles usines d'équipement automobile en France', *Dossiers du CEE*, new series, no. 7. 1995.

46 Labbé, Croizat and Bevort, *La Désyndicalisation*, p. 58.

47 Launay, *Le Syndicalisme en Europe*, pp. 444–5.

48 Antoine Lyon-Caen and Jean de Maillard, 'La mise à disposition de personnel', *Droit social*, no. 4, April 1981, pp. 320–35.

49 See Jacques Magaud, 'L'éclatement juridique de la collectivité de travail', *Droit social*, no. 12, December 1975, pp. 525–30.

50 See Spiros Simitis, 'Le droit du travail a-t-il encore un avenir?', *Droit social*, nos 7–8, July/August 1997, pp. 655–68.

51 Francis Ginsbourger and Jean-Yves Potel, 'La pratique de la négociation collective. Négociations de branches et négociations d'entreprises de 1972 à 1981', *Travail et emploi*, no. 20, June 1984, pp. 7–15.

52 See Caroline Grandjean, 'L'individualisation des salaires. La stratégie des entreprises', *Travail et emploi*, no. 32, June 1987, pp. 17–29.

53 'Peugeot … [is] really stingy where classifications are concerned, but on the other hand, it's big on bonuses: "if you stay until midnight, you'll get a bonus, you come in on Saturday, you'll get a bonus. …" And then there's medical control, they sit down with the workers, "you took such and such a day off, you have a given number of sick days and you've gone over the limit … you have to have a quality goal, you've just about made it … and then we ask you to come in every day just before work starts, five or ten minutes before, to listen to the briefings and you don't come… . That's over the top, I can't give you your bonus!" … [T]he stress comes from that, and then the section head made it clear enough, he said, "it's because of him that you're losing your bonuses," and people are so dumb they think that 50 francs is a big deal. … They just can't take losing out on 50 francs on account of that guy!': Michel Pialoux, 'The Shop Steward's World in Disarray', in Pierre Bourdieu *et al.*, *The Weight of the World*, p. 328.

54 Grégoire Philonenko and Véronique Guienne, *Au carrefour de l'exploitation*, Desclée de Bouwer, Paris 1997, p. 54.

55 Thirty-nine per cent of wage-earners in the private sector have great or reasonable trust in their superiors, while only 33 per cent say the same of trade unions (Duchesne, 'Le syndicalisme à venir', p. 218).

56 There are in fact more than ten of these 'Ten Commandments'. We might cite some of them: I maintain good relations with the group and with my superiors; my work attendance record is good; I am available and organize myself accordingly; at a minimum, I participate in a work group; I make an effort to be mobile (versatility, switching, etc.); on the outside, I contribute to the firm's good brand image (Pialoux, Weber and Beaud, 'Crise du syndicalisme et dignité ouvrière', p. 12).

57 Ibid., p. 14.

58 Analysing the reassertion of control in the Fiat factories in Turin at the end of the 1970s and beginning of the 1980s, after a decade of problems (hot autumn, shop stewards' movement, etc.), Giancarlo Santilli shows how the early implementation of measures heralding 1980s neo-management, combined with massive job reductions (from 164,352 in 1980 to 99,722 in 1985), caught the trade unions unawares and left them incapable of defining a new strategy, because these measures significantly transformed 'the composition of the working class', 'industrial relations' and 'the socio-technical environment'. Henceforth, unions 'experienced enormous difficulties interpreting the new trends that were emerging at the level of the working-class base as regards work and the firm. In contrast, the policy pursued in recent years by the FIAT

management represents a coherent, structured, complex strategy' ('L'évolution des relations industrielles chez Fiat, 1969–1985', *Travail et emploi*, no. 31, March 1987, pp. 27–36).

59 The CFDT's reorientation followed the break-up of the Union of the Left in 1977 and was to be reinforced by the left's electoral defeat in 1978, which entailed abandoning any hope of political change in the short term. The January 1978 Moreau Report contains a self-criticism of the politics pursued in the 1970s: 'Asserting a political outcome to struggles led us in the French context to privilege governmental and national action and had the effect of reinforcing tendencies to prioritize trade-union action at this level.' The same theme was taken up at the Brest congress in 1979: 'Too often, national initiatives, which were deemed to be unifying, intervened to telescope the gradual dynamic of struggles starting out from lived situations, inhibiting the creativity, the collective imagination of union teams' (quoted in Michel Branciard, *Histoire de la CFDT*, La Découverte, Paris 1990, pp. 293–4).

60 A. Borzeik, quoted in Gilles Margirier, 'Crise et nouvelle organization du travail', *Travail et emploi*, no. 22, December 1984, pp. 33–44.

61 See Antoine Lyon-Caen and Antoine Jeammaud, 'France', in Lyon-Caen and Jeammaud, eds, *Droit du travail, démocratie et crise*, Actes Sud, Arles 1986, pp. 19–49.

62 See Labbé, Croisat and Bevort, *La Désyndicalisation*.

63 Launay, *Le Syndicalisme en Europe*, p. 459.

64 Pierre Dubois, Claude Durand and Sabine Erbès-Séguin, 'The Contradiction of French Trade Unionism', in Colin Crouch and Alessandro Pizzorno, eds, *The Resurgence of Class Conflict in Western Europe since 1968*, Holmes & Meier, New York 1978, vol. 1, p. 66.

65 Labbé, Croisat and Bevort, *La Désyndicalisation*, p. 72.

66 Lyon-Caen and Jeammaud, 'France', p. 34.

67 Certain national campaigns by the CGT, like the campaign over the case of the Billancourt ten, were thus largely ignored by cells, which had other concerns (Piloux, Weber and Beaud, 'Crise du syndicalisme et dignité ouvrière', p. 14).

68 Labbé, Coisat and Bevort, *La Désyndicalisation*, p. 75.

69 In the thesis he has devoted to the reorganization of a large weapons factory in Belgium, Thomas Périlleux supplies considerable evidence about the sexual duress to which, as late as the 1960s, adjusters subjected female workers, over whom they exercised discretionary power, with the tacit backing of a management which was nevertheless very paternalistic and committed to respect for moral order, but closed its eyes to these 'inevitable' abuses: see *Le Travail des épreuves. Dispositifs de production et formes de souffrance dans une enterprise industrielle*, École des haute études en sciences sociales thesis, 1997.

70 Pialoux, Weber and Beaud, 'Crise du syndicalisme et dignité ouvrière', p. 8.

71 Agreements at enterprise level have developed continuously since the establishment of the obligation to negotiate annually on wages in the firm. Seventeen signatures were recorded in 1950, 658 in 1970, 6,198 in 1992, 9,109 in 1996 (Groux, *Vers un renouveau du conflit social*, p. 84), and 12,000 in 1997. However, these agreements cover only 3 million wage-earners out of the 7 million working in the 30,000 firms with more than 50. The high figure for 1997 is to be attributed to the Robien law of 1996, which made granting state aid dependent on an agreement. These figures are to be compared with the stability of sectoral negotiations: around 300 agreements concluded or altered a year since the mid-1980s (Michel Cézard and Jean-Louis Dayan, 'Les relations professionnelles en mutation', *Données sociales 1999*, INSEE, Paris 1999, p. 197).

72 See François Eymard-Duvernay, 'Droit du travail et lois économiques: quelques elements d'analyse', *Travai et emploi*, no. 33, September 1987, pp. 9–14.

73 Michèle Bonnechère, *Le Droit du travail*, La Découverte, Paris 1997, p. 62.

74 Alain Supiot, 'Du bon usage des lois en matière d'emploi', *Droit social*, no. 3, March 1997, p. 237.

75 Ginsbourger, *La Gestion contre l'entreprise*, pp. 73–4.

76 Bonnechère, *Le Droit du travail*, p. 72.

77 See Labbé, Croisat and Bevort, *La Désyndicalisation*.

78 There is an extreme example of the leftist critique of trade unions in a highly ambitious theoretical work published in 1978 by a jurist, Bernard Edelman, who at the time was influenced by Althusserianism: *La Légalisation de la classe ouvrière* (Christian Bourgois, Paris 1978). Edelman aims to show that labour law, secured following the social conflicts of the nineteenth and twentieth centuries, is in fact wholly 'bourgeois' in inspiration, such that 'the working class can be "corrupted" precisely by its own "victories"', which can also be presented as a process of integration into Capital' (p. 11). In this perspective, the union is 'an ideological state apparatus, which resembles the state apparatus as much as it does the ideological apparatus. Hence an apparatus that "administers" the working class: planning, efficiency, order and subordination – such are the key words of the technostructure' (p. 159). Thus, 'union power', as 'established' by the 'bourgeoisie', is comparable to that of an 'officer corps charged with training the army': the more the union is external to its rank and file, the more it is decentred from struggles, the more it escapes working-class "spontaneity", the more effective it is. The institutionalization of negotiations assumes a trade-union "machine" "concentrated" in the same fashion as state or capitalist concentration' (pp. 182–83). As for labour law, it is simply the germ of 'socialist law' – i.e. 'Soviet law' or, in other words, 'Stalinism' (pp. 191–7).

79 At the end of 1982, a journalist who had hitherto specialized in scientific popularization, François de Closets, published a work, *Toujours plus!*, which in a few weeks achieved a print run of 700,000 copies and had a major media impact (press articles, broadcasts, opinion polls). Written from the standpoint of a liberal justice (but, it seems, rather well received in Socialist circles, just arrived in power), the book attacked 'privileges' and 'corporatisms', while presenting itself as a plea on behalf of the weak against the strong, of isolated individuals against lobbies. It has the historical interest of bringing out the privileges of wage-earners and the role of trade unions in securing and defending these 'privileges', which – another argument with a very significant role in the first half of the 1980s – were preserved at the expense of jobs (de Closets, *Toujours plus!*, Grasset, Paris 1982). Three years later, the same author was to publish a 500-page lampoon against the unions: *Tous ensemble pour en finir avec la syndicatrie* (Seuil, Paris 1984), which perfectly reflects the reversal of the 1980s: without encountering much opposition, the main unions can now be presented not as the defenders of wage-earners against exploitation, but as the defenders of wage-earners as privileged figures, particularly public-sector wage-earners; the very fact that the latter enjoy job security begins to be presented as an exorbitant privilege. The main issue in de Closets's book, published during the negotiations on flexibility, was the struggle against the 'corporatism' and 'rigidities' preventing the adaptation of the production apparatus to the market.

80 Despite significant innovations in union practices *à la* CFDT and the construction of a Socialist Party composed of a plurality of currents. But these new structures (the CFDT emerged in 1964 out of the secularization of the CFTC, and the Socialist Party was founded at the Épinay Congress in 1971) were also caught up, albeit with a certain delay, in the general critique of the representative institutions of the industrial world. For example, the fact that the theme of working conditions appeared only in 1971, and then as a secondary issue, in the agreement on common action between the CGT and the CFDT (the previous agreement dated from December 1970, at a time when all commentators on the crisis were highlighting the importance of the theme for wage-earners) indicates the extent to which union organizations struggled to keep up with the new aspirations, which in any event they had not served to reveal (Claude Durand and Pierre Dubois, *La Grève. Enquête sociologique*, FNSP–Armand Colin, Paris 1975, p. 27). Moreover, one of the many reasons for disaffection with Communist institutions and neo-Leninist leftist movements – Maoist ones in particular, which were quasi-nonexistent after 1973 (see Jean-Pierre Le Goff, *Mai 1968. L'héritage impossible*, La Découverte, Paris 1998) – was their authoritarian and centralized *modus operandi*, which left little room for manoeuvre and autonomy for different

activists and local situations. Such organizational power over members – of which self-criticism sessions intended to purge Maoist militants of their petty-bourgeois egos represented an extreme example – was less and less accepted by the generation that had entered politics with the events of 1968.

81 Dominique Labbé, *Syndicats et syndiqués en France depuis 1945*, L'Harmattan, Paris 1996, p. 93.

82 Several examples are given in the investigation by Labbé, Croisat and Bevort (*La Désyndicalisation*, p. 73). Thus, that of technicians, senior *cadres* or engineers, who felt in an awkward position: 'The meetings were tedious. How can you get worked up about problems with canteens, or some workers' conflict with some boss for seemingly pathetic reasons?'; or, to take another example, '[t]he single group containing all wage-earners – from the roadsweeper to the management cadres – was a generous but impractical utopia. The CGT, which set up a "cadres" group, pinched our voters from us and attracted a lot of young people whom we had frightened off.'

83 The interviews recorded with CGT officials by Dominique Labbé and Jacques Derville (*Annexe du rapport 'La Désyndicalisation en France depuis 1945'*, CERAT, Institut des études politiques de Grenoble, 1995) are, in this respect, very enlightening: 'The CGT organizations messed quite a few engineers and *cadres* around. Firm intervention by the confederation was therefore required to transform this "workerist" vision and force them to take on board this problem of the increasing weight of engineers and *cadres* and their unease about manual workers' trade unions' (interview with René Lomet, p. 179). Or another example: 'Within it, there was a strong tendency which thought that schools were bourgeois schools. For a long time, the CGT thought it should train its *cadres* itself and not call upon graduates. These positions are explicable, but it was a serious legacy' (interview with Lydia Brovelli, p. 50).

84 Labbé, *Syndicats et syndiqués en France depuis 1945*, p. 95.

85 Michel Pialoux thus explains that at the Peugeot-Sochaux site, the socialization of Catholic rural workers was carried out largely by the JOC (Jeunesses Ouvrières Chrétiennes), which represented a breeding-ground for recruitment of young CFDT activists. In contrast, the Communist tradition was nonexistent in the region, and essentially developed around the factory, attracting workers from different backgrounds.

86 As for the CFDT, analysis of generations of union members permits the following observation: 'At the end of the 1950s, the project of a mass, non-Communist trade unionism was formulated by a single generation that led the organization for more than twenty-five years. Success seemed to be occurring in the 1960s and the beginning of the 1970s, and took the form of an influx of members and an expansion of its catchment area. But just at this time, the social mechanisms that had fashioned the founding generation in its youth (Christian-democratic current, Catholic movements, student unions) began to fade. The effects of this compounded the consequences of the crisis, threatening the survival of the organization, especially in private sector firms' (Labbé, Croisat and Bevort, *La Désyndicalisation*, p. 149).

87 Labbé, Croisat and Bevort's interviewees (ibid., p. 65) frequently refer to this generational conflict: 'I'm too old', 'my working life is over', 'make way for the young', 'people of my age (forty-eight) were thrown on to the scrapheap, youth believed it possessed the truth. Feeling I was a hindrance, I withdrew.' This is one of the explanations advanced by Launay (*Le Syndicalisme en Europe*, pp. 450–51), who constructs a marked contrast between the youth of the retired worker of today and that of his thirty-year-old son. On account of his standard of living, the former felt that he was part of the working class, whereas his son, born in the 1960s, cannot possess the same class consciousness. He spent longer at school, has the same sporting and music idols as his middle-class peers, has a hi-fi system and a motorbike. He is a member of a rock group. He goes to Bercy to hear concerts. 'If he differs from a student at Sciences-Po or the London School of Economics in his clothing, manners and way of interacting, his speech, his social practices and what he reads, he nevertheless shares a whole set of cultural references, which are interpreted differently but experienced in common and uniformly received. Class solidarities are

less important than general structures for this young worker, who does not have as precise a working-class memory as his father. If he is French, the great rebellion he hears people talking about is that of May 1968. Was it proletarian? June 1936 or August 1945 are far removed. ... In these conditions, how could trade unions be attractive? Read a page – a single page – of a union newspaper, whatever language it's in, and you'll see the distance that separates its presentation – today one refers to the "look" – from that of an adolescent magazine. Who can believe that a duplicated sheet will hold the attention of an *Actuel* reader?'

88   'The inquiries started in the 1970s into the psychopathology of work met with trade-union bans and leftist condemnation at the time. ... Any approach to psychological problems by psychologists, doctors, psychiatrists and psychoanalysts was tainted by a deadly sin: that of privileging individual subjectivity, of supposedly leading to individualistic practices and being detrimental to collective action. ... Supposedly anti-materialist, such concern with mental health was suspected of being deleterious for collective mobilization and class consciousness, favouring a "petty-bourgeois" navel-gazing of a necessarily reactionary kind' (Christophe Dejours, *Souffrance en France. La banalisation de l'injustice sociale*, Seuil, Paris 1998, p. 43).

89   'In a lot of branch organizations, one of the first tasks of activists (particularly workforce representatives) up to the end of the 1970s consisted in doing the "rounds" of offices and workshops. The collection of dues, but especially contact with union members, the gathering of information on the local situation and wage-earners' grievances were the essential aims of these tours. ... A large part of meetings was given over to accounts of them. Obviously, representatives sometimes had the feeling that they were wasting precious time – hours for branch work rapidly passed in sterile discussions – listening to the same mundanities on the filthy condition of the premises, the incompetence and authoritarianism of the supervisors, the inadequacy of the pay, the non-recognition of skills and qualifications. Activists often came back from these rounds with the sense that they had nothing more to learn from their workmates and, when you think about it, only an exacting ethic could lead them to repeat the exercise the following month. This presence of activists in the workplace generated a "union atmosphere" that was one of the primary justifications of membership' (Labbé, *Syndicats et syndiqués en France depuis 1945*, pp. 64–5).

90   Ibid., pp. 106–7.

91   Thus the CFDT was closely associated with the elaboration of the Auroux laws and the negotiations on flexibility in 1984. Numerous trade unionists were to be found in ministerial offices once the left arrived in power. To grass-roots membership, this sometimes looked like a betrayal: people were building a political career behind their backs.

92   After the 1929 crisis, and especially the 1936 strikes, no one – or virtually no one – denied that there were occupationally defined groups in society, endowed with different conceptions, lifestyles and interests. The resolution of the 'class problem' was therefore very generally regarded as being at the heart of the 'social question'. To be extremely schematic, we can say that the very wide range of positions adopted was distributed between Marxism and corporatism, which represented the official doctrine of the fascist regimes. The representations of social classes inspired by Marxism and corporatism were distinct in two key respects. The first concerns the *conflictual or complementary character* of social classes. In Marxism, the notion of class incorporates the idea not only of inequality, but above all of exploitation. It cannot be dissociated from that of class struggle, and has as its positive horizon, with the end of exploitation and the classless society (which will follow the climactic moment of class struggle represented by the revolution and a transitional phase of the dictatorship of the proletariat). In corporatism, classes are conceived not as necessarily antagonistic (even if they can sometimes have divergent interests) but as fundamentally complementary. It is the organization of classes, their representation in intermediate bodies and the harmonization of their interests under state auspices, which constitutes the positive horizon at which the revolution must aim. The second basic difference is this: in Marxism, the class system is articulated around the *central conflict between proletariat and bourgeoisie*, even if in the work of Marx and his subsequent commentators the existence of various secondary or

intermediate classes – subproletariat, peasantry, petty bourgeoisie, and so on – can be invoked, particularly to account empirically for crucial moments of struggle (as, for example, the 1848 revolution or the Commune in Marx). In corporatism, especially in the writings of the 1930s, it is the *middle classes* who constitute the linchpin of the class system. This option is bound up with a dual ideological opposition on the part of corporatism – on the one hand to 'collectivism' (associated, in this symbolic system, with the proletariat), and on the other to capitalism and liberalism (associated with the bourgeoisie and, in particular, with cosmopolitan capital owners), between whom a 'third way' must be found. To the conflict between the 'rootless' proletarian and the 'stateless' capitalist, shareholder in 'impersonal' companies, is thus counterposed the reconciliation of capital and labour that is supposedly embodied and realized in practice by the smallholder working in a family firm alongside his workers.

93 See Jean-Philippe Parrot, *La Représentation des intérêts dans le mouvement des idées politiques*, Presses Universitaires de France, Paris 1974.

94 See Alain Desrosières, 'Éléments pour l'histoire des nomenclatures socioprofession-nelles', in J. Affichard, ed., *Pour une histoire de la statistique*, vol. 2, INSEE-Economica, Paris 1987, pp. 35–56; and *La Politique des grandes nombres*, La Découverte, Paris 1993.

95 See Desrosières, *La Politique des grands nombres*.

96 In 1919, agreements had been reached in all sectors, notably for the application of the law limiting the working day to eight hours. But faced with employer intransigence, the CGT's weakness, and the CGTU's opposition to the principle of 'collaboration', the collective agreement fell into abeyance. Following the law of 1936, 8,000 agreements were signed, invariably not following a real joint agreement, but thanks to the intervention of 'overseers' selected by the state (Jean-Daniel Reynaud, *Les Syndicats en France*, Seuil, Paris 1975, p. 176).

97 Third electoral college for elections to works councils, superannuation funds, specific provisions of labour law in terms of payment for overtime, length of notice or probation period, and so on.

98 See Luc Boltanski, *The Making of a Class: Cadres in French Society*, trans. Arthur Goldhammer, Cambridge University Press/Éditions de la Maison des Sciences de l'Homme, Cambridge 1987. The classifications used in other countries, the English and German ones in particular, do not identify *cadres* in the sense of the French taxonomy. This is because the social history of these countries has not resulted in stressing the same type of separation between activities. German classifications are organized around the manual/non-manual distinction, corresponding to the identification at the end of the last century of a large class of white-collar workers; whereas English classifications divide things up in perpendicular fashion by dissociating engineers, experts, liberal professions (*professionals*) from senior managers (*managers*). See Jürgen Kocka, *Les Employés en Allemagne, 1850–1980. Histoire d'un groupe social*, Éditions de l'EHESS, Paris 1989, on the history of the category of white-collar workers in Germany, and Simon Szreter, 'The Genesis of the Registrar-General's Social Classification of Occupations', *The British Journal of Sociology*, vol. XXXV, no. 4, 1984, pp. 529–46, on the formation of the classification of occupations in Great Britain.

99 The construction of the 1982 nomenclature was also the occasion for struggles over the institutionalization of certain occupations, particularly paramedical ones, which wanted recognition of titles or the definition of criteria to determine the type of classification in the nomenclature (Alain Desrosières and Laurent Thévenot, *Les Catégories socioprofessionnelles*, La Découverte, Paris 1988).

100 The author of the 1954 classification, Jean Porte, also coined the term 'socioprofessional category', which has since become current. Desrosières and Thévenot (ibid., p. 191) recount that, often questioned subsequently about choosing this in preference to 'social category', he replied: 'If we had chosen that term, we would have been criticized by everyone. The left would have reckoned that they were not genuine social classes, while the right would have shouted that they were social classes. Whereas with "socioprofessional", no one said anything.'

101 Annette Jobert and Michèle Tallard, 'Diplômes et certifications de branches dans les conventions collectives', *Formation emploi*, no. 52, October/December 1995, p. 134.

102 See Luc Boltanski and Laurent Thévenot, 'Finding One's Way in Social Space: A Study Based on Games', *Social Science Information*, vol. 22, nos 4–5, 1983, pp. 631–80.

103 To the question 'Do you feel that you belong to a social class?', 61 per cent of people questioned replied 'yes' in 1966 – i.e. as many as in 1994 – but the number answering 'no' rose from 30 to 38 per cent (non-responses declining at the same time from 9 to 1 per cent): Dirn, *La Société française en tendances, 1975–1995*, p. 88.

104 Ibid.

105 We have also cited Launay's remarks (*Le Syndicalisme en Europe*, p. 451) on the lesser working-class consciousness of the young as a cause of deunionization.

106 This is what they said on the subject in 1998, proceeding to indicate that their predictions had not been realized given the reversal in trends observed subsequently: 'As for the overall structure of society, we had stressed two trends calling into question the image of a society divided into classes, which was still the most widespread image at the time. On the one hand, the sense of belonging to a social class was fading, since fewer and fewer people stated that they belonged to the working class or the bourgeoisie; and those who placed themselves in the middle class were becoming more numerous, to the point of becoming a majority of the whole population. This trend has continued. On the other hand, the intermediate social categories were proliferating to the point where the INSEE found itself compelled to alter its socioprofessional nomenclature. These two diagnoses heralded the effacement of the middle class itself, for, no longer being intermediate between two strong, antagonistic classes, it lost its specific characteristic of being "middle"' (Dirn, *La Société française en tendances, 1975–1995*, p. 21).

107 'If what is called the middle-class society corresponds in part to a tendency towards a homogenization of lifestyles, a disappearance of social hierarchy, we cannot make do with mere observation. Such a society is predominantly characterized by a formidable reorganization of modes of differentiation. These are not only collective (expressed in categories of income, qualifications, etc.): they are becoming more individualized' (Pierre Rosanvallon, *La nouvelle question sociale*, Seuil, Paris 1995, pp. 207–09).

108 According to Jean-David Fermanian ('Compte rendu de la journée d'étude à l'Observatoire sociologique du changement du 14 mars 1997', *Note INSEE*, Département de l'emploi et des revenues d'activité, 10 July 1997), such results no longer emerge with the two-figure socioprofessional category, which proves stronger for describing differences in income. The one-figure socioprofessional category used by Rosanvallon (*La nouvelle question sociale*) contains only seven posts (Farmers, Artisans-Shopkeepers-Heads of Firms, Liberal Professions, *Cadres* and Higher Intellectual Occupations, Intermediate Occupations, White-Collar Workers, Blue-Collar Workers), and in particular does not account for a number of distinctions, like private/public employment, that are obviously important when it comes to income. We know, moreover, that 'boundaries shift' between the three one-figure socioprofessional categories – i.e. 'white-collar workers', 'intermediate occupations' and '*cadre*' – the classifiers hesitating, for example, over whether to classify someone as 'middle *cadre*' rather than '*senior cadre*' (Alain Chenu, 'Le codage professionel à l'épreuve d'investigations réitérées, 1975–1990', communication to 'La journée de travail sur l'évolution de la catégorie socioprofessionnelle et des determinants de la stratification sociale', 14 March 1997, Observatoire sociologique du changement; 'La descriptibilité statistique des professions', *Sociétés contemporaines*, no. 27, 1997).

109 Rosanvallon, *La nouvelle question sociale*, p. 209.

110 'It makes no sense trying to understand those who are excluded as a category. What must be taken into account are the processes of exclusion. … It is disparities and differences that mark them, not ordinary descriptive positivities (income, occupation, educational level, etc.). There is therefore not much point in "counting" the excluded. That does not make it possible to constitute them as an object of social action. … The difficulty involved in mobilizing and

representing the excluded is explained by the fact that they are primarily defined by the failures in their lives, and hence by negativity. For this reason, they cannot constitute a social force that could be mobilized. They are not the new proletarians of the unemployment society. Strictly speaking, they have no common interests. They in no sense form an objective class, in the sense that the Marxist tradition gives this term (position in the productive process). Almost by virtue of their essence, the excluded even form a "non-class". They represent the shadow of society's dysfunctioning, are the product of a laborious process of decomposition, of desocialization in the strong sense of the term. ... The excluded are in a way "unrepresentable": they do not constitute a class that could have representatives or spokesmen. This is why there are no trade unions of the unemployed, and why all attempts to transform the millions of unemployed into an organized collective force have always failed' (Rosanvallon, *La Question syndicale*, pp. 202 f). It goes without saying that we do not share this analysis, if only because the chances of being 'excluded' are not uniformly distributed according to 'class'.

111 Yannick Lemel, Marco Oberti and Frédéric Reiller have carried out a count of terms connected with social stratification in the 1970–71, 1980–81 and 1990–91 issues of two French journals: *Sociologie du travail* and *Revue française de sociologie* ('Classe social, un terme fourre-tout? Fréquence et utilisation des termes liés à la stratification sociale dans deux revues', *Sociologie du travail*, no. 2, 1996, pp. 195–207). If, overall, the word 'class' appears in 50 per cent of articles, its occurrence has declined in recent years; there are both more articles that do not refer to it and fewer occurrences in the articles that do make use of it. The years 1970–71 are marked by the strong presence of a Marxist register, the beginning of the 1980s by a Bourdieusian register (*Distinction* dates from 1979), the years 1980–90 by simple use of socioprofessional categories or by recourse to stratifications of society according to certain variables, but without any reference to a framework that seeks to construct a theory of relations between classes. The authors are surprised that 'contrary to what we observe in other countries (the United States, Great Britain, Italy), we witness scarely any attempt at a "theoretical reconstruction" of the overall structure of society in terms of "classes", "social groups" or "strata"' (p. 205).

112 Dominique Sicot, 'Sous la fracture, les classes', *Alternatives économiques*, no. 29, special issue, July 1996. The evolution of the summary of *Données sociales*, published once every three years by the INSEE, is particularly interesting in this respect. This work, constructed on the basis of collecting the different work in progress at the INSEE, but also in the statistical departments of the ministries (Labour, Industry, National Education, Justice, etc.), or in research centres (Centre d'études de l'emploi, INED, CREDOC, etc.), is consequently fairly representative of the concerns of the circle of social statisticians. In 1990 and 1993, one could still find a section with a title referring to 'social groups' (on its own in 1993, combined with 'Population' in 1990). In 1996, this section disappeared, to be replaced by a new one on 'Poverty and Insecurity' that was continued in 1999. The work published in 1999 also marked the appearance of a section on 'Social Bonds' that was interesting as regards the growth in work referring to a conception of the social world in terms of networks. (We are grateful to Alain Desrosières for drawing our attention to these changes.)

113 The HEC graduate working at IBM was the paradigmatic representative, or 'good example', of the *cadre* in the 1960s – much more so than the self-taught production *cadre* working in a small or medium-sized firm. It can be demonstrated that the characteristics of the 'good representative' of a category are not statistically representative. Thus, the typical representative of *cadres* has more academic qualifications than the average *cadre* (see Boltanski, *The Making of a Class*; and Boltanski and Thévenot, 'Finding One's Way in Social Space'). On the analysis of the structure of mental categories in terms of focal points and periphery, see Eleonor Rosch, 'On the Internal Structure of Perceptual and Semantic Categories', in T.E. Moore, ed., *Cognitive Development and the Acquisition of Language*, Academic Press, New York 1973; and 'Classification of Real-World Objects: Origins and Representation in Cognition', in P.N. Johnson-Laird and P.C. Wason, eds, *Thinking: Readings in Cognitive Science*, Cambridge University Press, Cambridge 1977, pp. 212–22).

114   As François Eymard-Duvernay recalls, wages classifications, which in certain respects established the market by making it possible to designate what is exchanged, also constitute a fetter on a completely 'pure' operation of the market, because (a) 'they form groups for which wages are identical, while individuals can have different productivities'; (b) 'they are rigid whereas the market can reveal alterations in wages hierarchies'; and (c) 'they are frequently linked to procedures of advancement by seniority in the scale of classifications' ('Droit du travail et lois économiques: quelques éléments d'analyse', *Travail et emploi*, no. 33, September 1987, pp. 9–14).

115   See Eustache, 'Individualisation des salaires et flexibilité'.

116   In 1985, 80 per cent of branches with more than 10,000 wage-earners had at least one minimum inferior to the SMIC. The development by the state from 1990 onwards of incentives to negotiate made it possible to improve the situation somewhat, so that in 1993 more than half of the branches had wage schedules with minimum levels that were equal or superior to the SMIC. On the other hand, the guaranteed minima of the higher levels were scarcely altered, creating a flattening of branch-wage hierarchies, increasing the disconnection between the schedules and real remuneration practices, but also thereby legitimizing pay levels for skilled workers that were much closer to the SMIC and those of unskilled workers than before (Barrat, Coutrot and Mabile, 'La négociation salariale en France').

117   François Jeger-Madiot, 'L'emploi et le chômage des familles professionnelles', *Données sociales 1996*, INSEE, Paris 1996, p. 119.

118   See Jobert and Tallard, 'Diplômes et certifications de branches dans les conventions collectives'; Chenu, 'Une classes ouvrière en crise', p. 479.

119   See François Eyraud *et al.*, 'Les classifications dans l'entreprise: production des hiérarchies professionnelles et salariales', *Travail et emploi*, no. 38, 1989, pp. 64–78.

120   The second attitude was more prevalent in firms which believed that classification rules were a matter for negotiation by branches, which are weakly unionized and, as a result, under little pressure to negotiate whatever the subject. The wages in them are fairly close to the branch minima, or depend on the situation of the labour market. The third type of practice is more commonly associated with firms that are leaders in their market, and can bear the cost of redescribing jobs and practices. These initiatives occur at times of restructuring, the development of new business activities, and so on, which presuppose a significant reorganization of work.

121   See Jacques Lantin and Jean-David Fermanian, 'Présentation des conventions collectives', *Notes INSEE*, Départment de l'emploi et des revenues d'activité, 16 December 1996. What has nevertheless hitherto ensured the correspondence is that a majority of the schedules do not have 'pure' classificatory criteria, but have retained certain references to typical jobs or a segmentation of jobs where the old categories are still to be found. In order to make the transition, the social partners themselves need to preserve the link with the old forms of classification for a period of time.

122   Barrat, Coutrot and Mabile, 'La négociation salariale en France', p. 203. More than 50 per cent of firms still base themselves on the branch collective agreement for these various subjects, whatever their size. The only instance where this rate is not attained – and then only just – is by firms with more than 500 wage-earners and exclusively on subject of determining the basic wage: it is only 48.5 per cent when it comes to the role of the branch agreement, but to this must be added 27 per cent that base themselves on an agreement specific to the firm. The role of the branch agreement appears maximal for firms employing between 50 and 100 people, with 67 per cent using it for the basic wage, 69 per cent for the hierarchization of jobs, and 64 per cent for seniority increments (ibid.).

123   See Michel Cézard, 'Les classifications: les grande étapes', *Économie et statistiques*, Paris 1979.

124   Jobert and Tallard, 'Diplômes et certifications de branches dans les conventions collectives', pp. 142–3. The year 1990 witnessed the emergence of a new type of agreement with the

iron and steel industry agreement 'A. Cap 2000', set out in line with a logic of skills. This agreement organizes a framework that is likewise very flexible, where the classificatory hierarchies are based on people's accumulation of 'skills', and no longer on the 'weighting' of posts according to certain criteria, to the point where people can improve their qualifications without thereby really changing job. This kind of agreement typifies a desire to use collective agreements to promote internal change – in this instance, towards a greater versatility on the part of the workforce. It rests upon a complex set of descriptions of skills and jobs, as well as on the regular organization of individual interviews for appraising existing and desirable skills. See Kostas Chatzis, Frédéric de Coninck and Philippe Zarifian, 'L'évaluation des politiques de l'emploi', *Données sociales 1999*, INSEE, Paris 1999, pp. 117–27. For the time being, this agreement remains the only one of its sort and in fact involves only a single firm, Usinor-Sacilor, doubtless because it is relatively onerous to establish, and the branches that are negotiating seek instead to lay down the lightest possible frameworks, leaving their members room for potential innovation within a determinate format.

125 Entreprise et Progrès, *Cadre/non cadre. Une frontière dépassée*, Entreprise et Progrès, Paris 1992, p. 3.

126 Ibid., p. 18.

127 Ibid., pp. 29, 7.

128 Ibid., p. 29.

129 Confidence in the nomenclature is decreasing, as is attested by the INSEE assignment to some of its *cadres* to revise it. Nevertheless, the result of their investigation indicates that analysts of the social world, like their social partners, regard it as irreplaceable, and are content to propose a modest tidying-up operation (see Hedda Faucheux and Guy Neyret, with the collaboration of Jean-David Fermanian and Alain Ferragu, *Évaluation de la pertinence des categories socio-professionnelles (CSP)*, INSEE, Inspection générale, no. 49/B005, 1999). Similarly, a study day organized by the Observatoire Sociologique du Changement on 14 March 1997, on the theme of 'the waning of the socioprofessional category as an explanatory factor in behaviour and opinions', generally contradicted this opinion. Certainly, Alain Chenu ('La descriptibilité statistique des professions') suggested that the nomenclature was slightly less 'robust' in 1990 than in 1982 or 1975, inasmuch as the likelihood of coding the same individual twice in the same fashion had not altered, whereas coding methods had improved. He attributed this situation to 'the emergence of collective agreement with classificatory criteria and 'the tendency to an individualization of wages', which 'make the pinpointing of social status associated with such and such a job or occupation more problematic'. Instances were likewise found where the explanatory power of the socioprofessional categories seemed weak, as with sexual behaviour or students' attitude to their studies. In the round, however, the socioprofessional categories did not appear to have lost much of their power of discrimination. See Fermanian's report, 'Compte rendu de la journée d'étude à l'Observatoire sociologique du changement du 14 mars 1997'.

130 See, for example, Maurizio Gribaudi and Alain Blum, 'Des catégories aux liens individuels: l'analyse statistique de l'espace social', *Annales ESC*, no. 6, November/December 1990, pp. 1365–1402; Rosanvallon, *La nouvelle question sociale*.

131 One thinks here of the works, the majority of them historical, which against the mechanistic simplism of structuralist Marxism, have demonstrated the effort – especially the political effort – required to construct the equivalences on which social classes are founded, and to establish the instruments of their representations. See, in particular, E. P. Thompson, *The Making of the English Working Class*, Penguin, Harmondsworth 1980; and William H. Sewell, *Work and Revolution in France: The Language of Labor from the Old Regime to 1848*, Cambridge University Press, Cambridge 1980.

132 See Michel Callon and Bruno Latour, 'Unscrewing the Big Leviathan', in K. Knorr-Cetina and A.V. Cicourel, eds, *Advances in Social Theory and Methodology*, Routledge & Kegan Paul, Boston (MA) 1981, pp. 277–303.

133 François Dubet, *Sociologie de l'expérience*, Seuil, Paris 1994, p. 52.

134 See Ève Chiapello, *Artistes versus managers. Le management culturel face à la critique artiste*, Métailié, Paris 1998.

135 See Pierre-Michel Menger, 'Marché du travail artistique et socialisation du risque. Le cas des arts du spectacle', *Revue française de sociologie*, vol. XXXII, 1991, pp. 61–74; 'Appariement, risque et capital humain: l'emploi et la carrière dans les professions artistiques', in Menger and J.-P. Passeron, eds, *L'Art de la recherche. Essais en l'honneur de Raymonde Moulin*, La Documentation française, Paris 1994; and 'Être artiste par intermittence. La flexibilité du travail et le risque professionel dans les arts du spectacle', *Travail et emploi*, no. 60, 1995, pp. 4–22.

136 After more than twenty years of community efforts, a directive finally emerged on 22 September 1994 on European works councils, making negotiation compulsory for firms of EU dimensions. On the other hand, it left the partners a completely free hand to determine the content of the agreement (place, frequency and duration of meetings, material and financial resources, remits, information and consultation procedures), to choose between creating a European council or providing for a procedure for consulting and informing wage-earners at a European level (Bonnechère, *Le Droit du travail*, p. 109). In the event of the negotiations failing, provisions are applicable by default at the end of three years. But agreements already signed before the directive came into force provided for exemption from renegotiation, which gave rise to feverish manoeuvring on the part of the groups that were initially the most hostile, such as Unilever or Peugeot (see Udo Rehfeldt, 'Les syndicats face à la mondialisation des firmes: le rôle des comités d'entreprise européens', *Actes du GERPISA*, no. 21, December 1997, pp.35–8). Moreover, the agreements that have been signed can prove less favourable than the provisions by default, and it is even possible to negotiate to create neither procedures, nor a council. The employers represented at a European level by UNICE have always been hostile to any progress in this direction, have since 1972 caused the failure of other projects of the same type on several occasions, and contributed significantly to minimizing the impact of the directive in question, which nevertheless marks a first step towards a European representation of wage-earners. The employers' position is that multinationals must be allowed to experiment with mechanisms before there is any legislation, with some firms – mainly French, and then German – like Renault, Bull, Thomson, Danone or Volkswagen already being engaged in the creation of 'European group councils' whose remits vary greatly, do not necessarily cover the whole firm but only one branch, and so on (see the special issue of *Alternatives économiques*, no. 15, January 1993). For their part, the trade unions have been slow to recognize the need for European regulation, fearing that less favourable community provisions would be imposed on their wage-earners, and because they themselves would have to be initiated into transnational work.

137 See Alain Ehrenberg, *La Fatigue d'être soi*, Odile Jacob, Paris 1998.

138 See Georges Vigarello, *Une Histoire culturelle du sport. Techniques d'hier et d'aujourd'hui*, Revue EPS-Robert Laffont, Paris 1988.

139 Norbert Elias and Eric Dunning, *The Quest for Excitement: Sport and Leisure in the Civilizing Process*, Basil Blackwell, Oxford 1986.

140 François Chateauraynaud, *La Faute professionnelle. Une sociologie des conflits de responsabilité*, Métailié, Paris 1991, p. 166.

141 See François Eymard-Duvernay and Emmanuelle Marchal, *Façons de recruter. Le jugement des compétences sur le marché du travail*, Métailié, Paris 1996.

142 Ibid.

143 Moreover, it is interesting to see that this is exactly what Gribaudi and Blum do in an article ('Des catégories aux liens individuels') initially presented as a critique of the categories and a plea for a return to individual statistical data. Seeking to account for social mobility understood as a comparison between the occupations of sons and those of their fathers, they show that the categorical divisions used to account for transitions from one class to another or, contrariwise, for the reproduction of class allow us to see only what the categories have not erased.

On the other hand, they obscure the specific situations of 'marginal' beings who have been attached to a class in the context of a partition of space encompassing everyone, but whose characteristics are, ultimately, distinct from the beings who form the core of the category. If their critique of the disadvantages of categorization is perfectly valid, the alternative proposed for understanding the phenomenon under analysis is simply the realization of a different type of categorization. Thus, they construct classes of pairs of father–son occupations. Their catalogue of individual records is no longer composed of persons to whom a generational rank and occupation are attached, but of father–son links defined as links between occupations of the type butcher–baker, proprietor–solicitor, and so on. They end up with three classes of generational links between occupations, making it possible to bring out new phenomena as regards the issue of social mobility.

144 Readers will find a description of, and comparison between, three of these movements, which – with very different and, it must be said, far from equally acceptable ideologies and methods – have embarked upon resistance to liberalism or liberal modernity (the Zapatistas in Mexico, the militias of North America, and the Aum Shinrikyo sect in Japan), in Manuel Castells, Shujiro Yazawa and Emma Kiselyova, 'Insurgents against the Global Order: A Comparative Analysis of the Zapatistas in Mexico, the American Militia and Japan's AUM Shinrikyo', *Berkeley Journal of Sociology*, vol. XL, 1995, pp. 21–37.

145 See Chiapello, *Artistes versus managers*.

146 See Michael Piore and Charles Sabel, *The Second Industrial Divide*, Basic Books, New York 1984.

147 Production mechanisms in the fashion sector have formed the subject over the last ten years of several studies, the most relevant of which for our purposes have focused on Benetton (regarded as an example of a network firm) and the Sentier district in Paris, whose extremely adaptable mechanisms flexibly co-ordinate the work of designers at the leading edge of fashion and hip style, and the labour of workers who are often migrants – frequently illegal – and condemned to living conditions that approximate to slavery (see, in particular, Maurizio Lazzarato *et al.*, *Des entreprises pas comme les autres. Benetton en Italie, le Sentier à Paris*, Publisud, Aix-en-Provence 1993).

PART III

THE NEW SPIRIT OF CAPITALISM AND THE NEW FORMS OF CRITIQUE

6

THE REVIVAL OF THE SOCIAL CRITIQUE

Capitalism's displacements during the second half of the 1970s and in the 1980s did not only end up dismantling an earlier world, notably by weakening the mechanisms associated with the second spirit of capitalism, on which the definition and supervision of social selection tests was based (classificatory grids in collective agreements, wage-earners' trade unions, career advancement). They also contributed to the progressive installation (still ongoing) of a multitude of new mechanisms and selection tests (mobility, switching projects, versatility, ability to communicate during training courses), pertaining to a different logic that we have dubbed 'connexionist'.

This state of the world, which at the outset could be viewed purely negatively (the dissolution of the old conventions), or assimilated in postmodernist fashion to a chaos unamenable to any general interpretation, has finally found an instrument of representation in the language of networks. But because the tests it contained were novel, barely established and, in the absence of a labour of unification and establishment of equivalence, rather heterogeneous, they were difficult to identify – not only by critical bodies, but by the people obliged to submit to them. Consequently, it could become the locus of new forms of injustice and exploitation, facilitated precisely by the fact that they were based on tests that had not been identified and categorized. The forms of social critique that accompanied the construction of the second spirit of capitalism, with its unions, its analyses in terms of social classes, and its national negotiations under state auspices, proved largely ineffective when it came to acting on the new world.

Nevertheless, the growth in poverty and the increasing economic and social difficulties experienced by large numbers of people were bound to arouse indignation and act as a summons to action, even if those concerned with these changes – whether directly or out of altruism – did not always have a very clear idea of what was to be done. In these circumstances, a redeployment of social critique became possible. Its first task was a reformulation of critical categories to make it possible to get some purchase on the world again, in the hope of one day succeeding in reducing its injustice – that is to say, regulating and more effectively supervising the tests that people, especially the most deprived among them, now had to face.

We believe that, following the disarray of the 1980s, we are currently witnessing a period of revival of critique of this sort. Of the two forms of critique that were constructed in the nineteenth century – the *artistic critique*, which elaborates demands for liberation and authenticity, and the *social critique*, which denounces poverty and exploitation – it is the latter that is showing a new lease of life, however hesitant and modest it may currently be. Moreover, there is nothing surprising about this if we remember that when the fallout of the 1960s protest wave came, from the mid-1970s onwards, the fate of the two critiques was very different: whereas themes from the artistic critique were integrated into the discourse of capitalism, so that this critique might seem to have been partially satisfied, the social critique found itself nonplussed, bereft of ideological props, and consigned to the dustbin of history.

What we can expect of a renewal of the social critique is, in particular, an implantation in more robust mechanisms of forms and principles of justice specific to the projective city – a city we have hitherto registered at a theoretical level in management discourse. Without the formation of this city, the new spirit of capitalism would in fact lack the normative props it requires if the routes to profit in the new capitalist universe are to be justified.

We shall postpone to the next chapter the problems facing a revival of the artistic critique, which is still paralysed by the incorporation of part of its thematic into the new spirit of capitalism.

I. THE RESURGENCE OF THE SOCIAL CRITIQUE: FROM EXCLUSION TO EXPLOITATION

From social classes to exclusion

The notion of exploitation – which has hitherto received a developed theoretical formulation only in Marxism, and which for more than a century constituted the mainspring of the social critique – became blurred in the course of the 1980s, at the same time as the general class framework it was located in was abandoned.[1] Renunciation of this thematic – which, in the second half of the 1980s seemed rather 'old hat' – did not betoken unanimous support for the existing order and the abandonment of every species of critique. New categories have gradually been devised to express social negativity – in particular, exclusion (in contrast to inclusion). It was difficult for the notion of exploitation to find a place in this new manner of expressing indignation at growing poverty. In the Marxist critique, it was in fact bound up with class relations at work. Exploitation was predominantly exploitation through labour. But exclusion refers in the main to various forms of expulsion from the sphere of work relations. The excluded are primarily the 'long-term' unemployed (a statistical category constructed in the 1980s).

The first use of the term 'excluded' to refer to people who did not enjoy the beneficial effects of growth and economic progress because of their handicaps is usually attributed to René Lenoir, in his 1974 book *Les Exclus*.[2] The spirit in which Lenoir wrote remained the optimistic one of the 1960s. The consequence of inevitable growth was a general improvement and standardization in living conditions that would ultimately lead to the disappearance of social classes in their negative aspects – that is to say, as sources of exploitative relations – giving way to a division of labour whose only asymmetries would be functional. But there remained a dark zone in this radiant future: the handicapped. Incapable of contributing to the production of wealth, they could not share in the well-being it afforded either. In Lenoir, a handicap is primarily conceived as physical or mental, not as a 'social handicap'. The term was, however, already widely used at the time to refer to those who were subject to negative selection or discrimination on account of their social properties, or were rejects of the education system ('educational handicap'). The sidelining of the 'excluded' (from growth) thus had reasons other than their own failure. It could be imputed to the self-interested action of others.

Unlike the model of social classes, where explanation of the 'proletariat's' poverty is based upon identifying a class (the bourgeoisie, owners of the means of production) responsible for its 'exploitation', the model of exclusion permits identification of something negative without proceeding to level accusations. The excluded are no one's victims, even if their membership of a common humanity (or 'common citizenship') requires that their sufferings be considered and that they be assisted, particularly by the state in the French political tradition. Accordingly, the theme of exclusion pertains to what we have elsewhere called a 'topic of sentiment', rather than a 'topic of denunciation'[3] – something that is conducive to its reappropriation by the humanitarian movement ten years later.

According to Emmanuel Dixdier,[4] the theme of exclusion, which was very marginal in the ten years following publication of Lenoir's book (1974), really boomed in the very different circumstances of the mid-1980s. These circumstances were marked by the growth of unemployment and what was initially identified under the term 'new poverty', rendered increasingly conspicuous by the reappearance in the streets of large towns of *down-and-outs* in the nineteenth-century sense – people without means of subsistence or fixed abode, surviving courtesy of public or private charity. The term 'exclusion' was henceforth used to bring not only the bearers of handicaps, but all victims of the new social poverty, under an umbrella term.

In the meantime, it has passed in transit via humanitarian or charitable associations caring for the poorest, who were ignored by critical apparatuses and, in particular, trade unions. Among these associations, we must highlight the role played by Aide à toute détresse (ADT-Quart Monde), created in 1957 in the 'homeless camp' of Noisy-le-Grand by Father Wresinski, who himself came from a very poor background. For Father Wresinski, the term 'excluded' designated not the handicapped, but precisely those who were left on the margins of society, without any representation, abandoned, even by the critical bodies derived from working-class struggles, and reduced to humiliating, ineffectual assistance.[5]

Gradually integrated into state discourse via the Commissariat au Plan, notably through the discussions accompanying the establishment of the *Revenu minimum d'insertion* (itself heavily inspired by a report from Father Wresinski submitted to the Conseil économique et social in 1987), exclusion was to lose the orientation to protest it had in ADT-Quart Monde's texts. Coinciding with sociological and administrative discourse, it was to embody a new image of society of which we can identify two – compatible – expressions. The first still used the term 'class', but stripped it of any conflictual connotation; the second relied, often implicitly, on the metaphor of networks.

According to the first interpretation, formulated in macro-sociological terms, the old class society had been submerged by the expansion of a more or less uniform middle class occupying the bulk of the social space. At one extreme was to be found a very small fringe with superior wealth and power; at the other were the excluded, who were more or less numerous depending on the method of calculation used, composed in the main of the long-term unemployed, but also of men or women with various social or natural handicaps (children of marginalized families, single mothers, foreigners without identity papers, 'social misfits', etc.). Social work then consists in reintegrating these 'excluded' persons – that is to say, enabling their inclusion, so far as is possible, in the large middle class by helping them to overcome the handicaps which are responsible for their marginalization, but which their exclusion compounds.

A second, more micro-sociological interpretation is of interest to us because it is more clearly based on a representation of society constructed around the network metaphor. In this version of the exclusion paradigm, the included are those who are connected, linked to others – people or higher-level bodies such as public services, families, firms – by a multiplicity and diversity of bonds. By contrast, the excluded are those who have seen the ties that bound them to others severed, and have thus been relegated to the fringes of the network, where beings lose all visibility, all rationale, and virtually all existence. Thus, for example, in Robert Castel's elaboration of the notion of *disaffiliation* – undoubtedly the most important recent contribution to the analysis of phenomena of social marginalization – exclusion, like its opposite, inclusion, indirectly refers to forms of the social bond in a world conceived in the manner of a network.[6] A disaffiliated individual is someone whose connections have been successively broken, who is no longer integrated into any network, who is no longer attached to any of the chains whose intricate complex constitutes the social fabric, and who is consequently 'no use to society'.

In our view, the very rapid diffusion of a definition of the social world in terms of networks that accompanied the establishment of the connexionist world makes it possible to understand how the dynamic of exclusion and inclusion – initially associated with the fate of marginal groups – was able to take the place previously assigned to social classes in the representation of social misery and the means of remedying it.[7] One sign of this diffusion is the fact that in the course of the 1990s a growing number of actors (including *cadres*) saw 'exclusion' as threatening them personally. Consequently, they recognized something of their own fate in a social situation – very remote from their own – whose paradigmatic image – or, if you like, 'typical example' – was the 'SDF' (*Sans Domicile Fixe*), the vagrant without hearth or home.[8]

The construction of the notion of exclusion also allowed those on the bottom rung of the social ladder to find a place in the image of society offered by journalists, writers, film-makers, sociologists, statisticians, and so on. But this new image was no longer, as in the 1970s, that of proletarians or the exploited – that is to say, people belonging to social classes. Those whose condition is denounced take their place in the new picture as the poor, down-and-outs, those of no fixed abode or without identity papers, migrants, the inhabitants of suburbs that have been abandoned and condemned to violence. In the absence of a clear notion of exploitation and hopes for social change, the rejection of social injustice has in a sense regressed to its original stimulus: indignation at suffering. But this is also to say that all the positive features which a century of working-class struggles and revolutionary literature had attached to the figure of the man of the people – courage, candour, generosity, solidarity – tend to disappear from the representation of the most deprived. These qualities, now consigned to the market in mythological accessories (when not suspected of masking Stalinist violence), have been replaced by the piteous attributes of the excluded, defined primarily by the fact that they are *without*: without a voice, without a home, without papers, without work, without rights, and so on.

The humanitarian movement, which was in part the source of the concept, also initiated activity to combat the reality of exclusion. For a time, this kind of intervention also seemed the only feasible one.

Humanitarian action

Increased inequalities and the re-emergence of poverty in wealthy societies served to reawaken attention to the social question and social movements from the mid-1980s. However, in a situation characterized by the defeat, dissolution or discrediting of the critical bodies that had dominated the previous two decades, and in the absence of a critical theory that made it possible to transform indignation into argumentation or to ground rebellion rationally, such social concern and the movements accompanying it invariably adopted the form of humanitarian action.

This kind of activity, which in principle was nothing new (the Red Cross may be regarded as one of the first 'humanitarian' associations), had been given a new lease of life during the 1970s by associations of young doctors hailing from the left or the extreme left. They had abandoned the political struggle in France – deemed ineffectual and frivolous – to devote themselves to direct assistance to the victims of wars or natural catastrophes in the Third World, and also to seek to protect these populations by mediatizing their suffering and the aid delivered to them.[9] This form was a suitable one for embodying indignation about poverty in the conjuncture of the 1980s because it put all the emphasis on engaging in action and direct individual aid. It made it possible to dispense with going through the extensive chain required to point the finger at some far-off figure (for example, the employers or shareholders of multinational firms), or generalizing to the extent of incriminating a type of society. This retreat to humanitarian action was all the more surprising in that previously many critical bodies, while advocating solidarity with the victims of injustice, had roundly attacked 'charity' and even 'social work', denounced as hypocritical, complacent or perverse methods of diverting people from the only action that counted: political action.

The most celebrated example of the new charitable associations – born of leftism, not of a confessional milieu – was the Restaurants du coeur, founded by Coluche in the winter of 1985–86. Innumerable associations for helping people in difficulties saw the light of day in these years, and it was estimated in 1990 that eight million people had performed voluntary work (including 1.2 million volunteers in an aid association). The voluntary labour time devoted to these associations can be estimated at 120 million hours a month, representing approximately 700,000 full-time equivalent jobs, or 3.4 per cent of paid jobs.[10] Starting from the 1990s, these humanitarian associations, which increasingly hired young graduates as wage-earners for a limited period, discovered a common language in the idiom of exclusion and, whatever their immediate practical orientation, made the *reintegration* of the *excluded* their general objective. They intervene in very different spheres,[11] receive public funds, and often work in *partnership* with the state, social workers, or administrative personnel belonging to local communities in particular, with which they are associated in setting up fixed-term local *projects*.[12]

But this form of action soon seemed insufficient. Insecurity and poverty ceased to be treated exclusively as individual suffering whose alleviation was a matter of personal engagement, attaining the status of a social problem of the first importance and prompting the emergence of new social movements.

The new social movements

The politicization of exclusion can be dated to the beginning of the 1990s. It was encouraged by the debates surrounding the vote on the law on the *Revenu minimum d'insertion*, and perhaps above all by amazement at the number and variety of the people who qualified to benefit from it. The RMI thus served as a revelation of poverty, which then came to the awareness of those actors (journalists, sociologists, etc.) with a key role in representing the social world.[13]

Among the works that contributed to this belated awareness, the report published by the Centre d'études des revenus et des coûts (CERC) in the third quarter of 1993 on *Précarité et risque d'exclusion en France* played an especially important role, because it made it possible to translate into figures a wide-spread disquiet, attested to, among other indicators, by the success of *Le Misère du monde*, published at roughly the same time under Pierre Bourdieu's direction. In fact, this report, produced by Serge Paugam on the basis of the INSEE's 1986–87 survey of 'Situations défavorisées' (partially updated), assessed the percentage of those holding a 'secure, stable job' at 51.6 per cent and those holding a stable but threatened job at 28.5 per cent, with those holding unstable jobs and the unemployed comprising virtually 20 per cent of the working population. It also demonstrated very strong correlations between degree of job stability, and poverty and social vulnerability – that is to say, the 'risk of exclusion' and 'marginalization'.[14]

Signs of this mounting disquiet could be piled up, one of the most remarkable of them unquestionably being the tacit solidarity displayed by wage-earners in the private sector with public-sector wage-earners – who enjoy better protection against redundancy – in December 1995.[15] But one also thinks, for example, of the publication since the mid-1990s of a large number of works for a broad public, often with sizeable print runs, whose theme is the critique of economic society, whether their focus is on unemployment, work, exclusion, poverty, job insecurity, the new inequalities, neo-liberalism, the perils of globalization, the spread of violence, or extreme individualism.[16]

Even if, with the attempts to reconstruct a 'left of the left' since the 1995 strikes, humanitarian action is once again tending to fall into discredit on account of its 'apolitical' character, it remains the case that it was largely from the reorientation of political militancy towards humanitarian activity in the second half of the 1980s that a new milieu took shape, in which the revival of critique in the 1990s was rooted. This milieu is very diverse, heterogeneous even, yet it forms a continuous web where contacts can be established, opposition developed, and partial agreements concluded for selective operations on specific points. In this it is no doubt not so very different from the circles in which the foundations of what would become the welfare state were laid in the second half of the nineteenth century, through the combined efforts – even if those who contributed often clashed sharply – of social reformers, jurists, philanthropists, workers' mutual aid associations, and revolutionary trade unions or parties.[17] In the milieu constructed around the struggle against exclusion today, we find interaction between top civil servants, jurists, economists or sociologists of reformist inclination, members of movements that are religious in origin (like Secours catholique or CIMADE), and activists from associations of a new kind[18] – Droit au logement (DAL), Droits devant!! (Dd!!), Agir ensemble contre le chômage (AC!).[19] Constructed around a specific *cause* (like housing, those without papers, the unemployed, etc.), these movements have played an important role since the mid-1990s in reformulating the social critique – not only directly, through the actions they organize, but perhaps above all through the pressure that these actions and their mediatic visibility bring to bear on social reformers. The occupation of the building in the rue du Dragon and the 1995 strikes were the occasion for a *rapprochement* between these movements and trade unionists, particularly SUD, which emerged at the end of the 1980s out of a rebellion by CFDT activists.[20]

Without leading to the formation of a party (rejected because it recalls politicking forms of mobilization), these *rapprochements* are sufficiently close and constant for the activist scene likewise to have come to recognize itself in the metaphor of the network. In this network circulate people who are very different in many respects, with divergent opinions in many cases (the 'patchwork'), but are able to come together and aid one another in actions against exclusion based upon a minimal definition of rights, which are often demanded with reference to a 'citizenship' whose definition remains fluid.

It was in fact within these new movements that a conjunction was effected between the kinds of action (mediatized direct aid) and justification (human rights) developed by the humanitarian movements in the 1980s, and an oppositional know-how, a sense of the transgressive gesture aimed at provoking the authorities and revealing their bad faith, inherited from the struggles of the early 1970s.[21] These movements, whose most active members are often former union or political activists[22] disappointed by the ineffectiveness of established organizations, even disgusted by the games of political manoeuvring or personal interests they have witnessed in parties and unions, invented a *repertoire of protest* (to use Charles Tilly's term[23]) and forms of organization that contrast sharply with those which have dominated the workers' movement for a century. Thus, for example, they counterpose to *delegation*, which confers on spokesmen the power to operate *from a distance*, and exposes them to the accusation of usurping or abusing their authority, *face-to-face* action, direct aid to the oppressed, in a relation of proximity, which is understood as one of the conditions for authentic engagement, since it requires a sacrifice – particularly in terms of time – that is difficult to feign. Similarly, they contrast rigid organizations, whose *bureaucratization* risks passing off the organization's interests for those of the people it claims to be defending, with adaptable, *flexible* forms which, in connection with specific events (defined as so many *projects* and often deliberately mediatized, like, for example, occupations), call upon people who are involved to very different degrees and in various ways. Those who take a hand in these events are not asked for their total support on every detail, but simply for agreement on the validity of the particular action being undertaken. In fact, as against the ideological homogenization undertaken by traditional organizations, which is denounced as totalitarian, the movements demand respect for the heterogeneity and pluralism of the modes and motives of engagement.[24] Christophe Aguiton, one of the founders of SUD-PTT, defines this mode of action as follows: 'A form of organization symbolizes this situation: the network – a fluid system that people work together in, while retaining their own identity.'[25] It is because they describe themselves in terms of the logic of networks that the new movements formed around the defence of 'rights' are fairly indifferent to the question of the *number* of adherents – unlike traditional organizations, with their closed cells or branches, their membership cards, their rituals of renewing cards, and so on, where this issue became almost obsessive. For how can one know who is 'inside' or 'outside' when the issue of membership is replaced by joint action, which takes place only in conjunctural, local terms, on specific occasions?

On the basis of this brief description, we can recognize the morphological homology between the new protest movements and the forms of capitalism that have been established over the last twenty years. This homology affords these highly mobile movements the opportunity to recover some purchase precisely where the traditional organizations have lost their footing. But it also means that they must come to terms with the kinds of tension characteristic of the emergent forms of capitalism, not the least of which is the tension between flexibility, mobility and speed on the one hand, and the continuity of an engagement that is always vulnerable to becoming hazy if it is not continuously stimulated by events that can make it actual – that is, real – on the other.

One of the difficulties encountered by the new movements is the transition from the notion of exclusion – whose compatibility with a representation of the world in terms of networks we have noted, together with the fact that it pertains to a 'politics of sentiment' – to a theory of exploitation that would make it possible to relieve the 'excluded' of the burden of unilateral individual responsibility or inexorable fatality, and thus establish a link between their lot and that of the better-off, particularly those who occupy privileged social positions. Such an operation would make it possible to flesh out the responsibility of the latter, and constitute a better guarantee for the most deprived, than mere appeals to 'big-heartedness'. Moreover, transformation of the theme of exclusion could facilitate identification of the new causes of exclusion over and above a lack of qualifications, which is the explanation most frequently advanced at present.

The problems with exclusion as a critical concept

If exclusion is indeed a critical notion[26] – like social class which, in its principal meaning, is geared towards demanding the abolition of classes – these two
thematics pave the way for very different critical forms. Even after its generalization to society as a whole, the category of exclusion has retained
something of the manner in which it originally served to refer to those whose
handicaps excluded them from a share in social well-being. Not only does
exclusion, unlike exploitation, profit no one, so that no one can be deemed
responsible for it unless out of negligence or error, but it still resonates with
the negative characteristics attached to those who are its victims. Moreover,
such is indeed the meaning of the principal statistical works which, however
well-intentioned, identify groups or persons 'at risk' – that is to say, who find
themselves threatened with exclusion by virtue of their handicaps, now conceived as social as well as physical or mental handicaps. Yet it is precisely this
link between poverty and fault – or, to be more precise, between poverty and
personal properties – that can easily be converted into factors of individual
responsibility, which the notion of class, and especially that of the proletariat,
had succeeded in breaking.

Exclusion is thus presented as someone's misfortune (to be struggled
against), not as the result of a social asymmetry from which some people profit
to the detriment of others. Exclusion ignores exploitation. This argument is
explicitly developed by Jean-Baptiste de Foucauld, planning commissioner at
the beginning of the 1990s, and without a doubt one of the top civil servants
most strongly committed to the struggle against exclusion. While he acknowledges that residues of exploitation exist in our society, he aims to make a clear
distinction between exclusion and exploitation. Exclusion is of a different
nature. It cannot constitute exploitation, so he maintains, since exploitation
occurs at work and the excluded are primarily characterized by the fact that
they lack work.[27] This argument, which is often invoked, plays a highly significant role today because it breaks the link which, relating the good fortune
of the rich to the misfortune of the poor, preserved the reference to a balance
of justice in society conceived as an equilibrium between socioprofessional
groups on a national territory. But Western societies, unequal societies whose
ideal of justice rests on the principle of an equality of essence of all human
beings, cannot dispense with a justification of inequalities. Consequently, the
risk of a regression to explanations appealing exclusively to people's natural
abilities, even their genetic inheritance, however illegitimate, is not to be underestimated: some, endowed with many abilities, have proved capable of seizing
opportunities that others, less intelligent or cursed by handicaps (when they
are not vices), have squandered.

Must we conclude, for all that, that exclusion is a mere ideology (in the
Marxist sense of the term), seeking to mask the persistence of a society based

on class exploitation? On the contrary: we believe that the notion of exclusion should be taken seriously inasmuch as it points towards new forms of poverty corresponding to the capitalist forms that emerged in the 1980s. But we also think that it is appropriate to push the analysis further, in order to see how this notion is related to various contemporary mechanisms of profit creation.

In Marxism, exploitation is conceived with reference to the industrial and commercial worlds in which nineteenth-century capitalism expanded rapidly. But different forms of exploitation, tailored to different worlds, can exist. In the rest of this analysis, we shall develop the idea that the notion of exclusion is pertinent primarily with respect to *a form of exploitation that develops in a connexionist world* – that is to say, a world where the realization of profit occurs through organizing economic operations in networks. But something is lacking when it comes to isolating this connexionist form of exploitation, for it is not enough to define all the poverty peculiar to the new world as exclusion. We must also define the specific form assumed by egoism in this world, since theories of exploitation systematize the intuition that a relationship obtains between the misery of the poor and the egoism of the wealthy. The exploitation of some actors, even when it is unintentional, in fact assumes that other actors (or the same ones, but at different times) circumvent the requirement of aiming for a common good, considering only their private interests.

We shall thus seek to restore the link, loosened by the thematic of exclusion, between the two sources of indignation which, as we have seen, have sustained the social critique: indignation at *poverty* on the one hand, and indignation at *egoism* on the other.

Egoistic behaviour in a connexionist world

We are of the opinion that the new network mechanisms encourage the emergence and development of an original form of opportunism, which is different from market opportunism and more extensive – that is to say, able to find a place in a wide variety of situations, of which market transactions are only one possible scenario.

Since opportunism presents itself in the first instance as an individual aptitude, we shall start from the properties that people must possess in order to be comfortable in a connexionist world, and conduct themselves in such a way as to enjoy personal success, notably by shrewd management of their relational capital. These properties are not unfamiliar to us. We have already come across them in part when, in defining the model of the projective city, we enumerated the qualities whose possession prompts characterization of someone as a 'great man' in this city. They are, quintessentially, those of the manager or project head, who is mobile, streamlined, possessed of the art of establishing and maintaining numerous diverse, enriching connections, and of the ability to extend networks.

In the logic of the city (which is, let us remember, a model of justice, not an empirical description of the state of the world), these qualities are placed in the service of the common good. But this ideal also discloses, in a negative light, another possible form of behaviour, whereby the people who succeed in this world use their qualities only to serve their own personal interests in a selfish, even cynical fashion. To distinguish him from the great man in the projective city (to whom we shall give the generic term *network-extender*), we shall call the opportunistic character who, while possessing all the requisite qualities in this world, makes a purely selfish use of them, the *networker*. The distinction between the network-extender and the networker is based upon an analytical separation between the *characteristics that make for high status* in the logic of the city and the qualities and *actions that guarantee success* in a certain world – that is to say, access to better conditions. Thus, these two figures pertain to the same scale of values (network-extenders and networkers can succeed or fail for the same reasons); and, in order to succeed – that is to say, in this instance, to develop links – they must make the same sacrifices (in stability, continuity, etc.). They therefore share the main thing, with this difference – fundamental in the logic of the city – that the success of the networker benefits him alone, whereas the network-extender's attainment of better conditions benefits the whole city, and is thus a common good.[28]

In order to sketch the portrait of the networker, we draw on sociological literature that presents action in a network world as guided exclusively by strategic considerations and interests, and, in particular, on Ronald Burt's work. What is interesting about the American research on networks that has developed over the last twenty years is that it puts the emphasis not on small groups (cliques), characterized by a dense set of reciprocal relations where choices are mutual, information is shared, and each person communicates with everyone else, but on spaces bereft of links – what Burt calls 'structural holes' – and, more precisely, on the differential created by the contrast between masses of links and interstitial voids. Like Michel Callon's work,[29] but with a different approach, Burt's work paves the way for an analysis of the manner in which asymmetries and, in particular, asymmetries of information, are constructed in a network logic. In effect, if everyone communicates with everyone else in the same group, knowledge is pooled and information shared, which tends to limit the development of asymmetries. For the same reasons, however, no actor accumulates more than the others or, above all, at the expense of the others. A network whose meshing puts each node in communication with all the others does not generate any asymmetry. But nor does it furnish a differential that makes it possible to discharge benefits at certain points of the network, which profit thus from the accumulated capital, particularly information and relational capital.

This is the intuition developed by Ronald Burt in a series of writings,[30] whose interest stems in particular from their mixed character: somewhere between formal theory and an ambitious guidebook for managers. His main argument can be succinctly summarized as follows. Distinguishing between three types of capital, which he calls economic capital, human capital and social capital, he assigns the last the most important role, because it conditions the possibility of accumulating capital in the other two forms. By social capital is meant the set of personal relations that an individual can totalize. But the accumulation of social capital fairly rapidly runs up against limits, inasmuch as, since it relies on personal commitment, it demands investments of time and energy that are difficult to delegate. That is why, counsels Burt, it must be used with discrimination, avoiding redundant investments. If Pierre and Jacques hold similar positions in the same department, it is pointless to squander time engaging in a sustained relationship with both of them. The most profitable investments are not those made within the clique, but long-distance ones. It is by overcoming *structural holes* – that is to say, establishing relations with points or nodes that are not connected to the other points with which one is in contact – that an asymmetry can be formed. And on this basis, *differential* accumulation becomes possible. Without always being explicit, Burt's construction takes its place in a world where information plays a crucial role in wealth accumulation. The gains made by connecting points that were previously separated by structural holes are primarily gains in asymmetry of information. In this way, says Burt, it is possible on the one hand to access information that is not possessed by the other members of the clique or – which amounts to the same thing – to access it before them, and thus acquire a temporal advantage; and, on the other hand, to achieve gains in terms of *reputation* in spaces that are difficult to access, since the actors with whom relations have been established are liable to talk about you, and get your name known. Finally, let us add that Burt's model is open to empirical confirmation. The author puts it to the test, notably through a survey of the members of the senior and middle-ranking personnel of a large, high-tech firm, which reveals a close link between success and the number of structural holes at the disposal of each 'player', to adopt his terminology.[31]

What Burt (who, like all the authors of the same school, presents a totally reticular world from which other social forms have disappeared) does not say is that the profits accruing from strategies of surmounting structural holes would not be such if the actors were not separated by institutional boundaries. The existence of separate spaces, legal barriers or entrance fees increases the costs attached to forming links, and also the differential profits that those who succeed in overcoming these barriers may expect.[32] It is because actors are very unequally placed when it comes to extricating themselves from institutional affiliations – depending on the extent of their *loyalty*,[33] and also on the assets they possess – that the accumulation of a social capital rich in structural holes can be a source of profits for the opportunistic networker.

Similarly, the networker seeks to exploit asymmetries of information to the hilt. From his experience he derives an image of useful connections, but he keeps it to himself and (unlike the network-extender) does everything in his power to prevent those close to him constructing an effective topology of the network. He shrouds himself in secrecy and, above all, does not put the different arenas he manoeuvres in touch with one another. The object is to avoid these multiple contacts getting to know one another via him and, by linking up in durable fashion, having the chance to circulate useful information without going through him. Discretion is especially necessary with intimates (participants in the same project or, in network terms, members of the same 'clique'). Because the latter already possess much of the information capital that the networker uses to operate, they can get the most out of transfers of new information or new connections. Discretion makes it possible to neutralize potential rivals, without thereby being regarded as a traitor, in such a way as not to lose the advantages conferred by the trust and devotion of old friends and close collaborators. In fact, it is advisable to avert any suspicion of duplicity or strategic action. Likewise, if it is to inspire trust and prove genuinely profitable, each new encounter must be presented as fortuitous and disinterested. The same discretion is therefore indicated with new contacts, in order to avoid them either using the connection to extend their own network without paying the requisite price, or taking fright. Because different milieux separated by more or less rigid boundaries still exist, or because the people involved have an often conflictual history, not all connections are immediately compatible, so that the reputation of certain links ('bad company') can hamper establishing other connections. So it is by maintaining a separation between the different sections of networks which he has managed to bridge that the networker can become a *keyholder*. Consequently, his activity contributes to the creation of mafias,[34] networks of corruption, 'privilege', 'buddies', and so on. In the neo-management literature, these are so many terms designating bad networks, appropriated in a purely selfish way which cannot, therefore, form the basis of a projective city.

Not all positions are equally auspicious for developing networking activity. One interesting solution is to hold a post in an institution (firm, public service, association) in such a way as to dispose of resources (basic wage, work tools such as telephone, photocopier, computer, e-mail, etc.), an identity and legal guarantees, without encountering market constraints head-on (as is the case with the self-employed *entrepreneur*), or having direct responsibilities for subordinates (as is the case with the *manager*).[35] The opportunistic networker endeavours instead to get other people – entrepreneurs or those in charge of institutions – to bear the risks attaching to the operations he conducts, while he concentrates on seeking to rake in the profits. The best starting-point for developing operations as a networker thus seems to be that which provides access to the highest level of resources compatible with the lowest level of supervision, with a view to putting *company property* at the service of personal activity as a *networker*.

Take a *networker* participating in a collective endeavour, with access to resources and comparatively exempt from bureaucratic forms of supervision. He has given up the idea of a career, knows that the mechanism he is participating in is temporary, and is consequently not unaware that he will have to switch activities in the not too distant future. For him, a good strategy consists not, as management recommends, in sharing information and links with his team and benefiting the centre he depends on. Quite the reverse: it consists in exploiting the resources he has access to, and acquiring a social capital that will give him an advantage over the team's other members. Essentially, what is gained in the process is time. Thanks to his mobility, the networker steals a march on potential rivals – that is to say, collaborators and friends in many cases – and publicizes something original (product, idea, text, etc.) that is henceforth associated with his name and person. The networker has succeeded when, at the end of a project, something can be attributed to him and publicly associated with his name. This *something* does not necessarily possess the stability and objectivity that characterize an *œuvre*. As with the 'performance' artist, the important thing for the networker is to create a *happening* and to *put his name* to it. The shared skill and knowledge of the team are immediately devalued; this reduces the chances of the other members pursuing their activity or being employed on a different project. But even before this disastrous outcome, as a result of the relative isolation in which the networker tried to keep them, their skills were not being developed; they were learning nothing they did not already know, and were not being enriched through contact with others.

The activity of networkers can be a source of major problems for those they have connections with. It also creates supervision problems in the firms or organizations they operate out of. Encouraged in so far as they show a profit, they also provoke disquiet because their propensity to steer these profits towards the firm depends solely on their loyalty, which is uncertain. In fact, just as, in the case of bureaucratized firms, managers can develop different interests from those of the owners or shareholders (e.g. an interest in expanding the number of wage-earners under their authority), so networkers can develop interests that diverge from those of managers, whose power is exercised over the things required for institutions to function. They do not have the same temporal horizon. The transient, fluid character of the networker's activities prompts him to derive the maximum personal profit from each operation, without worrying unduly about the consequences for the institution from which he derives his resources. In a world regarded as extremely uncertain and fluctuating, the *self* is the only element worth the effort of identifying and developing, since it is the only thing that presents itself as even minimally *enduring*. Each of the operations that he transports himself through is thus an opportunity for the networker to aggrandize his self, to inflate it. He is 'his own entrepreneur'. For him, the value of the activity he participates in, of the 'mission' entrusted to him by a firm, will thus depend predominantly on how far it allows him to aggrandize himself by expanding and diversifying the universe of things and persons that can be associated with him, which represent the assets he will commit in new displacements. But in this logic, conflicts may develop with the unit – firm or administration – that initiated the project or provided the resources. These conflicts may centre on questions of property in particular, especially when the goods in dispute, being not objects but persons or immaterial goods, are difficult to protect – for example, customers, suppliers, ideas.

As we have seen, the development of opportunistic behaviour in a connexionist world harms the other members of work communities, whose employability diminishes, as well as the institutions that supplied the networker with resources he has not necessarily paid for. These observations indicate the possibility of forms of exploitation specific to a connexionist world. We must now construct a concept of exploitation tailored to a society in which, alongside the industrial and commercial worlds referred to by classical formulations of exploitation, the connexionist world assumes ever greater salience. This reformulation of exploitation will make it possible to bridge the gap currently separating this notion from that of exclusion.

Exploitation in a network world

A theory of exploitation must demonstrate that the success and strength of some actors are *in fact* attributable, at least in part, to the intervention of others, whose activity is neither acknowledged nor valued. Creating this critical perspective first of all presupposes the existence of a shared world. To relate exclusion to exploitation, we must, as a minimum, be in a position to found a principle of solidarity between the good fortune of the strong (great men) and the misery of the weak (little people). If, on one side, we have highly prosperous strong people and, on the other, little people in a miserable state, but there is no link between them and they move in completely different worlds, then the idea of exploitation has no meaning. They must at least share a common world. This common world can be identified here from an intuitive sense of the network. The network does indeed constitute the form which, revolving around relations, makes it possible to include within the same graph not only the strongest and the weakest but also, because the aggregates of relations can be more or less dense, the most connected and the least connected, the integrated and the unintegrated, the included, featuring at the centre of the diagram, and the excluded, expelled to its margins.

But can the strong and the weak not belong to a shared world without the good fortune of the one depending on the misfortune of the other, and vice versa? For us to be able to talk about exploitation, there must be an interdependence between them that is not merely structural (the supremacy the strong owe to the wealth of their links exists only differentially, by comparison with the poverty of the links connecting the weak to the rest of the world), but also substantial. In a world where the ability to forge relations is a source of profit, this must enable us to identify the missing portion without which the good fortune of the great man remains a *mystery* (as Marx puts it in connection with the valorization of capital); to clarify what this missing portion consists in; and demonstrate that it is, *in reality*, contributed by the little people, without the fraction of value added that should accrue to them being distributed accordingly.

So what is the missing portion, extracted from the little people, that explains the strength of great men in a connexionist world? To claim that the little people have contributed to the value-creating process, we must be in a position to show that they are useful in the construction of profitable links. If this is not the case, they are poor in links – which is a pity for them – but they contribute nothing. What the weak contribute must at once possess limited visibility, not be acknowledged in the framework of this world, and have meagre value (otherwise the injustice done to them would be obvious), while contributing to its enrichment. The following response may be offered: the specific contribution of little people to enrichment in a connexionist world, and the source of their exploitation by great men, consists precisely in that which constitutes their weakness in this framework – that is to say, their immobility.

In fact, in a connexionist world, mobility – the ability to move around autonomously not only in geographical space, but also between people, or in mental space, between ideas – is an essential quality of great men, such that the little people are characterized primarily by their fixity (their inflexibility). Once again, we should not attach too much importance to the distinction between specifically geographical or spatial mobility and other forms of mobility. In effect, connections of any significance are highly liable to be translated at some stage into geographical *rapprochement*; conversely, there is a strong likelihood that disconnections will result in a spatial distance. Obviously, this is even truer if we redefine geographical distance in the language of networks, where it is measured by the number and intensity of links. (In this case, someone who has always lived in the same town, but who has completely changed their set of relations, may be regarded as having made a move in the space of the network.) Geographical or spatial mobility may thus always be regarded as a paradigmatic expression of mobility.

Great men do not stand still. Little people remain rooted to the spot. It is by moving around that great men create new links. It is by remaining where they are that little people lose their potentially most profitable links (process of exclusion). A person is situated somewhere along with others; the others move on, and she stays behind. Ultimately, that person remains alone or connected by weak links to the core of the network.[36] That is why 'exclusion' may be envisaged as a process – that is to say, as an unintentional process that does not presuppose imputing to human beings a wish to exclude others from their circle.

But this is insufficient for an understanding of how those who do not move around (or move less) contribute to the formation of the value added of those who do (more). It may be argued that they do not move because they are stay-at-homes or are timid, that they have fixed ideas and habits, or because they are married, have children, or an elderly mother, and so on. But that is their business, even their fault. They are not prepared to make the sacrifices required to move. Certainly, this disadvantages them. But it in no way disadvantages those who do move. The exploitation has still not been detected. To identify it, it must be understood that *some people's immobility is necessary for other people's mobility*.

A connexionist world is haunted by a very acute tension between the proximate and the remote, the local and the global. And this tension weighs particularly upon great men, since they embody the truth of this world. To acquire high status in this world, it is advisable to move around incessantly, in order to cultivate new links. And it is preferable to move around in person (to attend the conference, to make contact with one's business partner, etc.). As we have seen, to designate the kind of active population to which strength is attributed in a connexionist world, Ronald Burt has used the term social capital, meaning by this that the relations established in a network are convertible into something else – in particular, into money, since otherwise the reference to 'capital' would be purely analogical.[37] But a characteristic of social capital by contrast, for example, with finance capital is that it possesses limited autonomy with respect to people. It is only weakly separated from them. It circulates poorly if people do not circulate with it. In this respect, social capital is comparable to human labour before the construction of the liberal divide between persons and their labour, labour and the labourer. This is why increases in social capital encounter a temporal limit. Hence the advice to investors to avoid forging superfluous links. But Burt also observes that one of the advantages we anticipate from relations with well-placed people is that they will say good things about us in our absence, when we cannot be present at an opportune moment (e.g. when it comes to finding a collaborator for a particular endeavour, or naming the head of some new project). Burt (who like most of those who think in network terms, adopts the standpoint of the strong) is obviously thinking exclusively about reputation. But this remark can put us on the track to identifying the contribution of the little people to the strength of great men in a connexionist world.

By remaining *in situ*, little people secure the presence of the strong there – the latter cannot be everywhere at once – and maintain the links they have cultivated for them. Thanks to them, the temporal (natural) limits to the expansion of social capital can be overcome. We shall say that in a connexionist world, the little people are *stand-ins*. The great man establishes a link from a distance. He connects a person (who is possibly herself at the centre of a clique) and he chooses or deposits someone to maintain the link in this place. The stand-in must remain in the place where he has been installed. His remaining in this node of the network allows the great man to move around. Without his aid, in the course of his displacements the great man would lose as many connections as he made. He would never manage to accumulate. Capital would escape him. What use would a mobile phone (a major connexionist object) be, if you could not be certain of finding someone at the end of the line, in place, on the ground, who can act in your stead, because he has what is to be acted on to hand?

In a connexionist world, where high status presupposes displacement, great men derive part of their strength from the immobility of the little people, which is the source of their poverty. The least mobile actors are a salient factor in the profits that the mobile derive from their displacements. In fact, in a world where everyone moved around, movements would be uncertain; and with the sites it is possible to move between losing all particularity, all singularity (since they would no longer be maintained in their specificity by actors who have remained *in situ*), the profits produced by displacement, and particularly by creating connections between beings or worlds that are distant because they are different, would tend to disappear.

If it is true that some people's immobility is the precondition for the profits others derive from their ability to move around, and that mobility procures incomparably greater profits than those who remain *in situ* can aspire to, then we may say that the immobile are exploited in relation to the mobile. They are exploited in the sense that the role they play as a factor in production does not receive the acknowledgement it merits; and that their contribution to the creation of value added is not remunerated at the requisite level for its distribution to be deemed fair.

The inequality seems even greater if it is considered over time, as a cumulative process. There is every chance that the least mobile will see the share of profit they could expect at the beginning of the period diminish; and that with time they will lose the relative security which, in another state of exploitative relations, could be anticipated in exchange for stability and loyalty (notably to oneself), which are highly prized in terms of foresight and prudence. In effect, little people who have remained *in situ* do not develop their ability to be mobile and establish new links (i.e., in the terminology being coined in firms, their 'employability'). As a result, their status depends upon the interest of their principal in maintaining the local connections they ensure. The value of little people who have remained *in situ* accrues to them from the link they have with some great man to whom it reverts. Stand-ins profit from the links they have with the great man. But little people do not profit from the relational capital amassed by the great man, since the latter, whose agent they are, is a *keyholder* for them. And they have no direct connection with the beings on whose relations the great man capitalizes. They are invariably oblivious of its very existence. The great man moves around (this is what accounts for his quality as a great man). The connections are not permanent. Firms come and go. Projects change. It can thus happen that the stand-ins become useless. They age with the investments in social capital on which their position depends. The link whose preservation they ensured *in situ* loses its relevance. The principal cuts the links (which cost nothing to maintain) with his agent. The stand-in is released, but his strength, and even his ability to survive, diminish accordingly. Cut off from those who represented the indispensable keyholder to more varied, remote connections, the *stand-in* is relegated to the edge of the network, and dragged into a process of exclusion.

In a network world, everyone thus lives in a state of permanent anxiety about being disconnected, rejected, abandoned on the spot by those who move around. This is why today local roots, loyalty and stability paradoxically constitute factors of *job insecurity* and are, moreover, increasingly experienced as such, as is indicated by the reluctance of young people in marginal positions – for example, doing jobs or living in regions in decline – to settle down in life, to borrow to buy accommodation (rather than renting), to marry (rather than cohabit), to have children (rather than an abortion in the hopes of keeping one's job), and so on. Thus, 'disaffiliation' can be initiated by self-defensive behaviour in a situation of job insecurity, the paradoxical result of which is to increase the insecurity.[38]

One effect of the new enterprise mechanisms especially relevant for our subject is that they thus increase the weight of inequalities stemming from the extent and diversity of the networks over which people can circulate. In contrast to those whose survival depends upon local, dense and compact networks, and who find themselves exposed to all manner of risks as soon as they stray from them, there are individuals and groups who, being able to circulate across extensive networks, owe their security not to the support of territorial protections, but to the preservation of the space on which the stability or, if you like, the interconnection of the circuits they move around depends on.

The remarks above do not, however, exhaust the charge of indignation contained in the idea of exploitation. Alongside those forms of exploitation that might be characterized as weak (they offend *only* the sense of justice, as it were), there exists *exploitation in the strong sense*, involving offence against the very dignity of human beings.[39] Critique relies here on the principle of dignity, in the sense of the impossibility of consigning people once and for all to a single form of status: someone who is a little person in one respect must always have every opportunity to be great in another. To diminish a human person so that she is no longer in a position to demonstrate her worth in any sphere is thus to attack what constitutes her dignity as a human being. Now, the treatment meted out to people in one world – here that of work – can be so unjust as to prevent them from showing what they are capable of in other worlds. How can exploitation (in the weak sense) in one world lead to exploitation in the strong sense in all possible worlds? By assuming such an intense form that it affects vitality itself – that is to say, all the reproductive capacities possessed by an individual. In the industrial world, this borderline form of exploitation consists in exhaustion through work. What about a connexionist world? Extreme forms of exploitation are expressed in an increasingly drastic privation of links and the gradual emergence of an inability not only to create new links, but even to maintain existing links (separation from friends, breaking of family ties, divorce, political abstentionism). Is it not this absence of links, this inability to create them, this complete jettisoning that constitute the condition of the 'excluded' as frequently described today?

We must nevertheless test this model of exploitation in a network world, in order properly to understand the world of work with its injustices as described in Chapter 4. To this end, we shall have to generalize the working diagram that has just been set out. For demonstration purposes, it was constructed exclusively on the basis of interindividual relations, so that it was able to describe with the same schema, exploiting mobility differentials, both the exploitation of some people on an individual basis and people in so far as they belong to collectives such as firms, countries and classes that are disadvantaged in respect of mobility.

Testing the exploitation of the immobile by the mobile

What is habitually condemned as one of the current sources of inequalities – that is to say, either the power of financial markets or globalization – does indeed pertain to the mobile/immobile differential such as we have analysed it above.

As has frequently been observed, *financial markets* move their investments around at a pace that is out of all proportion to the commodity exchanges that not so long ago underlay the basics of international financial fluctuations.[40] If our model is accepted, they are the premier exploiters, for the most mobile, in a long chain of sequential exploitation. The logic of their action encourages those of their victims who can do so to become as flexible as capital is mobile, in order to retain a greater share of the value added. This in turn triggers other phenomena of exploitation, with everyone except those situated at the two ends of the chain being simultaneously exploiter and exploited.

Financial markets may be regarded as exploiting countries or firms. They shift capital to a country (currency purchases, loans to the state,[41] acquisition of an interest in local firms), but can withdraw it at any moment (this possibility being stipulated as a condition of investment). The country involved, for its part, does not possess such mobility. It needs this money for development purposes, and its sudden withdrawal plunges it into crisis. Rather than being the gauge of its economic vitality, its currency instead reflects the confidence markets have in it, and the nature of their strategy for profit-taking at a given moment. Moreover, if capital is withdrawn, the currency nosedives, thus linking – contrary to the theory – the economic health of the country affected to the rate of its currency.[42] In order for investors to agree not to withdraw their funds, interest rates then rise, with the result that immobile agents – the states financed by the taxation of taxpayers who cannot flee taxation, like the indebted inhabitants – find themselves crushed under the debt burden, the weight of interest charges. Those who can unilaterally decide to withdraw dictate their price, their interest rate, to those who are left on the spot – 'stuck', to use the very term employed by financial dealers.

The extreme mobility of investors thus represents a constant threat to firms, whose capital is not, as they say, 'bolted down'. If the firm does not yield the returns they expect, they possibly sell it to an asset-stripper; if they sense that it could be run better, its lowish share price potentially makes it the victim of a takeover bid.[43] Industrialists who must invest long term, who possess assets that are not mobile – factories, machines – are in constant fear of losing the support of their financial backers, of no longer being able to realize the capital expansion they are intent on, or paying very dearly for it, since, in order to mobilize a certain sum, they will have to 'dilute' their capital significantly (since the price of shares is low, they will have to issue many more). They fear losing the confidence of their lenders, who are often the very people who hold their shares now that markets have been decompartmentalized,[44] and will impose high interest rates. Moreover, following a logic largely independent of that of firms, market fluctuations are always liable, as a result of changes in exchange or interest rates, to wipe out the industrial profits that have been achieved with such difficulty. Indeed, not content to use their greater mobility to demand higher returns, they can also tap profits directly in the chain of value: the turbulence they create prompts firms to cover themselves and, to that end, to buy financial products sold by the markets themselves, who have thus hit upon the means of being behind the ills for which they then sell the remedies.[45]

In response to this pressure, firms globalize themselves so that they become unavoidable.[46] Wherever investors go, they always come across the same actors, the same brands, the same products. There will soon be only four or five firms in each market. Their mobility is reduced accordingly. By becoming gigantic, firms liberate themselves from market tutelage, since above a certain size no candidate is large enough to buy them, so that the risk of a takeover bid recedes. For their part, shareholders, in line with market theory, demand that they be able to make the arbitrages themselves, to place their money where they wish, in trade and countries that are of financial interest to them. They desire, and sometimes obtain, this mobility: the chemicals giants, for example, are breaking up to give rise to two groups, one chemical, the other pharmaceutical. But the multinationals react in turn and, by globalizing, once again restrict the margins of arbitrage of the markets, which can no longer select their country of implantation. Firms seek to establish themselves in numerous countries, in order to make the arbitrages between regions themselves and secure the profit that the markets would otherwise wrest from them. And they also learn to play the markets directly, competing here with traditional actors for financial profits.[47]

Although they are less mobile than the financial markets, *multinationals* are scarcely more loyal to a country, region or site. In order to retain or attract them, it is now accepted that states or local communities will pay them, offer land, reduce taxes, and so on. The most mobile impose their price, but they do not really commit themselves to staying. They are always on the point of leaving.[48]

When the 'partner to exploit' is a country, global firms, although they are themselves victims of financial markets, may ally with them, as we have seen with the recent draft of the Multilateral Agreement on Investment (MAI) developed within the OECD.[49] This agreement was intended to ensure freedom of movement for direct foreign investment, which can be long-term industrial investment or the simple acquisition of financial holdings.[50] The draft was intended to complete the range of multilateral agreements on trade in goods (GATT) and services (GATS). Among the agreement's provisions, we find that 'payments linked to investments, particularly capital transactions, profits and dividends, must be able to be made freely to or from the host country'. The entry and residence of key personnel were likewise to be guaranteed. Moreover, the agreement sought to abolish most of the room for action by states on the investments made in their territory. The imposition of certain obligations on investors, such as minimal targets for the export of goods or services, was earmarked for proscription; equality between investors was to be guaranteed – a firm with national capital, for example, not being able to benefit from subsidies if foreign firms were excluded from them; the purchase of land, for example, could not be restricted to nationals; numerous clauses provided for compensation of investors and firms in the event of government intervention likely to limit their ability to profit from their investment, and to have a discriminatory effect on foreign capital in practice. Likewise, the political risk attaching to a country's situation was no longer to be the responsibility of investors, however desirous they might be of setting up there, but states. According to the draft, firms were thus to be entitled to compensation in the event of 'civil strife', 'revolution, states of emergency or other similar events'.

As the most mobile firms, *multinationals* can exploit this displacement differential to put pressure on firms that are smaller to start with. They have the financial power to close a factory in one place and reopen it elsewhere; or, even more rapidly, to sell a factory in one place in order to buy another in a different country. Relocation leaves all those who earned their livelihood from the closed factory out of a job: its wage-earners, its subcontractors, but also all those who derived their income from the latter (businesses, suppliers of the suppliers, etc.). In this way, part of the network dies, asphyxiated. In the case of the sale, not closure, of a factory, it leaves those who have remained *in situ* with the task of winning the new owner's favour.

The considerable switch to outsourcing and globalization that we have witnessed may thus be construed, at least in part, as the result of a wish to be streamlined, so as one can move more rapidly. An integrated firm that owns all its subcontractors will think twice before relocating. The problem is reduced when, wherever one is located, one buys 70 per cent of one's turnover from different suppliers.

To meet this risk, suppliers and subcontractors globalize and streamline in turn. Mobility must be met with mobility. If they are not to risk being left in the lurch themselves some day, they must be able to follow their client to the ends of the earth. They sometimes even manage to be more mobile than their clients – as we can see, for example, in the case of car parts manufacturers who today make larger profits than the manufacturers themselves. But this disparity is partially attributable to the fact that the manufacturers are owners of the appropriate equipment for making specific items for their different vehicles (e.g. the moulds with which their subcontractors make the dashboards). Such equipment can certainly be moved around the world, but it is not transferable from one vehicle to the next. By contrast, the subcontractors, relieved of these specific investments, enjoy a very low change-of-model cost. They are not penalized when market preferences alter, prompting the manufacturers to design other vehicles, since they continue to make the components without having pay the fixed costs for them. In an initial phase, the manufacturers succeeded in streamlining significantly by transferring production to the components suppliers. But they wanted to remain 'owners' of the vehicles (in conformity with the second spirit of capitalism), without realizing that they were thereby still overburdening themselves. Faced with the success of their suppliers, today they therefore envisage streamlining further by transferring the burden of ownership of the equipment to them.[51] As we can see from this example, mobility has a geographical dimension, but more generally it manifests itself in a detachment from anything that is too specific, too bound up with precise circumstances (with what cannot be transferred to other factories in the case to hand). Modular, flexible, non-specific industrial equipment is spreading. It is shifted around more easily geographically, but also from one output to another.

Consumers are another source of instability. Like the impersonal shareholder, the consumer decides whether to buy, and is not constrained by any loyalty.

Firms have sought to achieve a level of mobility tailored to the supposed volatility of consumer desires. They work on a just-in-time basis so that they do not risk being left with unsold stock. They produce exactly what consumers want when *they* want it – a feat they can bring off only by bearing down on the mobility of subcontractors, who invariably have larger stocks than their customers,[52] and use processes that are more labour-intensive (more personnel for less turnover). The subcontractors will themselves seek to streamline – that is to say, offload on to other actors the burden of minimum immobility required to conduct business. For it is clearly necessary to possess sites with a minimum of stability in which to set up factories for production, or marketing centres rooted in a territory, which the customer does not have to seek out every day, where they may have thought it good to move to. In these relatively stable sites, they must find a local workforce, at least while they are trading. But the less capacity for mobility this workforce has, the less it can go and find a job elsewhere, the easier it will be to impose casual status on it. Consequently, it is possible to reduce the plant's activity from one day to the next without resorting to redundancies and a redundancy scheme, simply by no longer using temporary workers from the country or region where it has been established – which makes it possible for other prior mechanisms to be as streamlined and mobile as possible.

This is why it is a significant error to include in the same category the flexibility and job insecurity of the temp with the mobility of the consumer or multinational. In one instance, flexibility is chosen, is a source of strength, is assertive; in the other, it is imposed, and turns out to be the reverse of freedom. The mobility of the exploiter has as its counterpart the flexibility of the exploited. Consigned to an agonizing job insecurity that does not afford freedom of mobility and does not allow them to develop their capacity for it – when it does not destroy it, that is – flexible workers are candidates for exclusion with the next displacement by the strongest (e.g. at the end of the temporary contract). So too are wage-earners who – for health reasons, for example – can no longer keep up with the furious tempo imposed on them.

Thus firms seek to reduce what might tie them to a territory or workforce that little bit more every day. Their efforts focus on production with the development of outsourcing and streamlined, modular equipment, but also on distribution, where an attempt is made to reduce physical sites. The development of mail-order sales using all available media (telephone, post, the Internet),[53] or of franchising networks, which mean that network heads do not have to bear the burden of all the assets, is indicative of this. A firm operating by mail-order selling and subcontracting manufacture possesses virtually no assets any more; it rents its registered office, and its value consists in its data files and the know-how of a handful of people who design, buy and sell. It can establish itself almost anywhere if its most indispensable personnel are ready to follow, but it has also become so streamlined that it might well stay where its key personnel want to live. Thus it is that the most mobile, the most employable, those who constitute the key personnel, are also those who can most easily compel their employer to allow them a settled way of life without the attendant risks.

These processes demonstrate that the experts are right when they urge people and firms to be mobile. What is at stake is being more mobile, less ponderous, than one's customer or employer: only then is the balance of forces restored. The well-informed specialist whom everyone is after is spoilt for choice. He can quit and find a new job the following day, and threats to resign will secure significant remuneration. The wage-earner who learns languages easily and switches jobs without too much difficulty can accompany his employer in his mobility; he is at one with the firm, and runs less risk of being left behind. All the rest will find themselves exploited on account of their lesser mobility. By threatening to break the link and abandon them – something that is easier if one is organized to move rapidly – employers force a lower wage out of them, and condemn them to putting up with the last links of the chain: market vagaries. The mobility imperative has been so well assimilated in practice that a firm which closes a site while offering redeployment five hundred kilometres away can claim to be making a closure without redundancies: if people do not follow, that, after all, is their own fault; if they are made redundant, it is because they wished it upon themselves.

In such circumstances, wage-earners whose knowledge or know-how is at once the most specialist and the least specific are the best paid, because they can switch rapidly from one firm to the next, and it is difficult to do without them. Thus, financial staff rely on skills that are relatively stable thanks to the financial markets, which use the same mathematical models everywhere, and to the standardization of accounting rules within a country and, increasingly, on a global scale, through multinationals that are all quoted on the same markets. Contrariwise, members of the industrial workforce responsible for managing factories employing several hundred people, and administering industrial assets, are badly paid, since their skills are bound up with encumbrances – that is to say, people and industrial plants. In addition, these *cadres* risk never being as useful as when they are involved in specific industrial processes that they know well, where they have made their whole career – heavy chemical industry, mechanical engineering, textiles, plastics, and so on. Their knowledge is less transferable. They have to remain in their sector. *Cadres* must therefore learn to standardize their knowledge in order to acquire transferability, by emulating financiers or consultants, who apply the same models of analysis and decision-making everywhere. It would therefore be in their interest to develop global certifications for occupations that are currently too specific, in order to enhance their mobility. Those who are very competent when it comes to a certain kind of product, business sector, or type of technology are indispensable, for without them machines break down, products cease to leave the factory, technical improvements do not get made. But because they are too local, too specific, they have depreciated in value. Only a handful of experts can hope to profit from their specialist knowledge. But there is a strong chance that they will be outstripped, that the day will dawn when their expertise will be outmoded. And in order to keep up to date, they must make considerable effort and investment, much more so than those who possess specialist but highly transferable – that is, non-specific – knowledge.

At all levels of the chain, those who are more mobile extort surplus-value from the less mobile, in exchange for a slackening in their own mobility. In exchange for a temporary suspension of the threat to relocate, the firm pays its workforce less, or casualizes it. Investors demand a higher return in exchange for a long-term commitment because – so they say – they run more risks if they cannot withdraw, and must be compensated for this risk. Countries subsidize multinationals to get them to accept being associated with their territory for a few years. Thus, in France, one and the same firm may be aided to close a factory in one place and create jobs in another.

The mobility differential is thus a highly valued commodity today. Its price is rising rapidly and is paid exclusively by the 'slow', who thereby get the 'rapid' to harmonize their pace and slow down somewhat. However, the rapid would not be able to survive without the aid of settled activities; and the network that they inspire cannot do without territorial inscription and the work of machines and human beings, those encumbrances *par excellence*. Their project is to get rich without supporting these burdens, by purchasing from subcontractors, affixing their brand, and reselling on the Internet, while collecting the greater part of the surplus-value produced by the whole of the chain in the process.

Thus there appear to be innumerable relations of exploitation based on mobility differentials: financial markets versus countries; financial markets versus firms; multinationals versus countries; large principal versus small subcontractor; world expert versus firm; firm versus casual workforce; consumer versus firm.

In so far as we are dealing with capitalism – a process striving for an ever greater accumulation of capital measured by a monetary value; and in so far as the tests for sharing value added between the different actors who are parties to the process (consumers, wage-earners, subcontractors and suppliers, financiers, etc.) take the form of contracts with a price, it might seem that the phenomena referred to above can be described exclusively in the terminology of commercial status (as is done by denigrators of 'neo-liberalism'). Yet nothing could be more incomplete, for an analysis in terms of the extension of market relations does not account for the generalization of a balance of forces bound up with mobility. Instead, commercial status everywhere enters into compromise with connexionist status, to the point where the relations established in markets are largely redefined.

The commercial balance of forces depends primarily on a difference in accumulated capital or credit at the point of the transaction (the wealthy person who can pay more wins out over the poor person, if both desire the product); or in desirability (some object or service costs more because it is more desirable; a supplier can dictate his price because he crafts things so distinctively that he makes himself indispensable). In a standard model of market dominance, it matters little that the supplier could move, or that the highly placed *cadre* could travel anywhere in the world, or that both are more mobile than their customers or their employers. For in and of itself, this variableness does not make them more desirable. They are simply more difficult to control. In a connexionist world, by contrast, it is not only the quality and scarcity of a product or service that are valued. The premium accruing from the mobility differential is added to the price paid. The most mobile can in fact threaten to 'exit' at any moment, in line with the opportunities open to them on account of their potential for variability; hence they are well placed to negotiate the price of the goods and services they offer.

A good example of the difference between a commercial justification and a connexionist justification is the nature of the reasons given to explain policies of flexibility and the development of organizational mobility. The argument most frequently invoked is the rapidity with which a new product is brought on to the market. What is at stake here is to be quicker than competitors in tapping the resources of the potential market. In this instance, the recommended mobility is legitimate, since the 'enemy' is the direct competitor. On the other hand, the idea that an advantage in terms of mobility constitutes a strength when it comes to bargaining with suppliers, wage-earners or customers is never mentioned. However, a firm that acquires the requisite mobility to bring a new product on to the market quickly has also gained in mobility on the other counts. For in order to achieve this, it has had to revise its organization thoroughly. More streamlined, it can then utilize this advantage in other situations. Legitimate market mobility is what makes it possible to move faster than competitors, not what makes it possible to 'blackmail' job-seekers. To justify a reduction in the pay of non-mobile wage-earners, recourse to a different justification – of a connexionist nature – is required, depreciating everything about them that is inflexible. This kind of justification is currently gaining in legitimacy.

2. TOWARDS CONNEXIONIST MECHANISMS OF JUSTICE?

In this section, we shall examine some mechanisms currently being proposed, notably by jurists, which are at the heart of debates about work. What they have in common, we think, is that their implementation would make it possible to realize the projective city by combining it with tests that allow us, in the name of the very principles this city is based on, to denounce unjust ways of

profiting from mobility, and thus restrict the level of exploitation in a connexionist world. But in order to consolidate the link between the problematic
of exploitation and that of the 'cities', we must first of all show how this very
specific form of exploitation, based on a mobility differential to which the
paragraphs above have been devoted, is only one particular instance of a more
general model: a model that can describe asymmetrical situations taking advantage of a multiplicity of differentials – including, obviously, the property
differential or the market differential of scarcity on which classical theories of
exploitation are based.

Elements of a general grammar of exploitation

In the context of capitalism that is of particular interest to us here, the idea
of exploitation can be formulated as follows. The test of strength typical of
capitalism, which is converted into a multitude of local tests, concerns the
remuneration of contributions to profit creation. Condemning exploitation
means that certain contributions have not received their just remuneration.

This operation, which is always open to challenge, presupposes establishing a vast mechanism of *accounting equivalences*, extending the range of
calculation in time and space. One characteristic of capitalism in comparison
with other regimes (like slavery or serfdom) is that exploitation under it does
not necessarily assume a patent, visible form. The existence of exploitation
always assumes some form of coercion. But whereas in pre-capitalist societies
exploitation is invariably direct, in capitalism it passes through a series of
detours that mask it. On the one hand, it is disclaimed juridically, since the
actors who contribute to production are in a contractual relationship. On the
other, it is not reducible to a relationship of duress that manifests itself in a
face-to-face situation, but possesses a systemic character. It involves actors
who operate from a distance, possibly in ignorance of one another and with
different intentions. Those who exercise close control (the *cadre* or administrator) are not necessarily those who derive the greatest profit from it (e.g.
shareholders). Accordingly, very long chains, comprising a large number of
mediations that are difficult to relate to one another, are often required to level
an accusation of exploitation (e.g. to relate the activity of a dealer in a trading
room in London to the poverty of street-children in the shantytown of an
African city).

The accounting framework that must be in place for a dispute over the existence of exploitation to arise must make it possible to identify the bodies
which contribute to profit-creation, and the contributions made by each of
them. In the first instance, this identification will revolve around beings, particularly people, between whom it must be possible to demonstrate a functional
interdependence. Next, it must state what each party has contributed and,
finally, what the level of remuneration of each contribution should be if it is

to count as just. The denunciation of exploitation – which can always be challenged from another accounting position and, as a result, issue in a dispute – can be based on each of these processes of identification. It may consist in demonstrating that beings contributing to the creation of the profit have been forgotten or neglected, or that their contributions have not been identified in full, or been underestimated. The strength of conviction of these denunciations will depend in large part upon the greater or lesser distance separating the beings between whom a relationship of exploitation is posited (asserting a relationship of exploitation between beings who are very distant, and at least one of whom disclaims any relationship with the others, will readily be deemed 'paranoid'), and upon the robustness of the system of accounting equivalences that orchestrates these denunciations.

But it is not enough to reveal a calculable injustice. To sustain an accusation of exploitation, it is equally necessary to specify the nature of *the strength on which the unequal division is based*, and also what makes it invisible (otherwise, unveiling it would be pointless). Thus, for example, in order to denounce a form of exploitation in pre-industrial societies, where social bonds rest largely on kinship, Marxist anthropology has sought to demonstrate that the strength differential making exploitation possible is based on relations of personal dependence grounded in membership of a lineage, and prescribed forms of subordination and fealty.

In classical Marxist denunciations of the exploitation prevalent in industrial society, the strength that makes the unequal division possible stems from a property differential (i.e. on a legal category): it is because some (capitalists) own the means of production (tools) that they can exploit those who, not possessing the means of production, can enter into production only as sellers of their labour-power.[54] In this instance, restoring a less unequal division assumes that those who own the means of production are equally dependent on those who own their labour-power. Given that ownership of the means of production is concentrated, whereas the ownership of labour-power is atomized, the route to greater social justice involves the workers combining in trade unionism.

The same kind of reasoning has been employed to denounce exploitation in socialist contexts and, more generally, in bureaucratic organizations that are controlled, not by owners, but by managers. In this instance, however, the differential called into question is no longer a property differential, but a power differential (likewise legally guaranteed), which makes it possible to extort a surplus of power.[55] In effect, those who occupy the higher echelons, whose status is guaranteed by a title (educational, functional, political, etc.), assume a decision-making power which, formally attributed to them, is in reality – in the words of Claude Lefort, from whom we borrow this analysis – 'composite' and 'distributed' at 'various lower levels'. This seizure of power is concealed by the identification of inferiors with the bureaucracy exploiting them.[56] In this second case, the return to parity occurs through a redistribution of official power corresponding to the distribution of real power – that is to say, through self-management.

We can also use the framework of justifications of cities to identify differentials which, while they are sources of high status in theory, can constitute sources of strength in the context of unsupervised tests, allowing for an unequal division. As a critical idea, exploitation is in fact perfectly consistent with the norm of justice contained in the concept of 'city'. Accordingly, there are not two logics – one directed towards dissension, the other towards consensus – but two viewpoints that can be brought to bear on the world as it is from one and the same normative position.[57] In effect, denunciation of exploitation effectively inverts the maxim that 'the good fortune of great men makes for the good fortune of the little people', which constitutes the keystone of the axiomatics of cities, by asserting, on the contrary, that *the misfortune of the little people makes for the good fortune of great men*. The mystery of their greatness is to be sought not in their personal merits, but in the fact that they profit from the misfortune of the little people.[58] Their high status is the result of a differential in good fortune. Therewith the maxim 'the good fortune of great men benefits the little people' can be seen as an ideology in the Marxist sense – that is to say, an illusion serving interests, which inverts the representation of what occurs in reality, and thus masks it. Counterposed to a vision of the world from above, by those whom the tests invariably benefit, is thus a vision of the world as seen from below, by those who, measured in the same light, have experienced only repeated failure.[59] But these different viewpoints on reality coincide at the level of ethics. In effect, great men, who cannot be persistently cynical without imperilling their own greatness, subscribe to the idea that their prerogatives are legitimate by dint of their contribution to the common good. As for the little people, they can persist in believing in a formula of inverted greatness, without succumbing to nihilistic despair, only by sustaining themselves with the utopia of a possible world where the tests would be genuinely just.

The inversion of the maxim that allows us to pass from cities to exploitation also indicates a way to fight exploitation. It consists in taking the norm of justice embodied by the city seriously, and organizing things so that the tests pertaining to this norm are actually geared towards justice. In terms of the form of exploitation specific to the connexionist world, which is rooted in the mobile/immobile differential, this involves clarifying tests of mobility as they currently are, and establishing mechanisms that aim to control their conduct, as well as cleaning up non-connexionist tests – for example, putative market tests that are in fact contaminated by unacknowledged, adjoining connexionist forces. Such a move assumes the construction of new mechanisms which, while they are isomorphic with the connexionist world, would make it possible to supervise it and limit its destructive effects – rather like classification grids in the industrial world. Although these grids accepted the principle of a hierarchy of qualifications, they nevertheless endeavoured to restrict the abuses that might have occurred in its name by fixing what were deemed to be acceptable wage differentials. The establishment of new accounting frameworks, permitting an inventory of the different contributors and their contributions in a network logic, would form part of the requisite mechanisms. It would prevent networkers – that is, the exploiters in a con-nexionist world – abstaining from remunerating those who have a share in their success, or remunerating them inadequately. In the industrial world, this inventory was created by all wage-earners belonging to one large integrated firm – a framework which, as we have seen, has lost much of its relevance today.

The conditions for establishing the projective city

Establishing the mechanisms of a projective city legitimating, but also limiting, the relations of force peculiar to the connexionist world remains an optimistic scenario. There is no reason to suppose that it will be realized – or not in the near future, at any rate, and not without a major crisis. As was the case in the past with other regulatory frameworks, its realization will depend on a con-junction of various agents the logics of whose action are different.

The first condition is the existence of a persistent, menacing, inventive critique. The new social movements – of which we have given a rapid descrip-tion, and whose development has accompanied the formation and diffusion of the notion of exclusion over the last twenty years – might represent its embryo. Their adoption of the thematic of networks and projects, situating them very close to the new world, means that they are particularly well placed to invent the mechanisms of the projective city. Moreover, while remaining outside the political world in the strict sense, they have exerted constant pressure on political officials and 'experts' (senior civil servants, jurists, econ-omists, sociologists, etc.) – other actors indispensable to the orientation towards a projective city, who, without sharing their radicalism, have laid plans for mechanisms to struggle against exclusion. The upshot is a revival of activity in the domain of social reformism, some of whose proposals we shall examine a little later.

Equally indispensable to any reformist action is the participation of senior civil servants, politicians, a fraction of management that is sufficiently autonomous of capitalist interests and shareholder tutelage, and even of cap-italists who are sufficiently detached from the imperatives of capital accumulation to see the eventual dangers of an increase in inequalities and insecurity, and also to be open to the shared sense of justice. In fact, these different actors are capable of playing a leading role in trying out new mech-anisms, giving their support to reforms of the regulatory framework, and putting their pragmatism and intimate knowledge of the machinery of capitalism at the service of the common good. The interests of senior civil servants may be regarded as the easiest to mobilize. Given that their task is administering the welfare state, they cannot watch unperturbed as firms maximize their profits by offloading on to the state – and to its detriment – costs bound up with maintaining the labour force. For as Jürgen Habermas had foreseen at the start of the 1970s, this induces a legitimation crisis of the state, which, 'because of a systematic overloading of the public budget', 'lags behind the programmatic demands *that it has placed on itself*': '[t]he penalty for this failure is withdrawal of legitimation'.[60] But businessmen, particularly those with power over large collections of things and people (directors), likewise have an interest in restricting the activity of networkers, who are parasitic upon the entities they manage, as well as in equalizing the conditions of competition between each other and *vis-à-vis* financial markets.

The problems posed by the development of opportunistic behaviour in a network world affect enough people – albeit in different forms, and in sufficiently alarming fashion – for an alliance between very disparate actors to be feasible. The opportunistic networker increases the personal profit he can derive from multiplying connections, but by damaging two types of actors: on the one hand, the entity he depends on (firm, project, profit centre, institutional space, state service, association), whence he derives some of the resources he needs, but to which he does not remit the returns from his activity expected by these instances; and, on the other hand, the less mobile actors whose exploitation he increases and whose exclusion he furthers. His victims, who have different interests, can nevertheless form an alliance on selected points to impose acceptance of a particular mechanism. More profoundly, it seems that the generalization of a connexionist world without checks of any sort upon exploitation is such as to destroy the social fabric, in a process some of whose main lines we are now going to present.

To realize his dual exploitation (of institutions and of the least mobile), the networker takes advantage of a mobility differential relative to actors who, for various reasons (moral, familial, institutional, patrimonial, etc.), remain attached to a place, and whose trust he has earned (whether they be close collaborators, principals on whom he depends institutionally, or remote actors with whom he manages to connect up). In this sense, the advantages he profits from are of the order of a breach of trust. It follows that the networker's opportunistic behaviour cannot be generalized to a whole world.

A world where everyone – or a large number of agents at least, not simply a few tricksters – sought to maximize their networks by selecting well-placed targets, and practising a separation between spaces and relations, would tend to collapse in on itself. On the one hand, no one would any longer assume institutional responsibilities, which would have become too costly in immobilized workers and impossible to exercise on account of a lack of authority and the impossibility of controlling the members. Even remotely enduring institutions would collapse, when such institutions are required to maintain resources and, in particular, the stock of objects to which the networker needs access in order to operate. And this would eventually entail a destruction of the fixed capital without which a capitalist world, even in its connexionist form, cannot survive. On the other hand, trust would tend to disappear to such an extent that not only would breaching it, which constitutes the networker's strength, become very difficult, but, above all, the emergence of generalized mistrust[61] would make the establishment of any arrangements between human beings extremely problematic. Such a phenomenon would be amplified by the emergence of reflexivity effects of which Ronald Burt's book, already cited, gives an idea. In effect, if the utility of maximizing networks, and the techniques used to achieve this, were to become common knowledge – based on sociological research, manuals, training exercises – everyone would forever be on the lookout for signs of opportunism by their partners. In such a world, daily life would become difficult, and the social fabric would tend to unravel.

It is likely that in a network world that is not subject to the control of a projective city, opportunistic behaviour, even if it were adopted only by a few people to start off with, would tend to spread rapidly. We may define opportunism as consisting in not acknowledging debts contracted with other persons, either individual or collective.[62] Now, the mechanisms associated with each city have, in particular, the function of ensuring the honouring of debts that have been contracted. In a commercial world, for example, opportunism must come to terms with the mechanisms on which the validity of exchanges rests, such as those which preserve monetary equivalence or, when the exchange is not immediate, guarantee the honouring of contracts. It may thus be thought that the emergence of a connexionist logic, escaping the control mechanisms associated with already established cities, paves the way for a marked growth in opportunistic behaviour – to the point where it will in turn be curbed by constraints which the projective city, if instituted, would make it possible to set.

Connexionist opportunism cannot, for one thing, be checked by the commercial city. Profitable network links do not systematically abide by market forms and, when they are the subject of contracts, these are incomplete or describe only part of the exchange, the rest being of an unspecified character and varying with the development of the relationship. Part of the interest of connections stems in fact from the inspection of resources that were not (at least until recently) regarded as commodifiable or amenable to contracts: ideas (which, as we know, cannot be subject to any legal protection); and information about other people's relations or, for example, their state of health, their political, aesthetic, intellectual, etc., inclinations. It is this incompleteness that explains the relative inoperability of the constraints that the commercial order rests on and the frequent recourse, in the case of the connexionist world, to the theme of trust in personal relations, which seems to be borrowed from the instrumentation of a domestic world. But the domestic world does not make it possible to avoid opportunistic network behaviour either. If the significance accorded to personal relations seems at first sight to assimilate the connexionist world to the domestic world, the former is distinguished by the absence of the mechanisms that guarantee debt enforcement in the latter. In a domestic world, honouring debts that have been contracted is based upon the coexistence of the same persons in the same space, and the reciprocal control they exercise over one another. Now, in a connexionist world, mobility, which constitutes a fundamental requirement, makes it largely possible to elude the collective reprisals entailed in the former domestic world by defaulting and displaying ingratitude towards those whose support one enjoyed. Similar remarks might be made about the inability of civic mechanisms to control connexionist opportunism. As Nathalie Sarthou-Lajus observes, the very notion of the social contract in Rousseau is based on the 'recognition of mutual debts',[63] so that it constitutes the basis for mechanisms of *assistance* (in this it is distinct from charity) as a 'social debt', a 'debt of society' to the poor inasmuch as they, simply by virtue of belonging to society, are possessors of 'rights-claims'.[64] But we must add that the actual realization of such mechanisms presupposes the definition of a framework in which a relationship between the misfortune of those who suffer and the good fortune of the prosperous can be established. Such a framework is precisely what was provided by the very notion of society, largely resting on a spatial conception of the nation-state, such as it was established in the nineteenth century.[65] Now, the logic of networks, on which the connexionist world is based, does not of itself make it possible to design such a framework. Despatialized, bereft of a representative body or overarching position, and dominated by the requirement of a boundless extension of networks, it does not permit integration into the same body of the networker who succeeds, and those whom his success helps to exclude, in such a way as to create a debt between them. As a result, this logic remains indifferent to justice and, more generally, to ethics.[66] Consequently, only the implementation of mechanisms pertaining to a form of justice, and similar to those modelled in the projective city, could subject such a world to tests incorporating the notion of debt.

In addition, the demand for autonomy and the individualistic ideal of self-begetting, of self-realization as a superior form of achievement, which represent the dominant values in a connexionist world, contribute to rendering those who are comfortable in networks largely inattentive to indebtedness as a legitimate source of social bonds. Hence, in particular, networkers succeed in exploiting others by establishing relations with them that can be interpreted in terms of the logic of a domestic world (trust), but in contexts where they can extricate themselves from the forms of control on which the stability of the domestic world was based.

For the networker himself, the danger comes from the stand-in, who can in turn take advantage of the situation and misappropriate links for his own benefit.[67] It is necessary to keep an eye on him. In this instance, industrial discipline, which capitalism was built on – often in a compromise with domestic discipline – is unavailing. It is too dependent on spatial and temporal proximity.

Among the many proposals debated since the beginning of the 1990s, some seem to us to foreshadow the establishment of mechanisms capable of giving substance to the projective city by rooting it in the world of objects, and also by inscribing it in legal texts. Let us once again stress the fact that, in the absence of a powerful critical intervention, we may also see insecurity, inequalities and generalized distrust (often interpreted as one facet of a 'triumphant individualism') continue to grow.

Overview of proposals for reducing connexionist exploitation

The mechanisms – or rather, proposed mechanisms – that we are going to examine do not counterpose domestic, civic or industrial forms of regulation to the expansion of network logics. On the contrary, what is interesting about them is that they rely on the network in order to limit the destructive effects of a connexionist world. In this sense, they are not derived from a 'conservative' critique seeking to restore a world that has gone for ever.

These proposals aim to tighten up the justice of connexionist tests of strength in order to transform them into tests of status in the projective city, not to replace them by tests of a different kind. This orientation explains why they must simultaneously maintain the flexibility of networks and, by recourse to law, secure better protection for social agents – in particular, those of them who are weak. The mechanisms envisaged are not intended to protect people by preventing them from being mobile, which would thwart the aspirations to autonomy or the requirement of flexibility that have become central in neo-capitalism, but to organize this mobility and the rounds of tests. What is at stake is making opportunities for displacement available to all, while accumulating fairly – that is to say, to start off with, being remunerated justly at each stage of the displacement. The mechanisms envisaged must therefore reconcile two temporalities: a short, discontinuous temporality, corresponding to the limited projects that temporary wage-earners must engage in to get paid; and a long, continuous temporality, which is that of people's lives.

How can people circulate while accumulating and taking with them what they have amassed? We shall entertain two possibilities, associated with different types of justice from the projective city, while showing that neither is appropriate to a connexionist world.

According to a first possibility, which might be called domestic, people circulate in a familiar environment accompanied by an aura of good repute. Other than escaping from domestic restraints, this does not allow people to circulate very widely. It is not conducive to circulation in a vast world. A second possibility, based on a civic–industrial compromise, makes access to the collectives, whether occupations or statutes, with which privileges are associated dependent upon an educational title certifying an initial level of education. For circulation to be possible, work spaces must be structured in such a way as to inscribe in them a series of hierarchical positions that people can pass through in a certain order. This formula, which we may call industrial, is what the system of collective agreements rests on. But this form demands, on the one hand, strenuous efforts to establish equivalence, in order to homogenize the different portions of space and make them interdependent; and, on the other, job stability within large, planned firms, of a sort that is no longer appropriate in a world which people want to see composed of heterogeneous, independent units, where the different entities – persons, jobs, firms, products – are defined as changeable.

Current discussions about notions like 'employability', 'skill', 'activity' and 'activity contract', or 'universal income', and so on, outline the possibility of a novel formulation of the problems involved in mobility, and suggest a new compromise between autonomy and security, compatible with the logic of a projective city.

The measures that we have grouped together are of two sorts. Most are situated at the point of contact between the social policy of firms and of the state. But they do not touch on the nature of the transactions between actors in firms, or the activities leading to profit creation, or even the organization of work, these aspects being treated as so many 'black boxes' obeying different logics that it seems pointless to their initiators to seek to intervene in. These measures derive from reformist currents that propose mechanisms to combat exclusion, and aim to defend people under threat, from a standpoint that may be characterized as macroeconomic. These currents take as their starting-point a situation that supposedly imposes the same constraints on everyone, as if no one had more or less willed it, and no one found it more or less in their interests. Unemployment and the casualization are treated as the outcome of impersonal forces acting at a global level and exercising a mechanical effect on enterprise strategy, whether the stress is laid on 'globalization' or 'technological' changes. Unemployment and casualization are regarded as externalities that can be dealt with socially. At the same time, however, what is going on inside firms, and the new types of social relations instituted there, are excluded from the field of inquiry. Thus, they invariably set aside analysis of the internal selection processes in firms that lead to the casualization of some actors, while others, subject to the same global constraints, see their advantages enhanced.

A second source of proposals is none other than management itself. This time, what is at the forefront of concerns is the more or less acceptable character of relations in firms. Because its favourite subject is increasing productivity with a view to maximizing profits, management literature cannot but interest itself in the issue of whether the remuneration of different actors is really justified by their contribution to value added. Despite the significant streamlining of firms, those administering the new, slimmed-down collectives must find an answer to the question of the justice of the different remunerations that are distributed. The persistence of unduly stark imbalances would risk demoralizing wage-earners, provoking disputes between them, thus reducing their productivity. Management literature thus possesses an ethical dimension that we relied on when we drew a picture of the projective city in Chapter 2.

We are going to classify these proposals in three categories suggested by our general grammar of exploitation: (a) proposals that seek to facilitate an inventory of the actors involved in a project; (b) those that attempt to elaborate just principles of remuneration in a network; and finally (c) a certain number of proposals that aim to equalize the opportunities (or strengths) of beings – that is to say, to equalize everyone's capacity for mobility.

New frameworks for inventorying contributions

The formulas we examine in this section tend to put an end to exploitation that is bound up with the low visibility of certain contributors, who are badly paid or not paid at all because of their marginal position in the network. These proposals aim to transform accounting frameworks modelled on the firm as legal entity, even on the plant, in an attempt to encompass all the component parts of sections of highly active networks more fully. They thus seek to introduce mechanisms of representation and reflexivity into network logics. Representation and, to a lesser extent, reflexivity presuppose activities of categorization, inherent in law, which tend to set some limits on the network system (to enable adjudication on membership or non-membership), and to fix it in forms that check its deployment and constant adjustment to external conditions.

As we shall see, the complex and – at least for now – sometimes rather abstract, even fluid, character of these formulas seems to stem from their authors' concern to confer legal status on networks. The aim is to restrict the possibilities of opportunism and exploitation that are currently developing in them, without imposing inflexible legal forms – something that would render them inoperative, because they would then not capture the specificity of the configurations to which they are intended to apply.

A sort of ideal of what an accounting framework adapted to a network world would look like is provided by the way film credits are constructed. A major project, associating for a fixed term a host of people from different firms and of varying status (permanent wage-earner, contract worker in the entertainment industry, liberal professional, service provider, etc.), the feature film is wholly integrated into a connexionist logic. Intended formally to associate everyone who has contributed, however minimally, to the production of the film, the credits, as is well known, present an exhaustive list of the contributors, whatever their employer or status. Every name, even that of the most minor and fleeting collaborator, appears.

According to Günther Teubner, it is possible to envisage giving *networks an official status in law*.[68] Largely because the 'quasi-firms' made up of networks of just-in-time suppliers, franchising networks, those transferring funds in the banking sector, strategic alliances in the domain of research, and so on, are concealed 'under a contractual veil', they can extricate themselves from the social controls and regulations established in the framework of the welfare state, and from the legal constraints of labour or consumer legislation. This dissimulation has, according to Teubner, been favoured by the spread of new economic theories of the firm (and especially the 'transaction costs' approach, which he calls a 'political weapon') which, assimilating the firm to a network of contracts, dissolve organizations into their commercial environment. Treating these quasi-firms as networks of contracts, not as legal entities with an official legal status, means, for example, that the customer of one of the numerous intermediate banks involved in a series of transfers of dematerialized funds, which has made a mistake, cannot pursue what amounts to the 'contractual or quasi-criminal responsibility of the bank involved, even though it has no direct contractual tie with the customer'. Similarly, 'the semiautonomous entrepreneur integrated into a network through a set of elaborate contracts concluded with the leading firm' cannot invoke 'the protection afforded by labour legislation' if things turn out badly. Lastly – a final example – the wage-earners of a franchisee cannot 'enjoy social protection from the franchiser at the centre of the whole franchise system', because, 'by virtue of the contractual set-up of the franchise, it appears that the franchisee is the sole employer'. And yet, adds Teubner, 'a franchise system is *de facto* a large firm' which, thanks to its network organization, can shirk its responsibilities and 'evade the law'. He proposes the formulation of a new law that would treat 'hybrid forms as a third order between contracts and companies, and would involve particular norms of protection, appropriate to networks'. He thus suggests, for example, establishing a 'representation of collective interests within networks' in the form not of 'rigid institutions', but of a 'centre of counter-power' possessing 'legal means of legitimation and control by virtue of flexible contractual agreements'.

Charles Sabel's work on what he calls 'constitutional orders' is another attempt, by equipping networks with specific rules, to circumscribe them periodically in order to disclose the persons or organizations engaged – the list of contributors – and bring out their rights and duties.[69] In particular, Sabel seeks to go beyond the reference to 'shared social rules' or 'shared beliefs and values' which act as a kind of unwritten law, and which he considers inadequate. Drawing on the experience of industrial zones, subcontracting relationships and project teams, he imagines a regulatory mechanism internal to the network that restricts opportunism. In so doing, he constructs an original form, consistent with the features of the projective city we have identified.

This form consists, on the one hand, in a constitutional order (thus named with a view to emphasizing its affinities with the political forms of democracy), composed of a heterogeneous set of units, and, on the other hand, of a 'superintendent'. The units may be made up of anything, on the sole condition that they are in a relationship of significant interdependence: individuals, teams, departments, firms, trade unions, schools, and so on. And the same applies to the superintendent, which can take the form of an arbitration committee comprising the parties themselves or their representatives, a court of justice, an elected agent, and so on. The superintendent must simply be part of a more general order. The superintendent's role is to define the role and responsibilities of the constituent units, to establish the rules by which they conduct their transactions, and to resolve their disputes in the event that the constituent units are unable to do so themselves. But this jurisdictional authority is itself limited. On the one hand, the rules that are valid for the constituent units must be consistent with the rules followed by the superintendent as a member of a larger whole. On the other hand, all the rules of arbitration must be established through consultation between the constituent units. Thus, the superintendent is limited to explaining and reinforcing the rules that the constituent parties derive from their own experience and history. His (or its) role consists predominantly in facilitating communication between them. But the superintendent is not the 'employer' of the other constituent parties, and the hierarchical positions of both are indeterminate. This form of governance is not constructed to define a stable order but, on the contrary, so that it is able continuously to adjust to shifts in co-operation – adjustment requiring a reorganization of the order itself. According to Sabel, institutional arrangements of this sort should make it possible to develop a 'deliberative', 'reflexive', or 'studied' trust. The kind of organization imagined thus assumes a way of inventorying contributors, in the form of keeping a list of the units that are 'members' of the network, even if this list changes from time to time. It is then a question of organizing for these different units interactive procedures conducive to the regulation of the network.

Towards fairer rules of remuneration

But it is not merely a matter of identifying those who have participated. The next step is to force the partners to offer them just remuneration, on the model of collective agreements in the industrial world. If, as François Eymard-Duvernay's analysis indicates,[70] work contracts are increasingly incomplete, a way must be found to tighten them up again, for contractual gaps in a context of very unequal forces leave the door wide open for greater exploitation of the weakest.

To be just, the remuneration due to a given contributor in a network world involving a succession of projects is not limited exclusively to the income he derives from his labour. In fact, it seems to be accepted that fair remuneration now is just as much a question of improving – or at least preserving – the worker's *employability*.

The remuneration of work cannot in fact be regarded as just if it is assessed solely by reference to the hours of labour performed, without equally taking into account the training and reproduction of the labour force. In modes of co-ordination that made a good deal of space for careers, lifelong employment, or permanent engagements at the very least, it was difficult, especially for *cadres*, to work out the share in the total wage between remuneration of the stipulated work and remuneration of labour-power; and also, secondarily, between the remuneration of current work and the deferred remuneration of sacrifices made at the beginning of their careers. In the new network mechanisms, the remuneration corresponding to each contractual engagement in a temporary project relates only to the particular job, which is defined as precisely as possible. This leaves the acquisition and maintenance of the qualities that make them capable of doing this job entirely up to individuals (or, should they falter, the state or humanitarian organizations). In this perspective, the notion of employability can be used as a pivot to outline a redistribution of the maintenance of labour-power between working people and employers, without affecting the requirement of mobility. Temporary employers have met their share of the upkeep of labour-power if they make a contribution to the development of the collaborator's employability during the limited period when the latter is participating in a particular project.[71] In practice, gains or losses in employability are revealed when, at the end of a project, people seek a new engagement. The surest sign that their employability has increased is when they are even more desirable to others than they were before their participation in the project they have just left, and when they find interesting new commitments with ease. By contrast, it can be said of those who have difficulty reintegrating themselves into a project, or who are directed towards less fulfilling projects, or relegated to marginal positions, that their employability has decreased. In this case, the main question that arises in terms of justice is which party bears responsibility for this loss of employability. In the absence of a recognized right to employability, and of a social duty on the part of firms to develop the employability of those they employ, the answer to this question inevitably assigns responsibility to individuals. If they are less employable, it is because they were not able to maintain their employability. Requiring firms to develop employability, and the progressive establishment of a *right to employability*,[72] would make it possible to envisage more complex tests (including hearings at industrial tribunals) with a view to determining who bears the responsibility in individual cases for a reduction in employability, resulting, for example, in a situation of long-term unemployment. In this way, responsibility for unemployment – which currently rests with the firm solely at the point of redundancies, and is otherwise mostly transferred on to the person who suffers the consequences – could be distributed between a multiplicity of bodies (the succession of employers) and spread over time.

The notion of *skill* is presented as an instrumentation of the notion of employability, redefined as the sum of skills accumulated by a given wage-earner, whose employability increases each time he acquires a new skill or progresses to the next level in the skills already listed. In this perspective, an employer's contribution to employability is certified by an improvement in people's skills profile.

The 'A. Cap 2000' collective agreement ('Agreement on the conduct of professional activities'), signed in 1990 by the Groupement des entreprises sidérurgiques et minières and the wage-earners' trade-union organizations, with the exception of the CGT, is a good example of an attempt to establish a form of justice based on an inventory and assessment of people's skills, as well as on an organization of career paths linked to the enrichment of the personal skills 'portfolio'.[73]

Other mechanisms are based on the notion of skill – like the 'skills appraisal' or the 'national reference system for qualifications' advocated by the Virville report.[74] What they have in common is that they aim to offer wage-earners a resource for being assigned a 'use-value' (in the terminology used by some of their supporters) and maintaining it during their displacements. Thus, the notion of skill was diffused at the same time as firms were seeking to organize the external mobility of their wage-earners (out-placement).[75] The recognition of 'skills' – acquired from initial education, continuous training or experience, and 'accredited' or 'approved' by public or private bodies,[76] in the form of abilities that are 'at once basic and very general',[77] and hence amenable to numerous recombinations – is thus conceived as an instrument for combating exclusion. For it allows people to equip themselves with a stock of qualifications and inspire potential employers with confidence in their *savoir faire*, while circulating over an extensive, heterogeneous space. Moreover, establishing such mechanisms would prompt a revival of efforts, currently in abeyance, in the direction of human-resources accounting, which explored a more just representation of wage-earners not only as costs, but also as 'resources' – that is to say, as possessors of skills that are useful to the firm.[78]

As Alain Supiot has shown, the idea of employability has two repercussions at a legal level. With respect to firms, it presupposes a new form of responsibility whose model might be mechanisms seeking to guarantee respect for environmental rights: 'just as in environmental issues the principle has been established that the polluter must pay (not the community), so what is becoming established is the idea of making the firms that transfer the maximum part of the cost of the "human resource" to the community pay more, and reducing the burdens on those who internalize this cost'.[79] Nor does Supiot neglect the fact that 'some firms ... externalize these costs not directly on to the community, but on to firms that depend on them economically or legally' – hence the necessity of introducing 'social clauses' into subcontracting contracts. Where the workforce is concerned, it leads to separating the 'worker's official status' from 'periods of contractual supply of work'. In effect, 'the execution of the contract is no longer wholly identified with the performance of work, but includes a growing proportion of training, which has become inevitable in order to adapt wage-earners to the changes in knowledge required to do the work'. It is therefore necessary to stop 'reducing labour to its exchange-value in the contract and to take account of the labour capacity embodied in the person of the worker', merging work in the wider notion of *activity*, which would acquire an official legal status.

Supiot sees these new legal forms emerging in various current developments in positive rights giving workers the 'right to move from one work situation to another'. The hourly credits attributed to wage-earners in possession of a *mandat d'intérêt collectif* doubtless represent the first expression of such rights. In recent years, different types of special leave and rights of absence have been added to it, such as training credits, time-saving accounts, grants to unemployed people who start up firms, training vouchers, and so on. We are in fact witnessing, insists Supiot, 'the appearance of a new type of social rights' referring to work in general (work in the family sphere, educational work, voluntary work, self-employed work, publicly useful work, etc.). He calls these new legal mechanisms, which 'facilitate the transition from one type of work to another' and, more generally, bolster a new kind of compromise between autonomy and security, *social drawing rights*. In fact, these new rights, whose realization is a matter to be freely determined by the relevant parties, are exercised 'within the limits of a previously accumulated credit'. They assume that 'sufficient provision' has been built up. According to Supiot, what must be developed on the basis of the mechanisms established in recent years is 'a coherent framework that would draw all the consequences from the principles of the continuity and mobility of people's occupational conditions, and which, in instituting these social drawing rights, would bring about a 'liberation of time', and make 'the financing of work outside the market' possible.

Widespread establishment of social drawing rights presupposes a change in the unit of time in which working hours are accounted and a transition from a short time unit (week, month or year) to a long time unit covering the whole of someone's working life. Consequently, it is bound up with programmes for reorganizing the life-cycle, with the replacement of a 'linear, inflexible life-plan' (education, working life, retirement) by a 'flexible model of existence'. This would be characterized by the possibility of flexibly distributing periods of work, education or leisure over a whole lifetime and in accordance with individual wishes; and 'social transfers not specified according to stages of life' would correspond to it.[80] Thus, for example, people might at any age take a prolonged leave of absence that would be counted as a down payment on retirement. Referring to this possibility, Gösta Rehn likewise talks about a 'drawing right' – that is to say, 'the right to exchange one form of existence for another during selected periods'.[81]

A new mechanism derived from the five-year law of 1994 – training-time capital – prefigures these social drawing rights in the sphere of training. This mechanism aims to encourage the 'continuous development of skills', to ensure 'professional maintenance' (a notion developed within the framework of the Commissariat general au plan to refer to maintaining people's qualifications in order to limit the risks of redundancy), by allowing wage-earners to benefit from 'time for training that may be accumulated in the course of their working life'. This capital is distinguished from individual leave for training in that it must be built up in the context of the firm's training plan, which derives from the 'the employer's plan, not the individual wishes of the wage-earner', and in that 'it does not suspend the work relation'. Nevertheless, it constitutes an individual right attaching to the person of the wage-earner and must be transferable from one firm to another, accompanying individuals in their moves; this would conduce to a mutualization of its financing.[82]

Bernard Girard integrates some forms of compensation for work, of the sort we have just referred to (gains in employability, the addition of new skills, enhanced social drawing rights), into what he calls a *'new social pact'*.[83] In this framework, submission to the firm is no longer justified by job guarantees or hopes of social advancement, but by the opportunity firms offer wage-earners, who know that they are 'bound to come back on to the labour market regularly', to 'build up a professional patrimony' in order 'to acquire the requisite skills to find another job'. He nevertheless observes that a 'pact' legitimating a form of social justice based on the circulation of people between different projects in a heterogeneous space poses new legal problems. These involve the division of property rights between mobile people and the firms or projects they move between – especially when scarce, sought-after goods are in significant measure made up of connections with persons, *savoir faire* or information. Without the establishment of such a 'pact', disputes are bound to proliferate between wage-earners who, no longer finding sufficient security in the firm, will use their specific capital – that is to say, their skills – to develop opportunistic behaviour, and firms, which will be tempted 'to take legal measures to prevent other companies poaching their *cadres*'.[84] From these developments, it is apparent that the renegotiation of work contracts in terms of the rights and duties of the two parties, in a world redefined around the metaphor of the network, should be able to check both the exploitation of workers by their employers and its converse – that is to say, the risk of opportunistic profit-taking by a wage-earner damaging the firm.

By analogy with the procedures used to ensure the reliability of systems containing a large number of components of diverse technological and geographical origin, we might also say that the mechanisms referred to hitherto must permit people's *traceability* throughout their careers in a heterogeneous, open space. Structurally, a network world is deterritorialized, and no longer makes it possible to identify beings by reference to their position in a structured space. On the other hand, they may retain the trace of the different projects they have passed through.

The contribution of management and organization theory to defining a fair exchange in a connexionist world lays more stress on the risks of opportunism to which firms are exposed than the risks of exploitation that firms can impose on wage-earners. But in some cases it may turn out that dealing with one risk impacts on another and, in addition, that setting limits on connexionist abuses helps to advance the legitimacy of such regulations. This is why the mechanisms invented by firms form part of the projective city. Moreover, firms have more leeway imposing control mechanisms on their members than the public authorities have controlling the dynamics of firms – so much so that today it would seem that they are more successful in curbing the exploitation to which they are vulnerable than countries and people are.

Reflection on the risks of opportunism has a long history in organizational economics. Thus the *theory of agency* basically seeks to account for the difficulties faced by the 'principal' in controlling the schemes and loyalty of its 'agent'. In this current of thought, based on a pessimistic anthropology which, in line with standard economic theory, knows only selfish motives for action, the mechanisms envisaged are control mechanisms acting either directly or via deterrence mechanisms (like reputation). The formation of mechanisms inspired by this theory presupposes strengthening systems of punishment/reward in order to inflect the action of networkers towards the good of the principal – here the firm – and, in addition, setting up monitoring mechanisms. The development of individual or small-group appraisal and remuneration, which developed in parallel with the relaxation of hierarchical constraints, can be interpreted in this perspective. Similarly, the generalization of various new communication and information technologies (portable computers, mobile phones, databases fed into from a distance, diaries posted on the Internet, ERP, etc.) makes it possible to support people's mobility without relaxing monitoring.

Organizational economics contains another current, however, based on an optimistic anthropology that endows human beings with the faculty of distancing themselves from their immediate interests for the purposes of joint action. In particular, this current seeks to overcome the drawbacks of theories centred on the paradigm of interests, which posit an absence of ethical preoccupations and exclude the possibility of altruistic behaviour.[85] The central concept in these new approaches is *trust*, which, as we have seen, is frequently adopted by neo-management. Trust is what makes it possible to relax control while banking on a form of self-control that is cheap for organizations, and does not seem to hamper mobility in any way. In our view, renewed investigation of control, such as that formulated by the theory of transaction costs and the theory of agency,[86] and the recent development of an enormous literature on trust,[87] are thus among the signs of the problems entailed by the emergence of new forms of opportunism. Bound up with new network forms of organization, these problems can no longer be construed in the framework established to define the norms governing market relations or hierarchical relations.[88] Analyses of trust have thus developed predominantly in connection with reticular forms of organization that are reducible neither to the market (the relations are enduring) nor to hierarchy (the units are not subject to authoritarian control).[89]

Yet instrumentation of the notion of trust is not straightforward. If firms want to see 'relations of trust' develop at a time when the world seems to offer premiums for opportunism each and every day, they must resort to mechanisms ensuring that the people they employ are 'trustworthy persons' rather than 'potential networkers'. The importance *attributed to educational qualifications* may be regarded as a relatively old mechanism used by firms to exercise tight control over access to positions that are ideal for networkers, where the degree of access to resources is considerable and the degree of control weak. Given that access to such positions depends more than ever today on the level of academic qualifications, the latter seems to act as a gauge of the good moral character of those who have attained it, especially inasmuch as it is thought to measure someone's ability to submit, in order to succeed, to external rules – those of the education system – which presupposes a certain obedience and contained opportunism.

The managerial vulgate that seeks to offer managers existential models for them to base their own behaviour on is another source of development of 'propensities for being trustworthy'. As we have seen, this literature sketches the ideal type of the great man in the projective city, whom we have called the *network-extender*. He shares with the *networker* all the qualities required to make useful connections and extend the network. But unlike the latter, he is deserving of trust – that is to say, he acts not on his own account but for the common good of all those engaged in a project. The morality of the network-extender acts as the guarantee that neither his team nor his firm will be exploited in the course of the project that he is heading up. In seeking to limit the opportunistic temptations of the project head, which result in the firm being asset-stripped, management authors have had to 'symmetrize' his behaviour towards the people who work with him.

The importance attributed to *business ethics* in recent years points towards other attempts to develop people's loyalty, something from which both firms and their collaborators would benefit. Analysis of the 'charters of values' and 'codes of ethics' established at the beginning of the 1990s, mainly in multi-national firms, indicates that two clauses crop up in all the documents. The first relates to the opportunistic use of the information to which wage-earners in a firm might have access. The charters formally prohibit its communication to the outside world, to people who could use it against the firm or for their own benefit. In the merchant banks whose *cadres* work on highly confidential operations involving mergers or takeovers of firms, the key issue is to avoid profit-taking derived from insider trading. Wage-earners' rights of self-expression on the subject of their firm outside it is guaranteed by law.[90] But organizations are well aware of the risks they run by allowing the diffusion of any information, and try to check such things by charters that sometimes involve ceremonies where pledges are made. The second constant of the codes of ethics is the prohibition of corruption, which is one of the networker's operational modes. Corruption can in fact be defined as the act of deriving personal benefit from an institutional position. It is because this institutional position confers a certain power on the person occupying it that he can convert it into cash, and derive personal benefits at the expense of the organization that appointed him, which, unawares, will, for example, be induced to pay a supplier more or accept the invoicing of fictitious services.[91]

The various mechanisms intended to organize just remuneration of contributions and format rules of fair exchange, by attempting on the one hand to establish additional remuneration in the form of a contribution to real employability (skills) or potential employability (drawing rights), and on the other to avoid the possibility of a partner evading obligations in the paradigmatic form of a breach of trust, are comparatively varied and numerous. Reformers seem more comfortable here than when it comes to developing accounting frameworks so as not to minimize or neglect certain people's contributions. This is because they take the value of mobility in the connexionist world seriously. And with a view to not making *structures* (a devalued category by dint of its association with industrial forms of organization) inflexible, they naturally end up attributing responsibility to *people* – either by making their *moral sense* bear the whole burden of correct conduct (as with 'business ethics'), or by transferring responsibility for their social lot on to their *cognitive capacities*, codified and certified on the model of the normalization of objects.[92] This focus on individual connections and particular persons seems to distance them from the search for an overarching position that would make it possible to regulate justice not only at the level of each node, but over the network as a whole. What is involved is a local approach to the network which, because it focuses on each of the connections taken individually, is blind to the specific forms generated out of the mass of connections, whose collective strength is superior to the sum of minor forces in play in each individual relation.

Towards equality of opportunity for mobility

The mechanisms studied in this section seek above all to offset the handicaps of certain people who, in the absence of compensation, will never be in a position to face a test where a capacity for mobility plays a significant role. For the connexionist test is fair only if everyone has a reasonable chance of tackling it with success, on condition that they make the requisite sacrifices. Certain people enjoy advantages related to their childhood (their parents having often moved house, they have, for example, developed a great capacity for adapting to different situations), or their income (they are not especially equipped for mobility, but can always pay for individual services: drivers, interpreters, etc.). Thus, they have an advantage when it comes to connexionist tests not because they have made a sacrifice (merit), but because they possess other resources. In these conditions, their victory cannot be legitimate. For it to be so, all those who do not enjoy the same resources must be given the opportunity to succeed despite everything. In the industrial world, if the testing of skills – which in France was based largely on educational success – was to be considered just, educational tests had to be regarded as measuring only scholarly performance, not the parents' economic resources or the child's social background. As is well known, this meritocratic exigency inspired a large number of critical works aimed at improving educational justice, and resulted in a number of reforms of the national education system.

Reintegration mechanisms are an initial example of formulas that seek to equalize opportunities in a network world. Policies to 'combat poverty' pertain to the mechanisms of projective city – not in so far as they aim to relieve poverty through public provision or social assistance, but because they are presented as more particularly intended to check exclusion by reintegrating people who have 'lost their links'. The overriding objective of these mechanisms is to help people forge new links, and to this end they often employ social technologies that directly refer to network logics. The project is what integrates or reintegrates, what makes it possible to develop a minimum employability in people – that is to say, a capacity to take the test of connection to an initial project successfully, followed by the test of mobility, or connection to another project once the first one is finished. Otherwise, it would not be possible to understand how the idea has grown up, notably among social workers and in the framework of urban policies, that participation in any activity constructed in the form of a definite project, whatever it might be – cultural, sporting, social – is preferable in terms of integration to a lack of activity.

The same could be said of the *Revenu minimum d'insertion*. On the one hand, one of the virtues attributed to its implementation is that it brought to light miseries that were hitherto ignored because those who experienced them were so isolated, so utterly disconnected from any institution, so definitively expelled to the margins of social networks, that their sufferings remained

beneath the threshold of visibility. On the other, one of the innovations introduced by the RMI was to make state aid conditional upon a policy of
'something in return'. With this, promoters of the RMI intended to differentiate this benefit mechanism from assistance in the traditional sense. They
believed that beneficiaries of the RMI contract a debt they can acquit only by
doing everything in their power to reconstruct the links they have lost.
Obtaining the RMI depends upon the decision of local integration commissions, made up of social workers, local government administrators, general
advisers, heads of firms or officials of associations, who make granting the
allowance dependent upon an 'integration contract' specifying the efforts that
the recipient is supposed to make to 'reintegrate' herself. 'Reintegration' primarily signifies obtaining regular work. But because in a large number of cases
this objective is unrealistic, any 'project' will be regarded as a (worthy) endeavour if it aims to help arrest 'marginalization' either directly, by re-creating links
with others (for example, by contributing voluntary help to others), or even
by doing the kind of work on oneself that is deemed to be a precondition for
reconstructing links – for example, undertaking to stop drinking and, more
generally, 'taking responsibility for one's health'.[93]

Equally pertinent with respect to the establishment of a projective city are
all the *grant-aided jobs aiming at professional integration* – government-sponsored
work contracts, local assignments, training courses, skills contracts, integration
contracts, and so on – whose promoters, while accepting that their record in
leading to stable employment is uneven, stress their beneficial aspects, not the
least of which is to provide 'stability for some months', 'offer[ing] the opportunity to reconstruct projects'.[94]

Various extremely diverse actors have proliferated around these mechanisms since the mid-1980s, dependent upon the state or linked to the new
humanitarian movement (local departments of the national employment
office, local services, training bodies, associations, integration enterprises, etc.).
These represent so many 'intermediaries for professional integration' whose
action – increasingly co-ordinated not in a hierarchical, planned fashion, but
in the form of '*local networks of integration*' – is defined by reference to the topic
of the network. The novelty of these mediating actors, by comparison with
long-distance administrative interventions operating on populations defined
in terms of criteria, is that they undertake action at a local level, taking account
of the particularities of job-seekers and potential suppliers. They seek to
'persuade employers and the unemployed to forge relations with one another',
to 'create the requisite relations of trust for employment', by highlighting 'particular qualities that are discounted in general forms of qualification, such as
educational diplomas' – to which they prefer the development of 'skills' like
'*savoir faire* and interpersonal skills not contained in curricula for acquiring
knowledge', but 'soon utilizable in a work situation' – and by 'negotiating the
content of the post' with those in charge of firms. Much of the training

dispensed by these types of bodies consists in developing in people cut off from the workplace a capacity to present themselves, to 'establish links', to 'make contacts', to 'obtain an appointment', and for this purpose to use communication tools – newspapers, Minitel, telephone. It also involves 'creating a network' of firms actively engaged in the mechanisms of integration.[95] At issue is increasing the chances of the unemployed taking the new connexionist tests with success, by helping them to develop their capacity for mobility and linking up with others.

But the designers of mechanisms are interested not only in those who, in respect of links, no longer possess any strength that they can mobilize – that is, the excluded – but also in all those who, less disadvantaged, still have the possibility of meeting new tests on condition that this specific strength is preserved. Here it is a question of developing the possibilities of mobility not only for the weak but for everyone.

François Eymard-Duvernay's proposals for constructing new intermediaries in the labour market – particularly between schools and firms, but also between firms and the labour market (the relational infrastructure is blocked today, and drains off only around one-fifth of job switches) – are part of the same spirit of putting the parties on an equal footing.[96] They would make it possible to reorganize what in this work we have called *selection rounds*, whose break-up over the last thirty years has resulted in very unequal recruitment tests since, when it comes to job switches made through intermediaries, a whole host of job-seekers enter into competition for a few job offers, paving the way for discriminatory processes; while in the case of changes without mediation (24 per cent by unsolicited application, 20 per cent by previous professional contacts, 23 per cent by personal or family connections), they are not offered to people on an equal basis. In particular, thanks to their associations the former pupils of the *grandes écoles* benefit from a network that is not available to the majority of university graduates. Associations of former pupils are, in addition, so many intermediaries on the labour market that university graduates do not possess. In Eymard-Duvernay's conception,[97] the new intermediaries should operate face-to-face modes of selection, as opposed to selection from a distance by CV, which tends to utilize discriminatory variables and prevents assessment of people's real skills.

The goal of other proposals is not only to allow occupational mobility, as in the case of the mechanisms of integration and recruitment mentioned hitherto, but also to offer everyone the autonomy and opportunities for personal development promised by the new world – that is to say, the possibility of involvement in a wide variety of projects, whatever they may be. Here it is a matter of equalizing opportunities for attaining the kind of good fortune afforded by the projective city.

The notion of *activity* is thus proposed in an attempt to legitimate any type of project and mobility, not only those that take the form of work. In this

perspective, the important thing is that people should be able to develop personally; and this, according to a number of reformers, is bound to develop
their employability. To 'labour time' performed 'in a contractual framework',
Alain Supiot thus counterposes 'human activities that can develop at other
levels'. Under this heading he includes 'training', 'consumption' and 'all forms
of freely undertaken activity', encompassing 'disinterested work' performed
in the framework of 'family activities, but also public or community ... cultural
or training activities'. The institution of an *activity status* must therefore guarantee the 'freedom to change work', but also a 'genuine freedom of choice
between work and non-work'. For 'what human beings experience as "work"
includes a portion of what the law today characterizes as "non-work", whether
it involves the labour of self-education (general or professional training) or
disinterested work (notably domestic labour)'. For Supiot, legal consolidation
of the notion of activity presupposes establishing a 'minimum work statute,
which would guarantee anyone who has worked for a certain amount of time
the chance during particular periods to devote themselves to activities they
have freely chosen', thus overcoming the distinction between, 'on the one side,
a social minimum guaranteed by the community and, on the other, remuneration of work confined to the framework of the contract'.[98]

But legal elaboration of the notion of activity poses not so much the issue
of accumulation (e.g. of skills) in the course of a career, as was the case with
the mechanisms mentioned in the previous section, as that of the persistence
of rights. It is this capacity to embrace the heterogeneous and attribute an
official status to it that gives the notion of activity a greater scope than that
of work. Whereas the notion of work is associated with subordination, the
wage-earning class, and the legal form of the work contract, activity is – as
François Gaudu stresses – neutral in terms of the legal form adopted, so that
this notion makes it possible to cover a whole range of heterogeneous situations.[99] This is the framework in which the proposal of an *activity contract*,
presented in the report of the commission 'Le travail dans vingt ans' chaired
by Jean Boissonat, is to be understood. Here we find the clearest current
outline of the mechanisms of justice suited to a projective city. The report
stresses the changes in the productive system, and particularly its 'network
organization' (partnership between large firms and subcontractors, proliferation of self-employed subcontractors and 'home-based firms', etc.); and the
necessity of altering the legal and institutional framework of work relations
in order to 'face up to the current mutations in capitalism' and permit, for
example, a smooth transition from the status of wage-earner to that of entrepreneur (and back again), change of occupation, location, and so on – in short,
in order to facilitate people's circulation across a vast, varied, heterogeneous
and changing space of activities.[100] An activity contract 'would encompass the
work contract without leading to its disappearance'. It would have a fairly long
temporal horizon (in the region of five years), 'covering periods of productive

work in firms, work in training,[101] and leave for social purposes (e.g. for family reasons), with a retention of social guarantees but a variability of modes and levels of remuneration'. The remuneration and protection of workers during non-productive periods could be 'ensured by the development of mutualized income funds, allowing for a smoothing-out of remuneration'.[102] The contract would be signed with a 'collective' comprising 'a freely constituted network of firms' and public or private training bodies, public agencies (from the state to local communities via the different categories of public institutions), associations, professional organizations of wage-earners and non-wage-earners.[103]

The activity contract thus clearly constitutes a compromise mechanism between, on the one hand, employers' demands for flexibility and mobility on the part of wage-earners and, on the other, requirements of justice aiming to 'counteract a one-sided distribution of employment risks',[104] and allow people to acquire employability and skills, and to transport these assets with them while circulating in the heterogeneous space of a network world – and this without breaks in projects relegating them to the margins and into exclusion.[105] In fact, firms enjoy great flexibility in the framework of the activity contract: 'a firm temporarily lacking a certain volume of orders could lend wage-earners to another firm, make them work part-time, place them in training, encourage them to undertake a self-employed activity for a period of time, or release them so that they have time for other social activities'. In this sense, the activity contract extends the increasingly frequent introduction of provisions for mobility, geographical or occupational, in the work contract, which, in reticular organizations, can lead to a *de facto* change of employer.[106]

But the activity contract is presented as both an institutionalization and a limitation of these practices. It must permit people impelled into mobility not to be thereby delivered over to the vagaries of the market: 'the wage-earner would retain the guarantees of an activity contract throughout, in return for performing specific tasks. He would not be consigned to the dustbin of unemployment' and, in the event of redundancy, 'could continue to be active within the terms of a new contract'.[107] The activity contract 'mutualizes risks' and 'periods of employment and non-employment' taken up with training, even voluntary work. In this framework, '*activity* encompasses socially useful activities'.[108] Thus the activity contract is supposed to make it possible 'to reconstruct a security in the work relationship by making its objective the construction of a long-term professional career path and social status, instead of the professional and social itinerancy to which all those without a permanent contract are condemned to today'.[109]

In some respects, the various proposals for a *universal income* – an egalitarian income paid to the rich as well as the poor,[110] which distinguishes it from compensatory social benefits – may be regarded as the monetary equivalent of the notion of activity. Accordingly, these proposals are worthy of consideration among the projective city's mechanisms, despite the fact that justification of them often appeals to other principles, particularly of an industrial kind, or even pertains to a liberal framework.[111] In effect, universal income aims to offset the 'disconnection between the economic and the social' by uncoupling income from work. The distribution of a basic income to everyone by social right (subsistence income), or political right (citizenship income), helps to attenuate the distinction between different types of work (waged, training, domestic, etc.), and especially the boundary that has hitherto separated waged work from voluntary work. Universal income must give everyone the freedom to work or not to work. Or rather, it must give everyone the freedom to choose their activity, defining 'independent activities' for themselves ('starting up a firm, trying out untypical activities that are not yet socially recognized'); and, in the case of waged work, the freedom to be better placed, given possession of a basic income, 'to negotiate conditions of work and pay'.[112]

Opponents of a universal income highlight the expense of an undifferentiated payment (estimated at 260 billion francs net, as opposed to 25 million for the RMI); the difficulty of recovering its payment to 'people who do not really need it' through taxation; and the enormous bureaucracy required to administer it. They advocate less radical solutions such as the 'second cheque': a compensatory payment, funded by resources that are part public and part derived from firms, paid to people who accept, on an individual basis, a reduction in their working hours and wages so that they can develop a 'socially useful' activity, or switch between different acitivities.[113]

The mechanisms referred to above aim predominantly to encourage the mobility of the maximum number of people. They are complemented by others that seek, on the contrary, to curb excessive mobility. The mobility of capital markets, for example, may be adjudged excessive if it comes into play in a test where the other participants can engage only the mobility of their industrial assets. By dint of its dematerialized character and the installation of a global economic network, capital is bound to win every time.

Thus, the *Tobin tax*, advocated by the recipient of the 1981 Nobel Prize for economics, James Tobin, known for his works on the relations between the financial sector and the real sector of the economy, aims to tax international financial transactions basically in order to reduce speculative flows – that is, those that are not bound up with the commercial trade in goods or services, or the financing requirements of states or firms. These speculative flows, especially on the currency markets, account for the major part of exchanges. The essential relevance of the tax would be to make short-term speculative flows particularly expensive. 'In fact, at the rate of 0.2 per cent a daily circuit on the currency markets would end up costing 48 per cent a year; however, the same rate would have only a negligible impact upon real trade or long-term investments.'[114] Such a tax would thus have the effect of slowing down financial mobility relative to other assets, and for this reason it forms part of the possible mechanisms of a projective city.[115]

The creation of the euro has also reduced capital mobility throughout the zone by abolishing exchange risks between eleven European currencies. By also permitting a reduction in interest rates, which no longer have to cover certain exchange risks, it has had the direct effect of reducing the drain on the real economy and slightly relaxing constraint on firms, which are expected to pay a return on capital higher than the interest rates.[116]

Recurrent appeals for the imposition of *more intensive controls on markets* also convey a desire for restrictions on potential mobility. At present only banks are subject to oversight, with the Cooke ratio in particular.[117] But this does not cover the off-balance-sheet commitments made with derivative products that have largely fuelled the growth in transactions in recent years. Other participants (fund managers, insurance companies, firms) are not subject to any 'prudential' regulation – that is to say, regulation that obliges them to take precautions.[118]

As for reductions in the mobility differentials between multinationals and wage-earners in different countries, we must add to the set of mechanisms of the projective city the rapidly expanding practice of *certifying* firms. This makes it possible to restrict the inequalities in labour and environmental protection from one country to the next, whereas such inequalities constitute one of the motives for relocation. Certification results in the issue of a label certifying that a firm respects a certain number of criteria combined in a norm. This label is awarded following an examination or audit conducted by an independent body. Moreover, even if this only partially checks relocation, these certifications should in theory make it possible to restrain the exploitation of human beings and nature by the countries that receive the investments. Certification proves a fairly suitable formula for control in a network world. It is based upon recurrent audits, systems charged with ensuring that practices within firms conform to a certain number of rules. Once the network heads have been certified, the tendency is to extend certification to the whole subcontracting chain. For in order to be credible in its certification (which is a sign of credit with its clients and final customers),[119] a firm seeks to supply itself from suppliers who are themselves certified, in order to block the escape route of transferring controversial activities to less closely monitored subcontractors. Certification thus makes its way step by step, from link to link within the network. An environmental certification ISO 14000 exists and is developing rapidly, but its drawback is that it merely confirms that firms are organized to respect a country's environmental laws, and is not based on a global frame of reference. In the social sphere, a norm called SA 8000 (Social Accountability 8000), aiming to guarantee basic rights for workers, was created in 1997, in dialogue with several international firms and organizations like Amnesty International.[120] But it is still too soon to tell whether it will have the same success as ISO 14000 or the model for both of them, the ISO 9000 quality norms.

CONCLUSION: THE PLACE OF LAW

Proposals for mechanisms which, in order to limit the abuses and dangers peculiar to the connexionist world, aim to inscribe the projective city in the domain of things and law (as opposed to giving it a merely 'ideological' discourse seeking to mask the existence of exploitation) have thus begun to flow. Reformists have been spurred into this by increased poverty, and under pressure from the social movements. Nevertheless, putting these mechanisms into practice, improving them as and when limitations and imperfections emerge (i.e. in the course of their use), and the speed with which they will be tried out, will depend largely upon the strength of the critique to which the capitalist process is exposed and the pressure exerted on governments to use the weapon that belongs exclusively to them: the law.

One sign of the formation of a new city is indeed the development of a specific system of law. Law, in fact, represents a mechanism for controlling the validity of tests, and is a recourse in the event of disputes over their result.[121] One aspect of the juridical nature of a norm is, as Antoine Lyon-Caen and Antoine Jeammaud put it, its 'debatability' – that is to say, 'the ability to challenge it, to debate its meaning, its scope, or its application to concrete situations in the context of a trial'.[122] Laws can be 'opposed' to the tacit forms of power. They make it possible to go beyond a purely formal usage of the pretension to justice, and put it to the test. In the logic we employ here, law may thus be regarded as the mode of public inscription, in the form of general rules, preserving the trace of the main regulations – that is to say, mechanisms of self-limitation in each of the worlds – pertaining to the different cities.[123] Law thus sets constraints on the way in which the resources specific to a world may be used, so as to limit excessively predatory conduct, which would imperil the logic on which this world is based. At the same time, it helps to ensure its legitimacy.[124]

Law's combination with a coercive apparatus makes for its specificity,[125] and allows it to form the link between normative requirements whose foundation is extra-juridical and executive means of coercion and punishment or – as Weber formulated it – violence. Without the need for an external sanction – in other words, policing to make people respect the just organization of tests and ensure that their verdicts are implemented – there would be no place for law in the architecture of cities. But that would assume that conventions are established by themselves, with sufficient force to guarantee the justice of the tests and agreement about the verdicts (with disapproval as the sole sanction), which is far from being the case. Thus, there is more likelihood of the legitimate order of cities being achieved if it has the backing of a legal order that must be abided by.

Consequently, two different viewpoints may be brought to bear on law (as on cities). In the first, the emphasis is put on the way in which it concludes tests that are deemed formally compliant, and thereby legitimates the inequalities which were apparent in them, favouring those whom these inequalities benefited.[126] In the second, the emphasis is placed on the way in which – repository, as it were, of the standard of the just test – it can serve as a recourse for those disadvantaged by a test, either because it is not based upon a legitimate principle of justice, or because its local conduct has contravened recognized valid (legal) procedures, or again because its unfavourable results are recorded *ad aeternum* and people are refused another chance to prove themselves.

Without ignoring the limits of legal regulation (the logic of displacements, which we have emphasized, precisely consists in circumventing well-ordered tests), here we shall nevertheless stress the role of law in protecting the weakest. Moreover, displacements that circumvent the tests most solidly based on legal norms, by transferring the balance of forces into zones of less legal resistance, indicate *a contrario* the force of law.

But it is in so far as law is not formalistic and regulated solely by an internal logic, but fulfils external normative requirements and relies on political definitions of the common good (cities), that it can serve to limit the use which the strongest make of their strength. That is to say: in the framework developed here, it is thus that it can identify and curb displacements (adjustments, exceptions, dispensations, etc.), by recalling the norm which, because it has been subject to categorization, opposes its inertia to the expansion of forces. Imposing norms could burden social existence with excessive inflexibility if law were not also the very site of compromise, because, not being inscribed in a particular city but retaining the trace of different legitimate definitions of the common good, it is led to work constantly – that is to say, to reduce the tensions between the heterogeneous requirements that make up its system.

In the next chapter, we shall examine the current state of the artistic critique of capitalism, and also the paths that might be pursued with a view to reviving it. The need to get restarted on the artistic critique may appear less urgent today than the reconstruction of the social critique, and also especially difficult given that it contributed to the advent of neo-capitalism. But we shall nevertheless seek to show that the artistic critique is indispensable when it comes to rectifying various current tendencies of capitalism which we regard as harmful, and which the projective city risks reinforcing if it is established, for in the process of regulating the new world it has also legitimated numerous aspects of it. Now, more than ever perhaps, we should to seek to combine the two critiques despite the contradictions that bring them into conflict.

Notes

1 The history of the term 'exploitation' in the various currents of French Marxism must be traced. Much used by the Communist Party and the trade-union movement from 1950 to 1970, it was gradually replaced in the different leftist currents that were influential in the years

leading up to May 1968 (*Arguments, Socialisme ou Barbarie*) by the theme of *alienation*, which predominantly refers to the young Marx, and shifts the misery of material poverty on to cultural poverty; and then, in the 1970s, by the theme of *domination*, which seemed better tailored to a society where the state had assumed a preponderant role and which, articulated with the critique of bureaucracy, made it possible to belabour the capitalist and socialist countries equally. The critique of domination, supported by a demand for liberation, also made it possible to build a bridge between the social critique and the artistic critique, between the denunciation of the treatment suffered by the most deprived and demands for autonomy on the part of the new intellectual wage-earners.

2 René Lenoir, *Les Exclus, un Français sur dix*, Seuil, Paris 1974. The term 'exclusion' seems to have made its first appearance in its current sense in 1964, from the pen of Pierre Massé (*Les Dividendes du progrès*), then Commissaire général au Plan. Michel Foucault had used it at the beginning of the 1960s. Thus, he declared to *Le Monde* in 1961, in an interview following publication of *L'histoire de la folie à l'âge classique*: 'In the Middle Ages, exclusion struck the leper, the heretic. Classical culture excluded from the general hospital, the *Zuchthaus*, the *workhouse*, all institutions derived from leprosy' (quoted in *Magazine littéraire*, no. 34, July/August 1995, headlined 'Les exclus', p. 22).

3 See Luc Boltanski, *Distant Suffering: Morality, Media and Politics*, trans. Graham Burchell, Cambridge University Press, Cambridge 1999.

4 Emmanuel Didier has gone through the catalogues of the libraries of the Conseil économique et social and the Ministère des Affaires sociales in order to identify works focusing on poverty and, among them, those including in their title or description by key words the term 'exclusion' (*De l'exclusion*, DEA thesis, GSPM/EHESS, Paris 1995). This sifting indicates that works on poverty, which were fairly rare from 1970–85 (around five to ten books a year), saw their number increase considerably from 1986, with a peak (thirty to forty-five titles a year) between 1987 and 1992. The term 'exclusion', virtually absent between 1975 and 1986, was abundantly employed at the end of the decade, and at the same time gradually rid itself of all qualifiers (social, economic, educational, etc.) – a sign of the category's increased legitimacy. If, up to 1983, people often spoke of the 'excluded' rather than 'exclusion', the proportions were subsequently reversed: 'exclusion', elevated to the rank of the new social question, now transcends the fate of those unfortunates who are its victims.

5 It is worth indicating that Father Wresinski chose the term social exclusion in order to distance himself from the notion of 'sub-proletariat', which he deemed too Marxist and, above all, too derogatory. However, he is happy to leave the paternity of the new category to Lenoir. The problematic of ATD's founder is predominantly social: people do not possess the culture required to belong to society and survive in civilization. In contrast to the Marxist approach, he does not stress their economic role in the transformation of the relations of production (it is also to Father Wresinski that we owe the expression 'Fourth World').

6 See Robert Castel, *Les Métamorphoses de la question sociale*, Fayard, Paris 1994.

7 Rapid diffusion of the theme of exclusion is not peculiar to France. The debate on exclusion, begun in France, soon extended to the rest of Europe. In 1989, the Council of Ministers of Social Affairs of the European Community adopted a resolution on combating exclusion. The official report of the European Commission on growth, competitiveness and employment, published in 1993, called for a 'fight against exclusion'. Denmark, Germany, Italy, Portugal and Belgium created new institutions charged with implementing measures against exclusion. But the term 'exclusion' has assumed different meanings in different socio-political contexts: thus, in the English-speaking countries, with their liberal tradition, it has centred on the idea of discrimination. The struggle against exclusion is then an element in the struggle against the different forms of discrimination (racial, sexual, etc.). In the European Union, the notion of exclusion is instead based upon the social-democratic idea of 'social citizenship', which 'links the word with notions of inequalities and social rights' (Hilary Silver, 'Exclusion sociale et solidarité sociale: trois paradigmes', *Revue internationale du travail*, vol. 133, nos 5–6, 1994, pp. 585–638).

8 Hélène Thomas, *La Production des exclus*, Presses Universitaires de France, Paris 1997.

9 See Boltanski, *Distant Suffering*.

10 See Serge Paugam, 'L'essor des associations humanitaires. Une nouvelle forme de lien social?', *Commentaire*, no. 68, pp. 905–12.

11 (1) The reintegration of the unemployed and job creation, in the case notably of intermediate associations and enterprises for reintegrating people into work to the tune of approximately 1,000 in 1994, and in which, in the same year, 46,000 people were got back to work; (2) aid to the 200,000 people excluded from housing (according to a 1992 survey) and the 470,000 people who occupy temporary accommodation (hostels, hotels, etc.); (3) aid to single mothers without work; (4) intervention in problem districts (between 500 and 800 depending on estimates), particularly through the organization of 'neighbourhood networks'; (5) aid to 'travellers'; (6) educational support for the children of problem families; (7) teaching adults to read and write (between 4 and 9 million adults are 'illiterate', according to the estimate of the Délégation permanente de lutte contre l'illetrisme); (8) aid to prostitutes who want to escape their situation (between 75,000 and 90,000 occasional or full-time prostitutes are registered in Paris); (9) intervention in prisons (57,400 people in prison in 1994); (10) aid to elderly and isolated people; (11) medical care (for example, the 300,000 consultations provided in seven years in the centres run by Médecins sans frontières to ill people without medical cover) and, in particular, help for people suffering from extremely disabling illnesses (associations for the protection of AIDS sufferers, etc.); (12) cultural activities, particularly in the theatre, or sporting associations to involve young people in problem areas in 'projects' requiring team work; (13) aid to migrants and, in particular, those without legal papers. (Source: special issue of *La Croix-L'Événement*, 23 November 1994, devoted to the fight against exclusion.)

12 See Paugam, 'L'essor des associations humanitaires'.

13 Without identifying a cause-and-effect relationship in it, it should be pointed out that it was also during this period that unemployment began to affect graduates from higher education, either as regards their own future or their children's, including those hailing from the bourgeoisie, who had hitherto been relatively immune. The unemployment of *cadres* began to increase sharply at the beginning of the 1990s (Valérie André-Roux and Sylvie Le Minez, 'Dix ans d'évolution du chômage des cadres, 1987–1997', *Données sociales 1999*, INSEE, Paris 1999, pp. 140–47).

14 See Serge Paugam, ed., *Précarité et risque d'exclusion en France*, document of the CERC, La Documentation française, Paris 1993.

15 See Alain Touraine *et al.*, *Le grand refus. Réflexions sur la grève de décembre 1995*, Fayard, Paris 1996.

16 *La Misère du monde*, a bulky volume published under Pierre Bourdieu's direction in 1993, sold 80,000 copies in a few months. There followed *J'accuse l'économie triomphante* by Albert Jacquard, published by Calmann-Lévy in 1995 (37,000 copies) and, in 1996, *L'horreur économique* by the writer Viviane Forrester, which has sold 300,000 copies and been translated into eighteen languages. Emannuel Todd's *L'imposture économique*, published in 1997, has sold more than 50,000 copies; and P. Labarde and B. Maris's *Ah! Dieu que la guerre économique est jolie*, published in 1998, 70,000 (see also the article by P. Riché, 'L'horreur économique', *Libération*, 21 May 1998). Attesting to the same critical reversal of fortune in social categories ignored by the university system (and, no doubt – though figures are lacking on this point – among a far from negligible section of young *cadres*) is the growing success of papers like *Charlie Hebdo* (80,000 copies a week) or *Le Monde diplomatique* (200,000 copies a month). We might also cite the proliferation of clubs: Merleau-Ponty, Marc Bloch, Pétitions, Raisons d'agir, Copernic, and so on (see Bernard Poulet, 'À gauche de la gauche', *Le Débat*, no. 103, January/February 1999, pp. 39–59). In addition, readers will find in *L'exclusion: L'état des savoirs*, published in 1996 under the direction of Serge Paugam, a reminder of the main evidence published at the end of the 1980s and the beginning of the 1990s on the subject of poverty or homelessness.

17 See, for example, Gertrude Himmelfarb, *Poverty and Compassion: The Moral Imagination of the Late Victorians* (A. Knopf, New York 1991) on the role of philanthropists in Victorian England; and Claude Didry, *La Construction juridique de la convention collective en France, 1900–1919*, thesis at the École des hautes études en sciences sociales, Paris 1994, on that of jurists under the Third Republic.

18 At the origin of these new forms of associations (called 'media-associations' by Jean-Marc Salmon), which are less intent on increasing the number of their members than on making their 'actions' conspicuous by mediatizing them, one finds notably the *coordinations* that were established in the social conflicts of the second half of the 1980s, and particularly during the action by nursing staff in October 1988, in response to the crisis of trade-union representation. Co-ordinations, which are not union-based, invented a new kind of demonstration focused on the professional dignity and moral aspects of the identity of nursing staff (in the service of others), and where symbolic gestures, stylized and expressive performance, are very striking characteristics (Olivier Fillieule, ed., *Sociologie de la protestation. Les formes de l'action collective dans la France contemporaine*, L'Harmattan, Paris 1993, pp. 94–107). These two features (moral dimension and theatricality) were also to be found in the demonstrations of the 1990s, when artists (visual artists and performing artists) played a significant role, as with the mobilization on behalf of those without legal papers in 1997–98.

19 DAL was formed in 1990 after the expulsion by the police of a squat in the rue des Vignoles. From the outset, it enjoyed the support of a 'network' of associations, including Médecins du monde, Emmaüs, the MRAP, CFDT trade unionists, and 'personalities' with potential access to the media: abbé Pierre, René Dumont, Albert Jacquard, Théodore Monod (Jean-Marc Salmon, *Le Désir de société. Des restos du coeur aux mouvements de chômeurs*, La Découverte, Paris 1998, pp. 173–4). But it was above all after the occupation of an empty building on the rue du Dragon in December 1994 that the importance of this movement, and those formed in its wake (Dd!!, AC!), increased; this helped to make the theme of exclusion a leitmotiv of the presidential electoral campaign in 1995.

Droits devant!! was created in 1995 during the occupation of the rue du Dragon with the support of Monseigneur Gaillot, Albert Jacquard and Léon Schwartzenberg. It was led by Philippe Chavance, who came from DAL. The aim of the movement was 'to generalize the struggle against exclusion' (Salmon, *Le Désir de société*, p. 187).

Agir ensemble contre le chômage was formed in the crucible of the trade-union journal *Collectif*, a network of trade unionists hailing from the left of the CFDT (like Claire Villiers, who was an activist in the JOC) and of SUD-PTT (like Christophe Aguiton). In October 1993, *Collectif* launched an appeal for a broad movement against unemployment. One of the first manifestations of the scale of AC! was the march against unemployment in spring 1994, in whose organization SUD-PTT participated (ibid., pp. 200–05; Marie-Agnès Combesque, *Ça suffit! Histoire du mouvement des chômeurs*, Plon, Paris 1998, pp. 112–13).

20 According to Christophe Aguiton, the expulsion of PTT trade unionists from the CFDT, which gave rise to SUD, like those of health workers (giving rise to CRC santé), at the end of the 1980s, was the continuation of the repression of the co-ordinations by the unions. SUD-PTT was created in 1989 with around 1,000 members. It has made strong progress in subsequent years, with 9,000 members in 1995. Its electoral audience at France Télécom has gone up from 5 per cent to 25 per cent in the same period. New SUD unions were set up after the 1995 strikes (SUD-Rail, SUD-education (Christophe Aguiton and Daniel Bensaïd, *Le Retour de la question sociale. Le renouveau des mouvements sociaux en France*, Éditions Page deux, Lausanne 1997, pp. 147–58).

21 One of the methods used by both DAL and AC! is discreetly to tip off the press and television that an action is being planned for some particular day at a particular hour, without indicating the precise location. An appointment is made for an underground platform. These actions take the form of the self-requisitioning of housing in the case of DAL, and temporary occupations in the case of AC!. For example, a firm is occupied and the management is called upon to explain

redundancies or the existence of unfilled posts. AC! established itself in the rue du Dragon in the winter of 1995 and is next to DAL. The co-ordination between AC! and CGT councils of the unemployed issued in the unemployed movement of winter 1997, marked by numerous occupations of ASSEDIC (the organization administering unemployment insurance payments).

22 Jean-Baptiste Eyraud, DAL's founder, was a Maoist at secondary school and then a CFDT activist. In 1982, he occupied a factory that had been closed and made contact with various associations, notably Emmaüs, founded by abbé Simon (Salmon, *Le Désir de société*, p. 171). Christophe Aguiton, one of SUD's founders, is a CFDT dissident (Combesque, *Ça suffit!*, p. 145). J. Dessenard, national representative of the Mouvement national des chômeurs et des précaires, was an LCR activist until 1997 (Poulet, 'À gauche de la gauche').

23 See Charles Tilly, *Class and Collective Action*, Sage, Beverly Hills 1981.

24 Thus, the same people can be mobilized under one acronym or a different one, depending on the cause being defended: 'Some members of SUD prefer AC!'s banner to that of their own union if they are marching against unemployment, or that of petitioners if they are demonstrating against the Debré law' (Aguiton and Bensaïd, *Le Retour de la question sociale*, p. 199).

25 Ibid., p. 200.

26 No one is *for* exclusion. All political tendencies are agreed in condemning it, except for the Club de l'Horloge. In 1995, the latter produced under the signature of P. Millan a text (*Le Refus de l'exclusion*, 'Lettres du Monde') which, criticizing the 'ideologies' of human rights, sought to differentiate between 'legitimate exclusions' and 'illegitimate exclusions'.

27 'Exclusion is to tomorrow's society what the working-class question was to yesterday's, and it must be extricated from its charitable or humanitarian coating in order to make it a political concept – that is to say, a concept of struggle.' 'Exclusion outside the firm often begins with exploitation inside it, particularly of poorly qualified workers or irregular workers.' But 'an "exploited" class at least has economic relations with the "exploiters" who oppress them. To adopt the famous enumeration of the 1848 *Communist Manifesto*, this applied to the slaves and plebs of Antiquity, the serfs of the Middle Ages or journeymen confronting master-artisans and, obviously, to the working-class proletariat of the nineteenth and twentieth centuries. The exploited are useful to the exploiters, because they are there and they work. Excluded people are perhaps equally "useful" to the excluders, if one reckons that in separating themselves from them the excluders have managed to to free themselves of people who are regarded as a dead weight. But they are then useful only by their absence. They are useful only because they have become useless. Exploiters and exploited, oppressors and oppressed, share the same economic and social sphere. They form a couple, even if it is inegalitarian and tempestuous. For their part, excluders and excluded have severed their ties, and their respective domains are divorced from one another' (Jean-Baptiste Foucauld and Denis Pivetau, *Une Société en quête de sens*, Odile Jacob, Paris 1995, pp. 13, 144–45).

28 The distinction between networker and network-extender is not defined by their respective ability to make a profit. Just as there are actors who, while developing a networking logic, fail in their undertakings and do not succeed in becoming indispensable keyholders for others (they are endlessly on the lookout for new connections, and have a quantity of names in their address books, but are not included in anyone's address book), so the network-extender's oblatory qualities are insufficient to ensure success. We shall say that a network-extender fails when, in the grip of boundless generosity, he passes on everything – people, information, and so on – without anything accumulating around him. He multiplies links, but does not succeed in co-ordinating them towards a goal for a limited period of time. He tirelessly constructs a network but without being able to establish the forms of provisional stabilization or, if you like, postponement of displacements and connections represented by projects.

29 See Michel Callon, 'Réseaux technico-économiques et irréversibilité', in Robert Boyer, ed., *Réversibilité et irréversibilité en économie*, EHESS, Paris 1991, pp. 195–230; and Callon, ed., *Ces réseaux que la raison ignore*, L'Harmattan, Paris 1993.

30 Ronald Burt, *Structural Holes*, Harvard University Press, Cambridge (MA) 1992; and 'The Social Structure of Competition', in N. Nohria and R. Eccles, eds, *Networks and Organizations: Structure, Form, and Action*, Harvard University Press, Cambridge (MA) 1992, pp. 57–91.

31 In a recent article, Burt undertakes on the basis of empirical work with fifty MBA students at Chicago University, who are also full-time employees in firms, to compare their positions in networks (focused on the contrast between those who have remained enclosed in cliques or rigid hierarchical structures and those who have broken through to structural holes) and their 'personality traits', assessed by means of a self-administered test perfected by a consulting agency. In those whose position in networks is rich in structural holes, he discovers many characteristics approximating to those that we have attributed to connexionist man, with this difference: the adjectives employed by Burt are always laudatory when speaking of people who are at ease in networks, and somewhat derogatory when speaking of those who have proved incapable of quitting their clique: the former see themselves as players, are profoundly independent, have an ability to create an aura of excitement around them, love change, are interested in others and the information they may be able to supply them with. They are independent *outsiders*. Contrariwise, those who live in cliques are repelled by risk, love security and stability, are obedient, concentrate on technical details, stress systems and procedures: they are conformist *insiders*. See Ronald S. Burt, Joseph E. Jannotta and James T. Mahoney, 'Personality Correlates of Structural Holes', *Social Networks*, no. 20, 1998, pp. 63–87.

32 The reasoning here is similar to that developed by economic analyses of corruption focused on the pursuit of unearned income. An economy of corruption is possible only if there exist boundaries and regulations the crossing and infringement of which are assigned a cost. It is the differential between an institutionalized space and a space of networks making it possible to surmount institutional separations and regulations that opens up the possibility of profit (Jacques Cartier-Bresson, 'Éléments d'analyse pour une économie de la corruption', *Revue Tiers-Monde*, no. 131, 1992, pp. 581–609).

33 See A.O. Hirschman, *Exit, Voice and Loyalty*, Harvard University Press, Cambridge (MA) 1970.

34 This is the principle that restricts the expansion of drug-trafficking networks. The person who manages to establish a chain must do everything he can to ensure that those below him in the channel do not possess his information about the sources of supply, so that they must go through him to be supplied, and so that those above him cannot come to a direct arrangement with the dealers. He must do anything, including using violence, to prevent newcomers establishing themselves. In this respect, drug-traffickers are conservative. They seek not to extend the network but, on the contrary, to close it: to form a mafia (Michel Schiray, 'Les filières-stupéfiants: trois niveaux, cinq logiques', *Futuribles*, March 1994). Given that information in a network of this sort is very fragmented and unequally distributed, the network as such exists only for the police who seek to accumulate the information and trace the chain of supply.

35 The occupation of a position of responsibility or power, while conferring on the occupier a certain visibility that is conducive to the development of connections, nevertheless curbs – if it is taken seriously – the creation of a social capital that is rich in structural holes. On the one hand, the official character of institutional power brings a constraint to bear on the nature of the links that can be forged. On the other hand, the power-holder – this guardian of things and of those who ensure their maintenance – is constrained by that over which his power is exercised.

36 The grief and nostalgia of emigration stem from a converse way of experiencing departure, which is doubtless a sign of the change in world and values. For the migrant who is moving far away, it is himself whom he finds alone, severed from his links, leaving everyone else behind, so that at the moment of departure he dreams of returning. By contrast, today's excluded person finds himself destitute because the others have left without even dreaming of returning, leaving him isolated.

37 See Burt, *Structural Holes.*

38 The relationship between capitalism and the family has thus altered considerably over the last thirty years. The combination of two types of value that formerly had a key position in the portrait of the bourgeois – family values and pecuniary values – when capitalism rested on a patrimonial basis and sought to stabilize and domesticate a mobile, unruly workforce, now tends to be replaced by a different scenario, where the stress on mobility renders attachment to the family a handicap. The fragmented family – 'reconstructed' in line with changes in situation and displacements and, if we may put it this way, 'flexible' – thus seems to have an affinity with a network form of capitalism.

39 It is this exploitation in the strong sense that is targeted, for example, by Simon Weil under the term 'oppression', and which she describes in her factory journal (*La Condition ouvrière,* Gallimard, Paris 1951). 'This', she writes in a letter to Albertine Thévenon published in the same volume, 'is what working in a factory meant. It meant that all the external reasons (previously, I thought they were internal) which the sense of my dignity and self-respect were based on for me have, in the space of two or three weeks, been radically shattered under the impact of a brutal, daily duress' (p. 27). And a few pages later, in a letter to an unknown correspondent, she writes: 'When you say, for example, that once he has left the factory the unskilled worker is no longer imprisoned in the domain of mass production, you're obviously right. But what do you conclude from this? If you conclude that every human being, however oppressed, still has the chance to act as a human being every day, all well and good. But if you conclude that the existence of an unskilled worker at Renault or Citroën is a satisfactory existence for a man who wants to preserve his human dignity, I cannot go along with you' (p. 44).

40 The sum total of transactions on the foreign exchange market linked to trade in commodities represented barely 3 per cent of total transactions in 1992 (see François Chesnais, *La Mondialisation du capital,* Syros, Paris 1994, p. 209). Whereas in 1980 movements bound up with the import and export of goods and services represented more than 70 per cent of the flows of the French balance of payments, this share had fallen to around 31 per cent in 1992, the rest comprising capital movements (measured here by variations in periodic outstanding debts, and hence not taking all the circuits into account). Already remarkable in themselves, these figures must be interpreted against the background of an enormous increase in the movement of capital of every type, which in the same period rose from 14 per cent of GDP to 89 per cent (ibid., p. 228).

41 Recourse by states to international financial markets to finance themselves sharply accelerated the process of the globalization of markets. In 1970, the American federal debt was 322 billion dollars, in 1992 4,061 billion, and in 1998 it was predicted to be 6,141 billion. These requirements were financed largely by resort to foreign capital (ibid., p. 221).

42 Immediately after the collapse of the Bretton Woods system under the impact of the suspension of dollar/gold convertibility in 1971, 'the consensus of the profession, basing itself on the theses of the monetarist Milton Friedman, was that the system of floating exchange rates discouraged speculation, since rates would automatically reflect the underlying "fundamentals" of economies' (Ibrahim Warde, 'Les maîtres auxiliaires des marchés. Le projet de taxe Tobin, bête noire des spéculateurs, cible des censeurs', *Le Monde diplomatique,* February 1997, pp. 24–5). The outcome was precisely the opposite. According to Chesnais (*La Mondialisation du capital,* p. 207), 'the exchange markets are now in a position to alter the relative rate of *all currencies without exception,* including the dollar, in order to collect the particular variety of speculative profits that they feed on'.

43 Takeover bids usually focus on firms whose price is adjudged low relative to potential profitability. An offer to buy the firm's shares at a price superior to its current price is made in order to try to take control of it. The firm, especially if it is acquired by a 'raider' – i.e. with a view to short-term profitability – and not, for example, by a competitor who thereby enhances its global weight, can then be broken up, sold in 'blocks', and in any case subject to restructuring

so as to extract the profitability it is considered capable of and to recoup the initial outlay on the operation. Because their capital is spread widely among the public, firms said to be 'liable to takeover' must offset this risk by reporting strong profitability.

44 The decompartmentalization of the various markets (foreign exchange, credit, bonds and shares) has been widely encouraged by the emergence of new financial products. In France, the most important decompartmentalizing measure was introduced by the 1984 law, which abolished the separation between long-term credit and loans and short-term credit (Chesnais, *La Mondialisation du capital*, p. 226). Moreover, disintermediation has allowed multinationals to make direct use of the markets without going through banks. These developments have helped to centralize all the sources of international financing in a very few hands. The actors in financial markets are in fact far fewer and much easier to identify than the impersonal term 'markets' suggests.

45 For a multinational group, any industrial decision, whether short-, medium- or long-term, must take into account a mass of financial variables: the evolution of exchange rates, the comparison between interest rates according to their term and country, and so on. And the stakes are considerable, for the financial costs bound up with exchange-rate risks can vary by as much as 100 per cent, unlike other exploitation outgoings. To take a single example: a group that makes out half of its receipts in dollars loses 5 per cent of its turnover (expressed in national currency) if the dollar falls by 10 per cent. According to the figures supplied by Claude Serfati ('Les groupes industriels acteurs de la mondialisation financière', *Le Monde diplomatique*, no. 23, special issue, January 1995), which were valid at the time he was writing, to cover oneself on the dollar at 5.30 francs at 6 months, it was necessary to pay 2.6 of the nominal sum total of the contract and 4.4 per cent at 2 years. On the market in interest-rate options, in order to guarantee an interest rate of 6.5 per cent, the option at 2 years cost 1.7 per cent and that at 5 years 6.5 per cent. Hence in order to to borrow at 6.5 per cent, augmented by the cost of the option guaranteeing this rate, it is necessary to post profitability at a still higher rate so as to be able to repay the loan and to satisfy the shareholders who, believing that their risk is higher than the lender's, want a higher yield.

46 Processes of industrial concentration carried out in the European Community developed at a faster pace above all after 1987, with the prospect of the single market and then a single currency. According to the figures quoted by Chesnais (*La Mondialisation du capital*, p. 70), there were four times as many mergers and acquisitions of majority interests in 1988–89 as in 1982–83. The sum total of mergers and acquisitions on a world scale reached a historical record in 1998. The previous record dated from 1997.

47 In order to take account of the fact that the opportunities and risks generated by financial markets (particularly the foreign exchange markets) are often greater than those created by industrial activities, a number of large groups possess trading rooms which have no cause to envy – except perhaps when it comes to size – those of banks and have established their own banks and credit institutions. They have also acquired the habit of placing a percentage of their funds on the financial markets (not in new industrial projects) in order more easily to satisfy financial dealers. Thus, they tap the remuneration demanded of them by the latter on the markets, which obviously does not greatly please the financial traders, who then bring all sorts of pressure to bear so that the firms release their funds to them (using the argument that it is exclusively their job to invest). One of the techniques permitting this transfer to be made is for a firm to buy its own shares. In so doing, it effectively transfers part of its funds into the hands of former owners of its shares, it helps to push up the prices, and ensures greater profitability for remaining shareholders, since the number of shares in circulation is lower relative to the profit to be distributed, which in theory is stable. In addition, from the standpoint of the markets this transfer of funds has the advantage of reducing the autonomy of firms, which will have to come to them to borrow in order to finance subsequent industrial projects.

48 In this respect, the Hoover affair was especially striking. At the beginning of 1993, the Maytag group took the decision to close its vacuum-cleaner factory at Dijon and concentrate all

production in its second factory – Longvic in Scotland – where more space was in fact available, even if the directors foregrounded lower wage costs in Scotland. What the official version does not say is that the management had threatened Scotland with closure in order to extract a downwards revision of the house agreement from the trade unions and, in particular, to impose recruitment conditions that were especially harsh for the new employees required for the transfer from Dijon (fixed-term two-year contract and exclusion from the company pension scheme for this period). It was only once agreement had been secured that the management announced the closure of the Dijon factory, which had doubtless been decided prior to the negotiations. In addition, this simple transfer of capacity, with the ultimate destruction of jobs at a European level, was regarded as a new start-up in Scotland, which allowed it to collect local subsidies (10 million pounds). According to the Hoover management, the French authorities offered the same amount in the event of a transfer in the opposite direction, which did not influence the final decision. But has anyone asked if the firm would quite simply have closed a factory had it not benefited from a subsidy on the occasion of this restructuring? See Pierre Sohlberg, 'Les leçons de l'affaire Hoover', *Alternatives économiques*, no. 106, April 1993.

49 Faced with the general outcry that greeted the publication of the draft agreement, the latter was handed over to negotiation in the World Trade Organization, which has the advantage, when it comes to amending the clauses that are most disadvantageous for countries, of representing only the rich countries.

50 The percentage of direct foreign investment deriving from the financial sector (banks, securities firms, insurance companies, pension funds) has in fact increased in the context of a general increase in direct foreign investment. In the Multilateral Agreement on Investment, 'investment' was defined in such a way as to encompass direct investment, but also portfolio investment, real-estate investment and royalties deriving from contracts.

51 Car manufacturers increasingly ask their suppliers to provide them with complete 'units' (an already assembled front compartment, the complete seating mechanism with the seat supports, fully equipped dashboard), which assumes transferring to the suppliers numerous processes involved in the collection and assembly of the components that make up the unit. The final assembly of the vehicles in the manufacturers' factories, which must still be done close to the final consumer, will progressively boil down to the assembling of various units. The car, an especially complex and 'heavy' product on account of the very large number of components required, will then have become a 'light' product industrially. It could even be that manufacturers will ask their subcontractors to finance part of their final assembly factories, since this is what we have observed with the construction in Lorraine of Mercedes' Smart (ex-Swatch) factory.

52 See Michel Amar, 'Les effets du "flux tendu"', *L'Entreprise*, no. 2518, special issue on 'La France des entreprises', 1992, pp. 234–5.

53 The recent success of Dell in the computing market is utterly exemplary. By selling its computers directly over the Internet, the firm economizes on distribution costs and, in addition, offers a better service since, being in direct contact with the customer, it can configure its computers in the factory directly with the desired software.

54 Because several forms of exploitation exist, the transition from one form to another can sometimes be experienced as a relative liberation, and sometimes as an unprecedented enslavement. In *Origins of Our Time: The Great Transformation* (Victor Gollancz, London 1945), Karl Polanyi thus observes that the new forms of exploitation established with the Industrial Revolution were rapidly regarded as unbearable by the English peasantry, which enjoyed a relative autonomy, but greeted with less hostility by the peasants of central Europe, whose condition had hitherto often approximated to serfdom. The same applies to current changes in the mode of exploitation, which can be experienced by those who undergo them as autonomization or casualization depending on the harshness with which industrial and bureaucratic forms of control are exercised over them.

55 Thus, against those who emphasize the 'abolition of private property', Claude Lefort observes that if the bureaucracy in the USSR is what it is 'by virtue of the planning and nationalization that guarantee it a material basis', its origin lies in a 'political bureaucracy' – that is to say, 'in the concentration of authority in the hands of a ruling minority, the exclusion of the masses from the sphere where information circulates and decisions are taken, the hierarchization of functions and wage differentiations, the rigorous division of tasks – in short, a scientific organization of inequality such that it becomes the principle of a new class oppression'. In this instance, 'participating in the appropriation of surplus-value is the same thing as participating in a system of domination' (*Éléments d'une critique de la bureaucratie*, Droz, Geneva-Paris 1971, pp. 308–9).

56 Ibid., pp. 298–9.

57 As Jon Elster has convincingly shown, the necessity of basing a critique of exploitation on a norm of justice and, consequently, on moral principles, also applies to Marx, despite the numerous passages in his work where moral claims are the target of his irony (*Making Sense of Marx*, Cambridge University Press/Éditions de la Maison des Sciences de l'Homme, Cambridge 1985, pp. 261 ff). See also the excellent clarification by Jacques Hoarau, 'La philosophie morale de Marx et le marxisme', in *Dictionnaire d'éthique et de philosophie morale*, Presses Universitaires de France, Paris 1996.

58 Thus, an exploited person in the domestic world is, for example, a younger brother compelled to serve the heir in a world governed by birthright. An exploited person in the commercial world is such because she is poor and consequently cannot buy the instrument of production she needs to exploit her labour. An exploited person in the industrial world is someone who does not obtain a wage that corresponds to his qualifications in so far as they help to produce value added. For this reason, in an industrial world the wages hierarchy is the subject of many disputes intended to settle fair remuneration. An exploited person in the civic world is the mere citizen without any power, whom his representatives exploit by imposing a tax that serves to enrich them. An exploited person in the reputational world is someone who helps to make the famous man known, without benefiting from it. The exploited person in the inspirational world is the assistant who whispers his ideas to the painter of genius without receiving any dividends. Given that exploitation is a notion bound up with capitalism, it is normal for it to be formulated on each occasion in terms of unfair monetary remuneration.

59 This means that we will encounter exploitation only by listening to critical actors denouncing it and accusing exploiters. But we will never encounter anyone who claims to be an exploiter. This is why the existence of some form or another of exploitation can always be denied, with the victims or their champions bearing the whole burden of proof.

60 Jürgen Habermas, *Legitimation Crisis*, trans. Thomas McCarthy, Heinemann, London 1976, p. 69.

61 Let us take the example of the introduction into the business world of a logic of the *signature*, hitherto reserved for intellectuals and artists. It fundamentally alters the conditions of competition between actors. In a hierarchical logic, it is in so far as the director holds a position and fulfils its obligations that he has the right to take credit for the success of the collective (service, department, administration, etc.). But the formal dimension of this attribution attenuates its personal character and confers on it some of the properties of representation: at the meeting where he is the only one to have been invited, the director *represents* his colleagues, who can control their sense of expropriation by regarding him as a kind of representative. However, in the case of the networker who mounts an operation, and who is already preparing for the next one, the attribution assumes the personal character of a signature. Competition then becomes a direct competition for the name – that is to say, either directly for the signature, or, when this goal is unattainable, for association with the success of a proper noun (I worked with such and such, I was so-and-so's assistant on some project, etc.). But therewith anxiety over identity, which was comparatively controlled by hierarchical subordination, re-emerges with all

its force and, with it, permanent suspicion of misappropriation and usurpation. The opportunistic posture appropriate to a connexionist world therewith finds itself, as Paolo Virno observes, 'tinged with fear': 'The fear of specific or merely potential perils *haunts* working time like an impression one cannot get out of one's mind.' But this fear, adds Virno, itself constitutes one of the motors of adjustment to the new working conditions: 'Insecurity about one's own availability for periodic innovation, fear of losing one's scarcely established prerogatives, anxiety about "being left behind" – all this translates into flexibility, obedience, promptness in redeployment' (*Opportunisme, cynisme et peur*, Éditions de l'Éclat, Combas 1991, pp. 16–17).

62 See Nathalie Sarthou-Lajus, *L'Éthique de la dette*, Presses Universitaires de France, Paris 1997.

63 Ibid., pp. 8–9.

64 See Pierre Rosanvallon, *L'État en France de 1790 à nos jours*, Seuil, Paris 1990.

65 See Peter Wagner, *A Sociology of Modernity: Liberty and Discipline*, Routledge, London and New York 1994.

66 Nicolas Dodier, *Les Hommes et les machines. La conscience collective dans les sociétés technicisées*, Métailié, Paris 1995, p. 35.

67 Stand-ins cannot be controlled directly, and their loyalty is a matter of trust. But when those who perform this role realize that they are the object of a breach of trust on the part of their principal (a realization that can only strengthen the diffusion of strategic knowledge about the forms of success in a network world), they can in turn seek to profit from their situation by appropriating to their own advantage the connections whose maintenance they ensure. A paradigmatic illustration of this scenario is to be found in Mankiewicz's film *All about Eve*. Eve is the stand-in for a great actress. Through guile, she succeeds in introducing herself to the actress's contacts and profiting from them (by playing on the rivalries in the circle her principal moves in), in such a way as to exaggerate her credits. At a propitious moment (the actress is away, removed from the scene by guile; one cannot be everywhere), she instigates the test of strength, and supplants the person whose power she has requisitioned. At the end of the film, a debutant actress, similar to what Eve was some months earlier, introduces herself. The cycle begins again.

68 See Günther Teubner, 'Nouvelles formes d'organisation et droit', *Revue française de gestion*, November/December 1993, pp. 50–68.

69 See Charles Sabel, 'Constitutional Ordering in Historical Context', in Fritz Scharpf, ed., *Games in Hierarchy and Networks*, Westview Press, Boulder (CO), 1993, pp. 65–123.

70 See François Eymard-Duvernay, 'Les marchés du travail: une approche institutionnaliste pluraliste', communication to the economic policy seminar, FORUM, University of Paris X, Nanterre, 1998.

71 The theme of the 'skilling organization' (developed following a report by Antoine Riboud in 1987) may be regarded as an attempt to shift the development of employability from the status of 'social objective' (i.e., in this context, benefiting wage-earners without contributing to profit creation) to that of 'economic stake'. In effect, among the management currents developing this approach (Philippe Zarifian, 'Compétences et organisation qualifiante en milieu industriel', in F. Minet *et al.*, eds, *La Compétence. Mythe, construction ou réalité*, L'Harmattan, Paris 1994), the skilling organization is what allows actors integrated into a project to develop their skills – not by withdrawing from production to go on a training course, but precisely through contact with more or less uncertain 'events' (breakdown of machinery, alterations to products, etc.), which punctuate the realization of the project and are put to use through cycles of reflexivity. These favour the diffusion of the learning experience and the ability to 'transfer what has been learnt in certain situations into other circumstances. Skills training is thus supposed to reconcile the bestowing of employability and the search for optimum performance. It is "the product that fires and maintains the dynamic", so that the "development of skills" is the result of "economic performance"' (Michel Parlier, Christian Perrien and Dominique Thierry, 'L'organisation qualifiante et ses enjeux dix ans après', *Revue française de gestion*, no. 116, November/December 1997, pp. 4–17).

72 Such a right is currently developing on the basis, in particular, of the Court of Appeal's judgement of 25 February 1992, which held that 'the employer, obliged to fulfil the work contract in good faith, has the duty to ensure that wage-earners are adapted to the development of their job'. This judgement restricts the principle, which had hitherto obtained, of the employer as 'sole judge of the aptitude' of the wage-earner, the common-law work contract not in principle giving rise to any obligation for training at the employer's expense. 'Training can henceforth be required by the judge, as a means used by the employer to perform his duty', the ground of professional inadequacy not being deemed valid in justifying termination of a contract if the employer has failed in his duty to provide training. Conversely, 'instances of rejection of training by the wage-earner, referred to the judge, are sanctioned by redundancy' (Jean-Marie Luttringer, "'L'entreprise formatrice" sous le regard des juges', *Droit social*, no. 3, March 1994, pp. 283–90).

73 In line with the 'skilling organization', the principle of the A. Cap 2000 agreement is the development of individual skills, defined as 'validated operational *savoir-faire*'. The notion of skill, institutionalized in this agreement, owes a lot to recent developments in cognitive psychology, the emphasis being put on training in action, in the face of unpredictable developments, and on the transferability of the acquisition of schemas rather than the learning of knowledge. It is accompanied by the establishment of a methodology of appraisal and validation, derived from work conducted over twenty years in educational circles, that is based on 'reference systems' – i.e. specifications of actions in post – which presupposes an exhaustive codification of forms of human action. The validation of a skill is subject to tests and based on an assessment of what is correct centred on the properties of individuals as disclosed by their performance ('to each according to his skills'), and not by their position in a cartographical representation of the division of labour ('same post, same pay'): see Lucie Tanguy, 'Compétences et intégration sociale dans l'entreprise', in F. Ropé and Tanguy, eds, *Savoirs et compétences. De l'usage des notions dans l'école et l'entreprise*, L'Harmattan, Paris 1994.

74 The right to a skills appraisal is written into the field of application of the clauses relating to professional training in Book IX of the *Code du travail*. It is similar to individual leave for training. It is an individual right that each wage-earner can activate in the context of their work contract, without the employer being able to oppose it. But this right really only took effect in 1993 and, according to the consulting firm CEGOS, remains relatively unknown to wage-earners, having been used by only 20,000 of them. In practice, the skills appraisal, made by psychologists, trainers or recruiters, is similar to coaching: those who undergo it derive no direct advantage apart from a better knowledge of themselves, their resources and desires, paving the way for greater realism. In this sense, it involves a kind of democratization of coaching, or the transformation of coaching into a universal right: A 'national reference system of qualifications constructed by occupational spheres and levels, comprising simple but capitalizable elements corresponding to basic occupational skills' (Michel de Virville, chairman, *Donner un nouvel élan à la formation professionnelle*, report of the assignment given by the Minister of Labour, Social Dialogue and Participation, Paris 1996). The function of the national reference system of qualifications is 'to place on an equal footing three ways of acquiring qualifications': initial training, continuous professional training, and professional experience.

75 See Myriam Campinos-Dubernet, 'La gestion des sureffectifs, la fin des illusions des ressources humaines?', *Travail et emploi*, no. 64, 1995, pp. 23–4.

76 Traditionally, certification in France is 'a prerogative of the public authorities'. Until recently, most diplomas were awarded by the state education system – something that is no longer the case today, with the proliferation of certifications redefined and recognized solely by professional sectors. Reference to diplomas (mainly CAP and BTS) features in most collective agreements. In the sample of sector agreements studied by Annette Jobert and Michèle Tallard, 88 per cent of grids cite at least one diploma and 41 per cent cited at least five. Since the beginning of the 1990s, new bodies – the national joint employment committees – have validated professional training certificates, breaking into the monopoly of the state education system.

These certificates are defined in terms not of content, but of objectives to be attained ('being capable of'), which is consistent with a logic of skills. They have developed primarily in the iron and steel industry (120 professional training certificates in the mid-1990s). See Jobert and Tallard, 'Diplômes et certifications de branches dans les conventions collectives', *Formation emploi*, no. 52, October/December 1995.

77 See Laurent Thévenot, 'Un gouvernement par les normes. Pratiques et politiques des formats d'information', in B. Conein and Thévenot, eds, *Cognition et information en société*, Éditions de l'EHESS, Paris 1997, pp. 205–42.

78 See Michel Capron, 'Vers un renouveau de la comptabilité des ressources humaines', *Revue française de gestion*, November/December 1995, pp. 46–54; Sonja A. Sackmann, Eric G. Flamholtz and Maria Lombardi Bullen, 'Human Resource Accounting: A State-of-the-Art Review', *Journal of Accounting Literature*, vol. 8, 1989, pp. 235–64. The human resources accounting current in fact covers a large range of works, some of which seem to tend in the direction of increasing the pressure on wage-earners, whereas others are inspired by the project of changing accounting tools in order to 'encourage employers to imagine employees as an assessable resource of the organization that can increase or depreciate in value depending on how it is managed' (Capron, 'Vers un renouveau de la comptabilité des ressources humaines', p. 46). Such an effort must be conceived in tandem with a reflection on the obligations on firms to publish information, of which the clauses on the 'social audit' communicated to works councils represented the first step (see Raymond Danziger, *Le Bilan social, outil d'information et de gestion*, Dunod, Paris 1983). The zenith of human resources accounting occurred in 1976 with the publication of a special issue of the journal *Accounting, Organizations and Society*. In France, mention must be made of the precursor book by Edmond Marquès, *La Gestion des ressources humaines* (Hommes et techniques, Paris 1980) and the works on hidden costs by Henri Savall (see Savall and Véronique Zardet, *Le nouveau contrôle de gestion*, Malesherbes, Eyrolles, Paris 1993), which instead illustrated the use of human resources accounting for productivity purposes. For its part, in the 1970s ANACT carried out work on the costs of bad working conditions (see *Les Coûts des conditions de travail. Guide d'évaluation économique*, 3 vols, Paris 1979; and Bernard Martory, 'Les coûts des conditions de travail. Fondements et outils', *Revue française de comptabilité*, no. 101, March 1980, pp. 136–41).

79 Alain Supiot, 'Le travail, liberté partagée', *Droit social*, nos 9–10, September/October 1993, p. 723.

80 Anne-Marie Guillemard, 'Emploi, protection sociale et cycle de vie: résultats d'une comparaison internationale des dispositifs de sortie anticipée d'activité', *Sociologie du travail*, no. 3, 1993, pp. 257–84.

81 Quoted in André Gorz, *Critique of Economic Reason*, trans. Gillian Handyside and Chris Turner, Verso, London and New York 1990, p. 210.

82 See Pascale Arbant, 'Le capital de temps de formation', *Droit social*, no. 2, February 1994, pp. 200–3.

83 See Bernard Girard, 'Vers un nouveau pacte social', *Revue française de gestion*, no. 100, September/October 1994, pp. 78–88.

84 The author gives the example of the German group Adam Opel SA, which had Volkswagen condemned on these grounds in 1993. It is the fear of seeing wage-earners leave with the skills capital they have acquired in the firm that has led to combining with 'skills-giving training' contractual loyalty clauses (so-called 'forfeit-training'), imposed on wage-earners selected to undertake training conducive to professional mobility (see Patrick Guilloux, 'Négociation collective et adaptation professionnelle des salariés aux évolutions de l'emploi', *Droit social*, no. 11, November 1990, pp. 818–32).

85 This restriction has generated numerous critiques (see, for example, Sabel, 'Constitutional Ordering in Historical Context' as regards transaction costs), which have recently prompted reflections aiming to reintroduce an 'ethical' concern into theories of agency, particularly by taking into account both the agent's obligations towards the principal (as in the standard theory)

and the principal's towards the agent (see Norman Bowie and Edward Freeman, eds, *Ethics and Agency Theory*, Oxford University Press, Oxford 1992).

86 See Oliver Williamson, *The Economic Institutions of Capitalism*, Free Press, New York 1985; John Pratt and Richard Zeckhauser, eds, *Principals and Agents: The Structure of Business*, Harvard Business School, Boston (MA) 1985.

87 See Diego Gambetta, *Trust: Making and Breaking Cooperative Relations*, Cambridge University Press, Cambridge 1988; Philippe Bernoux and Jean-Michel Servet, eds, *La Construction sociale de la confiance*, Montchrestien, Paris 1997.

88 These classical theories of agency feature only individuals pursuing their personal interests, who possess an interest in co-ordinating with one another in order to share risk, but also a tendency to deceive their associates. They lead in circular fashion from the market to hierarchy and from hierarchy to the market (Bernard Baudry, 'De la confiance dans la relation d'emploi et de sous-traitance', *Sociologie du travail*, no. 1, 1994, pp. 43–61). As we know, in Williamson the firm is in fact 'a functional substitute for trust' (Mark Granovetter, 'Economic Action and Social Structure: The Problem of Embeddedness', *American Journal of Sociology*, vol. 91, no. 3, November 1985, pp. 481–510). The potential for opportunistic behaviour associated with the impossibility of establishing *ex ante* complete contracts (limited rationality) makes authority and hierarchical control – based on an exchange of property rights – (costly) palliatives for market uncertainty. On the other hand, however, the agents who intervene in the bureaucratic firm (e.g. directors), not all of whose behaviour is observable or measurable (except at exorbitant cost), have specific interests and can interpret the instructions of the *principal* (e.g. shareholders) to their own advantage – but the same remarks apply to public bureaucracies – so that the search for palliatives for bureaucratic uncertainty returns, as in a swing of the pendulum, towards the market as a self-restraining mechanism. The analysis of trust itself does not avoid a conflict of anthropologies, which gives it an unstable character, either because it is reduced to clearly understood interest, as in the theory of agency where trust is the consequence of reputational effects, or because people seek to derive it directly from the altruistic predispositions of human beings, giving it an individual, voluntaristic character that is scarcely conducive to the search for stabilizing mechanisms.

89 See Walter Powell, 'Neither Market nor Hierarchy: Network Forms of Organization', *Research in Organizational Behavior*, vol. 12, 1990, pp. 295–336.

90 'The Clavaud case established the wage-earner's freedom of expression on his working conditions outside the firm. Alain Clavaud was made redundant by the Dunlop company following the publication by the newspaper *L'Humanité* of an interview where he spoke of his work. The Riom Appeal Court ruled that if no sanctions against the right of expression in the firm existed, it could not be otherwise outside the firm, and the Court of Cassation concurred with this reasoning.' ' More recently, wage-earners' freedom of expression outside the firm has been clearly based upon article 11 of the 1789 Declaration, which marks the intervention of constitutional rules in the work relationship' (Bonnechère, *Le Droit du travail*, p. 62).

91 Large firms have a collective interest in seeing a reduction in the corruption of their intermediaries, so that they no longer have to play the role of corrupter obliged to pay in order to secure certain markets in France or abroad, which unquestionably harms their profitability. But initiatives at this level seem limited and instead derive from financial markets unhappy about seeing some of the monetary funds they grant disappearing into the remuneration of intermediaries without creating value.

92 See Thévenot, 'Un gouvernement par les normes'.

93 Isabelle Astier, *Revenu minimum et souci d'insertion*, Desclée de Brouwer, Paris 1997.

94 The words of an association official, quoted in Denis Bouget *et al.*, *Les Politiques de lutte contre la grande pauvreté*, 4 vols, Centre d'économie des besoins sociaux, Nantes 1995, p. 17.

95 See Cécile Baron *et al.*, *Les Intermédiaires de l'insertion*, CEE, Paris 1994.

96 See Eymard-Duvernay, 'Les marchés du travail'.

97 See ibid. and Eymard-Duvernay, 'Les contrats de travail: une approche comparative', in C. Bessy and Eymard-Duvernay, eds, *Les Intermédiaires du marché du travail*, Cahiers du CEE, Presses Universitaires de France, Paris 1997, pp. 3–34.

98 Supiot, 'Le travail, liberté partagée', pp. 719, 721, 723. In a recent article ('Du bon usage des lois en matière d'emploi'), Supiot has returned to the notion of *activity*. He criticizes it inasmuch as, being 'inseparable from existence', it refers to the universal social rights that are those of existence and not 'of a sort to ground specific rights' and, consequently, permit redefinition of a 'professional condition' – that is to say, a different *employment statute*, constituted in France (Sapiot says) on the model of the civil service statute. He now prefers the term *work*, defined not by wage-earning, but by obligation. In this sense of the term, any activity subject to an *obligation*, whatever its contractual or statutory origin, is work, whether it is performed for pay or for free. The criterion here is the inscription of work in a legal bond involving sanction in the event of default. In an article echoing Supiot's, Dominique Méda poses the issue of the state's role in financing this new statute and the gradual transition to abandonment of the individualistic notion of work contract and wage, 'compensating the contribution of a particular individual', in order for 'the profoundly collective character of work' to be recognized ('Travail et politiques sociales', *Droit social*, no. 4, April 1994, pp. 334–42).

99 François Gaudu shows how, over the last twenty years, activity has penetrated the sphere of work via exceptional contracts 'whose purpose is the training or integration of workers', and also how work has fitted into activity with the inclusion of the work contract in 'personalized careers', requiring its articulation with other legal acts. He gives the example of the 'integration contracts' and 'career agreements' – mechanisms associated with the *Revenu minimum d'insertion* – which define a *progression* whose objective, 'ultimately, is the signature of a work contract', but also that of 'training credits', which provide entitlement to a 'personalized project of a programme of training', associated with 'skills appraisals' and a 'procedure for validating achievement' ('Travail et activité', *Droit social*, no. 2, February 1997, pp. 119–26).

100 Jean Boissonat, *Le Travail dans vingt ans*, Commissariat général du Plan, Odile Jacob et Documentation française, Paris 1995, p. 48.

101 The authors of the report regard the significance accorded in France to the initial education delivered by the education system as one of the main obstacles to such mobility (and, indirectly, one of the main causes of unemployment and also of inequalities in chances of unemployment, which are related to the level of academic qualification). They counterpose to it a 'plurality of educational paths', an education spread over the whole of people's lives, with a sequence of periods of study and periods of activity, which demands 'deep, organized and lasting involvement by firms in the education and training process', and a transition 'from the work contract to the work-training contract, or, in other words, an activity contract'.

102 See Jean-Yves Kerbourc'h, 'Le travail temporaire: une forme déjà élaborée de «contrat d'activité»', *Droit social*, no. 2, February 1997, pp. 127–32.

103 Gaudu, 'Travail et activité'. The activity contract is not an absolute utopia, and legal frameworks approximating to this formula exist. This is the case notably with the Groupement d'employeurs (established by the law of 25 July 1985, modified in 1993), which allows 'firms, small or medium-sized, to create a new legal entity, the employer of wage-earners who are then put at the disposal of members depending on their respective needs'. The group 'allows wage-earners to enjoy a stable job in the framework of a single work contract', and 'the wage-earner is covered by the collective agreement chosen when the group was created'. Other mechanisms offer comparable possibilities: local groups of employers (GLE) and groups of employers for integration and qualification (GEIQ). These forms all aim to offer the wage-earner 'a single statute', and avoid 'the multiplication of part-time and fixed-term work contracts'. They are accompanied by the definition of a code of ethics in order to 'exclude any thought of seeking cheaper manpower, as well as any practice contrary to existing legislation and remuneration'. Added to these formal mechanisms are numerous local initiatives for organizing multi-activity

in a given area (see Marie-Françoise Mouriaux, 'La pluriactivité entre l'utopie et la contrainte', *La Lettre du Centre d'études de l'emploi*, no. 51, February 1998).

104 Spiros Simitis, 'Le droit du travail a-t-il encore un avenir?', *Droit social*, nos 7–8, July/August 1997, pp. 655–68.

105 In a remarkable article dating from as early as 1980, Gérard Lyon-Caen offered a synthetic description of the new forms of casual jobs and objectives of flexibility: '[for employers] it is important to move towards a condition in which labour-power will *never* be *unproductive* and will be able to be excluded as soon as orders decline'. But – he added – 'it is important to observe that the compensation for this tendency has not materialized: *no statute of mobility* exists involving continuity underlying job insecurity, redeployment after each job' ('Plasticité du capital et nouvelles formes d'emploi', *Droit social*, nos 9–10, September/October 1980, pp. 8–18). The activity contract, as presented in its optimistic versions, might represent the beginnings of such a 'statute of mobility' (and, in its pessimistic version, a new form of hiring out of services)

106 Thus, the Court of Cassation recently decided that 'a clause anticipating the performance of assignments in France, and whose implementation was terminated when it was put at the disposal of a different company, did not constitute a substantial alteration [of the work contract]; even if being put at the disposal of another, as the wage-earner argued, involved a change of employer, the definition of the assignment in a unilateral internal norm made it possible to foresee this possibility' (Isabelle Daugareilh, 'Le contrat de travail à l'épreuve des mobilités', *Droit social*, no. 2, February 1996, pp. 128–40).

107 Boissonat, *Le Travail dans vingt ans*, p. 31.

108 Annie Fouquet, 'Travail, emploi et activité', *La Lettre du Centre d'études de l'emploi*, no. 52, April 1998.

109 See Thierry Priestley, 'À propos du «contrat d'activité» proposé par le rapport Boissonat', *Droit social*, no. 12, December 1995, pp. 955–60. As Jean-Yves Kerbourc'h remarks, the activity contract poses problems that have something in common with those of temporary work. They concern the continuous or discontinuous character of the service and the nature of the contract. The activity contract extends legal provisions prompted by the development of temporary work and aiming to 'mitigate the effects of discontinuity of employment, by reconstructing a professional continuity separate from the work contract' ('Le travail temporaire'). Yet, as in the case of temporary work, the circulation of people within a collective should not be assimilable to a sub-contracting of human beings or a hiring out of people. Most of the numerous critiques directed at the activity contract emphasize the risk of seeing this mechanism used to loan out manpower in a less restrictive framework than that of temping firms and, consequently, to reinforce and institutionalize the casualization of employment (Mouriaux, 'La pluriactivité entre l'utopie et la contrainte').

110 In some scenarios, however, universal income is subject to a proportional tax, and hence very unequally redistributed according to the wealth of the beneficiary.

111 Justifications of an industrial type can be found in Jean-Marc Ferry's work, where universal income derives from the need to offset crises of overproduction by requiring the state to allocate an unconditional basic income to households because, with the development of robotization, firms create wealth without any counterpart in wages, and no longer perform the function of distributing income in the monetary circuit that once fell to them (see Ferry, *L'Allocation universelle. Pour un revenu de citoyenneté*, Cerf, Paris 1995; and 'Pour une autre valorisation du travail. Défense et illustration du secteur quaternaire', *Esprit*, no. 234, July 1997, pp. 5–17). For Philippe Van Parijs, universal income is conceived as a compensatory mechanism, of civic-industrial inspiration, for the injustices consequent upon the formation of a new type of class division associated with a new form of exploitation (exploitation being defined by the possession of a scarce resource that affects the distribution of income). This new 'class struggle' opposes those who possess a stable, properly paid job to those who are deprived of access to employment – the rich-in-work and the poor-in-work. The struggle for universal income is to encourage the

organization of the poor-in-jobs into a self-conscious class. In effect, universal income has the power, according to Van Parijs, not to equalize the distribution of jobs between those who want to work (something that is possible only in a socialist system, but at the price of centralization and the abolition of freedoms), but to neutralize the effects of the unequal distribution of job assets ('A Revolution in Class Theory', *Politics and Society*, vol. 15, 1986, pp. 453–82). We shall attribute to liberal justifications the proposals for tax reform and redistributive mechanisms made by F. Bourguignon and P.-A. Chiappori who, while proposing 'a minimum income for all' (combined with taxation at a single rate paid at source, with a surtax on the highest incomes), are located in the tradition of works on negative tax introduced into economic literature by Milton Friedman (see their *Fiscalité et redistribution. Plans pour une réforme*, Notes de la Fondation Saint-Simon, Paris 1997).

112 Ferry, 'Pour une autre valorisation du travail'. On this last point, Robert Castel, in the course of a debate reproduced in the issue of *Revue du Mauss* devoted to universal income, provides an interesting counter-argument based on the experience of historical capitalism ('Débat sur le revenu minimum inconditionnel', *Revue de Mauss*, no. 7, 1996, pp. 174–87). He highlights the fact that in the pre-industrial society of the nineteenth century, the situation of rural artisans was always more disadvantageous than that of urban artisans because the merchants, possessors of capital, exploited the fact that rural artisans had a complementary income, bound up with agricultural activities, to exploit them 'mercilessly'. By analogy, he fears that employers will take advantage of the existence of a pre-wage to reduce the wages paid. In that event, universal income would facilitate 'an ultra-liberal reorganization of the labour market'. An argument of the same kind is to be found in Immanuel Wallerstein, who shows that maintaining a small agrarian yield creates surpluses that lower the threshold of the acceptable minimum wage accordingly.

113 See Jean-Michel Belorgey, interview with Didier Gelot and Serge Volkoff, *Collectif*, no. 24, December 1994.

114 See Warde, 'Les maîtres auxiliaires des marchés'.

115 A study was conducted in 1995 by a group of experts including some of the best specialists in international finance, who in particular analysed the ability of such a tax to stabilize financial flows (see Mahbub ul Haq, Inge Kaul and Isabelle Grunberg, *The Tobin Tax: Coping with Financial Volatility*, Oxford Univesity Press, Oxford 1996). With the exception of a few sceptics, the Tobin tax seemed to them 'full of promise' (quoted by Ward, 'Les maîtres auxiliaires des marchés'). The criticisms directed at it evoked the possiblity of circumvention by establishing markets in 'tax havens' that would refuse to collect the tax. But it appears that it would be possible to institute a system of sanctions by reforming the International Monetary Fund, which would prohibit, for example, these tax havens access to multinational loans. Another criticism stresses the fact that such a device would slow down only speculation aimed at making a small amount, but with a role in the formation of a single exchange rate for a currency the world over at each given moment. Contrariwise, the tax would have little deterrent effect on 'major coups' capable of destabilizing a currency. Rather than a tax on turnover, what is needed is a tax on value added – that is to say, on the profit of the relevant transactions. Others believe, moreover, that the interests of the United States and Great Britain, combined with the profits made by their markets, are too strong for states to collaborate on establishing this kind of mechanism, or that countries which have invested a percentage of their debts in the international financial markets are highly reluctant to go against the interests of the markets in any way whatsoever, for the sanctions on the interest rates demanded would be immediate. On the other hand, the financial resources they would derive from the collection of the tax, in the current period when their financial difficulties are irrefutable, would indeed constitute a real incentive.

116 See the article 'Stabiliser les changes', *Alternatives économiques*, no. 148, May 1997.

117 The Cooke ratio, developed in 1987 by a committee composed of the central banks and supervisory authorities of the ten countries sitting at the Bank of International Settlements,

defines the proportion of appropriate funds *vis-à-vis* outstanding credit, weighted by a coefficient from 0 to 100 per cent depending on the risks of non-payment. It is set around 8 per cent.

118 See Daniel Gervais, 'Contraintes internationales et démission des États. Les marchés financiers ou l'irresponsabilité au pouvoir', *Le Monde diplomatique*, January 1993, pp. 18–19.

119 See the fulsome publicity that features in the documents of firms when one of them has received some particular certification. In the case of the social certifications, they initially developed in the form of marketing policy aiming to satisfy consumers in Western countries disturbed, for example, by child labour in the Third World, whether this involved clothes brand names like Gap, sports shoes like Nike, or major distributors like Carrefour or Auchan.

120 See Martial Cosette, 'Les vertus du socialement correct', *Alternatives économiques*, no. 161, July/August 1998.

121 Law reinforces the quasi-juridical character of the cities, which can also express themselves in other ways. The procedural mechanism can remain largely informal and customary. But the regulation, the promulgation of codes of good behaviour (like manuals of civility), the accumulation of exempla (like the lives of saints), the composition of rules (rules of conduct for monks, workshop regulations, etc.), the inscription of series of procedural measures (like entrance conditions for an exam or competition), is one of their major tendencies. In the order of cities, juridical inscription is thus a form of completion.

122 Antoine Lyon-Caen and Antoine Jeammaud, 'France', in Lyon-Caen and Jeammaud, eds, *Droit du travail, démocratie et crise*, Actes Sud, Arles 1986, pp. 19–49.

123 Thus, it would be pointless to wish to inscribe the law in one world rather than another, even if its public character gives it a *civic* component or the regulations pertaining to different worlds are unequally represented in it at different points in time. As Günther Teubner reminds us ('*Altera pars audiatur*: le droit dans la collision des discours', *Droit et société*, no. 35, 1997, pp. 99–123), taking up the Weberian metaphor of the polytheism of values, law, particularly in complex modern societies, is an 'amalgam of heterogeneous social rationalities', deriving from various 'normative machineries of production' such as market relations, political relations, and scientific and technical practices, to which different definitions of justice correspond. And this is the case even if law – as Teubner puts it so well – 'observes, so to speak, the pluralism of the other social rationalities from the standpoint of its own rationality', which is centred on the distinction between the legal and the illegal.

124 These remarks equally apply to a commercial world. Against the liberal belief in the futility of regulation (other than contract law), and in the existence of a self-regulating market, it must be stressed that, as numerous works have shown (see, for example, Laurent Thévenot, 'Les investissements de forme', in *Conventions économiques*, Cahiers du centre d'études de l'emploi, Presses Universitaires de France, Paris 1985, pp. 149–89; Marie-France Garcia, 'La construction sociale d'un marché parfait: le marché au cadran de Fontaines-en-Sologne', *Actes de la recherche en sciences sociales*, no. 65, 1986, pp. 2–13), the very possibility of the market rests not only on restraining mechanisms (anti-cartel legislation, commission for supervising stock-market operations) and legal sanctions (fines, terms of imprisonment), but also on a multiplicity of conventions whose non-observance can have legal repercussions – in particular, on quality conventions. As has been demonstrated by the works of Eymard-Duvernay ('Conventions de qualité et pluralité des formes de coordination', *Revue économique*, no. 2, March 1989, pp. 329–59); and Thévenot ('Les justifications du service public peuvent-elles contenir le marché?', in A. Lyon-Caen and V. Champeil-Desplat, eds, *Services publics et droit fondamentaux dans la construction européenne*, Institut international de Paris-La Défense-Dalloz, Paris 1998), these conventions are necessary to 'identify the goods', to 'deliver a judgement on them', and to introduce a claim to 'justice in market relations' that monetary evaluation alone cannot guarantee. The extension of markets has thus been possible only because it has been supported by 'a whole apparatus of technical and conventional constructs' (e.g. 'brands'), protected by a property law (see the article by Thévenot). In short, as Supiot recalls ('Du bon usage des

lois en matière d'emploi'), 'law is not a tool external to the market; there is no market without law to establish it'.

125 See Max Weber, *Soiologie du droit*, Presses Universitaires de France, Paris 1986.

126 Weber takes the example of 'a worker's formal right to enter into whatever contract he chooses with any employer', which 'for the worker represents not the slightest freedom to determine his conditions of labour', because 'the person who is most powerful in the market – usually the employer – has the opportunity to fix the conditions as he chooses'. In this instance, 'contractual freedom ... offers an opportunity, through intelligent use of goods in a free market, to acquire power over others. The parties interested in power in the market are thus the interested parties in a legal order of this type' (ibid., p. 113). The principle of the equality of the parties to the contract, which 'has been at the very heart of the development of labour law', accordingly raises 'formidable legal difficulties. ... For the mere declaration of formal equality initially serves only to strip the weakest of their protections. It took a century, and the emergence of economic and social rights, for equality between workers and employers to become something other than a justification for the exploitation of the former by the latter' (Supiot, 'Du bon usage des lois en matière d'emploi').

7

THE TEST OF THE ARTISTIC CRITIQUE

In the 1990s, the resurgence of critique was especially evident in the social arena, where the deterioration in forms of existence associated with the growth of a capitalism freed from many of its constraints was patent. As we saw in Chapter 6, it is essentially in this sphere that palliatives have been explored in recent years to confront growing selfishness and poverty – as if reducing the economic insecurity of the most deprived sufficed to offer the members of developed countries, especially the young, 'stimulating' forms of existence in a society that has become 'open', 'creative' and 'tolerant'.

It is true that because the new spirit of capitalism incorporated much of the *artistic critique* that flourished at the end of the 1960s, the accusations formerly levelled at capitalism out of a desire for liberation, autonomy and authenticity no longer seemed to be soundly based. In its historical forms, the artistic critique subordinated the demand for authenticity to the demand for liberation: the manifestation of human beings in their full authenticity was regarded as difficult to achieve unless they were emancipated from the constraints, limitations, even mutilations inflicted on them by capitalist accumulation in particular. In this context, we might wonder if the gains in liberation secured following May 1968 have not given many people the opportunity to attain to the kind of authentic life that characterized the artistic condition, precisely in so far as it was defined by the rejection of all forms of disciplinary regulation, especially those associated with the pursuit of profit. Liberation, and especially sexual liberation; autonomy in personal and emotional life, but also in work; creativity; unbridled self-fulfilment; the authenticity of a personal life as against hypocritical, old-fashioned social conventions – these might seem, if not definitively established, at least widely acknowledged as essential values of modernity.

We may nevertheless wonder what it is about the new spirit of capitalism and the projective city that lends itself to a revival of this critique. Is it enough today to continue, as if nothing had changed, with the critique of the 'bourgeois mentality' and 'bourgeois morality' closely associated with the critique of capitalism since the mid-nineteenth century, in order to extend the project of emancipation inherent in it? Must we not instead start out from different bases – that is to say, ask if the forms of capitalism which have developed over the last thirty years, while incorporating whole sections of the artistic critique and subordinating it to profit-making, have not emptied the demands for liberation and authenticity of what gave them substance, and anchored them in people's everyday experience?

To pose this question, we must first of all set aside the aristocratic rejection of any democratization – denounced as a vulgarization – of the values of creativity, freedom and authenticity on which the distinctively artistic lifestyle rested when it was still generally regarded as exceptional. In reaction to the opening of the 1970s, a hardline elitism of this variety resurfaced strongly in the 1980s, evincing, for example, contempt for illegitimate cultural forms and their practitioners' demand to be recognized as 'creative', and, more generally, scoffing at today's widespread aspirations to 'fulfilling work', 'doing something interesting', 'expressing oneself', 'being oneself', 'breaking new ground', and so on.

What we shall do instead is to seek to bring out the potential for oppression contained in the new mechanisms of accumulation, and identify their perils for the possibility of authentic relationships, while taking the generalization of demands for liberation and authenticity as established.

In order to ground the need for a remobilization of the artistic critique, we shall begin by tracking down signs that the sources of indignation behind it have not dried up – not only by seeking to identify what remains problematic about the new capitalism from the standpoint of the aspirations articulated by the artistic critique, but also by reference to phenomena that can be read as expressions of a revulsion at existence. If we are to see a revival of the artistic critique, it will be on the basis not only of an 'intellectual' analysis of the phenomena associated with capitalism's current state, but of its conjunction with suffering that is diffuse – in the sense that those who experience it have difficulty pinning it down or attributing it to a source which can be denounced – and also the persistence of an aspiration to put an end to it.

I. THE SYMPTOMS OF AN ANXIETY

The problems of concern to the artistic critique are less directly accessible than those relating to the social critique, which are visible in the growth of begging and the proliferation of homeless people, or legible in the increase in unemployment, job insecurity and inequalities. We can nevertheless detect signs of distress, expressed in literature or the figurative arts, which in the writings of social reformers emerge in the theme of a 'loss of meaning'.[1] For our part, we shall use the term *anxiety* (borrowed from Laurent Thévenot's work[2]), which encapsulates an unease associated with the difficulty of identifying the origin of the threat and making plans to control it. No doubt it is in what Durkheim called the 'indicators of anomie' that we must seek the trace of the anxieties created by the emergence of a connexionist world.

Anomie in a connexionist world

The concept of anomie, which generally refers to the fading of the tacit norms and conventions regulating expectations, leading to a disintegration of social bonds, adequately describes a society in which, as we have sought to show, the former tests have been disrupted, while the new ones, established with the connexionist world, are poorly identified and minimally supervised.

The distinctions introduced by Durkheim in *Suicide* allow for greater clarity about anomie. In particular, he differentiates between the effects of *anomie* and those of the growth of *egoism*: whereas *egoistic* suicide is situated on an axis whose other pole is occupied by *altruistic* suicide, anomic suicide, deriving from the waning of rules and norms, is situated on an axis whose other pole is occupied by *fatalistic* suicide. It results from an 'excess of regulation' which Durkheim does not spend much time discussing, because he believes that it has become very rare in his society.[3] The usual indicators of anomie thus do not translate the increase in individualism, in the sense of egoism, into theory, but the increase in anomie in the strict sense – that is to say, *anxiety* about what to do, deriving not so much from a withering away of norms understood as 'mental' givens, as from their effacement from the situations and contexts in which they were rooted.

As we shall see, all the indicators in which Durkheim taught us to read the signs of anomie have been on the increase since the second half of the 1970s. This may be interpreted not only as a mechanical result of the growth in job insecurity and poverty, but also as the mark of an elimination of the purchase that people can have on their social environment, with a consequent fading of their belief in the future as a vanishing point which can orientate action and thus retrospectively confer meaning on the present.

Now, in our view, this 'difficulty projecting oneself into the future', as expressed by the indicators of anomie,[4] must be related to the experience of a connexionist world. The distress it creates can more specifically be attributed to the existence of a conflict between norms (particularly explicit in the domestic and industrial worlds), prioritizing what coheres over time, and the human condition in a flexible world, where beings alter themselves according to the situations they encounter. If people, or a majority of them, did not value what is supposed to last, they would not suffer from the ruptures associated with separations, and despondency when they are confronted with the task of having to re-create what seemed settled. Moreover, this is the distress the projective city aims to assuage by conferring legitimacy on that which presents itself as transitory, and also by organizing the tests that accompany transition. It remains the case that in many domains the value of a commitment, and the enthusiasm it elicits, continue to be associated, whether explicitly or implicitly, with its durability. This is obviously valid for marriage, which is not contracted for a fixed term (even if it can be broken up by divorce), but also for love affairs outside marriage. People accord more value to such affairs to the extent that they may be prolonged; at the very least, it is not customary to foresee their termination at the point of embarking on them. The same could be said of most of what are called personal relationships or friend-ships, whose charm derives from the fact that we look forward to seeing how they will turn out. Even in the sphere of work, where the temporary charac-ter of engagements is now an acknowledged fact, a satisfying experience usually prompts hopes of staying on (the renewal of a fixed-term contract, its conversion into a permanent contract, not to mention promotion or career development). It follows that a rupture in relations, the interruption of a project, are liable to be experienced as a failure (not a humdrum experience, as the logic of the projective city would have it). The emphasis placed on the values of autonomy and self-fulfilment, and neglect of the very unevenly dis-tributed character of the conditions for success in self-fulfilment, give this failure a personal character. Those who experience such failures bear the whole burden. What is called into question is their ability to 'fulfil themselves' in accomplishing any task (forming a relationship, securing a status at work, creating a family, etc.). By making the creation of new bonds more difficult, the ensuing self-depreciation helps to make isolation an enduring condition.

The various indicators of anomie referred to below clearly point towards the distress produced by anxieties bound up with the kind of 'liberation' asso-ciated with capitalism's redeployment, which, closely linking autonomy with job insecurity, unquestionably makes 'projecting into the future' more diffi-cult. But we may also see them as a sign of uncertainty about the value to be placed on the mechanisms and conventions that regulated the old world (family relations, educational qualifications, obtaining a work contract, the socioprofessional categories, etc.). Because of the de-categorization described in Chapter 5, in many situations it is becoming difficult to sub-scribe in the mode of *that-goes-without-saying* (as Schütz puts it) to what must be believed or done. In particular, the extension to an ever greater number of wage-earners of the lack of any distinction between time at work and time outside work, between personal friendships and professional relationships, between work and the person of those who perform it – so many features which, since the nineteenth century, had constituted typical characteristics of the artistic condition, particularly markers of the artist's 'authenticity'[5] – and the introduction of this *modus operandi* into the capitalist universe, can only have contributed to disrupt reference-points for ways of evaluating people, actions or things.

Indicators of anomie today

Without positing a direct cause-and-effect relation between the problem of establishing enduring professional links and phenomena marking a profound change in the sphere of private relations, we cannot but wonder about the concomitance of alterations in the life-cycle at work and affective and familial life-cycles. Late entry into working life and the substitution of *ad hoc* jobs for modes of integration that open up the prospect of a career have gone hand in hand with a development of *short-term commitments in private life*. This is indicated not only by the reduction in the number of marriages and the rise in divorce, but also by the growing fragility of relationships 'without legal documents' defined as 'cohabitation'.[6]

Changing trends in *suicide* statistics seem to be even more relevant. As is well known, since they were established in the nineteenth century they have displayed a strong correlation with matrimonial status (married people being less likely to commit suicide than those who are single, divorced or widowed), and with age, suicidal tendencies increasing regularly as people get older. The latter correlation, which until recently was very stable temporally and spatially,[7] has been interpreted in terms of people's relationship to the future. From this angle, it is the closing of the horizon of possibilities, the disappointment of aspirations, and the crumbling of social bonds as one gets older that are responsible for the intensification of suicidal tendencies.

Now, in this respect a lasting change in trends emerged at the turn of the 1970s and 1980s, marked by a general rise in the rate of male suicide, which increased by 45 per cent between 1977 and 1985 (rising from 22.9 to 33.1 per 100,000), followed by a drop up to 1990 (29.6 per 100,000), and a new rise thereafter (31.6 in 1994; 30.5 in 1995).[8] Moreover, the same years recorded a change in distribution according to age: a regular increase with age has been replaced by a bi-modal distribution, with a first peak in the 35–44 age group, followed by a reduction for subsequent age groups, the tendency to suicide rising again after 75.[9] The evolution in suicide rates and their age distribution is strongly correlated (correlation superior to 0.8) with other classic indicators of anomie: age at time of first marriage, primary marriage rate, rise in the youth unemployment rate, criminality, and so on.[10] According to Claudel, these changes are indicative less of a change in values than of a reconstruction of the life-cycle, a 'redistribution of the social status open to the different stages of life', and a corresponding alteration in people's relation to time at different ages: the young and people in the prime of life have greater difficulty 'projecting themselves into the future' on account of the *uncertainty* (in the sense of F. Knight, who contrasts it with calculable risk) affecting all the relations attaching them to the world and others. This is especially the case with work relations because of 'unemployment and job insecurity', which contribute in turn 'to the loosening of family ties and the moral or physical isolation of individuals'. Thus, we cannot fail to be struck by the fact that among adults aged 25–49 the contours of unemployment and suicide have the same profile.[11] These uncertainties entail 'a "void" of future, even of meaning, to use terms employed by Halbwachs and Durkheim'.[12]

This is how, following Alain Ehrenberg, the group of researchers under the name of Louis Dirn interprets the increase in the number of people stating that they have suffered 'depression' and the growth in the *consumption of psychotropic drugs*, where solitude constitutes one of the factors, which is three times higher among the unemployed than among those with a job.[13]

The indicators of anomie point to a paradoxical effect of liberation, since the increase in the number of people placed in anxiety-inducing situations has gone together with wresting autonomy, to the extent that it may seem that the promises of fulfilment have not been realized for everyone. It seems to us that the same figures, betokening a kind of confusion about the meaning of everyday existence, can also be related to unease about how to formulate the question of authenticity in a connexionist world – that is to say, in particular, the issue of how to assess the inherent worth of people and things.

We shall therefore seek to identify the extent to which, in being incorporated into the spirit of capitalism and making their contribution to profit creation, the demands of the artistic critique have, in their contemporary expressions, been integrated into cycles of recuperation – recuperation that paves the way for new forms of oppression on the one hand, and a rediffusion of the kind of anxiety which the quest for authenticity sought to assuage on the other. Thus, on the basis of demands for liberation and authenticity as expressed over the last thirty years, we shall examine the fate that has befallen them in a connexionist world.

2. WHICH LIBERATION?

Since its formation, the discourse of liberation has been one of the essential components of the spirit of capitalism.[14] Originally, the form of liberation offered by capitalism essentially derived its meaning from the reference to the contrast between 'traditional societies', defined as oppressive, and 'modern societies', the only ones capable of permitting individual self-fulfilment – a contrast that is itself an ideological construct constitutive of modernity. But in its subsequent formulations, the spirit of capitalism has been led to hold out a prospect of liberation that can also integrate critiques denouncing capitalist oppression – that is to say, the failure in practice to realize promises of liberation under the capitalist regime. This is to say that in its second expression, and in the forms it is assuming in our time, the spirit of capitalism pursues two different lines in this respect. The first always takes as its target the 'traditionalism' that is believed to menace modern Western societies with a virulent return, and which is denounced as a factual reality in the Third World.

The second, in at least implicit response to the critiques of capitalist oppression itself, contains an offer that presents itself as emancipatory with respect to capitalism's earlier creations. In the second half of the twentieth century, the spirit of capitalism consequently offered itself both as a way of achieving self-fulfilment by engaging in capitalism, and as a path of liberation from capitalism itself, from what was oppressive about its earlier creations.

Thus, as we have already seen in connection with the issue of justice, the dynamic of the spirit of capitalism seems to rest on 'cycles of recuperation'.[15] We can likewise identify them when it comes to liberation – that is, broadly with regard to what makes engagement in the capitalist process 'exciting'. Capitalism attracts actors, who realize that they have hitherto been oppressed, by offering them a certain form of liberation that masks new types of oppression. It may then be said that capitalism 'recuperates' the autonomy it extends, by implementing new modes of control. However, these new forms of oppression are gradually unmasked and become the target of critique, to the point where capitalism is led to transform its *modus operandi* to offer a liberation that is redefined under the influence of critique. But, in its turn, the 'liberation' thus obtained harbours new oppressive mechanisms that allow control over the process of accumulation to be restored in a capitalist framework. Cycles of recuperation thus lead to a succession of periods of liberation *by* capitalism and periods of liberation *from* capitalism. Below we shall analyse in more detail this dynamic since the constitution of what we have called the first spirit of capitalism.

The liberation offered by the first spirit of capitalism

In contrast to the societies defined in the second half of the nineteenth century as 'traditional', capitalism presents itself as emancipatory – that is to say, as encouraging the fulfilment of the promises of autonomy and self-realization regarded by the Enlightenment as basic ethical requirements. It does so in essentially two respects, both of which derive from the primacy accorded to the market: the possibility of choosing one's social condition (occupation, place and way of life, relations, etc.), as well as the goods and services owned or consumed.[16]

The expansion of the formal possibilities of *choosing one's mode of social affiliation*, essentially redefined by reference to place of residence and occupation – as opposed to being fixed by birth to a village and a station in life – was indeed one of the attractions of the original capitalism. Given the importance of the family in traditional societies, this form of liberation primarily takes the form of emancipation from the burden of domestic ties.[17] It is summed up in the opposition between 'status' and 'contract'. In contrast to societies where people are assigned a status that is practically impossible to alter in the course of their lives – at any rate, without changing village, which is difficult given that their worth and their very identity are dependent upon local

rootedness[18] – capitalism supposedly offers the possibility of voluntary deracination, which is protected by the importance it accords to the legal device
of the contract. For a contract, unlike status, can be established for a fixed
term, and does not engage the whole of a person, but stipulates the particular respect in which the person is bound by their promise in their relationship
with someone else. Thus the work contract, based upon the formal distinction between the worker's labour-power and their person, defines a form of
dependency which, unlike traditional dependencies, is not presented as total.
Consequently, the labour market offers itself as a mechanism conducive to
fulfilling an ideal of autonomy.

As for the *distribution of goods and services*, it is characterized in traditional
societies by long, complex circuits of gifts and return gifts. As a result, in the
absence of a recognized autonomous economic sphere – which, according to
Bartolomé Clavero,[19] was still far from being general in eighteenth-century
Europe, where it was only very gradually established in northern commercial
towns – exchange does not presuppose a clear distinction between goods and
the persons who own or acquire them.[20] Without entering into the debate
prompted by Marcel Mauss's *Essai sur le don*, let us simply note that this form
of exchange is based upon a system of obligations, the most constraining of
which is unquestionably the obligation to accept what is offered to you. This
is itself largely determined by statutory ties, whence derive other obligations,
particularly reciprocation, while respecting norms that are complex, unwritten, and capable of giving rise to a subtle casuistry of time-scales (not
reciprocating immediately, not reciprocating too late) and equivalences (giving
something in return which, while different, can be related to the thing that has
been given, and appreciated as such). Now, by comparison with these constraints, the market presents an opportunity for liberation, since it replaces a
system of obligations with a mechanism regulated by prices, where no one is
obliged to sell (at any price), or to buy (if the price is not suitable): individuals taken in isolation, but filled with the same desire for the same goods,
co-ordinate in the here and now around the focal points represented by prices,
which are supposed to encapsulate the qualities of the goods that they desire
and for whose appropriation they compete. If virtually every one of the terms
of this minimalist working sketch poses a problem, and has actually been challenged, it is a fact that the market ideal discounts the substantive qualities of
persons who, whatever their affiliations, are equally entitled to accede to it and
trade there as they wish, according to their financial means and their ability to
grasp the opportunities it offers at any given moment.

The critique of capitalism as a factor of liberation

The promise of liberation contained in capitalism came under strong challenge from the first half of the nineteenth century. The lines of argument

employed were different, and in part contra ory, although they could find themselves merged in a single critique.[21] The first attacks the disciplinary effects of capitalism, casting doubt on whether it can be a source of liberation, whereas the second challenges the possibility of constructing a viable social order on the basis of an unbridled quest for tonomy and self-fulfilment.

The first set of criticisms endeavours to nstrate how the new forms of oppression derive precisely from the way oitalism diverts the demand for liberation to its own advantage, so as e its discipline. Under the sway of capitalism, the promise of liberati ly functions as an ideology in the Marxist sense of the term, ensurir subjection to its order.

First and foremost, liberation from hich is supposed to be vouchsafed by engagement in the capitalist process, translates instead into deracination.[22] Separating people from their concrete spheres of existence, and the norms but also the protections bound up with them, this consigns them to factory discipline and the power of the labour market, with no possibility of resistance. Far from constituting a liberating factor, the separation entailed by deracination introduces universal competition for the sale of labour-power, reducing its price to the point where the workers are condemned to a condition in which the duration of work, enslavement to factory discipline, and meagre pay no longer allow for the realization of a properly human existence, which is precisely defined by self-determination and a multiplicity of practices. The promised liberation is in fact replaced by a new form of slavery. This is why the initial demands of the workers' movement involved a reduction in working hours without loss of pay, and the organization of the working day and week in such a way that existence could once again find expression in activities other than waged work: family life and the education of children, reading and access to a working-class culture and education, and so on.[23]

The illusory character of the liberation held out by capitalism thanks to the market in goods can also be denounced. Particularly in Marx's work, we find a critical argument that was to be one of the bases right up to the present day for the denunciation of what has been called the 'consumer society' since the 1960s, to which the development of marketing and advertising would give new vigour. It runs as follows: seemingly free, consumers are in fact completely in the grip of production. What they believe to be their own desires, emanating from their autonomous will as unique individuals, are, unbeknown to them, the product of a manipulation whereby the suppliers of goods enslave their imagination. They desire what they are led to desire. Supply subordinates and determines demand – or, as Marx puts it, '[p]roduction thus not only creates an object for the subject, but also a subject for the object'.[24] Given that the supply of goods through which profit is created is, by its very nature, unlimited in a capitalist framework, desire must be constantly stimulated so that it becomes insatiable.

According to the second line of argument pursued by the critique of the liberation that capitalism supposedly offers, the demand for autonomy cannot lead to genuine liberation unless it respects the limits imposed on it by another requirement: that of constructing a collective. Capitalism is thus condemned not in so far as it imposes a discipline more severe than the one it allowed people to escape from, but, on the contrary, inasmuch as it becomes impossible under its sway to instil sufficient discipline over individual aspirations and desires to prevent society dissolving.

This argument doubtless finds its consummate expression in the Durkheimian critique of economic liberalism, which rests upon a pessimistic anthropology. In Durkheimian anthropology, human beings are animated by unchecked desire,[25] which, unlike animal appetites, is not naturally limited by instinct: 'there is nothing within the individual to contain his appetites'. If they are not to become 'insatiable', they must therefore be 'contained by some force external to the individual'.[26] For Durkheim, this force is collective representations and, to be more precise, moral representations, which derive from society, from social being, from the group as supra-individual instance of practical reason. Only collectives, the site where morality is generated, possess the requisite authority to curb individual appetites, whose unbridled expression would reduce society to a state of disintegration and conflict approximating to Hobbes's state of nature, and to impose on each person the requisite 'sacrifice' if 'private utility' is to be subordinated to 'collective utility'.[27]

The emergence of the second spirit of capitalism is accompanied by a certain assimilation of these two sets of accusations, which challenge the oppressive (or disciplinary, in Peter Wagner's formulation[28]) character of capitalism associated with its first spirit on the one hand; and its inability to induce the formation of collectives capable of exercising normative constraints on individual appetites and egoism on the other.

From the second spirit of capitalism to its current form

In order to emerge from what Wagner calls 'the first crisis of modernity'[29] – at the end of the nineteenth century and in the first third of the twentieth – emphasis was placed, on the one hand, on mechanisms for stabilizing and coordinating actions, strengthening institutional boundaries, and planning and bureaucratization; and, on the other, on an improvement in the living conditions of wage-earners, an increase in their purchasing power (by redistributing productivity increases), and the establishment of mechanisms of security thanks to which the welfare state was gradually constructed.[30]

Having made possible increased security for workers, the institutions associated with the second spirit of capitalism could be presented as contributing to the development of real freedoms (in contrast to formal freedoms): they seemed to reduce subjection to work, and to make it possible to escape contingencies and the pressure of immediate needs. Security, frequently denounced in a liberal framework as a restriction of individual autonomy, especially when it derives from state action, can also be presented as the precondition for real liberation – that is to say, as the thing which allows people to live to the full in areas other than work. Moreover, to the extent that these new securities rested largely upon categorial mechanisms, they could serve as a focus for the emergence of new collective norms limiting destructive egoism.

But the appeasement of critique was short-lived, lasting only as long as it took to discover the new forms of oppression characteristic of the kind of capitalism associated with the second spirit. From the end of the 1960s, the denunciation of capitalism for not redeeming its promises of liberation was renewed with vigour. Not only were hierarchical constraints rejected, for stipulating preferential relations and the channels through which they were to be established (the organization chart) in favour of the freedom to construct any potentially enriching links, through systematic exploration of the network. But all the restrictions bound up with performing a task were refused, since each change of project affords an opportunity for redistributing tasks between people. The crisis of governability in the 1960s and 1970s would find expression in the incorporation of these demands into capitalism and the construction of the new, so-called 'network' capitalism, which served to ferment the emergence of the third spirit.

Having reached this point in the history of demands for liberation and their recuperation by capitalism, can it be shown that the promises have once again not been kept, and that new forms of oppression have emerged?

Imposed self-fulfilment and new forms of oppression

There is no question here of subscribing to a reactionary critique which, forgetting the intensity and validity of the denunciations of paternalism, the bureaucratization of organizations, and especially Taylorism, idealizes the forms of control associated with a 'Fordist' mode of regulation (to use the term popularized by the Regulation School). On the other hand, we cannot ignore those features of current forms of capitalism that tend to restrict and, to a certain extent, recuperate autonomy, which is not only presented as a possibility or right, but is as it were *demanded* of people, whose status is increasingly frequently assessed according to their capacity for self-fulfilment, elevated to the status of an evaluative criterion.

All the mechanisms associated with the new spirit of capitalism – outsourcing, the proliferation of autonomous profit centres within firms, quality circles, or new forms of work organization – have in one sense clearly arrived to meet the demands for autonomy and responsibility that made themselves heard at the beginning of the 1970s in an oppositional register. *Cadres* released from their chains of hierarchy to take responsibility for 'autonomous profit centres' or see 'projects' through, as well as workers freed from the most fragmented forms of assembly-line work, have indeed seen their level of responsibility enhanced, at the same time as their ability to act autonomously and demonstrate creativity has been recognized. But this recognition has not fulfilled all expectations – for several reasons.

First of all, despite the partial individualization of wages and payments, the reward for effort has consisted less in positive approval – such as rises or promotions – than in a suspension, often temporary, of negative sanction by redundancy. As we have seen, the new modes of organization have in fact rendered more or less obsolete the hopes for a 'career' which, long reserved for the higher echelon of wage-earners, were extended to middle and junior managerial staff, supervisory staff or even blue-collar skilled workers during the 1960s and 1970s. Thus it will be noticed that increased autonomy and responsibility were obtained at the price of a reduction in the protections enjoyed by wage-earners at the start of the period, which derived not only from economic conditions but also from a balance of power that was temporarily favourable to them. As we had occasion to indicate in Chapter 3, autonomy was exchanged against security, to the point where it is often a forced, involuntary autonomy, difficult to equate with freedom: 'wage-earners newly transformed into entrepreneurs' continue to depend upon their principal employer, and subordination is only formally masked by the transition from 'labour law' to 'commercial law'.[31] The most striking of the forms of oppression established since the second half of the 1970s is precisely the decline in job security deriving from the new methods of utilizing labour (temping, fixed-term contracts) and unemployment. Furthermore, in a connexionist world, where it is understood that the project into which actors have managed to integrate themselves must necessarily come to an end, the time devoted to the anxious search for new engagements and new connections is superimposed on working time in the strict sense, encroaching on periods that could be devoted to other activities.

Secondly, the work performed and the personal qualities mobilized invariably have a purely local visibility, with no generalizing mechanism (qualifications, certificates, media) making it possible to extend reputations far beyond the workplace.[32] As a result, in certain respects there is now less potential mobility because where national equivalences, like those measured by qualifications systems, once operated, it is based in the main on networks of personal acquaintances.

Finally, in the case of wage-earners who have not been casualized, the fact that autonomy has been granted in exchange for the assumption of greater responsibility, or in the context of a general recasting of working methods, results in a paradox revealed by surveys into working conditions: wage-earners are *simultaneously* more autonomous and more constrained.[33] In Chapter 4, we discussed the intensification of work as a result of the disappearance of slack periods, the development of constraints (bound up with the automatic tempo of machines, norms and tight deadlines, customer demands, etc.) weighing on workers, or of the monitoring facilitated by the new information technologies. As Michel Gollac explains,[34] in principle wage-earners have a choice of operating methods, but 'by virtue of the intensification of work, they are in fact compelled to use the quickest way of working. Yet this is not necessarily the one that suits them best.' He takes the example of 'a worker who has to manipulate heavy objects. If he has the time, he is going to choose a method of prehension adapted to his morphology, to possible muscular or rheumatoid problems ... in a rush, he will have to "choose" the fastest way of doing things, and that is not necessarily the same thing.'

This development is reinforced by the proliferation in the number of people liable to issue work instructions or directions, the percentage of colleagues and people outside the firm being on the increase (from 39 to 41 per cent and 19 to 22 per cent, respectively, between 1987 and 1993).[35] The growth in constraints has occurred in parallel with the development of wage-earners' initiative. Thus, the percentage of wage-earners who deal with an incident in their work themselves ('when something abnormal happens') rose from 43 per cent in 1987 to 54 per cent in 1993. The figure is rising for all social categories. Thomas Coutrot also shows that firms which have adopted at least three 'organizational innovations' (and are thus at the forefront of the new spirit of capitalism) offer more autonomy (no need to refer to superiors in the event of a minor accident) and versatility (practice of rotating work posts), but also more constraints (precise description of tasks to be performed, systematic control of individual performance) than those that have adopted fewer.[36] Similarly, wage-earners state that they are more often subject to tight deadlines, and can less frequently juggle with them. The creation of 'zones of autonomy' at work really does allow workers to experience a 'dignity at work' that was 'unheard of on the Taylorist assembly line'.[37] But it is accompanied by numerous new constraints associated with the reduction in stocks, versatility, and the creation of responsibility for maintenance, which tend to increase the mental burdens. In addition, these new zones of autonomy are narrowly framed by procedural constraints. The activities undertaken in them are in fact increasingly often monitored by computer systems that not only define the relevant categories recognized by the system, but give them a 'prescriptive force', which leads to structuring tasks through 'grammars of action'.[38] Moreover, there is no doubt that it was the computer revolution in control which helped to facilitate employers' conversion to the theme of autonomy.

Given that enhanced autonomy is accompanied by a growth in self-control and team work, with a corresponding reinforcement of peer-group control, it is even possible that workers are more highly controlled than they were previously. This is indicated in the study conducted by James Barker in a factory that introduced autonomous teams for the production of electrical circuits.

One of the author's informants summarizes the situation as follows: 'when the boss wasn't around, I could sit … and talk to my neighbour or do what I wanted. Now the whole team is around me and the whole team is observing what I'm doing.'[39] The union representative at Peugeot interviewed by Michel Pialoux stresses the same development. Numerous tasks previously undertaken by the bosses have been transferred to the team, which consequently exercises constant control over its members, notably as regards punctuality and attendance at work, prompting some workers not to take sick leave, at the expense of their health. When group bonuses are at stake, a kind of internal policing is established to crack down on those whose behaviour imperils everyone's bonus. The cohesion of the group of workers is inevitably affected: '[g]roup cohesion then was against the section heads, against the supervisors. Now the cohesion is workers against other workers.'[40]

On the basis these few indicators, the least that can be said is that duress has not disappeared from the world of work. On the contrary, it turns out to be extremely significant, even if it operates in novel forms today. The new forms of management are associated with *novel forms of control*. Involving less direct monitoring, exercised face-to-face by people vested with power over other people without power, they are less visible without thereby being absent: self-control, control via the market, and computerized control in real time but from a distance – these combine to exert quasi-constant pressure on wage-earners.

These transformations in control methods may thus be regarded as a response to the crisis of governability which, as we have seen, was a major aspect of labour disputes at the beginning of the 1970s.[41] To refer to these new forms of constraint, Michael Power talks about an audit society, which he distinguishes from a 'disciplinary society' in the Foucauldian sense by the switch in control techniques from 'direct supervision' to the 'control of control'.[42] Operating from a temporal and spatial distance, this move acknowledges the impossibility of the project of total surveillance associated with Taylorist organization.

The Durkheimian critique of liberation as conceived by capitalism could also be revived, in so far as the network presents itself as the negation of categories to which people are attached on a permanent basis, and thanks to which they can construct collective norms setting limits on their individual passions. This thematic is illustrated today by Charles Taylor in particular.[43] Self-fulfilment possesses meaning only as the achievement of something. Yet, however diverse the things it might tend towards, it nevertheless remains dependent upon the existence of ends that are worth fulfilling. According to Taylor, these ends cannot be purely individual; in order to be legitimate and worth the sacrifices they demand, they must be inscribed in a collective. Self-fulfilment in an activity presupposes that aims imbued with value have been set outside the self. Consequently, the exigency of self-fulfilment in discontinuous projects makes the construction of a community wherein diverse actions can be harmoniously co-ordinated highly problematic.

The idea of liberation can in fact be construed in at least *two senses* that are not equally mobilizable by the two lines of argument critical of capitalism as supposedly emancipatory. Thus it can be shown that the cycles of recuperation created in the framework of capitalism play on the confusion between these two different meanings, to the point where capitalism can seem to be making concessions and moving towards greater liberation – in the first sense of the term – while regaining a certain capacity for control and restricting access to liberation in the second sense.

The two meanings of 'liberation' on which its recuperation by capitalism plays

If capitalism does indeed incorporate an exigency of liberation in its self-description from the outset, the way it diverts it to support and stimulate the transformations that mark the development of the process of accumulation rests upon the confusion between two interpretations of the meaning of the term 'liberation'. Liberation can be understood as *deliverance* from a condition of *oppression* suffered by a people, or as *emancipation* from any form of *determination* liable to restrict the self-definition and self-fulfilment of *individuals*.

The first interpretation emphasizes historically situated forms of *dependency* wherein a collective suffers under the yoke of a group that dominates it. Construed in this sense, liberation is indissociably a political act of reappropriation of self-determination and a way of escaping cultural or religious oppression but also, in a number of cases, some form of exploitation. It points towards *specific alienations*, in the sense that these are specific to a group or category unjustly suffering oppression which other groups do not suffer, when they are not the ones exercising the oppression. According to Michael Walzer, this interpretation has its origins in the biblical text of Exodus, and has accompanied radical political movements for four centuries, from the English Puritans of the seventeenth century to the Latin American communities grouped around 'liberation theology'.[44]

The second interpretation, which has been particularly evident since the mid-nineteenth century in what we have called the 'artistic critique', inflects the project of liberation in the direction of an emancipation from all forms of necessity, whether these derive from settlement in a social environment stabilized by conventions (e.g. membership of a nation), or are inherent in inscription in an objective world (ties of filiation, type of work performed presupposing a specific skill), or the possession of a particular body (impossibility of being everywhere at once, age- or sex-related determinations). It therefore points in the direction of *generic alienations*. Here demands for autonomy and self-fulfilment assume the form given them by Parisian artists in the second half of the nineteenth century, who made *uncertainty* a lifestyle and a value:[45] being able to possess *several lives* and, correlatively, a *multiplicity of identities*,[46] which also presupposes the possibility of freeing oneself from any *endowment* and rejecting any *original debt*,[47] whatever its character. Viewed thus, liberation is predominantly conceived as setting free the oppressed desire to be someone else: not to be someone whose life-plan has been conceived by others (parents, teachers, etc.); to be who one wants to be, when one wants it. This leaves open the possibility of a multiplicity of identifications adopted in the way one adopts a look and, consequently, of escaping identitarian affiliation to a nation, region, ethnicity, and especially – at least from the mid-nineteenth century to the mid-twentieth – the family, which is invariably conceived as 'bourgeois' or 'petty-bourgeois'. Rejection of social inheritance as a condition of access to the artistic life,[48] and, in particular, rejection of membership of the provincial bourgeoisie, the trivial universe of notability and trade, and the adoption of a multiplicity of identities as a free choice or even a game, are recurrent experiences in late-nineteenth and early-twentieth-century literature. They appear in a multiplicity of figures: departing, tearing oneself away, journeying, wandering, drifting in the anonymity of great cities, conversion, treason, assertion of a usurped origin, the theatre – site *par excellence* of the multiplication of identities, of mystification, conspiracy, fraud, the dregs, where parallel lives can be led.

It can prove difficult to distinguish between the two types of alienation. Thus, in the case of alienations bound up with sex, some may be regarded as specific if *gender* (as Anglo-American sociology puts it) serves as a pretext for oppression by the other gender; others will be deemed generic if they involve rebellion against differences of physical constitution (muscular strength, the potential for bearing children, etc.). The case of class membership is even more complex: when, as in Marxist theory, the exploitation of one class by another is denounced, a specific alienation is being designated; but when the rebellion is against the constraints bound up with the exercise of a certain occupation or birth in a particular social milieu, a generic alienation is being pointed to, in the sense that individuals must be born somewhere and must have an occupation in their adult life. In fact, it is rare for demands for liberation not to merge the two, since the two forms of alienation are necessarily connected. Thus, the feminist movement, intent upon liberating women from the male yoke, has been led to denounce certain constraints bound up with women's physical constitution. Pregnancy and lesser bodily strength were the physical bases that made social oppression possible – hence the significance of liberating oneself from the generic alienation via the Pill and abortion in order to abolish the specific alienation. In the case of alienations connected with membership of social categories, generic and specific alienation are mixed indiscriminately when class reproduction is highlighted. Thus, being born in a certain milieu contributes to the oppression people will suffer in the course of their life, and largely determines the type of work they undertake, and the fact that they will not be able to change it should they so wish. These various observations explain why the characterization of an alienation as generic is soon suspect in the view of a social critique inspired by the desire to abolish oppression: faced with a demand for liberation in the sense of abolishing a specific alienation (e.g. the oppression of one sex by the other), the first reaction of those whose domination is being challenged is to redescribe the demand as one for generic liberation, and to mock it on that account ('so women want to have male bodies now?').

In contrast, denunciation of the disciplinary character of capitalism is based on a conception of liberation as the abolition of specific alienations (certain groups of people are particularly oppressed under the capitalist regime). But it can very easily spill over into demands for the abolition of forms of alienation that possess a generic character, like the demand for the abolition of work thanks to technological progress, which supposedly offers the prospect of abundance for all. (According to this schema, with the current level of technology human beings could reduce their centuries-long dependency on the search for food and the basic goods required for survival to a minimum. But because it presupposes the monopolizing of profit by a small elite, the capitalist system condemns the majority to having to work in order to survive.)

Contrariwise, the Durkheimian conception of a freedom that is real only when it is tempered by collective norms, which make it possible to denounce the 'false freedom' held out by capitalism, is compatible with the abolition of specific oppressions. But it represents a violent critique of the second interpretation of the idea of liberation.

Our hypothesis is that capitalism does not offer the two types of liberation in equal measure at every point in its development, and has a tendency to take back on one level what it offers on the other. However, given that the two forms of liberation are, as we have seen, highly interdependent, what is taken back or given on one level has a tendency to retroact on the other, resulting in a new relative state of the two forms of alienation.

Defined in opposition to traditional societies, capitalism seems to bring about liberation on both counts. It makes it possible for people to release themselves from the yoke of domestic constraints (specific alienation), and to test out liberation from spatial constraint understood as a generic alienation. But a new form of specific alienation is soon identified, with the emergence of a proletariat subordinated to a bourgeois class whose domination it endures. The proletarian nevertheless has the freedom of the vagrant, works one day and quits the next at will, to the extent that hunger affords him the leisure. The proletariat's 'generic' liberation (moving on) is checked by a 'specific' oppression (never being paid enough to be able to stop working, if only for the time it takes to move from one place to the next).

What the second spirit of capitalism offered was primarily a particular liberation from the specific alienation of the proletariat (its exploitation). But this occurred at the price of a recoupment on the generic liberation conceded earlier: job security and income from work were improved in exchange for working-class populations settling, and the development of factory discipline. In addition to the security it brought, the organization of practices within the framework of the bureaucratized firm opened up another space for demands for generic liberation by allowing for a certain multiplication of identities. On the one hand, it made it possible to differentiate clearly between life outside work (family life, private life) and life at work, between the person and the post held; on the other, especially for *cadres*, it offered the possibility of a career – that is to say, a change of duties in the course of one's life. In this context, duties were themselves defined in such a way as not to encroach unduly on people's unique qualities, by being indexed to established properties which, like educational qualifications, had been subject to social coding, resting in a number of instances on a state guarantee.

In the critiques of the late 1960s and early 1970s, both types of demands were prevalent and, what is more, frequently amalgamated. Demands focused on the need to liberate both the working class from the specific alienation to which it remained subject, and human beings from types of oppression that emerged in a generic form (as, for example, in the case of constraints on sexuality). The multiplication of identities offered by the second spirit of capitalism was deemed still too restricted, the range of possible roles being particularly limited for women, whose access to the identities deriving from work was impeded. But among young *cadres*, whose stylized representation was one of the archetypes of the 1960s, voices invoking psychoanalysis and the liberation of desire were raised to demand a breach in the narrow framework of the conventions and practices associated with the second spirit of capitalism. It was largely this second demand for liberation that was to be recuperated by capitalism and called on to support transformations conducive to pursuit of the accumulation process and render them desirable: now it was said that it was possible to change occupations as frequently as projects, and that all local ties and filiations could be severed because they were a source of inflexibility. It finally seemed as if the formal right to become who one wants to be, when one wants to be it, had been recognized.

But these gains in liberation were made at the expense of demands of the first type: far from finding themselves liberated, many people were instead casualized, subjected to new forms of systemic dependency, obliged to confront undefined, unlimited and distressing exigencies of self-fulfilment and autonomy in greater solitude,[49] and, in most cases, separated from the lived world where nothing helped them to fulfil themselves. For many people, the development of these new forms of specific alienation thus cancelled out the 'generic' liberation that seemed to have been achieved. Thus, for example, with the extension to periods and situations outside the work sphere proper of the kind of anxiety associated with working life or professional survival, the multiplication of projects paradoxically tends to abolish the minimal plurality of lives and identities (diversity of statuses and roles in different contexts – occupation, family, community, etc.), which was made possible by the relative security afforded by forms of organization based upon institutional anchorage. If all connections, however established, can be exploited in the search for employment or the construction of projects, the different spaces of existence become well and truly standardized in one network, geared towards activities aimed at guaranteeing people's economic survival.

Thus it seems as if it is extremely difficult under the capitalist regime to abolish the alienations disclosed by demands for liberation – on the one hand because the production of goods and services assumes a certain discipline, and on the other because it leads in its capitalist form to the accumulation of capital at certain privileged points. Yet it is always possible to judge the constraints and discipline excessive, and to denounce the distribution of profits at a given moment as both involving a form of oppression and deriving from domination, from a balance of forces. Although it incorporates the exigency of liberation into its self-description from the start, capitalism must therefore also always halt it at a certain point if it is to survive. But it can do so either in a negotiated way – as when, in interaction with critique, agreements are reached on acceptable ways of distributing wages and on working conditions – or by imposing its order, as is the case today, following its redeployment and the circumvention of tests supervised by critique.

On the other hand, there is one mode of liberation that capitalism has no need to curb, since it allows it to develop: this is the liberation offered by consumption. People's aspirations to mobility, to multiply their activities, to greater opportunities for being and doing, emerge as a virtually boundless reservoir of ideas for conceiving new products and services to bring to the market. Thus it could be shown that nearly all the inventions which have fuelled the development of capitalism have been associated with offering new ways for people to liberate themselves. This is obviously the case with the development of energy sources other than human beings and animals, with the automation of forms of work, including domestic labour (washing-machines, food-processors, ready-prepared meals, etc.), as well as with advances in the transportation of goods and services (railways, cars, planes), but also information (post, telephone, radio, television, computer networks). To this list must be added other products and services that have fuelled consumption in recent years, which can likewise be characterized in terms of mobility – whether they increase the speed and availability of displacements ('ready-to-consume' tourist products); or procure the illusion of a displacement (like the supply of exotic foodstuffs); or make it possible to acquire time and availability by pursuing an activity without being immobilized, as with the Walkman, the mobile phone and, recently, sight devices attached to glasses. These products, doubtless especially exciting because they engender the illusion of emancipation from space and time constraints, create their own chinks of consumption by freeing up the time slots required for their appropriation, which tends to push back the limits imposed by a shortage of time on the expansion of consumption among solvent but saturated social groups. The 'privatization of cultural consumption' made possible by the rapidly developing cultural industries today may also be regarded as a form of liberation via the commodity. Its archetypal form is listening to a recording when one wishes, where one wishes, courtesy of portable playing apparatuses – and hence access to the kind of music that one wants to hear precisely now, at this instant, and for a chosen length of time, as opposed to going to a concert.

This rapid overview of the different forms of incorporation of demands for liberation into the spirit of capitalism, depending on the epoch, has brought to light certain mechanisms whereby capitalism, while holding out a certain liberation, can by the same token deploy new forms of oppression. It thereby opens up paths for a revival of the artistic critique from the standpoint of the demand for autonomy, to which we shall return in the conclusion to this chapter. In particular, these will have to take seriously capitalism's vocation to commodify desire – especially the desire for liberation – and hence to recuperate and supervise it. On the other hand, a reformulation of the artistic critique should take account of the interdependence of the different dimensions of the demand for liberation, in order to be better equipped to foil the recuperative traps that have hitherto been set for it.

We shall now examine a second dimension of the artistic critique, which denounces the world's inauthenticity under the capitalist regime.[50]

3. WHICH AUTHENTICITY?

In order to understand the problems facing the critique of authenticity today, and the way in which it might be reformulated, we must take a look back and recall how it was directed – that is to say, towards a critique of *standardization and massification* – when the second spirit was dominant.

In contrast to the way we approached the issue of liberation, we shall not go back to formulations of the critique of inauthenticity associated with the first spirit of capitalism, which mainly took the form of a critique of the bourgeois mentality, its conventions and preoccupation with good manners, with 'what is done', regardless of the 'truth' of sentiments and 'sincerity' in relationships in particular. In effect, unlike what we observe in the case of demands for liberation, historical capitalism never claimed to respond to the critique of inauthenticity, which it only really took into consideration with the formation of what we have called the 'third spirit'. As a result, relevant changes in this respect occurred only at the end of the 1960s.

The critique of inauthenticity associated with the
second spirit of capitalism: a critique of massification

For this critique, loss of authenticity essentially refers to a standardization or, if you prefer, a loss of *difference* between entities, whether these are objects or human beings.

It derives first of all from the condemnation of mechanization and its corollary, *mass production*. The lack of difference concerns the proliferating objects that fill the lived world: cotton fabrics, furniture, knick-knacks, cars, household appliances, and so on. Technical objects or the products of technique, each of them has a distinct existence and is subject to personal appropriation. In another respect, however, each is utterly identical to all the others in the same series. Not only is there no difference between them, but each of them, in order to function, has to be used in precisely the same way.

Hence denunciation of mass production does not occur without a correlative denunciation of the *massification of human beings*. The standardization of objects and operations effectively entails a similar standardization of uses and, consequently, of users, whose practices are therewith massified, without them necessarily wanting it or being aware of it. With the development of marketing and advertising at the end of the interwar period, and especially after the Second World War, this massification of human beings as users via consumption extends to what seems to be among the most particular, the most intimate, of the dimensions of persons, rooted in their interior being: desire itself, whose massification is denounced in turn. There is no longer any relevant distance between my desire for some particular object and someone else's desire for an identical object belonging to the same series. Between libidos too, difference is abolished.

Similarly, in production, and especially in *forms of organizing work of a Taylorist type*, the difference between human beings vanishes: assembly-line workers lose all particularity, since workers at the same post are completely interchangeable. If a worker fails, he can immediately be replaced, just as in modern war – *mass warfare* – the infantryman who falls is immediately replaced in the post he occupied by some other.[51]

And the same goes for those domains that Enlightenment liberalism regarded as the very centre of autonomy: *political action* and the representations of themselves and the world, their ideas, their ideologies, that people adopt. The thesis that human beings are standardized and lose all particularity, all difference, when they are assembled in a crowd is unquestionably one of the commonest themes, taken up from very different perspectives, from the last third of the nineteenth century through to the 1960s. It culminates, from the 1930s to the 1960s, in the idea that we are witnessing the advent of an age of the masses and a massification of thought. Initially associated with the critique of democratic regimes,[52] accused of ceding power to the crowd and thereby encouraging the emergence of demagogues, it was to be adopted by the critique of *totalitarianism* and, in particular, of Nazism, in order to explain why the Germans put themselves in the 'Führer's' power as if they had abandoned any critical spirit, even any individuality. It re-emerged in the 1950s and 1960s in the shape of a critique of the *massification effected by the media*, accused of conditioning and standardizing consumers of mass cultural products by transforming them into passive recipients of a standard message, and hence predisposed uncritically to adopt the ideologies imposed upon them from above.[53]

Alongside this political thematic we find a philosopheme, likewise articulated in very different forms by very different authors (who may be at variance and opposed in other respects). It contrasts two ways, of unequal value, of living the human condition. The first, which confronts what is 'tragic' about it, may be declared 'authentic'. The second, dominated by the intention of fleeing it to take refuge in the inertia of a serial life, may be dubbed 'inauthentic'. On the one hand, then, we have the human being who, accepting her 'facticity' and 'contingency', courageously faces up to the 'anxiety' of 'being for herself', cast into a world that is 'already there'; who confers a 'meaning' on her existence by striving towards that which she has to be ('care' in Heidegger, the 'project' in Sartre) and, consequently, assumes her ontological 'freedom' and faces up to her 'responsibility'. On the other hand, we have the one who, fleeing anxiety by becoming submerged in everyday 'banality', takes refuge in 'chatter', as a debasement of speech, and allows herself to be entirely determined by others. (This is the tyranny of 'opinion', the conformist domination of the 'they', in the sense of 'they do', 'they say', 'they feel', in Heidegger; and in Sartre it is 'bad faith' as untruthfulness to oneself, or the *esprit de sérieux* through which an externalized constraint – be it submission to the determinations of the objective world or obeying transcendentally projected moral values – is substituted for the freedom of the responsible subject.)

In the late writings of members of the Frankfurt School still active after the war, like Theodor Adorno, Max Horkheimer and Herbert Marcuse, we find a critique of inauthenticity as a massification and standardization of persons. What it shares with the Sartreian synthesis of the 1960s is that it extends this thematic in a framework and idiom inspired by Marxism, which would help to encourage its reappropriation by the May 1968 movement.

These writers certainly intended to distance themselves from the use of the term 'authenticity' in Heidegger, to which Adorno devoted a violent tract, *The Jargon of Authenticity*, published in German in 1964.[54] But as one reads this attack, one cannot help thinking that it is primarily informed by a concern to exclude any assimilation of two rather compatible, even similar, ways of denouncing the modern condition and the grip of technology. Take, for example, *Dialectic of Enlightenment*, whose first edition dates from 1947. In language with Marxist echoes, but in a manner that is perfectly compatible with the Heideggerian thematic of inauthenticity (or at least, with the way this thematic has generally been understood), Adorno and Horkheimer condemn the consensual levelling, the conformist domination of a society that has made its goal the destruction of any difference. They aim to pursue the radical critique of the massification and standardization affecting every dimension of existence to a conclusion.[55] This standardization extends to language, transforming words, and even proper nouns, into 'capricious, manipulable designations, whose effect is admittedly now calculable', intended to provoke conditioned reflexes, as in the case of 'advertising trade-marks'.[56] Totalitarianism and fascism are thus treated as extremes of 'advanced capitalism' that disclose its truth. Thus, advertising is assimilated to propaganda, and totalitarian advertising proprietors in the service of omnipotent 'trusts' are identified with the masters of propaganda in the service of totalitarian states: in each instance, the individual, dissolved into the mass, is no longer anything but an 'illusion'.[57]

In the years around May 1968, this form of denunciation of inauthenticity enjoyed unprecedented diffusion and public success. The critique of the 'consumer society' brought out on to the streets, as it were, the denunciation of a world given over to the series, mass production, standardized opinion or, as Marcuse puts it, to a drugstore culture where 'Plato and Hegel, Shelley and Baudelaire, Marx and Freud' are on the same shelves as detective novels or romantic novels, and are thereby reduced to a function of sheer entertainment.[58] The utterly unexpected success in France of *One-Dimensional Man* – initially published in a small print run in the months preceding the May events, but then reprinted many times to meet demand – marked the high point, followed by a rapid decline, of this critique of inauthenticity. In effect, we find in Marcuse an opposition between a free consciousness, capable of knowing its own desires, and the man of 'advanced industrial civilization', 'cretinized' and 'standardized' by mass production and 'comfort', rendered incapable of acceding to the immediate experience of the world, wholly subject to needs manipulated by others.

The commodification of difference as the response of capitalism

Capitalism's response to the intense demand for differentiation and demassification that marked the end of the 1960s and the beginning of the 1970s was to internalize it.

This recuperation took the form of a commodification – that is to say, the transformation into 'products', allocated a price and hence exchangeable on a market, of goods and practices that in a different state of affairs remained outside the commodity sphere.[59] Commodification is the simplest process through which capitalism can acknowledge the validity of a critique and make it its own, by incorporating it into its own specific mechanisms: hearing the demand expressed by the critique, entrepreneurs seek to create products and services which will satisfy it, and which they will be able to sell. We have already seen this process at work in the satisfaction of demands for liberation with the invention of products and services with a supposedly 'emancipatory' quality. It has likewise operated on a wide scale to meet demands for authenticity: consumers would henceforth be offered products that were 'authentic' and 'differentiated' in such a way that the impression of massification would be dispelled.

Accordingly, alterations were made to mass production so as to be in a position to *offer more varied goods* destined for a shorter life-span and more rapid change (short production runs, multiplying the options offered to consumers, etc.), in contrast to the standardized products of Fordism. Entrepreneurs regarded this new source of supply as an opportunity to combat market saturation, intensifying consumers' desire by furnishing 'quality' products that were healthier and offered greater 'authenticity'.[60] This new output was stimulated by a growing interest in physical beauty and health, and encouraged by the denunciation, for which nascent ecology supplied some arguments, of the artificial, industrial character – especially in the case of food produce – of mass consumer products, which were not only insipid but also bad for the health. It was also furthered by an increase in consumer know-how in the developed countries. It proceeded in tandem with a commodification of *goods that had hitherto remained outside the commodity sphere* (the very reason they were deemed authentic): capitalism was to penetrate domains (tourism, cultural activities, personal services, leisure, etc.) which had hitherto remained comparatively external to mass commodity circulation.

Developments in the direction of an *increased commodification of certain qualities of human beings* also started, with the wish to 'humanize' services and, in particular, personal services, as well as work relations. The framework of personal services typically involves the proximity of direct contact, such that along with the actual 'service' other dimensions enter into the transaction, particularly those whose presence is most directly bound up with the body (not only inasmuch as it is offered to inspection, but also as regards smell, even touch). In eliciting, for example, sympathy or antipathy, attraction or repulsion, these influence customer satisfaction, and hence the profits that can be made. The personal dimensions involved in the transaction, without directly forming part of the definition of the service sold, may be present spontaneously, in unpremeditated fashion. Or, on the contrary, they may derive from specific selection or training,[61] to the point where the question of the actual nature of the relation (purely 'commercial' or also bound up with 'genuine' feelings) is always left in suspense, and invariably unanswered. Within a work collective, possession of these 'interpersonal qualities' is likewise recommended today – qualities that did not previously feature in the definition of what can be exchanged against a wage in the framework of a work contract.

The importance accorded to the role of mediators, personal relations, friendship or trust in profit creation in a connexionist world – and, correlatively, the fading of the distinction between private life and business life – thus tend to bring relations that were once defined precisely as 'disinterested' into the commodity sphere.

The supply of authentic goods and human relations in the form of commodities was the only possible way of responding to the demand for authenticity that was compatible with the imperatives of accumulation. But clearly, in this new sense the reference to authenticity no longer presupposed the ascetic rejection of goods, material comfort or 'materialism' that still permeated the critique of the consumer society in the years following May 1968.

The failures of the commodification of the authentic and the return of anxiety

Yet this response by capitalism to aspirations to what is authentic was doomed to failure, as we are going to seek to demonstrate. By comparison with the mass production of uniform objects intended for mass consumption, the commodification of authentic goods and services in fact possesses a paradoxical character.

On the one hand, to earn the label 'authentic' these goods must be drawn from outside the commodity sphere, from what might be called 'sources of authenticity'. The commodification of the authentic thus assumes reference to an original that is not a commodity good, but a pure use-value defined in a unique relationship to a user. Consequently, it acknowledges, at least implicitly, that non-commodity goods are superior 'in value' to commodity goods, or that use-value in its particularity is superior to exchange-value in its generic character. Commodification of the authentic consists in exploiting goods, values and means under the sway of capital which, while acknowledged to represent riches (or 'treasures', in Hideya Kawakita's formulation[62]), were nevertheless hitherto excluded from the sphere of capital and commodity circulation. In effect, at any one point only a limited portion of the entities – material or immaterial, real or virtual – that might be an object of desire, and hence a potential source of profit, is actually placed under the sway of capital. This is either because some of them have not been discovered as potential sources for satisfying a desire, and hence of profit; or because they are difficult to access and costly to transform; or again because they are deliberately excluded and protected by legally sanctioned moral prohibitions. In this sense, the commodification of the authentic made it possible to revive the process of transformation of non-capital into capital, which is one of the principal motors of capitalism, on new bases and, consequently, to meet the threat of a crisis of mass consumption that loomed in the 1970s.

On the other hand, however, in order for the circulation of goods drawn from the authenticity reserve of non-commodity goods to yield a profit, they had to fall within the sphere of control and calculation, be the object of transactions and, in the case of people, of 'target contracts', sanctions, and so on. The transition from non-capital to capital in fact follows a *series of operations* that may be called operations of production – since they have the effect of creating a 'product' out of diverse resources – even when they involve immaterial goods whose transformation is purely symbolic, or when they are applied to people.[63]

The commodification of the authentic first of all presupposes exploring sources of authenticity that are potential sources of profit, such as human beings, scenery, cafés where people feel comfortable, tastes, rhythms, ways of being and doing, and so on, which have not yet been introduced into the sphere of commodity circulation. This logic initially developed in what was for a long time the economically rather marginal domain of cultural enterprises – publishing, record production, orchestras, art galleries, and so on – where economic performance is basically a matter of the entrepreneur's ability in a personal relationship to sense creative potential and anticipate a public's tastes and desires. It has expanded considerably over the last thirty years with the growing importance of cultural and technological investments, and also with the development of services – in particular, tourism, the hotel business and catering, fashion and ready-to-wear clothes, interior decoration and design. It is a matter for 'managers', whose skills approximate to those of the artist, the organizer and the businessman. Seeking to exploit as yet unidentified sources, these people with a talent for sniffing things out cannot rely on existing standards, and must demonstrate what management literature calls 'intuition'. The chances of hitting the bull's-eye increase depending on how 'spontaneous' or 'natural' the intuition is – that is to say, the more it is rooted, not in a reflexivity developed in the course of professional activity, but in their own desire, which presupposes that they have shared tastes, interests and activities with the potential public whose demands they anticipate or, rather, elicit.

A second series of operations consists in analysing the good in question to control its circulation and make it a source of profit. In effect, with the exception of the borderline case of objects of Antiquity or artworks that circulate in a market without losing their substantial uniqueness,[64] entities – objects or persons – must, if they are to be incorporated into the accumulation process, be handled in such a way as to transform them into 'multiples', as art language puts it with reference to lithographs or photographs. The product or service intended for commodification is subject to an operation selecting the distinctive features to be preserved (in contrast to secondary features, which can be discarded or are too costly to reproduce) – that is to say, to 'codification', which is equally necessary for assessing the financial cost of the commodification of the authentic product and for serving as a device for marketing operations designed to enhance its prestige.

Codification is distinct from standardization, which was a prerequisite of mass production, in the sense that it permits greater flexibility. Whereas standardization consisted in conceiving a product from the outset, and reproducing it identically in as many copies as the market could absorb, codification, element by element, makes it possible to operate on a combinatory, and introduce variations in such a way as to obtain products that are relatively different, but of the same style. In this sense, codification allows for a commodification of difference that was not possible in the case of standardized production. That is why it is suitable for the commodification of the authentic, since it makes it possible to preserve something of the uniqueness that accounted for the value of the original. Take the example of the small café, which is fitted out any old how, intuitively, at random, but works. It works very well. It is always full. One is tempted to expand it. One could buy the adjoining house next door, but that would not go very far. To expand it, it must be reproduced elsewhere – in another district, another town. It needs to be transposed. But because it is not clear what accounts for its success, it is not clear what to take from it. The odd tables? The peasant dishes? The informal service? The friendly clientele that frequents it? The reasonable prices? (But wouldn't different customers elsewhere be willing to pay more?) To find out, it is necessary to analyse the café, see what gives it the truly authentic character that accounts for its value, select certain of its qualities – the most significant or the most transposable (for example, the clientele is the most difficult thing to transpose) – and ignore others, deemed secondary. This process is a process of coding.

The effect of capitalism's assimilation of the demand for authenticity, by means of a commodification whose highly contradictory character we have just noted, has been to introduce into people's relationship to goods and persons *rapid cycles of infatuation and disappointment* (modelled in other respects by A.O. Hirschman).[65] The desire for authenticity is principally focused on goods that are regarded as original – that is to say, on goods that may be regarded as having remained outside the commodity sphere and access to which, for that very reason, required a sacrifice irreducible to monetary expenditure (time, sustained physical effort, a personal investment in the establishment of a relationship of trust, etc.). The commodification of goods drawn from outside the commodity sphere has made these goods much more readily accessible for a monetary sum, and for those who possess the means. However, simply by virtue of the fact that to ensure their commodification these goods must be reproduced and copied, while undergoing a process of coding and calculation of profitability, they are bound to disappoint at least some of the expectations people had of them once they are on the market. The attraction of a product appreciated for its authenticity does not in fact stem exclusively from its ability to perform the specific functions it is intended for fully and more cheaply. It depends to a large extent on the open (and hence necessarily uncoded) character of its determinations, whose list is hypothetically unlimited – a property which, as N. Heinrich has noted in the case of the artwork, makes it comparable to the person. In the case of the authentic product, pleasure depends not only on the use that is made of it, but also on the disclosure of hidden meanings and qualities in the course of a unique relationship. Yet codification, on which reproduction depends, tends to limit the diversity of the meanings that can be extracted from the goods. Accordingly, once the significations intentionally introduced by means of the coding have been recognized, the goods tends to lose their interest and to disappoint, even if their use continues to perform a given function properly.

We can see a typical illustration of this phenomenon in the transition from mass tourism to so-called 'adventure' holidays, requiring a constant renewal of destinations as and when they become tourist attractions in their turn, losing the authenticity (of which an absence of tourists was precisely the sign) that made them so precious.[66] What are called 'natural' or 'authentic' commodity goods display a paradoxical character since, while circulating strictly as commodities (often even in the circuits of mass marketing), they must, in order to achieve prominence (and justify their price), present themselves in ways that refer to an earlier state of market relations: a state where the purchaser was face to face with an artisan, at once manufacturer and tradesman, in a marketplace. These objects are especially open to suspicion because it is difficult to brush aside the issue of whether they are distinguished from standard products exclusively by presentation (packaging) and selling points (advertising), or equally by substantial properties deriving from different manufacturing methods.[67]

Thus the possibility of commodifying differences ushers in a new era of suspicion. For if it was relatively straightforward to distinguish between an artisanal object and a mass product, between a 'massified' worker and a 'free' artist, how can we know if some particular thing, event or feeling is the expression of the spontaneity of existence, or the result of a premeditated process aimed at transforming an 'authentic' good into a commodity? Similarly, how can we tell if a particular author is an 'authentic' rebel or an 'editorial' product, whether a smile, a gesture of friendship, or a dinner invitation is the expression of a spontaneous, sincere friendship, or the product of training – a training course, for example, designed to make some service more attractive – or, worse still, a strategy designed to elicit trust or create appeal, so as to be surer of achieving a purely commercial objective?

As in the case of justice or liberation, we can thus bring out a cycle of recuperation in connection with the authentic. With the latter what we observed was, in a first stage, a critique of standard, conventional and impersonal goods and human relations. Capitalist mechanisms were amended to respond to these critiques by implementing a commodification of difference and supplying new goods, whose value precisely consisted in their original exclusion from the commodity sphere. We may say that capitalism has, in a way, recuperated the demand for authenticity in the sense that it has profited from it.

On the other hand, this form of recuperation is different from that effected in the cases of justice and liberation. In those two instances, the moment of recuperation was characterized not by satisfaction of the critical demand, as is the case here, but by recouping what had just been conceded in a different way. In the case of authenticity, what we have is a restoration of control by capitalism, in the sense that it disappoints the expectations which it earlier offered to satisfy. Commodification thus creates new forms of anxiety about the authenticity of things or persons; one no longer knows if they are 'authentic' or 'inauthentic', spontaneous or re-engineered for commercial ends. However, in contrast to what we observe in the case of the recuperation of justice or liberation, it cannot be said in this instance that the process of accumulation is liberated from the constraints which weighed on it. When what has earlier been conceded in terms of autonomy or control over tests is recuperated by other means, the accumulation process rediscovers a certain freedom and capacity to control the 'human resources' it engages. By contrast, when it fails to supply genuinely 'authentic' goods – something it is necessarily incapable of, since characterization as authentic refers to the uncalculated, the unintentional, the non-commodified – it comes up against limits to its development.

Suspicion of objects: The example of eco-products

The case of eco-products offers a good example of the way that recuperation of the demand for authenticity by capitalism leads to rapid cycles of infatuation and disappointment. This example demonstrates how consumer desire for 'natural' products, which are regarded as less polluting or less harmful to health, can be disappointed when the response of capitalism to this demand takes the form of marketing and advertising.

Green consumerism, which was often accompanied, at least in its formative stage in the 1970s, by a critique of capitalism and the consumer society, may be regarded as one of the current refuges of the artistic critique. It is based upon a thematic that, in its most general and widespread formulations, accords a value to nature as the locus of the authentic. On the one hand, it is the site of what is 'original', which must be preserved as such, and is always more or less threatened with being 'denatured' by copies assessed in terms of their fidelity to the model. On the other hand, it is a preserve of aesthetic differences (landscape) and organic differences (biodiversity), whose proliferation is a treasure in itself. From this standpoint, industrial products can be challenged on account of their contribution to environmental degradation.

The development of green consumerism at the end of the 1980s (the 'revolt of the shopping trolleys' referred to by marketing specialists) threatened a number of firms, by bringing about a sharp drop in the consumption of products condemned as polluting by environmentalist movements, or harmful to health (such as detergents containing phosphates, aerosols containing CFCs, or, in the United States, chemically treated apples or certain plastic wrappings). Initially, consumers' environmental concerns were expressed in the mode of what Hirschman calls defection (as opposed to protest). From 1988 to 1990, the percentage of green consumers (individuals stating that they preferred one product to another on ecological grounds) thus went up in Great Britain from 19 to 50 per cent.[68]

The first to become aware of the phenomenon were the distributors, who passed on the cost of the growth in green consumerism to producers, by encouraging suppliers offering products that were reputed to be less polluting. The producers themselves began to take a closer interest in the procedures used by their subcontractors; this helped to develop practices of traceability and contractual standardization. In order to respond to the threat represented by green consumerism, there were two further developments at the end of the 1980s and the beginning of the 1990s, especially in Anglophone countries: on the one hand, studies intended to reach a better understanding of consumer attitudes in this regard; and on the other, reflection aiming to integrate concerns about environmental protection into management (eco-management). From 1989 onwards, the manufacture of new products that were ecologically less open to attack – eco-products – and the development of marketing which emphasized environmental protection were stimulated by studies showing that green consumers possessed above-average purchasing power and educational levels; and that they were prepared to pay 25 per cent more for less polluting products or, in the case of food, for 'organic' products.[69] After the anxieties of the late 1980s, a number of firms optimistically discovered the potential for a new market at the top of the range.[70]

Ecological marketing developed in several directions. The first consisted in sponsoring campaigns for the protection of the environment, and publicizing the fact with a tag (ecological sponsorship). But it was also tempting to resort to ecological advertising, emphasizing the efforts under way either to make products less polluting and less harmful, or to improve their production in line with greater respect for the environment, or, finally, to facilitate their elimination at the end of their life-cycle. The arguments were of the following kind: the brand of beef used by such-and-such a restaurant chain has not encouraged deforestation; the way in which tinned tuna has been fished has not harmed dolphins;[71] these batteries do not use mercury; the lorries of one firm run on unleaded petrol; another firm uses recycled paper for its packaging.[72]

Consumers, however, fairly rapidly became sceptical about these kinds of arguments. The response of ecological marketing specialists was to try to decommodify their campaigns by appealing to outside experts, public authorities, mixed committees, environmentalist associations,[73] or labelling institutes, and by requesting ecological audits from agencies possessing eco-tools, in order to 'build up credibility' with 'environmental watchdogs'.[74] It appears, however, that the loss of credibility on the part of eco-marketing was not due only to the use of arguments that were largely unfounded, or to the fact that a product which was less polluting in one respect prioritized by the advertising could turn out to be more so in another respect that had been deliberately ignored. It also derived from the very fact of seeing the language of ecology turned into a commercial argument. *Commodification was enough to cast doubt on the reality and value of eco-products.* From the early 1990s, there followed a decline in the percentage of purchasers inclined to travel or pay more for green products.[75] Thus in France, for example, Monoprix, which was one of the first major distributors to launch 'green products' (in 1990), opting for eco-marketing rather than for environmental sponsorship, found itself charged with 'eco-freak-marketing'.[76] At the same time, more radical ecological movements (like Friends of the Earth) were criticizing green consumerism, in the belief that by encouraging the commodification of new goods it had helped to revive capitalism just when markets were reaching saturation point, thus deferring the possibility of an escape from the consumer society.[77]

A new demand for authenticity: The critique of fabrication

The way capitalism has incorporated the demand for authenticity by com-modifying it has prompted a redefinition of authenticity. A definition of the inauthentic as mass production and standardization dissolving difference, to which the authenticity of the singular as a principle of resistance to the uni-formity of standard models could be counterposed, was replaced by a definition of the inauthentic as *reproduction of a difference for commercial ends* – as copy – to which the authenticity of an original can be counterposed. The tension between the truth of the original and the artificiality of what has been 'fabricated' in its image inflects what it means to characterize something as authentic in a direction that makes reference not so much to the object itself, as to the *intentions* of those it is procured from. Now what is authentic is that which has been made without a secondary strategic intention – that is to say, without any other intention than making it (in contrast to the intention of getting it sold, as with eco-products), of making it (or oneself) loved, making it (or oneself) admired.[78] Likewise with relations between people, the fact that the connexionist world stresses the advantage to be derived from connec-tions, however established, tends to generalize suspicion about the intentions behind establishing a relationship. Consequently, the epithet 'inauthentic' tends to become attached to all forms of action suspected of being informed by a 'second-level' intention – that is to say, by a strategic or 'manipulative' design.

Rather than the problematic of massification, which dominated the first half of the twentieth century, the form currently taken by the critique of inauthenticity revives a different tradition. Deeply entrenched in it is the denunciation of artifice as opposed to the spontaneous, the mechanical in contrast to the living, the sincere in contrast to the strategic, and hence genuine emotion, which arises unintentionally, as opposed to its simulated imitation: a challenge to the 'spectacle'. As John Barish has shown in his monumental history of 'prejudices' against the theatre,[79] this tradition, which has followed its course since Greek Antiquity and culminated in the eighteenth century (particularly in Rousseau), is once again pervasive today. The art of the 'simulacrum' seems especially scandalous whenever, as was notably the case in the eighteenth century, critique of existing institutions transfers on to persons, in so far as they are susceptible to emotions and feelings, the whole burden of the ethical dimension. Detached from observance of an external norm, an imposed morality, the ethical dimension is disclosed as pure, spontaneous expressiveness.[80] The theatre is then attacked inasmuch as it relies upon actors' ability to produce the external signs of emotion. What is put in relief in the theatre is indeed difference – what the peculiarity of each character consists in, the sentiments that the human face alone is capable of expressing with its laughter or its tears, the uniqueness of gestures as the expression of a particular bodily *hexis*, and so on. But everything is simulated and premeditated; the realization of difference is subject to an external purpose – the pleasure of the spectator: everything is false.[81]

Thus, the commodification of everything, as the capitalist appropriation of difference to make a profit from it, can also indeed be denounced – by Debord, for example, or, in another respect, Baudrillard – as the transformation of everything into a spectacle: as the destruction of any authentic life force that, however faint, is immediately *encoded* in order to take its place in the commodity circulation of signs, which is then substituted for the experience of a genuine 'life' in contact with the world.[82] Suspicion of a generalized simulacrum, of a commodification of everything, including the seemingly most noble and disinterested sentiments, does indeed form part of our contemporary condition, as was illustrated, for example, at the beginning of the 1990s with the violent indictment of humanitarian action as a televisual spectacle.

This suspicion about the authenticity of people and things can be displayed in particularly explicit fashion today, because it is detached from the critique of mass society into which it was in some sense incorporated from the end of the nineteenth century. For example, for Marcuse, whose principal target is the North American society of his time, an important element in the critique of mass society integrates the thematic of recuperation via the commodification of everything, but without giving it real autonomy.[83] The capitalist self-criticism of mass society and the commodification of difference have paved the way for a denunciation of reality in its entirety as illusion and performance: as spectacle *qua* ultimate commodity form.

Nevertheless, as we are now going to seek to show, this new critique of inauthenticity cannot fully flourish, because it is neutralized by another ideological formation dating from the 1960s. Moreover, this is what makes for the specificity of the contemporary denunciation of inauthenticity as the fabricated, the spectacle or simulacrum: that it is constantly checked – from within, as it were – whenever it rediscovers autonomy.

4. THE NEUTRALIZATION OF THE CRITIQUE OF INAUTHENTICITY AND ITS DISTURBING EFFECTS

If we are to understand this neutralization, we must return to the years around May 1968. What we observe at this time is two contradictory dynamics. On the one hand, as we have seen, it was during these years that the critique of the inauthenticity of the world in the grip of capital enjoyed a kind of public success, leading to its recuperation by capitalism. On the other hand, however, it was during the same period, and likewise from positions associated with the May 1968 movement, that a *radical deconstruction of the exigency of authenticity*, as expressed in the first half of the century, was developed. The former figure of authenticity was denounced as an illusion in various respects: as bourgeois, reactionary, even 'fascist' elitism; as the illusion of presence and, in particular, of the presence to itself of an 'authentic' subject; as a naive belief in the existence of an 'original' whose representations could be more or less faithful, and hence more or less authentic, in the sense in which the truth is opposed to illusion (the simulacrum).

Initially formulated in relatively narrow circles, this critique, of which we shall give some examples below, was to be widely diffused in the following twenty years – a phenomenon not unconnected with the rise of the figure of the network. In effect, the deconstruction of the old notion of authenticity – as loyalty to self, as the subject's resistance to pressure from others, as a demand for truth in the sense of conformity to an ideal – goes hand in glove with the concept of a network world. In a connexionist world, loyalty to the self looks like inflexibility; resistance to others seems like a refusal to make connections; truth defined by the identity between a representation and an original is regarded as a failure to understand the infinite variability of the beings who circulate in the network, and change every time they enter into relations with different beings, so that none of their manifestations can be taken as a point of origin with which other expressions can be compared. In a network world, the question of authenticity can no longer be formally posed – either in the sense given it in the first half of the century, or even in the formulation that we have seen emerge following capitalism's attempts to recuperate the critique of standardization, which still assumes the possibility of a judgement whose assessments are grounded in reference to an origin.

Now – and this is one of the main arguments of this work – the redeployment of capitalism has been associated with the recuperation of the figure of the network, even if the emergence of this paradigm derives from an autonomous history of philosophy, and was not at any point directly and deliberately elaborated to confront the problems faced by capitalism from the 1960s onwards.

Hence it can be said, without exaggeration or paradox, that if capitalism attempted to recuperate the demand for authenticity underlying the critique of the consumer society (by commodifying it, as we have seen), in another respect – and relatively independently – it has, with the metaphor of the network, assimilated the critique of this demand for autonomy, whose formulation paved the way for the deployment of reticular or rhizomorphous paradigms.

This contradictory double incorporation tends both to acknowledge the demand for authenticity as valid and to create a world where this question is no longer to be posed. And this, as we shall see, underlies the existential tensions – inextricably psychological and ethical – felt by people engaged in the process of accumulation. But if this situation, on account of the tensions it entails, can be disturbing for those who are plunged into it, it must be recognized that it allows capitalism to circumvent the failure to which it seems doomed in its attempts to respond to the demand for authenticity. From the perspective of unlimited accumulation, it is preferable for the question to be cancelled and for people to be persuaded that everything is – or cannot now be anything but – a simulacrum; that 'genuine' authenticity is henceforth banished from the world; or that the aspiration to the 'authentic' was simply an illusion. They will then more readily accept the satisfaction to be had from the goods on offer, regardless of whether they are presented as 'authentic', without dreaming of a world that is not one of artifice and commodities.

Along with its incorporation into capitalism, the discrediting of the demand for authenticity has also had a certain effect on the way new demands for authenticity are expressed. Following the enterprise of deconstruction, they could no longer be (if we may put it thus) as 'naive' as they were in the past – as if there might somewhere still exist an authenticity that had been preserved. Accordingly, the new demand for authenticity must always be formulated in an ironic distance from itself.

It follows that the existential tensions deriving from the contradiction inherent in capitalism when it prides itself on being more 'authentic', while at the same time recognizing itself in a paradigm where the demand for authenticity is meaningless, are exacerbated by the absence of any possible solution on the part of critique, which is bound up with denouncing both the inauthenticity and the naivety of this denunciation.

Before examining these tensions, we must return in more detail to the way the former demand for authenticity was dismantled theoretically, before becoming discredited in its everyday expressions to the point where it appears anachronistic, even ridiculous.

The discrediting of the quest for authenticity

In the second half of the 1960s and the 1970s, the thematic of authenticity was subjected to a systematic labour of deconstruction by authors whose names are often associated, rightly or wrongly, with *la pensée 68*. No doubt this was prompted largely by a determination to have done with the different forms of existentialism (especially Christian existentialism, not to mention personalism) that had dominated academic philosophy in the 1950s. This radical critique was articulated from positions which, while they started out from different philosophical orientations, shared the aim of discarding the responsible subject to whom the alternative between authenticity and inauthenticity presents itself as an existential choice. This was denounced as sheer illusion, or as the expression of the bourgeois *ethos*. For simple descriptive purposes we shall give three examples of this critique in the work of Pierre Bourdieu, Jacques Derrida and Gilles Deleuze.

From a position close to what we have called the 'social critique', Bourdieu reveals an aristocratic contempt for the popular classes underlying the critique of massification. He takes as successive targets the sociology of the 'mass media', accused of ignoring the different interpretations that members of different social classes give of the same media message and the different uses they make of it;[84] Sartreian subjectivism and neglect of the 'social conditions of access' to 'authentic' forms of existence;[85] the Heideggerian opposition between authenticity and inauthenticity, between authentic speech and everyday chatter, which Bourdieu assimilates to an ideology – that is to say, in this specific instance, to one expression among others of the disgust inspired by the industrial masses in the prophets of the 'conservative revolution' in 1920s and 1930s Germany (and hence an anticipation of Nazism);[86] and, finally, the 'specifically aesthetic viewpoint' of 'pure aesthetics' and 'natural taste', unmasked as the expression of a 'charismatic ideology' seeking to dissimulate 'the hidden conditions of the miracle of the unequal class distribution of the capacity for inspired encounters with works of art', and to provide the privileged members of a culture with the advantages of distinction.[87] Thus, the relationship between the person with taste and the work of art that is presented as 'authentic' in the sense of sublime – the inspired encounter between a gaze and a work – is nothing other than the deciphering of a code that has been inculcated but does not know itself to be such.[88]

A second example, which is contemporaneous with the first, is Derrida. He does not directly criticize the opposition between the authentic existence of being for-oneself and flight into the everyday banality of the 'they'. But in assigning himself the task in *Of Grammatology*, published in 1967, of deconstructing the opposition on which (as he would have it) Western metaphysics in its entirety rests – the opposition between the 'voice' and 'writing' – he distances, and in a certain way relativizes, the simultaneously ontological and ethical primacy accorded to 'presence', and hence the aim of self-presence. Derrida questions the privilege accorded to the voice, to live speech as the expression without distance or intermediary of the truth of being, whose presence is thus unveiled in its authenticity – as opposed to writing as deferred presence and an operator of distance, as a supplement and contingent artifice that imperils the truth. He thereby dismantles a figure that has, since Rousseau, constituted one of the most fertile springs for sustaining a demand for authenticity.[89]

Finally, a third example is the Deleuzian enterprise developed in *Difference and Repetition* – published in 1968, and hence virtually at the same time as *Of Grammatology*. Deleuze develops a critique of representation in the sense of the correspondence between thing and concept, bound up with a metaphysics in which it is no longer possible to preserve the opposition between an original and a copy. In such a world, '[a]ll identities are only simulated, produced as an optical "effect" by the more profound game of difference and repetition'. For, adds Deleuze, '[m]odern life is such that, confronted with the most mechanical, the most stereotypical representations, inside and outside ourselves, we endlessly extract from them little differences, variations and modifications. Conversely, secret, disguised and hidden repetitions, animated by the perpetual displacement of a difference, restore bare, mechanical and stereotypical representations, within and without us.' The modern world is a world of 'simulacra'. Yet '[t]he simulacrum is not just a copy, but that which overturns all copies by *also* overturning the models'.[90] In the world of the 'simulacrum', it is no longer possible to contrast a 'copy' with a 'model'; an existence orientated towards authenticity, as self-identity, with an existence subjected by external forces to a mechanical repetition; an ontological difference, which would be that of the responsible subject, to its loss in the undifferentiated. The 'plane of immanence' knows only differentials of force whose displacements produce (small) differences, continual variations between which there is no hierarchy, and 'complex' forms of repetition.[91]

The various challenges to the thematic of authenticity whose main lines we have just evoked paved the way – opened up by the Frankfurt School, or even the Barthes of *Mythologies*[92] – from a Marxist critique of ideologies. The result was that social critique, and also literary criticism, was assigned as its main task deciphering and unveiling the codifying operations that secretly sustain (rather like theatre equipment operating from the wings) the claim of each being to authentic presence. This assertion of the absolute primacy of the code, and the unveiling of the illusion of presence as such, can help to support a critique of the inauthenticity of the world. But they do not allow for the contraposition of an authentic expression to an illusory representation.

Moreover, it was doubtless because it did not succeed in freeing itself from this deconstruction of the notion of authenticity, carried out as the 1960s passed into the 1970s, that the new critique of the inauthenticity of a world consigned to the sway of the commodity as generalized simulacrum easily collapsed into the aporia of denouncing the loss of any 'authentic' reality with the utmost radicalism, while undermining the normative and even cognitive position from which such a denunciation might be formulated. If everything without exception is now nothing but code, spectacle or simulacrum, from what external position can critique denounce an illusion that is one with the totality of what exists? The former critique of standardization and massification at least found a normative fulcrum in the ideal of the unique, authentic individual assuming responsibility, deaf to the chatter of the 'they say'. In the case of the critique of the world as spectacle, there is no remaining position from which an authentic relation to things, people and the self might be demanded. The radical aim of the new critique thus constantly threatens its own position of enunciation, for it has to be asked from what position the critique can be adopted if everything is now only simulacrum and spectacle; if, henceforth, any reference to an external world, and thus to a classical definition of truth, is cancelled ('[i]llusion is no longer possible, because the real is no longer possible');[93] if the 'system' we are immersed in, entirely 'encoded', 'is no longer itself anything but a giant simulacrum' – 'that is to say, never exchanged for the real, but exchanged for itself, in an uninterrupted circuit without reference or circumference'[94] – and, as a result, finds itself beyond, or behind, the true and the false.

The initial outcome of the tension between capitalism's dual assimilation of a critique of authenticity and a demand for authenticity had a particularly insidious impact on confidence in people's ability to reach mutual agreement.

Anxiety about relationships: Between friendship and business

If it is true that anxiety about relations with others plays an important role, alongside more easily observable factors like economic insecurity, in the formation of the behaviour traditionally taken to indicate anomie, we must focus particular attention on the unease generated in a connexionist world by the deletion of the distinction between disinterested relations, hitherto regarded as pertaining to the sphere of personal affective life, and professional relations that could be placed under the sign of interest.

As conceived in the framework of the projective city, the establishment of connections cannot be effected according to standardized procedures operating from a distance. Only in direct encounters can the radical uncertainty of the relationship be diminished and mutual expectations discovered, negotiated and co-ordinated. In this process, comparative factors are necessarily involved, whose description pertains to the language of friendly or affective relations, like affinity, the discovery of shared tastes, interests or ground, such as can produce the kind of trust often characterized as 'spontaneous'. The ways in which these bonds are established, the role played in them by affinity, are very similar to the way bonds of friendship are formed – particularly when the connection is remote, novel (innovative) and not finalized. Its function, as yet wholly potential, can be disclosed only in the dynamic of the relation itself, which, as it were, generates a utility whose content no one precisely knew before the connection was established. If the pursuit of profit remains the fundamental horizon in which these relations are formed, what ensues is a rather disturbing blurring of the distinction between friendly relations and business relations, between the disinterested sharing of common interests and the pursuit of professional or economic interests. How can we know if a particular invitation to dinner, introduction to a close friend, or participation in a discussion is disinterested or self-interested, contingent or part of a plan?[95] And how are people to distinguish the parts of the day or the year devoted to work from leisure time, private life from working life? Does not a notion like 'activity', at the centre of the construction of the projective city, precisely aim to blur the boundaries between these different states, which were hitherto clearly separated?

The strategic utilization of relations, which possesses certain features that in other contexts are attributable to friendship, is especially conducive to confusion when financial advantages may be derived from connections. Scarcely visible when the entrepreneur takes advantage of his relations to develop his own business, profits pertaining to connections are clearly apparent when the mediation is commodified – that is to say, when someone receives a wage, fees or commission for serving as an intermediary between people who go into business (e.g. for having contributed to the creation of a new product by putting an inventive scientist and the head of a firm open to innovation in contact during a dinner). Such activities pose a problem inasmuch as they may be subject to the accusation of infringing the prohibition on the commodification of human beings. Receiving a financial bonus for helping to extend a network by creating a new connection between people and groups who previously had no direct link; getting paid for putting someone whom one knows in contact with a third party desirous of meeting her – these bear a disturbing resemblance to the offence of subcontracting labour: the intermediary intervenes as if he had a property right over the person of the one whom he puts in contact with a third party, who anticipates some advantage from this liaison.

This confusion about the nature of the relationships one may have with others in a connexionist world derives from a basic contradiction between the requirement of adaptability and mobility on the one hand, and the requirement of authenticity (which assumes making connections in person, inspiring trust) that permeates the new world, and is duplicated in the projective city on the other.

On the one hand, then, there is the requirement to be mobile, to adapt to a variety of situations in order to take advantage of the opportunities for connections that present themselves. From the standpoint of a 'rhizomorphous' world, authenticity in the old existentialist sense – the solitary subject resisting spiritual massification – has become utterly obsolete. In an ontology based on the network, the quest for an authentic existence via separation from the crowd, voluntary solitude, and retreating into the self lose all value and even all meaning, since the relations precede the terms they are established between, and the substantial properties of persons themselves depend on the relations they are rooted in. Knowing nothing but *mediations*, the network ignores the opposition between beings characterized by the difference that defines what is most profound, intimate and specific about them, and the non-differentiation of the mass or series from which they should extricate themselves from in order to access what they really are. In such a world, a certain sense of freedom can flourish, but the requirement of authenticity is absent.

On the other hand, there is a requirement to be reliable, to be someone in whom one can trust. The challenge to institutions and institutional authority (condemned as bureaucratic), the critique of conventions in the sense of 'proprieties', 'conventional' relations, the prescriptions and rules governing 'conventional morality' (denounced as 'formal' in contrast to the spontaneity of 'ethics') and, more generally, of the conventions on which domestic orders and hierarchical relations rely, has resulted in reactivating a reference to 'authenticity' formulated in terms of 'sincerity', 'commitment' and 'trust', by making persons wholly responsible for relationships. Thus, to take only the most obvious examples, relations between couples are now deemed worthwhile experiences only if they are based upon an 'intense relationship' comparable to the state of affairs that obtained at the beginning of the relationship; relations between friends on spontaneous 'affinities'; and, in utterly paradoxical fashion, family relations, which are the most statutory relations that exist, on 'elective' choices.[96] In the business world, the same de-conventionalization has led to emphasizing the significance of what is 'personal' about relations, the need to base them on 'trust' – that is, on an internalized belief in the sincerity of the bond established for a certain length of time – while presenting the continual establishment of new connections as a prerequisite of profit creation. Thus, the old conception of authenticity as 'interiority', adopted in the face of the banality of the external world, manifests its persistence at the very heart of a new network world that has in a sense been constructed against it.[97]

In such a world, where the whole weight of relationships rests upon the authenticity of persons, it is particularly disturbing to see these relations utilized in strategies aimed at generating network profits, as recommended by neo-management.

Neo-management and denunciations of manipulation

The tension between a premium on authenticity in personal relations and the requirement of adaptability and mobility is at the heart of neo-management: either the two imperatives feature among the precepts dispensed by the same author, without the contradiction being explicitly registered; or, more rarely, the attempt to redefine the optimal forms of work organization is directed towards a search for mechanisms that aim to reduce the opposition between these different types of prescription.

Examples of the first type can be found in the writings of Bob Aubrey who, in a kind of apologue, relates the story of a 'client' who became a 'friend' during a discussion characterized as being at once 'frank' and 'effective': 'As soon as our relationship was transformed into a mutual understanding, I had the impression that I was at the heart of what is most genuine and noble in business – the decision to "make our way together", to trust one another and be concerned about each other. ... Since ... I have intuitively favoured during my decisions the possibility of creating a supportive relationship with my client.'[98] Yet the same author is one of the most enthusiastic promoters of the need for mobility, which he defines, notably, with the phrase 'self as enterprise'. Similarly, Rosabeth Moss Kanter simultaneously advocates 'empathy' ('good deal making depends on empathy – the ability to step into other people's shoes and appreciate their goals') and the adoption of a 'a logic of flexible work assignments' on the basis of 'sequential and synchronous projects of varying length and breadth, through which varying combinations of people will move, depending on the tasks, challenges, and opportunities'.[99] Finally – a last example – in the space of a few pages, Hubert Landier stresses the necessity of 'adapting rapidly' and developing 'informal relations' in a 'freely chosen co-operation based on trust'.[100]

Isabelle Orgogozo, in contrast, is inspired by a concern to reduce this tension when she counterposes two different forms to the old hierarchical modes of communication that she condemns: a first, ideal form (inspired, she says, by Jürgen Habermas and 'communicative ethics'), in which 'the universalization of interests does not descend from on high, but emerges from free, frank discussion between particular interests in a process of gradual construction'; the second, 'perverse' form, which 'in its modern aspects' consists in manipulating the firm's actors by means of 'mystifying communication'. In this instance, individuals are required to be 'loyal, sincere, enthusiastic', but while making them endure such pressure that they 'feel fear, mistrust and hatred', in contexts where 'the development of human resources simply means the art of squeezing more out of people'.[101] Here the consultant undertakes to denounce manipulative uses of the new management practices and to suggest ways of co-ordinating people at work that take the form neither of 'orders or information', issued from above, nor of personal, even emotional incentives, aiming to obtain the desired outcome in indirect, covert fashion.

Work situations in today's firms are in fact especially open to accusations of *manipulation*. If management always consists in *getting something done* by someone, manipulation and the suspicion of manipulation develop when it becomes difficult to resort to traditional forms of command, consisting in giving orders, which presuppose acknowledgement of subordination and the legitimacy of hierarchical power. However, the last twenty years have been marked by a decline in conventional orders and hierarchical relations, whether these pertain to an industrial world or a domestic world, denounced as authoritarian, and by the proliferation of demands involving autonomy. In such a context, there is a move to replace hierarchical command as often as possible by practices that aim to induce people to do what one wants them to do *by themselves*, as if under the influence of a voluntary, autonomous decision. Thus, as we saw in Chapter 1, '*cadres*' must turn themselves into 'sources of inspiration', 'coaches', or even 'leaders', whose trademark characteristic is that they formulate exciting 'visions' which make people aspire by themselves, since it is no longer legitimate to force them to do so.

There has thus been a particular spur to the development of techniques for getting people to do what one wants them to do in seemingly voluntary fashion. Think, for example, of the development of communication techniques (internal and external); of the current of organizational development (OD), which in particular aims to lead people to 'realize' the existence of 'problems', as already identified by management, so that a change in organizational methods is then easier to effect; or of participatory management, based on the wish of immediate superiors to take decisions while relying on the opinions of collaborators, which makes it possible for the latter then to support the decision.

Yet these mechanisms, which are based upon consent and agreement, can achieve their objective only by merging with forms that possess the typical features of a grammar of authenticity: spontaneous, friendly relations; trust; requests for help or advice; attentiveness to sickness or suffering; friendship, even love. Those who are caught up in these mechanisms cannot categorically refuse to participate in these exchanges; this would lead directly to their exclusion or dismissal. But nor – even on the occasions when they engage in them with the fewest reservations, or even with pleasure – can they be unaware that these more 'authentic' relations are reliant on techniques of 'mobilization' (as Crozier and Sérieyx put it, so that they are clearly distinguished from earlier 'infantilizing' forms of 'motivation' that no longer have 'any purchase on highly educated people').[102] And yet, without risking their self-esteem and their trust in the world, they cannot participate in an utterly cynical way, in pretend mode – or not for long, at least. For these new techniques, precisely in so far as they are dependent less on procedures or mechanisms involving objects (as with the assembly line) than on people, and the use they make of resources requiring their physical presence, their emotions, their gesticulations, their voice, and so on, form one body with those who implement them. The intrinsic qualities of the latter, as particular beings, end up interfering with the strategic use they make of themselves and always risk exceeding it, almost without them being aware of it, as when people pass from an emotion that was initially obligatory, and which they thought affected, to a genuine emotion that grips and overwhelms them quite unexpectedly. In such situations, virtually nothing is required for people to let themselves be taken in by focusing on the fact that the person responsible for getting things done, for persuading people, for leading them to want things, is really giving of himself; or, on the contrary, to withdraw and lose their fondness for him when they come to see his endeavours as merely a cynical use of manipulative techniques.

These tensions between engaging in relations interpreted in a grammar of authenticity and denouncing manipulative manoeuvres are at their greatest when, as is the case today, people are burdened by a strong need to distinguish themselves in the professional universe. This is valid for the rapidly expanding intellectual and artistic professions, marked by the need to acquire a particular reputation, but also increasingly for all professions characterized by casualization, where this value is a precondition for finding another project. In such situations, being the one who has done such and such, who has had some idea, and having it acknowledged, matters. Similarly, the fact that one might have been 'worked on' becomes intolerable, for what is then at stake is the ability to survive in a world where people must fulfil themselves by their own devices. With the increase in the demand for singularity, we can thus foresee an increase in paranoid behaviour by people who are forever fearful that they have been manipulated, plagiarized or hijacked. Consequently, the orders which can be established by reference to the projective city being formed are constantly undermined by the possibility that they will be denounced by people basing themselves on other worlds – for example, the domestic or inspired worlds – as a product of *manipulation*. In other words, they may be seen as deriving from a cynical use of the reference to authenticity in order to get people to do, seemingly voluntarily, what can no longer be dictated in hierarchical fashion – and hence as an instrument for developing 'voluntary servitude'.

This contradiction – between the exigency of adaptation and the demand for 'authenticity' once connections have been created – also creeps into the very core of the person. For human beings, whose identity is said to be dependent on the changing environment in which they are distributed (in contrast to the rejected figure of the unique subject), must nevertheless retain sufficient consistency and permanency in time and memory to be a medium of accumulation, without which they could not be enriched in the course of their encounters.

Being someone and being flexible

In a connexionist world, the tension between the requirement of *flexibility* and the need to be someone – that is, to possess a self endowed with *specificity* (a 'personality') and a certain *permanency* in time – is a constant source of anxiety. The slogan that sums up the ideal of a successful life as *becoming oneself* – that is, changing in order to bring out and discover what one potentially was, so that one is no longer the same person while nevertheless evincing conformity to an original self – is the typical expression of this tension.

To adjust to a connexionist world, people must prove sufficiently malleable to pass through different universes while changing properties. The logic of the temporary rental or loan can be extended from material properties to personal properties, to the attributes of persons – that is to say, to qualities which, stripped of their permanent character, are then assumed in particular situations. The skill to recognize what a situation consists in, and to activate the properties it requires of the self, is what primarily makes it possible to adopt modes of action tailored to this world. Adaptability – that is, the ability to treat one's own person in the manner of a text that can be translated into different languages – is in fact a basic requirement for circulating in networks, guaranteeing the transit through heterogeneity of a being minimally defined by a body and the proper noun attached to it. Considered from the standpoint of this new model of excellence, permanency and especially constancy to oneself, or enduring attachment to various 'values', are open to criticism as misplaced, even pathological inflexibility and, depending on the context, as inefficiency, rudeness, intolerance, and an inability to communicate.

But in another respect, the success of connexionist human beings does not depend solely on their plasticity. In fact, if they simply adjust to the new situations that arise, they risk passing unnoticed or, worse, being adjudged wanting in status and assimilated to the little people, the newcomers, the ignorant, the 'trainees'. To profit from the contacts they make, they must interest people and, to do that, they have to acquire a prominence that can derive only from their exteriority *vis-à-vis* the world they are coming into contact with. Here the ideal of adaptability comes into tension with that other – transactional – requirement of network activity. In effect, in order to attach himself to others – especially when they belong to worlds remote from his own – the networker must bring them something. To the extent that in his person, his personality, he possesses this 'something' which is likely to interest and win them over, he can attract their attention and obtain information or backing from them. But for that he must be *someone* – that is to say, come with elements foreign to their world and regarded as being specific to him. If he is merely his faculty for adapting, if he isn't someone, why attach oneself to him? The conjunction of the adaptability requirement and the transactional requirement can thus create insurmountable tensions.

These tensions specific to the connexionist world are not dispelled by the projective city; they are only exacerbated in it. In this city, the great man must be versatile and not shut himself up in a specialism, while at the same time having a specific skill to supply, for without it no one would call on him. He must have access to resources without thereby becoming a prisoner of the resources he relies on to make new connections. He must be capable of fully *engaging* in a project, while remaining sufficiently available to integrate himself into a different project. In fact, given that each of his projects and links is temporary in its structure, he must be able with equal dexterity to extricate, to release, to free himself, and to engage in a new relationship, a new project, which is more current and more profitable. Finally, he must inspire trust, which presupposes that he respects his commitments, while being sufficiently opportunistic to switch his links depending on the more or less profitable character of the connections that arise. Accordingly, Michael Piore regards the tension between the requirement of commitment and the uncertain, multiple, changing and temporary nature of projects as one of neo-management's key problems.[103] The happiness in prospect for the great man is self-fulfilment in the sense of discovering the potential he harboured within himself. The succession of projects is conceived as an opportunity to reveal something more of his essence to himself at each step, something more of the deepest identity that makes him what he is and distinguishes him (rather in the way that the succession of artistic avant-gardes was supposed to have the mission of progressively revealing the essence of art). But this quest for the self undergoes a series of ordeals that assumes both a variation in the identities adopted, depending on the project, and the preservation of a constant personality that makes it possible to capitalize assets during displacement in networks.

Accordingly, the possibility of striking a balance in such a world between a self-constancy that always threatens to turn into inflexibility, and continual adaptation to the demands of the situation at the risk of total dissolution into the fabric of transient links, is problematic, to say the least. An order of justice tacked on to the representation of a network world, the projective city, by simultaneously incorporating the requirement of authenticity as the guarantee of the personal relations on which work mechanisms are based, and the disqualification of authenticity in favour of the requirement of adaptability,[104] thus incorporates one of the main tensions that haunt a connexionist world.

In some respects, however, the projective city seems to be an attempt to overcome these difficulties – not by making the tension disappear, since it is incorporated into it, but by seeking to cancel its problematic character. This city is in fact supposed to abolish the issue of authenticity by reducing it to straightforward interactional exigencies that do not necessarily have to plumb a deep ego which they would somehow disclose. Consequently, the stakes in the establishment of the projective city are considerable. We have seen that in terms of the issue of justice, this city simultaneously presents itself both as a regulation of the connexionist world and as a legitimation of most of its features. When it comes to authenticity, the issue is legitimating a redivision between the spheres ruled by self-interest and those governed by disinterestedness – that is to say, a shift in the boundaries between what may be commodified and what may not.

The projective city and the redefinition of what may be commodified

The new enterprise practices and the new network morality accompanying them tend to challenge the division between activities and qualities of a personal kind and those that are professional – a division which played a considerable role in the formation of capitalism. It was precisely because they did not accept this division, among others, that literary and artistic activities remained on the margins of capitalism or came into conflict with it, the artwork being priceless in structure and principle, even if material exigencies made it necessary to offer it on a market.[105]

In the capitalist universe, this division is essential for at least two reasons. The first derives from the way a free labour market was constructed where the condition of wage-labour could develop. As is well known, in liberal categories the possibility of a labour market rests on the legal fiction (whose creation can be tracked from Roman law onwards) of a clear distinction between the person of the worker, which is inalienable, and their labour-power, which they can alienate contractually. As late as the nineteenth century, this distinction formed the basis for the contrast between the domestic condition, which establishes a personal bond between masters and servants presupposing not only subordination, but also loyalty and mutual aid (on the part of masters, for example, the duty to support elderly domestics and keep them in the family), and the working-class condition, which simply involves a contractual relationship, exclusively focused on work, between employer and employee.[106] Even today, this distinction likewise provides the basis for prohibiting the hire of people, which frames and checks the development of temping agencies and subcontracting. Finally, it stimulated a formalization of qualifications in certificates and degrees, which certify knowledge acquired via experience or at school, as opposed to aptitudes that are bound up with persons, and remain unknowable until and unless they are disclosed in tests.

The second reason is related to the way that the division between self-interest and disinterestedness is made. This division plays an especially important role in the sphere of personal relations. It makes it possible to establish a clear distinction, at least formally, between two categories of relationships. On the one hand, there are business relations where the partners, however cordial the links between them, may legitimately have the pursuit of their own interests (whether convergent or competitive) as their motivation;

on the other, there are relations of friendship, which deserve to be deemed such only if they are completely detached from any self-interested motives, and based exclusively on a mutual liking and shared tastes. As Alan Silver has shown, this comparatively recent conception of friendship was established precisely when, with the formation of a political philosophy of the economic, it became possible to conceive a specific domain governed entirely by competing interests.[107] It was the autonomization of interest and self-interested relations that then prompted a redefinition of friendship in terms of disinterestedness. Since then, this distinction has played a very important role in the moral judgements, often formulated in terms of 'authenticity' or 'inauthenticity', that people make about one another. Relations of friendship are deemed authentic when they are regarded as genuinely disinterested, whereas they are condemned as inauthentic when underlying motives of self-interest can be unmasked in at least one of the partners. In our society, *realizing* that the apparent affection of a dear friend, to whom one is devoted, *in fact* conceals self-interested motives and strategic designs is the paradigmatic instance – often dramatized in literature – of disillusionment, paving the way for disenchantment.

These two distinctions – between persons and their labour-power, and between disinterested relations and self-interested relations – play a key role in capitalism, because they are employed to effect the division between what may be commodified and what may not, and, consequently, to construct the contrast between capital and non-capital.

Thus, persons and personal relations alike are morally (and, to a great extent, legally) considered to be non-commodifiable; and those who are thought openly to transgress this norm are subject to virtually universal condemnation. Now, it is part of the logic of capitalism to place this norm under strain, the displacement of the boundary between capital and non-capital – that is to say, the commodification of goods and services that had hitherto eluded the market – playing a very significant role in the pursuit of accumulation. But if these displacements, which impinge on the principles on which everyday judgements are based, are to be made acceptable, they require *rearrangements in the relationship between profit and morality* (and, more profoundly no doubt, a redefinition of anthropology as a way of describing the specifically human), which in their turn contribute to changes in what we have called the spirit of capitalism.

A reorganization of this type, easing the tensions created by the new enterprise mechanisms and the displacement of profit towards new sectors of activity, accompanies the formation of a projective city. Characteristic of such changes is that they engage human persons as such more deeply than before in the profit dynamic.

As we shall see by way of a few examples, a number of mechanisms in keeping with the projective city (see Chapter 6) emerge as ways of reducing the existential confusion created by the tension between the contradictory requirements of adaptability and authenticity in the connexionist world. But this reduction rests largely on their ratification, and hence legitimation, of the displacement in the boundaries controlled by the two divisions, which are still relevant in the era of the second spirit of capitalism. In so doing, they sanction a displacement of the boundaries between the commodifiable and non-commodifiable and, as a result, pave the way for and legitimate greater commodification of human beings.

The argument used by André Gorz against the *Revenu minimum d'insertion*, which can be extended to universal income, is based upon a critique of this type: it is because, 'socially determined and remunerated', work 'confers upon me the impersonal reality of an abstract social individual', giving me 'a function which is impersonal in its essence, which I occupy as an interchangeable person among others', without having to 'engage the whole of my person, the whole of my life in it', that it is the condition of possibility of that other sphere – the 'private sphere' as the site of 'sovereignty and voluntary reciprocity'. However, by abolishing the compulsory and abstract character of social labour, the erasure of the separation between work and activity and mechanisms like universal income tend to deprive me of my 'private existence'.[108]

Similarly, the application of standardization procedures derived from product standardization to persons,[109] which is presupposed by the operationalization of the notion of 'skills' in managerial mechanisms, tends to confer an official form on the commodification of human persons. The reference-point is no longer the division of labour objectified in a structure of posts, but the qualities of the person: *'what can he do?'* replaces *'what does he do?'*[110] Whereas the qualifications associated with the classifications recognized by collective agreements were mainly directed to fixing relative wages – that is, to problems concerning the distribution of profits among workers, whose main demands were bolstered by the critique of exploitation – the logic of skills attributes a directly 'economic value' to human persons.[111]

Finally, the new mechanisms (job enrichment, improvement in working conditions) that are justified in particular by the intention of breaking with Taylorized forms of work, rightly regarded as inhuman, are also ambiguous in the respect considered here. The traditional Taylorization of work undoubtedly consisted in treating human beings like machines. But it did not make it possible to place the most specific qualities of human beings – their emotions, their moral sense, their honour, and so on – directly in the service of the pursuit of profit. Contrariwise, the new enterprise mechanisms, which demand greater engagement and are based on a more sophisticated ergonomics, incorporating the contributions of post-behaviourist psychology and the cognitive sciences, precisely because they are more human in a way, also penetrate more profoundly into people's interior being. The latter are expected to 'give themselves', as one says, to their work, and the mechanisms permit an instrumentalization and commodification of what is most specifically human about human beings.

Capitalism's assimilation after numerous detours of a paradigm – the network – derived from an autonomous philosophical history, and constructed in part against the notion of authenticity, has thus ended up today supplying arguments for, and even legitimating an increase in, commodification, particularly of human beings. The various critiques of authenticity diffused at the end of the 1970s, and especially in the first half of the 1980s, have thus helped to discredit the artistic rejection of consumer goods, comfort and 'everyday mediocrity', which is likened to an outmoded pose. More generally, they have released a number of intellectuals from what, in the postwar years, was both an ascetic constraint and a point of honour: scorn for money and the comfort it affords.[112] But if it is no longer acceptable to believe in the possibility of a more 'authentic' life at a remove from capitalism, and good form to mock those who remain attached to it; if one doubts the possibility of goods existing outside of the commodity sphere, endowed with a value that cannot be equated with the commodity and would be destroyed if they were introduced into the commodity circuit, then what is there to halt the process of commodification? Capitalism has thus wrested a freedom of manoeuvre and commodification it has never previously achieved since, in a world where all differences are admissible, but they are all equivalent precisely as equivalents, nothing is worth protecting from commodification by mere virtue of its existence and everything, accordingly, will be an object of commerce.

For these reasons, entrenching the values of the projective city in test mechanisms simply cannot be regarded as an adequate solution to the social problems produced by the new forms of capitalism, even though they would have the merit of reducing exploitation and the growth in inequalities. The artistic critique retains all its relevance when it comes to questioning the legitimations that the projective city effects as it regulates the new world. In particular, it would appear urgent to reconsider the issue of the limits that must be set on commodification. Likewise, the issue of the validity of the type of freedom that may be given free rein in a connexionist world, once framed by the conventions of the projective city, must be posed anew.

CONCLUSION: A REVIVAL OF THE ARTISTIC CRITIQUE?

The artistic critique is currently paralysed by what, depending on one's viewpoint, may be regarded as its success or its failure.

It was successful in the sense that, confined to minorities and avant-gardes until the 1950s, from the end of the 1960s it coincided with the aspirations of an enormous audience. This type of critique now possesses a base and spokespersons; and it occupies a significant place in the media.

It failed inasmuch as the liberation of desire has not sounded the death knell of capitalism, as heralded by Freudo–Marxism between the 1930s and the 1970s. Moreover, that belief entailed ignoring freedom's implication in the regime of capital and its profound complicity with desire, on which its dynamic to a great extent rests. By helping to overthrow the conventions bound up with the old domestic world, and also to overcome the inflexibilities of the industrial order – bureaucratic hierarchies and standardized production – the artistic critique opened up an opportunity for capitalism to base itself on new forms of control and commodify new, more individualized and 'authentic' goods.

Accordingly, the artistic critique is today caught in a dilemma both of whose horns reveal its impotence.

Either it can pursue the critique in the direction it embarked on in the nineteenth century (denunciation of bourgeois morality, censorship, the grip of the family and religion, constraints on the liberation of mores and sexuality, the conservatism of the dominant cultural institutions) without taking account of capitalism's displacements, and particularly the fact that it is no longer hand in glove with the family or religion, let alone morality. It can even (but in the columns of major newspapers or on television) attack the media conspiracy aimed at silencing freethinking. These are denunciations, incidentally, that the media are quite ready to accept as a commodity like any other which is likely to get people talking – that is to say, in this instance, to get things sold. In order to retain credence in itself, this line of conduct, which constantly tends to collapse in on itself for want of opponents – the most devastating proposals being almost immediately transposed into a well-ordered public debate, and then integrated into cultural supply in a dual dynamic of commodification of by-products and official celebration of their authors – must invent enemies, or credit remaining enemies with a power they have long since lost.

Alternatively, demonstrating a 'lucidity' presented as the only posture still worth adopting in the face of the impending apocalypse (in a tone that often recalls the catastrophist prophecies of the Weimar avant-gardes preceding and heralding the conservative revolution), one can register capitalism's ability to 'recuperate' anything and everything. One can announce the end of all value, and even of any reality (the domination of the virtual), the entry into an age of nihilism, and at the same time, in a rather paradoxical gesture, once again don the aristocratic but utterly threadbare garb of the lampoonist, the solitary 'conscience' confronting cretinized masses.[113] One can then steel oneself in reactionary nostalgia for an idealized past, with its warm human communities (as opposed to individualist isolation), its freely consensual discipline, often dubbed 'republican' (as opposed to educational anarchy and the disorder of the suburbs), its genuine and honest love (as against indiscriminate sexuality), its easel-painting (as against the installation of any old thing), its long-lost landscapes, its solid fare, its country produce, and so on.

To escape from this dead end, perhaps the artistic critique should, to a greater extent than is currently the case, take the time to reformulate the issues of liberation and authenticity, starting from the new forms of oppression it unwittingly helped to make possible.

Security as a factor of liberation

What purchase might there be for loosening the grip of capitalism as an oppressive instance? It is virtually the same as a century ago. Everything that enhances the security and stability of people at work today creates a margin of freedom and furnishes opportunities to resist the abusive expansion of self-control and, precisely relying on the ideal of autonomy acknowledged by the new spirit of capitalism, to contest the proliferation of the new control mechanisms, especially computerized ones.

One critical orientation, which is seemingly paradoxical given that mobility and liberation have hitherto been closely associated, is to be sought in challenging mobility as a prerequisite and incontestable value. Is the project of liberation still compatible with an unlimited extension of the exigency of mobility, contact and connection which, as we have shown, can be a source of new forms of exploitation and new existential tensions? The first problem, an absolutely concrete one, concerns the use made of time. Maybe a step in the direction of liberation today involves the possibility of slowing down the pace of connections, without thereby fearing that one no longer exists for others or sinking into oblivion and, ultimately, 'exclusion'; of deferring engagement in a project or publishing a work, and instead sharing it – for example, in an exhibition or at a conference – without thereby seeing the recognition to which one believes one is entitled appropriated by another; of lingering over an ongoing project, whose full potential one had not realized at the outset; of putting off the moment of the test and, more generally perhaps, not abolishing tests – which would be bound to provoke violent feelings of injustice – but spacing them out. If a world without tests is inconceivable, it is equally clear that a world of constantly renewed tests soon proves unbearable,[114] so that regulating the rhythm of tests is a very important component of justice.

The premium placed on mobility leads to assessing people according to a mode of existence which, in addition to being far from universally desired, presupposes access to resources that are very unequally distributed. On the one hand, the value conferred on mobility and the ability to make new links (which, time being a scarce resource, also assumes the ability to be shot of older links); and on the other, the preference in the construction of identities accorded to elective bonds forged with people's displacement in networks, over affiliations that depend upon already constituted collectives like nation, social class, or family – these tend to exclude at least one form of freedom, whose legitimacy is less and less assured. It is the form of freedom expressed in the option for stability, the prioritization of loyalty, and receipt of a heritage, accepted as such, without any consideration of the profits it might bring – simply because it is there. If a multiplication of identities and lived worlds is indeed a central element in expanded modernity,[115] it can represent a liberating factor only if the validity of aspirations to an existence wholly contained in a privileged identity and a non-fragmented space is acknowledged, even if this can be only one way of life among others today. Moreover, how could the range of identities, which in a radical logic of self-constitution actors (overused by sociology, the term finds its proper usage here) are free to assume at will, be preserved, if other people did not exist with a sufficiently stable affiliation for these identities to retain a substantial form and temporal continuity, without which they would tend to disappear into the multiplicity of ephemeral symbolic appropriations to which they are subject? Just as, as we saw in Chapter 6, the profit that can be obtained by circulating in networks would veer towards zero if boundaries did not persist between groups, institutions, fields, and so on, crossing which has a price, and if unchanging individuals did not exist to maintain the local links, so the paradox of fragmentation is that it assumes the existence of collectives attached to maintaining in good order the identities that others will adopt by way of simulacrum. Accordingly, it is equally in keeping with the requirement of liberation to defend the legitimacy and possibility of survival of such collectives, whose energy is mobilized in the struggle against deracination.

Proceeding thus would obviously bring the artistic critique closer to the social critique. Slowing down, deferring, delaying, spacing – these in fact presuppose constructing temporal spaces that are larger than the 'project', in the sense in which we found it defined in management literature, or providing people with the means to subsist between engagements in different projects. As Alain Supiot observes, workers' mobility and flexibility must not only mean 'greater and cheaper subservience to the needs of the firm', but be framed by regulations that make it possible to protect mobility and confer a 'status' on the 'mobile worker'.[116] In fact, there is scarcely any other way of equipping people with a relative freedom *vis-à-vis* the market, or when they are confronted with the new requirement of unbridled sociability, than to endow them with something resembling a *statute*. As a text regulating the situation of a group, in modern states the statute was initially conceived precisely as an instrument of liberation that aimed to emancipate individuals from personal dependence, petty political obedience, and strict, constant supervision conducted from without (e.g. with the notion of 'professional secret'). Hence it sought to guarantee freedom of thought and political freedoms, while specifying the kinds of tests to which people were required to submit in certain respects to preserve their state and material conditions of existence, in such a way as to protect them from undefined or unformalized tests whereby they might find themselves being assessed at any moment and in any respect.[117] Statutes express what can be established about the position of individuals for a certain length of time and in a certain space, independently of how their interaction with others unfolds at any given moment. They presuppose reference to something like *institutions* capable not only of organizing tests that last, in such a way as to stabilize expectations and define their rhythm, but also of exercising an external constraint in the form of obligations and sanctions. Only via a compromise with mechanisms that are at once constraining and reassuring, overarching with respect to everyday interaction and contractual relations, can the requirement of mobility conduce to a liberation that escapes the alternative of the bureaucrat's much-disparaged inflexibility and the innovator's now universally celebrated nomadism.

In this sense, the struggle to defend or obtain 'statutes', far from being a backward-looking battle, as neo-liberal discourse has it, is a wholly relevant objective from the perspective of liberation. Only statutory provisions can help to outlaw, or at least restrict, the new forms of real-time computer surveillance that are tending to proliferate in firms, workshops, offices, shopping areas, and so on.

But securing statutes can play only an emancipatory role *on two conditions*.

The first is that enhanced security is not bought at the cost of job impoverishment, as was the case during the transition from market capitalism to Fordist capitalism. It is to be hoped that the increased cultural component in work makes dispossession of the Taylorist variety more difficult than it was in the past, although the flexibility of computer mechanisms means that we cannot exclude this possibility.

The second is that the statute is not consolidated to the extent of excluding any form of test, regardless of its character. One of the important things about statutes is that they make it possible to space out the rhythm of tests by relying on clearly established test periods (inspections, interviews, appraisals), in between which trust is placed in the agents. There is little likelihood of the recognition of a statute enduring if it is not accompanied by recognition of the kind of convention that is generally called 'professional conscience'. It also presupposes the recognition of an authority capable of legitimating the tests and sanctions.

It remains the case that embarking on this road presupposes pretty much abandoning a quest for liberation defined as absolute autonomy, simultaneously free of any interference from others and any form of obligation laid down by an external authority.

The restriction of the commodity sphere

In the age of the commodification of difference, one task is obviously unavoidable on the authenticity front: restricting the extension of the commodity sphere, particularly in the direction of a commodification of the human. As we have seen, the commodification of the human was favoured in the framework of the projective city by the erasure of the boundary between the spheres of self-interest and disinterestedness, whether this involves generating profit by creating products obtained through the coding of personal human qualities, or even using the human body as one kind of material among others.

But this also presupposes restricting innovators' room for action and breaking with a reference to the demand for liberation sufficiently vague to allow it to pass, depending on the needs of the moment, from the critique of the market (against which protection is demanded) to a strictly market conception of free enterprise, even in the domain of science or culture. Moreover, the struggle against the commodification of new goods is particularly difficult not simply on account of the 'globalizing [character] of market coordination',[118] or the ability to convert one good into another inherent in the use of money.[119] It is also, no doubt, because it comes up against the libertarian interests of different groups, who may be at variance in other respects: innovators in the intellectual sphere and entrepreneurs in the sphere of capital, not to mention consumers whose only desire is to obtain the greatest comfort at the best price.

But why should it fall to an 'artistic critique' instead of – or alongside – a 'social critique' to attend to restricting commodification?

We may seek an answer to this question by running through the list of 'social goods' it is usually considered immoral to distribute as commodities, provided by Michael Walzer in the chapter of his *Spheres of Justice* devoted to money. The standpoint adopted on goods usually starts from *demand*: what is to be defended is, primarily, the equal dignity of persons, which allows them equal access to primary goods; and this defence is a priority among the tasks that fall to the *social critique*, since it involves remedying sources of inequality. Thus, numerous goods are shielded from the market because they are goods whose equal availability to all is regarded as morally necessary, and whose commodification would entail intolerable inequalities because of the inequality in people's financial resources. In Walzer this is the case, for example, with basic public services (such as the police), conscription for military service (buying exemption is now regarded as immoral and proscribed), with fundamental political rights like the right to vote, with love and access to marriage. Other prohibitions noted by Walzer are relevant by reference to a requirement not for equality but for security (e.g. dangerous second-hand cars). But in this case too, the standpoint adopted is that of the interests of demand.

Another standpoint on commodification exists that has been adopted, though invariably implicitly, only by an *artistic critique*. This standpoint is that of *supply*. Here it is not because its commodification would contravene the equal dignity of users that the good should be shielded from the market. Its commodification is to be excluded because it would contravene the *specific dignity* of the good were it to be 'denatured' through coding, transformed into a product or, if you like, 'alienated'. Moreover, it is precisely from the standpoint of supply that the commodification of human beings, in the form of slavery or procuring, has been outlawed. But such a prohibition can be extended to other goods: for example, aspects of persons or types of action that are thought to be degraded by their transformation into products allocated a price and offered on a competitive market; bodies – organs, foetuses, and so on; artefacts – artworks or places valued for their uniqueness, and so on; or, finally, natural entities such as animals (some of whom, Walzer observes, like human beings attach a value to 'freedom'), rivers, mountains, and so on. In this perspective, the revival of the artistic critique notably takes the form of an alliance with the ecological critique, which at present constitutes one of the only positions from which the multiplicity and particularity of beings – human beings, natural beings and, in some versions, artefacts – are assigned an intrinsic value.

Notes

1 See Jean-Baptiste de Foucauld and Denis Piveteau, *Une société en quête de sens*, Odile Jacob, Paris 1995.

2 See Laurent Thévenot, 'Émotions et évaluations dans les coordinations publiques', in P. Paperman and R. Ogien, eds, *La Couleur des pensées*, Éditions de l'EHESS, Paris 1995, pp. 145–74.

3 Philippe Besnard, *L'Anomie, ses usages et ses fonctions dans la discipline sociologique depuis Durkheim*, Presses Universitaires de France, Paris 1987, pp. 81–98.

4 See Louis Chauvel, 'L'uniformisation du taux de suicide masculin selon l'âge: effet de génération ou recomposition du cycle de vie?', *Revue française de sociologie*, vol. XXXVIII, 1997, pp. 735–58.

5 An artistic life in the nineteenth century could be deemed 'authentic', in particular because it was not compartmentalized but succeeded in unifying all the facets of the same existence, and gearing it towards the completion of an œuvre and the uniqueness of its creator.

6 Thus, 80 per cent of men between the ages of 25 and 44 were married in 1973, as opposed to only 54 per cent in 1995, while in the same period the number of single people more than doubled and that of divorces trebled. As for unions 'without legal documents', on the one hand they appear to be less durable than marriage, with 58 per cent of such unions that began in 1980 having broken down in less than ten years, as opposed to 12 per cent in instances where life together began with marriage; and on the other hand, their insecurity is tending to increase: '11 per cent of unions of this type formed in 1970, 23 per cent of those that began in 1980, and, according to a prospective calculation, 34 per cent of those initiated in 1990 have come to an end, or will have, in under ten years' (Alfred Nizard, 'Suicide et mal-être social', *Population et société*, no. 334, April 1998).

7 See Besnard, *L'anomie*.

8 Female suicide rates have undergone an analogous evolution, although at lower levels in absolute terms, with women making more attempts at suicide than men, but succeeding much less often.

9 See Chauvel, 'L'uniformisation du taux de suicide masculin selon l'âge'.

10 Ibid.

11 See Nizard, 'Suicide et mal-être social'.

12 See Chauvel, 'L'uniformisation du taux de suicide masculin selon l'âge'.

13 See Louis Dirn, *La Société française en tendances, 1975–1995*, Presses Universitaires de France, Paris 1998; Alain Ehrenberg, *La Fatigue d'être soi*, Odile Jacob, Paris 1998.

14 It is because it is constantly changing the conditions of production drastically that capitalism must make space for the idea of liberation. Here readers are referred to the work of Marshall Berman (*All That Is Solid Melts into Air*, Verso, London 1983) and the famous passage from the *Communist Manifesto* on which it offers a kind of vast commentary: 'Constant revolutionizing of production, uninterrupted disturbance of all social conditions, everlasting uncertainty and agitation distinguish the bourgeois epoch from all earlier ones. All fixed, fast-frozen relations, with their train of ancient and venerable prejudices and opinions, are swept away, all new-formed ones become antiquated before they can ossify. All that is solid melts into air, all that is holy is profaned, and man is at last compelled to face with sober senses, his real conditions of life, and his relations with his kind' (Karl Marx and Frederick Engels, *The Communist Manifesto*, Verso edition, London and New York 1998, pp. 38–9).

15 Their logic was as follows: various tests, which people concurred in regarding as central, are gradually tightened up under the impact of a critique that reveals respects in which they are unjust, to the point where a number of actors find it in their interest to circumvent these tests by effecting a series of displacements; these acts of circumvention constitute a moment of recoupment of the sacrifices made by the 'strong' at an earlier stage in order to be 'great' and of unrestrained redeployment of forces; then critique gradually starts up again, leading to the qualification and categorization of new tests that can in turn be criticized and tightened up with a view to greater justice. With this transformation, values emerge that are incorporated into the new spirit of capitalism.

16 We leave to one side the question of democracy and, more generally, the specifically political dimensions of the ideal of liberation and self-realization which, not being directly bound up with capitalism but liberalism (with which capitalism has complex links), cannot be tackled in the necessarily limited framework of this book.

17 Obviously, emancipation will not be complete since, if the first spirit of capitalism offers a certain liberation with respect to domestic bonds, as illustrated by the drift away from the land, its security dimension rests, as we have seen, on bourgeois morality (see Introduction).

18 See Élisabeth Claverie and Pierre Lamaison, *L'impossible mariage. Violence et parenté en Gévaudan, xviie, xviiie, xixe siècles*, Hachette, Paris 1982.

19 See Bartolomé Clavero, *La Grâce du don. Anthropologie catholique de l'économie moderne*, Albin Michel, Paris 1996.

20 See Marcel Mauss, *The Gift*, trans. W.D. Halls, W.W. Norton, London 1990.

21 See Peter Wagner, *A Sociology of Modernity: Liberty and Discipline*, Routledge, London and New York 1994.

22 Being uprooted is precisely what defines the *proletariat*. The genius of the young Marx notably consists in having, in a famous passage of his Introduction to 'A Contribution to the Critique of Hegel's Philosophy of Right' (1843), grounded hopes in the proletariat as an emancipatory force in this negative property: 'So where is the *positive possibility* of German emancipation? *This is our answer.* In the formation ... of a class [*Stand*] which is the dissolution of all classes, a sphere which has a universal character because of its universal suffering and which lays claims to no *particular right* because the wrong it suffers is not a *particular wrong* but *wrong in general*; a sphere of society which can no longer lay claim to a *historical* title, but merely to a *human* one.' (Karl Marx, *Early Writings*, Penguin/New Left Review, Harmondsworth 1975, p. 256).

23 See Georges Duveau, *La Pensée ouvrière sur l'éducation pendant la Seconde République et le Second Empire*, Domat-Montchrestien, Paris 1947.

24 Karl Marx, 'Introduction', in *Grundrisse*, trans. Martin Nicolaus, Penguin/New Left Review, Harmondsworth 1973, p. 92.

25 See Philippe Besnard, 'Durkheim et les femmes ou le *Suicide* inachevé', *Revue française de sociologie*, no. XIV, 1973, pp. 27–61.

26 Émile Durkheim, *Socialism and Saint-Simon*, trans. Charlotte Sattler, Routledge & Kegan Paul, London 1959.

27 This is why Durkheim, in the Preface to the second edition of *The Division of Labour in Society* (Macmillan, London 1984), indicated that he approved of the re-establishment of corporate bodies so that, constituting an intermediate body between individuals and the state, they could ensure the presence of the collective and revive an orientation towards communal action.

28 See Wagner, *A Sociology of Modernity*.

29 Ibid.

30 See Abraham De Swann, *In Care of the State*, Polity Press, Cambridge 1988.

31 Spiros Simitis, 'Le droit du travail a-t-il encore un avenir?', *Droit social*, nos 7–8, July/August 1997, p. 663.

32 See Nicolas Dodier, *Les Hommes et les machines. La conscience collective dans les sociétés technicisées*, Métailié, Paris 1995.

33 See Michel Cézard and Lydie Vinck, 'Contraintes et marges d'initiative des salariés dans leur travail', *Données sociales 1996*, INSEE, Paris 1996, pp. 217–24.

34 Michel Gollac, *À marches forcées? Contribution à l'étude des changements du travail*, University of Paris VIII, 1998, pp. 60–61.

35 See Valérie Aquain, Jennifer Bué and Lydie Vinck, 'L'évolution en 2 ans de l'organisation du travail: plus de contraintes mais aussi plus d'autonomie pour les salariés', *Premières synthèses*, no. 54, 16 June 1994, DARES.

36 See Thomas Coutrot, 'Les nouveaux modes d'organisation de la production: quels effets sur l'emploi, la formation, l'organisation du travail?', *Données sociales 1996*, INSEE, Paris 1996, pp. 209–16.

37 See Randy Hodson, 'Dignity in the Workplace under Participative Management: Alienation and Freedom Revisited', *American Sociological Review*, vol. 61, October 1996, pp. 719–38.

38 See Philip Agre, 'Surveillance et saisie. Deux modèles de l'information personnelle', in B. Conein and L. Thévenot, eds, *Cognition et information en société*, Éditions de l'EHESS, Paris 1997, pp. 243–66.

39 James R. Barker, 'Tightening the Iron Cage: Concertive Control in Self-Managing Teams', *Administrative Science Quarterly*, vol. 38, no. 3, 1993, p. 408.

40 Michel Pialoux, 'The Shop Steward's World in Disarray', in Pierre Bourdieu *et al.*, *The Weight of the World*, trans. P.P. Ferguson *et al.*, Polity Press, Cambridge 1999, p. 331.

41 James Beniger has shown how the development of control techniques, which has led to what is often called the 'information society', was driven by what he calls the 'crisis of control' created in the second half of the nineteenth century by the development of industrial mechanization in the domain of transport, production, distribution and consumption. According to Beniger, a crisis of control emerges when there is a growing disparity between the speed of transformation of technological systems and the capacity for dealing with information. For him, the development of large bureaucracies at the beginning of this century thus constitutes a response to the crisis of control at the end of the nineteenth century (*The Control Revolution: Technological and Economic Origins of the Information Society*, Harvard University Press, Cambridge (MA) 1986).

42 See Michael Power, 'The Audit Society', in A. Hopwood and P. Miller, eds, *Accounting as Social and Institutional Practice*, Cambridge University Press, Cambridge 1944, pp. 295–336.

43 Charles Taylor, *Sources of the Self: The Making of Modern Identity*, Cambridge University Press, Cambridge 1989, esp. pp. 495–521.

44 Michael Walzer, *Exodus and Revolution*, Basic Books, New York 1985.

45 See Jerrold Siegel, *Bohemian Paris: Culture, Politics and the Boundaries of Bourgeois Life, 1830–1930*, Penguin, New York 1986.

46 Alain Ehrenberg, *L'Individu incertain*, Calmann-Lévy, Paris 1995, thus interprets the development of drug use, whether illicit drugs or psychotropes, as 'a chemical short cut to manufacture individuality, an artificial means for multiplying the self' (p. 37).

47 See Nathalie Sarthou-Lajus, *L'Éthique de la dette*, Presses Universitaires de France, Paris 1997.

48 See Pierre Bourdieu, *The Rules of Art: Genesis and Structure of the Literary Field*, trans. Susan Emanuel, Polity Press, Cambridge 1996.

49 See Alain Ehrenberg, *La Fatigue d'être soi*, Odile Jacob, Paris 1998.

50 We must start with the issue of inauthenticity, not authenticity, because authenticity is – as Lionel Trilling observed in his analysis of the historical genesis of the modern notion of authenticity – a polemical notion, whose meaning is fixed only by its difference from, and opposition to, the accusation of inauthenticity directed at persons or objects (*Sincerity and Authenticity*, Harvard University Press, Cambridge [MA] 1971, p. 94).

51 On the relationship between the power of standardization and dehumanization of technique and the experience of the front during the 1914–18 war in the literary and artistic avant-gardes of 1920–30, see Dodier, *Les Hommes et les machines*, pp. 42–5.

52 For example, Gustave Le Bon, in *La Psychologie des foules*, published in 1895, gives systematic form to an interpretation traces of which can be found in numerous authors in the second half of the nineteenth century. Le Bon predicts the advent of what he calls 'the age of crowds', where the individual is going to find himself engulfed in the mass, and will lose all independence of mind in the grip of a 'mental contagion'. In Le Bon, the notion of 'crowd' covers a very wide set of different groups, including parliamentary assemblies (see Le Bon, *The Crowd: A Study of the Popular Mind*, Ernest Benn, London 1952). We find a similar vein in most of the authors who took up the theme of the crowd and the masses up to the 1930s – e.g. in J. Ortega y Gasset's work *The Revolt of the Masses*, published in 1930 and destined for great success – based upon the aristocratic contrast between 'mass-man' and the 'elite man'.

53 This theme was elaborated in France by Edgar Morin during the first half of the 1960s, in the context of the Centre d'étude des communications de masse and the journal published by this centre, *Communication*.

54 Adorno denounces in Heidegger a fetishized – i.e. ideological – use of language, which, severed from its history, transforms alienation under the dominion of capital into an ontological abyss lying in wait for being each time it dissipates itself in chatter. At the heart of his critique is the Heideggerian concept of 'mineness' ('gathered being' as 'condition of possibility of authenticity'), in which he reveals a 'disguised identity', a travesty of the bourgeois ideal of 'personality' (with its attributes of 'interiority', 'consciousness', etc.).

55 The most shocking standardization is obviously the one that affects intellectuals precisely inasmuch as they embody uniqueness, autonomy, resistance to banality. Thus, we read in aphorism 132 of Adorno's *Minima Moralia* (trans. E.F.N. Jephcott , Verso, London 1978, pp. 206–7): 'Even those intellectuals who have all the arguments against bourgeois ideology at their fingertips undergo a process of standardization. ... The good things they opt for have long been just as accepted. ... While they inveigh against official kitsch, their views, like dutiful children, are allowed to partake only of preselected nutrition, clichés against clichés. ... That all cultural products, even nonconformist ones, have been incorporated into the distribution-mechanisms of large-scale capital, that in the most developed country a product that does not bear the imprimatur of mass-production can scarcely reach a reader, viewer, listener at all denies deviationary longings their subject matter in advance.' The same theme (toleration of dissidence is advanced capitalism's form of totalitarianism) was to be developed by Herbert Marcuse in *One-Dimensional Man*.

56 Theodor Adorno and Max Horkheimer, *Dialectic of Enlightenment*, trans. John Cumming, Verso, London 1979, pp. 164–5.

57 'The way in which a girl accepts and keeps the obligatory date, the inflection on the telephone or in the most intimate situation, the choice of words in conversation, and the whole

inner life as classified by the now somewhat devalued depth psychology, bear witness to man's attempt to make himself a proficient apparatus, similar (even in emotions) to the model served up by the culture industry.' Thus, '[i]n the culture industry the individual is an illusion not merely because of the standardization of the means of production. He is tolerated only so long as his complete identification with the generality is unquestioned' (ibid., pp. 167, 154).

58 Herbert Marcuse, *One-Dimensional Man*, Beacon Press, Boston (MA) 1964, p. 64. Marcuse does not employ the categories of authentic and inauthentic. But he relies upon other contrasts that play approximately the same role in his construction. In particular, this is the case with the contrast between *sublimation* and *desublimation*. He associates sublimation with 'artistic alienation' and desublimation with 'technological reality'. The former, as 'mediated gratification', allows for withdrawal into an exteriority from which a critique of reality can be made; the second, as 'immediate gratification', ensures immersion in the viscosity of the everyday. Thus, the degeneration of high culture into 'popular culture' can be interpreted in the Freudian terms of sweeping desublimation (ibid., pp. 72 f.).

59 Some of the dynamic of capitalism and 'economic growth' must in fact be attributed to the 'transformation of activities that bring pleasure- or use-values into activities that also yield a profit to their organizers. ... The steady movement of such tasks as laundering, cooking, cleaning, and simple health care – not to mention recreation and entertainment – from the exclusive concern of the private household into the world of business testifies to the internal expansion of capital within the interstices of social life. Much of what is called "growth" in capitalist societies consists in this commodification of life, rather than in the augmentation of unchanged, or even improved, outputs': Robert Heilbroner, *The Nature and Logic of Capitalism*, Nortion, New York and London 1985, p. 60.

60 Capitalism has had to confront a dual, substantially contradictory demand: to supply more authentic goods (more unique goods that are also supposed to incorporate a degree of uncertainty) and to put on the market more reliable, more stable goods harbouring no surprises – a demand it has responded to by developing 'total quality' procedures.

61 Thus, for example, the young women who present themselves in McDonald's restaurants to work in the kitchen are systematically directed to reception when they are deemed particularly pretty by the person responsible for recruitment (Damien Cartron, 'Autonomie et contrôle dans un restaurant McDonald's', seminar paper, EHESS, 1998). As for training, we may cite the example of air hostesses studied by Arlie Russel Hoschild (*The Managed Heart: Commercialization of Human Feeling*, University of California Press, Los Angeles 1983). In the course of their training, they learn to control their emotions and to express them only in a stylized, codified way that is readily interpretable.

62 See Hideya Kawakita, 'The Dignity of Man', *Iichiko Intercultural*, no. 8, 1996, pp. 40–65. Charged with the promotion of a region of Japan (the prefecture of Fukui), Kawaki opted for starting from what was a 'source of pride' for the inhabitants. For that he organized a 'treasure hunt', intended to collect everything that constituted a 'value' for them, such as a 'beautiful view', 'old women speaking the old dialect well', a 'sunset' seen from the foot of the mountain, and so on. In particular, the 'treasures' were collected through organized compilations in the region's schools and among students. Four thousand five hundred 'treasures' were collected in this way. In order to deal with this collection and organize his promotional campaign, the author classified the items into categories such as 'relations between people', 'environmental treasures', 'events', and so on, which obviously led to them losing their unique character.

63 It will be noted that over the last twenty years the ordinary use of the term 'product' has undergone a major expansion, and that we commonly speak today of 'financial products', 'travel products', 'property products', referring not to material objects, but to specific assemblages of services. Sometimes one even hears people speak in certain scientific circles of a new theory or paradigm in terms of a 'product' (some particular theory is 'a product that works well').

64   This is so even though the value of artworks and objects of Antiquity depends upon their being connected in a symbolic series by art historians, whether amateurs or experts, who construct categories on which the identification and evaluation of the works is based, identify 'schools', institute a hierarchy among the artists, establish catalogues, and so on.

65   See A.O. Hirschman, *Shifting Involvements: Private Interest and Public Action*, Princeton University Press, Princeton 2002.

66   One form of innovation in this sector of economic activity consists in offering individualized services that are supposed to restore the sense of the 'journey' in contrast to mass tourism, and, for example, stays in 'authentic' places – that is to say, precisely spots that have not yet been affected by tourism: 'genuine Indian villages', 'ruins' that are accessible only on the back of a mule, and so on. Obviously, however, in introducing tourists into them, tour operators destroy the value of the goods they are offering.

67   A classic example is that of Camemberts, whose traditional packaging – a slatted poplar box invented at the end of the last century – can house a very wide range of products, differing in taste, but also in capacities for conservation and transport, and which are the outcome of different production processes (unpasteurized or pasteurized milk; mould filled automatically, ladled by hand or by means of a 'robot-ladler' that reproduces the gesture of the cheesemaker, etc.): Pierre Boisard and Marie-Thérèse Letablier, 'Un compromis d'innovation entre tradition et standardisation dans l'industrie laitière', in L. Boltanski and L. Thévenot, eds, *Justesse et justice dans le travail*, CEE-Presses Universitaires de France, Paris 1989, pp. 209–18.

68   Frances Cairncross, *Costing the Earth*, Business Books, London 1991. In September 1988, the *Green Consumer Guide* appeared in Great Britain, awarding stars to firms and products depending upon the extent to which they respected the environment. The book reached the top of the bestsellers for bookshop sales in four weeks.

69   Jean-Luc Bennahmias and Agnès Roche, *Des Verts de toutes les couleurs. Histoire et sociologie du mouvement écolo*, Albin Michel, Paris 1992, pp. 118, 125.

70   Two American specialists in the marketing of eco-products describe the enthusiasm generated by the discovery of this new market in the following terms: 'Back in the late 1980s when the environment suddenly rose to the top of the "cause" heap, entrepreneurs and marketers alike were quick to jump on what appeared to be the perfect greeen machine. "It's the greatest new business opportunity this century," people said. What could be easier? Turning clean, green deeds into big green bucks' (Bob Frause and Julie Colehour, *The Environmental Marketing Imperative: Strategies for Transforming Environmental Commitment into a Competitive Advantage*, Probus Publishing Company, Chicago 1994, p. 1).

71   In response to the boycott of tinned tuna, Heinz stated that it had conducted an investigation to ensure that the fishing tackle used did not harm dolphins. But this sales argument was challenged by Greenpeace, who supplied proof that Heinz's subcontractors were still using fish caught by older methods that were not 'dolphin-friendly', causing the firm to lose credibility (ibid., pp. 186–7).

72   Cairncross, *Costing the Earth*, p. 155.

73   McDonald's is a good example. When this firm realized that it was considered a 'bad guy' by environmentalists, it used as an argument for its sincerity the fact that the decision to recycle polystyrene packaging had been taken in agreement with the Environmental Defense Fund – an environmentalist association that had conducted a campaign against the waste occasioned by fast-food packaging (Frause and Colehour, *The Environmental Marketing Imperative*, pp. 184–5).

74   See Jacques Vigneron and Claude Burstein, eds, *Écoproduit. Concepts et méthodologies*, Economica, Paris 1993; Steven Bennett, Richard Frierman and Stephen George, *Corporate Realities and Environmental Truths: Strategies for Leading your Business in the Environmental Era*, John Wiley & Sons, New York 1993.

75   Cairncross, *Costing the Earth*, pp. 159, 163.

76   See Vigneron and Burstein, *Écoproduit*.

77   Gabriel Yiannis and Tim Lang, *The Unmanageable Consumer: Contemporary Consumption and its Fragmentation*, Sage, London 1995, p. 165.

78   In this sense, the authenticity of goods is an extension of the authenticity of persons. Going beyond sincerity as the desire to tell the truth – to speak things as they are, which assumes self-reflexivity – it refers to a condition where the person forms one body with what they express, without it being possible to distinguish what pertains to the order of being and what pertains to the order of communication, and hence without it being necessary to refer to a reflexivity and an intentionality. Taking the example of the protagonist of Wordsworth's poem 'Michael' in order to illustrate the difference, Lionel Trilling says that he seems to be one with his grief, so that we can apprehend his being only as the being of grief (*Sincerity and Authenticity*, p. 93).

79   John Barish, *The Antitheatrical Prejudice*, University of California Press, Berkeley 1981.

80   Thus, for example, for the Scottish Enlightenment authors, the moment of compassion expressed in an emotion when confronted with the spectacle of someone else's suffering is the point at which people's full humanity is disclosed. Given the role assigned the emotions in moral existence, it then becomes crucial to be able to discriminate between genuine emotions, going directly to the roots of the 'heart', and figurative, purely external, mimed emotions, that have no internal referent.

81   In the *Lettre à d'Alembert* (but also in *La Nouvelle Héloïse*), Rousseau counterposes to the 'opacity of the theatre', which imprisons the spectator fascinated by the illusion in his solitude, thereby removing him from real 'existence', the 'world of the transparency' of the festival, as 'self-affirmation of the transparency of consciousnesses', in which everyone is simultaneously 'actor and spectator' (see Jean Starobinski, *Jean-Jacques Rousseau*, trans. Arnold Goldhammer, University of Chicago Press, Chicago and London 1988).

82   In Jean Baudrillard's work, denunciation of the 'consumer society' in the 1970s is radicalized in the 1980s and 1990s into a critique of the 'simulation society', in which the domination of commodities results in an endless proliferation of images where nothing is made visible (computer-generated images, video, etc.). See, for example, his analysis of the Gulf War as a virtual orgy (*The Gulf War Did Not Take Place*, trans. Paul Patton, Indiana University Press, Bloomington 1995). This commodification does not spare the modern project of liberation – political or sexual – which henceforth becomes a commodity like any other, offered up for mediatization and commentary – i.e., in this logic, consumed. In Guy Debord, the opposition between the spectacle and life is central (see Julien Coupat, *Perspective et critique de la pensée situationniste*, DEA dissertation, EHESS, 1997). *The Society of the Spectacle* (trans. Donald Nicholson-Smith, Zone Books, New York 1994), written in the mid-1960s, prefigures the transition from the first critique of authenticity, which is still present on numerous pages – witness, for example, the denunciation of administrative centralization (pp. 19–20) or mass-produced commodities (p.120) – to the second, of which this text represents one of the first systematic expressions. The critique of the spectacle in Debord is in no sense reducible to the critique of the media, to which it is often reduced. It aims to be a radical critique of the state of the world under the ascendancy of a commodification that nothing escapes. The spectacle, sign of 'a generalized shift from *having* to appearing' (p. 22), 'caus[ing] a world that is no longer directly perceptible to be *seen*' (p. 23), is the negation of 'life': the more the spectator 'contemplates, the less he lives; the more readily he recognizes his own needs in the images of need proposed by the dominant system, the less he understands his own existence and his own desires' (p. 23). Henceforth he is 'cut off from … life' (p. 24). For Debord, the spectacle is the highest stage of the commodity, the moment when, everything being susceptible to being turned into a commodity, 'the commodity completes its colonization of social life' (p. 29): 'The world the spectacle holds up to view is at once *here* and *elsewhere*; it is the world of the commodity ruling over all lived experience' (p. 26). The spectacle, wherein everything is equivalent, has by the same token as money become 'the abstract general equivalent of all commodities' (p. 32).

83   Thus Marcuse makes the kind of tolerance and freedom offered by democratic society the very source of a new form of totalitarianism 'without terror'. For him, democratic society is not oppressive because it is assimilable to the blind will of the crowd attuned to the omnipotence of a demagogue, as in the work of Le Bon and his successors. It is oppressive precisely because it offers freedom by the same token, and in the same fashion, as any other mass consumer good. Tolerance – the absence of repression – nips in the bud the very possibility of transgression as a means of access to the truth of desire and, hence, to an authentic existence. Michael Walzer criticizes *One-Dimensional Man* by encapsulating Marcuse's thesis in the maxim 'the better, the worse' – and for this reason identifies Marcuse as 'an antidemocratic critic. Alone among twentieth-century leftists, he is fully capable of sounding like Ortega y Gasset' (*The Company of Critics*, Halban, London 1989, p. 184).

84   See Pierre Bourdieu and Jean-Claude Passeron, 'Sociologues des mythologies et mythologies des sociologues', *Les Temps modernes*, no. 211, December 1963, pp. 998–1021.

85   In a long note in his *Outline of a Theory of Practice* (trans. Richard Nice, Cambridge University Press, Cambridge 1977, pp. 74–5), Bourdieu criticizes what he calls the 'ultra-subjectivism' of Sartre who, ignoring the issue of the economic and social conditions of a true consciousness of economic and social conditions, 'confers on the awakening of revolutionary consciousness – a sort of "conversion" of consciousness produced by a sort of imaginary variation – the power to create the meaning of the present by creating the revolutionary future which negates it'. The 'world of action is nothing other than this universe of interchangeable possibles, entirely dependent on the decrees of the consciousness which creates it and hence totally devoid of *objectivity*'. Bourdieu adds that 'the only limit this artificialism recognizes to the freedom of the ego is that which freedom sets itself by the free abdication of the pledge or the surrender of bad faith, the Sartrian name for alienation, or the submission imposed on it by the alienating freedom of the alter ego in the Hegelian struggles between master and slave'.

86   '[T]he opposition between *Eigentlichkeit*, "authenticity", and *Uneigentlichkeit*, "inauthenticity", those "primordial modes of Being-there", as Heidegger says, around which the whole work is organized (even from the viewpoint of the most strictly internal readings), is a particular and particularly subtle retranslation of the common opposition between the "elite" and the "masses"' (*The Political Ontology of Martin Heidegger*, trans. Peter Collier, Polity Press, Cambridge 1991, p. 79). The rest of the passage is especially illuminating, because we can implicitly read in it the critique of other opponents whom Bourdieu has continued to combat – personalists (the allusion to 'the "person" here called *Dasein*') and sociologists of the mass media inspired by the Frankfurt School ('forces which "level down"'): 'One could list the commonplaces of academic aristocratism which recur throughout this oft-commented passage, replete with topoi on the agora as an antithesis of the *scholè*, leisure versus school. There is a hatred of statistics (harping on the theme of the "average") seen as a symbol of all the operations of "levelling down" which threatened the "person" (here called *Dasein*) and its most precious attributes, its "originality" and its "privacy". There is a contempt for all forces which "level down"' (ibid.).

87   Pierre Bourdieu, *Distinction: A Social Critique of the Judgement of Taste*, trans. Richard Nice, Routledge, London 1989, p. 29.

88   In fact, in *Distinction* something like a position of authenticity does indeed persist, but it is never explicitly stated as such: that of the 'popular aesthetic', 'based on the affirmation of continuity between art and life, which implies the subordination of form to function' (ibid., p. 32). It is from this position that two figures of the inauthentic can be unmasked: on the one hand, a primordial inauthenticity, that of 'pure taste' (p. 31); and, on the other, an inauthenticity that might be characterized as *derivative* – that of the 'petty-bourgeois' who, anxious to distinguish himself from popular taste without having the resources to accede to bourgeois taste, is condemned to 'imitations', 'a kind of unconscious bluff which chiefly deceives the bluffer who has most interest in taking the copy for the original, like the purchasers of "seconds",

"rejects", cut-price or second-hand goods, who need to convince themselves that "it's cheaper and creates the same effect'" (p. 323).

89 This is what Derrida calls *phonocentrism*, which he describes by means of a long commentary on Rousseau and, in particular, the *Essai sur l'origine des langues*, occupying the whole of the second part of *Of Grammatology* (trans. Gayatri Chakravorty Spivak, Johns Hopkins University Press, Baltimore and London 1977). In Rousseau, where we doubtless find the first systematic expression of the requirement of authenticity in its modern form, the voice as authentic presence and absolute proximity of the self to itself (and hence as truth) is opposed to writing as distance, mediation, loss of presence, paving the way for illusion, just as the immediacy of the popular festival is contrasted with the artificiality of the theatrical spectacle, or, in another respect, with the way the direct democracy realized by the assembly of citizens is opposed to representative democracy where the general will, confiscated by spokesmen, risks being diverted and degraded into particular interests.

90 Gilles Deleuze, *Difference and Repetition*, trans. Paul Patton, Athlone, London 1994, pp. xix–xx.

91 Nevertheless, something persists as the source of a moral position pointing in the direction of the more authentic: the primacy of *life* as openness (infra- or pre-individual) to the unlimited, to proliferation, to creativity and resistance to closed orders, to blockages; the Nietzschean prioritization of active forces over reactive forces (which in Nietzsche provoke *ressentiment* and, consequently, morality in the sense of the critique of 'moralism').

92 In numerous pages of Roland Barthes's *Mythologies* (trans. Annette Lavers, Jonathan Cape, London 1972), we find the prefiguration of a theme with a prosperous future ahead of it: that of the world as *look*. Take, for example, the chapter devoted to abbé Pierre, which dismantles the way he dresses in the way one would describe a theatrical costume intended to project a certain image of the character, where each piece of clothing is treated as a sign whose decipherment presupposes knowledge of a code. Abbé Pierre is not dressed as an abbot in accordance with the regulations of the institution he belongs to in the age in which he lives. He has given himself the *look* of an abbot. He has given himself a *new look*, as is said today of star singers, as a *high-powered parish priest*.

93 Jean Baudrillard, *Simulacra and Simulations*, trans. Sheila Faria Glaser, University of Michigan Press, Ann Arbor 1994, p. 19.

94 Ibid., p. 6.

95 An example of this kind of ambiguous relation is offered by the world of art. Analysis of the characteristics of the organizational contexts conducive to the emergence of artistic creations regarded as pathbreaking has brought out the crucial role of certain relations that mix the friendship and involvement of someone other than the artist (whom we might call a 'coach') in the artist's work, in the form of an empathetic critique – that is to say, a critique in theory conducted from the standpoint of the artist's project, not from that of the organization's concern for profitability. But this type of mechanism can appear to be a detour of production, friendship and 'affectionate criticism' *in fact* proving of use in the production of a quality good, to the point where they can come to be denounced as manipulation (see Ève Chiapello, *Artistes versus managers. Le management culturel face à la critique artiste*, Métailié, Paris 1998).

96 See Sabine Chalvon-Demersay, 'Une société élective. Scénarios pour un monde de relations choisies', *Terrain*, no. 27, September 1996, pp. 81–100.

97 Moreover, we encounter the same tension in the definition of the goods produced by a network world. We know that this world esteems innovation highly, but the innovation presents itself as the result of the encounters, connections and hybridizations that are constantly occurring in the network, to the point where it can never possess an absolute character: there is now nothing that makes it possible to assert the primacy of an 'original' over 'copies', since any change occurs under the auspices of multiplicity and infinite variation.

98 Bob Aubrey, *Savoir faire savoir*, InterÉditions, Paris 1990.

99 Rosabeth Moss Kanter, 'The New Managerial Work', *Harvard Business Review*, November/December 1989.

100 Hubert Landier, *Vers l'entreprise intelligente*, Calmann-Lévy, Paris 1991.

101 Isabelle Orgogozo, *Les Paradoxes du management, du château fort aux cloisons mobiles*, Éditions d'Órganisation, Paris 1991.

102 Michel Crozier and Hervé Sérieyx, eds, *Du management panique à l'entreprise du XXIème siècle*, Maxima, Paris 1994.

103 Michael Piore, *Beyond Individualism*, Harvard University Press, Cambridge (MA) 1995, pp. 76–8.

104 The same applies to the new uses of psychotherapy that aim not to treat psychic suffering, recognized in what is authentic about it, at root, but to teach ill people to distance themselves from their ills, to 'manage' themselves in such a way as to be able to adapt to situations involving interaction with others and satisfy transactional demands in relations with the other, which are regarded as normative demands *par excellence* (see Isabelle Baszanger, *Douleur et médecine. La fin d'un oubli*, Seuil, Paris 1995, pp. 343–56).

105 See Chiapello, *Artistes versus managers*.

106 The Constituent Assembly thus excluded servants (who, on the eve of the Revolution, formed 17 per cent of the working population of Paris), because they 'symbolized dependency on a third party' (Pierre Rosanvallon, *Le Sacre du citoyen. Histoire du suffrage universel en France*, Gallimard, Paris 1992, p. 120). Sieyès, quoted by Rosanvallon, referred to them as 'those whom a servile dependency binds, not to some work, but to the arbitrary wishes of a master'.

107 See Alan Silver, 'Friendship and Trust as Moral Ideal: An Historical Approach', *Journal européen de sociologie*, vol. XXX, 1989, pp. 274-97.

108 Gorz, *Critique of Economic Reason*, pp. 207–8.

109 See Thévenot, 'Un gouvernement par les normes'.

110 Michel Feutrie and Éric Verdier, 'Entreprises et formations qualifiantes. Une construction sociale inachevée', *Sociologie du travail*, no. 4, 1993, pp. 469–92.

111 The possibility of condemning the gulf between the nature of the post and its remuneration on the one hand, and the qualifications of those occupying it (the devaluation of academic qualifications) on the other, disappears with the employment of the notion of skill. Aiming in particular to avoid fixing knowledge in classifications that permit a stabilization of expectations, the notion of skill refers to potentialities inherent in people in their singularity, '*savoir faire*' or 'interpersonal skills', the fruits of particular experiences that can be brought out only in local contexts, so that their validation takes the form of observing behaviour and individual testing in real situations. In this framework, training no longer aims to transmit skills that can be validated by the award of a qualification, but to encourage professional transferability by stimulating predispositions that can be engaged in a multiplicity of different tasks (see Élisabeth Dugué, 'La gestion des compétences: les savoirs dévalués, le pouvoir occulté', *Sociologie du travail*, no. 3, 1994, pp. 273–92).

112 As regards cultural oganizations, the deconstruction of the aura attributed to the artist or author as the orginal subject of an authentic work owes much to the efforts of the sociology of art, particularly the current inspired by Marxism, in demonstrating that artists are simply workers like any others. This enterprise of disenchantment certainly contributed to a growth in the use of management techniques to control the production and marketing of artistic 'products', and the integration of an ever-increasing number of artists into the capitalist circuit, which no longer assumed a guise that was so negative and dangerous for the authenticity of creators and their works as in the past (see Chiapello, *Artistes versus managers*).

113 See Marc Angenot, *La Parole pamphlétaire. Typologie des discours modernes*, Payot, Paris 1983.

114 See Luc Boltanski, *L'amour et la justice comme compétences*, Métailié, Paris 1990, pp. 96–109.

115 See Wagner, *A Sociology of Modernity*.

116 Tending in this direction is what Alain Supiot ('Du bon usage des lois en matière d'emploi') calls 'professional freedom', within which he distinguishes between 'freedom of

enterprise' and 'freedom to work'. The general idea is to create rights that not only control the labour market but institute it, rights that are not only protective but also endowed with positive virtues. Thus, according to Supiot, the right to enterprise should lead to 'conferring particular rights on those engaged in business' (leave to set up a firm or grants to unemployed people who set up firms tend in this direction). Similarly, the right to work must not be conceived as a restrictive right, limiting wage-earners' opportunities for collective action (e.g. in the case of strikes), but a right endowed with 'positive virtues' providing 'a legal basis for people's autonomy at work … which, so administrators tell us, is a fundamental characteristic of new managerial modes'. Among these positive freedoms, whose legal recognition is under way, Supiot mentions the right to initiative (right to withdraw), to training (individual leave), to criticism (right of expression). The multiplication of such rights pertaining to the freedom to work could, according to the author, help 'check the new forms of subordination that are developing behind the screen of this autonomization. This is what is happening with many provisions for availability (being on call, work on demand, irregular work, etc.)', which allow the employer to ensure 'wage-earners' continual availability while being obliged to pay only periods that have actually been worked'. Such clauses 'obviously undermine the wage-earners' freedom to work, since they cannot hold another job during these periods of "free" time'.

117 In the case of primary-school teachers, for example, trade-union action at the end of the nineteenth century was aimed predominantly at securing a statute for members of the profession, in order to release them from the power of local notables and give them access to political freedom.

118 See Thévenot, 'Les justifications du service public peuvent-elles contenir le marché?'

119 On account of this, money is one of the principal media contributing to encroaching on the different spheres of justice, as Paul Ricoeur (*Le juste*, Esprit-Seuil, Paris 1995) notes, commenting on Michael Walzer.

CONCLUSION

THE FORCE OF CRITIQUE

In this conclusion, we have sought to condense in a comparatively limited space the historical transformations of capitalism over the last thirty years, as well as the concepts and model of change that we employ to account for them. This synthesis is presented in the form of a series of steps leading to the formation of the new spirit of capitalism.

Although it was no part of our ambition to construct a 'theory of change' proper, with a claim to general validity, we have nevertheless sought – by marking out sequences in the process that led to a change in the spirit of capitalism, and giving this history a schematic or stylized form[1] – to pave the way for a possible generalization in space as well as time.[2]

To begin with, we recall a certain number of axioms bearing on the relations between the main concepts on which the model of change proposed here is based – that is to say, capitalism, spirit of capitalism and critique.

I. THE AXIOMATICS OF THE MODEL OF CHANGE

The propositions that follow are so many premises underlying the model. In each instance, we touch on a number of reasons which lead us to think that it is possible on these bases to construct a pertinent interpretation of the events affecting society in its relations with capitalism over the last thirty years.

1. Capitalism needs a spirit in order to engage the people required for production and the functioning of business.

These people cannot be set to work and kept working by force. The first reason is practical: capitalism is not vested with the power of arms, since the state – always relatively autonomous with respect to capitalism, albeit to varying degrees – possesses a monopoly on legitimate violence. The second stems from the fact that freedom is, as it were, embedded in capitalism and would negate itself were it to rely exclusively on forcibly enlisting people: at the very least, it presupposes free labour (accepting a job and leaving it, and hence engaging or not engaging) and free enterprise (hiring, buying, selling and, more generally, combining various resources to derive a profit). Finally, if forced labour makes possible the performance of certain works that can be undertaken mainly using unskilled, plentiful manpower (earthworks, work in fields, simple factory or construction work, etc.), it is utterly inadequate when the tasks to be performed require a higher level of skill, autonomy and positive involvement from workers (intellectual work or work involving many decisions), or the use of sophisticated machinery; and when the product must satisfy stringent requirements in terms of innovation, reliability, quality of finish, respect of multiple manufacturing norms, and so on.

It is precisely because capitalism is hand in glove with freedom, does not have total sway over people, and presupposes the performance of a large number of tasks that cannot be carried out without workers' positive involvement, that it must furnish acceptable reasons for engaging. These reasons are contained in the spirit of capitalism.

2. To be capable of mobilizing people, the spirit of capitalism must incorporate a moral dimension.

This means that it must offer people the possibility, on the one hand, of appealing against the condition that is constructed for them by reference to *justice*, and on the other hand of legitimately aspiring to sufficient *security* of existence to maintain themselves (the conditions of their biological and social survival) and reproduce themselves in their children.

Even where capitalism is most strongly established, people continue to exist outside work and in other respects than as workers, so that they can always rely on this outside life (family, friendships, cultural, political or community life) to preserve a critical distance, at least when the level of exploitation is not at its maximum (exploitation *in the strong sense* of Chapter 6, defined by a degree of exhaustion such that those subject to it cease to be able to live to the full in non-work situations). The impact of this resistance leads capitalism, in order to remain desirable, to equip itself with an ideology that acts to maximum effect in furnishing justifications, pointing towards criteria of justice, and making it possible to respond to critiques.

Over and above the criticism to which capitalism is necessarily vulnerable because it does not engage people by force, and because in normal (i.e. non-totalitarian) regimes people can be sure of some space where they can distance themselves from the requirements of the accumulation process, there is another reason why capitalism needs regulations of a moral kind. It is as follows: whereas capitalism, by its very nature, is an insatiable process, people are satiable, so that they require justifications for getting involved in an insatiable process. It follows that capitalism cannot make do with offering nothing more specific than its inherent insatiability.

Thus, in contrast to Durkheim,[3] we transfer the full weight of such insatiability on to capitalism – that is, its systemic properties – not on to the anthropological properties of human nature. We think that one of the difficulties capitalism faces in getting itself accepted is that it addresses itself to people who are by no means ready to sacrifice everything to the accumulation process. This is precisely because they are not wholly identified with this regime, and have experience of different ones – for example, family attachments, civic solidarity, intellectual or religious life, and so on. And even those who seem to be most wholly identified with capitalism (a one-dimensionality that renders them somehow abnormal, even monstrous, in the eyes of the outside world) cannot completely forget having experienced different regimes, at least when they were children, and having been socialized in accordance with different values. By causing desires to be played off against one another as it were, the existence of a plurality of value orders and people's simultaneous or successive membership of several lived worlds thus tend to confer a satiable character on human nature. Or – to put it another way – they check the tendencies to insatiability Durkheim refers to. Perhaps these tendencies would be unbounded if human beings knew only one kind of goods and only one way of attaining them. But one-dimensional individuals of this variety – close to the fiction of *Homo oeconomicus* – would not grow indignant at anything, would have no compassion for anyone, or any critical spirit. There would no longer be anything distinctively human about them.[4]

Unable to discover a moral basis in the logic of the insatiable accumulation process (which in itself, on its own, is amoral), capitalism must borrow the legitimating principles it lacks from orders of justification external to it (here called *cities*). Through the intermediary of the spirit of capitalism, capitalism thus in a way also incorporates its own critique, since it incorporates moral principles on which people can depend to denounce those of its aspects which do not respect the values it has annexed to itself.

3. If it is to survive, capitalism needs *simultaneously* to stimulate and to curb insatiability.

As a process of unlimited accumulation, capitalism must constantly stimulate tendencies to insatiability and activate different forms of desire for accumulation: amassing property; concentrating power, which was particularly important in the forms associated with the second spirit of capitalism that accompanied the development of bureaucratized firms from the 1930s; or, as we observe today, the capitalization of resources conducive to mobility and creativity. In fact, capitalism can develop only by relying on human beings' propensities for accumulating profits, power, inventions, different experiences.

But this power is quite insufficient on its own, for without an external foundation the desire for accumulation itself becomes problematic and tends in the course of a life, or at least in the following generation, to exhaust itself. As we have seen, were human beings insatiable by nature, this would not be the case. But then the tendency would be to self-destruction, because the search for unlimited profits increases competition, which, if it is neither checked nor regulated, borders on violence. For example, what would become of capitalism without the interdiction of theft (i.e. respect for property rights)?

The spirit of capitalism may thus be conceived as a solution to this problem, since it activates insatiability in the form of excitement and liberation, while tethering it to moral exigencies that are going to restrict it by bringing the constraints of the common good to bear on it.

It is the site of a *permanent tension* between the stimulation of desire for accumulation and its limitation by norms corresponding to the forms that desire takes when it is embedded in other orders of status. Being an unstable compromise structurally, its mobilizing power can be strengthened or weakened. It can be weakened either because it loses its stimulating dimension, or because it is insufficiently orientated towards the common good, and people find the justifications for engagement it supplies rather thin. But the strengthening of any one of its components retroacts on the others. A perfectly just world would be singularly lacking in the capacity to generate the kind of pleasure that is experienced in confronting uncertainty, for all the *tests* on which the distribution of goods and responsibilities in a society depends (selection and recruitment tests, determination of pay levels, work appraisal, etc.) would be completely resolved in it and nothing, seemingly, would be left to chance. Would surprises still be possible in such a world? Conversely, a world where anything seemed possible, while it would be exciting, would also risk being highly demotivating, because people would no longer know what they could rely on.

4. The spirit of capitalism cannot be reduced to an ideology in the sense of an illusion with no impact on events in the world.

It must, to a certain extent, deliver on its promises. It is in fact constantly put to the test by people who, relying on it in the way that one evokes an ideal, denounce what in practice does not conform to the rule. This presupposes that people possess genuine critical capacities – that is to say, that they are never so alienated as to be incapable of establishing a critical distance. Critique has real effects for, in order to withstand the test, the justification of capitalism must be able to rely upon mechanisms – that is to say, collections of objects, rules, conventions, of which law is one expression. Developed in response to critiques, these mechanisms constrain the accumulation process.

5. Capitalism has a constant tendency to transform itself.

The search for new paths to profit is a potent force of transformation, whether it involves overcoming the effects of market saturation by creating new products and services – in particular, by commodifying spaces that have hitherto remained outside the commodity sphere – or restoring margins eroded by competition by gaining a temporary advantage over other competitors. Such an advantage ('competitive advantage' in the management literature) makes it possible to secure the benefit of a temporary revenue bound up with possession of a patent or manufacturing secrets, control over a new technology, or implementation of a new, more efficient organization. This indicates the role played in constant 'creative destruction', to use Joseph Schumpeter's phrase, by the very specific form of critique that is competition (an exit critique in Hirschman's typology, in the sense that it is expressed not in words but by defection). This constantly fuels the capitalist process by virtue of the fact that entrepreneurs are always seeking to escape the erosion of margins it entails.

On the other hand, changes in capitalism are largely independent of the *voice* critique in Hirschman's sense (public protest), although it may in some cases encourage them, slow them down, or prevent them occurring.

As they accumulate, the alterations can become so radical that a spirit of capitalism adapted to a given period can subsequently prove utterly incapable of performing its mobilizing function.

6. The principal operator of creation and transformation of the spirit of capitalism is critique (*voice*).

While the *voice* critique is not the main agent of change in capitalism, its role is central in constructing the spirit which, in different forms at different times, accompanies capitalism.

Through a reflexive endeavour on the part of those in charge of firms and their assistants, with a view to reproducing success and understanding failure, and on the part of critique, which seeks to understand the origins of its indignation and interrogates the former, obliging them to offer interpretations and justifications, a kind of cartography of the world in a certain state of capitalism is established, according to categories shared by both types of actors.

This cartography recognizes various important sites – focal points allowing for tacit co-ordination in a situation of uncertainty[5] – that will be regarded as privileged moments of judgement, of evaluation and hence selection, of remuneration, of positive or negative sanction. We have called them 'tests'. In part under the influence of critique, certain of these tests that are considered especially important are subject to a labour of institutionalization, and are scrutinized and controlled in respect of the extent to which the order derived from them – with its winners and losers, its great men and little people – is held to be just. This process allows the various partners to agree on the stress points that particularly merit elucidation and, as a result, helps to damp down conflicts. The more critique focuses attention on a test, the more chance there is that established mechanisms exist to improve it in terms of its more or less just character.

Thus critique plays several roles in this process: identification and categorization of the strengths that may legitimately be committed to the test; and protest when one of the protagonists is discovered exploiting strengths that are alien to the test format. It thus brings pressure to bear on the identified tests to make them more just by eliminating parasitic forces; in other words, it intervenes to *tighten* up the tests. Critique thus plays an important role in the formation of the spirit of capitalism, which, if it is to be credible, must have corresponding supervised tests.

Because critique makes it possible for capitalism to equip itself with a spirit which, as we have seen, is required for people to engage in the profit-making process, it indirectly serves capitalism and is one of the instruments of its ability to endure. This poses some serious problems for critique, since it easily finds itself faced with the alternative of being either ignored (and hence useless) or recuperated.

7. In certain conditions, critique can itself be one of the factors of a change in capitalism (and not merely in its spirit).

Three scenarios might be envisaged: (a) the critique of the established tests is so violent that capitalism seeks to elude them via displacements – that is to say, by wagering on terrain that has not as yet been subject to identification and categorization to the same degree, even at the price of imperilling the 'spirit' on which its legitimacy and mobilizing capacity rest. For example, one way of escaping the fixed links between job hierarchies and wage hierarchies guaranteed by collective agreements, which tends to pass on to the whole chain an increase at any of one of its points, has been to engage a casualized workforce that is not included in the classification and does not enjoy the established guarantees. Breaching the promise of career prospects associated with the second spirit, this helped to diminish its credibility; (b) because critique is plural, a change in the balance between its different critical components (which might be endogenous to the partially autonomous history of critique) leads to an emphasis on tests that have hitherto been weakly established, or even the establishment of new types of test through an identification-categorization of points of the map hitherto ignored or not qualified in autonomous fashion. Thus, the importance assumed by demands for liberation in the years following May 1968 shifted attention from the critique of the hitherto preponderant issue – the distribution of valued added – to hierarchical behaviour, to the point where those in charge of firms had to amend the old disciplinary forms; (c) by obliging capitalism to limit itself, critique constrains it to alter its forms of accumulation. For example, in the case of the second spirit of capitalism, the critique of exploitation made it possible to impose an accounting framework that disclosed value added and its distribution.

8. Critique derives its energy from sources of indignation.

Such indignation emerges in historically situated forms, while doubtless being rooted in anthropologies that possess very general validity. Forms of indignation may be regarded as emotional expressions of a meta-ethical anchorage, and concern infringements that are believed, at least implicitly, to affect people's possibilities of realizing their humanity. We have identified four main sources of indignation as regards the critiques directed at capitalism. Let us recall that the first has to do with the demand for *liberation*, which is grounded in the constitutive irreducibility of *persons*, whose *potential* (as opposed to *action*) cannot be confined to a finite list of properties. The second, which unmasks the *inauthenticity* of persons and objects, is based on the opposition between truth and illusion. The third incriminates *egoism* and points towards the exigency of a *common humanity*, expressing itself in solidarity within collectives. Finally, the fourth derives from sensitivity to *suffering* and, more precisely, forms of suffering which, not having a generic character (as is the case, for example, with mortality), can be attributed to human action – that is to say, in the case that concerns us, to the dynamic of capitalism. Unlike rebellion against the misery of the human condition as such, these sources of indignation point towards what is regarded as remediable in the human order.[6]

Although these forms of indignation may be regarded as possessing a relatively timeless character, critique, in the forms we are familiar with today, goes hand in glove with modernity and democracy. If there is certainly no form of society without critique, critique as a political exigency is a product of the Enlightenment.[7] For us, the right to condemn now forms part of human rights, to the point where we cannot imagine an acceptable life where there would be no place for the possibility of formulating critiques and getting them heard in the public arena.

No doubt Durkheim also had the development of critical capacities in mind when he contrasted mechanical solidarity with organic solidarity. Whereas critique in the framework of the former essentially consists in sanctioning transgressions that are deemed scandalous, the latter – which is associated with extended forms of the division of labour, a greater awareness of pluralism, and hence different claims to legitimacy – paves the way for a conflict of interpretations and, as it were, the institutionalization of social critique.

We can say that the development of capitalism would not have been possible without this unlocking of critique associated with a multiplication of practices, if only because it assumes free labour and free enterprise, and hence competition. As we have seen, in itself competition already represents a form of critique, which consists in defecting. However, in addition to the fact that it is rarely 'pure and perfect', it turns out that competition is a long way from possessing the regulatory power attributed to it by the classics, for which protests must implicate market imperfections. To the extent that prices cannot focus all the reasons for satisfaction or dissatisfaction, capitalism is also bound to give *voice* its due.

Having recalled the main capacities that we attributed to our 'macro-actors' – capitalism and critique – as well as certain features of the result of their interaction – the spirit of capitalism – we can now direct them in a sequenced history of the change in the components of the spirit of capitalism, such as we have been able to reconstruct it on the basis of the events of the last thirty years.

2. STEPS IN THE CHANGE IN THE SPIRIT OF CAPITALISM

In the discussion that follows, we shall alternate moments containing the model of change at its most general with others which, pointing towards features of the period studied, are as it were an illustration of it, or even offer examples from earlier epochs likewise marked by changes in the spirit of capitalism (indented passages).

Critique in the case of agreement on the important tests

Critique – at least in its public modes, and to the extent that it depends on justifiable expressions of the common good – is exercised as a matter of priority on tests that have already been subject to formalization, stabilization by means of procedures or rules, and at least the skeleton of an institutionalization, giving them an objectivity that makes it possible to share indignation. This contrasts with barely formalized tests that generate an 'unease' requiring interpretation,[8] which is difficult to induce others to share and which, when it is expressed, can easily be discredited as purely 'subjective', even as the fruit of a tendency to paranoia. Given the subject matter of our work, the formalized tests that interest us are in the main those through which capital accumulation and profit creation are pursued in forms that lay claim to legitimacy.

> We can distinguish three types of test among those that were confronted with the question of whether their conduct was just at the beginning of the period studied – that is to say, in the second half of the 1960s and the beginning of the 1970s:

(a) affected in the first instance were the tests on which the wages–profit relationship – that is, the division of value added – depended. These tests result in allocating people a certain number of characteristics, goods, rights and duties relative to work: the nature of the tasks they must perform (defined in terms of posts, for example); a remuneration; a type of work contract characterized notably, depending on its casual and flexible character, in terms of hours worked; and so on. Particularly since the 1930s, these tests had been subject to a formalization based on labour law, which led to the establishment of what is usually called 'industrial relations systems';

(b) likewise subject to close critical scrutiny were tests that legitimated asymmetries in terms of power, or positions of seniority, particularly when this asymmetry was of a domestic kind (that is, justified by seniority, family property, or gender), but also when it was based upon a claim to inequality in terms of merit as validated by the result of earlier selection tests (as when a 'mandarin' roots his authority in an academic title);

(c) finally, critique attacked all the more or less formalized and supervised tests, supposedly legitimate and just, on which social selection rested: obviously, educational tests in the first instance, but also professional recruitment tests, tests that career progress depends on, psychological tests, tests aiming to establish if a person at work is perfectly normal in the psychiatric sense, and capable of performing the tasks allotted to him (particularly detailed and legitimate in sectors where security requirements can be invoked – for example, on the railways),[9] not to mention a number of tests of a judicial kind aiming to determine the guilt or innocence of persons in different circumstances (from disciplinary committees to administrative tribunals or the courts of justice).

Critique unmasks infringements of justice in these tests. In particular, this unmasking consists in revealing the hidden forces that interfere with the test and exposing certain protagonists who, enjoying greater access to various resources, mobilize them unbeknownst to others, procuring an unwarranted advantage.

In the case of the division of value added, the demonstration consists in revealing the hidden assets that discreetly swell the employers' profits collectively or individually – that is to say, the exploitation of which the workers are the victims. This foils the employers' justifications, which draw on accounting results to show that it is impossible to meet particular demands without imperilling the firm.

In the case of selection, and especially educational tests, the typical form of critical exposure consists in showing how the competitors, placed in such conditions that their chances of success are formally equal – so that the success of some and the failure of others are due exclusively to merit – are in *fact* in radically unequal positions, because some of them benefit from parasitic forces alien to the character of the test. Also identified and unmasked are competitors who derive an advantage from these forces that is all the greater in that it is not officially taken into account. In principle, the forces unmasked can consist in anything. Theoretically, there is no property that cannot be the source of a positive or negative discrimination, even if those subject to challenge over recent decades have primarily revolved around social background, sex, age, ethnic origin, and physical or mental 'handicaps'. The challenge to these parasitic forces can be the subject of legal provisions (as in the proscription, which features in the electoral code, of putting members of the same family on the same list; or, in the opposite respect, anti-discrimination regulations).

On account of the institutionalization of certain tests that act as focal points, and are associated with repertoires of critique and justification incorporated into common knowledge, if critique seeks to proceed in different directions, it will have difficulty making itself heard, and is always liable to be dragged back to the recognized tests. This is particularly the case because the various actors do not know how to handle these new critiques, and wish to agree on negotiable points. In fact, consideration of critiques that are focused on themes whose definition is unstable, and on whose horizons no formalized tests appear, risks rendering the dispute interminable, or even inflecting it towards violence.

The 'social' critiques of 1965–70 taken seriously by employers (whether they were regarded as reasonable and rapidly taken into account, or rejected as unrealistic and dangerous), in contrast to the more 'artistic' critiques, which were rejected – at least to start off with – as incoherent, absurd or 'surreal', were above all those that pointed towards tests that had already (following earlier conflicts) been subject to a significant formalization and stabilization.

Thus, as we saw in Chapter 3, the spokespersons of parties to labour disputes addressed themselves in the first instance to formalized tests integrated into the system of industrial relations, in order to seek a solution to those disputes. Caught unawares by the violence of the disputes, they endeavoured, while remaining within a logic of competition and relations of force, to co-ordinate their efforts to reach a solution, by converging on the most robust of those tests. These tests, being particularly well supervised legally and institutionally, carried less risk of causing them to veer off into disconcerting, uncontrollable conflicts. This was the case *par excellence* with negotiations at confederal level between trade unions and employers' organizations, in which representatives of the state played a mediating role. These tests rested on the strong coupling between capitalism and the state characteristic of the second spirit of capitalism.

The tightening-up of tests under the influence of critique

Whether critique bears directly on the most conventionalized tests or is brought back to them, it cannot, if it is of significance, remain without an echo for very long (except at the price of interrupting the democratic operation of political and social debate: press censorship, banning of rallies and strikes, imprisonment of protesters, etc.). In fact, these tests (whose justification invariably appeals to the same normative positions as those invoked by critique) must be considered valid, even irreproachable, to guarantee the legitimacy of those who have something to gain from them, whom critique justly accuses of being unduly favoured. Those charged with responsibility for conducting them cannot therefore ignore the critiques directed at them for ever and must, if the tests are to remain legitimate, take notice of them.

After a more or less prolonged period of conflict, involving sequences of critique and justification, these tests often end up being more strictly supervised and fine-tuned than previously, in order to make them conform to the current model of justice.

The period considered offers numerous examples of measures that led to test formats being tightened up to respond to demands for justice. In addition to a reweighting of the wages/profits share in favour of wage-earners, the beginning of the 1970s was marked by agreements at the highest level issuing in laws or decrees which, extending the welfare state, sought to bolster wage-earners' stability and security (Chapter 3).

In the same years, selection tests were likewise examined more rigorously with regard to their ability to fulfil in practice the requirements of justice contained in their terms of reference. In the educational system in particular, a whole set of measures aimed to encourage access to secondary or higher education for children from social categories that had hitherto been excluded from it in practice.[10] The fact that many teachers subscribed to the belief that in covert fashion the education system favoured pupils or students who were privileged in other respects led them to be more careful than previously, when it came to the conduct of educational tests and their own behaviour towards children from different backgrounds, so as to control anything in their attitude that might be discriminatory.

As for the exercise of authority, it too was subject to a greater degree of control, with subordinates more often demanding that instructions and requests to them be justified. The development of an intensive critique of domestic bonds in the world of work – from the critique of the mandarinate in universities to the power of petty tyrants in workshops – at the time provided the basis for refining a large number of tests, in order to refocus tests on the strengths that specifically defined them: 'genuine' competence in a professional framework (or, in a political framework, civic qualities).

Following these various alterations to tests, it became rather more difficult to make wage-earners work over and above their contractual obligations
without compensation; to order people about in oppressive fashion; to rely
on the authority of academic titles to push through decisions that were unrelated to acknowledged competence; to sell products of dubious quality; to
make trade-union representatives redundant; and so on.

As the tests were refined and tightened up, the social world unquestionably
became rather more just – or, to use a different terminology, somewhat less
inegalitarian – in respect, obviously, of injustices or inequalities corresponding to the formats of recognized, established tests (other injustices and
inequalities could be maintained or even increased by relying on tests that had
been subject to little reflexive review).

Even if, for reasons bound up with the legitimacy of the social order, it is
difficult to oppose such a process head-on, it remains the case that greater
strictness in the established tests is not to everyone's advantage. Some gain
from it; others lose. Supervision of the forces actually engaged in the test
favours those who have received extensive training for that particular test and
not some other – professionals, specialists, and so on. In other words, it
benefits those who have made the greatest sacrifices in other respects and
who, for the same reasons, are often not very mobile and lose their comparative advantage as soon as they have to change terrain. Contrariwise, however,
it penalizes those who, having access to resources distributed in a multiplicity
of worlds associated with different ways of assessing persons and things, could
transfer them unconstrained from one test to another. The advantages they
used to enjoy tend to diminish.

As a result, the stricter the tests become under the influence of critique,
the greater the temptation to circumvent them. Those who hitherto benefited
from relatively unsupervised tests realize that the legitimacy gains brought by
more strict or more just tests are paid for by a decline in benefits in other
respects – for example, by a reduction in the chances of success for themselves or their children. They may not resign themselves to this loss of
advantages, and may use the assets they accumulated when tests were less strict
in order to seek new paths to profit. In order to avoid the loss of competitive advantage they enjoyed by virtue of being able to commit multiple
unidentified strengths, they move into situations containing tests where the
nature of the opposing forces is less subject to control.

The social gains of the end of the 1960s and the beginning of the 1970s made
it possible to alter the distribution of value added in favour of wage-earners.
But this situation – added to the economic problems of the second half of
the 1970s, which tended to reduce firms' profits still further – convinced the
employers that they should turn away from national negotiations and abandon

the 'corporatist policy', in order to explore new modes of organization and relations with wage-earners (Chapter 3).

How did people come to realize that the tests to which it had hitherto seemed normal to submit no longer offered the same possibilities as before, so that it was appropriate to seek other profitable routes, other opportunities? One hypothesis is that great men – those who have succeeded in a certain order – are the first to understand this point, because from a tacit knowledge which is difficult to communicate, especially publicly, they know that only a surplus of (illegitimate) force allows those who hold it to acquire a value superior to the minimum guaranteed by the test, when it is legitimately conducted. They suspect that they would never have 'succeeded' without this surplus strength, whose active potential would have been shattered by overly supervised tests, even if what this potential consists in often remains a mystery to them, and even if they believe that they have contributed in this way to the common good – which, in their view and the view of others, justifies the status accorded them.

Thus the great men of the capitalist world find themselves facing a tension that can be summarized as follows: inasmuch as they are hand in glove with the established tests – in particular so that they can punish those who seek to exempt themselves from them – they are hand in glove with the social order as it is, and readily prove 'conservative'; but given that they are always in search of new sources of profit, particularly as a result of the competition practised by those who lay claim to excellence, they cannot prevent the opening of the Pandora's box containing all the forces which had to be controlled if the state of the world – and, consequently, their own advantages as well – were to be less open to challenge from the standpoint of justice.

That is why, while they rarely go so far as to praise force in the 'pure' state – that is, precisely in so far as it remains indeterminate, and consequently open to all possible forms of qualification – they are always ready to criticize rules, regulations, moralism, and so on, as so many fetters on the performance of the great things to which they feel themselves summoned. Vulgar Nietzscheanism – derived from *The Genealogy of Morals*, and thematized in Scheler's *L'homme du ressentiment*, for example – finds an attentive ear among the strong: for them, the need to 'protect the strong from the weak' is a profound thought that mirrors their most intimate experience. Thus, to belong to the 'bourgeoisie', the 'dominant class' or the circle of 'notables', in the sense in which these terms feature in denunciations, is above all to share the knowledge, which is common to the happy few and cannot be entrusted to everyone, especially not made public, that nothing great is achieved – whether in art, politics or industry – without a surplus of force and without getting round the rules.[11]

Given that the established tests are invested with a high degree of legitimacy (from which the 'great' have hitherto benefited), the ability to realize that they have lost out on their interests, and that it is time to seek opportunities for alternative investment, other paths of profit involving different tests, thus presupposes a certain freedom with respect to morality – a variety of amoralism, often presented in the language of 'realism'.

'Immoralism' or 'amoralism', as a disposition favouring the primitive accumulation of capital, has since the beginning of the nineteenth century, and at least since Balzac, been a classical theme in literature that is critical of modernity and intent on understanding where the self-made – the new bourgeois dynasties – found the audacity to grasp the opportunities ignored or refused by existing elites, in profiting from confused political circumstances (the buying up of national property at low prices or speculative provisioning of the Empire's armies, etc.).

For the period that interests us – from the end of the 1960s to the mid-1980s – we may advance the hypothesis that innovators found the resources (the moral strength) required to liberate themselves from moralism at least in part in the diffusion of psychoanalysis and, in particular, Lacanian psychoanalysis, which was very widespread in these years. This played an important role in the deconstruction of customary morality (i.e. a morality primarily relevant in a domestic logic), by casting suspicion on the hidden motives of moralizing endeavours. More specifically, in these years the popularized version of Lacanianism was construed by a large number of young *cadres* in the public or private sector, who were receptive to the emancipatory themes of May 1968, as a school of realism.[12] What use is the psychoanalytic cure? For *cadres* (belonging mostly to the public sector or advanced tertiary sectors, like advertising), who undertook it in fairly sizeable numbers in the 1970s and 1980s, it first of all serves to enable one to look reality in the face – including, or especially, the reality of desire. But by the same token, it also aids one to acknowledge the limits that reality imposes on desire and, as a result, to make oneself better placed to tackle and control it (rather than interminably experiencing repeated failure because of an unrealistic search for fantastical solutions).

The vehemence of the artistic critique in the same period, combating all forms of convention and regarding morality and respect for the established order as unjustified oppression, likewise created an ideological context that was especially auspicious for all forms of subversion, including those practised by the employers' avant-garde. At a time when the watchword was to reinvent one's existence every day, heads of firms were able to enhance creativity and inventiveness in their organizational mechanisms, and thus emerge as men of progress.

Displacements and circumventions of the established tests

Displacements make it possible to restore strength by deriving less identified forces from the new circumstances in which those who bring them about are placed. The established tests of status are circumvented. All of a sudden, some people succeed in a different fashion. To start off with, no one knows what it is (it may be that they themselves do not know).

However unpredictable and daring they might appear, these displacements are simply the expression of the dynamic of capitalism, one of whose main properties – a source of fascination to Marx or Schumpeter – is, as we recalled at the beginning of this conclusion, to subvert the existing order while aiming for its reproduction. The systemic and mimetic effects of competition, by encouraging the adoption of innovations and hence reducing the advantages that they procure, in fact spur a constant search for new paths to profit.

> The period under consideration affords numerous examples of these displace-
> ments, which have taken very varied forms. They can be geographical in kind
> (relocation to regions where manpower is cheaper, labour law is undeveloped
> or flouted, and environmental regulations are less exacting), or organizational
> (the transformation of large structures into flotillas of small firms, casualiza-
> tion of a whole swathe of workers, etc.). They have affected the tests on which
> relations between firms depend (customer–supplier relations, subcontracting,
> partnership, formation of networks, etc.); the organization of work (develop-
> ment of multi-tasking or self-control); and the wages–profits distribution.
> They have led to the formation of new types of test (an ability to analyse
> quality problems by workers, the assessment of communication skills, etc.).
> The displacements have equally consisted in producing more varied goods in
> smaller runs, and commodifying objects and services that had hitherto
> remained outside the economic circuit, and which were presented on this
> account as more 'authentic', in order to satisfy critiques of the 'consumer
> society' while reviving consumption.

The accumulating displacements help to undo the established tests, which are not only circumvented but have also proved ineffective, since they are less and less capable of furnishing access to the good that they promised. Like their practical conduct, the principles they were based on thus become widely dis-credited. Displacements in capitalism thus dismantle the compromises between logics of action that the tests rested on, from the most established to the most informal.

> The forms of organizing production that led to the expansion of 1950–60
> rested, on the one hand, on the coupling of a Taylorist division of labour and
> state mechanisms for redistributing productivity increases (the 'Fordist

compromise' described by the Regulationists); and, on the other, on a compromise between requirements of an industrial type (planning, administrative control, etc.) and forms of justification and supervision of a domestic kind. The existence in firms of a large number of situations pertaining to a domestic logic was thus manifest. Where the employers were concerned, it took the form of preserving a family capitalism sustained by traditional bourgeois values in a world where the second spirit of capitalism was dominant. Where the wage-earning class was concerned, it expressed itself in forms of close supervision combining the discipline of the workshop (imposed by 'petty tyrants' recruited locally and promoted from the ranks), industrial control mechanisms (e.g. production indicators) and traditional – community or family – forms of social control outside the firm.

By means of the compromise between the industrial world and the civic world, economic mechanisms were connected with state orchestration and calculating centres favouring impersonal administration, justified by reference to a common good of a civic kind. But at the same time, by dint of the compromise between the industrial world and the domestic world, they also found themselves deeply imbricated in the social fabric, and bound up with the tests of everyday life and forms of personal experience.

Initially, at the beginning of the 1970s, the civic–industrial compromise seemed to emerge from the crisis strengthened. But the pursuit of demands prompted employers to embark upon a series of displacements that notably had the effect, ten years later, of recuperating the increased security obtained at the beginning of the period, thanks to measures that tended in the direction of a generalized flexibility. From the mid-1980s, the civic–industrial compromise emerged from these confrontations greatly weakened in practice and having lost much of its legitimacy. The period was equally marked by a considerable increase in the weight of multinational firms that reorganized themselves so that they were at once global and streamlined – that is to say, minimally dependent on their geographical location; this resulted in the consolidation of economic interest groups that were a good deal more autonomous *vis-à-vis* state requirements. Whereas the second spirit of capitalism operated in an era when the driving force was large national firms pursuing endogenous growth in a domestic market, which justified a stabilization of social relations by means of a national system of 'industrial relations' under state auspices, the new capitalism uncoupled itself from the state.

As for the domestic–industrial compromise, which from 1968 began to be uprooted from the academic world, it was maintained a little longer in the world of production, despite challenges to it from young *cadres*, engineers and qualified technicians, which more innovative employers (grouped, in particular, in Entreprise et Progrès), advised by management specialists and sociologists, sometimes echoed. It was only in the second half of the 1970s, when the managers of firms sought to put an end to the expansion of the civic world by encouraging a management style more attentive to demands for autonomy and creativity, that the legitimacy of domestic forms of arrangement in firms and, more generally, outside the closed space of the nuclear family, began to crumble.[13]

There is no doubt that the dismantling of the civic–industrial compromise helped to accelerate the dismantling of the domestic–industrial compromise. In effect, the durability of the domestic world outside the family and in work environments depended largely on the instruments of social control associated with this world. The long-term personal dependence of a subordinate on his employer, respecting relations between the generations and relations of seniority, presupposed that the superior was in a position to control the movements and contacts of his subalterns, and to inflect them in what he deemed to be the right direction. But in return for this consensual dependence, the employer had to ensure his protégé security and, in particular, open up a career path for him. In the large firms of the 1950s and 1960s, relations of domestic dependence thus found a relay in the bureaucratic forms of administration that offered young *cadres* from their 'reservoirs' the opportunity of a career in the organization. Why would they go elsewhere, at the risk of damaging their reputation for reliability and loyalty, in search of what was offered them on the spot? The durability of the domestic–industrial compromise was thereby linked to the existence of stable mechanisms and statutory preferences, which were incompatible with the search for maximum flexibility.

We must be careful not to see in these shifts the outcome of an overall strategy developed by occult bodies and implemented from on high. They are interpretable in terms neither of a plan preconceived, controlled and organized by an omniscient, omnipotent agent – the employers or capitalism – nor of an unconscious process, without a subject and bereft of reflexivity.

The organizational shifts of the 1970s were certainly prepared by much thought and many studies on the part of experts – economists, sociologists, administration specialists – and specialist consultants or journalists, concerned to confront criticism. The search for more robust mechanisms was also encouraged by employers' organizations. The same actors played a major role in pooling experience, stabilizing and transforming it into techniques or mechanisms that could be adapted and reproduced. But the *modus operandi* consisted instead in searching for new paths to profit by encouraging local, multiple, small-scale changes. This exercise in limited reflexivity stemmed from the concerns and actions of a considerable number of actors – employers, managers, human resources directors, *cadres*, and so on – each of whom sought to reassert control on their own particular patch, to get their subordinates back to work, to increase their margin of manoeuvre, and to restore profits. These actors were simultaneously in competition with one another and keen to co-operate, in order to understand what seemed to work for their competitors and, as far as possible, borrow it.

Competitive pressure led to a fairly rapid diffusion of displacements.[14] But an effort of interpretation, comparison and narration (often performed by consultants or in symposia, seminars, etc.) was required to define what seemed to have been beneficial, and to render local or circumstantial measures applicable elsewhere.

At the beginning of the sequence, when the displacements seemed heteroclite, accidental and local, the success of those whom they benefited could seem somewhat mysterious to the relevant parties themselves. Their striking success, in contrast to the inexplicable failure of those who delayed using the new recipes, could be attributed to circumstances or psychological peculiarities (e.g. their resourcefulness or lack of scruples).[15] But as these successes (or failures) persisted, a sense of what the success of those who had converted in time consisted in began to form in the consciousness of actors competing to create profits. Consequently, it began to be formulated and exchanged in co-ordinating bodies for those in charge of firms. A growing number of actors gave up the old tests and sought new ways of making a profit. The displacements then tended to proliferate. The polarization towards new tests and the abandonment of old tests tended to spread. Assets were devalued. Others saw their demand increase in significant proportions.

Let us point out that something other than displacement is possible when tests seem too strict to a number of actors. It consists in attempting to recover lost advantages by intervening in force in the order of categorization by 'deregulating', by doing everything to secure a change based on the stability and visibility of the legal order. However, there is little likelihood of this possibility being activated. For it would immediately encounter a critique strongly constructed around tests that had been openly attacked, and would probably have to take the form of political violence to achieve its ends, unless critique were itself, for one reason or another, greatly enfeebled or discredited. In certain historical circumstances, capitalism has certainly resorted to this, thanks to an alliance with authoritarian political forces – for example, in order to overturn a new communist regime that was challenging private property or free enterprise. But in so doing, it has transgressed its very strong bond with certain freedoms that are incorporated into it. Accordingly, this route, which blocks the dynamic of tests, is adopted only as a last resort because it is not conducive to innovation and mobility, which count among the mainsprings of capitalism. Whenever feasible, it is therefore preferable to opt for a course of low visibility in discreetly circumventing established mechanisms.

In the mid-1970s, one possible strategy would thus have been to attempt to dismantle the rights associated with permanent contracts. Given the wage-earners' high level of mobilization, such a strategy would have been very costly, notably in terms of legitimacy. It was preferable to opt for a multiplication of other forms of contract and possibilities of derogation from the rules of common law, which remained unchanged, while on the other hand strengthening the rights of those with permanent contracts. This created the impression that new social gains were involved, whereas this legal form was becoming less and less attractive to firms given the other possibilities open to them.

Displacements find their initial elements of legitimacy by exploiting differentials between the critical forces

Critique is not monolithic. Thus, we have identified two major critical registers that have pursued their course since the mid-nineteenth century, in different forms and subject to variation: the social critique and the artistic critique. Depending upon the historical conjuncture, they join together or experience tension. In the Introduction, we also saw that the critical emphasis could sometimes be placed on a test's nonconformity with the status order underlying it (a critique that we have called corrective); and sometimes on actually challenging the test, in that it is based on principles of equivalence whose validity is rejected in the kind of situation with which this test is associated (the so-called radical critique). Finally, critique is no more immutable than capitalism. It is displaced in accordance with procedures of extension to new subjects of anxiety as to the fair or unfair character of everyday situations. It can therefore be focused on moments that had not hitherto been formalized in terms of tests, engaging beings whose suffering or unjust condition had not been registered.[16]

Given this plurality, and the fact that critiques are sometimes contradictory, it is possible for displacements in capitalism to answer some demands while circumventing the tests that are of the utmost importance for another aspect of critique. This has the effect of winning a section of the oppositional forces over to the displacements that are under way, and making changes difficult to reverse.

In the period we have studied, it is fairly obvious that displacements in capitalism could not have come about so rapidly, or attained such scope, if they had not exploited the differential between the social critique and the artistic critique. As we have seen, one of the original features of the critical movement that developed in the second half of the 1960s and at the beginning of the 1970s was that it raised with the same intensity two sets of demands articulated by different groups, which were allies or rivals depending upon the circumstances. On the one hand, it demanded a reduction in exploitation and social inequalities, a consolidation of state mechanisms of security, and greater representation of wage-earners in the state – that is to say, an extension of what we have called the civic-industrial compromise. On the other hand, it demanded an abolition of domestic forms of subordination and judgement, of justification and social control, not only outside the family, in firms, but also in the world of private relations, even – particularly with the anti-psychiatry movement – in the family.

In order to circumvent the tests that the social critique had helped to toughen up, and wanted to strengthen further (the civic–industrial compromise), a number of displacements used the artistic critique. Thus, for example, faced with the growing demand for autonomy in work, the most realistic and profitable response consisted not in trying to raise the level of control by increasing the weight of hierarchy and accounting mechanisms but, on the contrary, in reducing the length of chains of hierarchy and proceeding in the direction of satisfying libertarian-looking demands, which helped to substitute self-control for external control. Translated into the terms of the artistic critique – autonomy, spontaneity, authenticity, self-fulfilment, creativity, life – many displacements could be interpreted, including by at least some of those who implemented them, as resulting from a recognition of the validity of the critical position by a capitalism that was finally enlightened, and whose openness and modernism conferred on it a novel legitimacy. This helped to mask the dismantling of the links between the world of work and the civic world. On the other hand, in order to eradicate domestic values from workplaces, new tests also had to be offered that did not refer to them, thus circumventing those established tests which relied on the recognition of hierarchical distances and personal dependencies or loyalties.

As we have seen (Chapter 3), circumvention of the tests that mattered for the social critique was also facilitated by changes affecting the autonomous history of critique when – at the end of the 1970s, and especially in the 1980s – the decay of the Communist Party assumed unprecedented proportions. This indirectly contributed to discrediting the social critique in the view of a large number of actors (including former Marxists), because its modes of expression and the kinds of organization it had relied on now appeared to be irredeemably bound up with the rhetoric and bureaucracy of the PCF, and hence found themselves proscribed. For a time the artistic critique remained the only legitimate critique.

If the artistic critique thus directly contributed to undoing the industrial-domestic compromise that had been preserved in the previous period, it also served as a lever for uncoupling capitalism from the state. Focused on the exigency of liberation and the demand for 'authentic' human relations, it equally helped – on the basis of a radical critique of that traditional institution *par excellence*, the family – to strengthen the anti-institutional dispositions of the protest forces, which could now direct their efforts to other subjects.

Thus the artistic critique was directed towards criticism of that other weighty institution: the state.

The social critique of the 1930s, which had contributed to the formation of the second spirit of capitalism, had taken the anarchic character of capitalism, dominated by private interests, as its main target. By way of remedy, it proposed planning and regulation under state auspices. The social circumstances of the 1960s and 1970s were quite different, since the demands of the earlier period had been partially satisfied, with the establishment in the postwar years of the Commissariat au Plan and, more generally, of the institutions of the welfare state. The 1960s were marked by Gaullist *dirigisme*, and the strengthening of the links between state personnel and that of the major firms. This *rapprochement* occurred in tandem with an optimistic belief in the convergence of economic progress and social progress, which was supposed to bring about a 'waning of ideology' in the face of increasing technical skills. This marked the zenith of the second spirit.

Accordingly, rather than contrasting the deregulation of private capitalism with state planning, one of the ways in which the revival of the social critique occurred from the mid-1960s to the mid-1970s was precisely by taking as its target the coupling of the state and capitalism (denounced under the term, notably, of 'state monopoly capitalism'). Capitalism had dissolved into the state and enlisted the welfare state in its service, with the result that the social advances derived from an earlier configuration of critique no longer represented an obstacle to the revival of critique. In this new perspective, which broke with the statist progressivism of the postwar years, Renault – symbol of the great national firm – was basically no better than Peugeot – embodiment of the old family capitalism.

But this new critique needed an external support other than liberalism, which was likewise opposed to 'unnatural' alliances between state and market. It was to find it in the ultra-left, in the anti-authoritarian and anti-hierarchical tradition of the artistic critique which, set upon denouncing 'domination' rather than 'exploitation', made it possible to merge in a single gesture a rejection of all institutions (including the established trade unions and the Communist Party). Rather than being regarded as an instrument of protection against the ('arbitrary') domination of the strongest, and hence also exploitation, the state was thus denounced not only as a servant of capitalism – a critique that Marxism had directed at the liberal state from the outset – but also as a central apparatus of oppression and exploitation, either directly or by means of 'ideological state apparatuses' – justice, cultural institutions, and especially schools and universities – according to Althusser's formula, oft repeated in the 1970s.

We may thus advance the hypothesis that capitalism's displacements relied mainly on demands for liberation – not only to the extent that circumvention of the tests hitherto regarded as essential in itself generated a liberating effect, especially among new entrants, but also as a result of the embedding of an emancipatory project in capitalism. These factors rendered the artistic critique particularly suited to accompany and legitimate the displacements, at least in its historical formulations, which privilege liberation over authenticity.

A displacement making use of a legitimacy derived from taking demands formulated in terms of justice into account seems less likely. For it would presuppose a heightened level of reflexivity, as well as a labour of categorization and codification, all of which takes time. Similarly, a response to demands for security seems difficult to deliver by means of a displacement, since such demands become established only when the risks associated with the new forms of freedom have been widely acknowledged.

The neutralization of the critique of established tests under the impact of displacements

Capitalism's displacements, and the many changes in the most daily of mechanisms that accompanied them, helped to disarm critique. On the one hand, they satisfied certain requirements articulated by one aspect of critique, without which, as we have seen, displacements would be more difficult and costly to implement. On the other hand, they baffled the critical forces attached to the defence of established tests. Displacements present critical forces with a world on which they have much less purchase: in the cognitive order, because they no longer know how to interpret it; and in the practical order, because they no longer know which mechanisms to attach themselves to in order to act on it.

Displacements have the particular effect of transposing tests from situations where there is a comparative symmetry of purchase between the different partners (the role of categorization and regulation is precisely to further the creation of such symmetry and, in particular, the purchase that depends on the level of information) to situations where purchase is distributed in highly asymmetrical fashion between the representatives of management and those of wage-earners. The critique and critical apparatuses associated with an earlier state of forms of social selection actually have little purchase on the new tests, which have not been subject to a labour of recognition, institutionalization and codification.

Initially relying on well-tried normative forms, corresponding to earlier orders of legitimacy, denunciation and rebellion consequently lag behind the state of the tests that have issued from displacements, and on this account can always be disqualified as conservative, reactionary and backward-looking.

Many commentators thus disqualified the strikes or protest movements of recent years, which sought to base their legitimacy on the defence of public services, collective agreements, qualification grids, or systems of social protection.

Working-class reactions to the rise of capitalist forms of exploitation in the nineteenth century likewise afford numerous examples of critique lagging behind, and its propensity to rely on outmoded forms to articulate resistance in periods of rapid change in modes of testing. Thus, as the meticulous analyses of William Sewell have shown, before 1848 it was primarily in the language of guilds, of the old solidarities of corporations, that French artisans and workers sought to interpret the deterioration in their condition accompanying industrialization, to formulate demands, and to establish mechanisms for mutual aid and (often violent) protest, such as friendly societies or guild societies, organizational forms whose boundaries were blurred. It was only in the weeks that followed the July revolution that 'they became clearly aware of the limitations of their [corporate] idiom', and that they undertook to fashion a new language by means of a 'creative adaptation of the rhetoric of the French Revolution',[17] notably by beginning to make a pejorative use, hitherto unknown, of the terms 'exploit', 'exploiter' and 'exploitation'.

Critical mechanisms are established with difficulty, at the cost of great sacrifices and with a delay, in an isomorphic relation with the institutions on which they are intended to have some purchase. This isomorphism is, in a way, the condition of their effectiveness. They thus find themselves caught unawares by any rapid change in the modes of organization and forms of justification of the world to which they had to stick closely in order to become a party.

> Mass trade unionism was thus established from the standpoint of the large firm, at once in opposition to and in tune with the bourgeois values of order, work and progress, coinciding with the major industrial concentrations of planned capitalism in its fascination with bureaucratic forms of administration. But when the people one is addressing are no longer concentrated in vast workshops in close physical proximity, no longer have the same official status, are not legally dependent upon the same employers, are caught up in chains of constraints such that their own survival depends on their ability to transfer the constraint on to others, who are possibly weaker, then it becomes very difficult to stage mobilizations on the basis of highlighting proximity in work, similarity of condition, and solidarity between workers.

For the same reasons, the calculation centres on which critique could rely to challenge the employers' justifications, or make counter-proposals, have likewise become ineffective. In fact, the reasons why capitalism's displacements lead to critical mechanisms losing their purchase are not only organizational in kind, but also – and inseparably – have to do with accounting. Among the numerous asymmetries that place wage-earners in a weak position *vis-à-vis* managements, one of the main ones stems from the ability to define account-ing parameters and orchestrate them into calculation centres, to use Bruno Latour's phrase.[18] The management of firms has a quasi-monopoly on this. Accounting frameworks, in which forces are converted into money, conse-quently represent one of the main subjects of dispute between capital and labour.[19]

Critical mechanisms succeed in influencing the accounting framework only at the cost of considerable struggle and – albeit to a very unequal degree, depending on the country and the state's role in regulating social relations – by taking the form of a generally valid legal change. This requires them to find allies in the state, or exert sufficient pressure on it. Yet this already presup-poses that the critical bodies possess calculation centres independent of those over which directorates and management exercise their power. The establish-ment of such alternative calculation centres is long and costly, the information is difficult to gather and to verify. Its collection therefore has to rely on observers who are differently placed and in a position to make concurrent reports, so as to construct a general picture, and on mechanisms for super-vising the way tests unfold on the ground. A test might formally conform to the rules while contravening them in practice, if no one is there to verify the relation between the test on paper, in the report on it made by management, and what actually transpired.

One of the most obvious effects of the displacements has been to render the supervision of tests on the ground much more difficult (for organizational reality has itself been diversified, particularized, fragmented – see Chapter 4). And it has also made the accumulation of data formated in such a way that it can be published in a reliable, convincing framework much more difficult.

The introduction of the welfare state cannot be dissociated from the estab-lishment of new accounting mechanisms that make it possible to employ the notion of value added, and facilitate calculation at a national level, as well as in the case of each firm, of the wages/profits division. But the fragmenta-tion of large, integrated firms into groups of small firms calling on numerous subcontracting services has made this accounting framework less effective. The multiplication of small calculation centres (as well as firms) has thus had the effect of obscuring the major divisions made over the whole of a pro-duction line (a 'branch', as it would be called in the language of the second spirit of capitalism). The 'breaking-up of capital into separate legal entities' has in fact proceeded in tandem with the preservation of a high level of inte-gration of the 'structure of information' on the managerial side.[20] For wage-earners, in contrast, the available information has become dispersed and the horizon restricted to the direct unit of integration, which is legally the direct employer, but without any decision-making autonomy. This situa-tion explains why we have introduced into the mechanisms of the projective

city those that aim to combine all the components of a network into an identifiable whole (see Chapter 6).

Similarly, it may be held that the accounting framework is likewise no longer
appropriate for financial institutions, as a result of the invention of 'derivative
products' that resemble so many displacements. For one of their advantages –
and by no means the least of them – for banks subject to the Cooke ratio is
that they represent so many off-balance-sheet commitments, which consequently escape supervision. Such is the information deficit on the markets that
no one is in a position precisely to evaluate the general risk that these new
financial products entail for the global economy, in particular as a result of
commitments that far exceed the creditworthiness of the signatories.

The development by large firms of branches abroad has also had the effect
of giving them a kind of invisibility and greatly complicating the attribution
of responsibility to bodies represented by readily identifiable persons, the
anticipation and identification of strategic decisions, and the traceability of
their effects.

Once in train, the displacements also contribute to dismantling critique by
mere virtue of the fact that they render it ineffective, which discredits bodies
invested with a counter-power in the view of the very people who expected
defence and protection from them. As the displacements occur, those who do
not follow, who do not understand, for whom nothing works any more, but
who still place their trust in the established tests, are amazed, distressed, or
wax indignant. The effects of this indignation are transferred on to the supervised tests of status (made extremely strict by a long cycle of critiques and
justifications) that have now been rendered obsolete, and on to their critical
mechanisms inasmuch as they continue to credit them with an importance
they no longer possess.

> This is how, at least in part, the decline of trade unionism over recent years
> is to be understood. Still focused on the key tests of a system of industrial
> relations that has been circumvented and outflanked on all sides, trade
> unionism loses its credibility, including among wage-earners. This then seems
> to confirm the view of those who regard it as now nothing more than the
> corporatist instrument of a small category of the privileged at work, cut off
> from the real world, the world as it is, the world such as it has become.

Critique is less mobile than capitalism. Critical bodies do not possess the initiative of displacement. They have weak calculating centres. Their mode of
action is direct, through strikes or a refusal to work – but also, and above all,
indirect, by means of the law, which imparts a certain inertia to them. Reliance
on the law to defend the interests of the weakest stamps the critical
organizations with a kind of conservatism that is alien to capitalism.

The recovery of accumulation and the redeployment of capitalism

The displacement of tests, the dismantling of critique, and the establishment of a new, asymmetrically distributed purchase on the world – these open up the opportunity for a recovery of accumulation and a restoration of profits. In circumventing the most categorized and supervised tests, capitalist accumulation emancipates itself from the fetters imposed on it by the constraint of the common good.

We see this process at work in the 1980s when, under the cover of a discourse on the 'crisis', the forms of the capitalist universe were reorganized at the same time as accumulation picked up again, which increased the share of profits in the distribution of value added.

The destructive effects of displacements and the imperilment of capitalism itself

Liberation from the constraints of the common good hitherto imposed by the prevailing spirit of capitalism, while it favours an unfettered resumption of accumulation, also has destructive effects. There is a strong chance that an unsupervised capitalism could be the source of different types of disaster: inequalities, unemployment, illness caused by work or by defective consumer products, and so on. Released from control, without constraints, capitalism knows no criteria except the private interests of the strongest, and has no reason to take account of the general interest. No 'invisible hand' now intervenes to guide it when the institutions and agreements without which the market cannot function collapse.[21]

Such historical moments, which may legitimately be characterized as 'revolutionary', are marked by profound alterations in the social world. Some groups disappear, while others form. Displacement of the tests brings sudden changes in social conditions: various worlds collapse, families break up, professions disappear, districts empty out, people leave, are ruined, commit suicide, fall into a decline, lose all their resources; while other actors, hitherto regarded as not being up to much, enjoy dazzling success.

Nineteenth-century literature has described all this a hundred times, haunted as it was by the effects, simultaneously mysterious (ever more poor in an increasingly wealthy world) and unbelievably destructive, associated with the development of industry and the rise of the 'liberal credo'.[22] The prevailing circumstances of the 1990s were likewise marked by the coexistence of a revived capitalism and a social world where the growth of inequalities, unemployment, poverty, uncertainty about the future (notably in the case of children), and difficulty in making sense of the present brought about a profound demoralization, whose expressions can be seen at work in the indicators of anomie (see Chapter 7).

Such a development, characterized by a disjunction between a growth in profits to the benefit of a limited number of people and an accumulation of problems that were sources of despondency for a majority of others, harbours a risk for capitalism.

The risks run by capitalism if its functioning is not once again framed by constraints established with reference to various external requirements of the common good are of several sorts. First and foremost, they involve the possibility of people disengaging. Even if it is temporarily stimulated by the surge in speculative profits, the accumulation process cannot proceed without the active participation of the greatest possible number of actors, mobilized either as workers or creators of new products, or as consumers, or as investors whose confidence can be maintained only if they reckon themselves sufficiently protected from systemic risks. For although it represents its own norm, in order to proceed, accumulation must – and this is its paradox – be deeply embedded in a social fabric that it is forever tearing apart when the logic it follows operates outside of any external control. This disengagement, however, is likely to affect different categories of wage-earners unequally, depending on the advantages they might derive from the reorganization of capitalism.

Thus, *cadres*, from whom (as we have seen) a high level of commitment was invariably demanded, can subscribe for a fairly extended period to a mode of operation which, in prioritizing entrepreneurial skills, offers them, especially when they are young, rather exciting prospects in terms of personal development (and also the hope of financial bonuses). And this is the case even if, in a number of instances, their present condition is predominantly characterized by an increased workload, without compensation in terms of wages. On the other hand, there is a risk that *cadres* today will be less attentive to the damage done by managerial practices than their predecessors were, in the forms of capitalism associated with the second spirit. With the autonomization of the units for which they are responsible, systemic constraints weigh on them more directly. Moreover – since they have fewer hierarchical responsibilities, and exercise direct control over subordinates less often on a face-to-face basis, but take on financial, design or sales responsibilities increasingly frequently – they are less subject to demands for justification.

Yet even in their case, especially when it comes to wage-earners with less autonomy, current levels of engagement – which, taken at face value, might seem high – derive from forces and mechanisms whose effects might very well diminish with time. These forces are, in the first instance, of the order of constraints – in particular, the constraint imposed by unemployment. But with the demoralization that it is bound to create, fear of unemployment risks ultimately inducing withdrawal. This may take the form either of retirement from the labour market and a retreat into not very lucrative activities situated outside the commodity sphere; or of a psychological withdrawal at work, entailing forms of 'resistance'[23] that are comparable, although they will certainly take different forms, to the braking processes which represented one means of resistance to Taylorism.

Moreover, many of the social technologies on which the engagement of human beings at work currently relies require workers to be replenished and the young to be recruited (see Chapter 4). Now, if the very rigour of the selection process at first glance constitutes a factor of engagement (those who have been selected, or survived, have the gratifying feeling that they have been chosen from out of a thousand), the aspirations created by the sense of election can only be disappointed in the more or less long term, when, in the absence of a career, the 'happy chosen few' realize that it is very difficult for them to improve their starting conditions. It is therefore very possible that resistance will be transformed into active protest, open revolt – individual or collective, depending upon the state of the critical organizations – or even into violence, of a sufficiently high level to fetter production.

A second type of risk derives from the dealignment of capitalism and the state introduced by the displacements. Capitalism has never been able to survive without relying on the state, and it cannot do so today either. It is political power, for example, that guarantees respect for property rights; it is the state that possesses the means of coercion which ensure respect – certainly for the recognized rights of workers, but also for the interests of firms and the contracts they sign.

The current crisis of the state is to be closely associated with recent developments in capitalism. In effect, one of the means by which capitalism emerged from the crisis that threatened it in the 1970s was to transfer responsibility for the damage and risks entailed by the accumulation process on to the state and, consequently, to increase the insurance role of the state as payer of last resort (see Chapter 4). This applies to unemployment, deterioration in the health of casualized workers, the increased insecurity bound up with the development of illegal markets,[24] but also, in other respects, to industrial and environmental risks.

The welfare state already represented a kind of 'last resort' for capitalism. On the other hand, however, it had at its disposal means of imposing significant constraints upon the forms of accumulation, such that the complementary character of capitalism and the state could be relatively balanced. It was this balance that was called into question when capitalism recaptured a margin of manoeuvre and put itself in a position to escape the coercive power of the state in large measure. This dynamic was based upon the deregulation of financial markets, which reduced the margin of financial manoeuvre possessed by states, and on the developing internationalization of large firms. The establishment of new 'network' forms of organization renders firms more flexible, and much less fragile than large national firms were and states still are.[25] Thus, in a large number of countries, we witness the development of a capitalism that is increasingly powerful and autonomous with respect to states which are ever weaker, containing a minority of citizens who are flourishing and a growing number of people in difficulty.

The impoverishment brought about by capitalism's displacements constitutes another risk factor, in the shape of a reduction in consumption (which is insufficiently compensated for by the growing market in luxury products), or the development of criminal activities presenting opportunities for enrichment no longer offered by capitalism. A capitalism that is no longer accompanied by an increase in the standard of living, especially of the poorest, loses its credibility. It can still rely on a promise of emancipation (or on the fear of a halt to, or regression in, the process of emancipation). But satisfaction of the demand for emancipation (understood in the broad sense, and not only with reference to political liberties) equally takes the form of goods, and hence the distribution of purchasing power.

In these conditions, the construction of a new spirit of capitalism becomes necessary not only from a humanist viewpoint – in order to limit the suffering produced by an unbridled capitalism – but also from a standpoint that is, as it were, internal to the accumulation process, whose continuation it is a question of ensuring.

However, the risks run by an unconstrained capitalism are mitigated by converse mechanisms, the main one being the constant entry of new actors as consumers or as producers, whose expectations have not yet been disappointed. These factors make it difficult to foresee a 'point of no return', beyond which the very pursuit of the accumulation process would find itself in question.

> The existence of a reserve army, available in the Third World, the emerging countries or the ex-communist countries, favours the displacements and revival of capitalism. For despite the despondency or rebellion of those whose hopes have been disappointed, others can always be found to embark on the adventure in their turn.
>
> As for insecurity, to take another example, its consequences for the functioning of capitalism can always be limited by inscribing networks in the materiality of the territory. Such is the case when protected residential districts are linked by means of private roads to office towers kept under close surveillance, from which capital can be moved around and the world acted on from a distance; or again, when closed-off luxury tourist 'paradises', under

the protection of paramilitary brigades, in poverty-stricken islands in the West Indies are linked to the rest of the world by private airports. The tolerance of the privileged for the decaying of public spaces can thus extend quite a long way.

The example of the interwar period in Europe indicates, however, that the continuation of the capitalist order is not necessarily inevitable, and that crises and political changes can occur which are so radical that the assets accumulated and the economic goods required for the pursuit of accumulation are endangered.

The role of critique in the identification of dangers

The dangers capitalism runs when it can deploy itself unconstrained, destroying the social substratum on which it thrives, have a palliative in its ability to listen to criticism. No doubt this is the main factor in its robustness since the nineteenth century. The critical function (voice), which has no place within the capitalist firm, where regulation is supposed to be performed exclusively by competition (exit), can be exercised only from without. Hence it is critical movements that inform capitalism about the dangers threatening it. Their role is made all the more necessary by capitalism's tendency to elude market regulation and hence regulation by competition (exit), which is expressed today by the construction of networks. But this type of regulation through conflict occurs at a very high price, predominantly paid by those who take responsibility for critique and lend it their voices.

Critique is all the more likely to be taken into account when capitalism's response cannot simply consist in flight, by moving to countries where the level of criticism is lower. The argument of the *border* – used by Sombart to explain why socialism had not developed in the United States, and according to which the transition to the status of farmer in the virgin lands of the American West absorbed the most oppositional working-class elements – is also valid for capitalism itself, which is prompted to listen to criticism only when it is impossible simply to flee it.[26] It will be noted, however, that the brakes on relocation are not only physical. They can also take the form of *loyalty* and – in the case of states, regions or local communities – an attachment that (without necessarily having the exclusive, aggressive and expansionist character of nationalisms) can tend to discourage flight, and consequently favour taking account of criticism.

Given the significance in neo-capitalism of the requirement of mobility, and the constant efforts by the different parties to offload the burden of economic activities on to less mobile actors who will bear all the risk (see Chapter 6), it may be thought that at the end of the twentieth century the capitalist firms controlled from France are less disposed to listen to criticism than they are in other places where collective values are stronger, or were during periods of the development of the productive apparatus and the domestic market (or, as exemplified by the postwar years, reconstruction). The price to be paid by critique for making itself heard is liable to be all the higher.

Even so, capitalism's reflexivity can be counted on to enable it to register the danger signals that are sent to it. It is in fact equipped with mechanisms of vigilance other than automatic market reflexes: bodies which supervise and orchestrate the market so that prices contain maximum information, calcula-tion centres that provide information on the state of critique, or co-ordinating bodies.

Employers' organizations, think tanks, management works, as well as the con-sultants who circulate organizational innovations – these act as so many co-ordinating bodies. As for calculation centres, it is sometimes those pertain-ing to critique that set off the alarm signals. Thus, in the 1970s, the sociology of work, trade unionism and social classes was denounced from leftist posi-tions, on the grounds that its main role was supposedly to inform bodies linked to the employers about the state of critique and, by providing expert infor-mation on wage-earners, to further the establishment of mechanisms for supervising and setting people to work. In Chapter 3, we saw that such a crit-icism was partially valid, even if the sociology of work has also made a significant contribution to the formulation of the critique of capitalism.

The way capitalism takes account of criticism therefore depends on the char-acter of the various bodies that make it possible to reduce the tension between the interests of entrepreneurs in so far as they engage in competition (which leads them to ignore criticism) and their interests inasmuch as they are united behind the functioning of the system as a whole (which prompts them to take account of protests in their political formulations).

The change over time in the main concerns of groups or bodies like employ-ers' federations and study circles, the OECD, the Trilateral Commission, the G7, and so on, is an excellent indicator of the efforts made by the reflexive bodies of the capitalist world to respond to criticism, either by integrating it or by dismissing it – which, even so, obliges them to construct justifications. At the international level, recent years have thus seen a proliferation of studies intended to invalidate any role of globalization in the decline in wages in the most industrialized countries, and to develop a concern with environmental risks and the protection of investments. These are so many 'risks' that have been taken on by capitalism's co-ordinating bodies, and on which they are working; this does not mean that they are in a position to identify them on their own, still less to resolve them.

The fact that capitalism hears the criticism does not, however, mean that it responds in concrete terms by changing its *modus operandi*. The initial reaction might simply consist in establishing arguments intended to dismiss criticism, rather than studying measures to amend the process it challenges.

The revival of critique

Through its displacements capitalism reorganizes itself, emancipating itself from critique. But the advantage thus secured consists in gaining time, not in a definitive victory. Even ignoring factors on the side of critique that favour its durability, the destructive effects of an unconstrained capitalism by themselves creative favourable terrain for the revival of critique. And this is so even if the moment and manner of the reversal depend upon the historical conjuncture and, consequently, are unpredictable, so that its manifestation is invariably greeted as a 'surprise' invalidating the predictions and projections of specialists in the future.

> We have seen (Chapter 6) how a kind of distressed astonishment, quickly transformed into indignation, was the response at the end of the 1980s and in the 1990s to the destructive effects of an evolution presented in the first half of the 1980s as simultaneously inevitable, because it was imposed by forces that were irrepressible and external to any political volition (globalization), and desirable, because it was orientated – all things considered, but in the long run – in the direction of progress.

The resumption of critique often occurs in the first instance from an anachronic position: by judging the present in the light of ideals that proved themselves in the past. More precisely, critique then takes the form of a conservative defence of the established tests that earlier social movements had helped to make stricter (or more just).

In a second stage, faced with the seemingly ineluctable character of this inversion in orders of status, critical vigilance is directed towards a search for the reasons for such a phenomenon – that is to say, more precisely, towards the identification of the new tests and the hidden surplus forces ensuring success. Gradually, interpretative schemas are reconstructed that make it possible to make sense of the changes that are under way, paving the way for a more precise critique of the new tests and the formulation of demands and proposals whose horizon is justice.

> Following the silence of the 1980s, the kind of social critique that tended to resurface in France at the beginning of the 1990s is thus not a direct logical extension of the 1970s critique, inspired in the main by Marxism – at least, not in its rhetorical methods. As for its most original aspects, it relies on the

humanitarian movement that developed at the turn of the 1980s and 1990s, and also on the thematic of *citizenship* and *rights*, in part inspired by radical Anglo-American thought, itself liberal in inspiration, which stresses an imperative of non-discrimination in access to those public goods that are regarded as basic, more than it does equality. Given the deconstruction of the forms of critique that had dominated the 1970s and the waning, even discrediting, of a number of the apparatuses that had provided its basis, critique was able to discover a new lease of life only in a sort of direct relationship with suffering (see Chapter 6).[27] In a period like the second half of the 1980s – marked by the arrival in positions of power of a number of critical actors from the 1970s, and by their social success in many spheres, from the academy to the media or even enterprise – reconstruction of a credible critique[28] in effect took the form of a relative refusal of discourse, particularly theoretical discourse, in favour of a direct engagement with those most profoundly affected by the destructive impact of capitalism's displacements.

This shift from a stance dominated by solidarity with the suffering of others, even by charity, to a stance of protest and struggle had already been witnessed in the case of the formation of the workers' movement in the second half of the nineteenth century, especially in Great Britain. This movement was constructed largely on the basis of friendly societies, cultural education associations, or even societies aiming at a moralization of behaviour (struggle against alcoholism, exhortation to save, etc.). Moreover, the intensification of social conflict in the years 1870–90 was to lead to police supervision of these associations, and often their proscription, in Great Britain, France and Germany.[29]

The search for new interpretative schemas was conducted together with the representatives of firms, consultants and those responsible for training the people who already worked there or would soon join them: they cannot retain their credibility for very long if they do not offer a map of the new world.

Thus, normative discourses and critical analyses gradually converged on the metaphor of the network which, although initially developed in complete autonomy from the capitalist process, found itself mobilized by it (see Chapters 1 and 2). On what remained of the civic–industrial and domestic–industrial compromise was established the kind of world that we have dubbed connexionist, rather than a market strictly speaking. Here, the network not only became a key support for connecting people in the labour market,[30] but was also the best metaphor for representing the condition that the social world seemed to be headed for. This was especially true in countries like France, which had no liberal tradition and did not possess enough of a liberal idiom to establish a coherent, justifiable interpretation of the changes over the last thirty years on such a basis.

If critique shares much of the representation of the world derived from capitalism's displacements with its representatives, its vocation is to point to what is unjust in this new world – that is to say, for example, how those who succeed in it possess more goods and resources than they would deserve in a just world, or how those who fail in it did not have the same chances of success at the outset. Critique's specific contribution is similar to a theory of exploitation tailored to the new world, which makes it possible to link the good fortune of the great men to the misfortune of the little people, and to instil in the former a sense of responsibility for the lot of the less privileged. In the absence of this link made by critique, it is not clear how a different world could be achieved that is less destructive of human destinies (not to mention 'resources').

> The difficulties in constructing such a theory of exploitation are especially significant today, as a result of the deindividualization of capitalism. Already appreciable in the case of managerial capitalism (in contrast to the readily identifiable employer in family capitalism), they are exacerbated by the importance of impersonal capital (for example, pension funds) and by the increase in the number of small shareholders (so-called 'popular' share ownership). Even if the number of those who exercise controlling power over financial circuits is still just as limited, the discretion of these servants of a system whose professionals they are (by the same token, for example, as meteorologists are specialists in climatic phenomena), and the proliferation of middlemen make it difficult to pinpoint the adversary – that is to say, those who are ultimately responsible for the misery of the most deprived.

The revival of critique accompanies – but always after some delay – the appearance of new kinds of protest mechanisms more attuned to the emergent forms of capitalism, in accordance with the principle that critique, in seeking to be effective, tends to become isomorphic with the objects it is applied to.

> This is the way to interpret the new movements, such as the 'co-ordinations' of the late 1980s, or Droits devant!!, AC!, Droit au logement, and so on, that sprang up in France in the 1990s, and which, in a break with the established forms of the workers' movement, developed by relying on schemas – particularly the figure of the network – that also underlay the new managerial regime that emerged in the 1980s (see Chapter 6).
>
> It might also be thought that the growing importance of multinational firms, of practices of direct relocation or relocation via the development of subcontracting, as well as the increasing interdependence of economic policies, would revive designs to internationalize critical movements, which faded in the postwar decades dominated by Keynesian policies within the framework of nation-states. The lagging of critique behind capitalism is still

patent here: capitalism internationalizes itself more readily and rapidly than the movements opposed to it, whose unification presupposes a prolonged, arduous effort to create parity between the forms of classification with which people identify and the values that set them in motion.

In phases of reorganization, the revival of critique is made more difficult by the fact that changes in capitalism have undermined the justifications which served as a mobilizing basis in an earlier state. The kinds of justification associated with the form taken by the spirit of capitalism in the preceding period are in crisis, without a new 'spirit' having as yet fully materialized.

Capitalist accumulation has indeed revived, but at the price of a legitimacy deficit. At the same time, deprived of the grounds and incentives that hitherto sustained their participation in the accumulation process and the pursuit of profit, a growing number of people find themselves plunged into a state of dissatisfaction and anxiety, which predisposes them to be receptive to critique.

The construction of new mechanisms of justice

When it exerts sufficient pressure, the revival of critique leads to the creation of new normative fulcra with which capitalism must compromise. This compromise asserts itself in the expression of a new form of the spirit of capitalism which, like those preceding it, contains exigencies of justice and which, in order to sustain its claims to legitimacy, must rely on very general orders of justification, which we have identified under the name of cities.

If new mechanisms of justice are to be established, and test procedures are to be respected, an external force is required – law, backed up by an apparatus of coercion that has hitherto belonged to states. In other words, the possibility of capitalism constraining itself does not depend only on the force of critique. It also depends on the force of the states on which it is reliant ensuring that those responsible for its functioning are bound to their promise of self-restriction, and respect contractual provisions that involve not only the interests of the parties, but also the common good.

Influenced by the revival of the social critique in the mid-1990s, a number of mechanisms are being discussed (see Chapter 6), whose implementation would, in all likelihood, render the connexionist world less unjust.

It might likewise be thought that a responsible public policy would be to help ensure the conditions of possibility for critique to exercise such vigilance, by allowing those who suffer most from the new conditions to be represented in political debate, and subsidizing independent centres of calculation able to construct and diffuse data about the effects of the dramatic change in the world in the sphere of neo-capitalism. The need for reliable information on the behaviour of multinationals, on the situation of the poorest in the developed countries and the Third World, on infringements of people's liberty and dignity produced by the commodification of everything, is felt more keenly than ever.[31] Over the last thirty years, such independent centres have, despite their feeble resources, played a vital role in the constitution of new rights.[32]

The formation of cities

Depending on the historical conjuncture – that is to say, depending on the direction taken by earlier displacements and the nature of the tests that are to be limited and justified – the establishment of new mechanisms of justice might be able to base itself upon the formation of new types of compromise between already established cities, deployed in arguments and inscribed in the world of objects (for example, a compromise between industrial and commercial worlds). Alternatively, it will have to be established and backed up by the formulation of new cities and their inscription in new mechanisms.

Inasmuch as new tests that cannot be described in the evaluative topics used hitherto (for example, in industrial, commercial, or domestic terms) have emerged, and new forms of exploitation have become apparent, the need to establish a different evaluative topic – a new 'city' – has made itself felt. It is thus that we have been led to model the projective city to account for the quite specific forms of justice that seem to us to be in the process of being established, in order to impart meaning and justice to everything in the world which refers to connexionist arrangements and which, in the absence of the formation of this city, cannot be controlled in terms of justice.

Cities are metaphysical political entities[33] which, by the same token as cultures or languages, have a historical existence, and can therefore be situated in time and space. Accordingly, it is relevant to grasp them in their life-span, their evolution, from the moment of their formation, via their entrenchment in mechanisms, objects and law, up to their recession.[34] At a given historical moment, a form of existence is identified and generalized in such a way as to serve as a support for a definition of the common good and a criterion for judgements about the value of beings, according to the contribution they make to the good of all thus conceived. Even when they are grasped synchronically, at a given moment in time, cities consequently bear the trace of the period when the form of existence that each of them takes as a model and evaluative criterion was autonomized and prioritized as such.

Take, for example, the commercial city. Commercial activities, which possess a universal character, obviously precede the emergence of legitimate justifications based on the market. For the market to serve as a yardstick of a form of the common good, commercial activity must be regarded as valid in itself, not simply for the contribution it might make to status in other worlds (the grandeur of the Prince, the power of the Church, etc.). Such an autonomization is furthered if people emerge whose activity is sufficiently specialized and equipped with specific mechanisms and objects, whose relations are sufficiently dense, and whose social role is sufficiently important for their form of existence to be subject to a collective labour of stylization and justification. For example, it is difficult to envisage the formation of a justification grounded in the market without an exceptional growth in commercial activities, and in the number and power of merchants relative to the other classes in society. Thus it was that the journeymen who extricated themselves from the power of the guilds in Paris at the end of the eighteenth century, to set themselves up as independent workers in the suburbs (exposing them to legal proceedings), developed arguments of a new type to defend themselves against the charge, levelled at them by the masters, that outside guild discipline there would be nothing to protect the quality of work. The justifications developed by the artisans, who knew nothing of what was in the process of becoming, under the name of political economy, the moral science of the market, referred to the commercial character of their activity, to the competition engaged in by manufacturers of the same products, to the freedom of choice enjoyed by buyers, and to their effect on quality, prices, and so on. Commercial activity thus achieves a dignity of its own by becoming autonomous *vis-à-vis* the principles of a domestic morality.[35]

A city thus has a chance of being established when a group of actors, relying on a stable world of mechanisms and objects, sees its power consolidated, in such a way that its members feel that they are in a position to demand exclusive recognition, and pride themselves on a specific contribution to the common good, without having to assert or even excuse the strength acquired in the sphere they excel in by undertaking other, more acceptable virtuous activities. They can then seek to elaborate for themselves, and get others to recognize, a value, a status, which specifically defines the way they have a grip on the world, and give it a moral dimension. It is only then that the work of theoretical formulation is carried out (formerly pertaining to moral and political philosophy, and today, in large measure, to the social sciences) which makes it possible to extend the validity of the values thus identified, and make them the basis for a new form of common good. To put it in the language of *De la justification*, worlds precede cities. And this is so even if the dynamic leading up to the formation of a city may be understood, somewhat in the logic of the hermeneutic circle, as a moment in a process of reflexivity whereby a certain form of existence acquires a meaning, and a certain world equips itself with a coherence and a style.

Thus – to return to the subject of our study – the development of a connexionist world preceded the definition of a projective city. Conception of the mechanisms relevant to a projective city has found support among professionals in mediation, who have proliferated in these last ten years, especially those of them who have developed an activity – whether paid or unpaid, professional or voluntary – as social integration intermediaries, employing techniques that call on network logic. These professionals, who are often led to adopt a reflexive stance on their own activity because they are confronted with a requirement to justify it by relying on an ethic of mediation that is still in gestation, certainly make an especially significant contribution to constructing the conventions on which a projective city rests, and to their entrenchment in reproducible mechanisms.

More generally, it might be thought that actors' specialization in a certain kind of activity is an important element in the formation of a new city. Think, for example, of engineers for the industrial city, or of state administrators for the civic city.

The formation of a city can be described at the most general level by the gradual transition to a regime of categorization. This process is a collective enterprise of regulation of the new tests of strength, derived from a more or less co-ordinated set of displacements, to which legitimacy constraints are then applied. A new city thus has a chance of being established only in historical circumstances where an increase in the speed and number of displacements brings about significant social changes. In this sense, the formation of a new city might equally – and just as validly – be regarded as an operation legitimating a new world and the new forms of inequality or exploitation on which it is based; and as an enterprise aiming to make this world more just by reducing the level of exploitation that it tolerates and, consequently, limiting the profits that those whom it favours can expect. Once a city is established, a more ordered world, comprising great men and little people, replaces a chaotic universe, with its strong and its weak.

Cities are thus simultaneously operators of justification and critical operators. On the one hand, each city serves as a fulcrum for criticizing tests organized in accordance with the logic of a different city. On the other, each displays a critical orientation directed against the bad practices of the specific world containing the reality tests that are pertinent from the standpoint of this city itself.

Thus, the projective city serves at once to criticize 'industrial' or 'civic' arrangements that are deemed insufficiently flexible, and to point out those features of the connexionist world that do not conform to the justice which this world claims as its own. For example, the projective city orchestrates denunciation of the fact that some project head has appropriated the reputation connected with the success of his project wholesale, and has not bothered about the re-engagement in other projects of his collaborators, whose employability he has even reduced by exploiting their skills without seeking to have them acquire others.

Hence the city appears as a *self-referential critical mechanism*, internal to and immanent in a world that is in the process of coming into being, and must limit itself if it is to last. One of the key characteristics of the order of cities is that it puts limits on the strength of the strong and declares them to be great (legitimate, authorized to exhibit and employ their strength) only if they internalize these limits and observe them.

In the domestic world, for example, the great king or good father is primarily he who does not abuse his generational strength, who demonstrates his fairness in the way he treats his sons (or daughters), who does not abuse them, who limits competition with and between them (rights of succession), who does not seek to destroy them in order to preserve his power. ... And the same goes for sons in their competition with fathers for the appropriation of women (of the mother in Freudian mythology). This is the price to be paid if a domestic world is to endure; if an order is to be based on it; if a common good is to be established.

And similarly, the establishment of a civic order, on the basis of the beings known to a political world, assumes that the strong one, whose asset is a capital made up of human beings, does not abuse his strength, which in this case is his capacity to obtain submission; that he employs it not by means of fear but of consent; that he does not behave like a tyrant, and so on. For an order based wholly on fear is not destined to last.

And likewise, the strong one in an inspired world, where the assets are the powers of the beyond, must not seek to control them in such a way as to place them entirely in his own service (magic). For were they to be unbridled, unchecked, they would destroy the very thing they give him power over. And so on and so forth.

In the current period, the constitution of a projective city takes responsibility for legitimating the tests that are effective in a connexionist world, and justifying the new forms of success and failure specific to this world. Thus, the new tests should be validated in all their generality while being subject to constraints. This would limit the level of exploitation.

For all that, this possibility is only one of the outcomes that can be envisaged for the ideological crisis of capitalism. Another possibility, which cannot be excluded either, is increasing degradation in the conditions of existence of the greatest number, rising social inequality, and the generalization of a kind of political nihilism. But in the event of the construction of a new spirit of capitalism, and its entrenchment in enduring mechanisms, the realism of this ideological formation and its mobilizing power will depend largely upon the pertinence and intensity of the pressures that critique has proved able to exert on the order or, to be more precise, the disorder that characterizes current forms of capitalist accumulation.

Notes

1 With respect to the classification of theories of social change undertaken by Raymond Boudon (*Theories of Social Change*, trans. J.C. Whitehouse, Polity Press, Cambridge 1986), the outline model presented here pertains to the *third type*, containing constructions whose particularity consists in emphasizing the *forms of change*. A celebrated example is Thomas Kuhn's *The Structure of Scientific Revolutions* (1962), which distinguishes three phases in the scientific dynamic. Moreover, it happens to be the case that the role assigned in this dynamic to 'anomalies' and conflicts whose subject is taking these anomalies into account, interpreting them and categorizing them, creates a parallel between our model and Kuhn's. Thus, like the anomalies in Kuhn's model, the changes provoked by capitalism's displacements, which favour some actors while plunging others into insecurity and poverty, are initially considered to be atypical, circumstantial and temporary, before being acknowledged in their novel aspects and becoming subject to a labour of interpretation prior to a revival of critique. On the other hand, we have not sought either to establish historical laws (in the sense of Popper's critique), whether tendential (*first type* in Boudon) or structural (*second type*), or even to claim to discover the causes of the change being analysed (*fourth type* in Boudon), as would have been the case, for example, had we undertaken to *explain* the construction of the world as a network by the development of instruments of communication or by the growth in trade.

2 Such a generalization in space seems all the more desirable in that we have deliberately restricted this work to the French case: even when our theoretical elaboration led us to embrace a broader horizon, as in our reflections on exploitation in a network world, our examples have in the main been selected from our own country. This focus on a single nation seemed to be the only way of examining the details of a history that was already highly complex. In addition, some analyses conducted directly at a global level tend to underestimate the significance for the development of economic practices, and the ideological forms of expression accompanying them, of traditions, institutions, law and political conjunctures, which depend mainly upon the framework of the nation-state. To suppress the country level is quasi-automatically to suppress the level that is most operative for thinking about political action in response to the changes affecting societies when the ways of creating capitalist profit are transformed.

3 Following the whole of Western political philosophy since Hobbes at least, Durkheim had already identified the problems posed by the insatiable character of modern societies.

4 For Durkheim, as we saw in Chapter 7, only collective norms can curb the insatiability of human beings, so that it is absolutely unrealistic and dangerous to seek to base a social order (that of capitalism) on the liberation of individual appetites. In order to reconcile our position with Durkheim's, let us state here that we believe that it is quite simply impossible for a person to be motivated exclusively by insatiable selfish interests, except perhaps in some pathological cases, precisely because she or he has been socialized. This is also to say that for Durkheim, the possibility of a world dominated by insatiable individual appetites, assimilated to a kind of mythical state of nature never encountered in reality, has the status of a pure thought experiment.

5 See Thomas Schelling, *The Strategy of Conflict*, Oxford University Press, New York 1960.

6 Unlike the Old Testament prophets invoked by Michael Walzer (*Exodus and Revolution*, Basic Books, New York 1985), who denounce the infidelity of their contemporaries to God's designs, Job is not a critic, even if his rebellion is doubtless the basis of any critical *ethos*.

7   It cannot be dissociated from the constitution of a new social form – the *affaire* form – whose appearance can be dated to the second half of the eighteenth century, during Voltaire's engagement in the defence of people accused of scandalous deeds: blasphemy in the case of the chevalier de la Barre and ritual crime in that of Calas (see Élisabeth Claverie, 'Procès, Affaire, Cause, Voltaire et l'innovation critique', *Politis*, no. 26, 1994, pp. 76–86; and 'La naissance d'une forme politique: l'affaire du chevalier de La Barre', in P. Roussin, ed., *Critique et affaires de blasphème à l'époque des Lumières*, Honoré Champion, Paris 1998).

8   See Laurent Thévenot, 'Un gouvernement par les normes. Pratiques et politiques des formats d'information', in B. Conein and L. Thévenot, eds, *Cognition et information en société*, Éditions de l'EHESS, Paris 1997, pp. 205–42.

9   See Philippe Corcuff, 'Sécurité et expertise psychologique dans les chemins de fer', in L. Boltanski and L. Thévenot, eds, *Justesse et justice dans le travail*, CEE–Presses Universitaires de France, Paris 1989, pp. 307–18.

10   In 1970, three-quarters of the working people from the families of blue-collar workers, farmers or white-collar employees (who had thus attended school between 1950 and 1960) had not progressed beyond the certificate obtained at the end of primary school. Twenty years later, a majority of them (who attended school in the 1970s) had a professional diploma at least, and one in five had the *baccalauréat*. Finally, 10 per cent of them were graduates from higher education. It is certainly true that the different social milieux have all benefited 'in roughly equivalent fashion from the attempt to open things up at each step of the educational system'. But one cannot retrospectively derive an argument from the comparative stability of disparities to deny all positive value to the democratizing efforts undertaken in the 1970s (see Dominique Goux and Éric Maurin, 'Éducation, expérience et salaire. Tendances récentes et évolutions à long terme', *Documents d'études*, no. 4, DARES, Paris 1997).

11   In the spheres of art or science, infringement of the communal rules is less illegitimate, because it can more readily be justified in terms of inspiration than in other domains.

12   This was completely contrary to the way psychoanalysis had been interpreted in the 1930s by writers and artists who had rubbed shoulders with it, particularly the Surrealists, who were fascinated by the forces of the unconscious precisely in so far as they promised liberation from bourgeois realism.

13   The dismantling of domestic arrangements did not, however, occur without meeting hostility from a number of wage-earners, older ones in particular no doubt. Wage-earners' resistance in the 1980s, supported by the trade unions, to the abolition of seniority increments, to which a majority of employers had become hostile (Caroline Grandjean, 'Modalités nouvelles de la rémunération à l'ancienneté', *Travail et emploi*, no. 41, 1989, pp. 7–17), is one indicator among others of the opposition that the elimination of domestic status from the main work situations encountered in the 1970s and 1980s. The early retirement of wage-earners over the age of fifty was the easiest way to deal with the problem posed by those who were formerly 'old servants of the firm', as people still used to say in the 1960s.

14   See Robert Boyer and André Orléan, 'Persistance et changement des conventions', in Orléan, ed., *Analyse économique des conventions*, Paris 1994, pp. 219–47.

15   William Sewell provides numerous examples for the early stages of industrial capitalism: 'Under the old regime, attempts to employ subcontractors, or to put work out to domestic workers, or to produce low-quality standardized goods, or to multiply the division of labor, or to introduce untrained workers into the trade were contrary to the statutes of the corporations and therefore illegal. This did not mean that these practices never occurred, but it did mean that they tended to occur ... on a small scale. ... It was ... because entrepreneurs wanted to evade the strict regulations and high labor costs of the urban corporations that weaving became a predominantly rural industry in the seventeenth and eighteenth centuries. But in the nineteenth century, thanks to the Revolution's abolition of corporations and redefinition of property rights, all these practices became exercises of the legitimate rights of individual proprietors. If an entrepreneur

wished to hire untrained workers to cut out standardized uppers for mass-produced shoes, there was no legal constraint to keep him from hiring them at whatever wage rate he could negotiate. … If such practices were to be limited at all, they could be limited only by the concerted action of workers, who might, of course, be supported in various ways by small masters fearful of the competition of more innovative rivals. But such concerted action was illegal and therefore difficult to organize and hard to sustain. In short, the tables were turned in the nineteenth century: What had been fraudulent practices became the legitimate exercise of individual industry, and what had been legitimate restrictions on the cupidity and fraud of dishonest masters became illegal conspiracies against the rights of property': *Work and Revolution in France: The Language of Labor from the Old Regime to 1848*, Cambridge University Press, Cambridge 1980, p. 159.

16 This was the case with natural entities – animals, landscapes, and so on – whose subjection to industrial constraints was viewed in its violent aspects, leading to the construction of new tests subject to a requirement of justification.

17 Sewell, *Work and Revolution in France*.

18 See Bruno Latour, *Science in Action*, Open University Press, Milton Keynes 1987.

19 We find several examples of these conflicts in the collective work published under the editorship of Anthony Hopwood and Peter Miller on the social history of accounting practices, inasmuch as they contribute to defining the basic social units – such as firms, establishments, departments, services – and relevant actors, and to structuring the framework into which the relations between these actors and their conflict are integrated, especially when it comes to calculating and distributing value added: see *Accounting as Social and Institutional Practice*, Cambridge University Press, Cambridge 1994.

20 See Günther Teubner, 'Nouvelles formes d'organisation et droit', *Revue française de gestion*, November/December 1993, pp. 50–68.

21 See Michel Callon, ed., *The Laws of the Markets*, Blackwell, Oxford 1998.

22 See Karl Polanyi, *Origins of Our Time: The Great Transformation*, Victor Gollancz, London 1945.

23 In transposing Christophe Hélou's analysis of resistance at school (*Entre violence et justice: une sociologie de la résistance à l'école*, sociology thesis, EHESS, Paris 1998), we shall define resistance by reference to the framework outlined by A.O. Hirschman in *Exit, Voice and Loyalty* (Harvard University Press, Cambridge (MA) 1970). Resistance may be defined as a refusal of *loyalty* in situations where criticism (*voice*) is not really possible and withdrawal (*exit*) proves too costly, because the market offers no alternative, as is currently the case in the labour market with the rise in unemployment.

24 See Marie-Angèle Hermite, 'L'illicite dans le commerce international des marchandises', in *L'illicite dans le commerce international, travaux du CREDIMI*, no. 16, 1996.

25 Compare the mobility differential between multinationals and states (Chapter 6). It will also be observed that because states have authority over a territory, they are much more vulnerable to criticism than firms organized in a network. For in such a framework, mobilizations are made easier by the existence of forms of equivalence, and those in charge are more readily identifiable (even if, in the French case, the combined impact of regionalization and the transfer of areas of competence to the European Commission equally tend to increase the opacity of decisions and responsibilities).

26 See Werner Sombart, *Why is there no Socialism in the United States?*, trans. Patricia M. Hocking and C.T. Husbands, Macmillan, London 1976. An example of flight when faced with critique is relocation whenever possible in the face of the environmentalist critique of polluting industries or the storage of waste (which explains, in particular, why critique has become polarized over nuclear energy that could not be sent outside of Europe on account of the non-storable character of electric current).

27 Highly significant in this respect was the work published in 1993 under the direction of Pierre Bourdieu, *The Weight of the World* (trans. P.P. Ferguson *et al.*, Polity Press, Cambridge 1999).

In the respect that interests us here, the main characteristic of this work, composed of a series of interviews preceded by introductory paragraphs presenting the characters and circumstances of the dramas disclosed by the interviews, is the fact that, unlike all the other works hitherto published by this sociologist, it is practically without any meta-discourse or obvious theoretical ambition. Destitution must be presented in its naked reality, in some sense in the singular, and provokes an indignation that is not mediated by a generalizing theoretical apparatus.

28 In effect, in order to be credible, critique must be related to a sacrifice. The existence of a sacrifice is, as it were, the test against which the validity of the critique is measured. Critique always exacts a cost, and those who conduct it often suffer the fate of martyrs. Low, self-interested motives are imputed to them; in interrupting the course of events, they are criticized for damaging the common good; they are accused of being insane (and sometimes driven to the brink of insanity – see Luc Boltanski, *L'amour et la justice comme compétences*, Métailié, Paris 1990). A critique for which no price is paid, or even a critique that seems to bring benefits to those who conduct it – not only financial benefits but also, for example, advantage in terms of official honours (institutional positions, literary or scientific prizes, etc.) or media fame – is scarcely credible, and easily open to denunciation. It can be suspected of being a merely verbal critique, of no consequence in the order of action.

29 See Dick Geary, *European Labour Protest, 1848–1939*, Croom Helm, London 1981, pp. 42–3.

30 See Mark Granovetter, *Getting a Job*, Harvard University Press, Cambridge (MA) 1974.

31 Today, for example, the surveys do not collect information on the percentage of staff who are temporary and/or on call used by each firm in each category of personnel. It is also very difficult to assess the levels of subcontracting and networks: even those of franchises, whose members nevertheless share at least one brand in common, are invisible (see Chapter 4). At an international level, the lack of information is even more significant. We know next to nothing about multinational firms, those superpower structures that create the bulk of world GDP, which lead international trade and dominate research. Whereas the investigative mechanisms should have been strengthened, we have in fact witnessed the sidelining of the United Nations' UNCTC, transferred with reduced means to UNCTAD (see the Prologue). The only information we possess, which is very incomplete, is based upon the financial communications these firms make to world stock markets, but to which unquoted firms are not subject. As for financial markets, they enjoy the utmost opacity.

32 Think only of the activity of Amnesty International in the field of human rights, of ATD–Quart Monde in exclusion, of CERC in the recognition of growing inequalities, not to mention associations with ecological sympathies, which – like CRII–RAD in the case of radioactivity, for example – conduct attentive surveillance of high-risk sites, substituting themselves for the dereliction of the bodies that are officially responsible.

33 In the sense that they rest upon constructions containing two levels: the first is occupied by individual things, whether human beings or objects; the second by conventions that make it possible to establish equivalences which transcend the particularities of persons and things. On the basis of a common axiomatic, each city thus proposes an architecture specifying the qualities of the beings it contains, and thereby defines the contours of a world.

34 In fact, cities contain several temporalities. The *first*, of very long duration, concerns the axiomatic on which the construction of the common good is based, of which we find traces throughout Western political philosophy. There is no reason to suppose that we are not still immersed in this long temporality. This axiomatic is founded on the tension between an axiom of common humanity (a fundamental equivalence between the members of a society in so far as they all belong by the same token to humanity) and a constraint of order (principle of dissimilarity), involving the possibility for people to accede to several orders of status, organized in a scale of values (for a development of this, see Luc Boltanski and Laurent Thévenot, *De la justification. Les économies de la grandeur*, Gallimard, Paris 1991). The *second temporality* concerns the

terms in which the different species of legitimate status (industrial, commercial or civic) are characterized, and the selection of the forms of existence that each of them highlights. These operators for the creation of equivalence are subject to variations according to a shorter temporality as a function of changes which, envisaged from the model of cities, may be regarded as contingent (it might, for example, be a question of changes in technology, in forms of power, in family organization, etc.). The social production of a new city is always possible inasmuch as the list of qualities capable of serving as a basis for a judgement cannot be closed, human beings possessing the capacity for a potential existence in a myriad of relations.

35 See Bartolomé Clavero, *La Grâce du don. Anthropologie catholique de l'économie moderne*, Albin Michel, Paris 1996.

POSTSCRIPT

SOCIOLOGY *CONTRA* FATALISM

We cannot tell, from the preceding analysis, whether capitalism will be induced to set limits to itself, or whether its untrammelled expansion will continue, with the attendant destructive effects. We believe we have shown that the answer to this question depends upon the action of those engaged in the tests of the present, and especially on the energy they put into liberating the force of critique, whose key role – including a negative one, when it is silent – we have observed.

We hope we have contributed to reviving critique and to reopening the paths that it is liable to take – not only by showing that its action is real, but also by trying to present a panorama of capitalist displacements that might provide a fulcrum for reconstructing critical forces. In so doing, our aim is to give the lie to fatalistic discourses that there will be no reason not to believe if nothing changes.

Arguably, no period has sacrificed so much to the belief in action without a subject as these last fifteen years, which were nevertheless often credited with a 'return of the subject'. But the subject in question was an individual agent, not a subject of history.

The subject of the economists was rational, completely taken up with his own affairs, absorbed, in particular, in the task of maximizing his individual interests. Such a perspective encourages fatalism about possible developments. From the standpoint of this anthropology, the only measures that may be deemed 'realistic' are those which act on individual behaviour through changes in incentives (reduction in the cost of labour to stimulate employment; the creation of 'free zones' to encourage firms to locate in reputedly 'difficult' areas, etc.). They exclude changes of format liable to alter the stakes to which the behaviour of actors is habituated. Sensible experts will thus hold that a thorough review of taxation, labour law, and ways of controlling financial circuits is unrealistic. For such measures presuppose winners and losers, and hence a challenge to interests liable, according to them, to block reforms, so that this obstacle could be overcome only by arresting the democratic process.

They forget that representations, which depend upon the available instruments of interpretation, have at least as much influence as personal interests on how people vote politically. Moreover, the way these interests are understood also depends on the available interpretative frameworks, whether these are derived from widely diffused theories or regulatory or accounting mechanisms. Theories indicate what an interest is, and mechanisms reveal them by putting them to the test. According to René Girard, interest no more possesses the privilege of transparency than desire. It must be pointed out in order to be recognized. Furthermore, it is at the very least hasty, and possibly even inappropriate, to characterize it as 'individual': its recognition by individuals in fact depends on the way in which they identify with groups by means of a labour of categorization and creation of equivalence that is collective and historical from start to finish. Thus it was that for something to be determined as an individual interest of *cadres*, each taken separately, the category of *cadres* had to be constructed as such by a whole historical labour of comparison, inclusion and exclusion, and also of institutionalization, to give the category substance.[1] As for the orientation of this individual interest, given as being necessarily egotistical, it too depends upon the frameworks it is inscribed in. This is demonstrated by the development of altruistic behaviour when individuals are offered *causes*: presenting themselves as if from without, these supply a goal for individuals' desire for self-fulfilment – an aim they cannot discover alone and for themselves.

The subject of social philosophy has also been depicted for us in the guise of inevitability: the rise of individualism, last of the 'meta-narratives' to have survived the rejection of philosophies of history. If a rise in individualism over the last fifteen years is indeed plausible, is it not manifestly the result, not of some evolutionary process that nothing could check, but of the deconstruction of groupings (classes, firms, unions, parties, but also, in another way, churches or schools) that formed the basis for people's ability to enrol in collective perspectives, and pursue what was recognized as the common good? These groupings, where people encountered one another physically and found themselves coming together on the basis of certain shared characteristics, and which offered a whole range of levels of participation, from simple attendance at meetings to full-time activist commitment, functioned as so many sites where the collective was constructed. Today, however, these sites are in such a state of decay that, shut in on themselves as it were, the only alternatives they offer are sceptical indifference or total commitment, which is rapidly disqualified as dogmatism. This has considerably increased the cost of membership and contributed to creating a prevalent sense of impotence, abandonment and isolation, conveyed, *inter alia*, by the indicators of anomie.

The legitimating effect that is bound to have been produced by the presentation of this 'rise of individualism', abundantly reiterated in numerous works, articles, table talk and television screens, should also be mentioned.

There too, it was easy to recognize individual interests as the only 'real' ones once the social world had been stripped of the institutions on which the possibility of collective affiliations and futures depended.

We could pursue a discussion of the doubts, even the malaise, that are bound to arise from close scrutiny of the various fashionable analyses of the present situation, deriving from different perspectives and identifying, in particular, with economic science.

The various models that the paradigm of the rational actor enables us to construct, which can obviously sometimes also be pressed into the service of a critical analysis of the contemporary capitalist world, are just as often vitiated by extreme schematism. This translates into seeking a single, totalizing cause for the changes that have affected capitalism and the societies it is embedded in over the last thirty years, be it the competition of 'low-wage countries', globalization, or technological innovation. Yet in placing all the emphasis on a determination operating, as it were, in accordance with an immanent logic, and holistically, the only conceivable interventions are either so radical (economic isolationism, a halt to productivity increases, abolition of private shareholding and state organization of work, etc.), or pursued at such a high level (a kind of global government) that they seem unrealistic in the short term or worse than the evil they purport to ward off. The same can be said of another image – 'complexity' – which, while it is not strictly compatible with the preceding one, is nevertheless to be found associated with it in certain documents. For if everything is so imbricated, inextricable and multi-factorial that it is impossible to untangle the skein of causes and effects, we are condemned to the same impotence. Moreover, we believe that there is no point looking for a single solution, or even a small number of solutions – which is frustrating for those who would like to build a campaign on the basis of one or two simple ideas – but that it is definitely more effective to create a multiplicity of changes that might seem small-scale from some overarching, grandiose viewpoint. If, in the space of thirty years, capitalism has been able to undergo such a transformation by exploiting minor displacements, is it not possible to employ the same tactic to revolutionize the world of work once more, but this time in the direction of greater justice and respect for what gives life its authenticity? Thus critique would have to be able to root itself once again in the local mechanisms it has gradually been driven out of. Only that which is practised can be well known. Critique will become realistic once again, and consequently effective, at the price of this reinscription in the interstices of everyday life.

Among the overarching causes, let us pause for a moment over references to the fierce competition economic actors are engaged in (which increased in tandem with globalization). This allegedly subjects the whole world to such systemic constraints that it is impossible to escape them, except by taking measures that are deemed reactionary. Competition appears in these discourses as an absolute, disembodied force; and the fact, in particular, that it pits firms of various sizes against multinationals invested with enormous power is generally ignored. The processes of merger and creation of global oligopolies, which are so many counter-examples to the theory of competition, are scarcely indicated, or are also put down to competitive pressures. Consequently, management literature is in many respects more 'realistic' about the nature of the processes under way than many works directly inspired by the discipline of economics. At least it does not blur the macro-actors constituted by firms. And we can read in it like an open book the many strategies for circumventing competition (securing 'competitive advantages' is nothing other than an opportunity to escape competition temporarily); the stakes of organizing and mobilizing human beings; ways to transform a factory into a centre of flexible production, particularly by casualizing the workforce and transferring constraints on to suppliers; various recommendations about good ways to manage the difficult relations of force that condition profits (with wage-earners, customers, suppliers, public collectivities) – the fact, for example, that one of the important things about achieving global scale is quite simply to be in an advantageous position in all negotiations (gaining strength); means of confronting problems in controlling, and even knowing, what is happening in firms, and so on. The term 'competition', because it points to the commercial status that might serve to construct a just social order – but only in conditions where competitors are on an equal footing, and when it is restricted to well-defined situations – conceals the unequal relations of force between those who concretely create supply and demand. In the current state of inequalities (between firms and workers, between firms themselves, between financial markets and states or firms, between territories and firms), this competition, about which there is nothing 'perfect', is indeed often merely the imposition of the law of the strongest – which is also to say, today, of the most mobile. If envisaging the existence of a number of ways for supply and demand to meet on a market was accepted, we could perhaps progress towards a reduction in the most unjust forms of competition. Even in a strictly market logic, to which the framework containing the mechanisms of justice is far from being reducible, this would be a first step towards attenuating the pure relations of force that currently prevail. Moreover, it is not clear what arguments the competitors, who have adopted liberal discourse, could easily use to oppose such a rebalancing, while preserving their good faith. For it would tend to equalize the conditions of competition and, consequently, to purify market tests. In approving it, liberals would simply prove faithful to their basic options.

In any event, if an ideology identifying with liberalism has indeed been imposed over the last twenty years,[2] by utilizing the 'benefits of competition' to legitimate a whole range of situations – some of them profoundly unjust, even from a liberal standpoint – it is by no means obvious that the major characteristic of the transformations of these years is the establishment of a more commercial world. As we have tried to show in this work, we believe instead that the specificity of recent developments consists in the development of a connexionist logic, which does not mean that it has invaded the totality of the social world or that, in particular, connexionist exploitation has replaced other forms of exploitation. In our view, however, it is precisely the shortage of descriptions tailored to the uniqueness of this world that has hitherto prevented critique from being more effective: the need for a form of justice adapted to this new logic has not been adequately taken into account, and critique has fallen back on principles of justice that have long been tried and tested, locking itself into a hackneyed, stereotyped debate over liberalism versus statism ('So, you want to re-create the Soviet Union?').

If the only hope for reopening the field of possibilities consists, in our opinion, in a revival of critique, supporting critique does not mean accepting the validity of all forms of accusation or invective, elevating protest and rebellion into a value in themselves, independently of their relevance or acuteness. In the first instance, criticizing signifies *distinguishing*, revealing differences in what, taken at face value, appears confused, obscure or difficult to grasp. Critique thus also needs analyses and equally, as we have said, means for amassing the original data on which analysis can be based, allowing it to be conducted in full possession of the facts. As we have seen, our work has frequently come up against an absence of data and information – partly because social statistics are in crisis, and the centres of expertise have been broken up; partly because some data collection is carried out in a format that renders the new relations of force invisible.

As for the projective city – which might appear to be 'our proposal', although we have merely sought to track its formation, and about whose completion there is nothing foreordained – it seems to us to possess political relevance. For it could serve to limit the violence that haunts the connexionist world as established over the last twenty years. It is nevertheless the case that the horizon of the projective city remains limited and, as we saw in Chapter 7, this leaves many of the problems raised by the critique of capitalism unresolved, when it does not actually exacerbate them. In particular, it does not enable us to engage in activity intended to restrict the extension of commodification. Yet it is arguably there that the only critical designs capitalism cannot recuperate are to be found, because it is as it were, in essence, bound up with the commodity.

Reviving the social critique and seeking to reduce inequalities and exploitation in the connexionist world are certainly vital. But there is no question, for all that, of burying the artistic critique on the pretext of its collapse – because over the last twenty years it has, rather, played into the hands of capitalism – and the urgent situation on the social front. The themes of the artistic critique are equally essential and still topical. It is on the basis of such themes that we have most chance of mounting effective resistance to the establishment of a world where, from one day to the next, anything could find itself transformed into a commodity product, and people would constantly be put to the test, subjected to an exigency of incessant change, and deprived by this kind of organized insecurity of what ensures the permanency of their self. We believe that it is necessary to preserve the possibility of leading a life whose particular dynamic could flourish without being subject to frequent, unforeseeable interruptions that are not only imposed, but supposed to be greeted with joy, as if discontinuity were the norm of a successful existence. It goes without saying that the artistic critique can see this task through to a conclusion only if it undoes the link that has hitherto associated liberation with mobility.

As a century and a half of the critique of capitalism has demonstrated, the two critiques – the social and the artistic – are at once contradictory on many points and inseparable, in the sense that, stressing different aspects of the human condition, they mutually balance and limit one another. It is by keeping both alive that we can hope to confront the destruction caused by capitalism, while avoiding the excesses that each of them risks inducing when it is given exclusive expression, and not tempered by the presence of the other.

Notes

1 See Luc Boltanski, *Les Cadres. La formation d'un groupe social*, Minuit, Paris 1982.
2 See Keith Dixon, *Les Évangélistes du marché*, Raisons d'agir Éditions, Paris 1998.

APPENDICES

APPENDIX 1
CHARACTERISTICS OF
THE MANAGEMENT TEXTS USED

These texts – between five and twenty-five pages long approximately, and all in French – were selected from Francophone management reviews or works published by specialist publishers. Given that our subject was the spirit of capitalism in France, we naturally restricted ourselves to French texts available in this country; some of them, however, are translations of works by foreign authors. Obviously, the French ideological scene is not insulated from representations elaborated in other European countries, the United States (the most important supplier of managerial innovations since the war), and even Japan, whose successes, studied and conveyed back by Western consultants, have been very significant sources of inspiration over the last two decades. On the other hand, it is equally clear that each country adapts internationally diffused ideas in accordance with its own history and 'national passions'. Moreover, far from being 'globalizing', management texts, like the capitalism they deal with, invariably have a geographical anchorage. They refer to countries, their particular spirit and problems, their progress or backwardness; they seek to adapt discoveries made in one country to a different one; they mention local traditions, and so on, as if the national frame of reference remained fully valid when it comes to supplying 'national' managers with reasons for engaging in a process that is said to be global.

All the texts selected deal, in whole or in part, with the question of *cadres*, even if they are referred to by various titles (manager, director, head, etc.). For example, in these extracts we find descriptions of the qualities demanded of *cadres*, portraits of the ideal manager, explanations of why the current development of firms is transforming the function and work of *cadres*, and so on. The texts employed possess a normative coloration and seek to promote what are deemed to be the most effective practices economically. Their aim is to be of direct use to firms; they seek to be constructive and they offer recommendations.

The texts selected were assembled on the basis of the HEC's library collection. They have been scanned in order to be processed, as set out below, using a textual analysis software program.

Table 1   Characteristics of the texts selected

	1960s	1990s
Number of texts[1] and size of corpus[2]	60 texts 1,393,988 octals	66 texts 1,398,444 octals
Number of source texts[3]	45 source texts	52 source texts
Number of authors	48 authors	49 authors
Some authors' names	Louis Allen, Louis Armand and Michel Drancourt, Robert Blake and Jane Mouton, Pierre Bleton, François Bloch-Lainé, Marvin Bower, Philippe De Woot, Octave Gelinier, Jean-Jacques Servan-Schreiber, André Malterre, Louis Salleron	Omar Aktouf, Bob Aubrey, Lionel Bellenger, Michel Crozier, Peter Drucker, Rosabeth Moss Kanter, Hubert Landier, Vincent Lenhardt, Meryem Le Saget, Pierre Morin, Isabelle Orgogozo, Tom Peters, Hervé Sérieyx, Alvin Toffler, Robert Waterman
Number of American source texts translated	11 source texts	7 source texts
Number of texts by French or France-based authors[4]	26 source texts	38 source texts
Year of publication[5]	1959 (3); 1960 (1); 1961 (1); 1962 (1); 1963 (7); 1964 (7); 1965 (5); 1966 (8); 1967 (7); 1968 (6); 1969 (14)	1989 (5); 1990 (7); 1991 (11); 1992 (9); 1993 (14); 1994 (20);

1   This is equivalent to the number of text files used by the analytical software program.

2   This is the size of the space taken up by all the 'text only' files, in no particular order. For this reason, although there are more texts in the 1990s corpus, the numerical volume of characters is more or less the same, because the 1960s texts are, on average, longer.

3   When too many passages of a given work came within our analytical field, we decided to cut the text up into several pieces in order to obtain text files of more comparable dimensions. There is a greater variety in the 1990s simply because of the increased supply of 'managerial products' available as a result of French journals and publishers specializing in this area.

4   Texts which are neither by French authors nor translations by American authors are by French-speaking Swiss, Belgian or Québecois authors, or translated from other languages (e.g. German).

5   The figures in brackets refer to the number of text files published in the relevant year. The 1960s corpus is particularly revealing of the late-1960s state of mind, around the time of the events of May 1968, while the 1990s corpus is representative of the early years of that decade.

APPENDIX 2
LIST OF SOURCE TEXTS IN
THE MANAGEMENT CORPORA

The 1960s Corpus

Allen, Louis, 1964, *Le métier de directeur*, Paris, Éditions d'organisation (translation of *The Management Profession*, McGraw-Hill, New York 1960).

Alluson, Roger, 1965, *Les cadres supérieurs dans l'entreprise*, Paris, Entreprise modern d'édition.

Armand, Louis and Drancourt, Michel, 1961, *Plaidoyer pour l'avenir*, Paris, Calmann-Lévy.

Aumont, Michèle, 1963, *Construire l'entreprise de demain*, Paris, Fayard.

Blake, Robert and Mouton, Jane, 1969, *Les deux dimensions du management*, Paris, Éditions d'organisation (translation of *The Managerial Grid*, Gulf Publishing Company, Houston 1964).

Bleton, Pierre, 1967, *Mort de l'entreprise*, Paris, Robert Laffont.

Bloch-Lainé, François, 1963, *Pour une réforme de l'entreprise*, Paris, Seuil.

Borne, Fernand, 1966, *Organisation des enterprises*, Paris, Foucher.

Bouquerel, Fernand, 1969, *Management: politique, stratégie, tactique*, Paris, Dunod.

Bower, Marvin, 1968, *Diriger c'est vouloir*, Paris, Hachette (translation of *The Will to Manage*, McGraw-Hill, New York 1966).

Carlson, Dick, 1963, *La direction moderne*, Paris, OECD (training manual).

Colin, A.T., 1964, *L'organisation rationnelle du travail dans l'entreprise*, Paris, Dunod.

Devaux, Guy, 1959, 'Synthèse des débats', *L'homme d'affaires de demain – les 75 ans d'HEC*, CCP Éditions, Paris, Hommes et commerces, pp. 167–74.

De Woot, Philippe, 1968, *Pour une doctrine de l'entreprise*, Paris, Seuil.

Drancourt, Michel, 1964, *Les clés du pouvoir*, Paris, Fayard.

Dubois, Jean, 1969, *Les cadres dans le société de consommation*, Paris, Cerf.

Froissart, Daniel, 1969, *Déléguer avec succès ses responsabilités*, Paris, Hommes et techniques.

Gabrysiak, Michel, Alquier, Jean-Yves, Antoine, Jacques, Grandmougin, Jean, de Mun, Pierre-Henri, Roulleau, Jean-Pol, and Roy, Maurice, 1968, *Cadres, qui êtes-vous?*, Paris, Robert Laffont.

Gélinier, Octave, *Fonction et tâches de la direction générale*, Paris, Hommes et techniques.

— 1965, *Morale de l'entreprise et destin de la nation*, Paris, Plon.

— 1966, *Le secret des structures compétitives*, Paris, Hommes et techniques.

Gutenberg, Erich, 1969, *La direction de l'entreprise*, Paris, Dunod.

Hughes, Charles, 1969, *Négocier les objectifs pour la réussite commune des hommes et de l'entreprise*, Paris, Hommes et techniques (translation of *Goal Setting: Key to Individual and Organizational Effectiveness*, American Management Association, New York 1965).

Hugonnier, René, 1964, *Former des chefs, promouvoir des hommes*, Paris, Dunod.

Humble, John, 1969, *Comment faire participer les cadres à la réalisation des objectifs*, Paris, Entreprise moderne d'édition (translation of *Improving Business Results*, McGraw-Hill, New York 1968).

Humblet, Jean, 1966, *Les cadres de l'entreprise: France, Belgique, Royaume-Uni*, Paris, Éditions universitaires.

Jaques, Elliott, 1965, 'Diagnostic de la capacité et de son développement en vue de la sélection et de l'appréciation du personnel', in ANDCP, ed., *Techniques modernes de choix des hommes*, Paris, Éditions d'organisation, pp. 231–45.

Jeannet, Maurice, 1967, *Le psychologue et la sélection des cadres*, Paris, Dessart.

Kootz, Harold, 1966, 'La formation des directeurs pour le profit', in Bloch-Lainé and Perroux, eds, *L'entreprise et l'économie du xxᵉ siècle*, vol. 3, pp. 917–28 (translation of 'Executives Who Can't Manage', *Atlantic Monthly*, vol. 210, July 1962).

Lambert, Paul, 1968, *Management ou les cinq secrets du développement*, Paris, Cercle du livre économique.

McCarthy, Dugue, 1962, *La conduite du personnel*, Paris, Dunod.

Malterre, André, 1969, *Les cadres et la réforme des enterprises*, Paris, France-Empire.

Massie, Joseph, 1967, *Méthodes actuelles de management des entreprises*, Paris, Éditions d'organisation (translation of *Essentials of Management*, Prentice Hall, Englewood Cliffs 1964).

Maurice, Marc, Monteil, Colette, Guillon, Roland, and Gaulon, Jacqueline, 1967, *Les cadres et l'entreprise*, Université de Paris, Institut de sciences sociales du travail.

Monsen, R.J., Saxberg, B.O. and Sutermeister, R.A., 1966, 'Les motivations sociologiques de l'entrepreneur moderne', in Bloch-Lainé and Perroux, eds, *L'entreprise et l'économie du xxᵉ siècle*, vol. 1, pp. 569–94.

Newman, William H., 1969, *L'art de la gestion. Les techniques d'organisation et de direction*, Paris, Dunod (translation of *Administrative Action: The Technique of Organisation and Management*, second edition, Prentice Hall, Englewood Cliffs, 1965).

Paterson, Thomas, 1969, *Théorie du management*, Paris, Gauthier-Villars (translation of *Management Theory*, Business Publications, London 1966).

Patton, Arch and Starcher, George, 1965, 'L'appréciation des cadres par la programmation des résultats', in ANDCP, ed., *Techniques modernes de choix des hommes*, Paris, Éditions d'organisation, pp. 163–80.

Rohan-Chabot, Guy de, 1959, 'La formation des cadres', *L'homme d'affaires de demain – les 75 ans d'HEC*, CCP Éditions, Paris, Hommes et commerce, pp. 328–32.

Salleron, Louis, 1965, *Le fondement du pouvoir dans l'entreprise*, Paris, Entreprise moderne d'édition.

Servan-Schreiber, Jean-Jacques, 1967, *Le défi américain*, Paris, Denoël (translated as *The American Challenge*, trans. Ronald Steel, Hamish Hamilton, London 1968).

Studders, Herbert, 1959, 'Comment adapter l'homme d'affaires au monde de demain', *L'homme d'affaires de demain – les 75 ans d'HEC*, CCP Éditions, Paris, Hommes et commerce, pp. 239–43.

Tronson, Jean, 1967, *Le développement de la carrière des cadres dans la grande entreprise*, Paris, Librairie générale de droit et de jurisprudence.

Vatier, Raymond, 1969, *Le perfectionnement des cadres*, Paris, PUF, 'Que sais-je?' collection.

Vidal, André and Beaussier, Jean, 1960, *Organisation des structures de direction top management*, Paris, Dunod.

The 1990s Corpus

Adam, Edmond, 1993, 'Le coaching ou le retour vers la personne', *Management France*, no. 86, November, pp. 12–14.

Aktouf, Omar, 1989, *Le management, entre tradition et renouvellement*, Montreal, Gaëtan Morin.

Archier, Georges, Elissalt, Olivier and Setton, Alain, 1989, *Mobiliser pour réussir*, Paris, Seuil.

Arpin, Roland, 1994, 'Diriger sans s'excuser', *Revue internationale de gestion*, vol. 19, no. 2, May, pp. 55–61.

Aubrey, Bob, 1990, *Savoir faire savoir*, Paris, InterÉditions (prix Dauphine 1990).
— 1993, 'Repensons le travail du *cadre*', *Harvard-L'Expansion*, August, pp. 56–64.
— 1994, 'La métamorphose du travail conduit à l'entreprise de soi' (presentation of *Le travail après la crise*), *Management France*, no. 87, February, pp. 22–3.
— 1994, *Le travail après la crise*, Paris, InterÉditions.

Baron, Xavier, 1993, 'Les enjeux de gestion des salariés travaillant dans les structures par projets', *Gestion 2000*, no. 2, pp. 201–13.

Bellenger, Lionel, 1992, *Être pro*, Paris, ESF.

Bonis, Jean, 1990, *Le management comme direction d'acteurs: maîtriser la dynamique humaine de l'entreprise*, Paris, CLET.

Crozier, Michel, 1989, *L'entreprise à l'écoute. Apprendre le management post-industriel*, Paris, InterÉditions.

Crozier, Michel and Sérieyx, Hervé, eds, 1994, *Du management panique à l'entreprise du XXIème siècle*, Paris, Maxima.

Cruellas, Philippe, 1993, *Coaching: un nouveau style de management*, Paris, ESF.

Desclée de Maredsous, Xavier, 1992, 'L'exercice du leadership ou la gestion de sa carrière au jour le jour', *Gestion 2000*, vol. 7, special issue: 'Gérer votre carriere', pp. 105–26.

Doyon, Christian, 1991, *L'intrapreneurship: la nouvelle génération de managers*, Montreal, Agence d'Arc.

Drucker, Peter, 1993, 'Le big-bang des organisations', *Havard-L'Expansion*, no. 69, Summer, pp. 35–42 (translation of 'The New Society of Organizations', *Harvard Business Review,* September/October 1992).

Ettighoffer, Denis, 1992, *L'entreprise virtuelle ou les nouveaux modes de travail*, Paris, Odile Jacob.

Gastaldi, Dino, 1990, 'Le métier de cadre: évolution et prise en compte du management', *Direction et gestion*, nos 126–127, pp. 57–62.

Genelot, Dominique, 1992, *Manager dans la complexité*, Paris, INSEP.

Girard, Bernard, 1994, 'Vers un nouveau pacte social', *Revue française de gestion*, no. 100, September, pp. 78–88.

Hammer, Michael and Champy, James, 1993, *Le reengineering*, Paris, Dunod (translation of *Reengineering the Corporation: A Manifesto for Business Revolution*, Nicholas Brearley, London 1993).

HEC (the professors of the groups), 1994, 'Management et ressources humaines: quelles stratégies de formation', *L'école des managers de demain*, Paris, Economica, pp. 245–68.

Landier, Hubert, 1991, *Vers l'entreprise intelligente*, Paris, Calmann-Lévy.

Lemaire, Bruno, 1994, 'Des entreprises sans hiérarchie?', *L'Expansion Management Revue*, Autumn, pp. 74–82.

Lenhardt, Vincent, 1992, *Les responsables porteurs de sens: culture et pratique du coaching and du team building*, Paris, INSEP.

Le Saget, Meryem, 1992, *Le manager intuitif*, Paris, Dunod (prix Dauphine 1993).
— 1994, *10 conseils pour le manager de demain*, brochure of the consulting firm Érasme International.

Midler, Christophe, 1993, 'La révoluton de la Twingo', *Gérer et comprendre*, June 1993.

Mingotaud, F., 1993, *La fonction d'encadrement*, Paris, Éditions d'organisation.

Moran, R. and Xardel, D., 1994, *Au-delà des cultures: les enjeux du management international*, Paris, InterÉditions.

Morin, Pierre, 1994, 'La fin du management romantique', *Management France*, no. 88, May, pp. 14–17.

Moss Kanter, Rosabeth, 1991, 'Les habits neufs du manager', *Harvard-l'Expansion*, no. 60, Spring, pp. 30–39 (translation of 'The New Managerial Work', *Harvard Business Review*, November/December 1989).
— 1992, *L'entreprise en éveil*, Paris, InterÉditions (translation of *When Giants Learn to Dance*, Unwin, London 1990).

Orgogozo, Isabelle, 1991, *Les paradoxes du management, du château fort aux cloisons mobiles*, Paris, Éditions d'organisation.

Orgogozo, Isabelle and Sérieyx, Hervé, 1989, *Changer le changement, on peut abolir les bureaucraties*, Paris, Seuil.

Peters, Tom, 1993, *L'entreprise libérée*, Paris, Dunod (translation of *Liberation Management: Necessary Disorganization for the Nanosecond Nineties*, Alfred A. Knopf, New York 1992).

Quinn Mills, D., 1994, *L'entreprise post-hiérarchique*, Paris, InterÉditions (translation of *Rebirth of the Corporation*, John Wiley & Sons).

Ramond, Philippe, 1993, *Le management opérationnel*, Paris, Maxima.

Raux, Jean-François, 1994, 'Management et mutations', *Futuribles*, no. 187, May, pp. 9–26.

Renaud-Coulon, Annick, 1994, *L'entreprise sur mesure*, Paris, L'Harmattan.

Sérieyx, Hervé, 1993, 'À propos du big-bang des organisations', *Management France*, no. 85, pp. 29–30.

— 1993, *Le Big-Bang des organisations*, Paris, Calmann-Lévy.

Sicard, Claude, 1994, *Le manager stratège*, Paris, Dunod.

Strebel, Paul, 1994, 'Comment faire évoluer les règles du jeu', *L'Expansion Management Review*, Summer, pp. 17–21.

Tapscott, Don and Caston, Art, 1994, *L'entreprise de la deuxième ère. La révolution des technologies de l'information*, Paris, Dunod (translation of *Paradigm Shift: The New Promise of Information Technology*, McGraw-Hill, New York 1993).

Tardieu, Michel, 1994, *Patrons–cadres: la crise de confiance*, Cahiers de l'Institut de l'entreprise, April, pp. 20–26.

Toffler, Alvin, 1991, *Les nouveaux pouvoirs*, Paris, Livre de Poche (translation of *Power Shift: Knowledge, Wealth and Violence at the Edge of the 21st Century*, Bantam Books, New York 1990).

Vermot Gaud, Claude, 1993, *Mobiliser pour gagner*, Paris, Éditions Liaisons.

Vincent, Claude-Pierre, 1990, *Des systèmes et des hommes*, Paris, Éditions d'organisation.

Waterman, Robert, 1990, *Les champions du renouveau*, Paris, InterÉditions (translation of *The Renewal Factor*, Bantam, London 1988).

Weiss, Dimitri, 1994, 'Nouvelles formes d'entreprise et relations de travail', *Revue française de gestion*, no. 98, March–May, pp. 95–103.

APPENDIX 3
GENERAL STATISTICAL PICTURE OF THE MANAGEMENT TEXTS

The software program

The two corpora were processed using the software program Prospero@, developed by Francis Chateauraynaud and Jean-Pierre Charriau. This combines a lexicographical with a hermeneutic approach, allowing for the codification and interactive construction of categories (characters, collective entities, objects, actions, etc.), and the elaboration of representations appropriate both to the texts concerned and the research problematic. To begin with, Prospero@ automatically labels the words encountered in a text by combining a morphological parser (which contains a certain number of rules, such as that words ending in *-ion* are *entities*) and reference to catalogues containing labelling operations performed on different texts by different users (which makes it possible to recognize words the parser does not know how to handle). The automatic labelling distinguishes *entities* (common nouns, proper nouns, compound nouns); *qualities* (adjectives or past or present participles that qualify the entities); *tests* (mainly verbs in the infinitive or conjugated); *grammatical words* (pronouns, conjunctions, etc.); *markers* (adverbs, but also forms that modalize the statement, such as '*il faut*', or '*pas toujours*', etc.); finally, *numbers* and *indeterminate terms* (entities that the program does not succeed in identifying). Once this stage is complete, the automatic processing can be corrected manually by the user to characterize the *indeterminate terms* or alter erroneous classifications. The analytical phase proper consists mainly in constructing categories (containing a series of terms or instances pinpointed below by the sign @), and working with these categories. In this way, for example, one can compare the presence of categories in different texts from the same corpus or different corpora; examine the instances or representatives that embody the category in different texts; make a list of the qualities attributed to an instance, come to know the terms most often associated with a category.

Validation of the general content of the two corpora

The software program allowed us to compare the two corpora systematically, and confirm that our analysis of their content, set out in Chapter 1, was an accurate enough reflection, not the result of some interpretative bias. To carry out this comparison, we constructed various *fictive entities* (to use the program's language), which take the form of lists of nouns grouped according to their similar meanings. Thus, for example, the fictive entity COACH@ combines all the terms used to refer to this new function of supporting and developing people to which the 1990s authors attribute so much importance. 'Fictive entities' have been constructed for all the categories of human beings pre-sented in the two corpora, which makes it possible, using the same indicators, to compare their relative presence in the representations of the two periods. We have likewise constructed certain 'fictive entities' to refer to various mech-anisms (like RÉSEAU@ or PROJET@). The list of contents of fictive entities is provided at the end of this appendix. On this basis, the program provides us with a count of the occurrence of each fictive entity and each entity. Table 2 reproduces the list of the foremost entities in each corpus, followed by the number of their occurrences and preceded by their rank in descending order.

It clearly reflects the striking differences between the two periods. In the 1960s corpus, *cadres* are the main concern. In the 1990s, interests are more varied, since we find among the corpus's foremost actors *cadres,* representa-tives of the old-style firm that needs reforming, as well as *managers,* the exemplary new figures destined to replace them;[1] but also *clients* [customers] and *fournisseurs* [suppliers], whose importance in the new mechanisms we have noted, whether the issue is integrating them into projects or gearing the whole organization to customers' expectations. Moreover, if the categories '*subordon-nés*' [subordinates] and '*dirigeants*' [directors], which refer to a hierarchical framework, persist, albeit not always in positive formulations, that of '*salariés*' [wage-earners] now occupies a preponderant position. This term – the most neutral imaginable – can take in the whole workforce, *cadre* and non-*cadre,* without distinction of statute or grade, in line with the new recommendations.[2]

In the 1960s, the other important actors in the corpus – besides '*chefs*' [heads], who in part function as synonyms for '*cadres*' – are shareholders (category of '*capital*'), whom we find in a very low ranking in the 1990s (72 as against 19) – not that their significance has diminished, but their existence is not the occasion for so much discussion. In the 1960s, in contrast, the sep-aration between management and ownership was still an issue, and an attempt was made to eliminate from business inefficient behaviour bound up with the exercise of power by owners.

The theme of freedom occupies a similar position in both periods, albeit, as we have seen, in different forms. The 1960s authors want to liberate *cadres*

---

1 The fact that in both cases '*cadres*' or '*cadres*' and '*managers*' are central reflects our way of constructing the corpus. Let us recall that we first and foremost selected extracts devoted to these figures.

2 The equivalent 'neutral' term in the 1960s was '*homme*', but in the plural it invariably refers to subordinates in line with a formulation, borrowed from the army, whose hierarchical, 'domestic' connotation is fairly clear.

Table 2 The leading entities in each corpus

1960s 6,146 different entities[3]		1990s 7,999 different entities	
1. ENTREPRISE@	1,330	1. ENTREPRISE@	1,404
2. CADRE@	986	2. travail	507
3. SUBORDONNÉS@	797	3. organisation	451
4. DIRIGEANTS@	724	4. RÉSEAU@	450
5. direction	549	5. ÉQUIPE@	392
6. travail	507	6. PROJET@	375
7. CHEF@	487	7. DIRIGEANTS@	369
8. cadre	361	8. CLIENT-FOURN@	363
9. organisation	343	9. SUBORDONNÉS@	343
10. autorité	316	10. MANAGER@	299
11. objectifs	308	11. mangement	265
12. fonction	274	12. temps	251
13. action	260	13. processus	227
14. formation	238	14. CADRE@	219
15. résultats	217	15. développement	213
16. fonctions	212	16. vie	205
17. système	207	17. SALARIÉ@	193
18. problèmes	195	18. pouvoir	192
tâches	195	19. changement	190
19. CAPITAL@	190	20. sens	188
20. responsabilité	189	21. HIÉRARCHIE@	185
21. hommes	188	22. compétences	185
22. LIBERTÉ@	185	23. système	184
23. temps	178	24. qualité	180
24. rôle	175	25. monde	175
25. l'homme	173	26. gestion	172
société	173	27. relations	170
26. groupe	167	28. action	167
gestion	167	29. LIBERTÉ	165

3 The variety of vocabulary measured by this figure is much greater in the 1990s. Recent authors use a great many references with scholarly and philosophical connotations; provide a lot of examples by citing particular situations and proper nouns; introduce a terminology bound up with new technologies, or with human sciences like psychoanalysis, and coin a large quantity of neologisms. Comparatively heteroclite, the whole set contains an abundance of common nouns and proper nouns.

from centralized control by employers, and never forget that the firms they are concerned with are representatives of the 'free world'. The 1990s want to liberate the whole workforce from hierarchy and bureaucracy in order to encourage creativity, flexibility, and individual self-realization (personal development). The 1990s consequently assign a preferential position to hierarchy, which is subjected to much criticism. In the 1960s, this fictive being comes rather further down (rank 45 against 22): its presence is significant, but unlike in recent years, we virtually never come across the references with a negative connotation to 'pyramids' and 'pyramidal functioning' that we have included in its construction.

The pervasiveness of a small number of proposals offered as solutions to the problems posed, and repeated from text to the next regardless of the epoch, is also very apparent from the table, whether *'direction'* [management] and *'objectifs'* [objectives] in the 1960s, or the trilogy *Réseau* [network]–*Équipe* [team]–*Projet* [project] in the 1990s. Entities with a marked presence in the 1960s evoke highly impersonal management (*fonctions, système, résultat, gestion*), whereas the 1990s accord significant space to *'vie'* and *'sens'* [meaning]. *'Pouvoir'* [power] in the 1990s (negatively connoted) corresponds to its supervised and bureaucratized doublets *'autorité'* and *'responsabilité'*, which were presented positively in the 1960s. Terms expressing movement and change (*processus, developpement, changement*) are likewise more prevalent in the 1990s, as one would expect.

Table 3, which contains the ranking order in each corpus of the *other* fictive beings constructed by us, provides a more precise idea of the contrast between the two periods. In particular, it indicates a diversification in the models intended to replace *cadres*. Above all, this is an index of terminological disarray among the 1990s authors, and their difficulties forging a new vocabulary. *'Manager'*, the term most frequently used in the texts, is in fact spread over a multitude of characters depending upon the characteristics the authors wish to highlight. Thus, as one might expect, in the 1990s corpus we come across the *expert* and the *consultant*, the *coach* and the *leader*, but also *formateurs* [trainers], *animateurs* [prime movers]–*coordinateurs–chefs de projet* [project heads], and *mailleurs* [network-extenders] (in this term we combine all the figures specifically responsible for connections in the network firm). The stress on innovation and flexibility equally gives creators and artists more than their due. The sporting metaphor, used, albeit marginally, in the 1960s, has now become standard. The bad subjects virtually all converge in *'bureaucratie'*. The category *'héros'* is more difficult to interpret in so far as it is composed, in part, of terms used in adulatory fashion referring to new model human beings like the *'champion'*, the *'battant'* [go-getter] and the *'bâtisseur'* [builder]; and in part of terms used pejoratively to denounce those who held power in firms in the 1960s, ironically characterized as *'surhommes'* [supermen] or *'demi-dieux'* [demi-gods], as opposed to the *'non-êtres'* [non-entities] (see the category *'alienated'*) subject to them.

Table 3 The relative position of other fictive beings in each corpus[4]

1960s		1990s	
45.	HIÉRARCHIE@	32.	EXPERT-CONSEIL@
59.	ÉQUIPE@	34.	VISION@
60.	EXPERT-CONSEIL@	46.	COACH@
		58.	COLLABORATEUR@
76.	ENTREPRENEUR@	59.	ALLIANCE@
79.	SALARIÉ@	60.	LEADER@
83.	SYNDICAT@	70.	CHEF@
97.	OFFICIER@		CRÉATEUR@
100.	COLLABORATEUR@	72.	CAPITAL@
104.	MANAGER@	81.	ENTREPRENEUR@
113.	CRÉATEUR@	84.	HÉROS@
117.	CLIENT-FOURN@		
		102.	BUREAUCRATIE@
		106.	SPORTIF@
		108.	ALIÉNÉ@
		111.	FORMATEUR@
			ANIMATEUR@
		114.	MAILLEUR@

4 Fictive beings with a ranking below 120 do not feature in this table. At 114, the category *'mailleur'* [network-extender] registers 40 occurrences in the 1990s, while in the 1960s the category *'client-fournisseur'* [customer-supplier], which ranks 117, registers 38. Given the some 500 pages of corpus for each period, we reckoned that the representation of a category was weak below this figure. In addition, the maximum rank occupied – i.e. that of all words cited just once – is 153 for the 1990s and 154 for the 1960s.

The category of actors other than *'cadres'* in the 1960s corpus is quite different from its 1990s counterpart: we find *syndicats* [trade unions], which are still a major source of concern in this period, as well as *officiers* [officers], who are still regarded as good examples, even when there are calls for greater decentralization.

Although they are present in both corpora, *entrepreneurs* in fact cover very different characters in the two periods. In the 1960s, the reference is above all to small employers, whereas in the 1990s the term refers to those who *'secouent la bureaucratie'* [shake up bureaucracy] and innovate, whom the large firm must learn to make use of and sometimes to moderate in their excesses (as in the case of the 'cowboy', a character created by Moss Kanter [1990]).

To conclude, readers will note the prevalence in the 1990s corpus of *'alliances'* and *'vision'*, whose central importance in the proposals made by neo-management we have observed.

Contents list of the fictive beings

ALIÉNÉ@: prisonnier(s), tiers monde, handicapés, marginaux, victime(s), infra-humains, infra-humain, impotent(s), bouc(s), émissaires, Tiers-Monde, aliéné(s), non-suject(s), non-personne(s), non-être(s), miséreux, sans abri(s), chômeur(s), exclu(s), exploité(s), prolétaire(s), larbin(s), gamin(s), esclave(s), nouveaux pauvres.

ALLIANCE@: alliance(s), joint-venture(s), joint venture(s), partenariat(s).

ANIMATEUR@: responsable(s), de projet, chef(s) de projet, coordinateur(s), animateur(s).

BUREAUCRATIE@: bureaucratie(s), bureaucrate(s).

CADRE@: Cette categorie vise à rassembler toutes les évocations des cadres d'entreprise au singulier et au pluriel et est constituée de façon à éviter d'être polluée par le <cadre> au sens de cadre d'analyse très fréquemment employé au singulier. Contenu: cadres, cadre-type, cadre retraité, cadre spécialisé, cadre chômeur, jeune cadre, cadre américain, cadre français, cadre inefficace, cadre incompétent, cadre subalterne, cadre intermédiarie, cadre hiérarchique, cadre, productif, cadre fonctionnel, cadre commercial, cadre administratif, cadre moyen, cadre supérieur, technico-commercial, ingénieur, ingénieurs, chefs d'agence, chef d'agence, chefs de produit, chef de produit, bon cadre, cadre plus âge, CADRE(S), Cadres, fonction-cadre, ingénieur-maître, ingénieurs-maîtres, cadre de talent, haut cadre, cadre de valeur.

CHEF@: sous-chef(s), chef(s).

CLIENT-FOURN@: client(s), fournisseur(s), franchiseurs, sous-traitant, partenaire(s).

COACH@: manager accompagnateur, formateur-éducateur, manger(s)-formateur(s), manager(s)-accoucheur(s), manager(s)-accompagnateur(s), impulseur(s) de vie, susciteur(s) de vie, accompagnateur(s), mentor(s), donneur(s), de souffle, coach(s), parrain(s), catalyseur(s), entraîneur(s), accoucheur(s), manager-accoucheur, facilitateur(s), manager(s)-coach(s), coach(s)-manager(s), maieuticien(s).

COLLABORATEUR@: collaborateur(s).

CRÉATEUR@: découvreur(s), chercheur(s), scientifique(s), concertiste, auto-createur(s), autocreateur(s), penseur(s), esprit(s) scientifique(s), chercheur(s), chef(s) d'orchestres, compositeur(s), musicien(s), romancier(s), poèt(s), peintre(s), génie(s), inventeur(s), créateur(s), innovateur(s), artiste(s), trouveur(s), écrivain(s).

DIRIGEANTS@: dirigeant-leader, PD.G, patrons-exemples, chef(s) d'entre-prise, capitaine(s) d'industrie, la Direction, directoire, Directoire, dirigeant(s), Président(s), président(s), Directeur(s), Directrice, directrice, directeur(s), grand(s), patron(s), grand patron, P.D.G., PDG, cadre(s), dirigeant(s), Président-Directeur général, président-directeur général, président directeur général, leader-chef-patron, ingénieur(s)-patron(s), président directeurs généraux,

Président Directeurs généraux. Il s'agit ici de rassembler tous les salariés qui exercent les plus hautes fonctions: président et premier rang de directeurs.

ENTREPRENEUR@: aventuriers entrepreneurs, self-made man, aventurier(s)-entrepreneur(s), entrepreneur(s), entrepreneur(s)-directeur(s), entrepreneur(s)-propriétaire(s), cowboy(s), intrapreneur(s).

ENTREPRISE@: regroupe toutes les occurrences du mot entreprise au singulier et au pluriel, en majuscules et en minuscules.

ÉQUIPE@: regroupe toutes les occurrences du mot équipe au singulier et au pluriel, en majuscules et en minuscules.

EXPERT-CONSEIL@: spécialiste(s), expert(s), consultant(s), conseiller(s) de direction, conseillers, expert(s)-compatable(s), avocat(s).

FORMATEUR@: pédagogue(s), formateur(s), enseignant(s), professeur(s), éducateur(s), formateur(s)-éducateur(s).

HÉROS@: mutant(s), vedette(s), immortel(s), suprapersonne, démiurge(s), battant(s), surhomme(s)-dirigeant(s), surhomme(s), legende-vivante, dirigeant(s)-héro(s), champion(s), demi-dieu(x), conquérant(s), héros, aventurieur(s), bâtisseur(s), star(s).

HIÉRARCHIE@: structure(s) pyramidale, pyramide(s), organigramme(s), hiérarchie(s), schéma pyramidal, entreprise pyramidale, organisation pyramidale.

LEADER@: meneur(s), dirigeant(s)-leader(s), leader(s), leader(s), meneur(s) d'hommes.

LIBERTÉ@: autonomie, Liberté, libérations, libération, libre-arbitre, libre arbitre, libertés, liberté, indépendance(s).

MAILLEUR@: négociateurs, négociateur, diplomate(s), passeur(s), stratégic brokers, networker(s), traducteur(s), portier(s), médiateur(s), entremetleur(s), homme(s) de réseau, homme(s) de contact, faiseur(s) de ponts, faiseur(s) de pont, interédiaire(s), communicateur(s), communicateurs, hommes-terminaux, ambassadeur(s), lobbyiste(s), passage obligé, gardien(s), portier(s).

MANAGER@: manager(s)-organisateur(s), MANAGER(S), manager(s), Manager(s), euromanager(s).

OFFICIER@: général d'armée, caporaux, carporal, le Général, le général, chef(s) militaire(s), captaine(s), commandant(s), sous-officier(s), officier(s), gradé(s), états-majors, États-major, army, armée, l'armée, Ármée, États-major, adjudants.

PROJECT@: regroupe toutes les occurrences du mot projet au singulier et au pluriel, en majuscules et en minuscules.

RÉSEAU@: regroupe toutes les occurrences du mot réseau au singulier et au pluriel, en majuscules et en minuscules.

SALARIÉ@: salarié(s).

SPORTIF@: champion de tennis, marathonien, sprinter, poulain(s), foot-balleur(s), jouer(s), sportif(s), athlète(s), équipe de football team, équipe de base-ball.

SUBORDONNÉS@: subalterne(s), dirigé(s), l'employé-réserve d'énergie, machiniste(s), super-machiniste(s), super-technicien(s), non-cadre(s), technicien(s), exécutant, travailleurs, employé(s), ouvrier(s), opérateur(s), exécutants, agents de maîtrise, subordonné(s), contre-maître, main-d'œuvre, un manœuvre. Cette catégorie rassemble toutes les appelations désignant les personnes au travail dans les entreprises qui étatient, dans les anées 60 encadrées par les cadres.

SYNDICAT@: syndicalisme, syndicat(s).

VISION@: regroupe toutes les occurrences du mot vision au singulier et au pluriel, en majuscules et en minuscules.

APPENDIX 4
RELATIVE PRESENCE OF THE DIFFERENT 'CITIES' IN THE TWO CORPORA

Tables 4 and 5 offer an overview of the corpora by text. Prospero can in fact determine which are the most important logics for each text.

The predominance of the industrial logic in the 1960s, which we have highlighted (Table 1, Chapter 2, pp. 000-00), is even more striking when analysis is carried out on a text-by-text basis, since it is the principal dominant in 85 per cent of the texts, the next logic (domestic) predominating in only 6 per cent of the texts. By comparison, in the 1990s the industrial logic is the principal dominant in 63 per cent of the texts, but the connexionist logic occupies that position in 28 per cent of the texts.

Analysis of the secondary dominants reveals that the domestic logic is indeed second in importance in the 1960s, whereas in our day this position is occupied by the network logic. On the other hand, these tables do not inform us as to the positive or negative evaluation of the logics concerned. But it should not be forgotten that if the domestic logic is often present in the 1960s texts, it is for the purposes of condemnation, the same role of foil being assumed by the industrial logic in the 1990s texts.

The nature of the other changes underlined in Chapter 2 is clarified here: if the inspirational logic, which was not dominant in any 1960s text, is in the position of principal dominant in three recent texts and second dominant in a further three, its breakthrough, noted on p. 000, thus corresponds to a mild profusion of the inspirational register in all the texts, rather as if the theme of creativity and innovation were 'sprinkled' over them without really being of the essence of the argument. The situation is exactly symmetrical for the civic logic, which is absent from the 1990s after having been fairly prevalent in the 1960s, but without being in position to exercise strong influence on a very large number of texts.

As for the commercial register, which, as we have seen (Chapter 2, pp. 000-00), has generally been appealed to rather more frequently in recent years, we note a decline in its importance in the last two tables: whereas it was in a position to exercise strong influence on more than a third of the corpus in the 1960s, it influences half as many texts today. We must therefore conclude

Table 4 Principal and secondary dominants in the texts of the 1960s corpus

1st dominant 2nd dominant	Commercial	Network	Inspirational	Industrial	Domestic	Reputational	Civic	Second dominant total (No. of texts)
Commercial				22				22
Network				4				4
Inspirational								
Industrial	2				3		2	7
Domestic				22			1	23
Reputational					1			1
Civic				3				3
First dominant total (No. of texts)	2			51	4		3	60

How to read the table: There are 22 texts where the first dominant is industrial logic and the second is commercial logic. In total, irrespective of the second dominant, 51 texts out of 60 are dominated by industrial logic. A text's dominant logic is the logic category containing the greatest number of occurrences.

Table 5 Principal and secondary dominants in the texts of the 1990s corpus

1st dominant / 2nd dominant	Commercial	Network	Inspirational	Industrial	Domestic	Reputational	Civic	Second dominant total (No. of texts)
Commercial				11				11
Network	1		1	26				28
Inspirational				3				3
Industrial	1	17	2					20
Domestic		2		2				4
Reputational								
Civic								
First dominant total (No. of texts)	2	19	3	42				66

How to read the table: See Table 4.

that the commercial logic was less diffuse and more concentrated in some authors in the 1960s. In the 1990s, by contrast, like the inspirational logic it is lightly sprinkled throughout the corpus, but is a strong influence on a much smaller number of texts. No doubt this corresponds to the greater legitimacy of the commercial world in the 1990s, where it is very widespread albeit low-grade in content, whereas the 1960s corpus was marked by a sharp divide in this respect. More legitimate and widely diffused, the commercial logic nevertheless does not end up dominating discourses, as if it was never sufficient in itself to justify the new mechanisms of capitalism and endow them with a power of attraction.

BIBLIOGRAPHY

Abramovici, Gérard, 'La protection sociale', *Données sociales 1999*, INSEE, Paris 1999.

Abrossimov, Christian and Gelot, Didier, 'La politique de l'emploi de 1990 à 1994 entre croissance économique et action publique', *Données sociales 1996*, INSEE, Paris 1996.

Adam, Gérard, *Le Pouvoir syndical*, Dunod, Paris 1983.

Adorno, Theodor, *The Jargon of Authenticity*, trans. Knut Tarnowski and Frederic Will, Routledge & Kegan Paul, London 1973.
— *Minima Moralia: Reflections from a Damaged Life*, trans. E.F.N. Jephcott, Verso, London 1978.

Adorno, Theodor and Horkheimer, Max, *Dialectic of Enlightenment*, trans. John Cumming, Verso, London 1979.

Afsa, Cédric and Amira, Selma, 'Le RMI: un dispositif en mutation', *Données sociales 1999*, INSEE, Paris 1999.

Aglietta, Michel, 'Nouveau régime de croissance et progrès social' (interview), *Esprit*, November 1998.

Agre, Philippe, 'Surveillance et saisie. Deux modèles de l'information personnelle', in B. Conein and L. Thévenot, eds, *Cognition et information en société*, 'Raisons pratiques' no. 8, Éditions de l'EHESS, Paris 1997.

Aguiton, Christophe and Bensaïd, Daniel, *Le Retour de la question sociale. Le renouveau des mouvements sociaux en France*, Éditions Page deux, Lausanne 1997.

Akerlof, George, 'The Market for "Lemons": Quality, Uncertainty and the Market Mechanism', *Quarterly Journal of Economics*, vol. 84, 1970.
— *An Economic Theorist's Books of Tales*, Cambridge University Press, Cambridge 1984.

Amand, Francis, 'Petit et grand commerce', *L'Entreprise*, no. 2518, 1992 (special issue on 'La France des entreprises' in collaboration with INSEE).

Amar, Michel, 'Les effets du "flux tendu"', *L'Entreprise*, no. 2518, 1992 (special issue on 'La France des entreprises' in collaboration with INSEE).

Amar, Michel and Bricout, Jean-Luc, 'La concentration financière', *L'Entreprise*, no. 2518, 1992.

ANACT, *Les Coûts des conditions de travail. Guide d'évaluation économique*, 3 vols, Paris 1979.

Andreff, Wladimir, *Les Multinationales globales*, La Découverte, Paris 1995.

André-Roux, Valérie and Le Minez, Sylvie, 'Dix ans d'évolution du chômage des cadres, 1987–1997', *Données sociales 1999*, INSEE, Paris 1999.

Angenot, Marc, *La Parole pamphlétaire. Typologie des discours modernes*, Payot, Paris 1983.

Ansart, Pierre, *Marx et l'anarchisme*, Presses Universitaires de France, Paris 1969.

Aquain, Valérie, Bué, Jennifer and Vinck, Lydie, 'L'évolution en 2 ans de l'organisation du travail: plus de contraintes mais aussi plus d'autonomie pour les salariés', *Premières synthèses*, no. 54, 16 June 1994, DARES.

Aquain, Valérie, Cézard, Michel, Charraud, Alain and Vinck, Lydie, 'Vingt ans d'évolution des conditions de travail', *Travail et emploi*, no. 61, April 1994.

Arbant, Pascale, 'Le capital de temps de formation', *Droit social*, no. 2, February 1994.

Arendt, Hannah, *The Human Condition*, University of Chicago Press, Chicago 1958.

Astier, Isabelle, *Revenu minimum et souci d'insertion*, Desclée de Brouwer, Paris 1997.

Audric, Sophie and Forgeot, Gérard, 'Le développement du travail à temps partiel', *Données sociales*, INSEE, Paris 1999.

Baechler, Jean, *Le Capitalisme*, 2 vols, Gallimard, Paris 1995.

Baktavatsalou, Ravi, 'Licenciements économiques et mesures d'accompagnement au début des années 90', *Données sociales 1996*, INSEE, Paris 1996.

Balazs, Gabrielle and Mathey, Catherine, 'Opinions sur le marginalisme: analyse d'interviews de spécialistes de la jeunesse', in Jean Rousselet *et al.*, *Les Jeunes et l'emploi*, Cahiers du CEE, no. 7, Presses Universitaires de France, Paris 1975.

Barish, John, *The Antitheatrical Prejudice*, University of California Press, Berkeley 1981.

Barjonet, André, *La CGT*, Seuil, Paris 1968.

Barker, James R., 'Tightening the Iron Cage: Concertive Control in Self-Managing Teams', *Administrative Science Quarterly*, vol. 38, no. 3, 1993.

Baron, Cécile, Bureau, Marie-Christine, Le Dantec, Eliane and Nivolle, Patrick, *Les Intermédiaires de l'insertion*, CEE, Paris 1994.

Barrat, Olivier, Coutrot, Thomas and Mabile, Sylvie, 'La négociation salariale en France: des marges de manoeuvre réduites au début des années 90', *Données sociales 1996*, INSEE, Paris 1996.

Barthes, Roland, *Mythologies* (1957), trans. Annette Lavers, Jonathan Cape, London 1972.

Baszanger, Isabelle, *Douleur et médecine. La fin d'un oubli*, Seuil, Paris 1995.

Baudelot, Christian and Gollac, Michel, 'La salaire du trentenaire: question d'âge ou de génération', *Économie et statistique*, nos 304–305, April 1997.

Baudrillard, Jean, *The Consumer Society*, Sage, London 1988.

— *Simulacra and Simulations*, trans. Sheila Faria Glaser, University of Michigan Press, Ann Arbor 1994.

— *The Gulf War Did Not Take Place* (1991), trans. Paul Patton, Indiana University Press, Bloomington 1995.

Baudry, Bernard, 'De la confiance dans la relation d'emploi et de sous-traitance', *Sociologie du travail*, no. 1, 1994.

Baumard, Maryline and Blanchot, Michel, *Crise du syndicalisme*, Hatier, Paris 1994.

Beaud, Stéphane and Pialoux, Michel, 'Étre OS chez Peugeot: changements techniques et usure au travail', *Critiques sociales*, no. 1, May 1991.

Becker, Gary, 'A Theory of the Allocation of Time', *The Economic Journal*, vol. LXXV, no. 299, 1965.

Bell, Daniel, *The Cultural Contradictions of Capitalism*, Heinemann, London 1976.

Belleville, Pierre, *Une nouvelle classe ouvrière*, Julliard, Paris 1963.

Belloc, Brigitte and Lagarenne, Christine, 'Emplois temporaires et emplois aidés', *Données sociales 1996*, INSEE, Paris 1996.

Belorgey, Jean-Michel, interview with Didier Gelot and Serge Volkoff, *Collectif*, no. 24, December 1994.

Bénéton, Philippe and Touchard, Jean, 'The Interpretations of the Crisis of May/June 1968' (1970), in Keith Reader, ed., *The May 1968 Events in France: Reproductions and Interpretations*, Macmillan, Basingstoke and London 1993.

Benghozi, Pierre-Jean, *Le Cinéma entre l'art et l'argent*, L'Harmattan, Paris 1989.

Beniger, James, *The Control Revolution: Technological and Economic Origins of the Information Society*, Harvard University Press, Cambridge (MA) 1986.

Benko, Georges and Lipietz, Alain, eds, *Les Régions qui gagnent. Districts et réseaux: les nouveaux paradigmes de la géographie économique*, Presses Universitaires de France, Paris 1992.

Bennahmias, Jean-Luc and Roche, Agnès, *Des Verts de toutes les couleurs. Histoire et sociologie du mouvement écolo*, Albin Michel, Paris 1992.

Bennett, Steven, Frierman, Richard and George, Stephen, *Corporate Realities and Environmental Truths: Strategies for Leading Your Business in the Environmental Era*, John Wiley & Sons, New York 1993.

Bénot, Yves, *L'autre Italie 1968–1976*, Maspero, Paris 1977.

Berger, Susan and Piore, Michael, *Dualism and Discontinuity in Industrial Societies*, Cambridge University Press, New York 1980.

Berggren, Christian, 'Lean Production: The End of History?', *Actes du GERPISA*, no. 6, February 1993.

Berle, Adolf and Means, Gardiner, *The Modern Corporation and Private Property*, Macmillan, London 1932.

Berman, Marshall, *All That Is Solid Melts into Air: The Experience of Modernity*, Verso, London 1983.

Bernoux, Philippe, *Les nouveaux patrons: le centre des Jeunes dirigeants d'entreprise*, Les Éditions ouvrières, Paris 1974.

Bernoux, Philippe, Motte, Dominique and Saglio, Jean, *Trois ateliers d'OS*, Les Éditions ouvrières, Paris 1973.

Bernoux, Philippe and Servet, Jean-Michel, eds, *La Construction sociale de la confiance*, Montchrestien, Paris 1997.

Besnard, Philippe, *Protestantisme et capitalisme: la controverse post-weberienne*, Armand Colin, Paris 1970.

— 'Durkheim et les femmes ou le *Suicide* inachevé', *Revue française de sociologie*, vol. XIV, 1973.

— *L'Anomie, ses usages et ses fonctions dans la discipline sociologique depuis Durkheim*, Presses Universitaires de France, Paris 1987.

— 'Mariage et suicide: la théorie durkheimienne de la régulation conjugale à l'épreuve d'un siècle', *Revue française de sociologie*, vol. XXXVIII, 1997.

Bessy, Christian, 'La sélection des salariés licenciés: économies d'une réglementation', *Travail et emploi*, no. 58, 1994.

— 'Cabinets de recrutement et formes d'intermédiation sur le marché du travail', in C. Bessy and F. Eymard-Duvernay, eds, *Les Intermédiaires du marché du travail*, Cahiers du CEE, Presses Universitaires de France, Paris 1997.

Bessy, Christian and Chateauraynaud, François, *Experts et faussaires. Pour une sociologie de la perception*, Métailié, Paris 1995.

Bessy, Christian and Eymard-Duvernay, François, eds, *Les Intermédiaires du marché du travail*, Cahiers du CEE, Presses Universitaires de France, Paris 1997.

Best, Fred, *Flexible Life Scheduling: Breaking the Education–Work–Retirement Lockstep*, Praeger, New York 1980.

Bihr, Alain and Pfefferkorn, Ronald, 'Peut-on définir un seuil de richesse?', *Alternatives economiques*, special issue no. 25, 'Les riches', Autumn 1995.

Bisault, Laurent, Bloch-London, Catherine, Lagarde, Sylvie and Le Corre, Valérie, 'Le développement du travail à temps partiel', *Données sociales 1996*, INSEE, Paris 1996.

Bloch-London, Catherine and Boisard, Pierre, 'L'aménagement et la réduction du temps de travail', *Données sociales 1999*, INSEE, Paris 1999.

Boisard, Pierre and Letablier, Marie-Thérèse, 'Un compromis d'innovation entre tradition et standardisation dans l'industrie laitière', in L. Boltanski and L. Thévenot, eds, *Justesse et justice dans le travail*, CEE–Presses Universitaires de France, Paris 1989.

Boissevain, Jeremy, *Friends of Friends: Networks, Manipulations and Coalitions*, Blackwell, Oxford 1974.

Boissonat, Jean (director), *Le Travail dans vingt ans*, Commissariat générale du Plan, Odile Jacob and Documentation française, Paris 1995.

Boltanski, Luc, 'Pouvoir et impuissance. Projet intellectuel et sexualité dans le Journal d'Amiel', *Actes de la recherche en sciences sociales*, vol. 1, nos 5–6, 1975.

— *Les Cadres. La formation d'un groupe social*, Minuit, Paris 1982.

— *The Making of a Class: Cadres in French Society*, trans. Arthur Goldhammer,

Cambridge University Press/Éditions de la Maison des Sciences de l'Homme, Cambridge 1987.

— *L'amour et la justice comme compétences*, Métailié, Paris 1990.

— *Distant Suffering: Morality, Media and Politics*, trans. Graham Burchell, Cambridge University Press, Cambridge 1999.

— 'Dissémination ou abandon: la dispute entre amour et justice. L'hypothèse d'une pluralité de régimes d'action', in P. Ladrière, P. Pharo and L. Quéré, eds, *La Théorie de l'action: le sujet pratique en débat*, Éditions du CNRS, Paris 1993.

Boltanski, Luc and Thévenot, Laurent, 'Finding One's Way in Social Space: A Study Based on Games', *Social Science Information*, vol. 22, nos 4–5, 1983.

— eds, *Justesse et justice dans le travail*, CEE–Presses Universitaires de France, Paris 1989.

— *De la justification. Les économies de la grandeur*, Gallimard, Paris 1991.

Bonnechere, Michèle, *Le Droit du travail*, La Découverte, Paris 1997.

Bordet, Gaston and Neuschwander, Claude, *Lip 20 ans après*, Syros, Paris 1993.

Boudon, Raymond, *Theories of Social Change*, trans. J.C. Whitehouse, Polity Press, Cambridge 1986.

Bouget, Denis, Cadio, Jacqueline, Guéry, Hervé and Noguès, Henry, *Les Politiques de lutte contre la grande pauvreté*, 4 vols, Centre d'économie des besoins sociaux, Nantes 1995.

Bourdieu, Pierre, *Outline of a Theory of Practice*, trans. Richard Nice, Cambridge University Press, Cambridge 1977.

— *The Political Ontology of Martin Heidegger*, trans. Peter Collier, Polity Press, Cambridge 1991.

— *Distinction: A Social Critique of the Judgement of Taste*, trans. Richard Nice, Routledge, London 1989.

— *The Logic of Practice*, trans. Richard Nice, Polity Press, Cambridge 1990.

— *The Rules of Art: Genesis and Structure of the Literary Field*, trans. Susan Emanuel, Polity Press, Cambridge 1996.

— et al., *The Weight of the World*, trans. P.P. Ferguson *et al.*, Polity Press, Cambridge 1999.

Bourdieu, Pierre, Boltanski, Luc and Maldidier, Pascal, 'La défense du corps', *Information sur les sciences sociales*, vol. X, no. 4, 1971.

Bourdieu, Pierre, Boltanski, Luc and Saint Martin, Monique de, 'Les stratégies de reconversion. Les classes sociales et le système d'enseignement', *Information sur les sciences sociales*, vol. 12, no. 5, 1973.

Bourdieu, Pierre and Boltanski, Luc, 'La production de l'idéologie dominante', *Actes de la recherche en sciences sociales*, nos 2–3, June 1976.

Bourdieu, Pierre and Passeron, Jean-Claude, 'Sociologues des mythologies et mythologies de sociologues', *Les Temps modernes*, no. 211, December 1963.

— *Reproduction in Education, Society and Culture*, trans. Richard Nice, Sage, London 1977.

—— *The Inheritors: French Students and their Relation to Culture* (1964), trans. Richard Nice, University of Chicago Press, Chicago and London 1979.

Bouretz, Pierre, *Les Promesses du monde. Philosophie de Max Weber*, Gallimard, Paris 1996.

Bourguignon, François and Chiappori, P.-A., *Fiscalité et redistribution. Plans pour une réforme*, Notes de la Fondation Saint-Simon, Paris 1997.

Bournique, Yves and Barry, Chantal de, 'Donneurs d'ordres et sous-traitants', *L'Entreprise*, no. 2518, 1992 (special issue on 'La France des entreprises' in collaboration with INSEE).

Bouveresse, Jacques, 'La vengeance de Spengler', *Le Temps de la réflexion*, vol. 4, Gallimard, Paris 1983.

Bouzonnie, Huguette, 'L'évolution des effectifs syndicaux depuis 1912: un essai d'interprétation', *Revue française des affaires sociales*, vol. 41, no. 4, October/December 1987.

Bowie, Norman and Freeman, Edward, eds, *Ethics and Agency Theory*, Oxford University Press, Oxford 1992.

Boyer, Robert, 'L'introduction du taylorisme en France à la lumière de recherches récentes', *Travail et emploi*, no. 18, October/December 1983.

Boyer, Robert and Orléan, André, 'Persistance et changement des conventions', in Orléan, ed., *Analyse économique des conventions*, Paris 1994.

Branciard, Michel, *Histoire de la CFDT*, La Découverte, Paris 1990.

Braudel, Fernand, *The Wheels of Commerce*, vol. 2 of *Civilization and Capitalism* (3 vols) trans. Sian Reynolds, Harper & Row, New York 1981–84.

—— *La Dynamique du capitalisme*, Arthaud, Paris 1985.

Bressand, Albert and Distler, Catherine, *La Planète relationnelle*, Flammarion, Paris 1995.

Bricout, Jean-Luc, 'La montée des services', *L'Entreprise*, no. 2518, 1992 (special issue on 'La France des entreprises' in collaboration with INSEE).

Bricout, Jean-Luc and Dietsche, M., 'Un bilan de santé favorable', *L'Entreprise*, no. 2518, 1992.

Broudic, Patrick and Espinasse, Jean-Michel, 'Les politiques de gestion de la main-d'oeuvre', *Travail et emploi*, October 1980.

Bruhns, Hinnerk, 'Économie et religion chez Werner Sombart et Max Weber', in Gérard Raulet, ed., *L'Éthique protestante de Max Weber et l'esprit de la modernité*, publication of the 'Groupe de recherche sur la culture de Weimar', Éditions de la MSH, Paris 1997.

Bué, Jennifer, 'L'expression des salariés avant la loi du 4 août 1982. Les expériences d'initiative patronale', *Travail et emploi*, no. 23, March 1985.

—— 'Les différentes formes de flexibilité', *Travail et emploi*, no. 41, 3, 1989.

Bunel, Jean, *La mensualisation. Une réforme tranquille?*, Les Éditions ouvrières, Paris 1973.

Bunel, Jean and Saglio, Jean, 'La redéfinition de la politique sociale du patronat français', *Droit social*, no. 12, December 1980.

Burnham, James, *The Managerial Revolution*, John Day, New York 1941.

Burt, Ronald, 'Models of Network Structure', *Annual Review of Sociology*, vol. 6, 1980.

—— *Structural Holes*, Harvard University Press, Cambridge (MA) 1992.

—— 'The Social Structure of Competition', in N. Nohria and R. Eccles, eds, *Networks and Organizations: Structure, Form, and Action*, Harvard University Press, Cambridge (MA) 1992.

Burt, Ronald, Jannotta, Joseph E. and Mahoney, James T., 'Personality Correlates of Structural Holes', *Social Networks*, no. 20, 1998.

Caire, Guy, 'La France est-elle encore à l'heure de Lip?', *Droit social*, no. 11, November 1973.

—— 'Précarisation des emplois et régulation du marché du travail', communication to the *IIes Journées d'économie sociale*, Faculté des sciences économiques de Dijon, 24–25 September 1981.

Cairncross, Frances, *Costing the Earth*, Business Books, London 1991.

Callon, Michel, 'Éléments pour une sociologie de la traduction. La domestication des coquilles Saint-Jacques et des marin-pêcheurs dans la baie de Saint-Brieuc', *L'Année sociologique*, no. 36, 1986.

—— *La Science et ses réseaux. Genèse et circulation des faits scientifiques*, La Découverte, Paris 1989.

—— 'Réseaux technico-économiques et irréversibilité', in R. Boyer, ed., *Réversibilité et irréversibilité en économie*, EHESS, Paris 1991.

—— ed., *Ces réseaux que la raison ignore*, L'Harmattan, Paris 1993.

—— ed., *The Laws of the Markets*, Blackwell, Oxford 1998.

Callon, Michel and Latour, Bruno, 'Unscrewing the Big Leviathan', in K. Knorr-Cetina and A.V. Cicourel, eds, *Advances in Social Theory and Methodology*, Routledge & Kegan Paul, Boston 1981.

Campinos-Dubernet, Myriam, 'La gestion des sureffectifs, la fin des illusions des ressources humaines?', *Travail et emploi*, no. 64, 1995.

Camus, Benjamin, 'Les débuts de la mesure', *INSEE Méthodes*, nos 67–68, 'Les réseaux d'entreprises: des collectifs singuliers', 20 November 1996.

Capron, Michel, 'Vers un renouveau de la comptabilité des ressources humaines', *Revue française de gestion*, November/December 1995.

Cartier-Bresson, Jacques, 'Éléments d'analyse pour une économie de la corruption', *Revue Tiers-Monde*, no. 131, 1992.

—— 'De la définition d'un marché de la corruption à l'étude de ses formes organisationnelles: un premier bilan des analyses économiques de la corruption', communication to the seminar on 'La corruption dans les systèmes pluralistes', Poitiers, November 1993.

Cartron, Damien, 'Autonomie et contrôle dans un restaurant McDonald's', working paper for the seminar of Luc Boltanski at the EHESS, 1998.

Castel, Robert, 'De l'indigence à l'exclusion: la désaffiliation', in Jacques Donzelot, *Face à l'exclusion: le modèle français*, Le Seuil-Esprit, Paris 1991.

—— *Les Métamorphoses de la question sociale*, Fayard, Paris 1994.

—— 'Débats sur le revenu minimum inconditionnel', *Revue du Mauss*, no. 7 (issue devoted to universal income), 1996.

Castel, Robert, Fitoussi, Jean-Paul and Freyssinet, Jacques, *Chômage: le cas français*, La Documentation française, Paris 1997.

Castells, Manuel, *The Rise of the Network Society*, Blackwell, Oxford 1996.

Castells, Manuel, Yazawa, Shujiro and Kiselyova, Emma, 'Insurgents against the Global Order: A Comparative Analysis of the Zapatistas in Mexico, the American Militia and Japan's AUM Shinrikyo', *Berkeley Journal of Sociology*, vol. XL, 1995.

Castoriadis, Cornelius, *L'expérience du mouvement ouvrier*, vol. 2, Union générale d'édition, Paris 1974.

—— *Capitalisme moderne et révolution*, vol. 2, Union générale d'édition, Paris 1979.

CERC-Association, 'Tendances de la distribution des revenus dans une perspective internationale', *La Note de Cerc-Association*, no. 1, October 1994.

—— 'Chiffrer le chômage', *Dossiers du Cerc-Association*, no. 1, 1997.

—— 'Les minima sociaux: 25 ans de transformation', *Dossiers du Cerc-Association*, no. 2, 1997.

Certeau, Michel de, *The Capture of Speech and Other Political Writings*, trans. Tom Conley, University of Minnesota Press, Minneapolis 1997.

Cette, Gilbert and Mahfouz, Selma, 'Le partage primaire du revenu: un constat descriptif sur longue période', *Économie et Statistique*, nos 296–297, June/July 1996.

Cézard, Michel, 'Les classifications: les grandes étapes', *Économie et statistiques*, Paris 1979.

Cézard, Michel and Dayan, Jean-Louis, 'Les relations professionnelles en mutation', *Données sociales 1999*, INSEE, Paris 1999.

Cézard, Michel, Dussert, F. and Gollac, Michel, 'Taylor va au marché. Organisation du travail et informatique', *La Lettre d'information du CEE*, no. 26, December 1992.

—— 'Conditions, Organisation du travail et nouvelles technologies', *Dossiers statisiques du travail et de l'emploi*, DARES, nos 90–91–92, 1993.

Cézard, Michel and Vinck, Lydie, 'Contraintes et marges d'initiative des salariés dans leur travail', *Données sociales 1996*, INSEE, Paris 1996.

CFDT, 'Pour la démocratie dans l'entreprise. Mai–juin 68, des expériences, des documents, des faits', *La Revue du militant*, no. 82, March–April 1969.

Chalvon-Demersay, Sabine, 'Une société élective. Scénarios pour un monde de relations choisies', *Terrain*, no. 27, September 1996.

Chandler, Alfred D., *The Visible Hand: The Managerial Revolution in American Business*, Harvard University Press, Cambridge (MA) 1977.

Charpail, Christine, Gelot, Didier, Gubian, Alain and Zilberman, Serge, 'L'évaluation des politiques de l'emploi', *Données sociales 1999*, INSEE, Paris 1999.

Chateauraynaud, Francis, *La Faute professionnelle. Une sociologie des conflits de respon-sabilité*, Métailié, Paris 1991.

Chatzis, Kostas, Coninck, Frédéric de and Zarifian, Philippe, 'L'accord A. Cap 2000: la "logique compétence" à l'épreuve des faits', *Travail et emploi*, no. 64, 1995.

— 'L'evaluation des politiques de l'emploi', *Données sociales 1999*, INSEE, Paris 1999.

Chauvel, Louis, 'L'uniformisation du taux de suicide masculin selon l'âge: effet de génération ou recomposition du cycle de vie?', *Revue française de sociologie*, vol. XXXVIII, 1997.

Chenu, Alain, 'Une classe ouvrière en crise', *Données sociales 1993*, INSEE, Paris 1993.

— 'Le codage professionnel à l'épreuve d'investigations réitérées, 1975–1990', communication to the working day on 'l'évolution de la catégorie socioprofessionnelle et des déterminants de la stratification sociale', Observatoire sociologique du changement, 14 March 1997.

— 'La descriptibilité statistique des professions', *Sociétés contemporaines*, no. 27, 1997.

Chesnais, François, *La Mondialisation du capital*, Syros, Paris 1994.

Chiapello, Ève, 'Les typologies des modes de contrôle et leurs facteurs de con-tingence – un essai d'organisation de la littérature', *Comptabilité–Contrôle–Audit*, vol. 2, no. 2, September 1996.

— 'Les organisations et le travail artistiques sont-ils contrôlables?', *Réseaux*, November–December 1997.

— *Artistes versus managers. Le management culturel face à la critique artiste*, Métailié, Paris 1998.

— 'Art, innovation et management: quand le travail artistique interroge le contrôle', in L. Collins, ed., *Questions de contrôle*, Presses Universitaires de France, Paris 1999.

Chiaramonti, Claude, 'L'asocialité dénoncée par ses victimes', *Données sociales 1990*, INSEE, Paris 1990.

Clairmont, Frédéric, 'Vers un gouvernement planétaire des multinationales. Ces deux cents sociétés qui contrôlent le monde', *Le Monde diplomatique*, April 1997.

Claverie, Élisabeth, 'Procès, Affaire, Cause, Voltaire et l'innovation critique', *Politis*, no. 26, 1994.

— 'La naissance d'une forme politique: l'affaire du chevalier de La Barre', in P. Roussin, ed., *Critique et affaires de blasphème à l'époque des Lumières*, Honoré Champion, Paris 1998.

Claverie, Élisabeth and Lamaison, Pierre, *L'impossible mariage. Violence et parenté en Gévaudan, xviie, xviiie, xixe siècles*, Hachette, Paris 1982.

Clavero, Bartolomé, *La Grâce du don. Anthropologie catholique de l'économie moderne*, Albin Michel, Paris 1996.

Clerc, Jean-Marie, 'Les conflits sociaux en France en 1970 et 1971', *Droit social*, no. 1, January 1973.

Closets, François de, *Toujours plus!*, Grasset, Paris 1982.

— *Tous ensemble pour en finir avec la syndicatrie*, Seuil, Paris 1984.

Clot, Yves, Rochex, Jean-Yves and Schwartz, Yves, *Les Caprices du flux. Les mutations technologiques du point de vue de ceux qui les vivent*, Éditions Matrice, Vigneux 1992.

CNPF, *Le problème des OS*, CNPF, Paris 1971.

— *L'amélioration des conditions de vie dans l'entreprise*, 4th 'Assises nationales des entreprises', 15–18 October 1977, 2 vols, CNPF, Paris 1977.

Coblence, Françoise, *Le Dandysme, obligation d'incertitude*, Presses Universitaires de France, Paris 1986.

Cohen, Daniel, *Richesse du monde, pauvreté des nations*, Flammarion, Paris 1997.

Coignard, Sophie and Guichard, Marie-Thérèse, *Les bonnes fréquentations: histoire secrète des réseaux d'influence*, Grasset, Paris 1997.

Combesque, Marie-Agnès, *Ça suffit! Histoire du mouvement des chômeurs*, Plon, Paris 1998.

Coninck, Frédéric de, 'Évolutions post-tayloriennes et nouveaux clivages sociaux', *Travail et emploi*, no. 49, 1991.

Corcuff, Philippe, 'Sécurité et expertise psychologique dans les chemins de fer', in L. Boltanski and L. Thévenot, eds, *Justesse et justice dans le travail*.

Coriat, Benjamin, *L'atelier et le chronomètre*, Christian Bourgois, Paris 1979.

— *Penser à l'envers – Travail et organisation dans la firme japonaise*, Christian Bourgois, Paris 1991.

— 'France: un fordisme brisé mais sans successeur', in R. Boyer and Y. Saillard, eds, *Théorie de la régulation. L'état des savoirs*, La Découverte, Paris 1995.

Cosette, Martial, 'Les vertus du socialement correct', *Alternatives économiques*, no. 161, July/August 1998.

Coupat, Julien, *Perspective et critique de la pensée situationniste*, DEA dissertation, EHESS (École des hautes études en sciences sociales), Paris 1997.

Courtois, Stéphane and Lazar, Marc, *Histoire du Parti communiste français*, Presses Universitaires de France, Paris 1995.

Coutrot, Thomas, 'Les nouveaux modes d'organisation de la production: quels effets sur l'emploi, la formation, l'organisation du travail?', *Données sociales 1996*, INSEE, Paris 1996.

Coutrot, Thomas and Mabile, Sylvie, 'Le développement des politiques salariales incitatives', *Données sociales 1993*, INSEE, Paris 1993.

Crosnier, Patrick, 'Les PMI dans le sillage des groups', *L'Entreprise*, no. 2518, 1992 (special issue on 'La France des entreprises' in collaboration with INSEE).

Crouch, Colin and Pizzorno, Alessandro, eds, *The Resurgence of Class Conflict in Western Europe since 1968*, 2 vols, Holmes & Meier, New York 1978.

Crozier, Michel, *La Société bloquée*, Seuil, Paris 1970.

Crozier, Michel, Huntington, Samuel and Watanuki, Joji, *The Governability of Democracies*, mimeo, The Trilateral Commission, 1975.

Danziger, Raymond, *Le Bilan social, outil d'information et de gestion*, Dunod, Paris 1983.

Daugareilh, Isabelle, 'Le contrat de travail à l'épreuve des mobilités', *Droit social*, no. 2, February 1996.

Debord, Guy, *The Society of the Spectacle* (1967), trans. Donald Nicholson-Smith, Zone Books, New York 1994.

Degenne, Alain and Forsé, Michel, *Les Réseaux sociaux*, Armand Colin, Paris 1994.

Dejours, Christophe, 'Pathologie de la communication. Situation de travail et espace public: le cas du nucléaire', *Raisons pratiques*, no. 3, 1992.

— *Souffrance en France. La banalisation de l'injustice sociale*, Seuil, Paris 1998.

Deleuze, Gilles, *Spinoza: Practical Philosophy*, trans. Robert Hurley, City Lights Books, San Francisco 1988.

— *Difference and Repetition* (1968), trans. Paul Patton, Athlone, London 1994.

Deleuze, Gilles and Guattari, Félix, *A Thousand Plateaus: Capitalism and Schizophrenia* (1980), trans. Brian Massumi, Athlone Press, London 1988.

Delors, Jacques, *Changer*, Stock, Paris 1975.

Derrida, Jacques, *Of Grammatology* (1967), trans. Gayatri Chakravorty Spivak, Johns Hopkins University Press, Baltimore and London 1977.

Descombes, Vincent, *Philosophie par gros temps*, Minuit, Paris 1989.

Desrosières, Alain, 'Éléments pour l'histoire des nomenclatures socioprofessionnelles', in J. Affichard, ed., *Pour une histoire de la statistique*, vol. 2, INSEE–Economica, Paris 1987.

— *La Politique des grands nombres*, La Découverte, Paris 1993.

Desrosières, Alain and Thévenot, Laurent, *Les Catégories socioprofessionnelles*, La Découverte, Paris 1988.

Dessors, Dominique, Schram, Jean and Volkoff, Serge, 'Du handicap de "situation" à la sélection–exclusion: une étude des conditions de travail antérieures aux licenciements économiques', *Travail et emploi*, no. 2, 1991.

De Swann, Abraham, *In Care of the State*, Polity Press, Cambridge 1988.

Didier, Emmanuel, *De l'exclusion*, DEA thesis, GSPM/EHESS, Paris 1995.

Didry, Claude, *La Construction juridique de la convention collective en France, 1900–1919*, École des hautes études en sciences sociales thesis, Paris 1994.

Dirn, Louis, *La Société française en tendances, 1975–1995*, Presses Universitaires de France, Paris 1998.

Disselkamp, Annette, *L'Éthique protestante de Max Weber*, Presses Universitaires de France, Paris 1994.

Dixon, Keith, *Les Évangélistes du marché*, Raisons d'agir Éditions, Paris 1998.

Dodier, Nicolas, *Les Hommes et les machines. La conscience collective dans les sociétés technicisées*, Métailié, Paris 1995.

Dubet, François, *La Galère. Jeunes en survie*, Fayard, Paris 1987.

—— *Sociologie de l'expérience*, Seuil, Paris 1994.

Dubois, Pierre, 'New Forms of Industrial Conflict', in Crouch and Pizzorno, eds, *The Resurgence of Class Conflict in Western Europe since 1968*.

Dubois, Pierre, Durand, Claude and Erbès-Séguin, Sabine, 'The Contradiction of French Trade Unionism', in Crouch and Pizzorno, eds, *The Resurgence of Class Conflict in Western Europe*.

Duchesne, Françoise, 'Le syndicalisme à venir', in J.-P. Durand, ed., *Syndicalisme au futur*, Syros, Paris 1996.

Ducrot, Oswald and Schaeffer, Jean-Marie, *Nouveau dictionnaire encyclopédique des sciences du langage*, Seuil, Paris 1995.

Dufour, Christian, 'Le repli sur soi des comités d'entreprise', *Alternatives économiques*, no. 125, March 1996.

—— 'Comités d'entreprise: le savoir sans le pouvoir', *Alternatives économiques*, no. 142, November 1996.

Dugué, Élisabeth, 'La gestion des compétences: les savoirs dévalués, le pouvoir occulté', *Sociologie du travail*, no. 3, 1994.

Dulong, Renaud, 'Les cadres et le mouvement ouvrier', in *Grèves revendicatives ou grèves politiques?*, Éditions Anthropos, Paris 1971.

Dumont, Louis, *Homo hierarchicus*, trans. Mark Sainsbury, Weidenfeld & Nicolson, London 1970.

—— *Homo aequalis*, Gallimard, Paris 1977.

—— *Essays on Individualism: Modern Ideology in Anthropological Perspective*, University of Chicago Press, Chicago and London 1986.

—— *German Ideology: From France to Germany and Back*, University of Chicago Press, Chicago and London 1994.

Durand, Claude, *Le Travail enchaîné. Organisation du travail et domination sociale*, Seuil, Paris 1978.

—— *Chômage et violence. Longwy en lutte*, Galilée, Paris 1981.

Durand, Claude and Dubois, Pierre, *La Grève. Enquête sociologique*, FNSP–Armand Colin, Paris 1975.

Durand, Michelle, 'La grève: conflit structurel, système de relations industrielles ou facteur de changement social', *Sociologie du travail*, no. 3, July/September 1979.

Durand, Michelle and Harff, Yvette, 'Panorama statistique des grèves', *Sociologie du travail*, no. 4, 1973.

Durkheim, Émile, *Socialism and Saint-Simon*, trans. Charlotte Sattler, Routledge & Kegan Paul, London 1959.

—— *The Division of Labour in Society*, trans. W.D. Halls, Macmillan, Basingstoke 1984.

Duveau, Georges, *La Pensée ouvrière sur l'éducation pendant la Seconde République et le Second Empire*, Domat–Montchrestien, Paris 1947.

Échardour, Annick and Maurin, Éric, 'La main-d'oeuvre étrangère', *Données sociales 1993*, INSEE, Paris 1993.

Edelman, Berard, *La Légalisation de la classe ouvrière*, Christian Bourgois, Paris 1978.

Ehrenberg, Alain, *Le Culte de la performance*, Calmann-Lévy, Paris 1991.

— *L'Individu incertain*, Calmann-Lévy, Paris 1995.

— *La Fatigue d'être soi*, Odile Jacob, Paris 1998.

Elias, Norbert and Dunning, Eric, *The Quest for Excitement: Sport and Leisure in the Civilizing Process*, Basil Blackwell, Oxford 1986.

Elster, Jon, *Making Sense of Marx*, Cambridge University Press, Cambridge 1985.

— *Local Justice: How Institutions Allocate Scarce Goods and Necessary Burdens*, Russel Sage, New York 1992.

Entreprise et Progrès, *Cadre/non cadre. Une frontière dépassée*, Entreprise et Progrès, Paris 1992.

Épistémon, *Ces idées qui ont ébranlé la France*, Fayard, Paris 1968.

Erickson, Bonnie H., 'Culture, Class and Connections', *American Journal of Sociology*, vol. 102, no. 1, 1996.

Eustache, Dominique, 'Individualisation des salaires et flexibilité. Le cas des entreprises chimiques et de leurs ouvriers de production au début des années quatre-vingt', *Travail et emploi*, no. 29, September 1986.

Eymard-Duvernay, François, 'Droit du travail et lois économiques: quelques éléments d'analyse', *Travail et emploi*, no. 33, September 1987.

— 'Conventions de qualité et pluralité des formes de coordination', *Revue économique*, no. 2, March 1989.

— 'Les contrats de travail: une approche comparative', in C. Bessy and F. Eymard-Duvernay, eds, *Les Intermédiaires du marché du travail*.

— 'Les marchés du travail: une approche institutionnaliste pluraliste', communication to the seminar on 'Politique économique', FORUM, University of Paris X, Nanterre, 1998.

Eymard-Duvernay, François and Marchal, Emmanuelle, *Façons de recruter. Le jugement des compétences sur le marché du travail*, Métailié, Paris 1996.

Eyraud, François, Jobert, Annette, Rozenblatt, Patrick and Tallard, Michèle, 'Les classifications dans l'entreprise: production des hiérarchies profession-nelles et salariales', *Travail et emploi*, no. 38, 1989.

Faucheux, Hedda and Neyret, Guy, in collaboration with Fermanian, Jean-David and Ferragu, Alain, *Évaluation de la pertinence des catégories sociopro-fessionnelles (CSP)*, INSEE, Inspection générale, no. 49/BOO5, 1999.

Favennec-Héry, Françoise, 'Le droit et la gestion des départs', *Droit social*, no. 6, June 1992.

Fermanian, Jean-David, 'Compte rendu de la journée d'étude à l'Observatoire sociologique du changement du 14 mars 1997', *Note INSEE*, Département de l'emploi et des revenus d'activité, 10 July 1997.

Ferry, Jean-Marc, *L'Allocation universelle. Pour un revenu de citoyenneté*, Cerf, Paris 1995.

— 'Pour une autre valorisation du travail. Défense et illustration du secteur quaternaire', *Esprit*, no. 234, July 1997.

Feutrie, Michel and Verdier, Éric, 'Entreprises et formations qualifiantes. Une construction sociale inachevée', *Sociologie du travail*, no. 4, 1993.

Fillieule, Olivier, ed., *Sociologie de la protestation. Les formes de l'action collective dans la France contemporaine*, L'Harmattan, Paris 1993.

Foucauld, Jean-Baptiste de and Piveteau, Denis, *Une société en quête de sens*, Odile Jacob, Paris 1995.

Fouquet, Annie, 'Travail, emploi et activité', *La Lettre du Centre d'études de l'emploi*, no. 52, April 1998.

Frause, Bob and Colehour, Julie, *The Environmental Marketing Imperative: Strategies for Transforming Environmental Commitment into a Competitive Advantage*, Probus Publishing Company, Chicago 1994.

Fremeaux, Philippe, 'Le bilan économique des années Mitterrand', *Alternatives économiques*, February 1995.

— 'Mondialisation: les inégalités contre la démocratie', *Alternatives économiques*, no. 138, June 1996.

Friedkin, Noah, 'Structural Bases of Interpersonal Influence in Groups: A Longitudinal Case Study', *American Sociological Review*, vol. 58, December 1993.

Friedman, Milton, *Capitalism and Freedom*, University of Chicago Press, Chicago 1962.

Friez, Adrien, 'Les salaires depuis 1950', *Données sociales 1999*, INSEE, Paris 1999.

Frigul, Nathalie, Bretin, Hélène, Metenier, Isabelle, Aussel, Lucette and Thébaud-Mony, Annies, 'Atteintes à la santé et exclusion professionnelle: une enquête auprès de 86 femmes au chômage de longue durée', *Travail et emploi*, no. 56, 1993.

Froidevaux, Gerald, *Baudelaire. Représentation et modernité*, Corti, Paris 1989.

Furet, François, *The Passing of an Illusion*, trans. Deborah Furet, University of Chicago Press, Chicago 1999.

Furjot, Daniel, 'Conflits collectifs: les conditions de travail en mauvaise posture', *Travail et emploi*, no. 61, 1994.

Galbraith, John Kenneth, *American Capitalism: The Concept of Countervailing Power*, Houghton Mifflin, Boston 1952.

— *The New Industrial State*, Hamish Hamilton, London 1967.

Gambetta, Diego, *Trust: Making and Breaking Cooperative Relations*, Cambridge University Press, Cambridge 1988.

Garcia, Marie-France, 'La construction sociale d'un marché parfait: le marché au cadran de Fontaines-en-Sologne', *Actes de la recherche en sciences sociales*, no. 65, 1986.

Gaudu, François, 'Les notions d'emploi en droit', *Droit social*, no. 6, June 1996.

— 'Travail et activité', *Droit social*, no. 2, February 1997.

Gaullier, Xavier and Gognalons-Nicolet, Maryvonne, 'Crise économique et mutations sociales: les cessations anticipées d'activité (50–65 ans)', *Travail et emploi*, no. 15, January/March 1983.

Geary, Dick, *European Labour Protest, 1848–1939*, Croom Helm, London 1981.

Gervais, Daniel, 'Contraintes internationales et démission des États. Les marchés financiers ou l'irresponsabilité au pouvoir', *Le Monde diplomatique*, January 1993.

Giarini, Orio, *Dialogue sur la richesse et le bien-être*, report to the Club of Rome, Economica, Paris 1981.

—— 'La notion de valeur économique dans la société post-industrielle: éléments pour la recherche de nouveaux pardigmes', *Économies et société*, February 1983.

Ginsbourger, Francis, 'Marie-Thérèse, le rendement et le Lectra', *Travail*, no. 10, November 1985.

—— ed., *Pour une gestion intentionnelle de l'emploi*, working document of the collective 'Instrumentation de gestion et emploi', ANACT, Paris 1996.

—— *La Gestion contre l'entreprise. Réduire le coût du travail ou organiser sa mise en valeur*, La Découverte, Paris 1998.

Ginsbourger, Francis and Potel, Jean-Yves, 'La pratique de la négociation collective. Négociations de branche et négociations d'entreprises de 1972 à 1981', *Travail et emploi*, no. 20, June 1984.

Girard, Bernard, 'Vers un nouveau pacte social', *Revue française de gestion*, no. 100, September/October 1994.

Giraud, Pierre-Noël, *L'inégalité du monde. Économie du monde contemporain*, Gallimard, Paris 1996.

Gollac, Michel, *À marches forcées? Contribution à l'étude des changements du travail*, document de synthèse en vue d'une habilitation à diriger des recherches, University of Paris VIII, 1998.

Gollac, Michel and Volkoff, Serge, 'Citius, altius, fortius. L'intensification du travail', *Actes de la recherche en sciences sociales*, no. 114, September 1996.

Gorgeu, Armelle and Mathieu, René, 'Recrutement et production au plus juste. Les nouvelles usines d'équipement automobile en France', *Dossiers du CEE*, new series, no. 7, 1995.

Gorgeu, Armelle and Mathieu, René, 'Les ambiguités de la proximité: les nouveaux établissements d'équipement automobile', *Actes de la recherche en sciences sociales*, 1996.

Gorz, André, ed., *The Division of Labour: The Labour Process and Class Struggle in Modern Capitalism*, Harvester Press, Hassocks 1976.

—— *Paths to Paradise*, trans. Malcom Imrie, Pluto Press, London 1985.

—— *Critique of Economic Reason*, trans. Gillian Handyside and Chris Turner, Verso, London and New York 1990.

Goux, Dominique and Maurin, Éric, 'La mobilité est plus forte, mais le chômage de longue durée ne se résorbe pas', *Données sociales 1993*, INSEE, Paris 1993.

Goux, Dominique and Maurin, Éric, 'Éducation, expérience et salaire. Tendances récentes et évolutions à long terme', *Documents d'études*, no. 4, DARES, Paris 1994.

Goux, Dominique and Maurin, Éric, 'Démocratisation de l'école et persistance des inégalités', *Économie et statistiques*, no. 306, 1997.

Goux, Dominique and Maurin, Éric, 'Les entreprises, les salariés et la formation continue', *Économie et statistiques*, no. 306, 1997.

Grana, Cesar, *Bohemian versus Bourgeois: French Society and the French Man of Letters in the Nineteenth Century*, Basic Books, New York, 1964.

Grandjean, Caroline, 'L'individualisation des salaires. La stratégie des entreprises', *Travail et emploi*, no. 32, June 1987.

— 'Modalités nouvelles de la rémunération à l'ancienneté', *Travail et emploi*, no. 41, 1989.

Granovetter, Mark, 'The Strength of Weak Ties', *American Journal of Sociology*, vol. 78, 1973.

— *Getting a Job*, Harvard University Press, Cambridge (MA) 1974.

— 'Economic Action and Social Structure: The Problem of Embeddedness', *American Journal of Sociology*, vol. 91, no. 3, November 1985.

Greffe, Xavier, 'La gestion du non-marchand', *Revue française de gestion*, September/October 1979.

Gribaudi, Maurizio and Blum, Alain, 'Des catégories aux liens individuels: l'analyse statistique de l'espace social', *Annales ESC*, no. 6, November/December 1990.

Grossein, Jean-Pierre, ed., Max Weber, *Sociologie des religions*, Gallimard, Paris 1996.

Groux, Guy, *Vers un renouveau du conflit social*, Bayard Éditions, Paris 1998.

Guéroult, François, 'Faut-il rétablir l'autorisation de licenciement?', *Alternatives économiques*, no. 140, September 1996.

Guillemard, Anne-Marie, 'Emploi, protection sociale et cycle de vie: résultats d'une comparaison internationale des dispositifs de sortie anticipée d'activité', *Sociologie du travail*, no. 3, 1993.

— 'Attitudes et opinions des entreprises à l'égard des salariés âgés et du vieillissement de la main-d'oeuvre', in *Emploi et vieillissement*, La Documentation française, Paris 1994.

Guilloux, Patrick, 'Négociation collective et adaptation professionnelle des salariés aux évolutions de l'emploi', *Droit social*, no. 11, November 1990.

Habermas, Jürgen, *Legitimation Crisis*, trans. Thomas McCarthy, Heinemann, London 1976.

— *The Theory of Communicative Action*, 2 vols, trans. Thomas McCarthy, Polity Press, Cambridge 1989.

Hannoun, Michel, 'Présentation d'une investigation', *INSEE Méthodes*, nos 67–68, 'Les réseaux d'entreprises: des collectifs singuliers', 20 November 1996.

Haq, Mahbub ul, Kaul, Inge and Grunberg, Isabelle, *The Tobin Tax: Coping with Financial Volatility*, Oxford University Press, Oxford 1996.

Heilbroner, Robert Louis, *The Nature and Logic of Capitalism*, Norton, New York and London 1985.

Hélou, Christophe, *Entre violence et justice: une sociologie de la résistance à l'école*, sociology thesis, EHESS, Paris 1998.

Hennion, Antoine, *La Passion musicale*, Métailié, Paris 1995.

Herault, Bruno and Lapeyronnie, Didier, 'Le statut et l'identité. Les conflits sociaux et la protestation collective', in O. Galland and Y. Lemel, eds, *La nouvelle société française. Trente années de mutation*, Armand Colin, Paris 1998.

Hermite, Marie-Angèle, 'L'illicite dans les commerces international des marchandises', in *L'illicite dans le commerce international, travaux du CREDIMI*, 16, 1996.

Himmelfarb, Gertrude, *Poverty and Compassion: The Moral Imagination of the Late Victorians*, A. Knopf, New York 1991.

Hirschman, Albert O., *Exit, Voice and Loyalty*, Harvard University Press, Cambridge (MA) 1970.

— *The Passions and the Interests: Political Arguments for Capitalism before its Triumph*, Princeton University Press, Princeton 1977.

— *L'économie comme science morale et politique*, Hautes Études–Gallimard–Seuil, Paris 1984.

— *The Rhetoric of Reaction*, Belnap Press, Cambridge (MA) 1991.

— *Shifting Involvements: Private Interests and Public Action*, Princeton University Press, Princeton 2002.

Hoarau, Jacques, 'La philosophie morale de Marx et le marxisme', in M. Canto-Sperber, ed., *Dictionnaire d'éthique et de philosophie morale*, Presses Universitaires de France, Paris 1996.

Hodson, Randy, 'Dignity in the Workplace under Participative Management: Alienation and Freedom Revisited', *American Sociological Review*, vol. 61, October 1996.

Holcblat, Norbert, Marioni, Pierre and Roguet, Brigitte, 'Les politiques de l'emploi depuis 1973', *Données sociales 1999*, INSEE, Paris 1999.

Hopwood, Anthony and Miller, Peter, eds, *Accounting as Social and Institutional Practice*, Cambridge University Press, Cambridge 1994.

Hoschild, Arlie Russel, *The Managed Heart: Commercialization of Human Feeling*, University of California Press, Los Angeles 1983.

Howell, Chris, *Regulating Labor: The State and Industrial Relations Reform in Postwar France*, Princeton University Press, Princeton 1992.

Illich, Ivan, *Tools for Conviviality*, Calder & Boyars, London 1973.

INSEE, *L'économie française. Édition 1998–1999*, Livre de Poche, Paris 1998.

— *Annuaire statistique de la France*, INSEE, Paris 1998 (CD-ROM version).

Jansolin, Paul, 'Une formation à deux vitesses', *L'Entreprise*, no. 2518, 1992 (special issue on 'La France des entreprises' in collaboration with INSEE).

Jeger-Madiot, François, 'L'emploi et le chômage des familles professionnelles', *Données sociales 1996*, INSEE, Paris 1996.

Jobert, Annette, 'Vers un nouveau style de relations professionnelles?', *Droit social*, nos 9–10, September/October 1974.

Jobert, Annette and Tallard, Michèle, 'Diplômes et certifications de branches dans les conventions collectives', *Formation emploi*, no. 52, October/December 1995.

Jobert, Bruno and Théret, Bernard, 'France: la consécration républicaine du néo-libéralisme', in B. Jobert, ed., *Le Tournant néo-libéral en Europe*, L'Harmattan, Paris 1994.

Johnson, Thomas and Kaplan, Robert, *Relevance Lost: The Rise and Fall of Management Accounting*, John Wiley & Sons, New York 1987.

Jourdain, Colette, 'L'intérim, une voie d'accès à l'emploi', *Données sociales 1999*, INSEE, Paris 1999.

Juillard, Michel, 'Régimes d'accumulation', in R. Boyer and Y. Saillard, eds, *Théorie de la régulation. L'état des savoirs*, La Découverte, Paris 1995.

Juillard, Michel and Boyer, Robert, 'Les États-Unis: adieu au fordisme!', in Boyer and Saillard, eds, *Théorie de la régulation*.

Karpik, L., 'L'économie de la qualité', *Revue française de sociologie*, vol. 30, 1989.

Kawakita, Hideya, 'The Dignity of Man', *Iichiko Intercultural*, no. 8, 1996.

Kerbourc'h, Jean-Yves, 'Le travail temporaire: une forme déjà élaborée de "contrat d'activité"', *Droit social*, no. 2, February 1997.

Kocka, Jürgen, *Les Employés en Allemagne, 1850–1980. Histoire d'un groupe social*, Éditions de l'EHESS, Paris 1989.

Kreye, Otto, Frobel, Folker and Heirichs, Jürgen, *The New International Division of Labour*, Cambridge University Press/Maison des sciences de l'homme, Cambridge and Paris 1980.

Kuhn, Thomas S., *The Structure of Scientific Revolutions*, University of Chicago Press, Chicago 1962.

Labbé, Dominique, *Syndicats et syndiqués en France depuis 1945*, L'Harmattan, Paris 1996.

Labbé, Dominique, Croziat, Maurice and Bevort, Antoine, *La Désyndicalisation. Le cas de la CFDT*, a study conducted for PIRTTEM-CNRS, Institut des études politiques de Grenoble 1989.

Labbé, Dominique and Derville, Jacques, *Annexe du rapport 'La Désyndicalisation en France depuis 1945'*, CERAT, Institut des études politiques de Grenoble 1995.

Lacan, Jacques, *De la psychose paranoïaque dans ses rapports avec la personnalité* (1932), Seuil, Paris 1980.

Lacroix, Michel, 'Les services aux entreprises', *L'Entreprise*, no. 2518, 1992 (special issue on 'La France des entreprises' in collaboration with INSEE).

Lagarenne, Christine and Marchal, Emmanuelle, 'Les recrutements sur le marché du travail de 1990 à 1994', *Lettres du CEE*, no. 9, May 1995.

Lallement, Michel, *Sociologie des relations professionnelles*, La Découverte, Paris 1996.

Lamour, Philippe and de Chalendar, Jacques, *Prendre le temps de vivre. Travail, vacances et retraite à la carte*, Seuil, Paris 1974.

Lantin, Jacques and Fermanian, Jean-David, 'Présentation des conventions collectives', *Notes INSEE*, Département de l'emploi et des revenus d'activité, 16 December 1996.

Latour, Bruno, *Les Microbes, guerre et paix*, suivi de *Irréductions*, Métailié, Paris 1984.

— *Science in Action*, Open University Press, Milton Keynes 1987.

— *We Have Never Been Modern*, trans. Catherine Porter, Harvester Wheatsheaf, London 1993.

Launay, Michel, *Le Syndicalisme en Europe*, Imprimerie Nationale, Paris 1990.

Lazzarato, Maurizio, Moulier Boutang, Yann, Negri, Antonio and Santilli, Gian-Carlo, *Des entreprises pas comme les autres. Benetton en Italie, le Sentier à Paris*, Publisud, Aix-en-Provence 1993.

Le Bon, Gustave, *The Crowd: A Study of the Popular Mind*, Ernest Benn, London 1952.

Lefort, Claude, *Éléments d'une critique de la bureaucratie*, Droz, Geneva–Paris 1971.

Le Goff, Jean-Pierre, *Mai 1968. L'héritage impossible*, La Découverte, Paris 1998.

Leifer, Eric, 'Interaction Preludes to Role Setting: Exploratory Local Action', *American Sociological Review*, vol. 53, December 1988.

Lemaire, Maryvonne, 'Les réseaux d'enseigne. Le cas de la distribution des articles d'habillement', *INSEE Méthodes*, nos 67-68, 'Les réseaux d'entreprises: des collectifs singuliers', 20 November 1996.

Lemel, Yannick, Oberti, Marco and Reiller, Frédéric, 'Classe sociale, un terme fourre-tout? Fréquence et utilisation des termes liés à la stratification sociale dans deux revues', *Sociologie du travail*, no. 2, 1996.

Lemieux, Cyril, *Le Devoir et la grâce*, Cerf, Paris 1999.

Lenoir, René, *Les Exclus, un Français sur dix*, Seuil, Paris 1974.

Lepetit, Bernard, ed., *Les Formes de l'expérience: une nouvelle histoire sociale*, Albin Michel, Paris 1995.

Linhart, Danièle, 'À propos du post-taylorisme', *Sociologie du travail*, no. 1, 1993.

Linhart, Danièle and Maruani, Margaret, 'Précarisation et déstabilisation des emplois ouvriers', *Travail et emploi*, no. 11, Janaury/March 1982.

Linhart, Robert, *The Assembly Line*, trans. Margaret Crosland, John Calder, London 1981.

Lorenz, Edward, 'Flexible Production Systems and the Social Construction of Trust', *Theory and Society*, vol. 21, September 1993.

Lorino, Philippe, *Comptes et récits de la performance. Essai sur le pilotage des entreprises*, Les Éditions d'organisation, Paris 1995.

Luttringer, Jean-Marie, '"L'entreprise formatrice" sous le regard des juges', *Droit social*, no. 3, March 1994.

Lyon-Caen, Antoine and Jeammaud, Antoine, 'France', in Lyon-Caen and Jeammaud, eds, *Droit du travail, démocratie et crise*, Actes Sud, Arles, 1986.

Lyon-Caen, Antoine and Maillard, Jean de, 'La mise à disposition de personnel', *Droit social*, no. 4, April 1981.

Lyon-Caen, Gérard, 'Plasticité du capital et nouvelles formes d'emploi', *Droit social*, nos 9–10, September/October 1980.

— 'La bataille truquée de la flexibilité', *Droit social*, no. 12, December 1985.

MacKinnon, Malcom H., 'The Longevity of the Thesis: A Critique of the Critics', in H. Lehmann and G. Roth, eds, *Weber's Protestant Ethic: Origins, Evidence, Contexts*, Cambridge University Press, Cambridge 1993.

Magaud, Jacques, 'L'éclatement juridique de la collectivité de travail', *Droit social*, no. 12, December 1975.

Maillard, Jean de, Mandroyan, Patrick, Plattier, Jean-Paul and Priestley, Thierry, 'L'éclatement de la collectivité de travail: observations sur les phénomènes d'extériorisation de l'emploi', *Droit social*, nos 9–10, September/October 1979.

Malleret, Véronique, 'Méthode d'évaluation des performances des services fonctionnels', *Revue française de comptabilité*, no. 259, September 1994.

— 'Les évaluations des situations complexes: des processus à maîtriser', in L. Collins, ed., *Questions de contrôle*, Presses Universitaires de France, Paris 1999.

Mallet, Serge, *The New Working Class*, trans. Andrée and Bob Shepherd, Spokesman, Nottingham 1975.

Marchand, Olivier, 'Population active, emploi, chômage au cours des années 90', *Données sociales 1999*, INSEE, Paris 1999.

Marchand, Olivier and Salzberg, Liliane, 'La gestion des âges à la française, un handicap pour l'avenir?', *Données sociales 1996*, INSEE, Paris 1996.

Marcuse, Herbert, *One-Dimensional Man*, Beacon Press, Boston 1964.

Margirier, Gilles, 'Crise et nouvelle organisation du travail', *Travail et emploi*, no. 22, December 1984.

Marin, Bernd, 'Qu'est-ce que le patronat? Enjeux théoriques et résultats empiriques', *Sociologie du travail*, no. 4, 1988.

Marquès, Edmond, *La Gestion des ressources humaines*, Hommes et techniques, Paris 1980.

Martory, Bernard, 'Les coûts des conditions de travail. Fondements et outils', *Revue française de comptabilité*, no. 101, March 1980.

— *Contrôle de gestion sociale*, Vuibert, Paris 1990.

Marty, Marie-Odile, Nehmy, Rosa, Sainsaulieu, Renaud and Tixier, Pierre-Éric, *Les Fonctionnements collectifs de travail*, 3 vols, mimeo, CSO, Paris 1978.

Marx, Karl, *A Contribution to the Critique of Political Economy*, trans. S.W. Ryazanskaya, Lawrence & Wishart, London 1971.

— 'A Contribution to the Critique of Hegel's Philosophy of Right', in Marx, *Early Writings*, Penguin/New Left Review, Harmondsworth, 1975.

— 'Economic and Philosophical Manuscripts', in Marx, *Early Writings*.

— 'Critique of Hegel's Doctrine of the State', in Marx, *Early Writings*.

— 'Introduction', in Marx, *Grundrisse*, trans. Martin Nicolaus, Penguin/New Left Review, Harmondsworth 1973.

Marx, Karl and Engels, Frederick, *The Communist Manifesto*, Verso, London and New York 1998.

Maurice, Marc and Cornu, Roger, *Les Cadres en mai–juin 68 dans la région d'Aix–Marseille*, rapport du Commissariat général au Plan, LEST, Paris 1970.

Maurin, Louis, 'Le bilan social des années Mitterrand', *Alternative économiques*, no. 123, January 1995.

— 'Le travail des femmes', *Alternatives économiques*, no. 127, May 1995.

— 'La grosse déprime de l'emploi', *Alternatives économiques*, no. 149, June 1997.

Mauss, Marcel, *The Gift*, trans. W.D. Halls, W.W. Norton, London 1990.

Mayere, Anne, 'Revalorisation qualitative des emplois et substitution de jeunes travailleurs français à des travailleurs immigrés: le cas d'une entreprise de collecte des ordures', *Travail et emploi*, no. 17, July/September 1983.

Méda, Dominique, 'Travail et politiques sociales', *Droit social*, no. 4, April 1994.

Menger, Pierre-Michel, 'Marché du travail artistique et socialisation du risque. Le cas des arts du spectacle', *Revue française de sociologie*, XXXII, 1991.

— 'L'hégémonie parisienne: économie et politique de la gravitation artistique', *Annales ESC*, no. 6, November/December 1993.

— 'Appariement, risque et capital humain: l'emploi et la carrière dans les professions artistiques', in Menger and J.-P. Passeron, eds, *L'Art de la recherche. Essais en honneur de Raymonde Moulin*, La Documentation française, Paris 1994.

— 'Être artiste par intermittence. La flexibilité du travail et le risque professionnel dans les arts du spectacle', *Travail et emploi*, no. 60, 1995.

— 'Les intermitttents du spectacle: croissance de l'emploi et du chômage indemnisé', *Insee-Première*, no. 510, February 1997.

Merckling, Odile, 'Transformation des emplois et substitution travailleurs français–travailleurs immigrés: le cas de l'automobile', *Sociologie du travail*, no. 1, 1986.

Meurs, Dominique and Charpentier, Pascal, 'Horaires atypiques et vie quotidienne des salariés', *Travail et emploi*, no. 32, June 1987.

Ministère du Travail, de l'Emploi et de la Formation professionnelle, 'Horaires de travail en 1991. Résultats de l'enquête Conditions de travail', *Dossiers statistiques du travail et de l'emploi*, nos 98–99, October 1993.

Mitchell, James Clyde, ed., *Social Networks in Urban Situations*, Manchester University Press, Manchester 1969.

Morazé, Charles, *Les Bourgeois conquérants*, Armand Colin, Paris 1957.

Moreno, Jacob Levy, *Who Shall Survive? A New Approach to the Problem of Human Interrelations*, Beacon House, New York 1934.

— 'La méthode sociométrique en sociologie', *Cahiers internationaux de sociologie*, vol. II (cahier double), 1947.

Mouriaux, Marie-Françoise, 'La pluriactivité entre l'utopie et la contrainte', *La Lettre du Centre d'études de l'emploi*, no. 51, February 1998.

Mouriaux, R., *Analyse de la crise syndicale en 1995*, working document no. 68, 1995.

Mucchielli, Jean-Louis, *Multinationales et mondialisation*, Seuil, Paris 1998.

Nelson, Richard and Winter, Sidney, *An Evolutionary Theory of Economic Change*, Harvard University Press, Cambridge (MA) 1982.

Nizard, Alfred, 'Suicide et mal-être social', *Population et société*, no. 334, April 1998.

Nohria, Nitin and Eccles, Robert, eds, *Networks and Organizations: Structure, Form, and Action*, Harvard University Press, Cambridge (MA) 1992.

OECD, *Les nouvelles attitudes et motivations des travailleurs*, Direction de la main-d'oeuvre et des affaires sociales, Paris 1972.

Padgett, John F. and Ansell, Christopher K., 'Robust Action and the Rise of the Medici, 1400–1434', *American Journal of Sociology*, vol. 98, no. 6, May 1993.

Parlier, Michel, Perrien, Christien and Thierry, Dominique, 'L'organisation qualifiante et ses enjeux dix ans après', *Revue française de gestion*, no. 116, November–December 1997.

Parrochia, Daniel, *Philosophie des réseaux*, Presses Universitaires de France, Paris 1993.

Parrot, Jean-Philippe., *La Représentation des intérêts dans le mouvement des idées politiques*, Presses Universitaires de France, Paris 1974.

Pastré, Olivier, 'Taylorisme, productivité et crise du travail', *Travail et emploi*, no. 18, October/December 1983.

Paugam, Serge, ed., *Précarité et risque d'exclusion en France*, document of the CERC, La Documentation française, Paris 1993.
— 'L'essor des associations humanitaires. Une nouvelle forme de lien social?', *Commentaire*, no. 68, 1995.
— ed., *L'exclusion. L'état des savoirs*, La Découverte, Paris 1996.

Périlleux, Thomas, *Le Travail des épreuves. Dispositifs de production et formes de souffrance dans une entreprise industrielle*, EHESS thesis, Paris 1997.

Philippe, Jérôme, 'Réseaux de commercialisation de l'habillement: l'imbrication des logiques de distribution et production', *Économie et statistique*, no. 314, 1998.

Philonenko, Grégoire and Guienne, Véronique, *Au carrefour de l'exploitation*, Desclée de Brouwer, Paris 1997.

Pialoux, Michel, 'The Shop Steward's World in Disarray', in Pierre Bourdieu *et al.*, *The Weight of the World*.

Pialoux, Michel and Beaud, Stéphane, 'Permanent and Temporary Workers', in Pierre Bourdieu *et al.*, *The Weight of the World*.

Pialoux, Michel, Weber, Florence and Beaud, Stéphane, 'Crise du syndicalisme et dignité ouvrière', *Politis*, no. 14, 1991.

Piketty, Thomas, *L'économie des inégalités*, La Découverte, Paris 1997.

Piore, Michael, *Beyond Individualism*, Harvard University Press, Cambridge (MA) 1995.

Piore, Michael and Sabel, Charles, *The Second Industrial Divide*, Basic Books, New York 1984.

Piore, Michael and Sabel, Charles, 'Le paradigme de la production de masse et ses alternatives: le cas des États-Unis and de l'Italie', *Conventions économiques*, Cahiers du Centre d'études de l'emploi, Presses Universitaires de France, Paris 1985.

Polanyi, Karl, *Origins of Our Time: The Great Transformation*, Victor Gollancz, London 1945.

Pommier, Philippe, 'Le monde des entreprises', *L'Entreprise*, no. 2518 (special issue on 'La France des entreprises' in collaboration with INSEE).

Poulet, Bernard, 'À gauche de la gauche', *Le Débat*, no. 103, January/February 1999.

Poulet, Pascale, 'Allongement de la scolarisation et insertion des jeunes: une liaison délicate', *Économie et statistique*, no. 300, 1996.

Powell, Walter, 'Neither Market nor Hierarchy: Network Forms of Organization', *Research in Organizational Behavior*, vol. 12, 1990.

Power, Michael, 'The Audit Society', in A. Hopwood and P. Miller, eds, *Accounting as Social and Institutional Practice*.

Pratt, John and Zeckhauser, Richard, eds, *Principals and Agents: The Structure of Business*, Harvard Business School, Boston 1985.

Priestley, Thierry, 'À propos du "contrat d'activité" proposé par le rapport Boissonnat', *Droit social*, no. 12, December 1995.

Procacci, Giovanna, *Gouverner la misère. La question sociale en France, 1789–1848*, Seuil, Paris 1993.

Raulet, Gérard, ed., *L'Éthique protestante de Max Weber et l'esprit de la modernité*, publication of the research group on Weimar culture, Éditions de la MSH, Paris 1997.

Rehfeldt, Udo, 'Les syndicats face à la mondialisation des firmes: le rôle des comités d'entreprise européens', *Actes du GERPISA*, no. 21, December 1997.

Reich, Robert, *The Work of Nations: Preparing Ourselves for 21st Century Capitalism*, Simon & Schuster, London 1991.

Reynaud, Jean-Daniel, *Les Syndicats en France*, Seuil, Paris 1975.

Ricoeur, Paul, *Freud and Philosophy*, trans. Denis Savage, Yale University Press, New Haven and London 1970.

—— *The Conflict of Interpretations*, Northwestern University Press, Evanston (IL) 1974.

—— *Le juste*, Esprit–Seuil, Paris 1995.

Roberts, Benjamin, Okamoto, Hideaki and Lodge, George C., 'Collective Bargaining and Employee Participation in Western Europe, North America and Japan', Trilateral task force on industrial relations (1979), in Trilateral Commission, *Task Force Reports: 15–19*, New York University Press, New York 1981.

Rosanvallon, Pierre, *Le Libéralisme économique. Histoire de l'idée d marché*, Seuil, Paris 1979.

—— *La Question syndicale*, Calmann-Lévy, Paris 1988.

— *L'État en France de 1790 à nos jours*, Seuil, Paris 1990.

— *Le Sacre du citoyen. Histoire du suffrage universel en France*, Gallimard, Paris 1992.

— *La nouvelle question sociale*, Seuil, Paris 1995.

Rosch, Eleonor, 'On the Internal Structure of Perceptual and Semantic Categories', in T.E. Moore, ed., *Cognitive Development and the Acquisition of Language*, Academic Press, New York 1973.

— 'Classification of Real-World Objects: Origins and Representation in Cognition', in P.N. Johnson-Laird and P.C. Wason, eds, *Thinking: Readings in Cognitive Science*, Cambridge University Press, Cambridge 1977.

Rothschild, Emma, 'Automation et O.S. à la General Motors', *Les Temps modernes*, nos 314–315, September/October 1974.

Rousselet, Jean, *L'Allergie au travail*, Seuil, Paris 1974.

Sabel, Charles, *Work and Politics: The Division of Labor in Industry*, Cambridge University Press, Cambridge 1982.

— 'Constitutional Ordering in Historical Context', in F. Scharpf, ed., *Games in Hierarchy and Networks*, Westview Press, Boulder (CO) 1993.

Sabel, Charles and Zeitlin, Jonathan, eds, *World of Possibilities: Flexibility and Mass Production in Western Industrialization*, Cambridge University Press and Éditions de la Maison des Sciences de l'Homme, Cambridge and Paris 1997.

Sackmann, Sonja A., Flamholtz, Eric G. and Bullen, Maria Lombardi, 'Human Resource Accounting: A State-of-the-Art Review', *Journal of Accounting Literature*, vol. 8, 1989.

Salmon, Jean-Marc, *Le Désir de société. Des restos du cœur aux mouvements de chômeurs*, La Découverte, Paris 1998.

Santilli, Gian-Carlo, 'L'évolution des relations industrielles chez Fiat, 1969–1985', *Travail et emploi*, no. 31, March 1987.

Sarthou-Lajus, Nathalie, *L'Éthique de la dette*, Presses Universitaires de France, Paris 1997.

Savall, Henri and Zardet, Véronique, *Le nouveau contrôle de gestion*, Malesherbes, Eyrolles, Paris 1993.

Schelling, Thomas, *The Strategy of Conflict*, Oxford University Press, New York 1960.

Scheler, Max, *L'homme du ressentiment* (1919), Gallimard, Paris 1970.

Schiray, Michel, 'La précarisation du travail', *Dossiers d'actualité mondiale*, La Documentation française, no. 575, January 1988.

— 'Les filières-stupéfiants: trois niveaux, cinq logiques', *Futuribles*, March 1994.

Schnapp, Alain, and Vidal-Naquet, Pierre, *Journal de la commune étudiante. Textes et documents, novembre 1967-juin 1968*, expanded edn, Seuil, Paris 1988.

Schumpeter, Joseph, *A History of Economic Analysis*, Allen & Unwin, London 1986.

— *Capitalism, Socialism and Democracy*, Allen & Unwin, London 1987.

Sennet, Richard, *The Corrosion of Character: The Personal Consequences of Work in the New Capitalism*, Norton & Company, New York 1998.

Serfati, Claude, 'Les groupes industriels acteurs de la mondialisation financière', *Le Monde diplomatique*, no. 23, January 1995 (special issue).

Serres, Michel, *Hermès ou la communication*, Minuit, Paris 1968.

— *Hermès II. L'interférence*, Minuit, Paris 1972.

Sewell, William, *Work and Revolution in France: The Language of Labor from the Old Regime to 1848*, Cambridge University Press, Cambridge 1980.

Shank, John and Govindarajan, Vijay, *La Gestion stratégique des coûts*, Éditions d'organisation, Paris 1995.

Shimizu, Koichi, 'Kaizen et gestion du travail chez Toyota Motor et Toyota Motor Kyushu: un problème dans la trajectoire de Toyota', *Actes du GERPISA*, no. 13, March 1995.

Sicot, Dominique, 'Cent ans de galère pour l'inspection du travail', *Alternatives économiques*, no. 104, February 1993.

— 'Sous la fracture, les classes', *Alternatives économiques*, no. 29, July 1996 (special issue).

Siegel, Jerrold, *Bohemian Paris: Culture, Politics and the Boundaries of Bourgeois Life, 1830–1930*, Penguin, New York 1986.

Silver, Alan, 'Friendship and Trust as Moral Ideal: An Historical Approach', *Journal européen de sociologie*, vol. XXX, 1989.

Silver, Hilary, 'Exclusion sociale et solidarité sociale: trois paradigmes', *Revue internationale du travail*, vol. 133, nos 5–6, 1994.

Simitis, Spiros, 'Le droit du travail a-t-il encore un avenir?', *Droit social*, nos 7–8, July/August 1997.

Sklar, Holly, ed., *Trilateralism: The Trilateral Commission and Elite Planning for World Management*, South End Press, Boston 1980.

Smith, Adam, *The Wealth of Nations*, Books I–III, Penguin, Harmondsworth 1976.

Sofri, Adriano, 'Sur les conseils de délégués: autonomie ouvrière, conseils de délégués et syndicats en 1969–1970', *Les Temps modernes*, no. 335, June 1974.

Sohlberg, Pierre, 'Les leçons de l'affaire Hoover', *Alternatives économiques*, no. 106, April 1993.

Sombart, Werner, *The Quintessence of Capitalism: A Study of the History and Psychology of the Modern Business Man*, trans. M. Epstein and T. Fisher Unwin, London 1915.

— *Why is there no Socialism in the United States?*, trans. Patricia M. Hocking and C.T. Husbands, Macmillan, London 1976.

Soubie, Raymond, 'Après les négociations sur la flexibilité', *Droit social*, no. 3, March 1985.

Spence, Michel, 'Job Market Signaling', *The Quarterly Journal of Economics*, vol. 87, no. 3, 1973.

Stark, David, 'Recombinant Property in East European Capitalism', *American Journal of Sociology*, no. 101, 1996.

Starobinski, Jean, *Jean-Jacques Rousseau*, trans. Arthur Goldhammer, University of Chicago Press, Chicago and London 1988.

Sullerot, Évelyne, *Le grand remue-ménage: la crise de la famille*, Fayard, Paris 1997.

Supiot, Alain, 'Le travail, liberté partagée', *Droit social*, nos 9–10, September/October 1993.

— *Critique du droit du travail*, Presses Universitaires de France, Paris 1994.

— 'Du bon usage des lois en matière d'emploi', *Droit social*, no. 3, March 1997.

Surault, Pierre, 'Nuptialité, divortialité et suicidité: des ruptures à rapprocher?', *Population*, no. 4, 1992.

Swedberg, Richard, *Economics and Sociology*, Princeton University Press, Princeton 1990.

Szreter, Simon, 'The Genesis of the Registrar-General's Social Classification of Occupations', *The British Journal of Sociology*, vol. XXXV, no. 4, 1984.

Taddei, Dominique and Coriat, Benjamin, *Made in France: l'industrie française dans la compétition mondiale*, Librairie générale française, Paris 1993.

Tanguy, Lucie, 'Compétences et intégration sociale dans l'entreprise', in F. Ropé and L. Tanguy, eds, *Savoirs et compétences. De l'usage de ces notions dans l'école et l'entreprise*, L'Harmattan, Paris 1994.

Taylor, Charles, *Sources of the Self: The Making of Modern Identity*, Cambridge University Press, Cambridge 1989.

Teman, Daniel, 'L'inégalité devant le chômage', *Alternatives économiques*, no. 21, July 1994 (special issue).

Terny, Guy, 'Éléments d'une théorie de la bureaucratie', *Vie et sciences économiques*, no. 87, 1980.

Teubner, Gunther, 'Nouvelles formes d'organisation et droit', *Revue française de gestion*, November/December 1993.

— '*Altera pars audiatur*: le droit dans la collision des discours', *Droit et société*, no. 35, 1997.

Théry, Irène, *Le Démariage*, Odile Jacob, Paris 1994.

Thévenot, Laurent, 'Les catégories sociales en 1975: l'extension du salariat', *Économie et statistique*, no. 91, July/August 1977.

— 'Les investissements de forme', in *Conventions économiques*, Cahiers du centre d'études d'emploi, Presses Universitaires de France, Paris 1985.

— 'Rationalité ou normes sociales: une opposition dépassée?', in *Le Modèle et l'enquête. Les usages du principe de rationalité dans les sciences sociales*, Éditions de l'EHESS, Paris 1995.

— 'Émotions et évaluations dans les coordinations publiques', in P. Paperman and R. Ogien, eds, *La Couleur des pensées*, *Raisons pratiques*, no. 6, Éditions de l'EHESS, Paris 1995.

— 'Un gouvernement par les normes. Pratiques et politiques des formats d'information', in B. Conein and L. Thévenot, eds, *Cognition et information en société*, 'Raisons pratiques' series, no. 8, Éditions de l'EHESS, Paris 1997.

— 'Pragmatique de la connaissance', in A. Borzeix, A. Bouvier and P. Pharo, eds, *Sociologie et connaissance: nouvelles approches cognitives*, CNRS Éditions, Paris 1998.

— 'Les justifications du service public peuvent-elles contenir le marché?', in A. Lyon-Caen and V. Champeil-Desplat, eds, *Services publics et droits fondamentaux dans la construction européenne*, Institut international de Paris-La Défense-Dalloz, Paris 1998.

Thollon-Pommerol, Vincent, 'L'armature des groupes', *L'Entreprise*, no. 2518, 1992 (special issue on 'La France des entreprises' in collaboation with INSEE).

Thomas, Hélène, *La Production des exclus*, Presses Universitaires de France, Paris 1997.

Thompson, E.P., *The Making of the English Working Class*, Penguin, Harmondsworth 1980.

Thurow, Lester, *Head to Head: The Coming Economic Battle among Japan, Europe and America*, Nicholas Brearley, London 1993.

Tilly, Charles, *Class and Collective Action*, Sage, Beverly Hills 1981.

Timbart, Odile, 'La délinquance mesurée par l'institution judiciaire', *Données sociales 1999*, INSEE, Paris 1999.

Touraine, Alain, Dubet, François, Lapeyronnie, Didier, Khosrokhavar, Farad and Wieviorka, Michel, *Le grand refus. Réflexions sur la grève de décember 1995*, Fayard, Paris 1996.

Trilling, Lionel, *Sincerity and Authenticity*, Harvard University Press, Cambridge (MA) 1971.

Trogan, Philippe, 'Nettoyage et sécurité', *L'Entreprise*, no. 2518, 1992 (special issue on 'La France des entreprises' in collaboration with INSEE).

UPRP (Union des organisations patronales de la région parisienne), *Combien de chômeurs?*, CNPF, Paris 1969.

Urlacher, Bernard, *La Protestation dans la usine et ses modes d'objectivation: des grafitti aux tracts*, Sociology DEA, EHESS (École des hautes études en sciences sociales), Paris 1984.

Uzzi, Brian, 'The Sources and Consequences of Embeddedness for the Economic Performance of Organizations: The Network Effect', *American Sociological Review*, vol. 61, August 1996.

Van Parijs, Philippe, 'A Revolution in Class Theory', *Politics and Society*, vol. 15, 1986.

Vaneigem, Raoul, *The Revolution of Everyday Life* (1967), trans. Donald Nicholson Smith, Left Bank Books and Rebel Press, London 1983.

Verdès-Leroux, Jeanine, *Le Réveil des somnambules. Le parti communiste, les intellectuels et la culture (1956–1985)*, Fayard–Minuit, Paris 1987.

Vergeau, Eric and Chabanas, Nicole, 'Le nombre des groupes d'entreprises a explosé en 15 ans', *INSEE Première*, no. 533, November 1997.

Verley, Patrick, *L'Échelle du monde. Essai sur l'industrialisation de l'Occident*, Gallimard, Paris 1997.

Vigarello, Georges, *Une Histoire culturelle du sport. Techniques d'hier et d'aujourd'hui*, Revue EPS–Robert Laffont, Paris 1988.

Vigneron, Jacques and Burstein, Claude, eds, *Écoproduit. Concepts et méthodologies*, Economica, Paris 1993.

Villey, Michel, *Le Droit et les droits de l'homme*, Presses Universitaires de France, Paris 1983.

Vindt, Gérard, 'Le salariat avant guerre: instabilité et précarité', *Alternatives économiques*, no. 141, October 1996.

Virno, Paolo, *Opportunisme, cynisme et peur*, Éditions de l'Éclat, Combas 1991.

Virville, Michel de (dir.), *Donner un nouvel élan à la formation professionnelle*, Report of the mission assigned by the Minister of Labour, Social Dialogue and Participation, Paris 1996.

Visser, Joëlle, 'Tendances de la syndicalisation', *Perspectives de l'emploi*, OECD, Paris 1991.

Voisset, Michèle, 'Droit du travail et crise', *Droit social*, no. 6, June 1980.

Wagner, Peter, *A Sociology of Modernity: Liberty and Discipline*, Routledge, London and New York 1994.

Wallerstein, Immanuel, *The Modern World-System*, 3 vols, Academic Press, New York and San Diego 1974–89.

— *Historical Capitalism*, Verso, London 1983.

Walzer, Michael, *Spheres of Justice*, Martin Robertson, Oxford 1983.

— *Exodus and Revolution*, Basic Books, New York 1985.

— *The Company of Critics: Social Criticism and Political Commitment in the Twentieth Century*, Halban, London 1989.

Warde, Ibrahim, 'Les maîtres auxiliaires des marchés. Le projet de taxe Tobin, bête noire des spéculateurs, cible des censeurs', *Le Monde diplomatique*, February 1997.

Washida, Kiyokazu, 'Who Owns Me? Possessing the Body, or Current Theories of Ownership', *Iichiko Intercultural*, no. 7, 1995.

Wasserman, Stanley and Faust, Katherine, *Social Network Analysis*, Cambridge University Press, Cambridge 1994.

Weber, Henri, *Le parti des patrons. Le CNPF, 1946–1986*, Seuil, Paris 1987.

Weber, Max, *General Economic History*, trans. Frank H. Knight, George Allen & Unwin, London 1927.

— *Economy and Society*, 2 vols, trans. Ephraim Fischoff *et al.*, University of California Press, Berkeley 1979.

— *Sociologie du droit*, Presses Universitaires de France, Paris 1986.

— *Sociologie des religions*, Gallimard, Paris 1996.

— *The Protestant Ethic and the Spirit of Capitalism*, trans. Stephen Kalberg, Fitzroy Dearborn, Chicago and London 2001.

Weil, Simone, *La Condition ouvrière*, Gallimard, Paris 1951.

Welcomme, Dominique, 'Mondialisation et emploi: les éléments du débat', *Lettre du CEE*, no. 24, November 1997.

White, Harrison C., 'Agency as Control in Formal Networks', in N. Nohria and R. Eccles, eds, *Networks and Organizations: Structure, Form, and Action*, Harvard University Press, Cambridge (MA) 1992.

White, Harrison C., Boorman, Scott A. and Breiger, Ronald L., 'Social Structure from Multiple Networks: 1. Blockmodels of Roles and Positions', *American Journal of Sociology*, vol. 81, no. 4, 1976.

Willener, Alfred, *L'image-action de la société et la politisation culturelle*, Seuil, Paris 1970.

Willener, Alfred, Gadjos, Catherine and Benguigui, Georges, *Les Cadres en mouvement*, Éditions de l'Épi, Paris 1969.

Williamson, Oliver, *The Economic Institutions of Capitalism*, Free Press, New York 1985.

Womack, James, Jones, Daniel and Roos, Daniel, *The Machine that Changed the World*, Rawson, New York 1990.

Yiannis, Gabriel and Lang, Tim, *The Unmanageable Consumer: Contemporary Consumption and its Fragmentation*, Sage, London 1995.

Zarifian, Philippe, 'Compétences et organisation qualifiante en milieu industriel', in F. Minet, M. Parlier and S. de Witte, eds, *La Compétence. Mythe, construction ou réalité*, L'Harmattan, Paris 1994.

Zegel, S., *Les Idées de mai*, Gallimard, Paris 1968.

NAME INDEX

AC! (*Agir ensemble contre le Chômage*) 352, 518
Adorno, Theodor 440
Afghanistan 189, 190
Africa 72–3
Aglietta, Michel 81
Aktouf, Omar 70n, 83n
Alberti, Leon Battista 59
Allen, Louis 70
Althusser, Louis *ix*
ANPE (*Agence National Pour l'Emploi*) *xxxviii*
Ansart, Pierre 62
Ansell, Christopher 150
Archier, Georges 115–8, 140
Armand, Louis 89n
Arpin, Roland 116
ATD-Quart Monde (*Aide à Toute Détresse*) 348
Atlan, Henri 139
Aubrey, Bob 73, 76n–77n, 83n, 90n, 92–4, 110, 115–6, 121–2, 123, 127, 134, 458
Aumont, Michèle 64n
Auroux, Jean 195–6, 276, 287

Baktavatsalou, Ravi 262
Balzac, Honoré de 498
Barish, John 450
Barjonet, André 206

Barker, James 431–2
Barthes, Roland 454
Bateson, Gregory 139
Baudelaire, Charles 38
Baudrillard, Jean 450, 478
Becker, Gary 152
Bell, Daniel 28, 30
Bellenger, Lionel 63, 76n, 78, 95n, 113–4, 119, 120, 123, 124, 127, 133
Belleville, Pierre 203
Belloc, Brigitte 232
Benetton 342
Benghozi, Pierre-Jean 271
Beniger, James *xxii*, 474
Berman, Marshall 473
Bessy, Christian 241
Bevort, Antoine 280, 282
Blake, Robert 63n
Bleton, Pierre 67n
Bloch-Lainé, François 64n
Boissonat, Jean 395
Boorman, Scott A. 150, 162–3
Borne, Fernand 62n, 65n, 86n, 87n, 88n, 89n
Boudon, Raymond *xx*
Bourdieu, Pierre *x*, 116–7, 453
Bouveresse, Jacques 162
Bové, José 467
Bower, Martin 62, 63, 65n, 66n, 67n, 68n

Braudel, Fernand *xxii*, 5, 62, 150–1, 163
Breiger, Ronald L. 150, 162–3
Bressand, Albert 139–40
Broda, J. 230
Burt, Ronald 116, 132, 378
    on types of capital 356–7

Caire, Guy 230
Callon, Michel 145, 310, 356
Cartron, Damien 245
Castel, Robert 126, 348
Castells, Manuel 156
Caston, Art 74n, 116
Catholicism 293, 297
CEE (*Centre d'Études de l'Emploi*) 174–5
Cegos 69
CERC (*Centre d'Étude des Revenus et des Coûts*) 186, 198, 240, 351
Ceyrac, François 181, 188, 191
CFDT (*Confédération Française Démocratique du Travail*) 171, 172, 176, 177, 182, 186, 189, 190, 197, 277–80, 286–8, 292, 295, 306
    SUD and 352
CFT (*Confédération Française du Travail*) 279
CFTC (*Confédération Française des Travailleurs Chrétiens*) 306
CGC (*Confédération Générale des Cadres*) 287, 294, 306
CGT (*Confédération Générale du Travail*) 171, 176, 178, 182, 186, 189, 190, 200, 275–80, 286–7, 289, 291–5, 306, 386
CGT-FO *see* FO
Champy, James 74
Chandler, Alfred 140
Chiaramonti, Claude 267
CIMADE (*Centre Inter Mouvement d'Aide aux personnes Déplacées*) 352

Clavel, Maurice 170
Clavero, Bartolomé 426
Clerc, Jean-Marie 186, 234
Closet, François de 291
Clot, Yves 247
CNPF (*Conseil National du Patronat Français*) 168, 181, 183, 184, 186, 187, 188, 192, 288, 302, 303
Colin, A.T. 65n
Coluche 350
Common Market 181
Common Programme (1972–7) 189
Cooke ratio 398
Coriat, Benjamin *xxxvi*, 81, 174, 194
Counter, Thomas 431
Coutrot, Thomas 219, 224
CPSU (Communist Party of the Soviet Union) 189
Croisat, Maurice 280, 282
Cronin, M. 140
Crozier, Michael 70n–71n, 76n, 83n, 112, 118, 191, 459
Cruellas, Philippe 76n, 95n

DAL (*Droit Au Logement*) 352, 518
Daugareilh, Isabelle 415
Dd!! (*Droits devant!!*) 352, 518
De Woot, Philippe 67n, 141
Debord, Guy-Ernest 450, 478
Debray, Régis 140
Dejours, Christophe 231, 240, 294
Deleuze, Gilles *xxiii*, *xxiv*, 107, 145, 156–7, 453–4
    A Thousand Plateaus (with Félix Guattari) 162
Delors, Jacques 181
Derrida, Jacques *xix*, 453–4
Descombes, Vincent 161
Desrosières, Alain 297
Devaux, Guy 66n, 87n, 88n
Didier, Emmanuel 401
Dirn, Louis 267, 300, 424

Distler, Catherine 139–40
Dixdier, Emmanuel 347
Drancourt, Michel 87n, 89n
Drucker, Peter 63, 71
Dubois, Pierre 173
Dugué, Élisabeth 481
Dumont, Louis xix, 3, 61
  on economics 12
  on ideology 20–1
Dupuy, J.-P. 139, 140
Dubois, Pierre 179
Durand, Claude 173, 179
Durkheim, Émile 325, 421, 424,
  428, 432, 435, 487, 491

Eccles, R. 140
Échardour, Annick 265
Edelman, Bernard 333
Ehrenberg, Alain 315, 424, 475
Elster, John 91, 150, 409
Enterprise et Progrès 185, 307
ERP (Enterprise Resources
  Planning) 248
Ettighoffer, Denis 90n
euro 398
Eurocommunism 189
Eymard-Duvernay, François 131,
  247, 319, 384, 394, 417
Eyraud, François 304

Faure, Edgar 191
Fayol, Henri 59, 71, 79
Ferry, Jean-Marc 415
FO (Force Ouvrière) 287, 295, 306
Fordism 81, 429
Foucauld, Jean-Baptiste de 354
Foucault, Michel 198, 401, 432
Frankfurt School 440, 454
Franklin, Benjamin 59
French resistance 141
Freud, Sigmund 170, 320

Freyyssinet, J. 230
Froissart, Daniel 63, 67, 68n, 88n
Furet, François xxiv, 17

Gabrysiak, Michel 141
Gadjos, Catherine 184
Garcia, Marie-France 417
GATS (General Agreement on
  Tariff and Services) 367
GATT (General Agreement on
  Tariff and Trade) 367
Gaudu, François 395
Gélinier, Octave 66n, 67n, 68n,
  69–70, 89, 141
Genelot, Dominique 63
Ginsbourger, Francis 237, 248, 284,
  289
Giono, Jean 63
Girard, Bernard 388
Girard, René 532
Giraud, P.-N. 290
Giscard d'Estaing, Valéry 186, 189
Gollac, Michel 431
Gorgeu, Armelle 225, 230, 238,
  240–1, 249
Gorz, André 203, 465
Granovetter, Mark 134, 140, 148
Grenelle agreements 179, 180
Grunberg, Isabelle 416
Gruson, Claude 198
Guattari, Félix 162

Habermas, Jürgen xxiv, 107, 139,
  163, 377, 458
Halbwachs, Maurice 424
Hammer, Michael 74
Handy, Charles 109–10
Hegel, Georg Wilhelm Friedrich
  153
Heidegger, Martin 440, 453
Heilbroner, Robert 5

Heinrich, N. 446
Heisenberg, Werner 139
Herzberg, F. 63
Himmelfarb, Gertrude 403
Hirschman, Albert O. *xiv*, 9–10,
    229, 445, 448, 489
    on 'exit' critique 42
    on cadres 15–6
Hoffman, Stanley *xxii*
Hofstadter, Douglas 139
Hong Kong 72
Hopwood, Anthony 187
Horkheimer, Max 440
Hughes, Charles 69n
Hugonnier, René 69n
human relations school 63
Humble, John 67n, 88n
Huvelin, Paul 87n

ICFTU (International Conference
    of Free Trade Unions) 279
Illich, Ivan 139, 159–60
INSEE (*Institut National de la
    Statistique et des Études
    Économiques*) 297, 299, 305, 303,
    307, 308–9
Internationale situationniste 170
Internet *xxiii*, 116, 118, 369, 371,
    389

Japan 72, 197
Jeammaud, Antoine 399
Jeger-Madiot, François 304
Jobert, Annette 306
Jobert, Bruno 198

Kant, Immanuel 149
Kaul, Inge 416
Kawakita, Hideya 443, 476
Keynes, Maynard 186

Knight, F. 423

Labbé, Dominique 280, 282, 283,
    294
Lacan, Jacques 498
Lagarenne, Christine 232
Landier, Hubert 79n, 84n, 90n,
    111, 115, 120, 127, 128, 458
Laslett, Peter 62
Latour, Bruno *xxix*, 140, 145, 310,
    508
Le Saget, Meryem 78, 80, 92n, 98,
    115–6, 122
Lefort, Calude 374, 409
Lemaire, Bruno 90, 115
Lenhardt, Vincent 95n
Lenoir, René 347
Linhart, Danièle 218
Lyon-Caen, Antoine 283, 399
Lyon-Caen, Gérard 225, 415

Magaud, Jacques 229, 284
MAI (Multilateral Agreement on
    Investment) 367
Maillard, Jean de 283
Mallet, Serge 203
Malterre, André 88n–89n
Maoism 178, 291
Marchal, Emmanuelle 131, 319
Marchand, Olivier 266
Marcuse, Herbert 440, 441, 450
Marx, Karl 153, 170, 325, 361
    on capitalism 7
    critique summarised 427
    on feudalism 163
    Proudhon and 62
    on 'social versus artistic' critique
    52, 469
    tests and 172
Marxism 87, 335–6, 454
    in 1960s 87

base/superstructure *xix, xxiv*
   structuralist *ix–x, xxvi,* 340
Maslow, Abraham 63, 88, 92
Mathieu, René 225, 230, 338,
   240–1, 249
Maurin, Éric 265
Mauroy, P. 198
Mauss, Marcel 426
May 1968 *xxxv–xxxvi,* 3, 97, 145,
   168–72, 178, 179, 184, 313
   capitalism's response to 441–3
   '*la pensée 68*' 453
   PCF and 189, 210–1
   trade unions and 278
McClelland, D. 63
McDonald's 245, 263, 476, 477
McLuhan, Marshal 140
McNamara, Robert 87n
Mead, G.H. 147
Medici, Cosimo de 150
Mendel, Gérard 170
Menger, Pierre-Michel 271, 312
Merckling, Odile 265
Midler, Christophe 75
Minitel 394
Moreno, Jacob Levy 143, 147–8
Morin, Pierre 74n
Morin, Edgar 139, 170
Moss Kanter, Rosabeth 71, 63n,
   74n, 76n, 78, 83n, 95n, 122, 123,
   458
   on security 93
Mouton, Jane 63n

N30 *see* Seattle protest
Nazism 440, 453
Nietzsche, Friedrich 170, 480, 497

OECD (Organisation for Economic
   Cooperation and Development)
   173, 168, 193, 367

Orgogozo, Isabelle 90n–91n, 119,
   458

Padget, John 150
Papert, S. 140
Park, Robert 147
Parrot, Jean-Philippe 297
Pastré, Olivier 175–6, 187
Patton, Arch 67n
PCF (*Parti Communiste Française*)
   189–90, 197, 200, 210–1, 295,
   504, 505
Péguy, Charles *xxxiii*
Peirce, C.S. 146
Périlleux, Thomas 241, 248
Peters, Tom 80
Peugeot 252, 285, 287, 505
Philonenko, Grégoire 227, 247
Pialoux, Michel 279, 285, 287, 432
Piore, Michael 462
Plato 59
Political and Moral Sociology
   Group *x*
Polyani, Karl *xiv, xix,* 41, 408
Porte, Jean 297
Porto Alegre (World Social Forum
   2001) *xvi*
Potel, Jean-Yves 284
Poulantzas, Nicos 162
Power, Michael 432
Prigogine, I. (physicist) 139
Prospero (software) 60
Proudhon, Pierre Joseph 62
PS (*Parti Socialiste*) 189, 295

Regulation School *xviii, xxxv,* 429
Rehn, Gösta 388
Reich, Robert 75
Renault 505
Restaurants du coeur 350
Revans, R.W. 173
Ricoeur, Paul *xxiv,* 482

RMI (*Revenu Minimum d'Insertion i.e.* universal income) 252, 392–3, 396–7, 465
Rochex, Jean-Yves 247
Ronsvallon, Pierre 275, 300–1
Rousseau, Jean Jacques 142, 296, 379, 450, 454
Rousselet, Jean 174

Sabel, Charles 383–4
Sade, Marquis de 38
Saint-Simon, Claude Henri 297
Sarthou-Lajus, Nathalie 379
Sartre, Jean-Paul 440, 453
Saussure, Ferdinand de 144
Scheler, Max 497
Schmidt, Carl *xxv*
Schumpeter, Joseph 42, 489
Schütz, Alfred 422
Schwartz, Yves 247
SDF (*Sans Domicile Fixe*) 349
Seattle protest (November 1999) *xvi*
Secours catholique 352
Séguin, Philippe 196
Sérieyx, Hervé 78, 80n, 83n, 90n–91n, 112, 118, 122, 140, 459
Serres, Michel *xxiii*, 140, 144
Servan-Schreiber, Jean-Jacques 67, 72, 87n, 89, 141
Sewell, William H. 340, 507
Shimizu, Koichi 246
Sicard, Claude 78n, 113
Silver, Alan 464
Singapore 72
Smith, Adam 108, 130
SNIP (*Syndicat National de l'Industrie Pharmaceutique*) 308–9
Socialisme ou Barbarie 170, 401
Sombart, Werner 59, 514
South Korea 72
Soviet Union 409
SP (Socialist Party) 301

Starcher, George 67n
Stengers, Isabelle 139
SUD (*syndicat Solidaire, Unifié, Démocratique*) 352, 353
Supiot, Alain 230, 251–2, 386, 417–8, 469, 481–2
on activity 395
Surrealism 170, 313

Taddeï, Dominique *xxxvi*
Taiwan 72
Tallard, Michèle 306
Tapscott, Don 74n, 116
Taylor, Charles 79, 432
Taylorism 80–1, 98, 175–6, 185, 195, 197, 217–9, 249, 429, 431, 432, 465, 512
Temps modernes, Les 38
Teubner, Günther 383
Thatcher, Margaret 168
Théret, Bernard 198
Thévenot, Laurent 417, 420
Thompson, E.P. 340
Tilly, Charles 352
Tirole, J. 140
Tobin, James 397
Tobin tax 397, 416
Toffler, Alvin 103, 128, 133, 140
Trilateral Commission 188
Trotskyism 178, 197
Turkle, Shelly 140

UIMM (*Union des Industries Métallurgiques et Minières*) 187
ul Huq, Mahbub 416
UNCTC (United Nations Centre on Transnational Corporations) *xxxvii*
UNEDIC (*Union Nationale pour l'Emploi Dans l'Industrie et le Commerce*) 252

Vaneigem, Raoul 101, 203
Varela, Francisco 139, 140
Verdès-Leroux, Jeanine 211
Vigarello, Georges 315–6
Vincent, Claude-Pierre 116
Virno, Paolo 410

Wagner, Peter 202, 410, 428
Walkman 438
Wallerstein, Immanuel 416
Walzer, Michael *xv*, 433, 471
Washido, Kiyokazu 152
Waterman, Robert 63, 127
Watzlawick, Paul 139
Weber, Florence 280
Weber, Max *xiv*, *xix*, *xlv*, 59, 100,
    154–5, 399, 418

on capitalism 7, 8–10
on moderation 25
Weiss, Dimitri 118
White, Harrison C. *xxiii*, 148, 150,
    162–3
Williamson, Oliver 84, 140
World Social Forum *xvi*
Wresinski, Father 348

Yugoslavia 197

Zapatistas 342
Žižek, Slavoj *xix*

SUBJECT INDEX

activity 394–7, 456
agency 389, 413
alienation 170, 401
  two types of 434–5
ambivalence 124
anomie 421, 423–4, 455
anti-capitalism *xvi*, 36
  see also new social movements;
  Seattle protest; World Social
  Forum
anxiety 420–1
audit society 432
authenticity (and inauthenticity)
  98–9, 326, 422, 424, 438–41, 449,
  450–1, 491
  as interiority 457
  critique of 451–3
  mobility and 456–8
autonomy 190–2, 199, 431

base (and superstructure) 162
'big bang' 71
business ethics 69, 95–6, 390–1,
  457–8

cadres 15–6, 18, 19, 141, 193, 204,
  511, 532
  attacks on term 306–9
  autonomy of 66, 174–5

careers and 87–8
creativity and 326
emergence of 59, 65
extinction of 76–9, 155
literature addressed to 57–9,
539–40
May 1968 and 184
mobility and 370–1
projects and 429–30
in rebellion 176
remuneration and 385
sackings of (1969–70) 88
transformation of 459
time and 152
capitalism
  contradiction of 215
  critique and 27–30, 32, 42,
  146–7, 427
  defined 4–7
  indignation about 37–8, 40, 97,
  355, 420, 491–2
  insatiability of 486–8
  military force and 485–6
  morals and 20
  new spirit of 467
  reflexivity of 515
  spirit of 8–11, 14, 19–21, 30, 485
    first 425
    second 487
    second and third 201, 238,
    345, 436

capitalism (cont'd.)
    dialectic of 67
    vision and 75–6
  state and 512
  youth and 36
  see also anti-capitalism
casualization 436, 460
categorization 315, 320–3,
  499–502, 522
certification 398
city 22–4, 26, 520–4
  commercial 105–8, 113–4,
  119–21, 520–1
  projective 139, 355, 372–3, 376,
  455–6, 522–3, 535
    connexionist world and 462
    justice and 462–3
    law and 399
    reputational world and 132
class *xii*, 296–303, 309–11
collective agreements 299, 303–5
commodification 441–7, 466
  green consumerism and 449
  of human beings 456, 465–6,
  470–1
  limits of 464
communism 65, 87
  collapse of 72
  see also PCF in PROPER NAME
  INDEX
competition 73, 492, 489, 494,
  533–4
connexionist logic/world 130–2,
  135, 345, 355, 362–3, 372, 449,
  522, 535
  authenticity and 451–2, 455
  flexibility and 461
  justice and 519
  law and 399
  opportunism and 378–9
consultants 197–8
consumers 368–9
corruption 121, 391

critique
  artistic 424, 466–8, 471–2, 535–6
  ecological 472
  everyday life and 533
  Freudo-Marxist 467
  social 346, 419
  social and artistic 38–9, 52, 97,
  99, 169, 171, 177–8, 190, 195,
  196, 200, 291, 293, 311–2, 324–7,
  400, 419–20, 433–4, 469, 503–6
customers 81, 91

decentralization 65–6, 70, 86
deconstruction 452–3
deregulation *xxxvii*, 194, 196, 314,
  505, 513
deterritorialization 389
dirigisme 21, 27
disability 347–8
disaffiliation 348–9
disenchantment 98–9
disinterest (and self-interest) 455–6,
  463–4
displacement 345, 462, 499–502,
  509
  tests and 508
  multinationals and 367–8
drugs 424, 475

eco-products *see* green consumerism
economics 12
empiricism 145–6
employability 93–4, 111, 119, 122,
  232, 385
employment policy 252–3
ethics *see* business ethics
ethos 11, 16, 453
exams 33
exclusion 233–4, 346–8, 353–5
  politicisation of 351
existentialism 453–4, 457

experts 79, 116–7, 197–8
exploitation 249, 346–7, 360, 364–5
  contrasted with exclusion 354–5
  denunciations of 373–5
  discovery of 507
  versus opportunism 389

family 133–4, 293, 457
family policy 252
fascism *xl*, 65, 87, 201
fatalism *xliii–xliv*, 531
feminism 434–5
financial markets 365–6
flexibility *xxxviii*, 112, 119, 190,
  192–5, 197, 217–8, 228, 231, 241,
  303, 306, 369, 396, 436
  new social movements and
  352–3
friendship 455–6, 459, 464

gender 7, 434
  see also labour, female
globalization *xvi–xvii*, *xxi*, 73,
  366–8, 516, 533
great men 112–4, 117, 122, 123–4,
  355, 462
  exploitation and 375
  Marx on 361
  mobility and 361–3
  tests and 497
green consumerism 447–9
habitus 117
hierarchy 70–1, 75
human beings
  as medium of accumulation 460
  commodification of 456, 465–6,
  470–1
humanitarian action 349–50, 351,
  450, 517
hypermarkets 222, 227

ideology *xx–xxii*, 3, 10–11, 454
immigration 187
indignation 37–8, 40, 97, 355, 420,
  487, 491–2, 516
  tests and 492–3
individualism 532–3
inflation 182
insider trading 33
internal accounting 246
investors 366

job insecurity 224, 233–5, 354
justice 28–9, 486, 516
  courts 493
  tests and 495

keyholders 358, 364

labour 131
  age and 238–9
  autonomy of 219, 254
  avoidance of 174–5
  capitalism and 7
  casualization of 225–9, 231–5,
  245
  female 187, 239–40, 241, 287–8
  health and 240
  immigrant 239, 265
  labour power 463, 464
  labour law 228, 243–5, 298, 314,
  399–400, 493
  as legal fiction 251
  part-time work 225
  temporary work 220, 224–5,
  226, 243, 244, 463
  wage individualization 250,
  284–5
leaders 75–6, 78, 91, 459
liberalism 534–5

liberation 424–38
loyalty 357

managers 8, 152–3, 358
  as artists 311–3
  emergence of 77–9
  management literature 57–101,
    103, 136–8, 141
manipulation 458–60
market services 220–1
massification 439–41, 450
meritocracy 65, 68, 88, 91, 297
  in sport 316–7
minimum wage 182, 195
mobile phones 363, 438
mobility 361–7, 370, 514, 536
  authenticity and 456–8
  critique of 468–9
  of investors 366
mobilization 459
morality x, 59, 123–4, 149, 326, 457,
  463, 486–7, 498, 521
  capitalism and 10
  profit and 464
  see also business ethics
multi-tasking 249
multinationals 367, 370–1

neo-management 457–8, 462
networks *xxii–xxiii*, 84, 103–8, 312,
  348, 513, 517
  adaptability and 461
  authenticity and 451–2, 466
  deterritorialization and 389
  family as 123
  historicist and naturalistic
    150–1
  history of term 104–5, 141–9
  informal 115–6
  justice and 105–6
  law and 383

leanness and 72–5, 218
  as natural 127–8
  networkers 356, 359, 377–80, 390
  as new paradigm 138–9
  ontology of 457
  as pro-capitalist 466
  projects and 111
  as quasi-firms 223
  sociology of 148–50
new social movements 351–2
new social pact 388
new technology 247

opportunism 355–6, 377–8, 410, 462
  versus exploitation 389
outsourcing 82, 221, 230, 236, 245,
  282, 368

planning 82–3
pollution 386–7, 448
postmodernism 345
poverty *xxxix*
pragmatism 146
private (versus professional) life 155,
  465
profit *xxxvi–xxxvii*, 172, 493
projects 73, 110–1, 312, 350
  cadres and 429–30
  Moss Kanter on 458
  new social movements and 352–3
  projective city *see* city, projective
proletariat 473
prostitution 472
psychoanalysis 436, 498

quality circles 219, 285
quietism 327

recession (1974–5) 184–5
recuperation 446–7

redundancy 69–70, 73
reform (versus revolution) *xiv*, 33, 229
rights 517
    social 387
risks 171

savings 152
security 88–9, 92–5, 93, 171, 176–7, 190, 199
    see also job insecurity
semiotics 146
signatures 409–10
simulacra 454
skills 386, 388, 465
slavery 472, 485–6
social class *see* class
social costs 251–2
social rights *see under* rights, social
sociology 301
spectacle 99, 450–1
sport 315–6
standardization 465
status 22–3, 31
statutes 469–70
streamlining 13–4, 369–70
strikes 169, 173, 175, 237, 277
    of December 1995 *xlii*
structuralism 144, 146
    Marxist *ix–x, xxvi,* 340
students 170
subcontracting 220, 230, 231, 245, 247, 368–9, 456, 463
suicide 421, 423

table manners 22–3
television 119
tests 30–5, 96, 106, 125, 171, 179–80, 183, 242, 313–4, 317–9, 373, 470, 488, 489, 492–4, 492–502

connexionist 392
    educational 493–4
    indignation and 492–3
    justice and 495
    sport and 315–7
theory of agency 389
time 129, 152
totalitarianism 87, 178, 440, 441
trade unions 494, 507–9
    as bureaucracy 278, 295
    deunionization 273–86, 288, 302
    in early 70s 179–81, 187–8
    left critique of 291–3
    malfunctions of 293–5
    militants 279–81
    unemployment and 282
training 237–8, 388
transparency 129–30
trust 83, 95, 130, 163, 390, 456, 457, 459, 462

unemployment *xxxviii–xli,* 91, 196, 235–6
    benefits 252
    suicide and 423–4
    trade unions and 282
    see also job insecurity
universal income *see* RMI (*Revenu Minimum d'Insertion*) in NAME INDEX

vision 73, 75–6, 91, 115, 459
vocation 9

welfare state 89, 201, 512
women *see* gender; labour, female
working class
    May 1968 and 169–70
    suppression of concept 168–9, 273, 295–303
works councils 276